T0178527

Lecture Notes in Computer Science　14596

Founding Editors

Gerhard Goos
Juris Hartmanis

Editorial Board Members

The series Lecture Notes in Computer Science (LNCS), including its subseries Lecture Notes in Artificial Intelligence (LNAI) and Lecture Notes in Bioinformatics (LNBI), has established itself as a medium for the publication of new developments in computer science and information technology research, teaching, and education.

LNCS enjoys close cooperation with the computer science R & D community, the series counts many renowned academics among its volume editors and paper authors, and collaborates with prestigious societies. Its mission is to serve this international community by providing an invaluable service, mainly focused on the publication of conference and workshop proceedings and postproceedings. LNCS commenced publication in 1973.

Isaac Sserwanga · Hideo Joho · Jie Ma ·
Preben Hansen · Dan Wu · Masanori Koizumi ·
Anne J. Gilliland

Editors

Wisdom, Well-Being, Win-Win

19th International Conference, iConference 2024
Changchun, China, April 15–26, 2024
Proceedings, Part I

 Springer

Editors
Isaac Sserwanga
iSchool organization
Berlin, Germany

Hideo Joho
University of Tsukuba
Tsukuba, Japan

Jie Ma
Jilin University
Changchun, China

Preben Hansen
Stockholm University
Stockholm, Sweden

Dan Wu
Wuhan University
Wuhan, China

Masanori Koizumi
University of Tsukuba
Tsukuba, Japan

Anne J. Gilliland
University of California
Los Angeles, CA, USA

ISSN 0302-9743   ISSN 1611-3349 (electronic)
Lecture Notes in Computer Science
ISBN 978-3-031-57849-6   ISBN 978-3-031-57850-2 (eBook)
https://doi.org/10.1007/978-3-031-57850-2

This Springer imprint is published by the registered company Springer Nature Switzerland AG
The registered company address is: Gewerbestrasse 11, 6330 Cham, Switzerland

Paper in this product is recyclable.

Preface

As we embark on the proceedings of iConference 2024, we reflect upon the changes since the iConference of 2023. This annual gathering represents a symbol of the resilience, adaptability, and innovation of the information community. Emerging from the challenges posed by the global COVID-19 pandemic, the iSchools community navigated the remote conference landscape, laying the foundation for a new normal where technology became the bridge connecting minds, ideas, and aspirations.

The success of the iSchools conference of 2023 reaffirmed the pivotal role of information technologies in fostering engagement and collaboration. It set the stage for the overarching theme of the 19th iConference: "Wisdom, Well-being, and Win-win." This theme encapsulates our commitment to exploring synergies, nurturing shared goals, and leveraging the power of information to enhance the well-being of individuals and communities. As we delve into the proceedings, we invite readers to witness the culmination of efforts aimed at not only advancing scholarly discourse but also contributing to the broader landscape of wisdom-driven innovation.

The virtual iConference 2024 took place from April 15–18, 2024 before the physical conference on April 22–26, 2024 at Changchun, China. Its hosts included Jilin University, China, and University of Tsukuba, Japan.

The conference theme attracted a total of 218 submissions with 109 Full Research Papers and 109 Short Research Papers.

In a double-blind review process by 319 internationally renowned experts, 91 entries were approved, including 36 Full Research Papers and 55 Short Research Papers. The approval rate was 33% for the Full Research Papers and 50.46% for the Short Research Papers. Additional submissions were selected for the Workshops and Panels, the Doctoral Colloquium, the Early Career Colloquium, the Student Symposium, Posters, and the Spanish-Portuguese and Chinese language paper sessions.

The Full and Short Research papers are published for the ninth time in Springer's *Lecture Notes in Computer Science* (LNCS). These proceedings are sorted into the following eighteen categories, reflecting the diversity of the information research areas: "Archives and Information Sustainability", "Behavioral Research", "AI and Machine Learning", "Information Science and Data Science", "Information and Digital Literacy", "Digital Humanities", "Intellectual Property Issues", "Social Media and Digital Networks", "Disinformation and Misinformation", "Libraries, Bibliometrics and Metadata", "Knowledge Management", "Information Science Education", "Information Governance and Ethics", "Health Informatics", "Human-AI Collaboration", "Information Retrieval", "Community Informatics" and "Scholarly, Communication and Open Access".

We greatly appreciate the reviewers for their expertise and valuable review work and the track chairs for their relentless effort and vast expert knowledge. We wish to extend our gratitude to the chairs and volume editors; Full Research Papers chairs, Hideo Joho from University of Tsukuba, Jie Ma from Jilin University, and Preben Hansen from

Stockholm University; Short Research Papers chairs, Dan Wu from Wuhan University, Masanori Koizumi from University of Tsukuba, and Anne J. Gilliland from University of California, Los Angeles.

The iConference lived up to its global representation of iSchools to harness the synergy of research and teaching in the field of information and complementary areas of sustainability.

February 2024

Isaac Sserwanga
Hideo Joho
Jie Ma
Preben Hansen
Dan Wu
Masanori Koizumi
Anne J. Gilliland

Organization

Organizer

Jilin University, People's Republic of China
University of Tsukuba, Japan

Conference Chairs

Yingtong Guo	Jilin University, People's Republic of China
Atsushi Toshimori	University of Tsukuba, Japan
Atsuyuki Morishima	University of Tsukuba, Japan
Jun Deng	Jilin University, People's Republic of China

Program Chairs

Local Arrangement Chairs

Yingtong Guo	Jilin University, People's Republic of China
Jun Deng	Jilin University, People's Republic of China

Proceedings Chair

Isaac Sserwanga	Humboldt-Universität zu Berlin (iSchools Organisation), Germany

Full Research Paper Chairs

Hideo Joho	University of Tsukuba, Japan
Jie Ma	Jilin University, People's Republic of China
Preben Hansen	Stockholm University, Sweden

Short Research Paper Chairs

Dan Wu	Wuhan University, People's Republic of China
Masanori Koizumi	University of Tsukuba, Japan
Anne J. Gilliland	University of California, Los Angeles, USA

Poster Chairs

Alex Poole   Drexel University, USA
Lei Pei   Nanjing University, People's Republic of China
Ellie Sayyad Abdi   Curtin University, Australia

Spanish - Portuguese Papers Chairs

Sara Martínez Cardama   Universidad Carlos III de Madrid, Spain
Josep Cobarsí Morales   Universidad Carlos III de Madrid, Spain
Alan César Belo Angeluci   Universidade de São Paulo, Brazil
Diana Lucio Arias   Pontificia Universidad Javeriana, Colombia

Chinese Paper Chairs

Xiwei Wang   Jilin University, People's Republic of China
Yang Zhang   Sun Yat-sen University, People's Republic of
                                      China
Gaohui Cao   Central China Normal University, People's
                                      Republic of China

Workshops and Panel Chairs

Ina Fourie   University of Pretoria, South Africa
Chengzhi Zhang   Nanjing University, People's Republic of China
Wonsik Jeff Shim   Sungkyunkwan University, South Korea

Student Symposium Chairs

Hui Yan   Renmin University of China, People's Republic of
                                      China
Elizabeth Eikey   University of California, USA
Romain Herault   Linnaeus University, Sweden

Early Career Colloquium Chairs

Charles Senteio   Rutgers University, USA
Jiangping Chen   University of North Texas, USA
Debbie Meharg   Edinburgh Napier University, UK
YuXiang Zhao   Nanjing University, People's Republic of China

Doctoral Colloquium Chairs

Widad Mustafa El Hadi	University of Lille, France
Howard Rosenbaum	Indiana University Bloomington, USA
Tina Du	Charles Sturt University, Australia

Doctoral Dissertation Award Chair

Pengyi Zhang	Peking University, People's Republic of China

Conference Coordinators

Michael Seadle	iSchools Organization
Slava Sterzer	iSchools Organization
Katharina Gudat	iSchools Organization
Ulrike Liebner	iSchools Organization
Isaac Sserwanga	iSchools Organization
Wei Feng	iSchools Organization

Reviewers Full and Short Papers iConference 2024 (319)

Jacob Abbott	Isak De Villiers {Diffie} Bosman
Naresh Kumar Agarwal	Theo J. D. Bothma
Daniel Agbaji	Guillaume Boutard
Aharony Noa Aharony	Sarah Elaine Bratt
Farhan Ahmad Ahmad	Paulina Bressel
Isola Ajiferuke	Jenny Bronstein
Mahir Akgun	Leonard D. Brown
Nicole D. Alemanne	Yi Bu
Daniel Gelaw Alemneh	Sarah A. Buchanan
Lilach Alon	Charles Bugre
Misita Anwar	Julia Bullard
Tatjana Aparac-Jelusic	Frada Burstein
Rhea Rowena Ubana Apolinario	Yu-Wei Chang
Lateef Ayinde	Haihua Chen
Dmitriy Babichenko	Hsin-liang Chen
Ananth Balashankar	Jiangping Chen
Sarah Barriage	Xiaoyu Chen
Ofer Bergman	Yi-Yun Cheng
Arpita Bhattacharya	Wonchan Choi
Jianxin Bi	Yujin Choi
Toine Bogers	Yunseon Choi

Miyoung Chong
Josep Cobarsí-Morales
Isabella L. Corieri
Julian D. Cortes
Andrew Cox
Amber L. Cushing
Mats Dahlstrom
Gabriel David
Nilou Davoudi
Jun Deng
Sanhong Deng
Shengli Deng
Leyla Dewitz
Junhua Ding
Karsten Donnay
Philip Doty
Liz Dowthwaite
Yunfei Du
Zhenjia Fan
Bruce Ferwerda
Rachel Fleming-May
Ina Fourie
Rebecca D. Frank
Viviane Frings-Hessami
Hengyi Fu
Yaming Fu
Jonathan Furner
Henry Alexis Gabb
Maria Gäde
Abdullah Gadi
Chunmei Gan
Yubao Gao
Zheng Gao
Stanislava Gardasevic
Emmanouel Garoufallou
Diane Gill
Fausto Giunchiglia
Dion Goh
Patrick Thomas Golden
Liliana Gonzalez Perez
Anne Goulding
Christopher Graziul
Elke Greifeneder
Jenifer Daiane Grieger
Melissa Gross

Ece Gumusel
Qiuyan Guo
Vibhor Gupta
Ayse Gursoy
Hazel Hall
Ruohua Han
Yue Hao
Noriko Hara
Jenna Hartel
Bruce Hartpence
Stefanie Havelka
Alison Hicks
Liang Hong
Lingzi Hong
Md Khalid Hossain
Jingrui Hou
Amanda Hovious
Xinhui Hu
Yuerong Hu
Zhan Hu
Ying Huang
Shezin Waziha Hussain
Isto Huvila
Aylin Imeri (Ilhan)
Sharon Ince
Jonathan Isip
Hiroyoshi Ito
Corey Jackson
Eunmi Jeong
Jie Jiang
Michael Jones
Heidi Julien
Nicolas Jullien
Jaap Kamps
Ijay Kaz-Onyeakazi
Mat Kelly
Rebecca Kelly
Heikki Keskustalo
Mahmood Khosrowjerdi
Jiro Kikkawa
Heejun Kim
Jeonghyun Kim
Kyungwon Koh
Masanori Koizumi
Kushwanth Koya

Adam Kriesberg
Maja Krtalic
Bill Kules
Mucahid Kutlu
Sucheta Lahiri
Glen Layne-Worthey
Chengyi Le
Gregory Leazer
Deborah Lee
Kijung Lee
Lo Lee
Tae Hee Lee
Wan-Chen Lee
Kai Li
Lei Li
Muyan Li
Ying Li
Yingya Li
Yuan Li
Shaobo Liang
Chern Li Liew
Louise Limberg
Zack Lischer-Katz
Chang Liu
Jieli Liu
Annemaree Lloyd
Kun Lu
Ana Lucic
Zhuoran Luo
Lai Ma
Linqing Ma
Shutian Ma
Xiaoyue Ma
Emily Maemura
Sara Martínez-Cardama
Matthew Mayernik
Diane McAdie
Kate McDowell
Claire McGuinness
Pamela Ann McKinney
David McMenemy
Debbie Meharg
Jonas Ferrigolo Melo
Shuyuan Metcalfe
Anika Meyer

Eric Meyer
A. J. Million
J. Elizabeth Mills
Yue Ming
Lorri Mon
Atsuyuki Morishima
Heather Moulaison-Sandy
Widad Mustafa El Hadi/Prunier
Hyeong Suk Na
Maayan Nakash
Ha Quang Thinh Ngo
Huyen Nguyen
Sarah Nguy˜ên
David M. Nichols
Kathleen Obille
Lydia Oladapo
Gillian Oliver
Felipe Ortega
Giulia Osti
Kathleen Padova
Nayana Pampapura Madali
Hyoungjoo Park
Jinkyung Park
Min Sook Park
William Christopher Payne
Lei Pei
Olivia Pestana
Alina Petrushka
Leonor Gaspar Pinto
Alex H. Poole
Widiatmoko Adi Putranto
Xin Qian
Rahmi Rahmi
Priya Rajasagi
Arcot Rajasekar
Alexandria Rayburn
Gabby Resch
Jorge Revez
Fernanda Ribeiro
Cristian Roman Palacios
Milly Romeijn-Stout
Vassilis Routsis
Carsten Rudolph
Sarah Elizabeth Ryan
Özhan Sağlık

Bin Zhang
Chengzhi Zhang
Chenwei Zhang
Jinchao Zhang
Mei Zhang
Xiaoqian Zhang
Yan Zhang

Yang Zhang
Yishan Zhang
Han Zheng
Kyrie Zhixuan Zhou
Lihong Zhou
Qinghua Zhu

Contents – Part I

Archives and Information Sustainability

Information Action Briefs: Advancing the United Nations Sustainable
Development Goals Through Information Research, Practice, and Policy 3
    Bharat Mehra, Jia Tina Du, and Clara M. Chu

Extraction and Visualization of Geographical Spatio-Temporal
Information from Chinese Historical Newspapers 12
    Shaodan Sun and Jun Deng

Identifying the Potential Users of Community Archives: A Case Study
of the History of the Chinese 30 Years Project 20
    Tianji Jiang and Jiarui Sun

Behavioural Research

What Motivates You to Use VR Exergames to Substitute for Real
Sports?—An Empirical Study Based on Technology Readiness
and Technology Acceptance Model 31
    Haodong Sun and Qing Ke

The Filtered Appeal: Evaluating the Impact of Appearance Enhancement
on Effectiveness of Donation Requests 53
    Susan C. Herring, Leo Yang, and Ashley R. Dainas

"If I Like BLANK, What Else Will I Like?": Analyzing a Human
Recommendation Community on Reddit 70
    Thi Binh Minh Cao and Toine Bogers

Can Chatbot Anthropomorphism and Empathy Mitigate the Impact
of Customer Anger on Satisfaction? 84
    Jian Tang, Yunran Wang, Xinxue Zhou, Jiayan Guo, and Chenguang Li

Understanding Users' Decision-Making on Privacy Disclosure
from a Configurational Perspective Perceived Values, Privacy Concerns,
Cognitive Style, and Trust 96
    Xiaoyu Chen and Ruoxi Yang

Genre Recognition: A Model of Behaviour 106
    Malcolm Clark and Ian Ruthven

"How I Form and Escape Information Cocoons": An Interview Study
of Users on Short Video Apps 129
   Manyu Sheng and Pengyi Zhang

Are Older People Battling with Digital Financial Services? 139
   Dain Thomas, Gobinda Chowdhury, and Ian Ruthven

Plant-Based Predictions: An Exploratory Predictive Analysis of Purchasing
Behavior of Meat-Alternatives by U.S. Consumers (2020) 147
   Grace Chmielinski and Sarah Bratt

AI and Machine Learning

AIGC-Enabled Interdisciplinary Science Measurement 161
   Jiangfeng Liu, Xiyu Wang, Dongbo Wang, and Lei Pei

Role of Emotional Experience in AI Voice Assistant User Experience
in Voice Shopping 171
   Xiwei Wang, Yutong Liu, Siguleng Wuji, and Ran Luo

A Contextualized Government Service Chatbot for Individuals with limited
Information Literacy 191
   Zhixuan Lian, Meiyin Huang, and Fang Wang

Detection Vs. Anti-detection: Is Text Generated by AI Detectable? 209
   *Yuehan Zhang, Yongqiang Ma, Jiawei Liu, Xiaozhong Liu,
   Xiaofeng Wang, and Wei Lu*

PrivacyChat: Utilizing Large Language Model for Fine-Grained
Information Extraction over Privacy Policies 223
   Rohan Charudatt Salvi, Catherine Blake, and Masooda Bahir

Information Science and Data Science

Reimagining Data Science Methodology for Community Well-Being
Through Intersectional Feminist Voices 235
   Sucheta Lahiri and LaVerne Gray

Participatory Observation Methods Within Data-Intensive Science: Formal
Evaluation and Sociotechnical Insight 253
   Elliott Hauser, Will Sutherland, and Mohammad Hossein Jarrahi

From Knowledge Representation to Knowledge Organization and Back 270
   Fausto Giunchiglia and Mayukh Bagchi

The Missing Linkage Between Science Technology and Innovation Policy
and the Scientific Workforce—Evidence from Colombia 288
    Julián D. Cortés and María Catalina Ramírez-Cajiao

Understanding Researchers' Data-Centric Tasks: A Classification
of Goals, Gaps, and Resources 298
    Guangyuan Sun, Chunfeng Liu, Siyuan Peng, and Qiao Li

Closing the Information Gap in Unidentified Anomalous Phenomena
(UAP) Studies 310
    Gretchen R. Stahlman

The Scholarly Age—Beyond the Academic Age Using Techno-Scientific,
Knowledge Appropriation and Mentoring Outputs 321
    Julián D. Cortés, Nicolás Robinson-García,
    Zaida Chinchilla-Rodríguez, and María Catalina Ramírez-Cajiao

Information and Digital Literacy

"Words Are not just Words; They Carry Experiences Within Them":
Navigating Personal Information Management in Multilingual Contexts 333
    Lilach Alon and Maja Krtalić

Data Curation Competencies, Skill Sets, and Tools Analysis 343
    Angela P. Murillo, Ayoung Yoon, Mitch Duncan,
    and Adam Thomas-Fennelly

The Effect of Digital Literacy on International Students' Adjustment
to University Life: Focusing on the Mediating Effect of ICT Self-efficacy 358
    Shuangling Cheng, Yeonhee Kim, and Jae-Hwang Choi

Data Wellness and Everyday Life Data Literacy 375
    Amanda Hovious and Sarah Sutton

Meeting People Where They Are: Customizing Digital Literacy Education 383
    Alison Harding, Jane Behre, and Mega Subramaniam

"Inclusion We Stand, Divide We Fall": Digital Inclusion from Different
Disciplines for Scientific Collaborations 398
    Wei Feng, Lihong Zhou, and Qinggong Shi

Developing Library and Data Storytelling Toolkits: Scenarios and Personas 410
    Kate McDowell, Xinhui Hu, and Matthew Turk

Nostalgia-Driven Design: Creating an Inclusive VR Experience for Older
Black Adults   421
    Kuo-Ting Huang

Correction to: "Inclusion We Stand, Divide We Fall": Digital Inclusion
from Different Disciplines for Scientific Collaborations C1
    Wei Feng, Lihong Zhou, and Qinggong Shi

Author Index   431

Contents – Part II

Digital Humanities

Evaluation of Ancient Chinese Natural Language Understanding in Large
Language Models Based on ACHNLU 3
 Die Hu, Guangyao Sun, Liu Liu, Chang Liu, and Dongbo Wang

A Problematic Dichotomy in the Perspective of Field Theory:
Hermeneutics and Quantitative Qnalysis in Distant Reading 19
 Mozhuo Chen

An Exploratory Study to Identify Research Interests and Analysis
Approaches in German Art History with a Potential for Digital Support 27
 Cindy Kröber

To Impress an Algorithm: Minoritized Applicants' Perceptions of Fairness
in AI Hiring Systems 43
 Antonio E. Girona and Lynette Yarger

Information Needs of and Information Sources Used by Individuals
with Social Anxiety Disorder 62
 Leyla Dewitz

Exploring Virtual Reality Through Ihde's Instrumental Realism 82
 He Zhang and John M. Carroll

Libraries as Partners for Emergency Preparedness and Response in Times
of Crisis: Survey Design and Development 94
 Kelda Habing and Lian Ruan

Intellectual Property Issues

Exploring Technology Evolution Pathways Based on Link Prediction
on Multiplex Network: Illustrated as CRISPR 105
 Zizuo Cheng, Juan Tang, Jiaqi Yang, and Ying Huang

Matching Patent and Research Field Classifications Using Lexical
Similarity and Bipartite Network—Evidence from Colombia 122
 Julián D. Cortés and María Catalina Ramírez-Cajiao

Mapping the Inventive Structure in Middle-Low Income Countries—The
Patent Network of Colombia 131
    Julián D. Cortés and María Catalina Ramírez-Cajiao

Social Media and Digital Networks

Evolving Definitions of Hate Speech: The Impact of a Lack of Standardized
Definitions 141
    Seul Lee and Anne Gilliland

Understanding the Motivations Behind Knowingly Spreading Rumors
on Social Media Using Q Methodology 157
    Xiao-Liang Shen, Qianwen Qian, and You Wu

Spatial Analysis of Social Media's Proxies for Human Emotion
and Cognition 175
    Anthony J. Corso, Nicolas C. Disanto, Nathan A. Corso, and Esther Lee

Exploring Influential Factors in Expert Advice Adoption on Social Media:
Insights from Weibo Trending Topics 186
    Jiaqi Liao

From Stickers to Personas: Utilizing Instant Messaging Stickers
for Impression Management by Gen Z 198
    Haoran Qiu, Dion Hoe-Lian Goh, Ruoxi Liu, and Peter J. Schulz

Disinformation and Misinformation

Arguing About Controversial Science in the News: Does Epistemic
Uncertainty Contribute to Information Disorder? 211
    Heng Zheng, Theodore Dreyfus Ledford, and Jodi Schneider

How Misinformation Manipulates Individuals: A Reflexive Thematic
Analysis Based on 185 Cases 236
    Yaning Cao and Qing Ke

Detecting the Rumor Patterns Integrating Features of User, Content,
and the Spreading Structure 254
    *Pengwei Yan, Guo Yu, Zhuoren Jiang, Tianqianjin Lin, Weikang Yuan,
    and Xiaozhong Liu*

Nudging Away Health Misinformation on Social Media: The Roles
of Social Influences and Power Distance 268
    Xinyue Li, Mandie Liu, Jingwen Lian, and Qinghua Zhu

Multidimensional Information Literacy and Fact-Checking Behavior:
A Person-Centered Approach Using Latent Profile Analysis 280
    Xiao-Liang Shen and You Wu

Libraries, Bibliometrics and Metadata

What Research Skills Do Scholars Excel at?—Based on Individual
Contribution and External Recognition 301
    Aoxia Xiao, Siluo Yang, Mingliang Yue, and Minshu Jin

Community Members' Perspective on Public Libraries as Places
to Overcome Social Divisions: A Case Study in Oslo 322
    Tomoya Igarashi, Jamie Johnston, and Masanori Koizumi

Unpacking Research Contributions: Investigation from Contextual
and Processual Perspectives 338
    Zhe Cao, Yuanyuan Shang, Lin Zhang, and Ying Huang

Micro Citation Importance Identification and Its Application to Literature
Evaluation 356
    Weimin Nie and Shiyan Ou

Exploring the Citation Lag in LIS: Trends and Correlations 376
    Hanqin Yang, Jingrui Hou, Qibiao Hu, and Ping Wang

Customer Service, Hard Work, and Normativity: Identity Standards
Encoded into Public Library Routines 392
    Darin Freeburg and Katie Klein

Will Affiliation Diversity Promote the Disruptiveness of Papers in Artificial
Intelligence? 407
    Xuli Tang, Xin Li, and Ming Yi

Platform, Visuals, and Sound: Webtoon's Immersive Romance Reading
Engagement 416
    *Hyerim Cho, Denice Adkins, Diogenes da Silva Santos,
    and Alicia K. Long*

Correction to: Arguing About Controversial Science in the News: Does
Epistemic Uncertainty Contribute to Information Disorder? C1
    Heng Zheng, Theodore Dreyfus Ledford, and Jodi Schneider

Author Index 425

Contents – Part III

Knowledge Management

A Network Portrait Divergence Approach to Measure Science-Technology
Linkages 3
    Kai Meng, Zhichao Ba, and Leilei Liu

Data Augmentation on Problem and Method Sentence Classification Task
in Scientific Paper: A Mechanism Analysis Study 23
    Yingyi Zhang and Chengzhi Zhang

Key Factors of Government Knowledge Base Adoption in First-, Second-
and Third-Tier Cities in China 35
    Jing Zhou and Li Si

Beliefs, Values and Emotions in Education Practitioners' Engagements
with Learning Analytics in Higher Education 54
    Itzelle Medina-Perea, Jo Bates, Monika Fratczak, and Erinma Ochu

Information Science Education

Promoting Academic Integrity Through Gamification: Testing
the Effectiveness of a 3D Immersive Video Game 65
    Xin Zhao, Haoyu Xie, Alec Roberts, and Laura Sbaffi

Information Governance and Ethics

Are We Practicing What We Preach? Towards Greater Transborder
Inclusivity in Information Science Systematic Reviews 79
    Stephanie Krueger and Rebecca D. Frank

Who Gets Left Behind in the Push for Smart Cities? Insights
from Marginalized Communities 90
    Sunyup Park and Jessica Vitak

Enhancing Ethical Governance of Artificial Intelligence Through Dynamic
Feedback Mechanism 105
    Yaqi Liu, Wenjie Zheng, and Yueli Su

Health Informatics

Digital Footprints of Distress: An Analysis of Mental Health Search
Patterns Across Socioeconomic Spectrums in Alabama Counties 125
    Hengyi Fu

Exploring Media Framing of the Monkeypox Pandemic in Mainstream
and Social Media: A Framing Theory Analysis 135
    Lin Yang

Prediction and Analysis of Multiple Causes of Mental Health Problems
Based on Machine Learning 150
    Shengli Deng, Fan Wang, Yunna Cai, Haowei Wang, Zhenyu Wang,
    Qianwen Qian, and Weiwei Ding

Automated Compliance Analysis on Clinical Notes to Improve Cancer
Lifestyle Management 161
    Yujia Hou and Javed Mostafa

Navigating Health Information: Understanding Conflicting Adoption
Mechanisms and Cognitive-Behavioral Paradoxes from the Patient's Lens 170
    Yan Jin, Di Zhao, Zhuo Sun, Chongwu Bi, and Ruixian Yang

Human-AI Collaboration

Does AI Fit? Applying Social Actor Dimensions to AI 195
    Chelsea Collier, Kenneth R. Fleischmann, Tina Lassiter,
    Sherri R. Greenberg, and Raul G. Longoria

Understandability: The Hidden Barrier and the Last Yard to Information
Accessibility 204
    Ian Y Song and Sherry L Xie

Differences in Knowledge Adoption Among Task Types in Human-AI
Collaboration Under the Chronic Disease Prevention Scenario 213
    Quan Lu and Xueying Peng

Influence of AI's Uncertainty in the Dawid-Skene Aggregation
for Human-AI Crowdsourcing 232
    Takumi Tamura, Hiroyoshi Ito, Satoshi Oyama, and Atsuyuki Morishima

Heuristic Intervention for Algorithmic Literacy: From the Perspective
of Algorithmic Awareness and Knowledge 248
    Jing Liu, Guoye Sun, and Dan Wu

Information Retrieval

An Exploratory Study on a Physical Picture Book Representation System
for Preschool Children 261
  Pianran Wang, Xuan Sun, and Yuting Wang

Challenges of Personal Image Retrieval and Organization: An Academic
Perspective 271
  Amit Kumar Nath, Forhan Bin Emdad, and An-I Andy Wang

Word Embedding-Based Text Complexity Analysis 283
  Kahyun Choi

Community Informatics

Towards a Better Understanding of Cyber Awareness Amongst Migrant
Communities in Australia 295
  Misita Anwar, Manika Saha, Gillian Oliver, Mohamed Ibrahim,
  and Carsten Rudolphr

Towards a Critical Data Quality Analysis of Open Arrest Record Datasets 311
  Karen M. Wickett and Jarrett Newman

Reading Habits and Inter-generational Influence of Women
with Child-Raising Obligations in Rural Areas 319
  Yi Xiao and Shijuan Li

Characterizing State Governments' Administrative Capacity for Broadband 329
  Caroline Stratton and Hanim Astuti

Assisting International Migrants with Everyday Information Seeking:
From the Providers' Lens 338
  Yongle Zhang and Ge Gao

Recordkeeping Practices of Grassroots Community Organizations:
Exploring the Potential Application of Push-Pull-Mooring Theory 356
  Md Khalid Hossain, Viviane Frings-Hessami,
  and Gillian Christina Oliver

Psychosocial Portraits of Participation in a Virtual World: A Comparative
Analysis of Roles and Motives Across Three Different Professional
Development Subreddits 365
  Subhasree Sengupta, Jasmina Tacheva, and Nathan McNeese

The Legacy of Slavery and COVID-19 Mortality in Southern U.S. States 382
   Mary Dalrymple and Vanessa Frias-Martinez

Scholarly, Communication and Open Access

A WOS-Based Investigation of Authors for English Predatory Journals 395
   Qian Tan, Xiaoqun Yuan, and Zixing Li

A Content-Based Novelty Measure for Scholarly Publications: A Proof
of Concept 409
   Haining Wang

Correction to: A WOS-Based Investigation of Authors for English
Predatory Journals C1
   Qian Tan, Xiaoqun Yuan, and Zixing Li

Author Index 421

Archives and Information Sustainability

Information Action Briefs: Advancing the United Nations Sustainable Development Goals Through Information Research, Practice, and Policy

Bharat Mehra[1]([✉]) [iD], Jia Tina Du[2] [iD], and Clara M. Chu[3] [iD]

[1] University of Alabama, Tuscaloosa, AL 35487, USA
bmehra@ua.edu
[2] Charles Sturt University, Bathurst, NSW 2795, Australia
tdu@csu.edu.au
[3] University of Illinois at Urbana-Champaign, Champaign, IL 61820, USA
cmchu@illinois.edu

Abstract. The Information Action Briefs (IAB) introduced in this paper use the format of a policy brief and serve as a resource and action guide to develop and create transformational actions using information to advance the United Nations Sustainable Development Goals (SDGs). The IAB is designed to inspire and mobilize library and information science (LIS) professionals (researchers, educators, scholars, students, practitioners, and policymakers) to act locally or globally, and personally or collectively in applying information-related work to promote community well-being and socioeconomic sustainability. LIS professionals are called to research, create, and use an IAB to advance the SDGs, by addressing the general aspects of a particular SDG as well as focusing on more specific topics at a granular level. LIS educators can use the IAB as a teaching tool, assigning the IAB for students to conduct research, propose solutions and write about sustainable development. In this manner, we hope readers will be similarly inspired as the authors to use the IABs in a variety of ways to conduct their research and practice and document their work while integrating the SDGs towards greater relevance and impact of their efforts in information work environments and beyond.

Keywords: Information Action Briefs · Information Research · Library and Information Science · UN Sustainable Development Goals (SDGs)

1 Context and Background

The Sustainable Development Goals (SDGs) (or *United Nations 2030 Agenda*) were adopted by all United Nations (UN) member states in 2015 to provide a "shared blueprint for peace and prosperity for people and the planet, now and into the future" [24]. Seventeen goals were identified as a call for action for every country to join in a global partnership to end poverty and employ strategies to "improve health and education, reduce inequality, and spur economic growth – all while tackling climate change and

I. Sserwanga et al. (Eds.): iConference 2024, LNCS 14596, pp. 3–11, 2024.
https://doi.org/10.1007/978-3-031-57850-2_1

working to preserve our oceans and forests" [24]. Library and information science (LIS) professionals (researchers, educators, scholars, students, practitioners, and policymakers) are in a unique position to facilitate the achievement of the SDGs. Information is needed to bring awareness to the issues, knowledge to design solutions, and data to monitor accountability, across various types of traditional and non-traditional information environments [5, 23].

We conceived a tool in the form of an *Information Action Brief* (IAB) to explicitly identify positive actions that the LIS professions can take to accomplish this task. Even though the focus of the application to identify actions can be directed at any aspects of information-related work, it is intentional in the *use of information* in this regard and the name of the tool. By organizing and working collaboratively, the information community of professionals, researchers, and educators can "join in the global effort to overcome poverty and inequality, tackle the climate crisis, empower women and girls, and build peaceful, just, and inclusive societies, free of discrimination and hate, in harmony with nature. To create a better future for all, we need information to bring awareness to the issues, knowledge to design solutions and data to monitor accountability. United in information, let's act together to meet the Goals" [5].

2   Theoretical Rationale: Collective Impact Framework

To tackle the critical issues identified in the SDGs, collective (or community) action not only by all nations, but across all sectors of society is fundamental [20]. North American researchers Kania and Kramer [11] first introduced *collective impact* in a *Stanford Social Innovation Review* article as appropriate to tackle complex social issues and defined it as "the commitment of a group of important actors from different sectors to a common agenda for solving a specific social problem" (p. 36). The core of the collective impact framework lies in the coordinated efforts of multiple stakeholders working towards a common goal of achieving long-term and meaningful social change [11, 22]. It emphasizes a systemic perspective that promotes cross-sector collaboration and provides a structured framework for implementation.

Christens and Inzeo [4] situated the collective impact framework in relation to similar approaches and collaborative frameworks among community organizing initiatives and provided recommendations for enhancing collaborative practice to address community issues via community action, i.e., community-led change efforts [7, 20]. Australian researchers Salignac, Wilcox, Marjolin, and Adams [22] sought to obtain insights into how the collective impact framework is applied and interpreted in collective impact initiatives by social enterprise organizations for issues of concern (e.g., health, aging, aged care, unemployment) in Australia. Factors for successful collaborative initiatives were found to refer to three overarching categories: organizational, relational and leadership. Collective impact is conceptualized as a cross-sector approach and is inclusive of diverse professions and organizations to achieve large-scale social impact through network-based interorganizational collaborations.

The collective impact framework guided the identification of a mechanism that LIS professionals can apply to contribute to achieving the SDGs and was critical in the development of the IABs to advance the 17 areas of sustainability related to the SDGs

[1]. Albright, Chu, Du, and Mehra [1] conceptualized the IAB as a collectivist approach and a multi-purpose tool that incorporates elements of a policy statement, research and education approach, and social awareness campaign, and as an instrument of transformation to foster actions (p. 267). LIS professionals are encouraged to utilize the IAB as a collaborative mechanism to identify issues, develop innovations and solutions from an information perspective to achieve SDGs and operationalize them in information-related work (i.e., transformational information actions), and to generate greater impact in practice, service/community engagement, education, and research [14].

An underlying consideration in the operationalization of the collective impact framework via the design and development of the IABs involves how diverse professionals and their organizations can build network-based interorganizational collaborations and measure them effectively. The International Organization of Standardization ISO 16439 (Information and documentation: Methods and procedures for assessing the impact of libraries, 2014, rev. 2019) contributes to the SDGs and can provide some directions in this regard for future consideration [10]. Currently, the sole initiative relies predominantly on the leadership and willingness of individuals and their networking, skills, and existing opportunities to draw synergies and collaborations related to SDG work across organizations. A strong approach emerging from the professional groupings and collectives (e.g., associations) in the development of committees and taskforces that intentionally apply their efforts around topics connected to the UN SGDs is needed. For example, the International Federation of Library Associations and Institutions (IFLA) (n.d.) has provided a modest start as reflected on its website "Powering Sustainable Development" that features important news, events, and resources. The American Library Association's [9] "ALA Task Force on United Nations 2030 Sustainable Development Goals" is planning a multi-year strategic effort to increase library participation in achieving the SDGs. One can surmise that these efforts will see libraries falling short of meeting the UN's agenda.

The development and authoring of an IAB requires social considerations of information research, education, and practice for the social good to make a difference at social, cultural, political, and economic levels, which are aligned within the framework of collective impact. In accordance with the collective impact concept, the IAB aims to promote and facilitate LIS professionals to engage in discussions and actions, intentionally and systematically, tackling society's grand challenges by shaping progressive changes and advancing the SDGs [2].

3   What and How: An IAB Example (SDG 16)

We designed the IAB to inspire and mobilize the library and information community to act locally or globally, personally, or collectively. The IAB uses the format of a policy brief and serves as a resource and action guide to develop and create transformational actions using information to advance the SDGs. We operationalized the format of the IAB as a 4-page document that consists of the following:

Page 1. What is the goal? [Authors write one clear and succinct phrase of the SDG goal/issue within an information context.]

Page 2. Why should we care? [Authors describe the issue/background (evidence, examples, etc.) in terms of what is creating the challenges in the goal/issue.]

Page 3. This consists of three parts:

- How is it related to information? [Authors discuss and select illustrative examples of how information is used/relevant to address the challenges in the goal/issue.]
- What can I (or the profession) do? [Authors identify strategic action items that the individual and/or groups can undertake. They list 10 actions that can then be grouped with relevant text into categories of practice, service/engagement (civic, professional, community, institutional), education, and research to reach/address the goal/issue.]
- Summary [Authors provide a closing summarizing statement.]

Page 4: Infographics [Authors identify graphics to create an infographic that will be created as the 4th page and can stand on its own to visually present the goal/issue].

This framework has been applied to produce four IABs for the following SDGs respectively: SDG 12: Responsible Production and Consumption; SDG 13: Climate Action; SDG 16: Peace, Justice and Strong Institutions, and SDG 17: Partnerships for the Goals. The following is an analysis of one SDG, SDG 16: Peace, Justice, and Strong Institutions, to spotlight the process and product of the efforts.

We first developed the title of the IAB for SDG 16 in an information context with the addition of "advancing" that served as an ongoing active verb [Title: Advancing Peace, Justice and Strong Institutions Within an Information Context]. The goal of the IAB for SDG 16 was created keeping in mind the inclusion of active verbs to "Create, provide access to, and manage information (e.g., acquire, organize, preserve, etc.) to advance and ensure peace, justice, and strong institutions for all" [1]. An opening narrative of why information professionals should care was developed around the idea that information can empower people and institutions via its role to "educate and inform" that can lead to "wise and judicious decisions" as compared to situations where there is a lack of information. The relationship of such scenarios to emerging threats in the advancement of peaceful and inclusive societies was discussed with specific examples. The team analyzed the connection to how this was related directly to information via illustrative cases discussing: 1) Information Access and Women; 2) Media and Information Literacy; 3) ICT Use and Civil Society. Actions for social transformation in various domains of application via information-related work were listed in actual actions that we can pursue in our various roles and capacities as information professionals. Appropriate and relevant graphics were also provided.

The published IABs are part of Libraries for Sustainable Development (LSD), a project of the Libraries for Peace Initiative of the Mortenson Center for International Library Programs at the University of Illinois at Urbana-Champaign, USA. Through its website Mortenson Center for International Library Programs [21], LSD promotes the UN SDGs by serving as a hub for resources on library efforts to advance sustainable development across the globe, and the access point to the IAB series. The IABs are freely available and can be used by library and information professionals to inform practice individually or collectively, by policymakers to enact policy or actions to ensure access to information to drive sustainability, by educators who teach information for social transformation and local and global impart, and by other stakeholders around the world interested in how information can deliver on the SDGs. To ensure access, the IABs may be translated into other languages.

The following are suggestions helpful in writing an effective IAB:

- Strategically reflect upon a focused area where information-related work is aligned with and advances the SDG(s) or their sub-topics and select it for developing the IAB.
- Identify and provide evidence-based information and rationale for a compelling and valid narrative.
- Use clear, succinct, and persuasive language, staying away from jargon.
- Identify quotes, graphics and illustrative content that is relevant to and can be understood by an international audience.
- Propose actions in the four different areas that are realistic and can be carried out in diverse contexts, globally, or if the IAB is for a targeted community, appropriate for the specific context.
- Work collaboratively or have others review your content.

4 Applying the IAB Framework in Global Contexts

The LSD website and IABs were launched on March 9, 2023, in the form of a webinar panel with the team and several authors presenting their experiences. Panelists illustrated how the IABs can be used in diverse ways in teaching, research, and practice [2], as shown below:

4.1 Reflective Practice of Global Content Integration

Mark Mattson (Head of Global Engagement Initiatives and International Partnerships Librarian, Penn State University), an IAB author, used the research and writing process to do big thinking in his academic librarian's position while developing partnerships for world betterment. He urged others to address questions like how librarianship (and/with others) can contribute to these issues in thinking about their place in a global society; how others can integrate IABs in LIS education; and in projects of data management (inter-related or separate). Through the process of authoring an IAB, he was able to distill the individual SDGs into relevant and actionable strategies, to recognize the connection through a facilitated process while developing a professional network and engage in creative collaboration especially across global contexts.

4.2 Classroom Integration in Teaching of Recordkeeping Informatics

In the application of the IABs in their own work, IAB author *Gillian Oliver* (Professor, Department of Human Centered Computing, Monash University) brought in a mixture of perspectives from a practitioner's and academic's point of view. She indicated that the IABs provided a practical tool giving her insight into the SDGs and how she could use them in teaching via creative strategies in assignment formulation. Discussing the experiences and applications in the classroom, she illustrated the example of her Recordkeeping Informatics course taught in the Master of Information Systems program at Monash University. Oliver discussed how the IABs had served as an excellent medium to connect with the mainly international students in the elective course while teaching communications and recordkeeping as evidence in decision-making. The key challenge was how to communicate the critical nature of records and archives in the workplace.

4.3 Connections to Social Justice and Action Research

For *Bharat Mehra* (EBSCO Endowed Chair in Social Justice and Professor, School of Library and Information Studies, University of Alabama), IAB team leader, Series Editor and author, "actions" in the framework builds on his past social justice research with underserved populations, e.g., African American women [13, 15] lesbian, gay, bisexual, and transgender communities [18, 20]; and rural libraries [16]. It connected him with co-conspirators to help shift the positionality of action research in resistance to the postpositivist hegemony in the information field [19]. Mehra described information actions in a newly released edited collection, *How Public Libraries Build Sustainable Communities in the 21st Century* [23]. He concluded with his current involvement in the *Civic Engagement for Racial Justice in Public Libraries* grant awarded by the Institute of Museum and Library Services that applies a logic model to further collective action [17].

4.4 Partnership-Building and Strategic Planning

Jia Tina Du (formerly Professional Lead, UniSA STEM, University of South Australia), IAB team leader, Series Editor, and author, used the IAB for both partnership- building in research and as a strategic planning tool in the workplace. Trust relationships and community-driven engagement are fundamental to her research with migrants for social capital development [6, 12] and Aboriginal communities for knowledge continuity [8]. As part of the research strategy to foster and strengthen research partnerships with industry, community, and end-users, the IAB is a useful tool outlining research goals, motivations, actions, and an infographic with potential research partners.

4.5 Knowledge Management in Community Context

Kendra S. Albright (Goodyear Endowed Professor in Knowledge Management, School of Information, Kent State University), IAB team leader, Series Editor, and author, used the IAB for SDG 17 to create a knowledge portal for Cleveland, Ohio. Working with multi-sectoral stakeholders, the portal will serve as the foundation for identifying and sharing community and knowledge resources to build a sustainable future. She uses the proposed actions from the existing IAB for SDG 17 as a checklist: Actively work with partners; identify the barriers of positive perception about the value of information professionals with external stakeholders; and aim to achieve collective social impact of research and practice both locally and globally, demonstrating that the IABs can be used by any professional to address the SDGs, create/propel action and guide one's work.

5 Call for Actions

We have published four IABs and plan to develop the remaining SDGs in relation to other social issues as we research and provide solutions using the IAB framework. The LSD website and IABs are public freely accessible resources to promote sustainable development within the LIS community and stakeholders, and for those wishing to learn and author an IAB, we invite LIS professionals to:

- Join a scheduled workshop in-person or online
- Invite us to present a workshop in-person or online
- Use the materials online and submit an IAB for publication
- Use the materials online, produce your own IAB, and let us know about your experience
- Use the IABs and take up the actions
- Use the resources to learn about libraries for sustainable development
- Use the IABs to teach the UN SDGs
- Author an IAB in non-English languages and submit for publication
- Translate existing IABs into other languages
- Propose to edit an IAB series on a specific scope, e.g., geographic area, a sub-topic of an SDG, action by a specific type of library and information organization.

This paper provides professionals with an opportunity to glimpse our conceptualization and implementation of the IABs as a tool to represent our information-related efforts in relation to the UN SDGs for generating greater collective impact within and beyond our local and global communities. We hope readers will be similarly inspired to use the IABs in a variety of ways to conduct their own research and document their work while integrating the SDGs towards greater relevance and impact of their efforts in their information work environments and beyond.

Acknowledgements. We appreciate the involvement and participation of IAB team leader Kendra S. Albright, and IAB authors Mark Allen Mattson (Penn State University), Gillian Oliver (Monash University), Bhuva Narayan (University of Technology), and Chris Cyr (OCLC) in the IAB development process and/or sharing their experiences noted in this paper.

References

1. Albright, K., Chu, C.M., Du, J.T., Mehra, B. (n.d.).: Advancing Peace, Justice and Strong Institutions Within an Information Context. Mortenson Center for International Library Programs. https://sdglibact.web.illinois.edu/wp-content/uploads/2023/03/SDG16.pdf
2. Albright, K., Chu, C.M., Du, J.T., Mehra, B., Mattson, M., Oliver, G.: Mobilizing libraries for sustainable development: A website and information action briefs. [Webinar]. Mortenson Center for International Library Programs (2023). https://mediaspace.illinois.edu/media/t/1_23kzlnr3/160939361
3. American Library Association. (n.d.): ALA Task Force on United Nations 2030 Sustainable Development Goals. https://www.ala.org/aboutala/ala-task-force-united-nations-2030-sustainable-development-goals
4. Christens, B.D., Inzeo, P.T.: Widening the view: Situating collective impact among frameworks for community-led change. Community Dev. **46**(4), 420–435 (2015). https://doi.org/10.1080/15575330.2015.1061680
5. Chu, C. (n.d.): Decade of Action: Ten Years to Transform Our World. [Video]. Mortenson Center for International Library Programs. https://uofi.app.box.com/s/2ia9fjtlvdkygyn iw7ov7xp7qvmhejb9
6. Du, J.T.: Understanding the information journeys of late-life migrants to inform support design: information seeking driven by a major life transition. Inf. Process. Manage. **60**(2) (2023). https://doi.org/10.1016/j.ipm.2022.103172

7. Du, J.T., Chu, C.M.: Toward community-engaged information behavior research: A methodological framework. Library Inf. Sci. Res. **44**(4) (2022). https://doi.org/10.1016/j.lisr.2022.101189
8. Haines, J., Du, J.T., Trevorrow, E.: Cultural use of ICT4D to promote Indigenous knowledge continuity of Ngarrindjeri stories and communal practices. Journal of the Association for Information Science and Technology (2022). Open Access from https://doi.org/10.1002/asi.24710
9. International Federation of Library Associations and Institutions. (n.d.). Powering Sustainable Development. https://www.ifla.org/units/sustainable-development/
10. International Organization of Standardization. (2014, rev. 2019). ISO 16439 (Information and documentation: Methods and procedures for assessing the impact of libraries). https://www.iso.org/standard/56756.html
11. Kania, J., Kramer, M.: Collective impact. Stanford Social Innovation Review. Winter 2011 (2011). www.ssireview.org/articles/entry/collective_impact
12. Khoir, S., Du, J.T., Davison, R., Koronios, A.: Contributing to social capital: an investigation of Asian immigrants' use of public library services. Libr. Inf. Sci. Res.. Inf. Sci. Res. **39**(1), 34–45 (2017)
13. Mehra, B.: An Action Research (AR) Manifesto for Cyberculture Power to "Marginalized" Cultures of Difference. In: Silver, D., Massanari, A. (eds.) Critical Cyber-Culture Studies, pp. 205–215. New York University Press, New York (2006)
14. Mehra, B., Albright, K., and Du, J.T.: President-Elect's international incubator: Transformational actions using information to advance the UN Sustainable Development Goals. Workshop presented at the 82nd Annual Meeting of the Association for Information Science and Technology, Melbourne, Australia, October 19–23 (2019)
15. Mehra, B., Bishop, A.P., Bazzell, I., Smith, C.: Scenarios in the afya project as a participatory action research (PAR) tool for studying information seeking and use across the "digital divide." J. Am. Soc. Inf. Sci. Technol. **53**(14), 1259–1266 (2002)
16. Mehra, B., Bishop, B.W., Partee, R.P., II.: A case methodology of action research to promote economic development: implications for LIS education. J. Educ. Libr. Inf. Sci. **59**(1–2), 48–65 (2018)
17. Mehra, B., Black, K.: Civic Engagement for Racial Justice in Public Libraries (RJ@PL) (funded grant). Institute of Museum and Library Services, National Leadership Grants for Libraries (NLG-L) – FY 2022 Guidelines (Implementation – Project Type), August 2022 – July 2025 (University of Alabama and Chicago State University) [PI: B. Mehra. Co-PI: K. Black]. [LG-252354-OLS-22] (2022). https://www.imls.gov/grants/awarded/lg-252354-ols-22
18. Mehra, B., Braquet, D.: Library and information science professionals as community action researchers in an academic setting: top ten directions to further institutional change for people of diverse sexual orientations and gender identities. Libr. Trends **56**(2), Fall 2007, 542–565 (2007)
19. Mehra, B., Gray, L.: An "Owning Up" of White-IST Trends in LIS to Further Real Transformations. Library Quarterly **90**(2), 189–239 (2020)
20. Mehra, B., and Srinivasan, R.: The library-community convergence framework for community action: libraries as catalysts of social change. Libri: Int. J. Libraries Inf. Serv. **57**(3), 123–139 (2007)
21. Mortenson Center for International Library Programs. (n.d.). "Libraries for sustainable development." https://sdglibact.web.illinois.edu/
22. Salignac, F., Wilcox, T., Marjolin, A., Adams, S.: Understanding collective impact in Australia: a new approach to interorganizational collaboration. Aust. J. Manag.Manag. **43**(1), 91–110 (2018). https://doi.org/10.1177/0312896217705178

23. Williams-Cockfield, K.C., Mehra, B. (ed.) How Public Libraries Build Sustainable Communities in the 21st Century. (Advances in Librarianship, Volume 53). Bingley, United Kingdom: Emerald Group Publishing (2023)
24. UN Department of Economic and Social Affairs. (n.d.). The 17 Goals. Accessed from https://sdgs.un.org/goals

Extraction and Visualization of Geographical Spatio-Temporal Information from Chinese Historical Newspapers

Shaodan Sun[1] and Jun Deng[2(✉)]

[1] School of Information Management, Nanjing Agricultural University, Nanjing 210095, China
[2] School of Business and Management, Jilin University, Changchun 130015, China
dengjun9722@163.com

Abstract. This research introduces a comprehensive framework for the extraction and visualization of geographical spatio-temporal information from Chinese historical newspapers. The framework categorizes geographical entities into five major classes and employs advanced deep learning techniques, including LSTM, BERT, CRF, Biaffine Decoder, and Boundary Smoothing, to enhance precision in extraction. Besides, geocoding, and state-of-the-art visualization tools are integrated to facilitate the display of geographical entities on interactive maps. This paper emerges as a cornerstone for enhancing the accessibility, precision, and contextual richness of historical newspapers, thereby fostering advancements in historical research, toponym resolution, toponym linkage, and the development of comprehensive toponym dictionaries.

Keywords: Digital Humanities · Geographical Spatio-temporal Information · Chinese Historical Newspapers · Information Extraction · Deep Learning

1 Introduction

Spatio-temporal information refers to all relevant data that possess characteristics of both spatial location and dynamic change. It represents the cognitive outcomes of humans regarding the distribution, evolution processes, and interaction patterns of people, objects, events, and phenomena in geographical space. The temporal dimension is an indispensable element in the narrative of historical events, aiding scholars in elucidating the temporal changes that occur during event evolution and deepening their understanding of the origins and outcomes of these events. Spatial information descriptions often involve toponyms, which are unique names given to places or geographical entities, including cities, countries, regions, streets, lakes and more. These toponyms encapsulate diverse content spanning history, geography, language, economics, ethnicity, politics, and more. They represent the legacy of human activities across historical epochs, serving as foundational geographic information that contributes significantly to public knowledge.

Historical newspapers contain abundant geographical and time-related information, documenting numerous Points of Interests (POIs) [1]. The value of these POIs data is

I. Sserwanga et al. (Eds.): iConference 2024, LNCS 14596, pp. 12–19, 2024.
https://doi.org/10.1007/978-3-031-57850-2_2

crucial for constructing historical information systems. By identifying and extracting toponyms, locations, dates, and other information from newspapers, we can help reconstruct the spatial distribution and time sequences of past events. This process reveals the connections and impacts among historical events, facilitating a better understanding of the geographical layout and societal activities of specific time periods. It is of significant value in researching urban evolution, political changes, economic development, social culture, and other aspects. Moreover, it holds important significance for accessing historical newspaper content, toponym resolution, linking knowledge bases, and toponym dictionaries [2].

Currently, there is a significant amount of research dedicated to the extraction of entities from historical newspapers. HIPE (Identifying Historical People, Places, and other Entities) is a specialized entity identification conference focused on historical newspapers [3]. It is part of the CLEF (Conference and Labs of the Evaluation Forum) subtask and evaluates named entity processing for French, German, and English historical newspapers. However, the task of extracting location-related entities is limited to administrative regions and does not encompass POIs data. Furthermore, it is not suitable for Chinese historical newspapers. Extracting entities from Chinese historical newspapers is more complex compared to general Named Entity Recognition (NER) tasks, and it involves several challenges: (1) The complexity of Chinese character composition and variants adds to the difficulty of the task, requiring models to handle these intricacies effectively. (2) The lack of standardized textual formats, including variations in punctuation, capitalization, and orthography, makes it challenging to accurately define entity boundaries and interpret context. (3) An important obstacle in Chinese historical NER is the scarcity of meticulously annotated datasets, especially for specific historical periods. This necessitates relying on domain expertise for effective data annotation.

To address these issues, this study uses the compilation of excerpts from the Chinese "*Shengjing Times*" as an example to build a framework for extracting and utilizing geographical spatio-temporal information. It constructs a multi-type geographical spatio-temporal information annotation structure and employs deep learning techniques to extract geographical spatio-temporal information. The study also focuses on parsing and visually presenting this information for research purposes.

2 Cultural Background

"*Shengjing Times*" was a Chinese newspaper founded by Nakashima Masao on the 1st day of September in the 32nd year of the Guangxu reign (October 18, 1906) in Shenyang. It had a wide circulation in Northeast China, North China, and even some cities in Southeast Asia with Chinese-speaking communities. The newspaper ceased publication in 1944. The publication primarily focused on domestic current affairs and commentary. It served as a comprehensive source of information on various aspects such as finance, commerce, transportation, education, literature, and more in the northeastern region. It is considered a precious historical document for researching the history of resistance against Japanese invasion by both civilians and the Northeast Army, the history of warlords in the Beiyang government, and Chinese history. The newspaper featured sections like editorials, news from the capital, news from the three northeastern provinces, international news, special reports, official documents, street interviews, and colloquial language. It contained a wealth of geographical spatio-temporal information. They hold significant importance for acquiring historical newspaper contents, toponym resolution, linking toponym knowledge databases, constructing toponym dictionaries, and even building historical spatio-temporal systems.

3   Method Framework

The study focused on data processing, construction of geographical spatio-temporal information framework, annotation of geographical spatio-temporal information, extraction of geographical spatio-temporal information, visualization of geographical entities (Fig. 1). This framework describes in detail the research process and the methodology basis of each step.

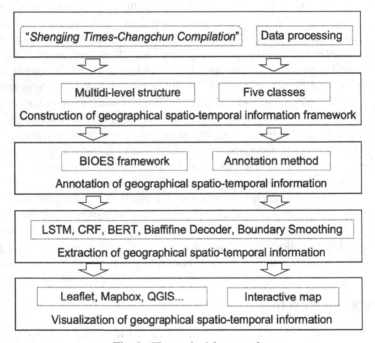

Fig. 1. The method framework.

3.1   Dataset and Processing

For our empirical research, we have selected the "*Shengjing Times-Changchun Compilation*", which spans from Issue No. 1 on September 1st of the 32nd year of the Guangxu reign (October 18, 1906), to Issue No. 1584 on December 29th of the 3rd year of the Xuantong reign (February 16, 1912). This dataset comprises approximately 727,978 words and was collaboratively compiled and meticulously edited over several years by academic institutions in Changchun. It was published in 2005 and chronicles the history of the late Qing dynasty, including the Guangxu Volume and the Xuantong Volume. According to this dataset, text cleaning was performed to eliminate noise, including special characters, punctuation, and any irrelevant information. Following this, the text underwent segmentation and tokenization to break it down into manageable linguistic units.

3.2 Construction of Geographical Spatio-Temporal Information Framework

Based on the categorization of geographical spatio-temporal entities [4] and considering the characteristics of historical newspaper resources, we have summarized and classified the following 5 major categories of spatio-temporal entities (Table 1). By organizing and categorizing this information into specific classes, we can gain a better understanding of the geographical context and spatio-temporal relationships of historical events. Such classification aids research in various fields including history, culture, society, and economics, while also providing valuable data for geographic information systems and the field of geography itself. Further subdividing the POI category allows for more precise tracking of developments in specific domains, such as healthcare, government, and cultural education, facilitating in-depth studies of the historical evolution and trends within each area.

3.3 Annotation of Geographical Spatio-Temporal Information

We have carefully selected a segment from the "*Shengjing Times-Changchun Compilation*," comprising around 350,000 words, which underwent meticulous manual proofreading and processing. Subsequently, we plan to involve a team of researchers specializing in archives, sociology, history, and literature for comprehensive training in annotating geographical spatio-temporal information. This training will occur across two rounds, aiming to establish consistent and standardized annotation methodologies through detailed guidelines. To validate the annotations, two separate annotators will independently review the texts, resolving any discrepancies through discussions. Our approach emphasizes continuous communication and rigorous quality control measures, including thorough proofreading, to ensure the final annotations exhibit high reliability, precision, and accuracy.

Table 1. Geographical spatio-temporal information framework.

Dimension	Description
[Country]	Include the names of various countries or regions. Countries are significant units in both geographical and political contexts, and they typically appear in historical newspapers under their official or common names
[Region]	Encompass various geographical areas such as states, provinces, counties, cities, and more. These regions are commonly used in historical newspapers to describe the locations of events or the geographic scope of related information
[Street]	Refer to specific street names, roads, or districts. This information helps us understand the specific location or path of events, especially within urban environments
POI	[POI-Med] Encompass information about hospitals, clinics, and other healthcare facilities, contributing to an understanding of developments in healthcare
	[POI-Gov] Cover government agencies, government offices, and departments, assisting in tracking political and administrative events
	[POI-Lif] Include information about stores, supermarkets, restaurants, banks, and other providers of life services, reflecting the characteristics of social and commercial activities
	[POI-Tra] Encompass information about train stations, airports, ports, and other transportation facilities, aiding in understanding developments in transportation
	[POI-Cul] Cover museums, schools, libraries, and other cultural and educational institutions, highlighting important events in the fields of education and culture
	[POI-Bus] Include various companies, enterprises, factories, and other business entities, helping to track business activities and industrial developments
	[POI-Bui] Encompass information about buildings, iconic structures, and architectural landmarks, crucial for understanding urban landscapes and architectural developments
	[POI-Nat] Include natural geographical landmarks such as mountain ranges, rivers, lakes, and more, providing insights into the evolution and impact of the natural environment
Time	Represent temporal information, such as dates, years, and time periods

Besides, in terms of the annotation framework selection, we have opted for the BIOES labeling system. This framework enables us to precisely annotate and categorize entities in the text with labels representing the beginning (B), inside (I), outside (O), end (E), and single (S) positions of entities. It precisely marks the start, end, and interior parts of entities within a sequence of words or characters, enhancing the accuracy of models in identifying entity boundaries and types. The samples are as illustrated in Table 2.

3.4 Extraction of Geographical Spatio-Temporal Information

We intend to use CRF, RNN, BiLSTM-CRF, BERT-BiLSTM-CRF [5] as the baseline models, which are the sequence labeling models commonly employed for extracting the

Table 2. Labels samples.

E/俄 O	Jin/近 S-Time	Zheng/正 B-POI-Bus
Bing/兵 O	Wen/闻 O	Jin/金 I-POI-Bus
Er/二 O	Chang/长 B-POI-Gov	Yin/银 I-POI-Bus
Wan/万 O	Chun/春 I-POI-Gov	Hang/行 E-POI-Bus
Yu/余 O	Fu/府 E-POI-Gov	Chao/钞 O
Ming/名 O	Di/地 O	Piao/票 O
Zhu/驻 O	Mian/面 O	Chang/常 O
Ji/吉 B-Region	Shen/甚 O	Tong/通 O
Lin/林 I-Region	Jue/觉 O	Xing/行 O
Sheng/省 E-Region	Huo/活 O	
Cheng/城 O	Po/泼 O	

aforementioned five major categories of geographical spatio-temporal entities. Building upon these models, we will incorporate the combination of the Biaffine Decoder and Boundary Smoothing methods [6] to enhance our entity extraction performance. In this combined approach, BERT will be utilized to capture bidirectional contextual information for each token. BERT's robust capabilities enable it to better comprehend the context and contextual relationships within the text, thereby facilitating more accurate entity recognition. Simultaneously, we will introduce the Biaffine Decoder and Boundary Smoothing methods. The Biaffine Decoder is a model architecture used for sequence labeling tasks that aids in better modeling relationships between labels. The Boundary Smoothing method aims to address the issue of discontinuous label boundaries by introducing a smoothing factor, encouraging the model to make smoother decisions regarding the placement of label boundaries, thereby improving the accuracy of entity recognition.

The entire process involves using BERT embeddings as features for each token, feeding them into a label prediction layer, typically implemented with the Biaffine Decoder, and then combining them with the Boundary Smoothing method to achieve smoother label transitions. Ultimately, the generated probabilities will be thresholded to assign final entity labels, resulting in a significant improvement in the accuracy of recognizing geographical spatio-temporal entities across various types of textual data. This approach leverages the strengths of BERT in understanding context while harnessing the consistency-enhancing properties of the Boundary Smoothing method, providing a powerful tool for enhancing entity recognition accuracy in diverse textual data.

4   Visualization of Geographical Spatio-Temporal Information

To visualize the distribution of geographical spatio-temporal entities extracted from historical newspapers on a map, we use map visualization tools such as Leaflet, Mapbox, QGIS and more to create an interactive map [7]. On this map, we can mark the geographical spatio-temporal entities extracted from historical newspapers as points and differentiate them using various markers or colors based on different types of place names and POIs. This kind of visualization allows users to explore the spatial distribution of locations, understand the density of place names, and observe distribution trends.

Additionally, we provide users with the option to access more information about these place names and POIs when needed. This interactive map can serve as a valuable tool for researchers and historians to gain insights into the geographical patterns and historical context of the spatio-temporal entities mentioned in historical newspapers.

5   Conclusion

This research is pivotal in constructing a robust framework for classifying geographical spatio-temporal information sourced from Chinese historical newspapers. It intricately categorizes geographical entities into five primary classes and harnesses advanced deep learning methodologies, including CRF, CNN, BiLSTM-CRF, BERT-BiLSTM-CRF, alongside innovative techniques like the Biaffine Decoder and Boundary Smoothing, to facilitate precise extraction. Additionally, the integration of geocoding and cutting-edge visualization tools empowers the creation of interactive maps that vividly display place-name entities. It bestows a structured approach to organize and analyze geographical spatio-temporal data within historical contexts, thus providing invaluable support for historical research. By adopting these advanced extraction methods, it enhances the quality and efficiency of data extraction, ultimately enriching the historical data available for analysis. Moreover, these techniques unveil intricate spatial and temporal patterns embedded within the historical newspaper data, enriching our understanding of historical events, place names, and their evolutionary trajectories.

However, it is essential to acknowledge certain limitations. Data quality remains a pertinent concern as the precision of geographical spatio-temporal information hinges upon the accuracy and consistency of historical newspaper archives. Furthermore, while geocoding is a valuable tool, it may not consistently provide precise coordinates for historical place names and POIs, especially if they have undergone changes over time. The complexity of historical data, characterized by nuanced language and archaic terminology, can also pose challenges to automated extraction methods, necessitating manual verification and correction in certain cases.

In summary, this research will provide some help in the structured extraction and visualization of geographical spatio-temporal information from Chinese historical newspapers. It offers valuable insights, tools, and methodologies to researchers and historians for deepening their understanding of geographical contexts.

Acknowledgments. This study was funded by the National Social Science Fund, China: "Research on archival data resources mining and intelligent service under the cultural digitization strategy"(23ATQ001).

References

1. Ardanuy, M.C., Hosseini, K., McDonough, K., Krause, A., van Strien, D., Nanni, F.: A deep learning approach to geographical candidate selection through toponym matching. In: Proceedings of the 28th International Conference on Advances in Geographic Information Systems, pp. 385–388 (2020)

2. Ardanuy, M.C., McDonough, K., Krause, A., Wilson, D.C., Hosseini, K., Van Strien, D.: Resolving places, past and present: toponym resolution in historical British newspapers using multiple resources. In: Proceedings of the 13th Workshop on Geographic Information Retrieval, pp. 1–6 (2019)
3. Boros, E., Pontes, E.L., Cabrera-Diego, L.A., Hamdi, A., Moreno, J. G., Sidère, N., Doucet, A.: Robust named entity recognition and linking on historical multilingual documents. In: Conference and Labs of the Evaluation Forum, Online, **2696**(171), 1–17 (2020)
4. Cadorel, L., Blanchi, A., Tettamanzi, A.G.: Geospatial knowledge in housing advertise-ments: Capturing and extracting spatial information from text. In: Proceedings of the 11th on Knowledge Capture Conference, pp. 41–48 (2021)
5. Labusch, K., Kulturbesitz, P., Neudecker, C., Zellhöfer, D.: BERT for named entity recog-nition in and historical German. In: Proceedings of the 15th conference on natural language processing, Erlangen, Germany, pp. 8–11. (2019)
6. Zhu, E.W., Li, J.P.: Boundary smoothing for named entity recognition, arXiv preprint arXiv: 2204.12031 (2022)
7. Hu, Y., Mao, H., McKenzie, G.: A natural language processing and geospatial clustering framework for harvesting local place names from geotagged housing advertisements. Int. J. Geogr. Inf. Sci. **33**(4), 714–738 (2019)

Identifying the Potential Users of Community Archives: A Case Study of the History of the Chinese 30 Years Project

Tianji Jiang(ID) and Jiarui Sun(✉)(ID)

University of California, Los Angeles, Los Angeles, CA 90095, USA
sunjiarui@ucla.edu

Abstract. This article employs ethnographic research methods, encompassing participant observation, informal conversations, and document analysis, to conduct a case study of the *History of the Chinese 30 Years* project, a digital archive project initiated by the Southern California Foundation for the Preservation of Chinese Literature and History. The primary focus of this article is to report on how the foundation identified and understood its potential users when initiating a digital archive project, as well as the challenges encountered in engaging them. The contribution of this article lies in enriching the discussion on the autonomy of community archives, delineating the considerations of community archives in relation to potential users at the outset of their establishment, and laying the groundwork for potential strategies proposed by archival professionals in the future.

Keywords: Community Archives · Archival users · Autonomy · Chinese Americans

1 Introduction

Autonomy is crucial for community archives, as it means that community members can independently decide what materials to collect, how to describe these materials, and who can use them. Among these issues, the question of who can have access to these materials reflects the concern of the users of community archives. In fact, from the inception of community archives, there has been consideration of identifying potential users, rather than after their establishment. In this study, we found that the autonomy of community archives also means that community members can independently determine who the potential users of archival materials are. This holds significant implications for the overall planning and development of community archives.

Although there is a considerable body of published work emphasizing the importance of being autonomous for community archives, there has been limited empirical research that investigate the identification of potential users by community members before the establishment of community archives, as well as the challenges they encounter in engaging these potential users. This paper aims to bridge this gap by presenting the findings of an ethnographic case study of the Southern California Foundation for the Preservation

I. Sserwanga et al. (Eds.): iConference 2024, LNCS 14596, pp. 20–27, 2024.
https://doi.org/10.1007/978-3-031-57850-2_3

of Chinese Literature and History as they endeavor to establish a digital archive. During the initial digital archive development, the board members of the foundation engaged in numerous discussions centered around a fundamental question: "Who could (and should) be our potential users?" Through their discussions and, at times, debates, we have the opportunity to observe and reflect upon the diverse users a community archive aims to engage, as well as the challenges faced in reaching and attracting them.

2 Background

Southern California Foundation for the Preservation of Chinese Literature and History is an independent nonprofit community-based organization which supports collecting, organizing, preserving, and providing access to materials focusing on the history and literature of Chinese Americans in Southern California. To collect, preserve and showcase the remarkable and transformative transformation of Chinese American communities in Southern California over the course of three decades, the foundation launched the *History of Chinese 30 Years* project in 2009. This project spanned four years, during which more than five hundred oral histories were created, over two hundred related books and publications were collected, along with thousands of newspaper clippings, over a thousand immigrant family surveys, and more than a thousand photographs, among other materials. All these archival materials were compiled into a comprehensive publication titled "*A Legacy Magnified: A Generation of Chinese Americans in Southern California (1980's – 2010's),*" preserving and showcasing the struggles and achievements of the Chinese community in Southern California over the thirty-year period from the 1980s to the first decade of the 21st century.

The foundation is in the process of planning the establishment of a digital archive for preserving and utilizing the archival materials (e.g., oral histories, newspaper clippings, photographs, and so forth) gathered throughout the *History of Chinese 30 Years* project, with the aim of increasing awareness of Chinese American history and stories and further expanding the project's impact.

3 Literature Review

Over the past two decades, the topics of community archives and community archiving practices have gradually garnered attention and discussion within the field of archival studies. In 2009, UK-based scholars Flinn, Stevens, and Shepherd [1] defined "community archives" as "collections of materials gathered primarily by members of a given community and over whose use community members exercise some level of control." In the US, the phenomenon of community archives is inextricably linked to power and oppression [2]. Caswell et al. [3] argued "those who have been disempowered by oppressive systems, those who have been 'symbolically annihilated', those whose histories have been ignored, maligned, misrepresented, and/or grossly distorted by mainstream memory institutions, feel the need to create their own autonomous community archives."

Current research revolves around topics such as community archives and identity, community archives and empowerment, and how community archives challenge traditional dominant archival theories and practices. Kaplan [4] argued that "it is critical that archivists and their collaborators consider the connections between archives and the construction of identity," which had laid a strong theoretical foundation for research on community archives and identity. However, the discourse of identity influenced by postmodernism has also been questioned by scholars. Paschild [5] believed that "an overarching emphasis on the questions of identity can distract community institutions from pragmatic evaluations of sustainable practice and can inadvertently mire archivists in a marginalizing rhetoric that blurs the issues at hand." Researchers also examined the intricate interplay between community archives and empowerment, shedding light on how archives have the potential to "empower community members to activate records and build corollary moments across space and time" [6]. In addition, scholars [7–9] have also investigated how community archives challenge the concepts, theories, and practices of dominant archival studies.

As a direct response to the failure of mainstream repositories in capturing a more accurate and comprehensive representation of society [10], community archives can be viewed as an endeavor to take control of the narrative of history and rectify or amend dominant stories about the past [11]. Therefore, autonomy, participation, activism, and so forth, are considered as community archives principles [12]. For community archives, maintaining autonomy is particularly crucial, as these materials "not only act as a resource for research but also as the context and backdrop for social activities, political organization, emotional responses in a space belonging to the community independent and separate from hostile or prejudiced external forces" [13].

While there is a significant amount of research on the autonomy of community archives, current research, and discussions on the identification of potential users at the outset of community archives are extremely limited. To address this research gap, this study uses the example of the *History of the Chinese 30 Years* project initiated by the Southern California Foundation for the Preservation of Chinese Literature and History to explore who their potential users are, and the challenges encountered in reaching and attracting them.

4   Methodology

This ethnographic research uses participant observation, informal conversations, and document analysis as primary methods of inquiry. In the late twentieth and early twenty-first centuries, ethnographic research methods began to be employed in archival studies [14–16]. Ethnography enables us to integrate "first-hand empirical investigation with the theoretical interpretation of social organization and culture" [17]. The first author of this paper has volunteered as a technology consultant for the Southern California Foundation for the Preservation of Chinese Literature and History since 2021. Throughout this period, he attended all regular board meetings and luncheons and had access to rich firsthand email correspondence and group social media chats. The foundation holds quarterly board meetings involving nine members. This study analyzes minutes from the last four meetings, which were initiated during deliberations about a digital archive project. Additionally, it integrates written conversations among board members conducted through email and group social media chats.

Furthermore, we undertook this research, focusing on a singular, information-rich case, to attain a comprehensive understanding and derive insights that can be generalized and applied to broader contexts. We anticipate that the findings from this study could also benefit the Southern California Foundation for the Preservation of Chinese Literature and History.

5 Findings

The study has illuminated various potential users of the *History of the Chinese 30 Years* project, based on meticulous observational research. The potential users, as identified by community members, can be initially categorized into two distinct groups: academic users and non-academic users. Among non-academic users, they can be further divided into the individuals within the Chinese American community and those outside of it. In addition to identifying potential users, the authors have also identified the obstacles that impede the foundation's accessibility to these individuals.

5.1 The Academic Users

Academic users are recognized by most of the board members as potential users of the *History of the Chinese 30 Years* project. The background of the board members likely accounts for this recognition, given that three of them have previous experience as faculty members in research institutions. Moreover, the remaining members have also had significant interactions with research institutions in the past. The archival materials are expected to provide a unique foundation upon which researchers can uncover new insights. For example, board member Mr. W said:

When we worked on our physical materials, many academic institutions were very interested and had high expectations for our work. I know some of them well. Some academic institutions have purchased the publication we have compiled. So, I'm confident that these academic institutions will also be interested in our digital archives. That's why I suggest we make academic research institutions our main users.

However, several obstacles emerged during the discussion. Firstly, community members lack the knowledge regarding archives and the expertise needed to ensure the quality of oral histories. This deficiency in knowledge and training has resulted in numerous inaccuracies, inconsistencies, formatting problems, and legal issues within archives.

As board member Mr. L pointed out during the discussion:

I talked to Ms. C, the director of the East Asian Library at University X, about our digital archive project. She was interested in our work but brought up some concerns we hadn't thought about before, such as the need to keep important context with our interview audio and getting consent from people who contribute to our archives. It made me realize that we don't have the necessary expertise to create high-quality archival materials for research purposes without professional help.

Board member Ms. CM, who is responsible for preserving all the existing materials for the digital archive, said in the discussion:

Ms. M (the secretary of the Foundation) and I have faced numerous challenges in our current work. Despite the East Asian Library at University X sharing their schema for describing digital items, we found some entries difficult to understand, let alone use them to describe our archive contents. Additionally, with the unfortunate passing of some of our members, we've lost valuable information (needed to describe certain archive contents). Moreover, considering my age (in my 80s) and Ms. M's age (over 60), it is impractical for us to maintain the energy required to continue working on the archive contents and bring them up to the academic standards.

Secondly, another challenge mentioned is raising the awareness within academia about this archive. Academics usually utilize their own platforms to access data, and the digital archive has limited opportunities to be integrated into these platforms and become visible to scholars. As Mr. L said:

Researchers have their own platforms for resource discovery. If our archives are not available on these platforms, how will researchers even become aware of our existence?

Thirdly, the archive predominantly contains content in Chinese. However, it is important to acknowledge that many scholars who might be interested in utilizing the archive, may have limited proficiency in the language. This language barrier can hinder their effective use of the archive as they may struggle to interpret the content.

5.2   Individuals Within the Chinese American Community

Board members have also identified non-academic users as their potential users of the archive, with the initial focus being on individuals within the Chinese American community. Chinese Americans encounter various identity-related challenges upon being part of this country. Since its inception, one of the foundation's central objectives has been to guide Southern California's Chinese American community in collectively preserving their entrepreneurial history and fostering a sense of identity deeply rooted in that history. This approach seeks to inspire them to embrace and celebrate their identities, recognizing them as sources of strength and richness in their lives. Consequently, it's unsurprising that Chinese Americans have been identified as primary potential users. As board member Mr. W said in the discussion:

We want (the digital archive) to demonstrate our community's contributions to the land we are living on and to answer simple inquiries (from people within our communities), such as: How is our political influence in Southern California? What is our contribution to the fields of education and philanthropy in Southern California? We need it to educate the younger generation about who we are, why we are here, our history of struggling for a better life on this land in Southern California, and to teach them to be proud of our identity.

Individuals within the Chinese American community are further divided into two generational subgroups. The board members anticipate that the senior generation, to which they belong, will be enthusiastic users of the digital archive, as these archives document their past lives. The primary barrier for some in this generation would be technological navigation skills. However, differing opinions exist among the board members regarding the younger generation as potential users of the digital archive. While some firmly believe that the younger generation will be eager to learn about the entrepreneurial history of their elders, others in the group hold a contrary view. Drawing from their own experiences, they feel that the history of the older generation has grown too distant from the lives of the younger generation. Consequently, even if the digital archive project is completed, it may face challenges in attracting a significant number of younger users. As board member Mr. L mentioned:

I don't believe that our younger generation will have much interest in delving into our past. Our previous life is quite distant from theirs, and they may struggle to understand or even imagine it. Even when I'm at home, my son and daughter rarely inquire about how my wife, and I came to the United States and how we established ourselves in this country. Therefore, I strongly suggest that we should not be overly optimistic about attracting a large number of younger users for our digital archive.

5.3 Individuals Outside the Chinese American Community

Individuals outside the Chinese American community are also proposed as potential users of the digital archive. Some board members expect the digital archive to attract the young people outside the Chinese American community. As board member Mr. L said:

We can also target young people learning Chinese as a goal of the digital archive. If our digital records also have both Chinese and English versions, just like the previous physical materials, by comparing and reading the Chinese and English versions, our digital archive can become ideal materials for young people to learn Chinese.

However, during the discussion, board members also highlighted several challenges that this proposal would encounter. Firstly, the content within the materials may lack inherent appeal, even among young individuals within the Chinese American community, making it even more challenging to attract youth from other communities. Secondly, despite the translation of all Chinese text materials into English through the "*A Legacy Magnified*" project, a substantial volume of interview videos, recordings, and historical photos – essential for inclusion in the digital archive – remain untranslated. Translating this extensive content would require a significant workload beyond the current foundation's capacity. Lastly, the translation of previous textual materials relied on volunteers. While these volunteers devoted considerable effort, the translations were occasionally inaccurate due to language limitations, resulting in inaccuracies and inconsistencies among the contents translated by different volunteers. Consequently, the current English version of the textual materials still contains numerous imperfections.

Some board members also envisioned the digital archive as a window to showcase the story of the Chinese American community to the broader public. They believed it had the potential to emphasize the community's contributions to the country and raise awareness among a wider audience, increasing visibility within mainstream society. However, it is acknowledged that the translation issue could pose a hurdle to achieving this goal. As Board Member Ms. X said:

If we want to attract individuals from the mainstream society to pay attention to and use our digital archive, we must undertake a significant amount of additional work to address language barriers ... We need to add subtitles to all Chinese audiovisual materials, provide English captions for all images, and translate all Chinese text materials into English ... Just thinking about the workload is already quite substantial, and ensuring quality is even more challenging.

6 Conclusion

In conclusion, while the prevailing perspective advocates for autonomy in community archives, as seen in the suggestion for archival professionals to step back, the challenges highlighted by the *History of the Chinese 30 Years* project underscore the potential drawbacks of limited professional involvement. The foundation, grappling with difficulties in identifying and engaging potential users for their digital archive, repeatedly emphasized the need for professional participation. This prompts a call to explore strategies that involve archival professionals in community archives while maintaining the autonomy of community members over the archive.

References

1. Flinn, A., Steven, M., Shepherd, E.: Whose memories, whose archives? Independent community archives, autonomy and the mainstream. Arch. Sci. **9**, 71–86 (2009)
2. Caswell, M., Douglas, J., Chow, J., et al.: "Come correct or don't come at all": building more equitable relationships between archival studies scholars and community archives (2021)
3. Caswell, M., Cifor, M., Ramirez, H.: "To suddenly discover yourself existing": uncovering the impact of community archives. Am. Arch. **79**(1), 56–81 (2016)
4. Kaplan, E.: We are what we collect, we collect what we are: Archives and the construction of identity. Am. Arch. **63**(1), 126–151 (2000)
5. Paschild, C.: Community archives and the limitations of identity: considering discursive impact on material needs. Am. Arch. **75**(1), 125–142 (2012)
6. Caswell, M.: Urgent archives: enacting liberatory memory work. Routledge, New York (2021)
7. Wurl, J.: Ethnicity as provenance: in search of values and principles for documenting the immigrant experience. Archival Issues, 65–76 (2005)
8. Cook, T.: Evidence, memory, identity, and community: four shifting archival paradigms. Arch. Sci. **13**, 95–120 (2013)
9. Zavala, J., Migoni, A.A., Caswell, M., et al.: "A process where we're all at the table": community archives challenging dominant modes of archival practice. Archives Manuscripts **45**(3), 202–215 (2017)
10. Caswell, M.: Seeing yourself in history: community archives and the fight against symbolic annihilation. Public Hist. **36**(4), 26–27 (2014)
11. Flinn, A., Stevens, M.: "It is noh mistri, wi mekin histri": Telling our own story: Independent and community archives in the UK, challenging and subverting the mainstream. In: Bastian, J.A., Alexander, B. (eds.) Community archives: the shaping of memory, pp. 3–27. Facet Publishing, London (2009)
12. Caswell, M.: Toward a survivor-centered approach to records documenting human rights abuse: lessons from community archives. Arch. Sci. **14**(3–4), 307–322 (2014). https://doi.org/10.1007/s10502-014-9220-6
13. Gilliland, A., Flinn, A.: Community archives: what are we really talking about? CIRN Prato Community Informatics Conference 2013 Keynote. https://www.monash.edu/__data/assets/pdf_file/0007/920626/gilliland_flinn_keynote.pdf. Accessed 13 Sept 2023
14. Yakel, E.: Record-keeping in radiology: the relationships between activities and records in radiological processes. Ph.D. Dissertation, University of Michigan (1997)
15. Gracy, K.F.: Documenting communities of practice: making the case for archival ethnography. Arch. Sci. **4**, 335–365 (2004)

16. Gilliland, A.J.: Moving past: probing the agency and affect of recordkeeping in individual and community lives in post-conflict Croatia. Arch. Sci. **14**(3–4), 249–274 (2014). https://doi.org/10.1007/s10502-014-9231-3
17. Hammersley, M., Atkinson, P.: Ethnography: Principles in practice. Routledge, New York (2019)

Behavioural Research

What Motivates You to Use VR Exergames to Substitute for Real Sports?—An Empirical Study Based on Technology Readiness and Technology Acceptance Model

Haodong Sun (ID) and Qing Ke(✉) (ID)

School of Information Management, Nanjing University, Nanjing Jiangsu 210023, China
sunhaodong@smail.nju.edu.cn, keqing@nju.edu.cn

Abstract. Virtual reality technology has brought about a new way of exercising through VR exergames. A critical and interesting question is whether users are willing to use VR exergames as an effective supplement to traditional exercise methods, or even as a complete substitute for some real sports. In this study, we aim to identify the factors that affect users' perception of VR exergames and intention to substitute them for real sports based on the Technology Readiness and Acceptance Model (TRAM). The proposed model and 16 hypotheses were tested by structural equation analysis using 248 validated questionnaires. Our results suggest that users' technological readiness and perceived interactivity significantly impact their perception of VR exergames and intention to substitute real sports. Perceived usefulness had a significant impact on substitution intention, while perceived ease of use did not. Our findings provide important recommendations for future VR exergames development to enhance user experience and promote national fitness.

Keywords: Virtual Reality Exergames · Technology Readiness and Technology Acceptance Model · Substitution Intention

1 Introduction

According to the latest report released by the World Health Organization (WHO), 81% of adolescents and 27.5% of adults do not meet the standard of physical activity [1], and the health risks caused by insufficient physical activity are becoming a global problem of great concern. The utilization of exergames has been demonstrated to have a positive impact on the physical and psychological well-being of individuals through gamified interventions [2–5]. With advances in virtual reality (VR) and augmented reality (AR) technology, immersive exergames have even greater potential in the field of human health, as they can enhance user perception and facilitate effective exercise. [6, 7]. In fact, VR exergames have become a trendy new form of exercise, offering a novel approach towards health management, and presenting significant opportunities for growth in both the gaming and VR industries.

I. Sserwanga et al. (Eds.): iConference 2024, LNCS 14596, pp. 31–52, 2024.
https://doi.org/10.1007/978-3-031-57850-2_4

The concept of VR exergames involves the utilization of computer-generated simulations to create an interactive environment that promotes both physical and mental exercise, thus enhancing the user's sense of presence [7]. With the onset of the COVID-19 pandemic in early 2020, social distancing policies curtailed outdoor activities globally, which increased the popularity of VR exergames among users [8]. They have the potential to alter individuals' initial exercise routines and emerge as an effective means of maintaining physical fitness, partially replacing, and in some instances, entirely substituting for real sports. Figure 1 shows some of the VR exergame screenshots.

Studies on technology acceptance have shown that individual differences in psychological characteristics towards new technology can be decisive in predicting users' acceptance and use of new technologies [9, 10]. Models like the technology readiness and acceptance model (TRAM) have been proposed to elucidate the influence of technology readiness on users' adoption of new technologies [11]. TRAM assesses users' inclination to use new technologies across four dimensions: optimism and innovativeness (positive), as well as discomfort and insecurity (negative). As VR exergames are a new technology, it is highly applicable to use the TRAM to study users' perceptions and intentions to substitute them for real sports.

Despite the rising popularity of VR exergames as a means of physical activity and amusement, there still exist some research gaps that require further investigation. More specifically, the impact of various individual traits on users' perception of VR exergames remains unclear. And furthermore, the factors influencing users' inclination towards substituting real sports with VR exergames have yet to be thoroughly analyzed. To address these above gaps, we posed the following research questions based on TRAM:

RQ1: How do users' psychological characteristics on technology readiness impact their perceived ease of use and perceived usefulness of VR exergames, respectively?

RQ2: What factors influence users' intention to substitute VR exergames for real sports?

The primary objective of this study is to examine the synergistic development between VR exergames and real sports, emphasizing the substitution effect exhibited by VR exergames. This research can serve as a foundation for the promotion and advancement of VR exergames for a diverse population.

Fig. 1. Screenshots of VR exergames.

2 Literature Review

2.1 Technology Readiness and Technology Acceptance Model

Various theoretical models have been proposed to study the decision-making process of users adopting new technology. Proposed by Davis et al. [12], TAM is one of the most significant models in the field of information behavior, as it analyzes the influence of perceived usefulness and perceived ease of use on users' intention to use and usage behavior toward new technologies. Parasuraman and Colby [13] expanded the technology readiness (TR) to include four dimensions of technology readiness: optimism, innovativeness, discomfort, and insecurity. TRAM, which combines TR and TAM, offers a more comprehensive understanding of the decision-making process behind users' acceptance of new technologies [11]. As shown in Fig. 2, it analyzes the perceived ease of use and usefulness of new technologies based on users' different TRI, providing insight into the basic psychological processes of users. Seong and Hong [14] argued that TR only provides a limited discussion of users' behavior in using new technologies at the psychological level, while the limitation of TAM is that it can only address the systemic features of new technologies, while TRAM can address all these limitations.

Previous studies have already shown the effectiveness of the TRAM in explaining how users' perceptions and usage behavior are influenced by technology readiness in various domains [14–17]. However, no study has been conducted to examine the substitution intentions of VR exergames based on TRAM, showing a research gap in this area. Therefore, our study will adopt the TRAM model to investigate VR exergames.

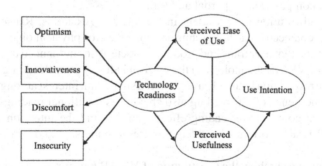

Fig. 2. Technology Readiness and Acceptance Model (TRAM) [11].

2.2 VR Exergames

Exergame can be defined as a video game that promotes players' physical movements beyond sedentary activities, incorporating strength, balance, and flexibility activities [18]. The definition of VR exergame refers to a computer-generated VR game that combines elements of exercise and physical activity. VR exergames have attracted attention for their ability to improve embodiment and immersion, increasing user enjoyment [19]. VR technology has been considered a new way to promote physical activity and healthy behavior [2, 20, 21].

Research on the comparison of the effects of VR exergames and real sports is the focus of scholars' attention. Comparisons of physical activity [6, 22–24], psychological outcomes [3, 6, 23], and physical performance [6, 21, 22, 25] between exercise on VR and traditional equipment showed VR to be more effective. Ng et al. [26] conducted a meta-analysis and found that VR-based training was considerably more robust in promoting physical activity and performance than the traditional way. Many scholars have further validated the role of VR exergames in motivating users to exercise by enhancing self-efficacy and pleasure [27, 28].

VR exergames have emerged as an exciting new form of sports that seamlessly integrates state-of-the-art technologies. Despite being a relatively young field, its potential for effective application in professional sports training has already garnered widespread recognition.

2.3 Substitution Research

Porter's [29] five-factor model, which identifies the key factors that influencing a company or industry's success, is widely regarded as the most famous theoretical framework for analyzing the situation of a company. Among these factors, substitution stands out as a critical one, marking the first introduction of the concept of substitution. Substitution often involves the adoption of new technologies, resulting in the replacement of the previous [30]. And it has been argued that some innovations are simply better than their predecessors, while others may have additional features. This substitution process can be referred to as partial substitutability [31]. In comparison, VR exergames' substitution of real sports encompasses both partial and full.

Studies on substitution are prevalent in the VR and AR fields. Rauschnabel [32] explored the acceptance of AR holograms as substitutes for physical objects in various countries and found that user traits and product characteristics influenced user intentions. The utilization of VR/AR technology in the tourism industry, its influencing factors, and its impact on the motivation to travel have garnered significant interest among researchers [33–35]. The emergence of VR reading also challenges traditional reading habits, with scholars studying comparative reading effects [36–38] and the intention to use [39]. They found VR reading offers a heightened sense of immersion and a more enjoyable experience.

In conclusion, research on the substitution of VR/AR has primarily concentrated on analyzing the user experience and its effects on traditional ways. However, there is still a need for research on fostering a synergistic development between VR and traditional ways.

2.4 Perceived Interactivity and Perceived Substitution

The interaction function in VR refers to the seamless interaction between individuals and the system, as well as the interpersonal interactions within the system. The real-time feedback provided by the system enhances its attractiveness and motivates users to engage. And these interaction functions foster a sense of connection and emotional engagement. The perceived interactivity in VR exergames can bring users a stronger sense of engagement and motivation to exercise, which also has a greater impact on users' sports performance and intention [7, 40–42]. Collectively, these aspects demonstrate the heightened interactivity of VR exergames compared to real sports.

Perceived substitution is the perception of a new technology as a substitute for the original technology, which is affected by the objective function of the new technology on the one hand, and by the individual's subjective needs and perceptual abilities on the other [43, 44]. When users perceive a higher degree of substitution, they are more likely to adopt the new technology [16]. Perceived substitution in VR exergames refers to when users perceive that certain functional settings or features in VR can be substitutive for real sports. This is an important influencing factor that may directly affect the subsequent intention to use and substitute.

Therefore, perceived interactivity and perceived substitution will be studied as potential influencing factors in the present research.

3 Research Design

3.1 Research Hypothesis

The Impact of Positive Technology Readiness. Positive technology readiness refers to a person's positive attitude towards technology, including their belief that technology can enhance control over their life (Optimistic), and their inclination to adopt new technology (Innovative). Optimistic and innovative individuals are more likely to have an open and optimistic attitude toward new technologies [9, 45]. Previous research on TRAM has shown that optimism and innovativeness have a positive effect on perceived ease of use and perceived usefulness [14, 16, 17, 46]. Therefore, we propose the following hypotheses:

- H1a: Optimism positively affects perceived ease of use.
- H1b: Optimism positively affects perceived usefulness.
- H2a: Innovativeness positively affects perceived ease of use.
- H2b: Innovativeness positively affects perceived usefulness.

Impact of Negative Technology Readiness. Negative technology readiness encompasses two key factors – discomfort and insecurity. Discomfort refers to the feeling of being overwhelmed and out of control when presented with new technologies, while insecurity refers to distrust in new technologies due to security and privacy concerns [46]. These factors can significantly impact user behavior, as discomfort can reduce the willingness to use new technologies. In contrast, insecurity may lead to resistance behaviors [47, 48]. The impacts of discomfort and insecurity on the perception of new technologies have been confirmed through various studies [15, 17, 49, 50]. Thus, we propose the following hypotheses:

- H3a: Discomfort negatively affects perceived ease of use.
- H3b: Discomfort negatively affects perceived usefulness.
- H4a: Insecurity negatively affects perceived ease of use.
- H4b: Insecurity negatively affects perceived usefulness.

Impact of Perceived Ease of Use and Perceived Usefulness. The relationship between perceived ease of use and perceived usefulness has been consistently shown to be significant in previous studies investigating new technologies [14, 49, 50], as both factors play a key role in determining user acceptance of technology [51]. For instance, Seong and Hong [14] demonstrated that perceived usefulness had a significant positive impact on the intention to use sports game screen golf. Similarly, Cui [15] found that perceived ease of use and perceived usefulness for mobile sports apps both had a significant and positive effect on users' attitudes towards using. So, we propose the following hypotheses:

- H5: Perceived ease of use positively affects perceived usefulness.
- H6: Perceived ease of use positively affects substitution intention.
- H7: Perceived usefulness positively affects substitution intention.

Impact of Perceived Interactivity. The utilization of interactive functions in VR exergames has been observed to significantly impact user performance and exercise effectiveness [28, 52, 53]. Furthermore, researchers have analyzed the role of different interaction settings in influencing the intention to use VR exergames [40, 55–57]. These studies have demonstrated that interactivity can positively affect the perception of VR exergames. Therefore, we propose the following hypotheses:

- H8: Perceived interactivity positively affects perceived ease of use.
- H9: Perceived interactivity positively affects perceived usefulness.
- H10: Perceived interactivity positively affects perceived substitution.

Impact of Perceived Substitution. Rauschnabel [32] found that the extent to which users perceive AR holograms as a replacement is influenced by their perceived levels of usability. Helm et al. [43] highlighted the high perceived value of e-books as a substitute for paper books, as expressed by users. Chang and Chen [16] discovered that users are more likely to use smart stores when they perceive significant improvements in their shopping experience and efficiency. Pogrebnyakov and Buchmann's [44] study on the substitution process of e-newspapers for print newspapers found that the perception of substitution positively affects the intention to use and perceived usefulness. Thus, we propose the following hypotheses:

- H11: Perceived usefulness positively affects the perceived substitution.
- H12: Perceived substitution positively affects the substitution intention.

3.2 Research Model

Figure 3 presents the theoretical model utilized in this study, which encapsulates the TRAM. The dashed box on the left exemplifies the TRI measures employed in the research. Specifically, we evaluated two optimistic technology readiness measures (innovativeness and optimism) alongside two negative technology readiness measures (discomfort and insecurity) and their relation to perceived ease of use and perceived usefulness. Additionally, we investigated their effects on eventual substitution intention. Moreover, the study examined perceived interactivity and perceived substitutability as potential variables in VR exergames to assess their influence.

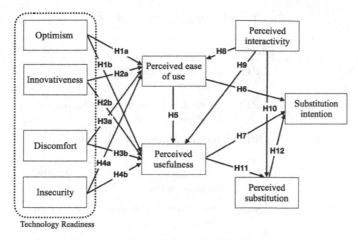

Fig. 3. Research Model

3.3 Questionnaire Design

The questionnaire in this study comprises two sections. The first section, demographic information, consists of nine questions designed to gather information on participants' gender, age, education level, weekly exercise time in reality and VR exergames, familiarity with VR technology, vision for the development of VR exergames, and commonly used VR devices and applications. The second section is based on well-established scales used in relevant research (Table 1), namely, four technical readiness dimensions, four perception dimensions, and the final substitution intention. Participants responded to all questions in the second section using a Likert-7 scale, where 1 denotes strong disagreement and 7 indicates strong agreement.

3.4 Data Collection and Analysis

The questionnaire for this study was conducted online and went through a preliminary survey process involving 30 participants. To ensure the accuracy of the research, a purposive sampling method was employed. Social media groups were identified as potential research groups, and users with experience in VR exergames were invited to participate. Additionally, users who had posted about VR exergames topics on some well-known Chinese social media platforms like Bilibili and Xiaohongshu were also invited. Through targeted questionnaire forwarding using the snowball method, 283 questionnaires were collected between March 27 and April 6, 2023. After eliminating 35 invalid questionnaires based on validity questions, response time (less than 100 s), and similar responses, 248 valid questionnaires remained, representing an 87.63% questionnaire recovery rate. The sample size of our research meets the quantitative requirements for PLS analysis [58]. The collected data was then processed using SPSS 24 and Smart PLS 4 software.

Table 1. Measurement Items

Constructs	Items	Contents	References
Optimism (OPT)	OPT1	New technologies contribute to a better quality of life	[13, 14, 16]
	OPT2	Technology gives me more freedom of mobility	
	OPT3	Technology gives people more control over their daily lives	
	OPT4	Technology makes me more productive in my personal life	
Innovativeness (INN)	INN1	Other people come to me for advice on new technologies	
	INN2	In general, I am among the first in my circle of friends to acquire new technology when it appears	
	INN3	I can usually figure out new high-tech products and services without help from others	
	INN4	I keep up with the latest technological developments in my areas of interest	
Discomfort (DIS)	DIS1	When I get technical support from a provider of a high-tech product or service, I sometimes feel as if I am being taken advantage of by someone who knows more than I do	
	DIS2	Technical support lines are not helpful because they don't explain things in terms I understand	
	DIS3	Sometimes, I think that technology systems are not designed for use by ordinary people	
	DIS4	There is no such thing as a manual for a high-tech product or service that's written in plain language	
Insecurity (INS)	INS1	People are too dependent on technology to do things for them	
	INS2	Too much technology distracts people to a point that is harmful	

(continued)

Table 1. (*continued*)

Constructs	Items	Contents	References
	INS3	Technology lowers the quality of relationships by reducing personal interaction	
	INS4	I do not feel confident doing business with a place that can only be reached online	
Perceived ease of use (PE)	PE1	Learning how to use VR exergames is very easy to me	[12, 46, 51]
	PE2	The method of using VR exergames is simple and clear	
	PE3	It is very easy to enjoy the fun of VR exergames	
	PE4	Overall, I find the VR exergames are very easy to use	
Perceived usefulness (PU)	PU1	VR exergames can improve my sports skills	
	PU2	Exercising through VR exergames is an effective way	
	PU3	VR exergames will allow me to achieve exercise	
	PU4	Overall, I think VR exergames are very useful	
Perceived interactivity (PI)	PI1	I can experience interaction with other characters in VR exergames	[14]
	PI2	I can exercise with other characters in VR exergames	
	PI3	I can receive real-time feedback from the VR exergames	
	PI4	I'm exercising with a group of people who share a common interest in using VR	
Perceived substitution (PS)	PS1	VR exergames can have a similar effect to real sports	[44]
	PS2	VR exergames can have a similar experience to real sports	
	PS3	VR exergames are an alternative to real sports。	

(continued)

Table 1. (*continued*)

Constructs	Items	Contents	References
Substitution intention (SI)	SI1	I'll be augmenting the exercise with VR exergames	[32]
	SI2	I will realize the sports experience through VR exergames	
	SI3	I'll be fulfilling exercise needs through VR exergames	
	SI4	I would like to substitute VR exergames for real sports	

4   Results

4.1   Respondents Demographic Characteristics

Table 2 presents the demographic characteristics of the participants. The largest group in this study was 31 to 35 years old (26.2%). Additionally, 71% of the sample consisted of individuals aged 21–35. Most participants held a bachelor's degree (63.3%). Interestingly, the group of participants who exercised for less than one hour per week in reality was the most prominent (25.8%), whilst the largest proportion of those who exercised with VR for five hours or more a week was 25.4%. Hence, the selection of participants in this study more accurately represents the current VR exergames user group, primarily comprising the younger demographic that possesses a greater familiarity with emerging technologies.

Table 2. Characteristics of participants (N = 248)

Item		Frequency (%)	Item		Frequency (%)
Gender	Male	188(75.8)	Average weekly exercise time in real world	Under 1h	64(25.8)
	Female	60(24.2)		1-2h	59(23.8)
Age	Under 20	12(4.8)		2-3h	31(12.5)
	21–25	55(22.2)		3-4h	30(12.1)
	26–30	56(22.6)		4-5h	18(7.3)
	31–35	65(26.2)		Over 5h	46(18.5)
	36–40	27(10.9)	Average weekly time using VR exergames	Under 1h	57(23.0)
	Over 40	33(13.3)		1-2h	42(16.9)
Education Levels	High school or below	17(6.9)		2-3h	26(10.5)

(*continued*)

Table 2. (*continued*)

Item		Frequency (%)	Item		Frequency (%)
	Associate degree	46(18.5)		3-4h	40(16.1)
	Undergraduate degree	157(63.3)		4-5h	20(8.1)
	Postgraduate degree	28(11.3)		Over 5h	63(25.4)

4.2 Common Method Bias (CMB)

To mitigate common method bias, an online survey platform was used to collect a diverse range of responses. The Harman one-way test was also used to detect potential CMB. After conducting factor analysis, a cumulative variance of 70.549% was explained by multiple factors. The first principal factor accounted for 30.71%, which is within the accepted standard of less than 35% [59]. Thus, the CMB was not found to be severe in this study.

4.3 Measurement Model Evaluation

The analysis revealed that the overall correlations between the scale's items were greater than 0.5, indicating a strong internal consistency. However, to improve this dimension's Cronbach's alpha coefficient, the PU1 item was excluded. Subsequently, DIS1, DIS2, and INS1 were removed due to their outer loadings being less than 0.7. As presented in Table 3, Cronbach's α coefficients for all constructs ranged from 0.769–0.925, and the combined reliability (CR) ranged from 0.874–0.952, exceeding the suggested threshold of 0.7 [58]. Additionally, the range of average variance extracted (AVE) was 0.652–0.869, surpassing the recommended threshold of 0.5. Furthermore, all outer loadings ranged from 0.752–0.935, were significant at the P < 0.001 level, and met the model measurement criteria suggested by Hair et al. [58].

Table 3. Reliability and convergent validity tests

Construct	Item	outer loading	M	SD	Cronbach's α	CR	AVE
Optimism	OPT1	0.837	6.222	0.987	0.88	0.916	0.732
	OPT2	0.846	6.246	1.010			
	OPT3	0.891	5.734	1.314			
	OPT4	0.846	5.895	1.199			
Innovativeness	INN1	0.809	4.794	1.736	0.823	0.882	0.652

(*continued*)

Table 3. (*continued*)

Construct	Item	outer loading	M	SD	Cronbach's α	CR	AVE
	INN2	0.858	5.464	1.566			
	INN3	0.752	5.843	1.157			
	INN4	0.805	5.593	1.310			
Discomfort	DIS3	0.869	3.589	1.684	0.769	0.895	0.809
	DIS4	0.929	3.762	1.843			
Insecurity	INS2	0.832	3.859	1.756	0.786	0.874	0.699
	INS3	0.847	3.661	1.872			
	INS4	0.829	3.536	1.868			
Perceived ease of use	PE1	0.862	5.851	1.239	0.888	0.922	0.747
	PE2	0.867	5.794	1.254			
	PE3	0.824	5.952	1.165			
	PE4	0.902	5.883	1.145			
Perceived usefulness	PU2	0.931	4.984	1.556	0.925	0.952	0.869
	PU3	0.935	5.468	1.425			
	PU4	0.93	5.210	1.521			
Perceived interactivity	PI1	0.831	5.415	1.389	0.861	0.905	0.705
	PI2	0.843	5.427	1.424			
	PI3	0.826	5.508	1.519			
	PI4	0.858	5.460	1.450			
Perceived substitution	PS1	0.926	5.097	1.797	0.887	0.93	0.815
	PS2	0.904	4.935	1.542			
	PS3	0.878	4.911	1.522			
Substitution intention	SI1	0.92	5.157	1.593	0.922	0.945	0.812
	SI2	0.904	5.298	1.476			
	SI3	0.94	5.077	1.659			
	SI4	0.839	4.387	1.974			

To test the discriminant validity of the model, three criteria were considered. First, each construct corresponds to a factor loading of the latent variable that exceeds the factor loading of that variable on the other constructs. Second, the square root of the AVE arithmetic was greater than the factor correlation coefficient [60], as shown in bold on the diagonal of Table 4. Finally, the heterotrait-monotrait ratio (HTMT) of the discriminant validity was counted, and as shown in Table 5, it was less than the suggested threshold of 0.9 [61]. Overall, the model demonstrated excellent discriminant validity between its constructs.

Table 4. Factor correlation and AVE arithmetic square root matrix

	INS	DIS	OPT	INN	PI	PE	PS	PU	SI
INS	**0.836**								
DIS	0.477	**0.9**							
OPT	−0.159	−0.062	**0.855**						
INN	−0.039	−0.069	0.41	**0.807**					
PI	−0.157	−0.149	0.219	0.222	**0.84**				
PE	−0.213	−0.283	0.406	0.235	0.462	**0.864**			
PS	−0.181	−0.176	0.253	0.226	0.516	0.456	**0.903**		
PU	−0.262	−0.224	0.177	0.239	0.498	0.56	0.746	**0.932**	
SI	−0.123	−0.13	0.213	0.266	0.416	0.482	0.722	0.744	**0.901**

Note: The diagonal bold numbers in the table are the square root of the arithmetic of AVE

Table 5. Heterotrait-monotrait ratio

	INS	DIS	OPT	INN	PI	PE	PS	PU	SI
INS									
DIS	0.623								
OPT	0.183	0.068							
INN	0.114	0.107	0.496						
PI	0.19	0.182	0.248	0.267					
PE	0.241	0.336	0.445	0.273	0.519				
PS	0.214	0.207	0.275	0.266	0.583	0.497			
PU	0.306	0.261	0.18	0.263	0.551	0.598	0.822		
SI	0.137	0.148	0.226	0.296	0.46	0.515	0.799	0.804	

4.4 Structural Model Evaluation

The results of hypotheses testing and path analysis using PLS are presented in Table 6, with 11 out of the 16 proposed hypotheses being supported. Specifically, it has been observed that optimism has a significant positive effect on perceived ease of use ($\beta = 0.308, p < 0.001$), innovativeness has a significant positive effect on perceived usefulness ($\beta = 0.125, p < 0.05$), discomfort has a significant negative effect on perceived ease of use ($\beta = -0.207, p < 0.01$), and insecurity has a significant negative effect on perceived usefulness ($\beta = -0.149, p < 0.05$). This supports hypotheses H1a, H2b, H3a, and H4b. Additionally, perceived ease of use significantly and positively influences perceived usefulness ($\beta = 0.423, p < 0.001$), and perceived usefulness significantly and positively influences substitution intention ($\beta = 0.425, p < 0.001$), supporting hypotheses H5 and H7. Furthermore, perceived interactivity significantly and positively influences perceived ease of use ($\beta = 0.358$, $p < 0.001$), perceived usefulness ($\beta = 0.281$, $p < 0.001$), and perceived substitutability ($\beta = 0.192$, $p < 0.001$), thus supporting hypotheses H8, H9, and H10. Perceived usefulness significantly influences perceived substitutability ($\beta = 0.651$, $p < 0.001$), and perceived substitutability significantly influences substitution intention ($\beta = 0.371$, $p < 0.001$), hence supporting hypotheses H11 and H12. However, hypotheses H1b, H2a, H3b, H4a, and H6 are not supported.

Table 6. Hypothesis Testing

Hypothesis	Path	β	T	P	Results
H1a	Optimism → Perceived ease of use	0.308	4.306	0.000	Supported
H1b	Optimism → Perceived usefulness	-0.131	2.000	0.046	Not supported
H2a	Innovativeness → Perceived ease of use	0.014	0.207	0.836	Not supported
H2b	Innovativeness → Perceived usefulness	0.125	2.000	0.046	Supported
H3a	Discomfort → Perceived ease of use	-0.207	3.001	0.003	Supported
H3b	Discomfort → Perceived usefulness	0.01	0.145	0.885	Not supported
H4a	Insecurity → Perceived ease of use	-0.007	0.096	0.923	Not supported
H4b	Insecurity → Perceived usefulness	-0.149	2.443	0.015	Supported
H5	Perceived ease of use → Perceived usefulness	0.423	6.111	0.000	Supported
H6	Perceived ease of use → Substitution intention	0.075	1.589	0.112	Not supported
H7	Perceived usefulness → Substitution intention	0.425	5.860	0.000	Supported
H8	Perceived interactivity → Perceived ease of use	0.358	6.693	0.000	Supported
H9	Perceived interactivity → Perceived usefulness	0.281	4.317	0.000	Supported
H10	Perceived interactivity → Perceived substitution	0.192	3.632	0.000	Supported
H11	Perceived usefulness → Perceived substitution	0.651	12.630	0.000	Supported
H12	Perceived substitution → Substitution intention	0.371	5.012	0.000	Supported

The model validation results, as depicted in Fig. 4, indicated that the explanatory power of the constructs in the model was moderate to substantial. Specifically, the R^2 values of perceived ease of use, perceived usefulness, and perceived substitution were 35.4%, 41.9%, and 58.4%, respectively. These values were all greater than the critical value of 33% for moderate explanatory power [62], while the R^2 value of substitution intention was 62.0%, which was close to the substantial explanatory power critical value of 67% [62]. This suggests that the structural model holds a strong explanatory power.

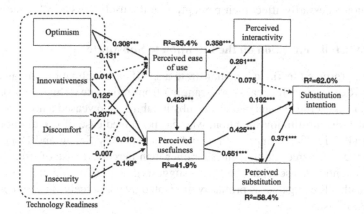

Fig. 4. Structural equation modeling results.

In terms of the control variables, only the vision for the development of VR exergames had a significant effect on substitution intention ($\beta = 0.133$, $p < 0.01$). Gender, age, education, familiarity with VR, weekly realistic exercise time, and weekly VR exergames time had no significant impact on substitution intention. Furthermore, correlation analysis has revealed that all control variables, except age, are significantly correlated with the vision for the development of VR exergames.

5 Discussion

In the present study, we developed a research model to examine the factors that influence users' perception and intentions to use VR exergames as a substitute for real sports based on the TRAM. We found:

5.1 There is a Significant Effect of Positive and Negative Technology Readiness

We found that optimism significantly enhances users' perceived ease of use, while innovativeness contributes to the perceived usefulness. These results are consistent with previous studies by Seong & Hong [14], Kuo et al. [17], and Chang & Chen [16]. While innovativeness had a positive effect on perceived ease of use in our study, it was not statistically significant. We also found a significant negative effect of optimism on perceived usefulness, which contradicts some previous studies [14, 15]. This may be due to that optimists have a more positive outlook on the development of new technologies, leading to higher expectations for VR exergames.

Discomfort and insecurity were found to have a significant negative influence on perceived ease of use and perceived usefulness, respectively. These findings are consistent with previous research conducted by Kuo et al. [17] and Chang & Chen [16]. However, we did not find a significant effect of discomfort on perceived usefulness or insecurity on perceived ease of use, which is consistent with Sivathanu's [63] study. Users who experience discomfort may feel a greater sense of losing control over new technology, but it does not necessarily affect their perception of the usefulness of VR exergames.

5.2 The Effect of Perception on the Intention to Substitute

The findings presented in Table 3 demonstrate a significant inclination among users to substitute VR exergames for real sports, ranging from moderate to high (4.98). Importantly, perceived usefulness and perceived substitutability showcased a noteworthy positive influence on substitution intention, whereas perceived ease of use did not exhibit any statistically significant impact. In a study conducted by Seong and Hong [14], it was confirmed that perceived usefulness, rather than perceived ease of use, positively impacts the intention to use screen golf. This suggests that users' inclination to substitute real sports with VR exergames is primarily motivated by the perceived usefulness rather than the ease of use.

The expectations of exercise outcomes are strongly associated with adopting new fitness technologies [55]. Consequently, users who view VR exergames as a complete or partial substitute for real sports are more concerned with their effectiveness and functionality. In contrast, those who view VR exergames primarily as entertainment are less likely to substitute them for real sports.

5.3 Interactivity is the Key Setting Element of Perception

The significance of interactive features in VR exergames has been highlighted in this study, with perceived interactivity shown to have a positive influence on users' perceived ease of use, perceived usefulness, and perceived substitution of VR exergames. Previous research has supported the idea that interactive functions play a critical role in enhancing the overall user experience of games [40, 41]. According to the self-determination theory (SDT) proposed by Deci and Ryan [64], fulfilling individuals' autonomy, competence, and relatedness needs can lead to internal motivation, resulting in more positive and long-lasting effects. SDT provides a framework for understanding individual participation, effort, and persistence in a specific activity [28]. The interactive function in VR exergames helps users experience a sense of connection with others, which has a direct impact on their motivation to exercise.

5.4 Influence of the Individual Background

Aside from the perception factors, the individual vision of VR exergames development also has a significant positive effect on substitution intention. This finding is consistent with Rauschnabel [32]'s research. Users who have a robust vision for the development of VR exergames will have a longer-term perspective and will be more likely to adopt them as a substitute for real sports. Furthermore, correlation analysis reveals that men, users with higher levels of education, and those with greater familiarity with VR generally exhibit a more visionary outlook regarding the development of VR exergames. This finding aligns with prior research on VR exergames [65]. Similarly, users who spend more time on average engaging in physical exercise and using VR exergames also tend to possess a more visionary perspective.

6 Implications

6.1 Theoretical Implications

First, this study identifies the influence of users' different technology readiness on the perceived ease of use and usefulness of VR exergames. It also introduces new variables such as perceived interactivity and perceived substitutability, enriching the theoretical application of TRAM in the field of VR. Second, this paper explores the concept of substitution in the five-factor model proposed by Potter [29] in the VR exergames field, which can provide implications for future research on substitution in areas such as VR and AR. We conducted deeper research on the behavior of substitution and found it goes beyond technology adoption and acceptance, and it is a further expansion of usage behavior. Finally, this paper analyzes the influence of user psychological characteristics in VR exergames to increase the knowledge of new technology usage behavior based on individual differences. Returning to user psychology to explore the adoption and substitution behavior of new technologies can enrich the existing theories and models.

6.2 Practical Implications

The findings of this study suggest that it is essential to implement precise strategies for promoting VR exergames to individuals with varying psychological characteristics. A daring and avant-garde marketing approach can be used to attract users who exhibit optimistic and innovative technological readiness. In contrast, individuals with a sense of discomfort and insecurity in technology readiness tend to be skeptical of new technologies. Thus, a more cautious approach focused on simplifying usage methods, highlighting effectiveness, and addressing safety concerns is necessary to promote this group's adoption of VR exergames.

It is also crucial to continue improving the interaction function of VR exergames. This can include providing real-time feedback based on users' performance. By incorporating features such as cooperation, competition, guidance, and supervision, users can establish a sense of connection, thereby triggering both internal and external motivation, increasing their sense of self-efficacy and pleasure, and ultimately facilitating long-term use of VR exergames.

Furthermore, ongoing research should focus on improving the effectiveness of VR exergames and enhancing the overall experience to simulate real sports. Through the development of supporting equipment and applications, the exercise mode can be continuously improved to cover the whole body. Moreover, differentiated modes may be established, such as entertainment-focused and exercise-focused or entertainment and professional, to cater to the varying needs of users. Additionally, it is essential to bolster the promotion of the advantages of VR exergames over real sports, thus reinforcing the perceived substitutability of VR among users.

Finally, this study finds that users' overall intention to substitute VR exergames for real sports is moderately high. With their potential to produce better exercise effects on the physical and psychological, and stronger motivation and exercise experience, institutions can use VR exergames to replace some real sports. In schools, for example, VR exergames can be used to allow students to experience sports that may be difficult to access while reducing the danger of some high-risk kinds. For individuals, VR exergames can provide an exciting and effective way to work out.

Overall, the findings of this study provide valuable insights for designing and developing VR exergames to improve users' experience and explore their potential as substitutes for real sports.

7 Conclusions

In this paper, we aimed to explore the factors that influence users' perception of VR exergames and their intention to substitute them for real sports. By constructing a research model based on the TRAM, we discovered that the effects of individual psychological characteristics on VR exergames perception vary. Additionally, the intention to substitute was influenced by various factors such as individual background and platform characteristics.

While the study provides important theoretical and practical implications for the promotion and development of VR exergames, there are some limitations that need to be considered. One of the main challenges of conducting this research was the limited population of VR technology users, which made it difficult to collect a substantial number of questionnaires. Moreover, the questionnaire-based research method constrained our ability to gather more in-depth data from users. To address these limitations, future studies could employ alternative research methods such as in-depth interviews and grounded theory, which would improve our understanding of the factors influencing users' intention to substitute VR exergames for real sports. Meanwhile, different types of sports and different users' exercise preferences may also be factors influencing users' substitution intentions, which could be a direction for further research.

References

1. WHO. Global status report on physical activity 2022 (2022). https://www.who.int/publicati ons/i/item/9789240059153
2. Cheng, C., Ebrahimi, O.V.: A meta-analytic review of gamified interventions in mental health enhancement. Comput. Hum. Behav.. Hum. Behav. 141, 107621 (2022). https://doi.org/10. 1016/j.chb.2022.107621
3. Zheng, H., Li, J., Salmon, C.T., Theng, Y.: The effects of exergames on emotional well-being of older adults. Comput. Hum. Behav.. Hum. Behav. 110, 106383 (2020). https://doi.org/10. 1016/j.chb.2020.106383
4. Alsawaier, R.S.: The effect of gamification on motivation and engagement. Campus-wide Inf. Syst. 35(1), 56–79 (2018). https://doi.org/10.1108/ijilt-02-2017-0009
5. Huang, H., Wong, M., Lu, J., Huang, W., Teng, C.: Can using exergames improve physical fitness? a 12-week randomized controlled trial. Comput. Hum. Behav.. Hum. Behav. 70, 310–316 (2017). https://doi.org/10.1016/j.chb.2016.12.086

6. Trewick, N.A., Neumann, D.L., Hamilton, K.: Effect of affective feedback and competitiveness on performance and the psychological experience of exercise within a virtual reality environment. PLoS ONE **17**(6), e0268460 (2022). https://doi.org/10.1371/journal.pone.0268460

7. Neumann, D.L., et al.: A systematic review of the application of interactive virtual reality to sport. Virtual Real. **22**(3), 183–198 (2018). https://doi.org/10.1007/s10055-017-0320-5

8. Demers, M., Martinie, O., Winstein, C. J., Robert, M. T.: Active Video Games and Low-Cost Virtual Reality: An Ideal Therapeutic Modality for Children With Physical Disabilities During a Global Pandemic. Front. Neurol. 11 (2020) https://doi.org/10.3389/fneur.2020.601898

9. Parasuraman, A.: Technology Readiness Index (Tri): a multiple-item scale to measure readiness to embrace new technologies. J. Serv. Res. **2**(4), 307–320 (2000). https://doi.org/10.1177/109467050024001

10. Agarwal, R., Prasad, J.: Are individual differences germane to the acceptance of new information technologies? Decis. Sci.. Sci. **30**(2), 361–391 (1999). https://doi.org/10.1111/j.1540-5915.1999.tb01614.x

11. Lin, C., Shih, H., Sher, P.J.: Integrating technology readiness into technology acceptance: the TRAM model. Psychol. Mark. **24**(7), 641–657 (2007). https://doi.org/10.1002/mar.20177

12. Davis, F.D., Bagozzi, R.P., Warshaw, P.R.: User acceptance of computer technology: a comparison of two theoretical models. Manage. Sci. **35**(8), 982–1003 (1989). https://doi.org/10.1287/mnsc.35.8.982

13. Parasuraman, A., Colby, C.L.: An updated and streamlined technology readiness index. J. Serv. Res. **18**(1), 59–74 (2015). https://doi.org/10.1177/1094670514539730

14. Seong, B., Hong, C.: Corroborating the effect of positive technology readiness on the intention to use the virtual reality sports game "Screen Golf": Focusing on the technology readiness and acceptance model. Inf. Process. Manage. **59**(4), 102994 (2022). https://doi.org/10.1016/j.ipm.2022.102994

15. Cui, H.C.: Research on the usage willingness of mobile fitness app—based on technology readiness and technology acceptance model (TRAM). China Sport Sci. Tech. **58**(6), 104–113 (2022)

16. Chang, Y., Chen, J.: What motivates customers to shop in smart shops? The impacts of smart technology and technology readiness. J. Retail. Consum. Serv.Consum. Serv. **58**, 102325 (2021). https://doi.org/10.1016/j.jretconser.2020.102325

17. Kuo, K., Liu, C., Ma, C.: An investigation of the effect of nurses' technology readiness on the acceptance of mobile electronic medical record systems. BMC Med. Inform. Decis. Mak. **13**(1) (2013). https://doi.org/10.1186/1472-6947-13-88

18. Oh, Y., Yang, S.: Defining exergames & exergaming. Proc. Meaning. Play, 1–17 (2010)

19. Yu, K., Wen, S., Xu, W., Caon, M., Baghaei, N., Liang, H.: Cheer for me: effect of non-player character audience feedback on older adult users of virtual reality exergames. Virtual Real (2023). https://doi.org/10.1007/s10055-023-00780-5

20. Grosprêtre, S., Marcel-Millet, P., Eon, P., Wollesen, B.: How exergaming with virtual reality enhances specific cognitive and visuo-motor abilities: an explorative study. Cogn. Sci. **47**(4) (2023). https://doi.org/10.1111/cogs.13278

21. Chen, P., Hsu, H., Chen, K., Belcastro, F.: VR exergame interventions among older adults living in long-term care facilities: a systematic review with Meta-analysis. Ann. Phys. Rehabil. Med.Rehabil. Med. **66**(3), 101702 (2023). https://doi.org/10.1016/j.rehab.2022.101702

22. Li, J.: The influence of virtual reality sports game mode on energy consumption and heart rate variability of schoolboy. Genom. Appl. Biol. **37**(11), 5050–5056 (2018)

23. Murray, E., Neumann, D.L., Moffitt, R.L., Thomas, P.R.: The effects of the presence of others during a rowing exercise in a virtual reality environment. Psychol. Sport Exercise **22**, 328–336 (2016)

24. Plante, T.G., Aldridge, A., Bogden, R., Hanelin, C.: Might virtual reality promote the mood benefits of exercise? Comput. Hum. Behav.. Hum. Behav. 19(4), 495–509 (2003). https://doi.org/10.1016/s0747-5632(02)00074-2

25. Howard, M.C.: A meta-analysis and systematic literature review of virtual reality rehabilitation programs. Comput. Hum. Behav.. Hum. Behav. 70, 317–327 (2017)

26. Ng, Y.P., Ma, F., Ho, F.K., Ip, P., Fu, K.: Effectiveness of virtual and augmented reality-enhanced exercise on physical activity, psychological outcomes, and physical performance: a systematic review and meta-analysis of randomized controlled trials. Comput. Hum. Behav.. Hum. Behav. 99, 278–291 (2019). https://doi.org/10.1016/j.chb.2019.05.026

27. Gao, Z., Chen, S.J., Pasco, D., Pope, Z.: A meta-analysis of active video games on health outcomes among children and adolescents. Obes. Rev.. Rev. 16(9), 783–794 (2015). https://doi.org/10.1111/obr.12287

28. Ijaz, K., Ahmadpour, N., Wang, Y., Calvo, R.A.: Player Experience of Needs Satisfaction (PENS) in an immersive virtual reality exercise platform describes motivation and enjoyment. Int. J. Hum.-Comput. Interact. 36(13), 1195–1204 (2020). https://doi.org/10.1080/10447318.2020.1726107

29. Porter, M.E.: How competitive forces shape strategy. Harv. Bus. Rev. 57(2), 137–145 (1979)

30. Huh, Y., Kim, S.H.: Do early adopters upgrade early? role of post-adoption behavior in the purchase of next-generation products. J. Bus. Res. 61(1), 40–46 (2008). https://doi.org/10.1016/j.jbusres.2006.05.007

31. Steffens, P., & Kaya, M.: Drivers of technology substitution: Successive generations of high tech products. GSE International Entrepreneurship Research Exchange (2009)

32. Rauschnabel, P.A.: Augmented reality is eating the real-world! the substitution of physical products by holograms. Int. J. Inf. Manage. 57, 102279 (2021). https://doi.org/10.1016/j.ijinfomgt.2020.102279

33. Lai, Q., Qian, L.L., Ying, T.Y., Chen, Y.W.: A review of virtual tourism research: bibliometrics and content analysis based on scopus database. Tour. Sci. 6(01), 16–35 (2022)

34. Van Nuenen, T., Scarles, C.: Advancements in technology and digital media in tourism. Tour. Stud. 21(1), 119–132 (2021). https://doi.org/10.1177/1468797621990410

35. Chung, N., Han, H., Joun, Y.: Tourists' intention to visit a destination: the role of augmented reality (AR) application for a heritage site. Comput. Hum. Behav.. Hum. Behav. 50, 588–599 (2015). https://doi.org/10.1016/j.chb.2015.02.068

36. Li, Y.Q., Wang, X.W., Luo, R., Liu, X.: A comparative experimental study on the comprehension effect and the flow experience between virtual reality and traditional reading devices. Inf. Stud. Theory Appl. 46(02), 127–135 (2023)

37. Rau, P.P., Zheng, J., Guo, Z.: Immersive reading in virtual and augmented reality environment. Inf. Learn. Sci. 122(7/8), 464–479 (2021). https://doi.org/10.1108/ils-11-2020-0236

38. Danaei, D., Jamali, H.R., Mansourian, Y., Rastegarpour, H.: Comparing reading comprehension between children reading augmented reality and print storybooks. Comput. Educ.. Educ. 153, 103900 (2020). https://doi.org/10.1016/j.compedu.2020.103900

39. Wang, D., Wang, X.W., Wang, Y.: Study on the influencing factors of virtual reality readers' use willingness. J. Mod. Inf. 41(08), 66–75 (2021)

40. Seong, B., Hong, C.: Decision-making in virtual reality sports games explained via the lens of extended planned behavior theory. Int. J. Environ. Res. Public Health 20(1), 592 (2023). https://doi.org/10.3390/ijerph20010592

41. Rufi, S., Wlodarczyk, A., Páez, D., Javaloy, F.: Flow and emotional experience in spirituality. J. Humanist. Psychol. 56(4), 373–393 (2016). https://doi.org/10.1177/0022167815571597

42. Walker, C.F.: Experiencing flow: Is doing it together better than doing it alone? J. Posit. Psychol. 5(1), 3–11 (2010). https://doi.org/10.1080/17439760903271116

43. Helm, S., Ligon, V., Stovall, T., Van Riper, S.: Consumer interpretations of digital ownership in the book market. Electron. Mark. **28**(2), 177–189 (2018). https://doi.org/10.1007/s12525-018-0293-6
44. Pogrebnyakov, N., Buchmann, M.: The role of perceived substitutability and individual culture in the adoption of electronic newspapers in scandinavia. Inf. Res. **19**(3), 639 (2014). https://dblp.uni-trier.de/db/journals/ires/ires19.html#PogrebnyakovB14
45. Lin, J., Chang, H.: The role of technology readiness in self-service technology acceptance. Manag. Serv. Qual.. Serv. Qual. **21**(4), 424–444 (2011). https://doi.org/10.1108/096045211 11146289
46. Walczuch, R., Lemmink, J., Streukens, S.: The effect of service employees' technology readiness on technology acceptance. Inf. Manage. **44**(2), 206–215 (2007). https://doi.org/10.1016/j.im.2006.12.005
47. Oh, J.J., Yoon, S., Chung, N.: The role of technology readiness in consumers' adoption of mobile internet services between South Korea and China. Int. J. Mob. Commun.Commun. **12**(3), 229 (2014). https://doi.org/10.1504/ijmc.2014.061460
48. Lu, H., Hsu, C., Hsu, H.: An empirical study of the effect of perceived risk upon intention to use online applications. Inf. Manage. Comput. Secur. **13**(2), 106–120 (2005). https://doi.org/10.1108/09685220510589299
49. Chen, M., Lin, N.: Incorporation of health consciousness into the technology readiness and acceptance model to predict app download and usage intentions. Internet Res. **28**(2), 351–373 (2018). https://doi.org/10.1108/intr-03-2017-0099
50. Dong, X.W., Ye, Z.J., Xu, N.N., Wang, Y.L., Guan, J.J., Chen, J.: Tourists'intention to book freelance tour guide online based on technology acceptance model and technology readiness index. Tour. Trib. **35**(7), 24–35 (2020)
51. Venkatesh, V., Davis, F.D.: A model of the antecedents of perceived ease of use: development and test. Decis. Sci.. Sci. **27**(3), 451–481 (1996). https://doi.org/10.1111/j.1540-5915.1996.tb01822.x
52. Far, I.K., et al.: The interplay of physical and social wellbeing in older adults: investigating the relationship between physical training and social interactions with virtual social environments. PeerJ **1**, e30 (2015). https://doi.org/10.7717/peerj-cs.30
53. Anderson-Hanley, C., Snyder, A.M., Nimon, J.P., Arciero, P.J.: Social facilitation in virtual reality-enhanced exercise: competitiveness moderates exercise effort of older adults. Clin. Interv. AgingInterv. Aging **6**(1), 275–280 (2011). https://doi.org/10.2147/cia.s25337
54. IJsselsteijn, W.W., De Kort, Y.Y., Westerink, J.H.D.M., De Jager, M.M., Bonants, R.: Fun and sports: enhancing the home fitness experience. In Lect. Notes Comput. Sci., pp. 46–56. Springer Science+Business Media (2004). https://doi.org/10.1007/978-3-540-28643-1_8
55. Yadav, R. a. K., Yadav, M., Mittal, A.: Effects of gain-loss-framed messages on virtual reality intervened fitness exercise. Inf. Discov. Deliv. **50**(4), 374–386 (2021). https://doi.org/10.1108/idd-04-2021-0051
56. Westmattelmann, D., Grotenhermen, J., Sprenger, M., Rand, W., Schewe, G.: Apart we ride together: the motivations behind users of mixed-reality sports. J. Bus. Res. **134**, 316–328 (2021). https://doi.org/10.1016/j.jbusres.2021.05.044
57. Sanz, F., Multon, F., Lécuyer, A.: A methodology for introducing competitive anxiety and pressure in VR sports training. Front. Robot. AI **2** (2015). https://doi.org/10.3389/frobt.2015.00010
58. Hair, J.F., Ringle, C.M., Sarstedt, M.: PLS-SEM: indeed a silver bullet. J. Mark. Theory Pract. **19**(2), 139–152 (2011). https://doi.org/10.2753/mtp1069-6679190202
59. Podsakoff, P.M., MacKenzie, S.B., Lee, J., Podsakoff, N.P.: Common method biases in behavioral research: a critical review of the literature and recommended remedies. J. Appl. Psychol. **88**(5), 879–903 (2003). https://doi.org/10.1037/0021-9010.88.5.879

60. Fornell, C., Larcker, D.F.: Evaluating structural equation models with unobservable variables and measurement error. J. Mark. Res. **18**(1), 39–50 (1981). https://doi.org/10.1177/002224 378101800104

61. Shiau, W., Yuan, Y., Pu, X., Ray, S., Chen, C.C.: Understanding fintech continuance: perspectives from self-efficacy and ECT-IS theories. Ind. Manage. Data Syst. **120**(9), 1659–1689 (2020). https://doi.org/10.1108/imds-02-2020-0069

62. Chin, W.W.: The partial least squares approach for structural equation modeling. Adv. Hosp. Leis. **8**(2), 295–336 (1998). https://psycnet.apa.org/record/1998-07269-010

63. Sivathanu, B.: An empirical study on the intention to use open banking in India. Inf. Resour. Manag. J.Resour. Manag. J. **32**(3), 27–47 (2019). https://doi.org/10.4018/irmj.2019070102

64. Deci, E.L., Ryan, R.M.: Intrinsic Motivation and Self-Determination in Human Behavior. In Springer eBooks. (1985). https://doi.org/10.1007/978-1-4899-2271-7

65. Xu, W., Li, Z., Yu, K., Wen, S., Baghaei, N., Tu, H.: Acceptance of virtual reality exergames among Chinese older adults. Int. J. Human-Computer Interact. **39**(5), 1134–1148 (2022)

The Filtered Appeal: Evaluating the Impact of Appearance Enhancement on Effectiveness of Donation Requests

Susan C. Herring(✉) ⓘ, Leo Yang ⓘ, and Ashley R. Dainas ⓘ

Indiana University Bloomington, Bloomington, IN 47405, USA
{herring,leoyang,ardainas}@indiana.edu

Abstract. This study investigates how appearance enhancement using AR video filters affects the perceptions and outcomes of an online video donation request, including the authenticity and trustworthiness of the requester. Results of a survey experiment in which the attractiveness of a male and a female actor was manipulated using filters show that perceived attractiveness and trustworthiness positively influenced donation willingness, as did previous donation experience and the demographics of the study participants. Filter use also enhanced perceptions of the quality of the request. Surprisingly, the filtered video versions were not rated as less authentic than unfiltered video. Participant gender interacted with actor gender, producing mixed findings as regards the halo effect of filtered appearance enhancement.

Keywords: AR Filters · Crowdfunding · Halo Effect · Social Media · Trust

1 Introduction

Video-mediated communication (VMC), which has become increasingly popular since the Covid-19 pandemic forced the world online, affords new possibilities for visual self-presentation. One such affordance is video face filters, augmented reality (AR) three-dimensional animations overlaid on the image of a face. Using computer vision and facial mapping technology, these filters track movements of the face and head in real time, modifying the user's appearance in various ways, ranging from beautifying to silly to radically transformative [11]. The animations are easy to apply and are very popular on mobile apps such as Snapchat, Instagram, and TikTok. Deloitte Digital (2021) estimates that more than 4.5 billion AR photos and/or videos are taken daily by Snapchat users alone.

In this study, we investigate the effects of beauty filter use on the perception and effectiveness of a common online act: donation requests such as those seen on crowdfunding platforms like Kickstarter and GoFundMe [29]. The success or failure of these requests has real-world consequences for the requester as regards their ability to support their cause. Therefore, requesters will typically use persuasive means to achieve their ends. Physical attractiveness is known to produce "halo effects" such as perceived trustworthiness (e.g., [31] and may contribute to the persuasiveness of requests. We investigated

I. Sserwanga et al. (Eds.): iConference 2024, LNCS 14596, pp. 53–69, 2024.
https://doi.org/10.1007/978-3-031-57850-2_5

this proposition by conducting an online survey experiment in which we applied filters to a female and a male actor to manipulate their attractiveness in a video request for donations. We examined the influence of degree of perceived attractiveness, along with other qualities of the requester and of the request, on how the video donation request was received and the study participants' willingness to donate money, drawing on halo effects from psychology (e.g., [6]) and the literature on charitable donation behavior [2].

The findings show that perceived attractiveness positively influenced donation willingness, albeit less strongly than the requester's perceived trustworthiness, and only for the male actor. The strongest predictors were the demographics and previous donation experience of the study participants. Surprisingly, the filtered video versions were not rated as less authentic than unfiltered video; some filtered versions were even rated as more natural. Participant gender interacted with actor gender: Women were more willing than men to donate to the extremely beauty enhanced female actor, and participants tended to rate extremely (as opposed to moderately) beauty-enhanced same-sex actors as more trustworthy than extremely beauty-enhanced opposite-sex actors. This contrasts with previous halo effect studies, which found that men evaluated attractive women more positively than women did [1, 12]. Taken together, the findings suggest that beauty filter use may provide some advantage when making online video requests, particularly if it also makes the requester appear more trustworthy, and that beauty filter use does not necessarily make users appear inauthentic. However, extreme beauty enhancement could be counter-productive when appealing for donations to mixed-gender audiences.

2 Background

2.1 Attractiveness

Halo effects for facial beauty and for gender are often reported in the psychological literature. Numerous experimental studies have found that "beautiful is good," in that attractive people are assumed to possess more socially desirable personality traits and to be more trustworthy [6, 31]. Halo effects have also been found for female gender, especially when the evaluator is male [1, 12]. In some contexts, however, such as among physicians, attractiveness is disadvantageous [28], and males sometimes enjoy a greater halo effect than females [22]. Thus, although varying in their particulars, these findings demonstrate that possessing a certain appearance and a contextually appropriate gender can bestow individual advantages. The "beautiful is good" stereotype has been found to operate even when participants' attention is not explicitly directed to a person's appearance [27]. One study [1] found an attractiveness bias even when the evaluator was told that the visual representation (a photo) did not actually portray the person – that is, even when they believed the representation to be inauthentic. The present study investigates whether video filter use can also produce halo effects.

The halo effect literature raises the question of what facial features are considered attractive. Based on a review of the facial literature, Little [15] reports that younger, thinner faces; healthy skin; redness or yellowness of the skin; averageness; and symmetry are generally associated with attractiveness regardless of sex. Men and women typically have similar intuitions about what makes someone attractive, but they differ in what criteria they prioritize (e.g., men tend to value youth and attractiveness more highly than women do). Mature male faces tend to have larger jawbones, more prominent cheekbones, and thinner cheeks, features which are associated with high dominance and lower attractiveness [15]. Additionally, multiple studies have found that perceptions of attractiveness and trustworthiness are correlated [21]. Traits of trustworthy faces include a higher brow ridge, a slightly upturned mouth, shorter distance between the nose and upper lip, and a wide chin, whereas untrustworthy faces have the opposite features [25]. However, Stirrat and Perett [24] found that people were less likely to trust males with wide rather than narrow faces, independent of their attractiveness.

2.2 Donation Requests

Increasingly, requests for donations are made in videos posted to social media such as Instagram and TikTok, and they are often made by and for the benefit of individuals. Popular crowdfunding platforms like GoFundMe enable individuals, as well as organizations and businesses, to raise funds for various causes, including medical expenses, education costs, disaster relief. On these platforms, individuals set their goals and explain their reasons for seeking funding through narrative, images, and video [16], then promote their campaign to their social networks in order to find potential donors. In a study of a large multimodal crowdfunding platform, Zhao et al. [35] found that the verbal modality (text descriptions) was superior to the visual modality (images of the beneficiary's face) in explaining campaign success, or the amount of money raised in a campaign.

From a social science perspective, McGuire's [18] attractiveness model proposes that the effectiveness of a message depends on the source's likability, similarity, and attractiveness to the respondent. Source traits influence the outcome of donation requests. For example, in a study of celebrity product endorsements, Wymer and Drollinger [32] found that the endorser's admirability and expertise influenced the audience's intention to donate directly, while the endorser's perceived attractiveness, perceived likeability, and perceived trustworthiness had indirect effects. Moreover, physically attractive people tend to be more effective negotiators [23], and females tend to be more successful than males at collecting funds through crowdfunding sites [26].

As for who donates, many factors have been found to correlate with the decision to donate money to charitable causes, including the donor's wealth, age, education, race/ethnicity, and previous donation experience [2, 19, 30]. For example, a number of studies found increased age to be correlated with increased philanthropy, although some found that the relationship diminishes after the ages of 65–75 [2]. Studies have also found that women are more likely to give, while men are more likely to give larger donations [30]. Properties of the donation request, such as credibility and rationality, can also affect whether people choose to donate [9].

2.3 Video Face Filters

Research on AR filter use thus far has focused mostly on direct effects of filter use. Marketing research has analyzed customer satisfaction with AR technology dedicated to improving consumers' experiences by allowing them to virtually try on products [33]. Research from psychology has focused on the effects of beauty filter use on mood and self-concept [4]. In videoconference systems, image-filtering techniques can improve user comfort, with users preferring subtle changes to their appearance over distortion filters or using an avatar [7]. However, while several studies have noted that there can be social rewards associated with filter use, such as increased interactivity and acceptance by one's peers (e.g., Chua & Chang, [5]; Javornik et al. [11]), few have investigated how filter use affects outcomes in social interaction, particularly when participants are unaware that someone is using filters. An exception is Leong et al. [14], who found that people who feel anxious about public speaking can benefit from the use of private filters or filters that are only visible to the speaker in online environments.

Herring et al. [10] examined video face filter use in the context of trust and deception and found that filter users generally do not consider the use of AR beauty filters by strangers to be a mark of untrustworthiness. However, female participants across cultures were more sympathetic towards the "deceptive" use of filters compared with male participants, who were more skeptical. In the present study, we focus on the perception of faces experimentally modified through AR beauty filters, including their trustworthiness, in the context of online donation requests.

3   Research Goals

The goal of this research was to analyze the effects of video beauty filters on the reception and success of online donation requests. Specifically, we asked:

> RQ1: How does beauty enhancement via filters affect viewer perceptions and evaluation of donation *requesters* in VMC? What traits are associated with positive evaluations (i.e., attractiveness, trustworthiness, likability, naturalness) of the requester? Does this vary by gender of the viewer?

> RQ2: How does beauty enhancement via filters affect viewer perceptions of, and responses to, *requests* for donation in VMC? What factors are associated with positive responses to requests (i.e., the credibility of the request, how well it is justified, how persuasive it is)? Does this vary by gender of the viewer?

Based on previous literature, we expected to find halo effects of perceived attractiveness, perceived trustworthiness, and perceived likeability on request effectiveness (cf. Rosenblat [23], Wymer & Drollinger, [32]), operationalized as participants' willingness to donate some amount of money. We also expected to find increased willingness to donate to requests that are perceived as more credible, justified, and persuasive (cf. Goering et al. [9]).

We included naturalness as a construct, because negative evaluations and negative request outcomes could be more likely if the participants suspect that the speaker's appearance is unnatural or artificially enhanced – they might then perceive the speaker to be less credible overall (but cf. Bak. [1]). We also expected that extreme attractiveness enhancement would be less effective than subtle enhancement, consistent with findings that users prefer subtle filters [7]. Finally, we expected that female participants more than male participants would agree to donate regardless of filter condition overall (cf. Wiepking & Bekkers [30]), but that male participants would be more likely than female participants to donate to attractive female requesters (cf. Bak [1]; Kaplan [12]).

4 Methods

4.1 Data Collection

In the experiment, participants responded to a short (about one minute) video featuring either a male actor (Marco) or a female actor (Kendra) delivering the same script (see Appendix) asking for a donation.[1] The actors presented themselves as art students in need of donations to replace a broken laptop that would allow them to continue creating digital art commissions to support themselves through art school.

To generate a realistic script, we collected and examined a sample of existing donation requests from multiple platforms (e.g., TikTok, Instagram). A list of common scenarios was generated, and pilot tested (n = 59) to determine a relatively neutral cause that participants would be equally likely to donate or not donate to. According to the pilot study, asking money for a laptop was likely to generate a moderate degree of sympathy, compared to very sympathetic causes such as disaster relief, on the one hand, and causes that generated less sympathy, such as cosmetic surgery, on the other. Three versions of a laptop script were drafted by the researchers and pilot tested (n = 61). For all three versions, participants were less likely to donate than expected. The best-received version was edited to be more persuasive based on the feedback received, for example, by specifying that the request had been shared by a close friend. In addition, to add legitimacy to the request, we added a graphical background to the video illustrating the "student's" digital art, as well as a link to a (fake) gofundme page.

The actors were chosen to be average in appearance, ethnically ambiguous, and around the same age (mid-20's). After rehearsing the script, the actors individually recorded the video on their phones using Instagram, after which they were paid. To modify the appearance of the actors, we used the Chinese mobile app Meitu, which allows fine-grained customization of the appearance of a person in a photograph or video. Based on the literature on attractiveness and trustworthiness (e.g., Little [15]; Todorov et al. [25]), modifications were made to the actors' faces, including their eyes, eyebrows, mouth (smile), forehead, face shape, and skin tone.[2] Fifteen-second clips of the original and modified videos of each actor were created and shown to different online pilot testers (n = 63). Each pilot participant rated nine of 18 versions that appeared in a random order on aspects such as attractiveness, trustworthiness, likeability, and naturalness. All three pilot surveys were created using Qualtrics, and the survey links were shared with the researchers' friends, students, colleagues, and families, as well as through snowball sampling. The pilot respondents in all three surveys tended to skew older, well educated, middle class, and White or Asian.

Based on the attractiveness ratings from the third pilot, three versions of each actor were selected such that there was a low, intermediate, and highly attractive version of each, for a total of six conditions. For the male actor, the least attractive version according to the pilot respondents was the unmodified baseline (m_LOW). The intermediate attractive version involved subtle attractiveness modifications (m_MID), and the high

---

[1] The actors' names are pseudonyms assigned by the authors.

[2] The skin tone modifications were made to the female actor to make her skin color more similar to that of the male actor. This was done to avoid potential confounds in the results due to perceived racial/ethnic differences between the actors.

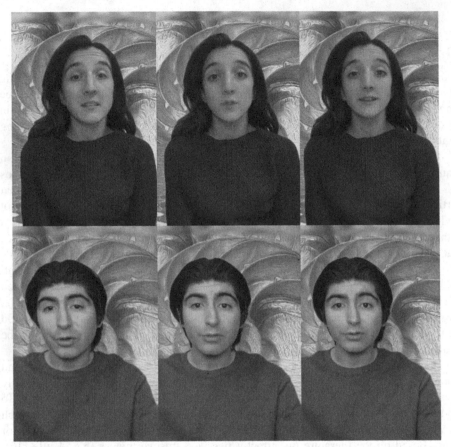

Fig. 1. The six video conditions. Top row, from left to right: f_LOW, f_MID, f_HIGH. Bottom row, from left to right: m_LOW, m_MID, m_HIGH.

attractive version involved more extreme attractiveness modifications (m_HIGH). For the female actor, the pilot respondents found the least attractive version to be one that was originally modified to appear extremely untrustworthy (f_LOW).[3] The intermediate attractive version involved subtle attractiveness modifications (f_MID), and the most attractive version involved more extreme attractiveness modifications (f_HIGH).[4] Each condition is illustrated with a screenshot from the video in Fig. 1.

In the final survey, participants were presented twice with one of the six possible versions of the request video and were asked to rate the request (how credible, justified, persuasive it was) and the requester (how attractive, trustworthy, likable, natural they were) on Likert scales from 1 (not at all) to 7 (extremely). Participants were also asked

---

[3] These modifications included lowering the eyebrows, making the eyes smaller and closer together, making the edges of the mouth turn down slightly, and narrowing the face.

[4] The subtle attractiveness versions were created by reducing by half the degree of the modifications used to create the extreme attractiveness versions.

how much money they would donate and how certain they were of their donation amount
[3]. Information was collected about the participants' demographics, prior donation
history, and social media use.

The experiment was conducted through the Qualtrics online survey platform. Participants were recruited through the company Centiment. Quotas were set to balance
the participant population on several factors: 1. Gender (only individuals identifying as
male or female were included in the study, with the goal of achieving an even gender
balance), 2. Age (based on US census data), and 3. Race/Ethnicity (based on US census
data). Out of 873 completed surveys, 860 surveys were usable after removing outliers
(e.g., individuals who said they would donate more than $500) and otherwise suspicious
respondents (e.g., an 18-year-old claiming to have a Ph.D.). The remaining participants
skewed female (409 male, 451 female) and ranged in age from 18 to 90 (mean 48.05;
sd 16.81). The majority were white (67.9%) and non-Hispanic (80.8%), and the most
common education level was a high school diploma or equivalent (48.4%), with the most
common annual income level being $25k or less (32.8%).

4.2 Analytical Methods

All data were coded, entered, and transformed in SPSS 28. Binary logistic regression
analysis was conducted to explore the association between willingness to donate and
multiple predictors Adjusted odds ratios, along with their corresponding 95% confidence
intervals, were employed to assess the strength of the relationship between the variables.
Analysis of variance was used to investigate the influence of filter conditions on perceived
attitude towards the actor characteristics and the message characteristics. Chi-squared
statistics were used to test the association between categorical variables and donating
behavior. All analyses were performed separately for the female and the male actor. A
p value of less than 0.05, two-tailed, was considered statistically significant. P values
between 0.05 and 0.10 were considered marginally significant.

5 Results

Each of the six video conditions elicited enough total donations for the "art student"
to be able to purchase their $1200 laptop. Section 5.1 describes factors that influenced
study participants' willingness to donate some amount of money. Section 5.2 describes
the effects of the filtered manipulations on participant perceptions of the actor and
the actor's message. Section 5.3 describes the relationship between the attractiveness
manipulations and the participants' ratings of the actors' attractiveness.

5.1 Factors Associated with Donation Willingness

A preliminary analysis suggested that the assumption of multicollinearity was met for
all variables (tolerance above .1). The model was statistically significant for both actors
(Marco: $\chi2$ (12, N = 429) = 171.572, p < .001; Kendra: $\chi2(6, N = 426) = 143.271$, p <
.001), suggesting that it could distinguish between those who donate and those who do
not. For Kendra, the model explained between 28.6% (Cox & Snell R square) and 38.1%

(Nagelkerke R square) of the variance in the dependent variable and correctly classified 73.2% of cases. For Marco, the model explained between 33% (Cox & Snell R square) and 44% (Nagelkerke R square) of the variance in the dependent variable and correctly classified 74% of cases. The variables included in the model are demographic information such as gender, white or non-white, education level, political party, frequency of filter use, similar experience to scenario, and perception of the prevalence of online scams. Other variables are related to the actors' qualities (i.e., trustworthiness, attractiveness, likability, and naturalness) and those of the donation request (i.e., how credible, justified, and persuasive it is). Tables 1 and 2 show the remaining variables that significantly contribute to the models and their odds ratios for each actor. Values in the exponential beta (Exp(B)) column that are less than 1.0 indicate decreased odds.

Table 1. Variables associated with willingness to donate to Kendra.

Variables	Exp(B)	95%CI		p
		Lower	Upper	
Non-white	1.959	1.205	3.185	.007
Male	.596	.376	.942	.027
Justified	1.400	1.167	1.680	<.001
Persuasive	1.439	1.203	1.721	<.001
Past donation behavior	3.082	1.797	2.286	<.001

Table 2. Variables associated with willingness to donate to Marco.

Variables	Exp(B)	95%CI		p
		Lower	Upper	
Non-white	1.770	1.030	3.044	.039
Trustworthy	1.305	1.048	1.624	.017
Attractive	1.195	.993	1.438	.059
Credible	1.349	1.117	1.628	.002
Past donation	3.268	1.814	5.888	<.001
Income: $100k or more	.306	.127	.738	.008
Age	.969	.955	.983	<.001

Note: Baseline for income level: $25k or less

Respondent Demographics. Overall, demographic factors predicted donation willingness more strongly than use of filters. Past donation experience was the strongest predictor for both the male actor ($p < .001$) and the female actor ($p < .001$). Non-white race was also significant for both actors (Marco: $p = .039$; Kendra: $p = .007$). Additionally, younger age was a significant predictor of willingness to donate to Marco ($p <$

.001), as was lower income level. The $25k or less group was significantly more likely to donate than the $100k or more group (p = .008).

Male respondents were less likely than female respondents to donate to Kendra overall (p = .027). Chi-square statistics were used to examine the association between gender of participants and donation. For Kendra, there is a significant association at the 5% significance level ($\chi 2 = 5.639$, df = 1, p = .018). The major difference was for the f_HIGH condition ($\chi 2 = 4.259$, p = .039). However, the association between gender and donation was not significant for Marco ($\chi 2 = .321$, df = 1, p = .630). See Figs. 2a and 2b.

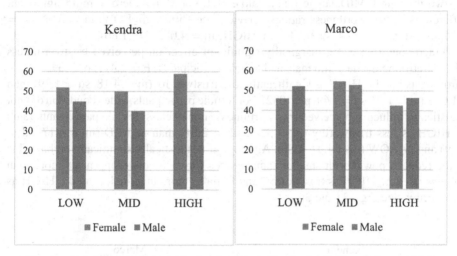

Figs. 2a & b. Percent of respondents who donated to Kendra (left) and Marco (right).

Requester (Actor) Characteristics. Perceived attractiveness had a marginally positive association with donation willingness for Marco (p = .059). Perceived trustworthiness was also positively associated with donation willingness for the male actor (p = .017), and the exponential beta coefficients for Marco in Table 2 show that higher trustworthiness increases the odds of donation more strongly than attractiveness. None of the requester characteristics remained significant in the final model for Kendra.

Request Characteristics. Request credibility (p = .002) was significant for Marco. For Kendra, ratings of the request as justified (p < .001) and persuasive (p < .001) were both significant predictors of willingness to donate.

Other Factors. Surprisingly, participant judgments of the prevalence of online donation scams did not correlate with willingness to donate. Other factors that did not significantly predict donation willingness are the actor's perceived likeability and naturalness, and the participant's political party, experience with being similarly in need as the actor, and experience with and judgments about filters.

5.2   Other Effects of Filtered Manipulations

Trustworthiness. Holding all other variables in the model constant, trustworthiness was a strong overall predictor of willingness to donate, especially for Marco. The effect of trustworthiness for Kendra is significant up to a certain point but loses its effectiveness after including several models (backward listwise regression).

When ratings are broken down by video condition, f_LOW (m = 4.58, sd = 1.84) was rated as more trustworthy than f_MID (m = 4.01, sd = 1.84, p = .008), despite f_LOW having been created with features that previous literature identified as untrustworthy [25]. However, f_HIGH (m = 4.39, sd = 1.80, p = .078) was rated as marginally more trustworthy than f_MID, suggesting a halo effect. For Marco there were no significant differences in trustworthiness ratings per video condition (m_LOW: m = 3.94, sd = 1.86; m_MID: m = 4.14, sd = 1.87; m_HIGH: m = 4.08, sd = 1.86).

Video condition had a marginally significant effect on perceived trustworthiness when stratifying the data into male and female participants (F = 2.417, p = .092). Male participants rated f_HIGH as significantly less trustworthy (m = 4.18, sd = 1.79) than f_LOW (m = 4.63, sd = 1.69, p = .032). For female participants, video condition did not statistically influence perceived trustworthiness; nonetheless, female participants rated m_HIGH as less trustworthy (m = 3.93, sd = 2.01) than m_MID (m = 4.17, sd = 1.79) and m_LOW (m = 4.04, 1.80). Although not statistically significant, perhaps due to the reduced power with smaller sample sizes for each condition, males more than females rated m_HIGH as trustworthy, and females more than males rated f_HIGH as trustworthy. See Figs. 3a and 3b.

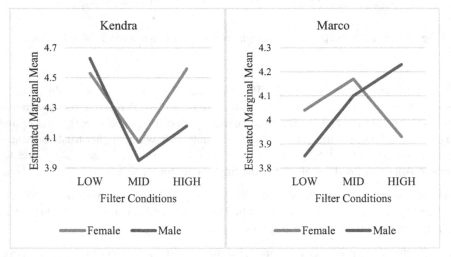

Fig. 3a & 3b. Mean trustworthiness ratings for Kendra (left) and Marco (right) by participant gender.

Likeableness. Likeableness did not significantly improve donation willingness for either actor in the final models. However, video condition had a significant effect on perceived likeableness (F = 4.03, p = .018) overall. f_LOW (m = 4.78, sd = 1.64) was rated as more likable than f_MID (m = 4.23, sd = 1.81, p = .007) or f_HIGH (m = 4.65, sd = 1.70, p = .498). Video condition did not significantly affect Marco's perceived likeableness (F = .466, p = .498. m_LOW: m = 4.10, sd = 1.95; m_MID: m = 4.26, sd = 1.97; m_HIGH: m = 4.30, sd = 1.83).

Naturalness. Increased naturalness did not improve the odds of donation willingness for either actor in the final models. For Marco, perceived naturalness was not affected by filter use (F = .515, p = .598. m_LOW: m = 4.13, sd = 1.86; m_MID: m = 4.35, sd = 1.90; m_HIGH: m = 4.2, sd = 1.86). Filter use had a significant effect on perceived naturalness for Kendra (F = 30.70, p = .006): f_LOW was rated as more natural than both f_MID and f_HIGH (p = .002 and .025, respectively; f_LOW: m = 4.86, sd = 1.61; f_MID: m = 4.22, sd = 1.76; f_HIGH: m = 4.41, sd = 1.77). However, although f_LOW serves as the analog to m_LOW in this study because it was rated as least attractive by our pilot study participants, f_LOW was created using filters (originally, to appear untrustworthy). Therefore, this finding does not support our expectation that filtered videos would be perceived as less natural.

Message Characteristics. Video condition did not statistically affect Marco's message credibility (F = 1.708, p = .182), justifiability (F = 1.363, p = .257), or persuasiveness (F = .625, p = .536). For Kendra, however, video condition significantly affected message credibility (F = 3.134, p = .045). f_LOW (m = 4.58, sd = 1.70) was perceived as significantly more credible than f_MID (m = 4.06, sd = 1.80, p = .014). The mean difference in justifiability was marginally significant (F = 2.787, p = .063), where f_LOW (m = 4.47, sd = 1.722) was significantly more justified than f_MID (m = 3.99, 1.834, p = .027) and marginally more justified than f_HIGH (m = 4.08, sd = 1.82, p = .074). Persuasiveness approached marginal significance (F = 2.215, p = .110), where the largest difference was between f_LOW (m = 4.22, sd = 1.77) and f_MID (m = 3.78, sd = 1.93). There were no significant differences in ratings of message characteristics according to the gender of the study participants.

5.3 Attractiveness Manipulations and Participants' Ratings of Attractiveness

Our filtered manipulations approached marginal significance (F = 2.209, p = .111) in the predicted direction for participants' attractiveness ratings for Marco. However, they were not associated with participants' attractiveness ratings for Kendra (F = .212, p = .809), because ratings for f_LOW were different than we expected.

Specifically, f_LOW (m = 4.01, sd = 1.62) was not rated as significantly more or less attractive than f_MID by either male (m = 4.00, sd = 1.54) or female (m = 4.03, sd = 1.69) respondents. We expected f_LOW to be rated as less attractive, based on the ratings of the pilot study participants. However, as expected, f_MID (m = 3.97, sd = 1.72; males m = 3.98, sd = 1.61, females m = 3.96, sd = 1.82) was rated as less attractive than f_HIGH (m = 4.10, sd = 1.72; males m = 4.07, sd = 1.81, females m = 4.13, sd = 1.77). See Figs. 4a & 4b.

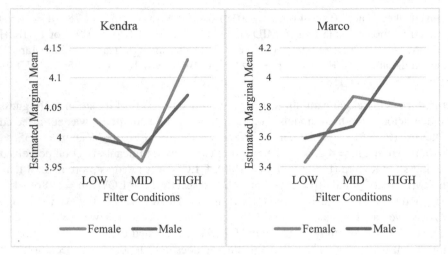

Figs. 4a & b. Mean attractiveness ratings for Kendra (left) and Marco (right) by participant gender.

6   Discussion

Our first research question asked: How does beauty enhancement via filters affect viewer perceptions and evaluation of donation *requesters* in VMC? What factors are associated with positive evaluations (i.e., attractiveness, trustworthiness, likability, naturalness) of the requester? Does this vary by gender of the viewer?

Attractiveness enhancement was marginally significantly associated with increased donation willingness for the male actor, and trustworthiness was significantly associated, consistent with previous research that found that attractiveness and trustworthiness are often correlated [21, 31]. Interestingly, our study participants did not appear to notice the use of filters, even in the extreme attractiveness enhanced versions, as the filtered videos were not rated as less natural than any other versions. This suggests that filters could be used to obtain halo effects when making video donation requests without risking appearing inauthentic.

Willingness to donate was also strongly predicted by previous donation experience and respondent demographics – in particular, being non-white, and for Marco, being younger and having a lower income. Previous research into charitable donations found that donors were more likely to be white, older, and wealthier [2, 19]. The differences in our results can be partially explained by the situation of our request – an individual requesting donation for himself or herself, rather than for a charitable organization, on social media. Younger people use social media more than older people, and thus they are more likely to have encountered social media requests of this sort and to be comfortable with them; young people also tend to have lower incomes. Although Marco and Kendra are similar in age, younger survey respondents appeared to relate more to Marco, for reasons that are unclear. Conversely, nonwhites donated more to both actors. This could be because the actors are ethnically and racially ambiguous: A survey by Osili et al. [20] found that donors of color give to their ethnic communities. They are also more likely than white donors to engage in informal giving or giving through crowdfunding sites to strangers [20].

Survey respondent gender significantly affected the results. Women were more willing to donate to Kendra, partially consistent with our expectation that women would be more likely to donate overall [30]. This finding could also be a reflection of gender-based homophily [13]. Relatedly, we found a nonsignificant tendency (Figs. 3a & 3b) for participants to rate the extreme beauty filtered version of the opposite sex actor as less trustworthy than the extreme beauty filtered same-sex actor. These findings are consistent with findings that men view very attractive women with suspicion (e.g., McGloin & Denes [17]), although it is the opposite of what the halo effect literature predicts (e.g., Bak, 2010). Relatedly, more respondents chose to donate to Marco than Kendra overall (cf. Ullah & Zhou [26]), mainly because males were significantly less likely to donate to f_HIGH.

In addition to the above, we encountered unexpected findings as regards the f_LOW version of the female actor. In the pilot study, f_LOW was rated as the least attractive version, less attractive than the original unedited version of Kendra. However, in the final study, f_LOW was not rated as less attractive than f_MID. One reason for this difference may be differences between the pilot population and the study population. The survey participants' levels of education and income were lower than those of the pilot test participants, and the survey participants were more ethnically diverse. The two populations may have different beauty standards.

The results for f_LOW present other paradoxes. Despite being created originally to exhibit less trustworthy traits, f_LOW was rated as the most trustworthy version and more likeable than f_MID. Moreover, although filtered, f_LOW was rated as significantly more natural than any other version. It is possible that untrustworthy-looking faces are believed to be commonplace and hence perceived as natural. Relatedly, f_LOW's plain looks may have inspired trust because she looks like a real person. An average-looking woman may also have been perceived more positively and even as being more attractive when requesting help.

Our second research question asked: How does beauty enhancement via filters affect viewer perceptions of, and responses to, *requests* for donation in VMC? What factors are associated with positive responses to requests (i.e., the credibility, justifiability, and persuasiveness of the request)? Does this vary by gender of the viewer?

Different request qualities influenced willingness to donate to each actor. Request credibility was significant for Marco, whereas for Kendra, justified and persuasive were significant factors. This shows that the halo effect can extend beyond the individual to the contents of their communication (see also Kaplan [12]). Indeed, it is difficult to separate request qualities from requester qualities. It seems that for Marco, whether he seemed believable was most important to the participants, whereas Kendra was judged based on whether her need was valid or convincing. This suggests that the same request conveyed by different genders may be judged by different criteria, regardless of the individuals' attractiveness. It is also possible that factors such as perceived ethnicity[5] or social class played a role in which message characteristics were oriented to by potential donors.

---

[5] Marco is Hispanic and, as such, his appearance could have triggered stereotypes about Hispanic males.

However, male and female viewers did not evaluate message characteristics differently, regardless of filtered condition.

7   Conclusions

7.1   Contributions

This study extended research on halo effects by applying AR facial filters to actors requesting donations in a modality that has recently seen an upsurge in popularity, video-mediated communication. The investigation also breaks new ground regarding the interaction of filter effects and participant demographics.

Main take-aways of the study are as follows:

1) Filter users were not perceived as fake or artificial. Appearance-enhancing filter use mainly went undetected (as such) in the study context, which involved communicating with strangers.
2) Using appearance enhancing filters can make one appear more trustworthy, likable, and (paradoxically) more natural. It can also enhance the perception of the quality of the request itself.
3) Using appearance enhancing filters can increase the likelihood of getting donations in requests on social media, especially if it makes one appear more trustworthy.
4) However, this may depend on the perceiver's gender. Men distrusted the very attractive version of the female actor and were less likely to donate to her. An implication of this finding is that extreme beauty filter use can be counter-productive when communicating with mixed-gender audiences.
5) The case of f_LOW illustrates that making oneself look less conventionally attractive with filters may also increase the likelihood of getting a positive response to social media donation requests.

7.2   Broader Implications

Empirically demonstrating to what extent and in what ways digital modification of faces affects the outcomes of common social actions has the potential to facilitate strategic filter use by individuals and organizations in order to optimize outcomes, including raising money for charitable causes, garnering favors, influencing voters, and striking up online relationships. However, it could also facilitate deception and fraud, as in the use of filters to appear more trustworthy in charity scams [34]. Thus, the ethical implications of video face filter use also need to be considered.

7.3   Limitations and Future Directions

A limitation of this study is that Kendra's (filtered) baseline turned out not to be equivalent to Marco's (unedited) baseline in terms of attractiveness ratings, despite being rated as the least attractive version in our pilot study, and this affected the overall findings for Kendra. Future work on video filters should ensure that stimuli are comparable. It should also endeavor to match the demographics of the pilot population with the intended study population.

Due to the number of conditions in our study, we only used one male and one female actor, which limits the generalizability of our findings as regards requester gender effects. Future research could try to replicate our findings using multiple actors and actors of different ethnicities. Additionally, we used a single scenario designed to be moderately effective in eliciting donations; however, scenarios that elicit greater or lesser sympathy could be explored in future research.

Another limitation is that currently available video beauty filter apps are designed primarily to amplify and improve feminine facial features (e.g., making lips fuller, softening the jawline) as opposed to enhancing masculine features (e.g., squaring the jaw, adding facial hair). Thus, our ability to make Marco appear more traditionally handsome was limited; the enhancements tended to make him look younger and more feminine. Although Little [15] reports that male feminized faces may be considered more attractive because they can mitigate the perception of negative personality traits associated with male features, a traditionally handsome man may be perceived differently from an attractive man with feminine features in the context of charitable giving.

Finally, requests for donations are increasingly made in videos posted to social media, and they are often made by and for the benefit of individuals, rather than charitable organizations. There is a need for more research along the lines of the present study to understand this trend, as well as how people strategically exploit self-presentational resources such as filters to optimize request outcomes.

Appendix: Donation Request Script

"Hi, guys, those of you who know me, know I don't like to ask anyone for help. But I'm in a tough situation and I don't know what else to do.

I'm a digital artist, and I've been supporting myself with commissions to get through art school. My old MacBook Pro has been on its last legs for about a year, and yesterday it completely died.

Luckily I had most of my work backed up, but I need to finish a big commission that's due in a couple of weeks.

I really need a laptop with a hi-rez screen and a powerful graphics card to make my art. I found a refurbished MacBook Pro that would be perfect for my needs, but it's still $1200, and I don't have that kind of money right now.

I've got a part-time job, but it's barely enough to pay my rent. My commissions are what's been paying for my groceries and gas. My parents can't help, they had to close their restaurant because of covid. I'm not sure what else to do except reach out to all of you.

So, if you guys have ever enjoyed or shared any digital art, please consider donating to help me support myself through my art. [Looks down] Uh, there's a link below you can click on that'll take you to my GoFundMe page with examples of my work.

I would really appreciate any amount you can give. Thanks so much, guys!".

References

1. Bak, P.: Sex differences in the attractiveness halo effect in the online dating environment. J. Bus. Media Psychol. **1**(1), 1–7 (2010)
2. Bekkers, R., Wiepking, P.: Who gives? A literature review of predictors of charitable giving part one: religion, education, age and socialisation. Voluntary Sector Rev. **2**(3), 337–365 (2011)
3. Champ, P.A., Bishop, R.C.: Donation payment mechanisms and contingent valuation: an empirical study of hypothetical bias. Environ. Resource Econ. **19**(4), 383–402 (2001)
4. Chen, J., et al.: The Zoom boom: how video calling impacts attitudes towards aesthetic surgery in the COVID-19 era. Aesthetic Surg. J. **41**(12), 2086–2093 (2021)
5. Chua, T.H.H., Chang, L.: Follow me and like my beautiful selfies: Singapore teenage girls' engagement in self- presentation and peer comparison on social media. Comput. Hum. Behav.. Hum. Behav. **55**, 190–197 (2016)
6. Dion, K., Berscheid, E., Walster, E.: What is beautiful is good. J. Pers. Soc. Psychol. **24**(3), 285–290 (1972)
7. Filho, J.E., Inkpen, K.M., Czerwinski, M.: Image, appearance and vanity in the use of media spaces and videoconference systems. In: Teasley, S., Havn, E. (eds.) ACM International Conference on Supporting Group Work 2009, pp. 253–262. Sanibel Island Florida, USA (2009)
8. Fribourg, R., Peillard, E., Mcdonnell, R.: Mirror, mirror on my phone: Investigating dimensions of self-face perception induced by augmented reality filters. In: 2021 IEEE International Symposium on Mixed and Augmented Reality (ISMAR), pp. 470–478. Italy (2021)
9. Goering, E., Connor, U.M., Nagelhout, E.: Steinberg, R: Persuasion in fundraising letters: an interdisciplinary study. Nonprofit Volunt. Sect. Q. Volunt. Sect. Q. **40**(2), 228–246 (2011)
10. Herring, S.C., Dedema, M., Rodriguez, E., Yang, L.: Gender and culture differences in perception of deceptive video filter use. In: HCI International 2022 - Late Breaking Papers. Interaction in New Media, Learning and Games. Lecture Notes in Computer Science, vol. 13517. Springer (2022)
11. Javornik, A., et al.: 'What lies behind the filter?': uncovering the motivations for using augmented reality (AR) face filters on social media and their effect on well-being. Comput. Hum. Behav.. Hum. Behav. **128**, 107–126 (2022)
12. Kaplan, R.M.: Is beauty talent? sex interaction in the attractiveness halo effect. Sex Roles **4**(2), 195–204 (1978)
13. Lanido, D., Volkovich, Y., Kappler, K., Kaltenbrunner, A.: Gender homophily in online dyadic and triadic relationships. EPJ. Data Sci. **5**(1), 19 (2016)
14. Leong, J., Perteneder, F., Rajvee, M. R., Maes, P.: "Picture the audience...": Exploring private AR face filters for online public speaking. In: Proceedings of the 2023 CHI Conference on Human Factors in Computing Systems, pp. 1–13. Germany (2023)
15. Little, A.C.: Facial attractiveness. In: Shackelford, T.K., Weekes-Shackelford, V.A. (eds.) Encyclopedia of evolutionary psychological science, pp. 2887–2891. Springer, Cham (2021)
16. Manning, S., Bejarano, T.: Convincing the crowd: Entrepreneurial storytelling in crowdfunding campaigns. Strateg. Organ.. Organ. **15**, 194–219 (2016)
17. McGloin, R., Denes, A.: Too hot to trust: examining the relationship between attractiveness, trustworthiness, and desire to date in online dating. New Media Soc. **20**(3), 919–936 (2018)
18. McGuire, W.J.: Attitudes and attitude change. In: Lindzey, G., Aronson, E. (eds.) Handbook of social psychology, vol. 2. Random House, pp. 233–346 (1985)
19. Mesch, D.J., Rooney, P.M., Steinberg, K.S., Denton, B.: The effects of race, gender, and marital status on giving and volunteering in Indiana. Nonprofit Volunt. Sect. Q. Volunt. Sect. Q. **35**(4), 565–587 (2006)

20. Osili, et al.: Everyday donors of color: diverse philanthropy during times of change. Report: Lilly Family School of Philanthropy (2021, updated December 2022). https://scholarworks. iupui.edu/server/api/core/bitstreams/829fe636-91b6-4ea1-a683-e501148e2620/content, last accessed 2023/09/17

21. Oosterhof, N.N., Todorov, A.: The functional basis of face evaluation. Proc. Natl. Acad. Sci. **105**(32), 11087–11092 (2008)

22. Reis, H.T., Wheeler, L., Spiegel, N., Kernis, M.H., Nezlek, J., Perri, M.: Physical attractiveness in social interaction: II. Why does appearance affect social experience? J. Personality Soc. Psychol. **43**(5), 979–996 (1982)

23. Rosenblat, T.S.: The beauty premium: physical attractiveness and gender in dictator games. Negot. J.. J. **24**(4), 465–481 (2008)

24. Stirrat, M., Perrett, D.I.: Valid facial cues to cooperation and trust: Male facial width and trustworthiness. Psychol. Sci. **21**(3), 349–354 (2010)

25. Todorov, A., Baron, S.G., Oosterhof, N.N.: Evaluating face trustworthiness: a model based approach. Soc. Cogn. Affective Neurosci. **3**(2), 119–127 (2008)

26. Ullah, S., Zhou, Y.: Gender, anonymity and team: What determines crowdfunding success on Kickstarter. J. Risk Financial Manage. **13**(4), 80–106 (2020)

27. van Leeuwen, M.L., Macrae, C.N.: Is beautiful always good? Implicit benefits of facial attractiveness. Soc. Cogn.Cogn. **22**(6), 637–649 (2004)

28. Wang, Q., Perlmutter Bowen, S.: The limits of beauty: Effects of physician attractiveness and biological sex on patient trust, satisfaction, and disclosure. Commun. Res. Rep.. Res. Rep. **31**(1), 72–81 (2014)

29. Waters, R.D., Auger, G. A.: Crowded but not crowded out: comparing the solicitation strategies and outcomes of nonprofits' and individual's GoFundMe campaigns. J. Philanthropy Mark., e1766 (2022)

30. Wiepking, P., Bekkers, R.: Who gives? a literature review of predictors of charitable giving. Part Two: Gender, family composition and income. Voluntary Sector Rev. **3**(2), 217–245 (2012)

31. Wilson, R.K., Eckel, C.C.: Judging a book by its cover: beauty and expectations in the trust game. Polit. Res. Q. **59**(2), 189–202 (2006)

32. Wymer, W., Drollinger, T.: Charity appeals using celebrity endorsers: celebrity attributes most predictive of audience donation intentions. Voluntas: Int. J. Voluntary Nonprofit Organizations **26**, 2694–2717 (2015)

33. Yim, M.Y.-C., Park, S.-Y.: "I am not satisfied with my body, so I like augmented reality (AR)": consumer responses to AR-based product presentations. J. Bus. Res. **100**, 581–589 (2019)

34. Zenone, M., Snyder, J.: Fraud in medical crowdfunding: A typology of publicized cases and policy recommendations. Policy Internet **11**(2), 215–234 (2019)

35. Zhao, K., Zhou, L., Zhao, X.: Multi-modal emotion expression and online charity crowdfunding success. Decis. Support. Syst.. Support. Syst. **163**, 113842 (2022)

"If I Like BLANK, What Else Will I Like?": Analyzing a Human Recommendation Community on Reddit

Thi Binh Minh Cao[1] and Toine Bogers[1,2](✉) ⓘ

[1] Department of Communication & Psychology, Aalborg University, Copenhagen, Denmark
tobo@itu.dk
[2] Department of Computer Science, IT University of Copenhagen, Copenhagen, Denmark

Abstract. While there have been several studies on how users experience algorithmic recommendations and their explanations, we know relatively little about human recommendations and which item aspects humans highlight when describing their own recommendation needs. A better understanding of human recommendation behavior could help us design better recommender systems that are more attuned to their users. In this paper, we take a step towards such understanding by analyzing a Reddit community dedicated to requesting and providing for recommendations: /r/ifyoulikeblank. After a general analysis of the community, we provide a more detailed analysis of the prevalent music requests and the example items used to ask for these recommendations. Finally, we compare these human recommendations to algorithmic recommendations to better characterize their differences. We conclude by discussing the implications of our work for recommender systems design.

Keywords: Human Recommendation · Music Recommendation · Reddit · Narrative-driven Recommendation · Mixed Methods

1 Introduction

Recommender systems help users make decisions by suggesting and presenting content in a relevant way. Before the advent of algorithmic recommendation, this role used to be fulfilled by other people through various channels, such as printed media, radio and TV, bestseller lists and word-of-mouth recommendations between friends. Many of these channels have since served as inspiration for and potential input sources to different recommendation algorithms. Over the years, there have been several studies of how people interact with algorithmic recommendations [2,10,11,15], and how to craft understandable explanations for these recommendations [12,21,24].

However, very little of this work has focused on *human recommendations* (i.e., recommendations between two individuals without any algorithmic intervention), and which item attributes humans highlight when describing their

I. Sserwanga et al. (Eds.): iConference 2024, LNCS 14596, pp. 70–83, 2024.
https://doi.org/10.1007/978-3-031-57850-2_6

own recommendation needs or explaining recommendations to others. A deeper understanding of how human recommendation works could help in designing better recommender systems that are more attuned to their users.

In order to better study how people both request and provide recommendations to each other, we turn to a specific subcommunity on Reddit with over 944,000 subscribers: the /r/ifyoulikeblank subreddit. The self-described[1] purpose of this subreddit is to solicit and provide *"recommendations of any relevant media—whether it be music, television, video games, movies, or anything else"*. Subscribers to /r/ifyoulikeblank can post either requests for recommendations (e.g., *"If I like the vibrant musical experimentation and catchiness of Hip Hop acts like Kid Cudi and Kanye West, what other Hip Hop would I like?"*) or offer recommendations to others (e.g., *"If you like 'Arrested Development', you might like 'Agents of Cracked'."*). Other users can react to these posts and contribute with their own recommendations. In 2022 alone, /r/ifyoulikeblank received over 23,000 posts and close to 87,000 comments, and was in the top 1000 of most popular subreddits, which suggests that it offers its users a popular way of addressing their recommendation needs that other popular streaming services such as Spotify, Netflix and Disney+ cannot seem to fulfil.

In this paper, we present an analysis of a random sample of 300 /r/ifyoulikeblank posts and their 1,620 comments to learn more about the types of recommendations being provided and requested, and which item aspects are highlighted in doing so. We find that close to 80% of all posts focus on music, so we explore the characteristics of human music recommendation in more detail. Finally, we compare these human music recommendations to algorithmic recommendations from Spotify in order to learn whether and how they differ from each other. In sum, we address the following research questions:

RQ1 What characterizes the human recommendations and recommendation needs shared on /r/ifyoulikeblank?

RQ2 What characterizes the music requests and the recommendations provided by other users?

RQ3 How do human music recommendations compare to those provided through algorithmic means?

Our study does not only provide an overview of an interesting online community, but it can also be used to inform the algorithmic and interface design of future recommender systems, in particular conversational recommenders.

The rest of this paper is organized as follows. In the next section, we highlight some of the relevant related work, after which we describe our methodology in Sect. 3. We present our results in Sect. 4 and conclude in Sect. 5.

---

[1] Available at https://www.reddit.com/r/ifyoulikeblank/, last visited May 1, 2023.

2   Related Work

2.1   Human Recommendation

While there has been plenty of work on how people experience algorithmic curation [11,15], relatively little attention has been paid to how people experience
recommendations from family, friends, or strangers, compared to recommendations from an algorithm. To the best of our knowledge, the only direct comparison
between human and algorithmic recommendations is the work by Yeomans et
al. [23], which also comes closest to our own work. They conducted a set of four
different studies on joke recommendation where they asked paired-up participants who knew each other well to predict which jokes the other would like,
based on a small set of jokes rated by their partner. Yeomans et al. found that
recommender systems outperformed humans, regardless of how well they knew
each other. However, their study also showed that people are averse to relying
on recommender systems, which they suggest stems from the perception that
the human recommendation process is easier to understand. Further evidence
for this was uncovered by Kunkel et al. [14], who found that human explanations were seen as more trustworthy and of higher quality than algorithmically
generated explanations. Park and Kenshiro [17] presented similar findings for
collaborative playlist creation. While not the same as direct recommendation,
creating a playlist together involves recommending songs to one's collaborators.
Park and Kenshiro [17] found that people were more willing to engage with
human-contributed recommendations compared to algorithmic ones in the case
of successful collaborative playlists.

2.2   Narrative-Driven Recommendation

There is precedence for analyzing recommendation requests posted to online discussion fora: in the past, researchers have investigated which content, metadata,
contextual, and experiential aspects users describe when asking for help with
their recommendation needs for books [7,13], games [5], and movies [3,4]. These
requests—like those on /r/ifyoulikeblank—are an example of *narrative-driven recommendation*, a recommendation scenario defined by Bogers and Koolen [6],
where historical data on user preferences is combined with a narrative description of the aspects of items desired by the users, along with an optional context
of use. They analyzed a set of book recommendation needs posted to the Library-
Thing forums and identified seven different aspects that users refer to as relevant
for them in their narrative descriptions: content, metadata, familiarity, engagement, accessibility, novelty, and socio-cultural relevance. After its introduction
in 2017, has seen slow adoption by others due to its similarities with and application to conversational recommenders [1,9,18,19]. Eberhard et al. [9] focused
on narrative-driven recommendation for the movie domain and constructed a
dataset of human requests and recommendations based on a different Reddit
community, while Afzali et al. [1] took a similar approach to tourism/POI recommendation.

2.3 Conversational Recommendation

Narrative descriptions of recommendation needs are also a common staple of conversational recommendation, where the user describes their preferences to a conversational agent who uses questioning and feedback mechanisms to build up an understanding of the user needs [8,16,18]. Radlinski et al. [19] argue that developing natural language representations of user's recommendation needs—such as those posted to /r/ifyoulikeblank—could provide several benefits. Representing user needs using clear and concise language instead of numerical representations in the form of embeddings could offer greater transparency and allow for better, more practical over recommendations. Related to this is the work by Schnabel et al. [20], who developed a taxonomy of different aspects in natural language expressions of recommendation needs.

3 Methodology

In this section, we discuss how we collected, annotated and analyzed the human recommendations contained in posts from the /r/ifyoulikeblank community.

3.1 Data Collection

The /r/ifyoulikeblank subreddit was created on March 31, 2011 to provide a place for Reddit users to request and offer recommendations of any relevant media. The admins describe two different types of allowed posts in the posting guidelines: (1) posts where the user is looking for recommendations (to be prefixed with the [IIL] tag for "If I like"), and (2) posts where the user is offering recommendations (to be prefixed with [IYL] for "If you like"). Users are encouraged to include at least one example item and a description of why they like it, with a maximum of 9 examples.

While historical data on subreddits is not available from Reddit itself, the service SubredditStats[2] provides a reasonably complete picture of subscriber, post and comment counts[3] On April 30, 2023, /r/ifyoulikeblank had 944,629 subscribers and 20,797 posts and 76,554 comments were posted to the subreddit in the last 365 days, which ranked it 813 out of all 3.4 million subreddits, indicating a level of activity. This amounts to 57.0 posts and 209.7 comments per day, suggesting that many people have recommendation needs they cannot (or do not want to) have fulfilled by a recommender system. Figure 1 visualizes the development of (a) post, (b) comment and (c) subscriber statistics over the past years, and shows a peak in activity coinciding with the pandemic and subsequent increase in number of subscribers. Activity levels have since returned to pre-pandemic levels.

---

[2] Available at https://subredditstats.com/r/ifyoulikeblank, last visited May 1, 2023.

[3] Only 2.0% of all 3,760 data points were missing from the subscriber counts collected between October 29, 2012 and April 30, 2023. This suggests these data can be used to provide a reliable indication of subreddit activity levels and popularity for /r/ifyoulikeblank.

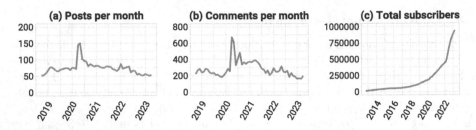

Fig. 1. Change in activity levels for (a) posts, (b) comments, and (c) subscribers on the /r/ifyoulikeblank subreddit.

To collect posts and comments from /r/ifyoulikeblank, we adapted an existing Reddit crawler[4] to continuously crawl all threads and comments posted to these three subreddits from June 1, 2018 to August 3, 2018, resulting in 4,957 discussion threads. From this sample, we randomly selected 300 threads consisting of the initial post and all associated comment posts ($n = 1,620$) for analysis. For each of these 1,920 posts, we have the post title and text, the user ID of the poster, the rank of a post in the thread, and the post score (= the number of upvotes minus downvotes).

3.2   Data Annotation

The presence of the [IIL] and [IYL] tags allowed us to automatically detect whether an initial post was a recommendation request or an offer in 257 of the 300 cases. The remaining 43 posts were categorized manually. One post was spam and was filtered from the dataset, leaving 299 original posts and 1,620 comments for annotation and analysis. With our research questions in mind, one of the authors then performed open coding on the title and text of 50 random posts to develop an initial set of codes. During the subsequent axial coding phase by both authors, we settled on the final set of codes shown in Table 1. We then applied this coding scheme to the 299 original posts and 1,620 comments[5]. Whenever we encountered new codes or examples of media type, we updated our coding scheme, with the final version shown in Table 1.

4   Results

4.1   Analyzing /r/ifyoulikeblank

In this section, we answer our first research question: what characterizes the human recommendations and recommendation needs shared on /r/ifyoulikeblank?

---

[4] Available at https://github.com/lucas-tulio/simple-reddit-crawler, last visited May 2, 2022.

[5] Our annotated dataset along with our R code for analysis is available from Zenodo at https://doi.org/10.5281/zenodo.10413359.

Table 1. Overview of the coding scheme.

Code	Description
Seed item	The seed item(s) in the initial posts for which recommendations were requested or offered
Recommended item	The recommended item(s) mentioned either in the initial post or by other users in the comments
Recommendation quality	Feedback from the original requester on the quality of a recommendation, translated to a binary scale
Positive attributes	Positive attributes of a recommended item according to the user writing the post or comment
Negative attributes	Negative attributes of a recommended item according to the user writing the post or comment
Media type	The type of media recommendations are requested or offered for, further subdivided into six categories: (1) **Music** (e.g., song, artist, album, genre), (2) **Books** (e.g., book, author, manga, story); (3) **Movies** (e.g., movie, actor, director, producer); (4) **TV shows** (e.g., TV show, cartoon, anime); (5) **Games** (e.g., game, gamer); and (6) **Miscellaneous** (e.g., car, food, podcast, YouTube channel, website)

The majority of the posts in our sample ($n = 299$) are requests for recommendations at 97.0% ($n = 290$) with only 9 posts offering recommendations (3.0%). There does not appear to be any difference between these two post types in terms of how many replies they garner with a mean thread length of 8.4 and 8.1 comments respectively, which is not significant according to a Mann-Whitney U test ($U(N_{request} = 219, N_{offer} = 9) = 940.5$, $z = 0.23$, $p = 0.82$)). When comparing the types of comments on both post types, both tend to be a mixture of feedback on the recommendation(s) and other recommendations in the same vein. Because of the small number of threads offering recommendations, we will focus exclusively on the 290 recommendation requests and their 1,561 associated comments in the rest of this paper.

Requests and Comments. Requests have an average length of 41.3 words ($Md = 30$, $SD = 39.7$), but with a long tail of longer requests as shown in Fig. 2a. Comments tend to be shorter on average ($M = 24.3$, $Md = 13$, $SD = 45.9$). Out of all 290 requests, 219 received at least one reply (75.5%), indicating an active community, with the mean number of replies a request received (i.e., the thread length) at 6.4 ($Md = 3$, $SD = 9.1$). Figure 2b shows the positively skewed distribution of thread length (in comments received). Post length was neither correlated with thread length ($r(288) = 0.062$, $p = 0.294$) nor with the total number of items recommended in a thread ($r(288) = 0.073$, $p = 0.212$). In other words, writing more words in one's request is not necessarily a recipe for more interaction with or receiving more recommendations from other users.

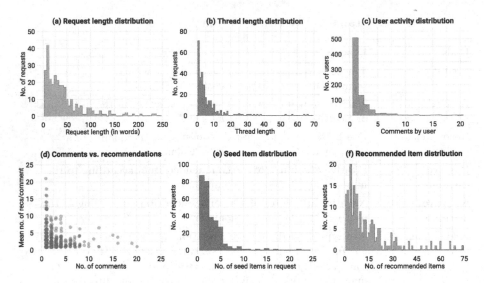

Fig. 2. Distributions of (a) request length in words, (b) thread length as number of comments received, (c) user activity level in terms of comments posted, (e) seed items, and (f) recommended items mentioned per request. Subfigure (d) shows the relation between the number of comments a user has posted and the mean number of recommendations they include per post.

Users. There is one user in our sample who has posted four requests to the /r/ifyoulikeblank subreddit, nine who each posted two requests, and the remaining 280 posts come from different users. There are 799 different users who have left at least one comment in our sample ($n = 290$) with an average of 1.95 comments per user ($Md = 1$, $SD = 2.05$). The distribution of comments per user in Fig. 2c is long-tailed. Users post comments in 1.54 different threads on average (with a maximum of 15 different threads), suggesting that most users only react to requests where they feel knowledge and where their specialized knowledge could be of use. As Fig. 2d shows, there is no relationship between the number of comments a user posts and how many recommendations they include: some users provide many recommendations in a single comment, while other provide only a few but in many different threads.

Seeds and Recommendations. Users are thorough in describing their recommendation need with regard to providing example items: the original poster (OP) offers more than one seed item in 89.8% of all requests, with a mean of 3.0 items included in each request ($Md = 2$, $SD = 2.6$). The distribution of seed items in Fig. 2e shows that while most people provide between 1–5 examples, providing additional examples is not uncommon. Asking for recommendations appears to be a fruitful strategy: on average, a request receives 12.1 recommendations ($Md = 6$, $SD = 18.8$) and 75.5% of all requests get at least one recommendation with one requests even receiving 143 different recommendations. Figure 2f shows the distribution of recommended items. Providing more seed items is positively correlated with receiving more recommendations ($r(288) = 0.385$, $p = 0.000$).

Recommendation Quality. The OP behind a request is the final judge of recommendation quality. Our crawl does not contain data on which comments an OP has upvoted in their own thread—and this could also be a sign of encouragement instead of approval—so instead we consider the explicit comments an OP leaves in their own thread. A majority of threads (55.5%) does not ever receive OP comments or feedback, so it can be hard to assess for other users (as well as us researchers) whether their recommendations were correct. 17.2% of OPs comment at least once in their own thread. We manually assessed each OP comment and assigned a binary score if the comment represented feedback instead of something else, e.g., additional information about their recommendation need. The OP provided feedback on at least one of the recommendations in 23.7% of the requests ($n = 290$). Feedback is almost overwhelmingly positive: 129 out of 145 cases of feedback were positive (89.0%).

Media Type. Figure 3a shows the distribution of top- and lower-level media types requested by users. A majority are for music (80.3%), which we examine in more detail in the next section, with movies and TV shows a distant second. Due to the small sample size for media types other than music, it is difficult to come up with a conclusive explanation for this big difference, but one possible explanation for this is that current music streaming services make it hard for (or less visible to) their users to get recommendations based on a single artist or song than movie and TV streaming services do. Given the small sample sizes for the non-musical media types, Table 2 shows some interesting differences in activity levels. Movie and TV requests receive the most comments on average, but requests for movies tend to be twice as verbose as TV shows. Books seem to be the most difficult to solve with the least responses from other users despite having the longest requests. Music requests tend to see the most active dialogue between OP and other users in terms of OP feedback, although these differences remain small.

4.2 Analyzing Human Music Recommendations

In this section, we answer our second research question: what characterizes the music requests and the recommendations provided by other users? Because of the prevalence of music requests, we will analyze this subset of the data ($N = 233$) in more detail in this section. Figure 3a shows that music requests most commonly provide songs (70.0%) and artists (35.2%).

Genres. Eight users (or 3.4%) explicitly provided one or more example genres when requesting music recommendations whereas two users (0.9%) provided an example song to describe the genre instead. To compare the different music requests, we used the Spotify API[6] to look up the genres for each of the artists

---

[6] Available at https://developer.spotify.com/documentation/web-api, last visited April 4, 2024.

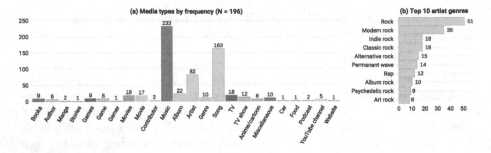

Fig. 3. Distributions of (a) different top-level and lower-level media types over all 290 requests, and (b) the top 10 genres attached to the 196 artist seeds mentioned in 82 different music requests.

Table 2. Request activity levels split by media type. The numbers in the four right-most columns are all calculated on a per-request basis, e.g., books receive 3.8 comments per request on average of which 0.1 contain feedback from the OP, who receives 4.7 recommendations on average per request.

Media type	n	Length	Comments	Feedback	Recommendations
Books	9	50.6	3.8	0.1	4.7
Games	9	43.9	5.6	0.2	9.6
Movies	18	43.0	9.3	0.4	19.2
Music	233	41.8	6.0	0.6	12.0
TV	18	24.3	7.2	0.3	14.2
Miscellaneous	10	42.9	4.5	0.1	6.3

provided as seed items. 196 different artists examples are mentioned in 82 different requests that describe their need by mentioning an artist, and these artists together represent 383 different genres. Fig. 3a shows the top 10 most frequent genres, which suggests a big chunk of /r/ifyoulikeblank music requests are dominated by rock music and its different subgenres.

Links. Some OPs choose to include links to example songs or albums to aid other users in the recommendation process: even when unfamiliar with an example artist or song, listening to it might still allow a user to provide recommendations. Links are used in 66 (28.3%) of all 233 music requests, and 26.6% ($n = 332$) of all 1,246 comments. YouTube is by far the most popular domain as it is used for 1,182 of 1,341 (88.1%) of the links included in all posts and comments. Other common domains include Reddit ($n = 79$), Spotify ($n = 31$), SubtleTV ($n = 24$), BandCamp ($n = 17$), SoundCloud ($n = 10$), and Vimeo ($n = 4$). When zooming in on Spotify links, 15 were song links, 14 links to other playlists, and two single links to an album and an artist. All other domains are used less than five times. Providing links appears to increase the chances of success and interaction: the number of links included in a requests is significantly positively correlated with the number of comments a request receives ($r(231) = 0.501$, $p = 0.000$), with the number of recommendations received ($r(231) = 0.488$, $p = 0.000$), and with the feedback received ($r(231) = 0.391$, $p = 0.000$).

Positive/Negative Attributes. We annotated our 1,462 music requests and comments for any clearly positive and negative descriptions of the recommendations in the thread by the OP or other users. Only 55 posts contained positive descriptions and 13 contained negative attributes. Skimming these descriptions revealed that off-the-shelf sentiment analysis tools may not be useful here, as a majority of the descriptions refer to specific musical properties that would not be detected be a sentiment analyzer (e.g., *"catchy melodies"*, *"lacking cool element"*). While positive remarks will often describe what a user likes about a song (e.g., *"scifi vibe"*, *"weirdly chipper stoner rock"*, *"upbeat music"*), the negative comments usually describe what is lacking from a recommendation (e.g., *"lacking positive atmosphere"*, *"chorus not powerful enough"*, *"lacking cool element"*). When we generated a unigram frequency list for all the positive attribute descriptions and filtered out stopwords, the most frequent words included many genres (e.g., *"pop"*, *"rock"*, *"doom"*), musical properties (e.g., *"atmospheric"*, *"catchy"*, *"melodic"*), and moods (e.g., *"dark"*, *"upbeat"*, *"free-feeling"*), although the sample size remains too small for any definitive conclusions. Nevertheless, our initial analysis of these positive and negative attributes suggests that there is a need for domain-specific sentiment analyzers for the music domain that can identify when such descriptors reflect positively or negative about a song or artist.

4.3 Comparing Human to Algorithmic Recommendations

For our third research question, we focus on whether and how the human-provided recommendations differ from algorithmic recommendations. We use the Spotify API to request 10 recommendations for each of the seed songs mentioned in requests. There appears to be very little overlap between the human recommendations and the ones provided by Spotify: the average Jaccard similarity between the two sets of recommendations is only 0.000281, suggesting that human and algorithmic music recommendation provide very different experiences.

In addition to requesting recommendations from the Spotify API, we also retrieved the popularity scores for each seed song, each song recommended by a Reddit user, and each Spotify recommendation. Spotify's proprietary popularity of a song is a value between 0 and 100, with 100 being the most popular. The popularity is based on *"the total number of plays the track has had and how recent those plays are"*[7]. Given that each OP turned to Reddit to have their recommendation needs fulfilled for a reason, one might expect humans to produce better recommendations and perhaps more off-the-beaten-path suggestions that commercial streaming services are not able to provide. One might also expect that OPs turn to /r/ifyoulikeblank because their seed songs are not in the musical mainstream, necessitating help from others.

---

[7] https://hexdocs.pm/spotify_web_api/Spotify.Tracks.html.

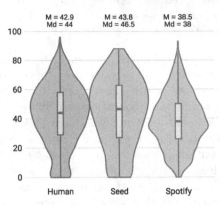

Fig. 4. Distributions of popularity scores for seed songs versus the human and Spotify recommendations.

While we cannot evaluate the quality of the Spotify recommendations using our observational study, we do see that, in terms of popularity bias, the human recommendations tend to contain more popular songs on average than those provided by Spotify. However, both hypotheses do not seem to be true. Figure 4 shows the popularity score distributions for seed songs, human-recommended songs and songs recommended by Spotify. It shows that, of these three categories, seed songs have the highest popularity scores, followed by human recommendations, with Spotify recommendations being the lowest on average. This popularity difference between Spotify recommendations and human recommendations is statistically significant according to a Mann-Whitney U Test ($U(N_{human} = 1149$, $N_{Spotify} = 3724) = 2457307.5$, $z = 7.63$, $p = 0.000$). This lower popularity bias for Spotify matches the findings of Turnbull et al. [22], who showed that commercial streaming services exhibit less popularity bias than state-of-the-art recommendation models.

5   Discussion and Conclusions

In this paper, we presented an analysis of the human recommendation behavior in the /r/ifyoulikeblank Reddit community. In this subreddit, users can both post requests describing a recommendation need they have or offer recommendations of their own, both prompted and unprompted. Our analysis of 300 requests and 1,920 comments suggests that seeking human recommendations is a fruitful strategy, as they receive around 12 recommendations on average. When describing their recommendation need, users that provide more example items and links to those examples for easy inspection by other users are more successful in having their needs met. There appears to be an influence of media type on how successful the human recommendation process is, but the sample size for most media types was to small to draw any definitive conclusions.

Previous work has shown that people trust human recommendations more than algorithmic recommendations [14,17,23], and we suspect this is also a major reason for turning to this online community instead of using the recommendation functionality provided by modern media streaming services. Another reason could be that current-generation recommender systems are simply not able to handle these narrative-driven requests [6], both algorithmically and in terms of the user interface. Finally, another possibility could be that users turn to /r/ifyoulikeblank with particular 'niche' needs, although most seed items appear to fall solidly in the musical mainstream, so this is not the only reason.

Implications. Beyond providing an overview of an interesting online community, our analysis also has value for the design of future recommender systems. Recommendation on /r/ifyoulikeblank revolves around providing example items and a more careful comparison of the seed and recommendation items could possibly reveal interesting similarity dimensions that could be modeled algorithmically for generating better item-to-item recommendations.

In general, a better understanding of how people describe their recommendation needs—such as in the music domain—could result in better interfaces for music browsing, search and recommendation. Knowing which item attributes are important to users could lead to interfaces that offer affordances for prioritizing some of the attributes over others in music recommendation.

The recommendation needs posted to /r/ifyoulikeblank could be especially useful in training and designing better conversational recommenders. The discussions that take place in the Reddit threads mimic the turn-taking in conversational interaction with initial specification of the user's need, clarification questions, and critiquing of the provided answers. Many subreddits exist in addition to /r/ifyoulikeblank that could provide such training data, such as /r/musicsuggestions, /r/moviesuggestions, /r/gamesuggestions, /r/tipofmytongue, /r/namethatsong, and /r/tipofmyjoystick to name but a few. To this end, we also need to develop better domain-specific information extraction tools that understand how music is described textually. This would be essential for a conversational music recommender to understand what a user is looking for and how to map this to properties of the songs in the catalog.

Limitations. While we have attempted to characterize a representative sample of threads posted to /r/ifyoulikeblank, it is dominated by music requests. As a result, our conclusions on non-music requests cannot be seen as generalizable; only our music subset is large enough for a reliable characterization. Another skew in our dataset is that, despite the posting guidelines for the /r/ifyoulikeblank subreddit, only a handful of original posts offer recommendations. The overwhelming majority request them, which as a result are more representative.

We also believe more in-depth analysis of textual feedback is needed. Content analysis using musically-trained experts could be beneficial here in identifying which properties of songs and artists are most relevant. Finally, our popularity analysis in Sect. 4.3 was only conducted on songs, but we do not know how artists popularity compares to this.

Future Work. Possible future work could include a more thorough analysis of the textual feedback that users provide on recommendation, as well as an in-depth analysis of the (dis)similarities between the human and Spotify recommendations and the example items provided by the OP. Another fruitful option would be to develop a proper coding scheme for annotating the requests and comments, similar to the work on categorizing and analyzing information needs related to books [7,13], games [5], and movies [3,4].

References

1. Afzali, J., Drzewiecki, A.M., Balog, K.: POINTREC: a test collection for narrative-driven point of interest recommendation. In: SIGIR 2021: Proceedings of the 44th International ACM SIGIR Conference on Research and Development in Information Retrieval, pp. 2478–2484. ACM, New York, NY, USA (2021). https://doi.org/10.1145/3404835.3463243
2. Alvarado, O., Abeele, V.V., Geerts, D., Verbert, K.: "i really don't know what 'thumbs up' means": algorithmic experience in movie recommender algorithms. In: Lamas, D., Loizides, F., Nacke, L., Petrie, H., Winckler, M., Zaphiris, P. (eds.) INTERACT 2019. LNCS, vol. 11748, pp. 521–541. Springer, Cham (2019). https://doi.org/10.1007/978-3-030-29387-1_30
3. Bogers, T.: Searching for Movies. In: iConference 2015 Proceedings. iDEALS (2015). http://hdl.handle.net/2142/73689
4. Bogers, T., Gäde, M., Koolen, M., Petras, V., Skov, M.: "What was this movie about this chick?". In: Chowdhury, G., McLeod, J., Gillet, V., Willett, P. (eds.) iConference 2018. LNCS, vol. 10766, pp. 323–334. Springer, Cham (2018). https://doi.org/10.1007/978-3-319-78105-1_36
5. Bogers, T., Gäde, M., Koolen, M., Petras, V., Skov, M.: "Looking for an amazing game i can relax and sink hours into...": a study of relevance aspects in video game discovery. In: Taylor, N.G., Christian-Lamb, C., Martin, M.H., Nardi, B. (eds.) iConference 2019. LNCS, vol. 11420, pp. 503–515. Springer, Cham (2019). https://doi.org/10.1007/978-3-030-15742-5_48
6. Bogers, T., Koolen, M.: Defining and supporting narrative-driven recommendation. In: RecSys 2017: Proceedings of the Eleventh ACM Conference on Recommender Systems, pp. 238-242. ACM, New York, NY, USA (2017). https://doi.org/10.1145/3109859.3109893
7. Bogers, T., Koolen, M.: "I'm looking for something like ...": combining narratives and example items for narrative-driven book recommendation. In: Anelli, V.W., et al.. (eds.) Proceedings of the Workshop on Knowledge-aware and Conversational Recommender Systems 2018 co-located with 12th ACM Conference on Recommender Systems, KaRS@RecSys 2018, Vancouver, Canada, October 7, 2018. CEUR Workshop Proceedings, vol. 2290, pp. 35–43. CEUR-WS.org (2018). https://ceur-ws.org/Vol-2290/kars2018_paper7.pdf
8. Christakopoulou, K., Radlinski, F., Hofmann, K.: Towards conversational recommender systems. In: Proceedings of the 22nd ACM SIGKDD International Conference on Knowledge Discovery and Data Mining, pp. 815–824. ACM (2016)
9. Eberhard, L., Walk, S., Posch, L., Helic, D.: Evaluating narrative-driven movie recommendations on reddit. In: IUI 2019: Proceedings of the 24th International Conference on Intelligent User Interfaces, pp. 1-11. ACM, New York, NY, USA (2019). https://doi.org/10.1145/3301275.3302287

10. Freeman, S., Gibbs, M., Nansen, B.: 'Don't mess with my algorithm': exploring the relationship between listeners and automated curation and recommendation on music streaming services. First Monday **27**(1), 1–19 (2022)
11. Freeman, S., Gibbs, M., Nansen, B.: Personalised but impersonal: listeners' experiences of algorithmic curation on music streaming services. In: CHI 2023: Proceedings of the 2023 CHI Conference on Human Factors in Computing Systems. ACM, New York, NY, USA (2023). https://doi.org/10.1145/3544548.3581492
12. Karimi, A.H., Barthe, G., Schölkopf, B., Valera, I.: A survey of algorithmic recourse: contrastive explanations and consequential recommendations. ACM Comput. Surv. **55**(5), 1–29 (2022)
13. Koolen, M., Bogers, T., van den Bosch, A., Kamps, J.: Looking for books in social media: an analysis of complex search requests. In: Hanbury, A., Kazai, G., Rauber, A., Fuhr, N. (eds.) ECIR 2015. LNCS, vol. 9022, pp. 184–196. Springer, Cham (2015). https://doi.org/10.1007/978-3-319-16354-3_19
14. Kunkel, J., Donkers, T., Michael, L., Barbu, C.M., Ziegler, J.: Let me explain: impact of personal and impersonal explanations on trust in recommender systems. In: CHI 2019: Proceedings of the 2019 CHI Conference on Human Factors in Computing Systems, pp. 1-12. ACM, New York, NY, USA (2019). https://doi.org/10.1145/3290605.3300717
15. Lee, J.H., Pritchard, L., Hubbles, C.: Can We listen to it together?: Factors influencing reception of music recommendations and post-recommendation behavior. In: ISMIR 2019: Proceedings of the 20th International Society for Music Information Retrieval Conference, pp. 663–669 (2019)
16. Mahmood, T., Ricci, F.: Improving recommender systems with adaptive conversational strategies. In: Proceedings of the 20th ACM Conference on Hypertext and Hypermedia, pp. 73–82. ACM (2009)
17. Park, S.Y., Kaneshiro, B.: Social music curation that works: insights from successful collaborative playlists. In: Proceedings of the ACM on Human-Computer Interaction, 5(CSCW1), April 2021. https://doi.org/10.1145/3449191
18. Pramod, D., Bafna, P.: Conversational recommender systems techniques, tools, acceptance, and adoption: a state of the art review. Expert Syst. App. **203**, 117539 (2022)
19. Radlinski, F., Balog, K., Diaz, F., Dixon, L., Wedin, B.: On natural language user profiles for transparent and scrutable recommendation. In: SIGIR 2022: Proceedings of the 45th International ACM SIGIR Conference on Research and Development in Information Retrieval, pp. 2863–2874. ACM, New York, NY, USA (2022). https://doi.org/10.1145/3477495.3531873
20. Schnabel, T., Ramos, G., Amershi, S.: "Who doesn't like dinosaurs?": finding and eliciting richer preferences for recommendation. In: RecSys 2020: Proceedings of the 14th ACM Conference on Recommender Systems, pp. 398-407. ACM, New York, NY, USA (2020). https://doi.org/10.1145/3383313.3412267
21. Tintarev, N., Masthoff, J.: A survey of explanations in recommender systems. In: Proceedings of the 2007 IEEE 23rd International Conference on Data Engineering Workshop, pp. 801–810. IEEE (2007)
22. Turnbull, D.R., McQuillan, S., Crabtree, V., Hunter, J., Zhang, S.: Exploring Popularity Bias in Music Recommendation Models and Commercial Steaming Services (2022)
23. Yeomans, M., Shah, A., Mullainathan, S., Kleinberg, J.: Making sense of recommendations. J. Behav. Decis. Mak. **32**(4), 403–414 (2019)
24. Zhang, Y., Chen, X., et al.: Explainable recommendation: a survey and new perspectives. Found. Trends Inf. Retr. **14**(1), 1–101 (2020)

Can Chatbot Anthropomorphism and Empathy Mitigate the Impact of Customer Anger on Satisfaction?

Jian Tang[1][✉] ⓘ, Yunran Wang[1] ⓘ, Xinxue Zhou[2][✉] ⓘ, Jiayan Guo[1] ⓘ, and Chenguang Li[3][✉] ⓘ

[1] School of Information, Central University of Finance and Economics, Beijing, China
jiantang@cufe.edu.cn
[2] School of Business, Guangxi University, Nanning, China
zhouxinxue@gxu.edu.cn
[3] School of Insurance, Central University of Finance and Economics, Beijing, China
lichenguang@cufe.edu.cn

Abstract. When customers initiate inquiries with negative emotions following a service failure, whether chatbot service agents can alleviate the undesirable outcomes resulting from negative emotions poses significant challenges for researchers and practitioners. Drawing upon computers are social actors (CASA) framework, this study examines how chatbot anthropomorphism and empathy features function as emotion-focused service recovery to mitigate the adverse effect of customer anger on satisfaction. The model is validated through a three-way factorial between-subjects experiment. The results demonstrate that anger negatively affects satisfaction. Chatbots with empathy features can mitigate this negative impact, whereas chatbots with anthropomorphism features cannot. The findings provide theoretical and practical implications for designing chatbot service agents to achieve emotion-based service recovery.

Keywords: Service Recovery · Customer Satisfaction · Chatbots · Computers are Social Actors

1 Introduction

Chatbots have been widely applied in various fields such as e-commerce, financial services, and healthcare [1]. Chatbots have advantages such as extended availability and fast response time. Customer service employees need to serve customers with different emotions. Particularly, when service failures occur, customers initiate inquiries with negative emotions. How chatbots handle customer' negative emotions and mitigate their adverse effects is a crucial issue that needs to be addressed in service recovery [2].

Customer negative emotions represent a subjective, unpleasant experience. Anger, as the most typical representation of negative emotions, is an activated, high-intensity emotion [3, 4]. Compared to other negative emotions, anger is more likely to trigger users' unfavorable responses. If chatbots cannot effectively handle customer anger, customer satisfaction may be further hampered, potentially leading to severe consequences for the business. Service recovery can adopt problem-focused or emotion-focused strategies [5]. The problem-focused solutions rely on chatbots' intelligence levels and problem-solving capabilities to ensure the effectiveness of service recovery [6]. Emotion-focused solutions, built on service personnel' emotional intelligence, regulate customers' negative emotions and enlighten a new direction for chatbot service. Currently, only a few studies have considered the role of chatbot emotional remediation, particularly when faced with customer negative emotions such as anger [2].

The computers are social actors (CASA) framework [7–9] suggests humans may treat media agents as human-like beings and use social scripts evolved from human-human communication in human-computer interaction. Chatbot is a type of media agent that can display social cues and become a source of social interaction [7]. In the customer service context, customers may perceive chatbots as real social entities and apply corresponding social norms to their interactions with chatbots. How social features of chatbots may impact customer experience and behavior has become a prominent problem [10].

Among these features, anthropomorphism and empathy have garnered significant attention [11], with existing research yielding inconsistent findings. Anthropomorphic features of chatbots can elicit positive responses from customers [12, 13]. Conversely, high anthropomorphism may cause negative consequences [14]. While some research suggests that empathy expressed by chatbots can make them appear more friendly to humans [15], others contend that chatbots with empathy might lead humans to perceive emotional manipulation [11]. In this study, building on the CASA paradigm, we focus on two critical social features of chatbots, anthropomorphism and empathy, and investigate the following research questions: (1) What is the impact of customer anger on satisfaction? (2) How do chatbot anthropomorphism and empathy mitigate the impact of customer anger on satisfaction?

2   Related Work

2.1   Customer Anger

Customer negative emotions can have detrimental effects on businesses. Westbrook and Oliver [16] define customer negative emotions as unpleasant experiences that customers have after using or consuming products or services. When products and services provided by a company do not meet customer expectations, customers are likely to experience negative emotions, lose trust in the company, and opt for other brands or providers [17, 18]. When customers are assisted by chatbots, leaving them with negative emotions can further intensify their unfavorable feelings and make them reluctant to engage with the brand [19].

2.2   Chatbot Anthropomorphism

Chatbot anthropomorphism refers to features that make chatbots appear and behave similarly to humans [20, 21]. Chatbot anthropomorphism can be manifested in visual cues, conversational cues, and behavioral cues [22]. For example, a chatbot with an avatar, a human-like name, and a vivid conversation style is perceived to be more similar to a human agent. Existing literature shows the mixed effects of anthropomorphism. Incorporating anthropomorphism features into chatbot design can lead to positive customer responses [12, 13]. Han [23] found that consumers' perception of chatbot anthropomorphism can increase their enjoyment and promote their purchase intentions. Yen and Chiang [24] found that anthropomorphism features can increase consumer trust in chatbots and their willingness to make purchases in the e-commerce context. However, a growing body of literature has found anthropomorphism features negative effects. For example, Crolic et al. [2] discovered that if a chatbot with a high level of anthropomorphism fails to address customers' problems, customer satisfaction becomes much lower due to violated expectations. Therefore, the improper deployment of anthropomorphism may cause negative results [25].

2.3 Chatbot Empathy

Empathy refers to the ability to recognize, understand, and respond to the emotions of others [26]. Empathy is another social feature that manifests a chatbot's emotional intelligence [11]. Existing research has identified the positive influence of chatbot empathy. For instance, Jiang et al. [27] found that empathy is a key mechanism in improving information processing in human-AI interactions. Diederich et al. [28] found that conversational agents with empathy can lead to higher customer service satisfaction. Lv et al. [29] explored chatbot service failures and discovered that empathetic chatbots can reduce the psychological distance between customers and brands and increase the willingness to continue using the service.

3   Research Hypotheses

According to the CASA framework, humans can naturally and mindlessly apply social scripts evolved from human-human interaction to human-computer interaction [9]. Especially when a technological artifact has sufficient social cues and indicates its potential to be a source of social interaction, humans respond to the human-like artifact in a social manner. Anthropomorphism and empathy are two social features that signify the emotional intelligence of chatbots. Chatbots with anthropomorphism and empathy features display human-like social cues and make customers perceive them as human counterparts. The social affordances of chatbots in customer service enable them to conduct emotion-based service recovery. The specific effects of emotion-based service recovery may depend on what social features the chatbots have and in what context the chatbots are used. Next, we propose the research hypotheses on the impact of customer anger on satisfaction and how chatbot anthropomorphism and empathy may alter their relationships.

3.1   The Impact of Customer Anger

Anger is a stimulating and intense emotion [30]. Compared to other emotions with lower arousal and intensity, anger is more likely to trigger human decision-making and behavioral responses [31]. When customers are angry, the aroused negative feelings can lead to damaging consequences, such as reduced customer satisfaction and an increased likelihood of service termination [32]. Satisfaction reflects a customer's subjective and overall feelings in service encounters, referring to the degree of contentment and fulfillment experienced by a customer with a product, service, or overall interaction with a business. When customers are assisted by chatbot agents, the stimulated anger emotion remains to generate unfavorable outcomes. For example, Crolic et al. [2] suggest anger emotion can lead to lower satisfaction ratings. Therefore, we propose the following hypothesis:

Hypothesis 1: Customer anger negatively impacts satisfaction.

3.2 The Role of Anthropomorphism and Empathy

Anthropomorphism is defined as attributing human characteristics, mental states, and emotions to non-human entities. Benbya et al. [11] pointed out that the degree of chatbot anthropomorphism is crucial, as inappropriate anthropomorphic design can make users switch between treating a chatbot as a human and constantly exploring a chatbot's capability, which diminishes the customer service experience. Puzakova et al. [33] suggested that anthropomorphism can reduce customer engagement and brand preference. The CASA paradigm suggests users perceive robots as having social attributes, thoughts, and awareness, and thus apply interpersonal interaction norms to human-machine interactions [34], thereby generating higher expectations for their social and problem-solving capabilities. If an anthropomorphic chatbot fails to address customers' problems, customers' expectation of chatbot service is violated and therefore results in lower customer satisfaction with the service [2]. Hence, we propose the following hypothesis:

Hypothesis 2: Chatbots with more anthropomorphic cues can strengthen the negative impact of customer anger on satisfaction.

Chatbot empathy refers to its ability to recognize, understand, and respond to customer emotions [26]. Chatbot empathy may have a positive impact on user attitudes and behavior. For example, empathy can lead to friendly perception of human-robot interaction [15] and higher customer service satisfaction [28]. Empathy is a critical mechanism in human-AI interactions, contributing to emotional responses and well-being [27]. Empathetic responses from AI chatbots after service failures can induce customers' emotional transformation and significantly enhance their willingness to continue using the service [35]. Considering the role of empathy in transforming customer emotion, this paper argues the positive effect of empathy when the customer is angry. Therefore, this paper proposes the following hypothesis:

Hypothesis 3: Chatbots with empathy can weaken the negative impact of customer anger on satisfaction.

4 Research Design

4.1 Experiment Design

This paper employs a between-subjects experiment with 2 (Anger: Presence vs. Absence) × 2 (Anthropomorphism: High vs. Low) × 2 (Empathy: Presence vs. Absence) factorial design (see Table 1). Anger is stimulated by the experimental scenario, which is adapted from Crolic et al. [2]. The scenario is as follows: "You rent a camera from an online store for an upcoming trip. After receiving the camera, you find the photos and videos taken by the camera are blurry. You want to make an exchange. The store policy states that you need to return the camera for troubleshooting and then receive a replacement. The new delivery date is estimated to be later than your departure date. To receive the exchange before your leave, you contact the customer service for help". In the condition of anger, additional texts are provided to simulate anger (see Table 1). A pilot study was conducted to ensure that the anger is triggered and the chatbot design does not exhibit any gender bias.

Table 1. Experiment treatments

Variable	Presence or High	Absence or Low	References
Anger	• After trying the camera many times, you realize the camera is broken • The store requires you to provide proof that the camera is broken • You call the customer service number on the store homepage, but no one answers • You feel frustrated and angry	• No additional texts	Crolic et al. [2]
Anthropomorphism	• Using a human-like avatar as a profile photo • Human-like nicknames • Social-oriented communication style	• Using the store logo as a profile photo • No nicknames • Task-oriented communication style	Go and Sundar [22], Miao et al. [36], Chattaraman et al. [37]
Empathy	• Using social interaction words to show compassion and comfort • Displaying responsibility • Using a perspective-taking approach	• Absent any of these empathetic cues	Shum et al. [38], Portela and Granell-Canut [39], Clark et al. [40]

4.2 Experimental Procedures

Participants were recruited from a crowdsourcing platform named Credamo. They gave informed consent and voluntarily attended the study. Upon entering the experiment, participants first read the experiment instructions and were then randomly assigned to one of eight experimental groups. Participants viewed the corresponding experimental materials for their assigned group, which were presented in the form of images depicting a simulated interaction between the chatbot and the customer. Subsequently, participants answered questions related to their experiences and perceptions. Participants received monetary incentives upon completing the experiment.

4.3 Measurements and Manipulation Questions

Five items measuring user satisfaction were adapted from Cheng and Jiang [41]. Individual characteristics, including age, gender, education, prior experience with chatbot, and the frequency of chatbot usage were measured as control variables. Manipulation questions about customer anger, chatbot anthropomorphism, and empathy were asked to ensure the treatments were effective. Besides, four attention check questions were included at different stages of the experiment to filter participants who were not paying close attention. A pilot study was conducted to assess the effectiveness of the experimental materials, the experimental procedure, and the measurements. Adjustments were made based on the results of the pilot study.

5 Results

5.1 Descriptive Analysis

The formal experiment recruited 447 participants from the same platform. Among them, 19 subjects failed the attention check questions, and three subjects were under the age of 18, resulting in a total of 425 valid participants. Table 2 shows the demographic information of participants. This study used Kruskal-Wallis analysis to examine the individual characteristics of participants. Except for the frequency of chatbot usage in the past year ($p = 0.023$), participants in the experimental groups did not differ significantly in terms of age ($p = 0.139$), gender ($p = 0.732$), education level ($p = 0.122$), and prior experience with chatbot ($p = 0.412$). These variables were all included as control variables in the regression analysis for hypothesis testing.

5.2 Hypotheses Testing

The measurements of satisfaction show good reliability and validity, with Cronbach's α value of 0.953, the composite reliability value of 0.964, and the average variance extracted value of 0.842. Table 3 shows the results of multiple regression analysis of the impact of customer anger on satisfaction. Model 1 only includes control variables. Model 2 includes the effect of anger, showing a negative impact on satisfaction ($\beta = -0.082, p < 0.1$), thus providing support for H1.

Table 2. Descriptives of demographic information

Variable	Value	Frequency	Percentage (%)
Age	19–25	85	20.0
	26–30	116	27.3
	31–35	120	28.2
	36–40	65	15.3
	More than 40	39	9.2
Gender	Male	171	40.2
	Female	254	59.8
Education	Middle school or below	3	0.7
	High school	16	3.8
	College/ Undergraduate	323	76
	Master	79	18.6
	Doctoral	4	0.9
Prior experience with chatbot	Zero	0	0.0
	One to five	76	17.9
	Six to ten	158	37.2
	More than ten	191	44.9
The frequency of chatbot usage	Never	0	0
	Occasionally	119	28
	Often	283	66.6
	Every time	23	5.4

Table 3. The Impact of Anger on Satisfaction

Dependent Variable	Satisfaction	
Independent Variable	Model 1	Model 2
Anger		$-0.082(-1.721) +$
Control		
Age	0.117(2.456) *	0.123(2.576) **
Gender	$-0.058(-1.210)$	$-0.061(-1.282)$
Education	0.115(2.382) *	0.108(2.225) *
Prior experience	$-0.075(-1.396)$	$-0.070(-1.291)$
Frequency	0.201(3.728) ***	0.202(3.756) ***

(*continued*)

Table 3. (*continued*)

Dependent Variable	Satisfaction	
Independent Variable	Model 1	Model 2
Adjusted R^2	0.055	0.060
F-value	5.980	5.500

Note: The coefficients are standardized, and the T-values are in parentheses
+p<0.1, *p < 0.05, **p < 0.01, ***p < 0.001. ($N = 425$)

Table 4 presents the impact of chatbot anthropomorphism. In Model 1, anger has a significant negative impact on customer satisfaction ($\beta = -0.093, p < 0.1$). The interaction term between anthropomorphism and anger has a negative impact. Although the interaction term is not significant ($\beta = -0.083, p = 0.45$), which means H2 is not supported, the negative coefficient of the interaction term suggests that high anthropomorphism exacerbates the negative impact of anger emotions on chatbot satisfaction.

Table 5 presents the impact of chatbot empathy features. In Model 1, empathy has a significant positive impact on satisfaction ($\beta = 0.127, p < 0.01$). In Model 2, the interaction term between empathy and customer anger has a significant and positive impact, indicating that chatbot empathy can mitigate the negative impact of customer anger on satisfaction ($\beta = 0.149, p < 0.1$). Thus, H3 is supported.

Table 4. The moderating role of Chatbot anthropomorphism

Dependent Variable	Satisfaction	
Independent Variable	Model 1	Model 2
Anger	−0.093(−1.953) +	−0.049(−0.757)
Anthropomorphism	0.102(2.143) *	0.148(2.282) *
Anger × Anthropomorphism		−0.083(−1.036)
Control		
Age	0.116(2.430) *	0.116(2.434) *
Gender	−0.058(−1.214)	−0.06(−1.258)
Education	0.102(2.115) *	0.107(2.198) *
Prior experience	−0.07(−1.311)	−0.066(−1.218)
Frequency	0.19(3.539) ***	0.185(3.433) ***

(*continued*)

Table 4. (*continued*)

Dependent Variable	Satisfaction	
Independent Variable	Model 1	Model 2
Adjusted R^2	0.068	0.068
F-value	5.411	4.870

Note: The coefficients are standardized, and the T-values are in parentheses
+p < 0.1, *p < 0.05, **p < 0.01, ***p < 0.001. ($N = 425$)

Table 5. The Moderating Role of Chatbot Empathy

Dependent Variable	Satisfaction	
Independent Variable	Model 1	Model 2
Anger	−0.07(−1.471)	−0.169(−2.367) *
Empathy	0.127(2.694) **	0.047(0.734)
Anger × Empathy		0.149(1.854) +
Control		
Age	0.129(2.721) **	0.137(2.881) **
Gender	−0.056(−1.184)	−0.061(−1.288)
Education	0.105(2.188) *	0.098(2.033) *
Prior experience	−0.068(−1.265)	−0.069(−1.302)
Frequency	0.195(3.659) ***	0.202(3.793) ***
Adjusted R^2	0.074	0.079
F-value	5.822	5.554

Note: The coefficients are standardized, and the T-values are in parentheses
+p < 0.1, *p < 0.05, **p < 0.01, ***p < 0.001. ($N = 425$)

6 Discussion and Future Research

This study investigates the role of chatbots in emotion-focused service recovery when customer anger is simulated. Our research findings show that chatbots featured with empathy can alleviate the negative effects of anger on satisfaction, but chatbots with anthropomorphism have no effects. The study suggests that when using chatbots for service recovery, it's essential to be mindful of using social features to cope with customers' needs, especially when customers experience negative emotions such as anger. One possible explanation is that excessively high anthropomorphism in design may raise customer expectations, and when the chatbot cannot meet these expectations, it may lead to expectation violations and, consequently, exacerbate customers' negative reactions. Additionally, chatbots with empathy may be effective emotional remediation methods to mitigate the consequences of customer anger.

The study has several limitations. First, this paper studies a specific condition of emotion-focused service recovery, which is how chatbot anthropomorphism and empathy affect the relationships between customer anger and satisfaction. Future research should investigate the underlying mechanism. Second, anger is only one type of negative emotion. Customers may experience more complex emotions which causes additional challenges for chatbot design. Third, the characteristics of service failure such as service severity and service urgency may change the effectiveness of server recovery [42]. Last, the experimental materials used in the study are text-based scenarios, which have limitations in their fidelity to fully represent real-world scenarios. Future research could consider conducting field experiments in real-world settings and engaging participants in interactive dialogues.

Acknowledgement. This work was partially supported by the National Natural Science Foundation of China (71904215, 72072194), the Social Science Fund Research Base Project of Beijing (19JDGLB029), and the Young Talents Support Program from the Central University of Finance and Economics (No: QYP2211).

References

1. Følstad, A., Araujo, T., Law, E.L.-C., Brandtzaeg, P.B., Papadopoulos, S., Reis, L., et al.: Future directions for chatbot research: an interdisciplinary research agenda. Computing **103**(12), 2915–2942 (2021). https://doi.org/10.1007/s00607-021-01016-7
2. Crolic, C., Thomaz, F., Hadi, R., Stephen, A.T.: Blame the bot: anthropomorphism and anger in customer-chatbot interactions. J. Mark. **86**(1), 132–148 (2022). https://doi.org/10.1177/00222429211045687
3. Gelbrich, K.: Anger, frustration, and helplessness after service failure: coping strategies and effective informational support. J. Acad. Mark. Sci. **38**(5), 567–585 (2010)
4. Lerner, J.S., Keltner, D.: Beyond valence: Toward a model of emotion-specific influences on judgement and choice. Cogn. Emot.. Emot. **14**(4), 473–493 (2000). https://doi.org/10.1080/026999300402763
5. Van Vaerenbergh, Y., Varga, D., De Keyser, A., Orsingher, C.: The service recovery journey: Conceptualization, integration, and directions for future research. J. Serv. Res. **22**(2), 103–119 (2019)
6. Hsu, C.-L., Lin, J.C.-C.: Understanding the user satisfaction and loyalty of customer service chatbots. J. Retail. Consum. Serv.Consum. Serv. **71**, 103211 (2023)
7. Gambino, A., Fox, J., Ratan, R.A.: Building a stronger CASA: extending the computers are social actors paradigm. Hum.-Mach. Commun. **1**, 71–85 (2020)
8. Nass, C., Steuer, J., Tauber, E.R.: Computers are social actors. In: Proceedings of the SIGCHI Conference on Human Factors in Computing Systems, 1994, pp. 72–78 (1994)
9. Reeves, B., Nass, C.I.: The media equation: How people treat computers, television, and new media like real people: Cambridge University Press (1996)
10. Song, M., Zhang, H., Xing, X., Duan, Y.: Appreciation vs. apology: Research on the influence mechanism of chatbot service recovery based on politeness theory. J. Retailing Consumer Serv. **73**, 103323 (2023)
11. Benbya, H., Pachidi, S., Jarvenpaa, S.: Artificial intelligence in organizations: implications for information systems research. J. Assoc. Inf. Syst. **22**(2), 281–303 (2021). https://doi.org/10.17705/1jais.00662

12. Schanke, S., Burtch, G., Ray, G.: Estimating the impact of "humanizing" customer service chatbots. Inf. Syst. Res. **32**(3), 736–751 (2021). https://doi.org/10.1287/isre.2021.1015

13. Toader, D.-C., Boca, G., Toader, R., Măcelaru, M., Toader, C., Ighian, D., et al.: The effect of social presence and chatbot errors on trust. Sustainability **12**(1), 256 (2019). https://doi.org/10.3390/su12010256

14. Hill, V.: Digital citizenship through game design in minecraft. New Library World **116**(7–8), 369–382 (2015). https://doi.org/10.1108/NLW-09-2014-0112

15. Leite, I., Pereira, A., Mascarenhas, S., Martinho, C., Prada, R., Paiva, A.: The influence of empathy in human–robot relations. Int. J. Hum. Comput. Stud.Comput. Stud. **71**(3), 250–260 (2013)

16. Westbrook, R.A., Oliver, R.L.: The dimensionality of consumption emotion patterns and consumer satisfaction. J. Consumer Res. **18**(1), 84–91 (1991). https://doi.org/10.2307/2489487

17. Lou, C., Kang, H., Tse, C.H.: Bots vs. humans: how schema congruity, contingency-based interactivity, and sympathy influence consumer perceptions and patronage intentions. Int. J. Advertising **41**(4), 655–684 (2022). https://doi.org/10.1080/02650487.2021.1951510

18. Bougie, R., Pieters, R., Zeelenberg, M.: Angry customers don't come back, they get back: the experience and behavioral implications of anger and dissatisfaction in services. J. Acad. Mark. Sci. **31**(4), 377–393 (2003)

19. Kull, A.J., Romero, M., Monahan, L.: How may I help you? driving brand engagement through the warmth of an initial chatbot message. J. Bus. Res. **135**, 840–850 (2021). https://doi.org/10.1016/j.jbusres.2021.03.005

20. Diederich, S., Brendel, A.B., Kolbe, L.M.: Designing anthropomorphic enterprise conversational agents. Bus. Inf. Syst. Eng. **62**(3), 193–209 (2020). https://doi.org/10.1007/s12599-020-00639-y

21. Pfeuffer, N., Benlian, A., Gimpel, H., Hinz, O.: Anthropomorphic information systems. Bus. Inf. Syst. Eng. **61**, 523–533 (2019)

22. Go, E., Sundar, S.S.: Humanizing chatbots: the effects of visual, identity and conversational cues on humanness perceptions. Comput. Hum. Behav. **97**, 304–316 (2019). https://doi.org/10.1016/j.chb.2019.01.020

23. Han, M.C.: The impact of anthropomorphism on consumers' purchase decision in chatbot commerce. J. Internet Commerce **20**(1), 46–65 (2021). https://doi.org/10.1080/15332861.2020.1863022

24. Yen, C., Chiang, M.-C.: Trust me, if you can: a study on the factors that influence consumers' purchase intention triggered by chatbots based on brain image evidence and self-reported assessments. Behav. Inf. Technol. **40**(11), 1177–1194 (2021). https://doi.org/10.1080/0144929X.2020.1743362

25. Hill, J., Randolph Ford, W., Farreras, I.G.: Real conversations with artificial intelligence: a comparison between human–human online conversations and human–chatbot conversations. Comput. Hum. Behav. **49**, 245–250 (2015). https://doi.org/10.1016/j.chb.2015.02.026

26. Levenson, R.W., Ruef, A.M.: Empathy: a physiological substrate. J. Pers. Soc. Psychol. **63**(2), 234–246 (1992)

27. Jiang, Q., Zhang, Y., Pian, W.: Chatbot as an emergency exist: Mediated empathy for resilience via human-AI interaction during the COVID-19 pandemic. Inf. Process. Manage. **59**(6), 103074 (2022). https://doi.org/10.1016/j.ipm.2022.103074

28. Diederich, S., Janßen-Müller, M., Brendel, A., Morana, S.: Emulating empathetic behavior in online service encounters with sentiment-adaptive responses: insights from an experiment with a conversational agent. In: Proceedings of the Fortieth International Conference on Information Systems, vol. 2 (2019)

29. Lv, X., Yang, Y., Qin, D., Cao, X., Xu, H.: Artificial intelligence service recovery: the role of empathic response in hospitality customers' continuous usage intention. Comput. Hum. Behav. **126**, 106993 (2022). https://doi.org/10.1016/j.chb.2021.106993
30. Bodenhausen, G.V., Sheppard, L.A., Kramer, G.P.: Negative affect and social judgment: The differential impact of anger and sadness. Eur. J. Soc. Psychol. **24**(1), 45–62 (1994)
31. Averill, J.R.: Studies on anger and aggression: Implications for theories of emotion. Am. Psychol. **38**(11), 1145–1160 (1983)
32. Funches, V.: The consumer anger phenomena: causes and consequences. J. Serv. Mark. **25**(6), 420–428 (2011)
33. Puzakova, M., Kwak, H.: Should anthropomorphized brands engage customers? the impact of social crowding on brand preferences. J. Mark. **81**(6), 99–115 (2017)
34. Aggarwal, P., McGill, A.L.: When brands seem human, do humans act like brands? automatic behavioral priming effects of brand anthropomorphism. J. Consumer Res. **39**(2), 307–323 (2012)
35. Lv, X., Liu, Y., Luo, J., Liu, Y., Li, C.: Does a cute artificial intelligence assistant soften the blow? The impact of cuteness on customer tolerance of assistant service failure. Ann. Tour. Res. **87**, 103114 (2021)
36. Miao, F., Kozlenkova, I.V., Wang, H., Xie, T., Palmatier, R.W.: An emerging theory of avatar marketing. J. Mark. **86**(1), 67–90 (2021). https://doi.org/10.1177/0022242921996646
37. Chattaraman, V., Kwon, W.-S., Gilbert, J.E., Ross, K.: Should AI-Based, conversational digital assistants employ social- or task-oriented interaction style? a task-competency and reciprocity perspective for older adults. Comput. Hum. Behav. **90**, 315–330 (2019). https://doi.org/10.1016/j.chb.2018.08.048
38. Shum, H.-Y., He, X.-D., Li, D.: From Eliza to XiaoIce: challenges and opportunities with social chatbots. Front. Inf. Technol. Electron. Eng. **19**, 10–26 (2018)
39. Portela, M., Granell-Canut, C.: A new friend in our smartphone? observing interactions with chatbots in the search of emotional engagement. In: Proceedings of the XVIII International Conference on Human Computer Interaction, pp. 1–7 (2017)
40. Clark, M., Robertson, M., Young, S.: "I feel your pain": A critical review of organizational research on empathy. J. Organ. Behav.Behav. **40**(2), 166–192 (2018). https://doi.org/10.1002/job.2348
41. Cheng, Y., Jiang, H.: How do ai-driven chatbots impact user experience? examining gratifications, perceived privacy risk, satisfaction, loyalty, and continued use. J. Broadcast. Electron. Media **64**, 592–614 (2020)
42. Zhang, J., Zhu, Y., Wu, J., Yu-Buck, G.F.: A natural apology is sincere: Understanding chatbots' performance in symbolic recovery. Int. J. Hosp. Manag.Manag. **108**, 103387 (2023)

Understanding Users' Decision-Making on Privacy Disclosure from a Configurational Perspective Perceived Values, Privacy Concerns, Cognitive Style, and Trust

Xiaoyu Chen(✉) 🆔 and Ruoxi Yang🆔

School of Cultural Heritage and Information Management, Shanghai University, Shanghai, China
{xiaoyu-chen,yangruoxi}@shu.edu.cn

Abstract. Based on the privacy calculus model, users traditionally made decisions about privacy disclosure by weighing perceived values against privacy concerns. However, recent studies indicate that users' cognitive style and trust also play significant roles in a social media context. This study examines how these factors collectively influence users' privacy disclosure behavior from a configurational perspective. Through an online survey, we collected data from 452 respondents on a Chinese social media platform. The results reveal that users' decision-making on privacy disclosure is a complex process with various configurations. For individuals with a field-dependent cognitive style, cognitive style is more important than the trade-off between perceived values and privacy concerns. On the other hand, for field-independent individuals, decisions are not only influenced by the trade-off between perceived values and privacy concerns but also by trust. We finally discuss the theoretical and practical implications of these findings.

Keywords: Cognitive style · Configurational perspective · Privacy disclosure · Social media · Trust

1 Introduction

Nowadays, users are leaving more digital traces than ever before by sharing private information in this highly connected world. The increase in users' privacy disclosure is happening alongside growing privacy concerns. Despite being concerned about their privacy being compromised, users still choose to share their personal information in order to enjoy various social media services. This phenomenon, known as the "privacy paradox," has attracted attention from both academia and practitioners [1].

This study attempts to contribute to the ongoing scholarly debate on the privacy paradox in social media. Typically, this decision-making process involves weighing the benefits a user would receive against the privacy concerns they may face. The privacy calculus model (PCM) suggests that users are more likely to disclose their privacy if

I. Sserwanga et al. (Eds.): iConference 2024, LNCS 14596, pp. 96–105, 2024.
https://doi.org/10.1007/978-3-031-57850-2_8

they perceive greater benefits than privacy concerns. Conversely, they may reduce their privacy disclosure when they have heightened privacy concerns [2].

However, the PCM fails to adequately explain how users make informed decisions when both their perceived values and privacy concerns are high. Previous research suggests that users' decision-making regarding privacy disclosure may depend on their perceptions of values across different dimensions [3]. Taking into account related literature and our research context, we identify three key dimensions of perceived values: utility value, emotional value, and cognitive value. Utility value refers to the extent to which users perceive social media as useful [4]. Emotional value refers to the extent to which users derive enjoyment and pleasure from social media [5]. Cognitive value refers to the extent to which users can acquire specific knowledge from social media [5].

Furthermore, users' calculus of perceived values and privacy concerns is also contingent on individual factors such as one's personality. Based on related literature [6, 7], this study proposes two significant constructs to capture user differences in the privacy disclosure decision-making process: cognitive style and trust. Cognitive style describes how one thinks, perceives, and processes information. It is generally classified into *field independence* and *field dependence* [8]. In this study, trust can be defined as the extent to which one perceives a social media platform as possessing credibility and reliability [9].

Despite the importance of perceived values, privacy concerns, cognitive style and trust, the knowledge of how they collectively work to influence users' decision-making on privacy disclosure on social media platforms remains largely unknown. Users may weigh them disproportionately when deciding to disclose information or not. In particular, past research tends to adopt a variance-based view that primarily focuses on each factor's respective effect on users' privacy disclosure [10]. For instance, the variance-based view suggests that when perceived values are high, one's privacy disclosure will be high; when privacy concerns are high, one's privacy disclosure will be low. In brief, this view assumes the symmetric causality between influencing factors and privacy disclosure behavior [3].

In fact, any individual factor may not lead to the outcome sufficiently. In other words, multiple configurations of influencing factors exist that conjunctively lead to high or low privacy disclosure. Unlike prior research using the variance-based view to decipher the causality between potential factors and privacy disclosure, this study employs a configurational perspective that powerfully reflects the trade-off between perceived values and privacy concerns as well as the contingency of cognitive style and trust. The perspective assumes that multiple configurations of these factors can lead to users' high and low privacy disclosure respectively. In this paper, we thus propose two research questions here.

RQ 1: *What are the configurations for users' high privacy disclosure in social media?*
RQ 2: *What are the configurations for users' low privacy disclosure in social media?*

2   Decision-Making Tree Model and Hypotheses Development

2.1   Decision-Making Tree Model

To address the two research questions, we construct a decision-making tree model and formulate five hypotheses to identify the causal conditions and configurations associated with high and low privacy disclosure. We propose that users' decision-making regarding privacy disclosure on social media platforms can be categorized into five scenarios (see Fig. 1).

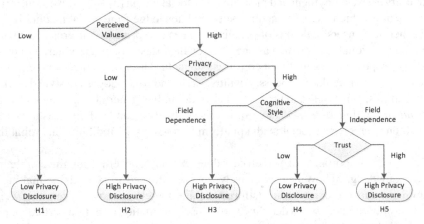

Fig. 1. Decision-making tree model of users' privacy disclosure in social media

2.2   Hypotheses Development

Based on the PCM, two hypotheses are proposed here.

H1: *When perceived values are low, individuals have a low degree of privacy disclosure.*

H2: *When perceived values are high and privacy concerns are low, individuals have a high degree of privacy disclosure.*

Besides, when both perceived values and privacy concerns are high, we propose that cognitive style and trust may play a role. Users may have different cognitive styles that influence their privacy disclosure [7]. Field-dependent (FD) individuals tend to view the social media platform they frequently use as a comfortable space for sharing private information [11]. They often rely on the behavior of others on the platform as a reference when making decisions. Social media platforms, by design, encourage users to create and publish social information [12], and the act of self-disclosure and self-presentation on social media is often seen as a norm [13, 14]. Therefore, FD individuals on social media platforms are likely to have a higher degree of privacy disclosure.

On the other hand, field-independent (FI) individuals rely on their critical thinking abilities when determining their privacy disclosure [8]. In this case, the level of trust they have in the platform becomes crucial in their decision-making process. For example, if they have low trust in the platform, they may hesitate to disclose private information, and vice versa. Hence, we propose three hypotheses below.

H3: *When perceived values and privacy concerns are both high, FD individuals have a high degree of privacy disclosure.*

H4: *When perceived values and privacy concerns are both high, FI individuals have a low degree of privacy disclosure if their trust is low.*

H5: *When the perceived values and privacy concerns are both high, FI individuals have a high degree of privacy disclosure if their trust is high.*

3 Research Design

3.1 Data Collection

Xiaohongshu (www.xiaohongshu.com) was selected as the research setting. It is a fast-growing and popular social media platform in mainland China and other regions with a significant number of young overseas Chinese users. Xiaohongshu allows users to create and discover high-quality content tailored to their preferences, making it an ideal venue for researchers to analyze users' privacy disclosure behavior [15].

Data was gathered using Credamo (www.credamo.com), a professional Chinese survey platform. Credamo has more than 3 million registered samples in China and also allows for the collection of global sample data from the United States, Canada, the United Kingdom, India, and Singapore. Through Credamo, we recruited numerous volunteers who were regular users of Xiaohongshu.

Before the formal research, a warm-up survey was conducted to examine the users' frequency of use of the Xiaohongshu platform. We included users who used the platform at least 5 times per week in the "sample pool." The formal research was conducted in the "sample pool" to ensure that the respondents were loyal users of the Xiaohongshu app and fully understood the app. We collected research data from a total of 452 valid respondents. Among the sample, 59.96% of the respondents were between the ages of 21 and 30, and the majority (65%) were female. The majority of respondents (85.84%) had a bachelor's degree or higher.

3.2 Measures

The measures for the proposed constructs were adapted from established scales in the existing literature. Perceived values items were taken from Krasnova et al. [16], privacy concerns were measured based on the study by Malhotra et al. [17], trust items were sourced from Milberg et al. [18], the classification of FD and FI was based on the cognitive style questionnaire designed by Witkin et al. [19], and users' privacy disclosure was measured using the scales developed by Chellappa and Sin [20].

We evaluated the measurement model by checking for reliability and validity with the SmartPLS 3.0 tool. After removing some items, the CR and AVE of all constructs were above 0.7 and 0.5, respectively, indicating good reliability [21]. We assessed convergent validity by examining the loadings of the items on their corresponding constructs. The results showed that all items had loadings greater than 0.7 on their respective constructs, thus ensuring the convergent validity of these constructs. Finally, we assessed the discriminant validity by comparing the square root of AVE and the correlation coefficient. Table 1 shows that the square root of the AVE was higher than the correlation coefficient for all of the constructs, indicating that the discriminant validity of these constructs was relatively good [22].

Table 1. Measures of related constructs

Construct	Cronbach's α	CR	AVE	Loading range	UV	EV	CV	PC	TT	PD
UV	0.59	0.83	0.71	[0.83–0.84]	**0.84**					
EV	0.76	0.86	0.68	[0.82–0.84]	0.51	**0.82**				
CV	0.66	0.81	0.59	[0.72–0.80]	0.56	0.48	**0.77**			
PC	0.89	0.93	0.76	[0.82–0.90]	0.26	0.26	0.20	**0.87**		
TT	0.84	0.89	0.68	[0.78–0.85]	0.51	0.49	0.41	0.53	**0.82**	
PD	0.70	0.83	0.62	[0.74–0.84]	0.49	0.53	0.49	0.33	0.61	**0.79**

Note(s): UV = Utility Value; EV = Emotional Value; CV = Cognitive Value; PC = Privacy Concerns; TT = Trust; PD = Privacy Disclosure. CR = Composite reliability, AVE = Average variance extracted. Composite reliability, AVE = Average variance extracted. Bold numbers on the diagonal were the square roots of AVEs

4   Data Analysis and Results

Fuzzy-set qualitative comparative analysis (fsQCA) method is adopted to analyze users' decision-making on privacy disclosure on Xiaohongshu from the configurational perspective. We used the fsQCA software tool for the analysis.

4.1   Descriptive Statistical Analysis

We established anchor points to calibrate all constructs (refer to Table 2). Based on relevant literature [23, 24], three anchor points were set in this study: 0.95, 0.5, and 0.05, representing full membership, crossover, and no membership, respectively. The anchor points were determined by calculating the proportions of corresponding demarcation points in numerical sequence.

4.2   Analysis of the Necessity of Each Signal Condition

We performed a necessary conditions analysis for each condition to determine if they are necessary for generating high or low privacy disclosure. Consistency is a key indicator to assess necessity, and typically, a minimum consistency value of 0.9 is considered necessary [25]. The results did not reveal any potential single-factor necessary conditions (refer to Table 3), indicating that none of the factors were necessary for high/low privacy disclosure.

Table 2. Calibration Process

Construct		Anchor point		
		Fully-in(0.95)	Cross-over(0.50)	Fully-out(0.05)
Condition	UV	52.00	47.00	37.00
	EV	26.00	23.00	18.00
	CV	27.00	24.00	18.00
	PC	27.00	20.00	8.00
	TT	26.30	23.00	16.00
	CS	1.00	/	0.00
Outcome	PD	26.00	23.00	17.00

Note(s): CS = Cognitive style, Fully-in denotes field dependence, Fully-out denotes field independence, PD = Privacy disclosure

Table 3. Analysis of the necessity.

Condition	Consistency		Condition	Consistency	
	PD	~ PD		PD	~ PD
UV	0.79	0.51	~UV	0.51	0.80
EV	0.83	0.58	~EV	0.46	0.72
CV	0.78	0.55	~CV	0.54	0.78
PC	0.59	0.70	~PC	0.68	0.57
TT	0.83	0.54	~TT	0.49	0.78
CS	0.55	0.42	~CS	0.46	0.58

Note(s): "~" represents that the condition does not exist (i.e., the negation of the specified condition)

4.3 Adequacy Analysis of Conditional Configuration

In the configurations analysis, we anchored the existing literature [25, 26] to establish the following parameters: raw consistency of 0.8, PRI consistency of 0.75, and a frequency cutoff of 1. Our analyses led to 4 configurations of high disclosure and 5 configurations of low disclosure, as summarized in Table 4. The table showed strong support for H1, H3, and H4, while H2 and H5 had a mix of supported and unsupported configurations. We discuss these results in the subsequent section.

102 X. Chen and R. Yang

Table 4. Configurations of high and low privacy disclosure

Condition	High privacy disclosure				Low privacy disclosure				
	C1	C2	C3	C4	C5	C6	C7	C8	C9
UV	●	●	●		⊗	⊗			⊗
EV		●	●	●		⊗	⊗		
CV		●		●			•	x	⊗
PC	⊗							•	•
TT	●	●	●	●	⊗		⊗	x	
CS	●		●	●	⊗	⊗	⊗	x	⊗
Raw coverage	0.30	0.63	0.33	0.32	0.36	0.34	0.19	0.28	0.29
Unique coverage	0.02	0.33	0.01	0.02	0.03	0.03	0.01	0.01	0.01
Consistency	0.95	0.93	0.95	0.96	0.95	0.93	0.96	0.94	0.93
Overall solution coverage	0.71				0.44				
Overall solution consistency	0.91				0.91				

Note(s): UV = Utility Value; EV = Emotional Value; CV = Cognitive Value; PC = Privacy Concerns; TT = Trust; PD = Privacy Disclosure; CS = Cognitive style. Large circle (●) indicates core condition and present; Circle with a cross (⊗) indicates core condition and absent; Small circle (•) indicates peripheral condition and present; Cross without circle (x) indicates peripheral condition and absent. In particular, in cognitive styles, the circle denotes field-dependence, and the cross denotes field-independence. Blank elements demonstrate that the condition does not matter.

5 Conclusions

5.1 Key Findings

Based on the results of the above analysis, we draw the privacy decision tree of FD and FI individuals, as shown in Fig. 2 and Fig. 3, respectively. We summarize the following key findings.

First, users' privacy decision-making on social media platforms is influenced by various situational factors and individual differences rather than being solely determined by a simple trade-off between perceived values and privacy concerns.

Second, individuals with a need for firm identity (FI) exhibit a more intricate decision-making process regarding privacy disclosure compared to individuals with a fluid identity (FD). As depicted in Figs. 2 and 3, FD individuals tend to engage in direct trade-offs between perceived values and privacy concerns. In contrast, FI individuals must also consider the extent of trust.

Third, FD individuals tend to have higher levels of trust and engage in more privacy disclosure compared to FI individuals. According to the findings presented in Table 2, FD individuals consistently demonstrated a high level of trust, while all configurations associated with low privacy disclosure were attributed to FI individuals. This suggests a tendency among FD individuals to trust the platform, thereby leading to higher levels of privacy disclosure.

Last, it appears that FI individuals may require a higher degree of perceived values than FD individuals in order to disclose private information. As evidenced in Figs. 2 and 3, FD individuals tend to exhibit a substantial level of privacy disclosure even when their perceived values are not exceptionally high. Conversely, FI individuals are more likely to engage in high levels of privacy disclosure only when all three dimensions of perceived values are present.

In summary, these findings provide insights into the complex nature of users' decision-making on privacy disclosure on a social media platform. They empirically demonstrate the respective importance and sequences of situational factors, individual differences, and varying levels of trust in the decision-making process.

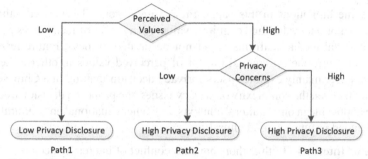

Fig. 2. Decision-making tree for field-dependence users

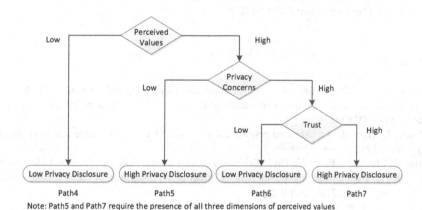

Fig. 3. Decision-making tree for field-independence users

5.2 Theoretical and Practical Implications

Our research has both theoretical and practical implications. Theoretically, it expands the Privacy Calculus Model (PCM) by adopting a configurational perspective to examine the roles of perceived values across different dimensions, privacy concerns, cognitive styles, and trust. These findings contribute to the existing literature by presenting diverse configurations of users' privacy decision-making beyond the simple trade-off between perceived values and privacy concerns.

Practically, this study offers insights for social media platform providers and privacy policymakers. It highlights the need to revise and adapt current privacy regulations to accommodate individuals with varying cognitive styles and levels of trust. For instance, cultivating trust among individuals with a need for firm identity (FI) is crucial if stakeholders aim to gain their acceptance of privacy regulations on a particular platform.

5.3 Limitations and Future Work

There are some limitations in this paper. First, we categorized perceived values into utility value, emotional value, and cognitive value. As a matter of fact, values perceived by users on social media platforms might not be limited to these. Future research is suggested to explore the differential impact of perceived values in other dimensions. Second, this paper mainly explores users' privacy decision-making in a Chinese social media context. Given the complexity of privacy issues, the proposed decision tree model may not be applicable in other cultural contexts, and other situational and cultural factors must be included in future cross-cultural studies.

Disclosure of Interests. Both authors have no conflict of interest to declare.

Acknowledgments. An earlier version of this manuscript was orally presented at the 2023 ASIS&T annual meeting in London, UK. This research is financially supported by the Shanghai Pujiang Program (grant number: 23PJC047).

References

1. Masur, P.K.: Understanding the effects of conceptual and analytical choices on 'finding' the privacy paradox: a specification curve analysis of large-scale survey data. Inf. Commun. Soc. **26**(3), 584–602 (2023)
2. Dinev, T., Hart, P.: An extended privacy calculus model for e-commerce transactions. Inf. Syst. Res. **17**(1), 61–80 (2006)
3. Sun, Y., Zhang, F., Feng, Y.: Do individuals disclose or withhold information following the same logic: a configurational perspective of information disclosure in social media. Aslib J. Inf. Manag. **74**(4), 710–726 (2022)
4. Slade, E.L., Dwivedi, Y.K., Piercy, N.C., Williams, M.D.: Modeling consumers' adoption intentions of remote mobile payments in the United Kingdom: extending UTAUT with innovativeness, risk, and trust. Psychol. Mark. **32**(8), 860–873 (2015)
5. Sheth, J.N., Newman, B.I., Gross, B.L.: Why we buy what we buy: a theory of consumption values. J. Bus. Res. **22**(2), 159–170 (1991)
6. Lo, J.: Privacy concern, locus of control, and salience in a trust-risk model of information disclosure on social networking sites. In: AMCIS 2010 Proceedings, p. 110 (2010)
7. Sun, R., Chen, J.R., Wang, Y.X., Zhou, Y.R., Luo, Y.Y.: An ERP experimental study about the effect of authorization cue characteristics on the privacy behavior of recommended users. J. Adv. Comput. Intell. Intell. Inform. **24**(4), 509–523 (2020)

8. Witkin, H.A., Goodenough, D.R.: Cognitive styles: essence and origins. Field dependence and field independence. Psychological Issues (51), 1–141 (1981)
9. Pavlou, P.A., Dimoka, A.: The nature and role of feedback text comments in online market-places: Implications for trust building, price premiums, and seller differentiation. Inf. Syst. Res. **17**(4), 392–414 (2006)
10. Yang, R., Chen, X., Fu, S.: Unlocking privacy paradox in social media from a configurational perspective. Proc. Assoc. Inf. Sci. Technol. **60**(1), 1197–1199 (2023)
11. Nosko, A., et al.: Examining priming and gender as a means to reduce risk in a social net-working context: can stories change disclosure and privacy setting use when personal profiles are constructed? Comput. Hum. Behav. **28**(6), 2067–2074 (2012)
12. Ibrahim, Y.: The new risk communities: social networking sites and risk. Int. J. Media Cultural Politics **4**(2), 245–253 (2008)
13. Nosko, A., et al.: Examining priming and gender as a means to reduce risk in a social net-working context: can stories change disclosure and privacy setting use when personal profiles are constructed? Comput. Hum. Behav. **28**(6), 2067–2074 (2012)
14. Tufekci, Z.: Can you see me now? audience and disclosure regulation in online social network sites. Bull. Sci. Technol. Soc. **28**(1), 20–36 (2008)
15. Chen, X., Simchi-Levi, D., Wang, Y.: Privacy-preserving dynamic personalized pricing with demand learning. Manage. Sci. **68**(7), 4878–4898 (2022)
16. Krasnova, H., Veltri, N.F., Günther, O.: Self-disclosure and privacy calculus on social network-ing sites: The role of culture: Intercultural dynamics of privacy calculus. Wirtschaftsinformatik **54**, 123–133 (2012)
17. Malhotra, N.K., Kim, S.S., Agarwal, J.: Internet users' information privacy concerns (IUIPC): The construct, the scale, and a causal model. Inf. Syst. Res. **15**(4), 336–355 (2004)
18. Milberg, S.J., Smith, H.J., Burke, S.J.: Information privacy: corporate management and national regulation. Organ. Sci. **11**(1), 35–57 (2000)
19. Reid, J.M.: Learning styles in the ESL/EFL classroom. Heinle & Heinle Publishers, Florence (1995)
20. Chellappa, R.K., Sin, R.G.: Personalization versus privacy: an empirical examination of the online consumer's dilemma. Inf. Technol. Manage. **6**, 181–202 (2005)
21. Fornell, C., Larcker, D.F.: Evaluating structural equation models with unobservable variables and measurement error. J. Mark. Res. **18**, 39–50 (2018)
22. Bock, G.W., Zmud, R.W., Kim, Y.G., Lee, J.N.: Behavioral intention formation in knowl-edge sharing: examining the roles of extrinsic motivators, social psychological forces, and organizational climate. Manag. Inf. Syst. Q. **29**, 87–111 (2005)
23. Ordanini, A., Parasuraman, A., Rubera, G.: When the recipe is more important than the ingredients: a qualitative comparative analysis (QCA) of service innovation configurations. J. Serv. Res. **17**(2), 134–149 (2014)
24. Pappas, I.O., Woodside, A.G.: Fuzzy-set Qualitative Comparative Analysis (fsQCA): guide-lines for research practice in Information Systems and marketing. Int. J. Inf. Manage. **58**, 102310 (2021)
25. Ragin, C.C.: Redesigning social inquiry: Fuzzy sets and beyond. University of Chicago (2008)
26. Park, Y., Fiss, P.C., El Sawy, O.A.: Theorizing the multiplicity of digital phenomena: the ecology of configurations, causal recipes, and guidelines for applying QCA. Manag. Inf. Syst. Q. **44**(4), 1493–1520 (2020)

Genre Recognition: A Model of Behaviour

Malcolm Clark[1]([✉]) [iD] and Ian Ruthven[2] [iD]

[1] Computing and Digital Media, University of the Highlands and Islands Moray,
Elgin IV30 1JJ, Scotland
malcolm.clark.moray@uhi.ac.uk
[2] Department of Computer and Information Sciences, University of Strathclyde,
Glasgow G1 IXH , Scotland

Abstract. This paper studies the behavioural processesinvolved in the decision-making process when detecting the genre of Wikipedia pages. We analysed qualitative data collected from a study of Wikipedia search behaviour to evaluate the importance of textual features in these decision-making processes. We discuss how and why genre should be included in current information models, including the decision-making processes. We redefine a literary document selection model to demonstrate the decision-making processes and by contrasting the document information elements, criteria, and values by re-framing it in the context of genres within the Wikipedia domain.

Keywords: Genre · Wikipedia · Information Behaviour

1 Introduction

In this study we examine the ways in which humans use form, the visual appearance of a document, and a document's purpose to determine the 'genre' or categories of texts. We explore the historical meaning of genre, related work, such as evolution [1, 2], on the smaller and holistic features of genre, and discuss genre-related information behaviours on Wikipedia genres. We also discuss how and why genre should be included in current information models and cognitive frameworks [3], including the decision-making processes.

Genre may form the origin of text recognition and in digital text layout - as hypothesised by [4]. The readers then determine the occurrences and situations in which the characteristics of genre serve as a 'basic level' in the process of recognition. Computational linguists, for example, are using a wide array of methods to predict the category a document should belong; however, human formed text categories are there already to assist people in making the judgements they need about texts, and in text classification, it is an extensive problem because some categories, as well as consensus, can diverge broadly.

In this and our previous studies [5, 6], information seeking participants appeared to perform an initial 'scan' and/or 'skim' of emails and documents. This is in agreement with [4], who noted that information seekers construct a document visually as a "whole"

[7] but also suggest that the categorisation decision occurs at a basic-level structure psychologically, and there is some evidence to support this in the study that follows.

We then propose a redefinition to an existing model of decision-making behaviour of journals' features [8] to highlight the importance of genre to the scholastic model of decision making, that is, in this case, the Document Selection Model by Wang & Soergel [8].

2 Background

In this section we discuss the two main areas of knowledge related to this research, namely prior knowledge of genre and perception and Wikipedia as a source of information. Our research questions are as follows:

1. What are the information behaviours involved in detecting genre during an information search task?
2. How are formatting, shapes, and visual cues, such as information boxes, lists, image texts, utilized when assessing Wikipedia pages?

2.1 Genre and Perception

Genre work is a thriving scholarly community of practice with a long history. Contemporary approaches to genre have included analysing authorial identity construction [9, 10]. Identified problems, like genre, connected to information classification in theory and to put those problems into the context of experiences from practice [11] mapped new and evolving news genres by factuality and formality. Salamon [12] examined media unions' online resistance rhetoric where the unions reproduced social movement genres of organisational communication.

Most authors are still inspired by scholars like Toms & Campbell, Dewdney, Yates & Orlikowski and Spinuzzi [4, 13–15]. The renowned genre scholars [13] suggested that *"Genres (for example, the memo, the proposal, meeting minutes etc.) are typified communicative actions characterized by similar substance and form and taken in response to recurrent situations"*. Further, they say that '*genres are social institutions that are produced, reproduced, or modified when human agents draw on genre rules to engage in organizational communication.*' Genre therefore acts a social tool to help people recognise and make sense of the documents with which they are interacting. Social rules lead to documents of particular types that have distinct structures that enhance the ability of a reader to understand the document and its purpose. One author [16] from the sphere of intertextuality referred to texts in terms of two axes, i.e., a *horizontal axis* linking the author and reader of a text, and a *vertical axis*, which relates the text to other texts, c.f., Chandler [17].

Our interest begins by examining how a document's genre is determined by its *purpose* (sometimes synonymous with substance) and mainly by *form* (or layout). The purpose is determined by many attributes, such as arguments, and discourse structure. The form (the readily observable features) contains visual attributes including text-formatting devices, such as lists and headings. Visual cues e.g., frames of structured text, keywords and formatting options in text allows the reader to perceive [18, 19], any distinguishable visual features, which then help the reader to interpret features leading to finding relevant information more efficiently. Substance and form are clearly discussed in [15] which document genre is seen as a particular label which conveys a set of information presented by conventions, such as style and formatting of the language utilised.

Genres shape our knowledge of the world says [20]. For example, in a newspaper article, the title and emboldened summary are present to reduce cognitive load there is no need for an individual to scan the whole text unless searching for specific keywords or quotes, the genre provides these filtering cues in its structural makeup. When viewing the texts, the reader cannot help but pay attention to the '*embedded assumptions*' and '*understandings*' [20]. These attentive behaviours are structured by genre.

In this view, genres behave as 'affordances' [19] or actionable properties. The theory of affordances is an attempt to restructure how perception and meaning are relatable because it posits that instead of perceiving things (in our case texts) and then adding substance later, there are visual combinations of invariant properties of objects which cue the reader how to act and interpret in relation to these objects [20–22]. As explained in [22] genre is not just a set of texts or a list of the important '...*features of texts but an interpretative process called into being by the fact that 'all understanding of verbal meaning is necessarily genre-bound'.*' Basically, when hypothesising on the genre of a text an instinctual assumption is made, until the initial interpretation is reformed because of an informed decision through further analysis, which then allows the viewer to re-evaluate the understanding of the purpose and form of the text.

Others, e.g., [4, 23] have demonstrated how the genre features, for example, the shapes of information and semantic content are useful to show how the textual object can be used. Our study looks at how what features of Wikipedia articles lead to the determination of genre.

2.2 Wikipedia

Wikipedia first appeared in January 2001 and has articles in more than 119 languages. The English version alone consists of 6,676,047 articles and has 45,772,068 active editorial users and 898 administrators [24]. Indeed 'Editors' of the English Wikipedia have established some ideas as conventions, policies, or features, including featured articles, the neutral point of view policy, navigation templates, reorganisation of short stub articles into sub-categories, dispute resolution mechanisms which can be viewed in the Discussion tabs on each page. Other democratic mechanisms like mediation, arbitration, and weekly collaborations are also active.

Wikipedia is a thriving community of practice (COP), as defined by [25], where literary evolutionary processes occur in which editors to develop new and old variants of genres. A theoretical introduction is presented by [26] into the concept of web genres, provides a detailed overview of the types of encyclopaedic websites that exist, offering the features of their content, form and functionality. A previous analysis of developing genres in Wikipedia show that the online encyclopaedia contains a wide array of socially constructed genres; some are classic forms such as Reviews, News Articles, Events, Discography, Filmography, whilst others are more contemporary, such as Frequently Asked Questions [2].

Scanning and skimming patterns were explored when participants viewed Wikipedia pages and showed that people extensively interacted with layout features, such as tables, titles, bullet lists, contents lists, information boxes, and references [2, 6]. This study demonstrated how textual features and formatting were used when examining Wikipedia pages. In this study we now show how these patterns differ for distinct types of proposed Wikipedia genres.

3 Methodology

3.1 Overview

The study was a task-based study involving thirty participants who were each asked to search Wikipedia for information on three allocated topics. All participants were students, from a variety of disciplines, of whom 18 were male and 12 were female. They were aged between 18 and 42, with a mean age of 23.5. Eight had edited Wikipedia articles, and two participants had edited Wikipedia many times (P8 estimated that they had submitted circa 20 edits and P28 estimated 10 edits).

The starting point of each task was the main page of the English language Wikipedia. Each participant was asked to use the Wikipedia search engine to find relevant information, including reformulating queries and browsing from retrieved pages, until they felt that they had completed the tasks. The first 15 participants were allocated tasks 1–3 from the list at the end of this paper, the second 15 participants were allocated tasks 4–6.

The tasks were framed as an information need scenario with a task background and indicative information goals. The tasks were conducted one at a time and participants were allocated a maximum of 20 min for each task. The participants' eye movements were recorded using the Tobii T-60 system which recorded the fixation, saccadic and scanpath data for each page viewed. We used the IBM Statistical Package for the Social Sciences (SPSS) software for testing in the analysis by a one-way ANalysis of VAriance (ANOVA).

3.2 Analysis

The 30 participants viewed 711 pages, including duplicates as some participants viewed the same pages, which were all analysed. Many pages were showing search results, whole page imagery (jpg or png), whole page Lists, definition pages and so on. These non-content pages were excluded, including 26 pages resulting from typo query errors in the Wikipedia search page.

The remaining articles were manually classified by genre giving the following breakdown (unique pages, not including duplicates): biographical pages (footballers/ philanthropists/politicians) (119), lists articles (55), football clubs (46), football grounds (16), events/timelines (111) like revolutions/uprisings and air crashes (19), airlines (18), aircraft types (7), category (5), country (18) and city (5).

We then examined what formatting, cues and shapes were used through eye fixations and saccades as shown in Fig. 1 and what information was saved in Word files as part of the search exercise. As means of examples, formatting can be emboldened text, cues can be symbols of meaning and shapes can be the layout. These can be on their own or indeed grouped together to aid interpretation. The fixations denote an area of interest fixated on by a participant (circles), and the saccades which show the direction of travel and sequence of the eye movements (lines) and are also known as scanpaths. The bigger the circle signifies that the participant fixated on that area for a longer duration, so it is understood that the area viewed intensively by the participant got closer cognitive attention.

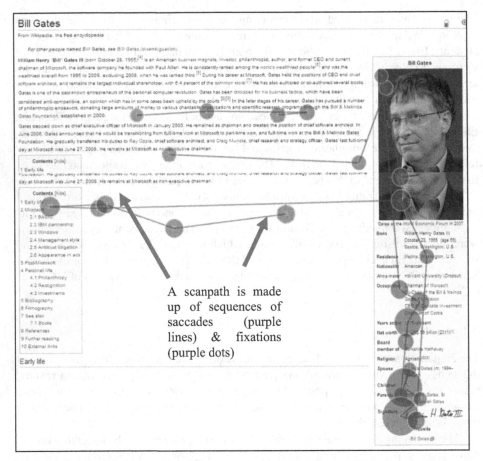

Fig. 1. Fixations and saccades on a Wikipedia biography for William 'Bill' Gates page. The image readability is slightly affected because of the rendering by Tobii Studio during the screenshot capture from the video, however, it does show the scanpaths (in purple) as intended.

The number of Whole articles was 711. This total includes articles that were seen multiple times, for example, the Arab Spring page was viewed 15 times. The areas of interest were codified into the following labels and are shown in Fig's. 3, 5, 8, 9 & 11. In this study we focus on the pages which were retrieved by the participants in the search and the most fixated textual feature sets listed below:

Main Title (711)
Subtitles (24)
Contents List (Left 32)

Contents List Title
Contents List Text (31)
Contents List Title (30)

Summary Box (35)

Bullet Lists (14)
Bullet Lists in Paragraphs (6)

Tables (18)

Table Headers (18)
Table Contents (8)

Information Box (top right 13–29)

Information Box Image (14)
Information Box Image Banner Text (22- e.g., Fig. 4)
information Box Image Text (13)
Information Box Title (28)
Information Box Content (29)
Information Box Contents Title (29)

References Sects. (11)

Contents (11)
Left Indices (11)
Paragraphs and Sects. (8)
Large Bullet Lists (15)
Emboldened text (3)
Indices (9)
Links n = 18

From these smaller granular feature sets we then sought to understand how the information behaviour decisions were made.

4   Findings

In each section below, we take a Wikipedia genre and analyze how the features were used in the search task. We concentrate on five genres: biography, lists, football clubs, events/timelines, countries. Some are identifiable by structure alone, content and some only identifiable with both the purpose and form features.

4.1 Biographical Genres

The task in this case was asking the participants to find information regarding famous philanthropists. Wikipedia biographical pages typically centre on a person and contain standard information such as date of birth, nationality, children, spouse, etc. However, they can also evolve into what could be argued are sub-genres, for example, in [2] the biography of Spike Milligan (satirist/author/soldier) was compared with that of Bill Gates. Whilst some features are similar, other attributes were different, e.g., Spike Milligan now contains details on military service, whereas the Bill Gates article mentions company details and awards received.

A biography shows the life of person. The key structured information in this profile is a date of birth, date of death (if applicable), notable achievements, spouse, parents and so on. There are some notable differences in the biographies depending on the person being profiled. As an example, a person known for being a president will have a date of birth, and then the structure will deviate to more contextual information regarding the role and other related presidential information in the Summary, Contents List, and Information Box. This area was key to user identification of biographies (Fig. 2).

A one-way repeated-measures ANOVA was used to assess time until first fixation per areas of interest for each user and revealed a main effect of $F(1, 13) = 18.078$, $p < .001$ (statistically significant differences between the Areas of Interest (AOI) on the Wikipedia pages. Bonferroni post-hoc tests revealed some interesting findings:

1. The 'Information Box Image' was viewed more than the 'Information Box Banner Image Text' ($p = .002$) (Fig. 3).
2. 'Information Box Title' and 'Information Box Content' were both looked at more than the 'Information Box Image Text' ($p = .005$).
3. 'Information Box Contents Title' was looked upon more than 'Information Box Image Text' ($p = .005$).

From analysing the scan paths, the smaller textual elements, such as textual bannersthat highlighted text, sub-titles and the information box contents were particularly important for the users compared to the information titles in this task. The biographical content that appeared in summary seemed to be more important than the main text and the image was important to quickly identify the person being described in the biography.

Contents [hide]

(Top)

Early life

Second World War

> Career

> Personal life

Humour with the Prince of Wales

Campaigning

Death

Legacy

Radio comedy shows

Other radio shows

Television comedy shows

Other notable television
involvement

Theatre

Filmography

> Books

Recordings

Notes

References

> Further reading

External links

Terence Alan "Spike" Milligan KBE (16 April 1918 – 27 February 2002) was an Irish[a] comedian, writer, musician, poet, playwright and actor. The son of an English mother and Irish father, he was born in British Colonial India, where he spent his childhood before relocating in 1931 to England, where he lived and worked for the majority of his life. Disliking his first name, he began to call himself "Spike" after hearing the band Spike Jones and his City Slickers on Radio Luxembourg.[1][2]

Milligan was the co-creator, main writer, and a principal cast member of the British radio comedy programme The Goon Show, performing a range of roles including the characters Eccles and Minnie Bannister. He was the earliest-born and last surviving member of the Goons. He took his success with The Goon Show into television with Q5, a surreal sketch show credited as a major influence on the members of Monty Python's Flying Circus. He wrote and edited many books, including Puckoon (1963) and a seven-volume autobiographical account of his time serving during the Second World War, beginning with Adolf Hitler: My Part in His Downfall (1971). He also wrote comical verse, with much of his poetry written for children, including Silly Verse for Kids (1959).

Early life [edit]

Terence Alan Milligan was born in Ahmednagar, India on 16 April 1918[3] during the British Raj,[4] the son of an Irish father, Leo Alphonso Milligan, MSM, RA (1890–1969), a regimental sergeant-major in the British Indian Army,[5][6][7] and English mother, Florence Mary Winifred (née Kettleband; 1893–1990). He spent his childhood in Poona and later in Rangoon, capital of British Burma. He was educated at the Convent of Jesus and Mary, Poona, and later at St Paul's High School, Rangoon. His father remained in the Indian Army after the end of the First World War, steadily promoted till "the family's lifestyle became almost lavish"; Milligan considered that "My old man lived the life of a gentleman on sergeant's pay".[5][8]

After Army cuts meant his father's position was no longer required, Milligan travelled by sea, from India to England for the first time. He arrived on a winter's morning and was bemused by the climate, so different from India's, remembering the dock's "terrible noise, and everything so cold and grey."[4] The Milligan family lived in England in somewhat straitened circumstances, Leo Milligan only being able to find "a poorly paid job in the Associated Press photo library"; Milligan recalled his mother being "often tense and angry... a domestic tyrant" due to having to manage on "next to no income".[5] After moving to Brockley, south east London from the age of 12 in 1931, Milligan attended Brownhill Road School (later to be renamed Catford Boys School) and St Saviours School, Lewisham High Road. Disliking his first name Terry, he began to call himself "Spike" after hearing the band Spike Jones and his City Slickers on Radio Luxembourg.[3]

Spike Milligan KBE	
	Milligan, c. 1990
Born	Terence Alan Milligan 16 April 1918 Ahmednagar, British India
Died	27 February 2002 (aged 83) Rye, East Sussex, England
Resting place	St Thomas's Church, Winchelsea, East Sussex, England
Occupations	Comedian · writer · musician · poet · playwright · actor
Years active	1951–2002
Spouses	June Marlow (m. 1952; div. 1960) Patricia Ridgeway (m. 1962; died 1978) Shelagh Sinclair (m. 1963)
Children	6
Military career	
Allegiance	United Kingdom
Service/ branch	▬ British Army
Years of service	1940–1945
Rank	Lance bombardier
Unit	Royal Artillery
Battles/wars	Second World War

Fig. 2. Spike Milligan biography article in Wikipedia 2023 which seems to indicate his short duration in the military rather than being a satirical genius that influenced many contemporary comedians. The article has evolved since 2009 when first examined [2].

4.2 List and Lists of Lists Genre

Lists are a quite common genre and a very commonly used structure. Wikipedia contains many types of lists including timelines, reference lists, gazetteer (list of geographic places and information about them), and even lists of lists. The lists our participants used most often were of the two types: Index and Timelines, for example, in the Aircrash task the timelines were retrieved and on many occasions the Indices at the bottom of articles were used to find information.

Fig. 3. Bill Gates biography 2022 on Wikipedia with labelled Areas of Interest (AOI) feature sets

A one-way ANOVA was used to assess time until first fixation per areas of interest for each user and revealed a main effect of F (10, 285) = 3.487, p < .000. Bonferroni post-hoc tests were again utilised to test for effects between Areas of interest.

1. The 'Summary Box' was more used rather than the 'Contents List,' 'Information Box' and 'Main Title' (p = .042).
2. The 'Main Title' was looked on more than all other 'Contents List' and 'Information Box' areas (p = .010).
3. The 'Summary' was used more than the 'Contents List' (p = .010) and the 'Information Box' (p = .005).
4. The 'Contents List' was used more than the 'Information Box' (p = .001).
5. Bullet icons were used predominately more rather than numerics or alphabetical characters (p = .004).

In most cases, by observing the scanpath data the decisions of relevance were made using the 'Information Box,' 'Contents List' or 'Summary Text' rather than scrolling down each long page. These are bigger structural features which help with navigation on the page.

The participants navigated and used more bullet-type lists rather than numeric-type lists in the articles. Overall, at the top of the articles, the only major difference between all the features pertained to the Summary Box rather than to the Contents List, Information Box and Main Title, for example, Fig. 4 shows a Table List of years which could be argued as a chronology. The Wikipedia authors have not decided on the best way to show some information like the list in table in Fig. 4, however, they seem to have settled on a table which is especially useful, because the users can easily skim by years (1919–2023), then choose to filter.

Contents									
									1919
1920	1921	1922	1923	1924	1925	1926	1927	1928	1929
1930	1931	1932	1933	1934	1935	1936	1937	1938	1939
1940	1941	1942	1943	1944	1945	1946	1947	1948	1949
1950	1951	1952	1953	1954	1955	1956	1957	1958	1959
1960	1961	1962	1963	1964	1965	1966	1967	1968	1969
1970	1971	1972	1973	1974	1975	1976	1977	1978	1979
1980	1981	1982	1983	1984	1985	1986	1987	1988	1989
1990	1991	1992	1993	1994	1995	1996	1997	1998	1999
2000	2001	2002	2003	2004	2005	2006	2007	2008	2009
2010	2011	2012	2013	2014	2015	2016	2017	2018	2019
2020	2021	2022	2023						

Fig. 4. Example of a Table of Years from a Contents List (left of page)

4.3 Football Club Genre

The task on football clubs asked participants to identify South American Football Clubs and associated star players and grounds were the quickest and easiest to identify from all our tasks [6]. A football club article is structured (Fig. 5) which shows information on the team crest, team kit colors (home and away), tables of players names along with positions played/number of games etc.

Maybe, because many types of features afforded the identification, the images for the Football Club, badge icon and different strips for home, away and third colours were especially useful as 'signalling devices' [27].

A one-way ANOVA was used to assess time until first fixation per areas of interest for each user and revealed a main effect of $F(1, 14) = 18.012$, $p < .000$. Bonferroni post-hoc tests were again utilised to test for effects between AOIs.

1. Once the club was found, the 'Information Box titles' directed the participants to the information because it was rich in features (p = 0.002). The box also contained text which may have been useful for disambiguation if the team was not known or identified by images alone.
2. The 'Information Box Images' (football strips' graphics), without any text was arguably the most useful, however, the emboldened 'information box' titles: Founded, Ground, Capacity, Manager & League were also key indicators (p = 0.002).

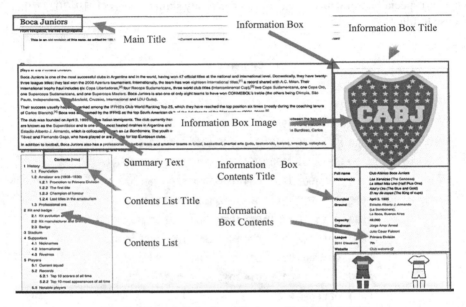

Fig. 5. The article for Boca Juniors with AOIs labelled.

The smaller textual elements, such as those shown in Fig. 5, structural (invariant) cues/formatting features document information elements, devices, and some shapes like small images of football strips, like Fig. 5, above, were vital, and this is supported by comparing the non-structured text with the structured text. The importance of form and semiotics gave valuable clues as to their usefulness in the decision-making behaviour of differentiating the genres.

4.4 Events/Timelines Genre

The task asking for articles on the Arab Spring and Aircrashes (Fig. 6 & Fig. 8 respectively) led to the retrieval of many articles on the genre of Events and Timelines. These genres layout and discuss the narrative of each event from how it began, to the eventual outcomes and any further repercussions. However, it became apparent during the analysis that Timelines and Chronologies were also closely related in form. It can be argued that a similar structure to these genres exists in other areas, such as True Crime that purports to examine an actual crime, lists the details of the actions of real people associated with and affected by criminal events. In some cases, Aircrash investigations do eventually become criminal investigations, leading to a whole new genre, mainly due to a judgement of errors involving airline manufacturing or human.

The Information Box in the page on the Arab Spring was vital as it contained titles intricately linked to the 'timeline' genre, such as dates, locations of events that triggered social unrest, goals of the unrest, methods of unrest, such as silent protest and violent activity, and the outcomes, e.g., an autocrat was overthrown. In the Arab Spring task, the pages are long with large tables of text, so they led to some intense searching for specific information to successfully achieve the task.

The main page has linked to some quite interesting other alternative genres, like: List by Country and Live Blogs. A sub-genre of Events has also evolved in Wikipedia, such as Self Immolation, Silent Protests, Hunger Strikes and Civil Disobedience. The search data also included some interesting findings where Wikipedia has some slightly different articles, which were similar representative types, i.e., Event, Timelines and Chronology. A Revolution, for example, is an Event with a Timeline which also lays out Types, Methods, and Causes in a Chronological structure (Fig. 6). The methods shown in the figure appeared in the data, but some articles had main titles using the nouns: revolt, unrest or uprising as synonyms to describe the 'event.' (Fig. 7)

Fig. 6. In amongst the data on the Information Box was the smaller box on 'Revolution'. This was linked to the Event and Timeline articles, so is slightly ambiguous, however, it does link to other related concepts on Revolution.

Figure 8 (below) is a less ambiguous event, where the Information Box and Titles were the most prominent. One thing to note is although this was an event, it would

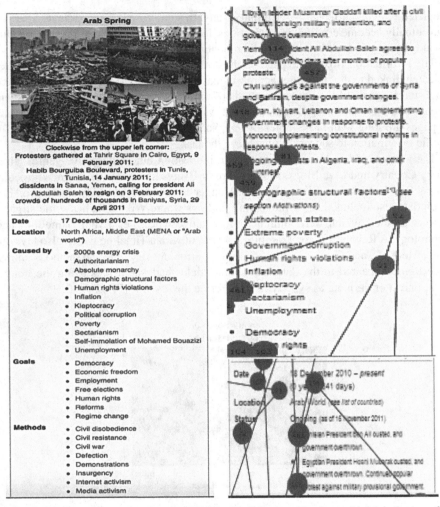

Fig. 7. (left) is the Information Box detailing the Arab Spring. The figure (right) is the top of an information box whereas it shows the information box titles and content with some scanpath data (saccade-fixation-saccade sequences). The scanpath shows the user fixating and skimming certain elements of the text rather than intensive reading.

undoubtedly trigger genres like chronological and timeline structures of further events, such as investigations, outcomes, and potential changes to actual aircraft mechanisms, which would need updates to the article on the Tupolev TU-154B-2 type, list of Air-crashes and update to the Airport information. In this case, however, it was a pilot error so the report would layout the chronology of the conditions of their employment because the crash was caused by pilot fatigue.

A one-way ANOVA was used to assess time until first fixation per areas of interest for each user and revealed a main effect of $F (1, 14) = 41.783$, $p < .000$. Bonferroni post-hoc tests were again utilised to test for effects between Areas of interest.

Aeroflot Flight 5143   文A 15 languages ˅

Article Talk   Read Edit View history Tools ˅

From Wikipedia, the free encyclopedia

Aeroflot Flight 7425 was a Tupolev Tu-154B-2 airliner on a July 10, 1985 flight from Tashkent, Uzbek SSR to Leningrad, Russian SFSR, with stops in Qarshi and Orenburg. The aircraft was cruising at 11,600 metres (38,100 ft) with an airspeed of only 400 kilometres per hour (250 mph), close to stalling speed for that altitude. The low speed caused vibrations which the aircrew incorrectly assumed were engine surges. Using the thrust levers to reduce engine power to flight idle, the crew caused a further drop in airspeed to 290 kilometres per hour (180 mph). The aircraft stalled and entered a flat spin, crashing into the ground near Uchkuduk, Uzbekistan, which at that time was in the Soviet Union. There were no survivors among the 191 passengers and 9 crew.

Vasily Ershov, a veteran Tu-154 pilot and aviation writer, speculates that the reason for crash might be the lack of an adequate crew rest. The Tashkent Airport at the time was in half-finished state and lacked proper crew rest facilities. The aircrew in question has flown from Leningrad for a return flight, and, despite ostensibly having rested in Tashkent, couldn't get an adequate sleep in those conditions. Fatigue finally took its toll after the takeoff from Qarshi, with the crew falling asleep during climb, without turning on a stall warning system. They were waked by the shaking of the stalling plane, which surprised crew mistook for engine surges. They then reduced the engine power, sending the plane further into a deep stall and unrecoverable flat spin.

Aeroflot Flight 7425	
Accident	
Date	10 July 1985
Summary	Pilot error
Site	Near Uchkuduk, Uzbek SSR, Soviet Union 🌍 42°9′24″N 63°33′20″E
Aircraft	
Aircraft type	Tupolev Tu-154B-2
Operator	Aeroflot
Registration	CCCP-85311
Flight origin	Tashkent
Destination	Leningrad
Passengers	191
Crew	9
Fatalities	200
Injuries	0
Survivors	0

It is the deadliest air disaster in Soviet and Uzbek aviation history, and as of 2011 has the highest worldwide death toll of any accident involving a Tupolev Tu-154.

References

- UK CAA Document CAA 429 World Airline Accident Summary
- Accident description ↗ at the Aviation Safety Network

External links

- Air Disaster database record ↗
- Plane Crash Info ↗

V·T·E	Aviation accidents and incidents in 1985		[hide]
Jan 1	Eastern Air Lines Flight 980	Aug 12	Japan Air Lines Flight 123
Jan 21	Galaxy Airlines Flight 203	Aug 22	Manchester Airport disaster
Feb 1	Aeroflot Flight 7841	Aug 25	Bar Harbor Airlines Flight 1808
Feb 19	China Airlines Flight 006	Sep 4	Bakhtar Antonov An-26 shootdown
Feb 19	Iberia Flight 610	Sep 6	Midwest Express Airlines Flight 105
Feb 24	Polar 3	Sep 23	Henson Airlines Flight 1517
May 3	1985 Zolochiv mid-air collision	Nov 10	Teterboro collision
Jun 14	Trans World Airlines Flight 847	Nov 23	EgyptAir Flight 648
Jun 21	Braathens SAFE Flight 139	Nov 25	Aeroflot Antonov An-12 crash
Jun 23	1985 Narita International Airport bombing	Dec 12	Arrow Air Flight 1285R
Jun 23	Air India Flight 182	Dec 19	Aeroflot Flight 101/435
Jul 10	**Aeroflot Flight 5143**	Dec 31	Ricky Nelson plane crash
Aug 2	Delta Air Lines Flight 191		

Categories   1984 ◄ ► 1986

➢ *This article about an aviation accident is a stub. You can help Wikipedia by expanding it.*

Categories: Aviation accidents and incidents in 1985 | 1985 in the Soviet Union | Aviation accidents and incidents officially attributed to pilot error | Aviation accidents and incidents in the Soviet Union | Aeroflot accidents and incidents | Aviation accidents and incidents in Uzbekistan | Accidents and incidents involving the Tupolev Tu-154 | Aviation accident stubs

Fig. 8. The article naming conventions have changed so the Aeroflot flight 5143 is also now known as 7425, but was an example of the event data found during the Aircrash information seeking task. Note the example of the 'Categories' at the bottom of the article which were also viewed by the participants to help with filtering for information (Fig. 9).

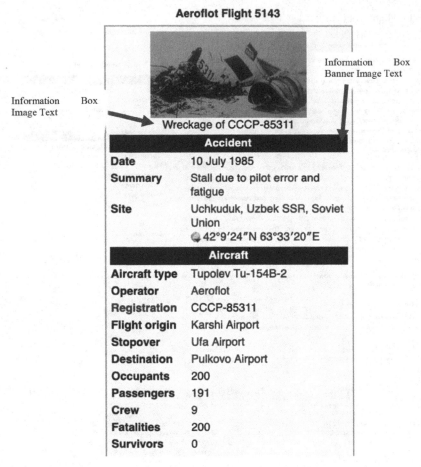

Fig. 9. Aircrash partial information box and sub sections

1. The 'Information Box' on the right of the page on the Arab Spring was the main feature used (p = .001).
2. In articles for Aircrashes the tables were particularly important for navigation, e.g., the numeric table 'device' in Fig. 10 provided expedient perceptual clues. This was particularly important for this task as it contained an emphasis on numerics which listed years which are often contained within tables, which helped the participants filter Aircrashes by year.

4.5 Country/City Genre

A "gazetteer" is defined by [28] as a geographical index or directory used in conjunction with a map or atlas. The Wikipedia pages for Countries and Cities are relatable to the

1910s and 1920s [edit]

1919 [edit]

- July 21 – The Goodyear dirigible *Wingfoot Air Express* catches fire and crashes into the Illinois Trust and Savings Building in Chicago, Illinois, while carrying passengers to a local amusement park, killing thirteen people: three out of the five on board and ten others on the ground, with 27 others on the ground being injured.
- August 2 – A Caproni Ca.48 crashes at Verona, Italy, during a flight from Venice to Taliedo, Milan, killing all on board (14, 15, or 17 people, according to different sources).

1920 [edit]

- December 14 – A Handley Page O/400 hits a tree and crashes at Golders Green, London, after failing to gain height following takeoff, killing four out of eight on board.

Fig. 10. Example of a List page retrieved by participant 19 List of Accidents or Incidents by Commercial Airliner. The page lists all the 'events' up to the current year.

gazetteer, as country as a Wikipedia genre, generally involve a structure regarding geolocation (latitude/longitude), flags, capital city, languages spoken, currency, population, position on globe, history, and contemporary standing.

The task on countries asked participants to find information about the legislature of Namibia. The pages they found were well formed, interactive with good purposeful features and useful format with tabular layout. Figure 11 affords its purpose through the form with key signals to the perceiver being the Information Banner with the granular Information Banner Titles: Capital, Anthem, Motto and pictorially, the location of the country on the African content and the Flag icon were informative and important. The unstructured text areas of the page were very unhelpful and vague which was evidenced by the free text comments by the participants later in this paper, so the participants gaze, and attention made the most of the structured areas to locate the relevant information, rather than reading intensely (Fig. 12).

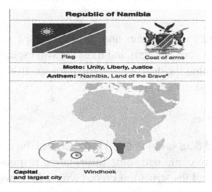

Fig. 11. Namibia information box experimental data.

A one-way ANOVA was used to assess time until first fixation per areas of interest for each user and revealed a main effect of $F (1, 14) = 15.872$, $p < .001$. Bonferroni post-hoc tests were again utilised to test for effects between Areas of interest.

1. The 'Information Box' with the granular 'Information Box Title' were most important overall ($p = .001$).
2. The iconography (Fig. 11 & 12), such as geographical outline, flags and mottos were also important.

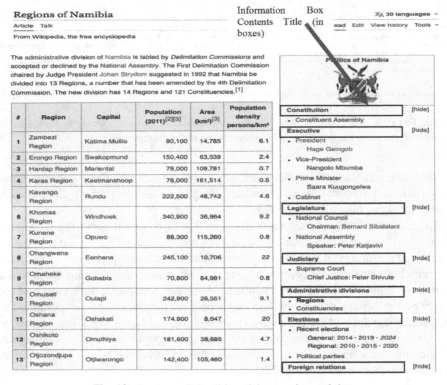

Fig. 12. Regions of Namibia article experimental data.

3. Despite the archaic links with indices and directories, the Information Banner and iconographic detail (e.g., coat of arms and flag) are still especially important clues to the perceiver when making the decisions on the purpose, even though overall the text was statistically the most important.

4.6 Participant Responses

In addition to the retrieved data saved in the Word files and the eyetracking data our post task and exit questionnaire contained some informative responses that indicated how useful the participants found the structural layout within Wikipedia.

1. 'I enjoy the structure of the pages, so finding relevant information was easy.'
2. 'Layout was very useful and helpful.'
3. 'Use of boxes to highlight key facts was helpful to finding information.'
4. 'Wikipedia makes searching very easy as the layout of every page is simple to work with and they all have very useful structures. By providing reference/footnote links it makes the site more reliable.'

5   Discussion

In our study, searchers appeared to perform an initial 'scan' and/or 'skim' of the document. This is in agreement with [4], who noted that 'users develop a sense of the document as a visual whole' [7] also suggests that the act of categorisation occurs at a basic-level structure psychologically, and there is some evidence to support this in our Wikipedia study.

Genre forms the origin of text recognition and in digital text layout - as hypothesised by [4]. They then determine the occurrences and situations in which the characteristics of genre serve as a 'basic level' in the process of recognition. Contemporary computational linguists are using a wide array of methods to predict the category a document should belong; however, human formed text categories are there already to assist people in making the decisions they need about texts, and in text classification, it is an extensive problem because some categories can diverge broadly.

In their longitudinal study of the users of a bibliographic system, Wang and Soergel examined decision making during document use. In particular, they asked: "what are the processes and factors involved in arriving at a decision once a document has been retrieved in a system?" [8] Firstly, excluding the Document input, they highlight the 'Document Information Elements' (DIE) which in their study had examples such as title, author, abstract for a journal which assumes some contextual knowledge like the document type and organisation. Secondly, they highlight the importance of 'Criteria' which can be topicality, authority, and relation amongst others. The Document 'Values' were used from consumer theory which incorporates the five Values (Fig. 13) as: Epistemic, Functional, Conditional, Social and Emotional. [8] unfortunately have omitted the importance of the perceptual processes within the Values column, such as affordances of genre, which are vital to the decision making.

They also asked the following questions [8]:

- What are the [user] criteria derived from the document information elements in the assessment of the document values?
- What document information elements are used and how are they used in judging document criteria?
- What personal knowledge do users bring to bear on interpreting document information elements?
- What are the decision rules used in document selection?

As a result of their study and above questions they formulated the cognitive model in Fig. 13.

Based on our findings, we can therefore redefine their model to demonstrate the importance of genre during the Wikipedia tasks.

Many important published articles examining genre can be aligned with the cognitive skills and Document Information Elements; e.g., Interpretation [29], formal cues [27], shape/metaphor [23], shape/interpretation [22] and frames [20].

It has direct relationships with the position by [4] asking how does the form of a document affect the user in those first seconds? In those first few moments, the structural aspects are especially important and, as [14] suggests, genres do act as textual affordances: the unique shapes may trigger the user's mental model and this 'interpretation'

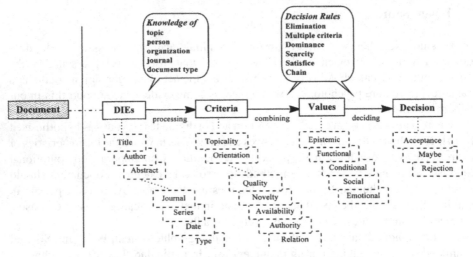

Fig. 13. Document Selection Model proposed by [8].

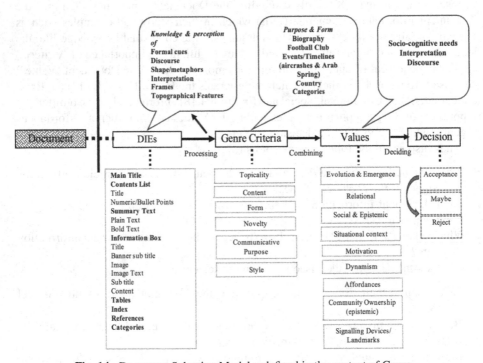

Fig. 14. Document Selection Model redefined in the context of Genre.

of the 'shapes', 'frames' and 'cues' may lead the user to develop a set of expectations about the article before reader surveys the formatted content to confirm what was predicted.

The model presented above (Fig. 14) is an adaption showing the document selection method, along with the processing of the document information elements, which are then amended with genre criteria and values. This also demonstrates the authors beginning to answer the question: how can genre be included in theories of decision-making? The decision-making processes for the participants should not only involve the document information elements, but also demonstrates how the signals, cues, shapes, and landmarks for the whole document genre are useful for completing the tasks. There is a debate to be had, however, how much of the genre decision comes before the document information elements, as awareness or expectations of the genre may influence the readers expectations of the shape of the Wikipedia item to be perceived. This is a question of the perception to act (affordances) or perceiving to recognition actions. As [30] point out, perception for recognition and perception leading to action are different mechanisms which may involve different neural processes.

The two perception processes were difficult to detect but some clues were found in the data collected, for example, when the participant was not aware of the genre type, he/she did not know what to expect in terms of attributes or layout nor did he/she have any previous knowledge to draw from. Therefore, if during the task, the genre was identified, it could be assumed that the article had possibly afforded its purpose or, indeed, gained the reader's attention and/or directed the reader to the salient properties of the particular type. For example, the blocks of features (layout and format features) *afforded* the information/action, e.g., the feature sets were informative enough they allowed the decision to be made regarding whether it was in a certain category. These are created affordances, created partly because the human visual system is outstanding at pre-conscious processing. This is an accumulating evidence strategy, with people using features based on immediacy for attention, relevance, and building up evidence to a point where a decision can be made, however, unlike constructivism (without cognition). Now, if the reader was fully familiar with a type of genre, again, this could lead to an 'expectation of purpose/form' with the result that the reader would compare knowledge expectation to visual attributes and thus recognise the purpose and form.

6   Conclusions

We show the value of genres to Information Seeking (IS) scholars, where this work has highlighted the value of a small subset of genres (biographies, lists, timelines/events, football clubs and genres) because our participants information behaviour conducted effective information filtering using genres and small granular features sets, essentially distinguishing by perceptual structural cues and features that acted as affordances to the user to cognitively filter and access information in the decision making behaviour, thus also redefining the model originally shown in [8].

Appendix

A1 Footnotes

[1]http://www.prweek.com/article/1074122/fixer-cleans-wikipedia-entries-senior-business-figures.
[2]http://www.bbc.co.uk/news/technology-16084861.

A2 Tasks

1. You are joining a debating society and need some notes to make a PowerPoint presentation on the first topic, which is: "Cannabis: Good or Bad?" Since being made illegal in the UK in 1928 and since the introduction of the 1971 Dangerous Drugs Act, the use of cannabis for medicinal reasons has been restricted. However, in recent years, some countries (for example, Austria) have legalized the smoking/ingesting of cannabis by certain patients for pain relief and other medicinal benefits. Thus 'medical cannabis' has become a topic of hot debate. You want to understand the arguments for and against the use of marijuana for medical purposes. Therefore, you decide to do some preliminary research on this subject using Wikipedia. What are the possible health benefits and health problems that may entail from smoking/ingesting cannabis for medical reasons?

2. You have been tasked to write an essay on the Arab Spring which started to be reported in late 2010. The beginning of the so-called 'Arab Spring' led to a huge wave of demonstrations and uprisings in at least 17 countries that has resulted in many long-standing military regimes being overthrown and, in some cases, in civil war. Use Wikipedia to find out some useful information that you feel is appropriate and can be used later to form a basis for the essay. For example, the countries involved and so on.

3. You are in the third year of a social studies degree and have been given coursework on the topic of 'Philanthropy.' On the 4th August 2010, thirty-eight US billionaire philanthropists pledged at least 50% of their wealth to charity through a campaign started by the investor, Warren Buffet, and the Microsoft founder, Bill Gates. Some of those who have signed the pledge include Michael Bloomberg and George Lucas. Many mentioned in 'The Giving Pledge' project are among the most influential people in the contemporary United States and debatably the world. Your coursework states that you have to carry out an investigation to find out who you think is the most influential philanthropist in the pledge group.

4. You are working for ITN news as an intern. There has been a major air crash at an international airport. The news editor wants you to search for background information on the previous top two worst air disasters in history, such as the numbers of fatalities, casualties and so on. She also wants to know the names of airlines with the best and worst safety records.

5. You are on work experience at the sports desk at The Guardian newspaper and have been asked by the editor to collect information on the two rival teams, Boca Juniors, and River Plate, as they face each other in the Argentine Cup Final. Use Wikipedia to find out appropriate information about each club, such as the stadiums, star players and the managers of each team.

6. You are in the third year of a political studies' degree course and have been given coursework on studying the legislature in an African country. You decide to focus on Namibia. Collect information about the Parliament, National Council of Namibia, National Assembly, and any other information you think is relevant to form the basis of your work.

References

1. Miller, C.R.: Genre innovation: evolution, emergence, or something else? J. Media Innov. **3**(2), 4–19 (2016)
2. Clark, M., Ruthven, I., Holt, P.: The evolution of genre in Wikipedia. J. Lang. Technol. Comput. Linguistics **25**(1), 1–22 (2009)
3. Ingwersen, P., Järvelin, K.: The Turn: Integration of Information Seeking and Retrieval in Context. Springer, Dordrecht, The netherlands (2005)
4. Toms, E.G., Campbell, D.G.: Genre as interface metaphor: exploiting form and function in digital environments. In: Proceedings of the 32nd Annual Hawaii International CONFER-ENCE on System Sciences: Digital Documents Track (HICSS-32), pp. 2008–2024. IEEE Computer Society, Hawaii, US (1999)
5. Clark, M., Ruthven, I., Holt, P., Song, D., Watt, S.: You have e-mail, what happens next? tracking the eyes for genre. Inf. Process. Manage. **50**(1), 175–198 (2014)
6. Clark, M., Ruthven, I., Holt, P.O.B., Song, D.: Looking for genre: the use of structural features during search tasks with Wikipedia. In: Fourth Information Interaction in Context CONFERENCE (IIiX) (Year)
7. Lakoff, G.: Women, Fire and Dangerous Things: What Categories Reveal About the Mind. University of Chicago Press, Chicago (1987)
8. Wang, P., Soergel, D.: A cognitive model of document use during a research project. Study I. Document selection. J. Am. Soc. Inf. Sci. **49**(2), 115–133 (1998)
9. Azar, A.S., Hashim, A.: Analysing authorial identity construction in the review article genre in Applied Linguistics. Stud. English Lang. Educ. **9**(1), 94–114 (2022)
10. Andersson, S.: Problems in information classification: insights from practice. Information & Computer Security (2023)
11. Lin, Z., Welbers, K., Vermeer, S., Trilling, D.: Beyond discrete genres: mapping news items onto a multidimensional framework of genre cues. In: Proceedings of the International AAAI CONFERENCE on Web and Social Media, pp. 542–553 (Year)
12. Salamon, E.: Media unions' online resistance rhetoric: reproducing social movement genres of organizational communication. Manag. Commun. Q.. Commun. Q. **37**(2), 368–395 (2023)
13. Yates, J.A., Orlikowski, W.J.: Genres of organizational communication: a structurational approach to studying communication and media. Acad. Manag. Rev.Manag. Rev. **17**(2), 299–326 (1992)
14. Spinuzzi, C.: Four ways to investigate assemblages of texts: genre sets, systems, repertoires, and ecologies. In: Proceedings of the 22nd Annual International CONFERENCE on Design of Communication - the Engineering of Quality Documentation, pp. 110–116. ACM Press, New York (2004)
15. Dewdney, N., VanEss-Dykema, C., MacMillan, R.: The form is the substance: classification of genres in text. In: Proceedings of the Workshop on Human Language Technology and Knowledge Management, vol. 2001, pp. 1–8. Association for Computational Linguistics Toulouse, France (2001)

16. Kristeva, J.: Desire in Language: A Semiotic Approach to Literature and Art. Columbia University Press, New York (1980)
17. University of Wales. http://www.aber.ac.uk/~mcswww/Documents/intgenre/intgenre.html
18. Wertheimer, M.: A source book of Gestalt psychology. In: Ellis, W.D. (ed.), p. 11. Kegan Paul, Trench, Trubner & Company. (1938)
19. Gibson, J.J.: The Theory of Affordances. The ecological approach to visual perception, p. 127. LEA, Hillsdale, New Jersey (1979)
20. Frow, J.: Genre. Routledge Taylor & Francis Group, Oxon, UK (2006)
21. Watt, S.N.K.: Text categorisation and genre in information retrieval. In: Göker, A., Davies, J. (eds.) Information Retrieval: Searching in the 21st Century, pp. 159–176. John Wiley & Sons, Chichester, U.K. (2009)
22. Hirsch, E.D., Jr.: Validity in Interpretation. Yale University Press, New Haven (1967)
23. Toms, E.G., Campbell, D.G.: Utilizing information "shape" as an interface metaphor based on genre. In: Proceedings of the 27th Annual CONFERENCE of the Canadian Association for Information Science, pp. 370–386. QB: The CAIS, Quebec (1999)
24. Wikimedia. https://en.wikipedia.org/wiki/English_Wikipedia
25. Wenger, E.: Communities of practice a brief introduction. Cambridge University Press, North San Juan, CA (2009)
26. Wenger, E.: Communities of practice and social learning systems. Organization 7(2), 225–246 (2000)
27. Lorch, R.F.: Text-signaling devices and their effects on reading and memory processes. Educ. Psychol. Rev. 1(3), 209–234 (1989)
28. Dictionary, T.O.E.: Gazetteer. The Oxford English Dictionary. Oxford University Press, Oxford (2021)
29. Bazerman, C.: Intertextuality: How texts rely on other texts. In: Bazerman, C., Prior, P. (eds.) What writing does and how it does it: An introduction to analyzing texts and textual practices, pp. 83–96. Lawrence Erlbaum Associates, Mahwah, NJ (2004)
30. Pike, G., Edgar, G.: Perception. In: Braisby, N., Gellatly, A. (eds.) Cognitive Psychology, pp. 71–112. The Open University, Milton Keynes (2005)

"How I Form and Escape Information Cocoons": An Interview Study of Users on Short Video Apps

Manyu Sheng[1,2] and Pengyi Zhang[3(✉)]

[1] National Science Library, Chinese Academy of Sciences, Beijing 100190, China
shengmanyu@mail.las.ac.cn
[2] Department of Information Resources Management, School of Economics and Management, University of Chinese Academy of Sciences, Beijing 100190, China
[3] Department of Information Management, Peking University, Beijing 100871, China
pengyi@pku.edu.cn

Abstract. The advancement of big data driven recommendations reinforces information cocoons, where people only access information that conforms to their existing views or interests. However, little is known about how information cocoons are formed in short video applications. In this study, we conducted semi-structured interviews with 22 users of short video apps such about their viewing experiences. We used thematic analysis to identify the main themes and patterns in their responses. The results suggest that 1) users form information cocoons purposefully, but they sometime take an explicit effort to escape information cocoons for diversity and serendipity purposes. 2) users use various strategies to escape the information cocoons, such as following or unfollowing certain accounts, interacting with algorithms, and exploring different hashtags or categories; 3) the phases of information cocoons vary from topic to topic, including exploratory information seeking, information filtering, opinion consolidation, and continuous self-verification. We discuss the implications of our findings for short video application design, information literacy education, and future research.

Keywords: Information Cocoons · Information Behavior · Short Video Platforms

1 Introduction

Short video applications have emerged as a new type of media platform and even a distinct lifestyle, especially for young people. For instance, short video platforms such as Douyin (TikTok) and Kuaishou have attracted more than one billion users (95.2% of all mobile users) by August 2023 in China [1]. They are increasingly trapped in "information cocoon" and exposed to content that is tailored to their preferences [2]. This phenomenon has caused polarized points of view and has had a significant impact on people's thinking, culture, and political life. Previous studies have explored the factors that lead to the information cocoons and their impact on individuals' perceptions. However, little is known about the significant role of users within both forming and breaking information cocoons.

I. Sserwanga et al. (Eds.): iConference 2024, LNCS 14596, pp. 129–138, 2024.
https://doi.org/10.1007/978-3-031-57850-2_10

One of the causes of information cocoons lies in the loss of users' ability to access diverse information, and this study investigates how users form and escape information cocoons on short video apps, focusing on their motivations, information behaviors and strategies during different phrases of video viewing. It emphasizes user awareness and guidance in unconscious information behavior. This research contributes to our understanding of users' information behavior and its relationship in the short video platform. It assists users in self-regulating their behavior and enhancing their ability to seek diverse information. It also helps the platform to recognize and fulfil users' potential needs. Finally, it also provides recommendations for solving the various problems caused by automated recommendation technologies.

This paper is organized as follows: Sect. 2 introduces the current research on information cocoons and behaviors on short video platforms. Section 3 presents the entire process of our study. Section 4 discusses how information cocoons form and how users attempt to escape them. Finally, Sect. 5 summarizes the main findings, identifies limitations and directions for future research.

2 Literature Review

2.1 Information Cocoon, Filter Bubble, and Echo Chamber

Information cocoon means the narrowing of individual's exposure to information, while echo chamber refers to a closed social circle trapped by homogeneous information in the group, leading to wild errors, undue confidence, and unjustified extremism [2]. In contrast, filter bubbles arise because recommendation algorithms are blindly focused on to users' interests, ignoring the diversity of information, such as Google's PageRank [3]. However, they all emphasize the increasing homogenization of information access. As for their influences, researches have focused on its negative impact on the formation of individual opinion, group polarization and political tendencies. Bessi's research indicates that continuous exposure to echo chambers slightly affects users' psychological characteristic on Facebook [4]. Yu and Wang [5] argue that information cocoons can make information receiving singular, repetitive, and self-centered.

Factors contributing to the formation of information cocoons include four dimensions, they are technology (platform and its automated recommendation tools et al.), user (information behavior and selective exposure et al.), information environment (source, content, quality et al.) and social environment (policy and social network et al.). Information service tools can influence individuals' thoughts and attitudes, and users' selective exposure further exacerbates this tendency [6]. Li et al. [7] conducted a correlation analysis study to explore the influencing factors of information cocoons, confirmed that users with narrower preferences are more likely to form information echo cocoons.

Strategies for escaping information cocoons include both technological and user perspectives. At the technical perspective, it is essential to improve recommendation mechanisms in order to provide users with a broader range of content. Grossetti, Du, Travers and Constantin indicate that content recommendations from social networks may help reduce the impact of filter bubbles [8]. In addition, it is crucial to improve product design by visualizing recommendation systems. Lo, Dai, Xiong, Jiang and Ku [9] suggest that the visualization of the distribution of political ideologies in news could help users identify whether they are trapped in an echo chamber. On the user side, improving the ability to access diverse information is key to overcoming information narrowing. For instance, Fu and Jiang [10] suggest using thematic analysis to manage information sources.

2.2 Information Behavior on Short Video Sites

Taylor defines information behavior as the "sum of actions that make information useful" [11]. And Wilson indicates that information behavior can be categorized as active and passive information seeking and use [12]. Users' information behavior in short video platforms includes the generation of information needs, information retrieval, selection, processing, sharing, storage, utilization and creation [13]. Users' willingness to use short video platforms, browsing, sharing and creation behavior are core topics. Zhu and Wei [14] explored users' information dissemination behavior on Douyin, showed the music community on Douyin is characterized by community, small world and scale-free. Zhang, Wu and Liu [15] explored the factors influencing users' browsing and creative behavior, found that users' narcissistic traits and desire to belong positively influence their creation behavior, while the need for popularity and the documentation function positively influence their browsing behavior.

Research has been conducted to understand how users' active and passive information behavior may reduce the influence of information cocoons. Peng and Liu interviewed 13 users of short video sites, revealing the importance of individuals' subjective motivations in searching for opposing viewpoints and breaking information cocoons [16]. Passive, aimless information behavior was also essential to escape the information cocoons. Erdelez defines passive information behavior as opportunistic encounters with information, that is, stumbling upon useful information unexpectedly while engaged in other activities [17]. Zhao and Xue [18] suggest that passive information behaviors such as information encounters are characterised by non-linearity and mobility, which may help to reduce algorithmic barriers. Prior research also proposed the importance of system design on users' passive information behavior. Reviglio [19] suggests that serendipitous system design, such as providing buttons for "random discovery of information", can facilitate the dissolution of filter bubbles.

In summary, the research on information cocoons has delved deeply into their nature and influencing factors, emphasizing the role of users' information selection tendencies in cocoon formation, and explored how to reduce the negative impact from various aspects. However, limited research has been conducted into user's interaction with automated recommendation systems and the entire process of their information behavior. Additionally, there has been little consideration towards users' awareness and control of unconscious information behavior. We need to explore more effective measures to enhance users' ability and reduce the negative effects of information restriction.

3 Method

3.1 Data Collection

This research employed a semi-structured interview approach for data collection, conducted from 10th to 23rd April 2023. Participants were recruited through distributing questionnaires on a wide range of platforms including Douyin, Kuaishou, etc. In the first stage, a total of 22 respondents were recruited, constituting a diverse demographic, including gender, education, age groups and viewing durations (see Table 1).

Interviews were conducted either in person or over the phone. Participants were informed before the interviews to prepare experiences on three topics: a topic they had recently encountered on the short video platform, a topic they had become more informed about, and a topic they browsed every day. The interviews asked about the users' motivation, usage behaviors, and strategies for information cocoons.

Table 1. Basic characteristics of interviewees

Categories	Subcategories	Quantity	Categories	Subcategories	Quantity
Gender	Male	12	Education level	Secondary vocational	1
	Female	10		Junior college	4
				Bachelor's degree	11
Age group	18–25 Years	12		Master's degree	1
	26–30 Years	3		Ph.D	5
	31–40 Years	4	The short video platform used	TikTok	51%
	41–50 Years	2		Kuaishou	48%
	51–60 Years	1		Xiaohongshu	48%
				Xigua Video	23%
Average daily browsing time	Less than 1 h	6		WeChat Video	18%
	1–2 h	5		QQ World	15%
	2–5 h	10		Tencent Weishi	12%
	More than 5 h	1		Bilibili	3%

3.2 Data Analysis

We analyzed the interview data through qualitative thematic coding with Nvivo 14, to extract concepts, categories, and their connections. The stages of users' information cocoons were determined based on factors such as durations of topic browsing, whether users had firm opinions or specific preferences, whether they were willing to explore new perspectives, and whether they faced challenges in accessing comprehensive information. Users' information behaviors on short video platforms have been identified based on previous researches. This includes the entire process of information processing and using [13]. The coded concepts, categories, and relationships are presented in Tables 2.

To ensure coding process was reliable, two samples were independently coded by another researcher in the field. We calculated the inter-coder agreement and reached a Kappa value of 0.75.

Table 2. Concepts and categories derived from qualitative coding (Shortened version)

Themes	Categories	Concepts	Codes
Different information behaviors of users	Information Encounter	Content	Medical Knowledge, etc
		Behavior after Encounter	Information Utilization, etc
		Frequency	More frequent encounters, Less frequent encounters
	Information Selection	Following	Regulate algorithms, etc
		Blocking	Lack of interest, etc
		Favoriting	Retrieve information, etc
	...	...	...
Specific stages of information cocoons	Cocoon Formation Stage	Fixed Style of Information	Most viewed information
	Established Cocoon Stage	Reflection and Perspective Change	New reflection
	...	...	...
Different aspects of users' perceptions of information cocoons	Crisis Awareness	Being In It	Attempt to break, no change required
		Not Being In It	Trust in recommendation system, etc
	Knowledge of Automated Recommendation Systems	Unfamiliar	No idea
		Preliminary Understanding	Understand what it is
		...	...

(*continued*)

Table 2. (*continued*)

Themes	Categories	Concepts	Codes
	...	...	...
Strategies for escaping information cocoons in different dimensions	Platform	Algorithm Transparency	Product design
		...	...
	User	Recipient	Stop using, etc
		Producer	Create high-quality content
	Regulator	Publish powerful Policies	Restrain the platform

4 Findings

4.1 Users' Perception and Motivation

Users Have Limited Understanding of Automated Recommendation Systems. Most interviewees have a basic understanding of these systems, while some have a lack of knowledge. Users with backgrounds in computer science or related fields tend to be more familiar with the algorithmic principles.

Some Users Are Content within the Cocoons. The majority of interviewees recognized the negative influence of information cocoons and desire to break out of them. However, some users are still satisfied with the content provided by short video platforms and are unwilling to change, even though they are aware of their cocooned state. As interviewee N said, "It caters to my taste and I'm already tired from work, I just want to have some fun when I come home." Additionally, some interviewees have faith in recommendation systems and consider short video platforms to be secondary information sources. For example, Interviewee P said, "I know that what short videos present is not the whole world, and that's enough, I won't get caught in it."

Some Users Have a Clear Awareness of their Selective Exposure. Users primarily consider factors when analyzing the reasons for information cocoons: themselves, the platform, and regulatory authorities. They said that individuals who receive information tend to have selective cognitive tendencies, pursuing personal interests to reduce cognitive load, which enhances the impact of information cocoons. As Interviewee D noted, "Many of the topics promoted are unhealthy, such as the belief that having square shoulders is attractive, causing everyone to hurry to imitate it."

4.2 Users' Information Behavior on Short Video Platforms

Users' Information Behavior on Short Video Platforms Includes Different Stages of Information Processing. There are information needs generation, information acquisition, filtering, processing, dissemination, utilization, and production. Information needs arise for entertainment, relaxation, or efficient information seeking. In addition to browsing and searching, serendipitous encounters also play a vital role in information acquisition and escaping from information cocoons due to its non-linear and infinite nature. Serendipitous topics may be the dissemination of knowledge such as academic researches or games skills. When processing information, the majority of respondents believe that content of short videos is highly homogeneous and opposing viewpoints are less common. Nevertheless, some users still mentioned that when they find opposing viewpoints, they may take a more dialectical view. They might follow, marking, comment or sharing the content.

Users' Information Cocoon States Vary Over Time and Across Topics. We asked users about their information behavior on topics at different stages of information cocoon. The differences of users' information behaviors at different stages are as shown in Fig. 1. Users' selective behaviors play an important role in the formation of information cocoons.

Pre-cocoon Stage (free Information Acquisition). It is evident that browsing is less when the cocoons has not been formed. Since the main content is news and skills, the frequency of information search and processing of opposing views is higher, which is more likely to encounter and further usage. The information selection, transmission and publishing are few at this stage, but users will share many of the views they encounter.

Cocoon Formation Stage (Information Filtering and Perspective Consolidation). During this phase, users' browsing topics are based on knowledge and personal interests, leading to more focused information gathering. Information selection behaviors, such as following, saving, and blocking, become prominent. Users begin to focus on specific pieces of information rather than on the entire site.

Established Cocoon Stage (Continuous Self-verification). Users in this stage primarily engage with topics related to their personal interests. Information retrieval is less frequent and users are more likely to encounter and publishing content that confirms their existing views. However, it is worth noting that as users spend more time browsing, they may also encounter videos or comments with more diverse perspectives.

Post-cocoon Stage (Reflection and Inspiration). During this stage, certain users may experience a heightened sense of self-awareness. They reflect on their information cocoon and realize its impact on their lives. These individuals engage in self-regulation and interaction with algorithms through various behaviors, including browsing, searching, commenting, sharing and so on.

Users' behavior becomes increasingly involved browsing, following, and marking, commenting, homogeneous information processing and production. There is a gradual decrease in information seeking and encountering, and homogeneous information processing is evident at all stages, validating the trend of information narrowing again. The behavior of information blocking initially increase and followed by a decrease, conversely and logically, the frequency of encountering conflicting views shows a decrease followed by an increase.

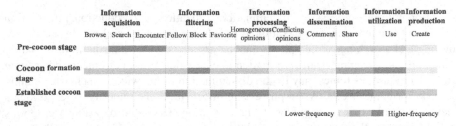

Fig. 1. Differences of users' behavior at various stages of information cocoon

4.3 Users' Strategies

Users Used a Variety of Strategies to Interact with Algorithms. There are multiple ways to reduce the impact of information cocoons which include promoting algorithm visibility, improve recommendation algorithms and publish powerful rules. Moreover, Users should create quality content, engage in independent critical thinking, and seek information from alternative sources. Most importantly, explore their potential information needs and critical thinking, and take active measures to regulate algorithms by controlling their active and passive information behavior consciously to engage themselves within particular topics. As Interviewee K suggests, "I know my phone is tracking me, so if I want to see something, I will intentionally talk about that topic with someone nearby, and then some apps will recommend content related to that."

5　Conclusion and Discussion

Focusing on short video platforms, this research examines the process of information cocoon formation from three perspectives: user motivations, information behaviors, and strategies. It shows that users actively contribute to the formation of information cocoons. They may trust their own judgment or the recommendation system, and some may willingly accept these cocoons, enjoying the efficient information retrieval environment. Meanwhile, some users express a desire to break out of information cocoons and have attempted to control the algorithms by actively interacting with them. Importantly, information cocoons can change dynamically over time and across topics, and users' information-selection behaviors play a key role in the formation of them. It is worth noting that some users can still access multiple viewpoints and engage in continuous self-reflection, which is a key factor in awakening during the later stages of information cocoons.

More attention should be paid to users' ability to lead themselves out of the information cocoon, and many scholars are aware of this. For example, Li, Gao and Huang et al. analyzed users' records on Kuaishou and showed that users' personal preferences play a more vital role in the formation of the information cocoon than the recommendation algorithms [20].

This research also has limitations. While the sample selection included a diverse range of respondents from different regions, occupations, education levels, their distribution may not have been balanced. Future research could explore how users can manage their behavior, improving their ability to access diverse information, and cultivate information literacy. In addition, it would be valuable to explore how to improve algorithm design to assist in identifying the stage of cocoons and recommend different content. Finally, future research could explore the causes of users' reflection and inspiration, and how to promote them effectively.

Acknowledgment. This research is supported by National Science Foundation of China Grant No. 72174014.

References

1. CNNIC Report. https://www.cnnic.net.cn/n4/2023/0828/c88-10829.html. Accessed 28 Aug 2023
2. Sunstein, C.R.: Infotopia: How many minds produce knowledge. Oxford University Press, Cambridge (2006)
3. Pariser, E.: The Filter Bubble: What the internet is hiding from you. Penguin UK (2011)
4. Bessi, A.: Personality traits and echo chambers on Facebook. Comput. Hum. Behav.. Hum. Behav. **65**, 319–324 (2016)
5. Yu, X., Wang, J.P.: Reconceptualizing the "Information Cocoon": a study on the symbiotic mechanism between instrumental and value rationality in the age of intellectual Media. News Writing **39**(3), 65–78 (2022)
6. Wang, R., Feng, B.Y., Li, M.: Mechanisms of selective attention and factors influencing it. Psychol. Tech. Appl. **5**(9), 567–573 (2017)
7. Li, N., et al.: An exploratory study of information cocoon on short-form video platform. In: Proceedings of the 31st ACM International Conference on Information and Knowledge Management, ACM, pp. 4178–4182. ACM, New York (2022)
8. Grossetti, Q., Du Mouza, C., Travers, N., Constantin, C.: Reducing the filter bubble effect on Twitter by considering communities for recommendation. Int. J. Web Inf. Syst. **17**(6), 728–752 (2021)
9. Lo, K. C., Dai, S. C., Xiong, A., Jiang, J., Ku, L. W.: Escape from an echo chamber. In: Companion Proceedings of the Web Conference 2021, ACM, pp. 713–716. ACM, New York (2021)
10. Fu, S., Jiang, T.: Motivations, purposes, and means of creating information cocoons intentionally for oneself: looking on the bright side. In: International Conference on Information 2023, LNCS, vol.13972, pp. 123–130. Springer, Nature Switzerland (2023)
11. Taylor, R.S.: Information Use Environments. In: Dervin, B., Voight, M.J. (eds.) Progress in Communication Sciences, pp. 217–255. Ablex, Norwood, NJ (1991)
12. Wilson, T.D.: Human information behavior. Informing. Science **3**(2), 49–56 (2000)
13. Song, X.Y., Wang, P.: A review of research on user information behavior. Inf. Sci. **28**(4), 625–629+636 (2010)
14. Zhu, H., Wei, H., Wei, J.: Understanding users' information dissemination behaviors on Douyin, a short video mobile application in China. Multimed Tools Appl. (2023). https://doi.org/10.1007/s11042-023-17831-3
15. Xing, Z., You, W.: Analysis of factors influencing browsing and creation behaviors of mobile short video users. Library Intell. Work. **63**, 103 (2019). https://doi.org/10.13266/j.issn.0252-3116.2019.06.013
16. Peng, H., Liu, C.: Breaking the information cocoon: when do people actively seek conflicting information? Proc. Assoc. Inf. Sci. Technol. **58**(1), 801–803 (2021)

17. Erdelez, S.: Information encountering: it's more than just bumping into information. Bull. Am. Soc. Inf. Sci. Technol. **25**(3), 26–29 (1999)
18. Zhao, Y.Z., Xue, T.Y.: A study of "Information Chance Encounter" behavior in social media: a perspective on solving the "Information Cocoon" problem. Friends of the Editor **5**, 38–43 (2020)
19. Reviglio, U.: Serendipity as an emerging design principle of the infosphere: challenges and opportunities. Ethics Inf. Technol. **21**(2), 151–166 (2019). https://doi.org/10.1007/s10676-018-9496-y
20. Li, N., et al.: An exploratory study of information cocoon on short-form video platform. In: Proceedings of the 31st ACM International Conference on Information & Knowledge Management. pp. 4178–4182. ACM, Atlanta (2022). https://doi.org/10.1145/3511808.3557548

Are Older People Battling with Digital Financial Services?

Dain Thomas[✉] ⓘ, Gobinda Chowdhury ⓘ, and Ian Ruthven ⓘ

University of Strathclyde, Glasgow, UK
dain.thomas.2015@uni.strath.ac.uk, {gobinda.chowdhury,
ian.ruthven}@strath.ac.uk

Abstract. The proliferation of technology is the cause of converting many of the services to digital form which pressurizes everyone to adopt the internet. Online services which consist of financial transactions are required in this digital realm to gain benefits which would result in leading a convenient life in various ways. However, older people aged 65 and over are encountering obstacles that exclude them from the use of digital financial services, for example, fear, lack of experience/knowledge and interface issues. We discovered how older people interact with these services and some explanations for why older people in Scotland do not leverage these services. Data was collated from 14 semi-structured interviews with older people (those aged 65 and over) and intermediaries. Consequently, the hidden costs of not using digital financial services were revealed. Not only do these costs produce an impact on the everyday lives of older people but also on people who aid them with digital financial services.

Keywords: Online Financial Services · Older people · Benefits · Challenges

1 Introduction

Online banking, booking online cinema tickets, buying flight tickets, online shopping or any other digital services which include financial transactions are considered as online financial services [1]. In the UK, older people aged 65 and over rarely use the internet compared to younger age groups [2]. A report stated that 32% of adults aged 65+ are internet non-users [3]. This clearly indicates that they use online financial services infrequently [1]. A number of papers have declared the challenges that older people are confronting with these services, for instance, lack of equipment [4, 5], language [6] and lack of confidence [7].

A recent study has reported the preliminary findings of some of the challenges gathered from five interviews that hinder older people (those aged 65+) from using digital financial services; the main factors are fear of scams, lack of skills and lack of help [1]. This paper discusses the challenges obtained from some semi-structured interviews and aims to address two specific research questions. Firstly, how do older people in Scotland aged 65 or over conduct online financial services? Secondly, are older people losing benefits from not using these services? These questions are answered through the data procured from interviews with older people and intermediaries.

I. Sserwanga et al. (Eds.): iConference 2024, LNCS 14596, pp. 139–146, 2024.
https://doi.org/10.1007/978-3-031-57850-2_11

The first question focuses on older people's interactions with online services and the assistance acquired from intermediaries to use these services. The second question intends to identify the advantages of digital financial services and how this could impact the day-to-day lives of older people.

2 Literature Review

2.1 Digital Divide

Some people have access to technology and some don't; this is often known as the 'digital divide'[8]. There are three factors which contribute to digital divide in older people: information access (i.e. the right equipment to access internet), information capability (i.e. possessing the capability to utilize technological devices), information utilization (i.e. possessing the capability to make use of the obtained information) [9]. In terms of information access, older people are experiencing issues associated with accessibility. A report stated that internet access is not available at the residence of 34% of older adults aged 65+ in the UK [10]. Not having access to internet could indicate that older people may have financial limitations if they are on low income and as a result, they significantly lack digital skills; this reinforces digital divide and the exclusion of older people from technology.

2.2 Older People's Use of Online Financial Services

The Office for National Statistics (ONS) in the UK declared that only 49% of older people aged 65+ used online banking in 2020 whereas over 65% of people in each of the other age groups were online banking users [11]. This clearly suggests that any benefits which could be derived from online banking are not being received by majority of the older people. Furthermore, only 65% of those over 65s used online websites for shopping and only 13% of older people (those aged 65+) purchased online transport service tickets (bus, train or flight); other age groups have a significant proportion of users who utilize online financial services [11].

All these statistics validate that over 65s are beginning to segregate from younger age groups due to the accumulation of technological services. Hence, it is vital to bridge this gap through effective interventions which would assist older people with digital financial services.

2.3 Older People's Challenges in the Use of Online Financial Services

As briefly mentioned, a variety of reasons are related to older people's low usage of digital financial services. For instance, trust, perceived ease of use and perceived usefulness have an impact on adults' intention to adopt online shopping [12]. Some older people try to avoid digital services where they have to enter personal information as they do not fully trust these services [13]. These types of behavioral challenges prohibit older people from using online financial services to some extent.

Furthermore, some older people are frustrated about the time required to learn digital skills and some are having difficulties with finding information they have already retrieved [13]. This could be a result of inadequate design of the interfaces; older people are digitally excluded due to accessibility issues. Although there are web guidelines, most designers do not follow these guidelines when designing interfaces [14].

In addition to these issues, some older people are not aware of online banking [15]. This indicates that they are not aware of online financial services. Hence, they perceive that technology is not useful to them [16]. On the other hand, some people have worries regarding security because websites or transactions that are not sufficiently protected can cause major problems [17]. Financial scams are increasing in society. Personal information is collected by fraudsters through fake websites [18]. This increases fear in older people which negatively influences their intention to use online financial services.

2.4 Help Provided to Older People

Marginalized individuals often receive help with digital services from digital carers; these carers could be family, friends or relatives [19]. This clearly indicates that older people rely on people who they fully trust to help them with online services. They often seek support from libraries to obtain digital skills [20] and from people or organisations to assist them with digital financial services. For example, post offices help people to carry out a few banking tasks such as withdrawing, paying cash into an account and checking account balance [21]. This is beneficial for older people who lack digital skills and who cannot travel to a nearby bank branch.

2.5 Benefits of Online Financial Services

Since a lack of awareness of the internet is evident in older people [22], they are not aware of the benefits they are losing by not using online financial services. Online banking was created to enable users to have convenient access to their account information [23]. Online banking would stimulate eco-friendliness as there will be a reduction in the use of paper and the journey to a bank can be avoided [24]. Environment sustainability would not only be improved via online banking but through the use of all the other online financial services.

Leveraging online financial services has many other benefits as well. For instance, online purchases are cheaper and individuals can save up to 13% when compared to in-person shopping [25]. This is financially beneficial for older people as they could save money on travel expenses and various products including flight tickets and insurance policies. Moreover, time spent on in-person activities can be saved through the use of digital financial services; individuals can conserve around 30 min per transaction [25].

3   Method

Although the previous section mentions that older people are encountering several obstacles with online financial services and they are losing benefits from not using such services, this study aims to provide a theoretical contribution to knowledge by elevating our understanding of the key challenges that older people face in the use of online financial services and how this impacts them and others in the society. In order to achieve this, 14 semi-structured interviews were carried out; 7 interviews with older people (those aged 65 and over) and 7 interviews with intermediaries including employees and digital carers. Participants were gathered through communication and organisations such as Glasgow's Golden Generation, Glasgow Women's Aid, the Well Multi-Cultural Resource Centre, Hindu temple, and university students who have helped or are currently aiding older people with digital financial services. It was not mandatory to take part in the interview or provide a response to all the questions.

Older people's challenges and interactions on online financial services were determined by asking around 7–8 questions to each participant and the duration of each interview was approximately 30 min. Older people were asked about the challenges they experience on online banking, online shopping, insurance policies, transport/event tickets and other financially related tasks that they carry out online. Intermediaries were asked about their experiences on working with older people, the type of help they provided and the challenges they noticed while assisting them with digital financial services. Interviews were recorded using a phone and were transcribed using a transcription software called Otter. A data analysis software (NVivo) was utilized to carry out thematic analysis on the transcripts. Various themes and codes were produced from thematic analysis such as challenges, hidden costs, help provided, implications etc.

4   Results

4.1   Challenges Faced by Older People

The most common challenges identified from the analysis were fear followed by lack of experience/knowledge and interface issues. These three codes were formed under the main theme – 'Challenges'.

Older people have a fear of carrying out transactions on digital financial services due to scams in society. One participant stated, "I don't want to lose my money". This fear prevents older people from adopting such services. An employee mentioned that "when it comes to buying things online…our service users are quite put off because they think it's quite a dangerous thing to give out bank details online." Also, they need reassurance from their family members prior to clicking the last button.

Another factor confronted by older people in the use of digital financial services is a lack of experience/knowledge. Since they were not born in the digital realm, they have difficulties in understanding the whole concept of technology: "…they're just kind of uncertain, like, what is the internet? What does that mean? What is a website?". They do not have prior experience or knowledge to boost their confidence to use online services: "…there's no computers or anything when I was working…I've been retired for a long time."

Along with the challenges disclosed above, interface issues were also reported during the interviews. For instance, one digital carer stated, "Some of the processes are a little too complicated, for example, the two-factor authentication." Also, "phone font size" is an issue; they increase font size on phones which becomes harder to control as they have to scroll up and down many times to view the text. Another issue is the online shopping basket; some older people may not understand icons and they are not sure about how to remove added items from the basket: "My friend told me…. She ordered something…instead of one item she ordered 10 items. She didn't know how to delete it."

4.2 Older People's Interactions

With regard to interactions with online financial services, a number of questions were asked about five digital financial services: online shopping, buying/renewing insurance policies, tickets for events, transport service tickets and online banking. It was noted that older people rarely used these services. Some older people utilized these services independently or with the assistance of family members or friends: "…he usually uses the app for like to check the balance and then to transfer money as well."

Others did not use these services at all due to fear or because they have family members to deal with these services on their behalf. One participant mentioned that she has an online banking app on her phone, but she never uses it as her husband is handling all these services: "Not scared…. It's just because he does it". Another participant said that she learned to add items to the basket but she didn't have the confidence to move forward as she had a fear of losing money. Lack of digital skills was also evident in most of the older people: "I don't have the skill to use the app."

4.3 Hidden Costs Linked to Intermediaries

Digital carers aid older people with digital financial services in different ways: "I demonstrate it to him…. he writes it down. And then he tries it himself with the instructions he has written down." Another digital carer said that her parents don't have Wi-Fi so she does the tasks for them at her own home. Sometimes, they feel frustrated when they have to repeat the instructions and they lose patience: "It can be difficult. I do sometimes lose patience with my mother. Just because she's kind of, you know, like repeating things." Sessions could last for "45 min or an hour" or "two or more hours per week".

However, there are some indirect costs associated with this, for example, digital carers can otherwise spend this time for leisure activities or for their personal work-related tasks. One participant mentioned that she's losing time by helping her parents, but she needs to do it; she doesn't have a choice. In addition, they spend a lot of effort into helping these marginalized people which can be considered as another hidden cost (theme).

Employees working at non-profit organisations also aid older people with online services. Some employees do become frustrated: "It was very frustrating to kind of teach them how to identify what was safe and what wasn't on online." Also, sometimes it is difficult for them to deal with their personalities: "They just keep talking over you while you're trying to do the things for them."

However, they tend not to lose patience while working with vulnerable people as they are being paid for their job. This implies that the monetary aspect is a direct cost linked to the help provided by digital carers. The minutes or hours they spent with older people were free of charge; they could use this time for another job where they could easily obtain remuneration, but they decided not to as they prefer to support older family members, friends, and relatives.

In terms of help provided by employees, they deliver training on online services including instructions on how to stay safe online: "So it's been my job to get out to our service users with the tablets and kind of teach them…do tutorials, do one to one sessions, build up their confidence and then I also do group sessions as well." They usually provide them with instructions or as they're going through a task, they'll write specific instructions: "If there's a little symbol, like, say the basket symbol or the love heart. I'll draw out what symbol it is and then what that means when they click on it." They spend around "one hour with either an individual or a group of people." Employees also put a lot of effort into training older people: "I think online safety was kind of the hardest part… I need to make sure that they are not being financially abused in any way. It was very worrying for me that I don't take the time to explain this, they could potentially buy something online or be scammed. And because I taught them how to do it, I would be in trouble." This denotes that effort is another hidden cost faced by employees as well as digital carers.

4.4 Hidden Costs Linked to Older People

Older people who receive help from intermediaries experience a number of direct and indirect costs. An employee stated, "She has to travel into the city center if she ever wants to go into a physical bank." This clearly suggests that they spend time and effort (indirect costs) on travelling to the nearest branch for banking tasks since they do not utilize online banking. This finding was also revealed in previous research [1]. Moreover, they spend money (direct cost) on travel expenses. If these costs are reduced to some extent, older people could have an improved lifestyle in the context of everyday life.

Two employees did mention that there's a higher percentage of females who attend the organisation for assistance whilst another two employees stated that they worked with roughly an equal number of male and female older adults. Although the gender aspect cannot be verified through the conducted interviews, majority of the participants were not aware of the implications of not using digital financial services: "I'm still old fashioned. I just think to myself, why do I need online banking? I just keep saying this. Why do I need it?" It is explicitly evident from this that older people lack knowledge of the benefits of online financial services and therefore they face hidden costs.

5 Conclusion

Findings from this research exhibited deeper insights by addressing the two research questions. This study divulged that fear, lack of experience/knowledge and interface issues were the main factors that act as barriers to older people's (those aged 65 and over) use of online financial services. These factors have been revealed in previous studies [1, 26–28]. Those who face challenges or those who do not utilize online financial services seek help from intermediaries such as digital carers and organisations. They interact more with such services once they receive assistance. However, hidden costs such as time, effort and money were revealed which corroborates that older people are losing many benefits from not using these services. As highlighted earlier, using digital financial services provide positive impacts on the environment and public in the form of benefits, for example, lower pollution and lower online prices. Intermediaries especially digital carers are also being affected by the hidden costs. Ofcom report indicated that 46% of 16–24-year-olds digitally helped someone weekly [10]. Hence, it is vital to reduce the costs through potential solutions.

As part of upcoming work, additional interviews would be conducted to contribute knowledge to the public especially financial service providers on the challenges encountered by older people and the necessity of performing amendments to existing products and developing inclusive interventions such as digital tools and training sessions.

References

1. Thomas, D., Chowdhury, G., Ruthven, I.: Exploring older people's challenges on online banking/finance systems: early findings. In: Proceedings of the 2023 Conference on Human Information Interaction and Retrieval (2023). https://doi.org/10.1145/3576840.3578324
2. ONS. Internet users, UK:2020. 2020 [cited 2021 14 December]. https://www.ons.gov.uk/bus inessindustryandtrade/itandinternetindustry/bulletins/internetusers/2020
3. Finance, U. Financial Inclusion in a Digital Age. 2018 [cited 2021 15 December]. https:// www.ukfinance.org.uk/system/files/UK-Finance-Financial-Inclusion-AW-web.pdf
4. Polasik, M., Wisniewski, T.P.: Empirical analysis of internet banking adoption in Poland. Int. J. Bank Marketing (2009). https://doi.org/10.1108/02652320910928227
5. Onyia, O.P. and S.K. Tagg, Effects of demographic factors on bank customers' attitudes and intention toward Internet banking adoption in a major developing African country. J. Financial Serv. Mark. 16(3), 294–315 (2011). https://doi.org/10.1057/fsm.2011.28
6. Annamalah, S.: Factors determining consumer adoption of Internet Banking. Available at SSRN 1021484 (2007). https://doi.org/10.2139/ssrn.1021484
7. Lam, J.C., Lee, M.K.: Digital inclusiveness–Longitudinal study of Internet adoption by older adults. J. Manag. Inf. Syst.Manag. Inf. Syst. 22(4), 177–206 (2006). https://doi.org/10.2753/MIS0742-1222220407
8. Gunkel, D.J.: Second thoughts: toward a critique of the digital divide. New Media Soc. 5(4), 499–522 (2003)
9. Jun, W.: A study on cause analysis of digital divide among older people in Korea. INT J ENV RES PUB HE 18(16), 8586 (2021). https://doi.org/10.3390/ijerph18168586
10. Ofcom. Adults' Media use and Attitudes report. 2022 [cited 2022 25 October]
11. ONS. Internet access-households and individuals, Great Britain: 2020. 2020 [cited 2021 4 November]. https://www.ons.gov.uk/peoplepopulationandcommunity/householdcharacter istics/homeinternetandsocialmediausage/bulletins/internetaccesshouseholdsandindividuals/ 2020
12. Guritno, S., Siringoringo, H.: Perceived usefulness, ease of use, and attitude towards online shopping usefulness towards online airlines ticket purchase. Procedia Soc. Behav. Sci.Behav. Sci. 81, 212–216 (2013). https://doi.org/10.1016/j.sbspro.2013.06.415
13. Gatto, S.L., Tak, S.H.: Computer, Internet, and e-mail use among older adults: benefits and barriers. Educ. Gerontol.Gerontol. 34(9), 800–811 (2008). https://doi.org/10.1080/036012 70802243697
14. Milne, S., et al.: Are guidelines enough? an introduction to designing Web sites accessible to older people. IBM Syst. J. 44(3), 557–571 (2005)
15. Omotayo, F.O., Akinyode, T.A.: Digital Inclusion and the Elderly: The Case of Internet Banking Use and Non-Use among older Adults in Ekiti State, Nigeria. Covenant Journal of Business and Social Sciences, 2020. 11(1)

16. Ameme, B.: The impact of customer demographic variables on the adoption and use of internet banking in developing economies. J. Internet Bank. Commer.Commer. **20**(2), 1 (2015)

17. Jun, M., Cai, S.: The key determinants of internet banking service quality: a content analysis. International journal of bank marketing (2001)

18. Finance, U. 2021 Half year fraud update. 2021 [cited 2021 29 December]. https://www.ukf inance.org.uk/system/files/Half-year-fraud-update-2021-FINAL.pdf

19. Harvey, M., Hastings, D.P., Chowdhury, G.: Understanding the costs and challenges of the digital divide through UK council services. J. Inf. Sci., 01655515211040664 (2021). https://doi.org/10.1177/01655515211040664

20. GlasgowLife. Digi-PALS. 2023 [cited 2023 5 December]. https://www.glasgowlife.org.uk/event/1/digi-pals

21. Barclays. Post Office Banking. 2021 [cited 2021 14 November]. https://www.barclays.co.uk/ways-to-bank/post-office-banking/

22. Morris, A., Goodman, J., Brading, H.: Internet use and non-use: views of older users. Univ. Access Inf. Soc. **6**(1), 43–57 (2007). https://doi.org/10.1007/s10209-006-0057-5

23. Aldas-Manzano, J., et al.: Key drivers of internet banking services use. ONLINE INFORM REV **33**(4), 672–695 (2009). https://doi.org/10.1108/14684520910985675

24. Koskosas, I.: The pros and cons of internet banking: a short review. Bus. Excellence Manage. **1**(1), 49–58 (2011)

25. CEBR. The economic impact of Basic Digital Skills and inclusion in the UK. 2015 [cited 2023 13 August]. https://www.goodthingsfoundation.org/wp-content/uploads/2021/02/the_economic_impact_of_digital_skills_and_inclusion_in_the_uk_final_v2.pdf

26. Bhattacharjee, P., Baker, S., Waycott, J.: Older adults and their acquisition of digital skills: A review of current research evidence. In: Proceedings of the 32nd Australian Conference on Human-Computer Interaction (2020). https://doi.org/10.1145/3441000.3441053

27. Mukhtar, M.: Perceptions of UK based customers toward internet banking in the United Kingdom. J. Internet Bank. Commer.Commer. **20**(1), 1–38 (2015)

28. Kaijanen, S., Stenberg, L.: How to empower old people to join the digitalization of services? Gerontechnology **17**(s), 58 (2018)

Plant-Based Predictions: An Exploratory Predictive Analysis of Purchasing Behavior of Meat-Alternatives by U.S. Consumers (2020)

Grace Chmielinski and Sarah Bratt[✉]

School of Information (iSchool), University of Arizona, Tucson, USA
{gchmielinski,sebratt}@arizona.edu

Abstract. Despite the recent increase of plant-based diets, animal-based product consumption remains a major environmental concern. Present information science research is focused on the role of consumer perception in meat-alternative purchasing behavior and its marketing implications. This paper shifts from the profitability aspect of consumer behavior and seeks to understand how external variables such as urban residency, poverty, grocery store access, household income, food expenditure, and grocery costs relate to a county's likelihood to purchase meat-alternatives. Using consumer survey responses from MRI Simmons and statistics from the U.S. government, we developed a logistic regression model, a support vector machine, and a generalized additive model to predict the likelihood of households in a county purchasing meat-alternatives. All features except for grocery access proved to be significant, positively correlated predictors. We conclude that features of physical and financial accessibility are useful in identifying, with roughly 68% accuracy, a U.S. county's tendency for purchasing meat-alternatives. This identification might further sustainability initiatives and local efforts to incentivize environmentally conscious food decisions.

Keywords: Meat-Alternative · Accessibility · Predictive Model · Consumer Behavior

1 Introduction

Plant-based diets have gained popularity in recent years due to increasing awareness of the climate crisis, ethical concerns for animal welfare, and personal health considerations. These diets emphasize minimizing or avoiding animal-based products such as meat, dairy, and eggs. In addition to whole foods like fruits, vegetables, legumes, and grains, plant-based diets might include meat alternatives such as soy, seitan, and other plant-based products.

According to the 2022 "State of the Industry Report: Plant-based meat, seafood, eggs, and dairy", the United States (U.S.) market for plant-based foods has grown to a value of 8 billion dollars [8]. Even still, major inhibitors for the

© The Author(s), under exclusive license to Springer Nature Switzerland AG 2024
I. Sserwanga et al. (Eds.): iConference 2024, LNCS 14596, pp. 147–157, 2024.
https://doi.org/10.1007/978-3-031-57850-2_12

consumption of plant-based products remain: e.g., perceived preference, taste, cost, texture, and the level of processing involved in production [8]. The current state of the literature is focused on these individual, cognitive influences on consumer behavior. One study tested how individuals responded to products labelled "vegan" or "vegetarian" versus "plant-based" with a clear objective to evaluate "how subtle strategies may be effective at shifting consumer intentions" [14]. Another study explored how personal habits, individual feelings, and 'social influence' related to inclinations toward purchasing meat alternatives to mitigate climate change [7].

There is comparatively less research on the external influences of plant-based diets that take into account the broader contexts that shape meat-alternative purchasing habits. A 2006 study of neighborhoods in Sacramento and Los Angeles established that communities with low-income or limited access to grocery stores face difficulties in eating healthy [10]. While valuable, these studies tend to focus on the environmental factors related to purchasing grocery items to promote healthful eating, rather than a focus on meat alternatives. Likewise, the current state of the literature on COVID-19 impacts are fragmented across disciplines and have reported conflicting results. For example, one paper concluded that general consumer spending decreased following March 2020, including grocery spending [3]. Another set of research, however, points to an increase in spending within food and beverage store categories [5]. Our study aims to contribute to clarifying the conflicting results with additional empirical data analysis. Namely, the study reported in this demonstrates the feasibility for predicting consumer behavior related to plant-based purchasing.

In this paper, we join the small but growing body of information science literature that examines the trends in use meat alternatives, including counties across the nation. Of immediate concern to information science scholars, we identify data sets available to address this issue, highlighting the challenges and opportunities for information science scholars to examine the relationship of U.S. consumer purchasing behavior of meat-alternatives.

Understanding the broader limitations of plant-based consumerism is crucial to counteracting the environmental consequences of animal-based eating and promoting access to healthy eating. Plant-based eaters, vegans, vegetarians, and "flexitarians" deserve well-researched product development so that they might have foods that align with their values. In the global community at large, propounding accessible, enjoyable meat alternatives is a necessity due to the unsustainability of widespread meat consumption [6]. That is, successfully addressing climate change is dependent not just on those who personally choose to eat plant-based but also on encouraging non-plant-based eaters to do the same.

This exploratory study was guided by the research question (RQ): "How do county-level environmental factors—rather than cognitive and individual influences—including urban population, grocery store access, consumer expenditure, food price indices, and household income in the U.S. influence a population's tendency to purchase meat alternatives?" By building a predictive model based on nationally representative survey data and government statistics, we hope to address this question and, ultimately, inform policy choices that benefit sustainability and food accessibility initiatives.

Based on prior literature that indicates a positive relationship of the accessibility and proximity of foods and consumer purchasing [10], we expect that the removal of barriers, such as distance from a grocery store and the cost of meat-alternative products, will increase consumers' purchasing of plant-based meat alternatives. We hypothesize that financial freedom and physical accessibility encourage increased purchasing behavior. In this study, we test several hypotheses and examine the strength of the relationship using multiple features from a large-scale longitudinal survey of consumer purchasing behavior.

2 Data and Methods

To initiate our exploration, we searched multiple University of Arizona library databases within business and managements disciplines, seeking out specific data on consumer behavior and perception or product pricing of meat-alternatives. We considered consumer analytics platforms such as Mintel, but found they were limited in important details. For example, they did not provide consumer-specific survey responses or geographies more granular than the major U.S. regions. We also consulted The Good Food Institute, MarketResearch.com, and IBISWorld's industry reports. These offered summary statistics of entire product categories (e.g. non-dairy milks, frozen products) or crops (e.g. soy, peas) which were insufficient for our exploratory and predictive purposes.

Ultimately, our data was collected from multiple U.S. government resources and MRI Simmons USA, a consumer insights platform [1]. We chose MRI Simmons for their household purchasing behavior data aggregated by ZIP code and U.S. government sites based on their reliability and U.S. county granularity. We used the following data sets in the study:

2.1 MRI Simmons USA

MRI Simmons conducts nationally representative, annual surveys with a methodological approach that boasts "stability of insights and ... the most accurate view of the American Consumer" [1]. The 2020 National Consumer Study employed a probabilistic sampling

Geographies	Target Sample ▼
43701 - ZANESVILLE	2,315
78046 - LAREDO	2,020
78040 - LAREDO	1,973
47906 - WEST LAFAYETTE	1,884
85364 - YUMA	1,868
78041 - LAREDO	1,747
78043 - LAREDO	1,709
56001 - MANKATO	1,691

Fig. 1. Example MRI Simmons data where Target Sample is 'MEAT ALTERNATIVES - HH USES? YES.' Geographies represent ZIP Codes and values are ordered according to Target Sample, ascending. [11]

approach of American adults and presented them with questions regarding "Media", "Demographics", "Lifestyle/Psychographics", "Retail Shopping" and "Products/Services". This study represents the most recent data available; we expect that COVID-19 impacted survey responses and our results are generalizable only to this year. For each ZIP Code, the number of 'Yes' and 'No' survey responses to the question "Does anyone in your household use [meat alternatives]?" were downloaded (See Fig. 1).

2.2   U.S. Bureau of Labor Statistics

Statistics from the U.S. Bureau of Labor Statistics (BLS) were collected through Social Explorer's 2020 Market Profile Data report. Values were measured for each county, as described by a FIPS code [13].

- (FOODCPI) Food Consumer Price Index: The [Food] CPI is a measure of the average change in prices over time in a fixed "market basket" of [food and beverages] purchased either by urban wage earners and clerical workers or by all urban consumers.
- (TOT_POP1) Total Population: Total civilian non-institutional population of the United States.
- (URBANPOP) Urban Population: All persons living in ... densely developed territories that contain at least 2,500 people.
- (FOODHOME) Food at home: The total expenditures for food at grocery stores (or other food stores) and food prepared by the consumer unit on trips. It excludes the purchase of nonfood items.

2.3   U.S. Census Bureau

Two statistics from the U.S. Census Bureau were also pulled from Social Explore 2020 Market Profile Data report, per FIPS code.

- (MEDHHINC) Median household income: Median household income was chosen to best reflect the central tendency of income. A right-skewed metric, average income would provide an inflated view of county earnings.
- (POV_TOTAL) Total population in poverty: the total number of households living below the poverty threshold as defined by the Current Population Survey [15]

2.4   USDA Food Access Research Atlas

The USDA Food Access Research Atlas provided data regarding a census tract's proximity to grocery stores [16].

- (LAPOPHALF) Low access, share of people at one-half mile: Percentage of tract population living more than one-half mile from the nearest supermarket, supercenter, or large grocery store.
- (LAPOP1) Low access, share of people at 1 mile: Percentage of tract population living more than 1 mile from the nearest supermarket, supercenter, or large grocery store.

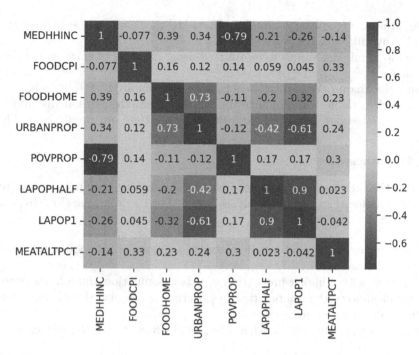

Fig. 2. Heat map demonstrating pairwise Spearman's correlation coefficients for each numeric variable

2.5   Pre-processing

We consolidated all data sources into a single data frame, with each record representing a county, its corresponding FIPS code, and relevant features for exploration. To achieve this, we performed a series of transformations:

- After converting the "Yes" and "No" samples of each ZIP Code to the corresponding county, we summed the values to obtain a total number of households for each county and respective response [4]. A new variable, MEATALT-PCT, was calculated as $\frac{yeses}{yeses+nos}$; this proportion acted as a measure of a population's tendency to purchase meat alternatives, independent of its size.
- To measure the effect of poverty and urban populations on purchasing tendencies, two proportion variables, URBANPROP $= \frac{URBANPOP}{TOT\_POP1}$ and POVPROP $= \frac{POV\_TOTAL}{TOT\_POP1}$ were similarly calculated.
- Features of grocery accessibility, LAPOPHALF and LAPOP1, were transformed from Census Tracts to their broader counties, by taking the last 5 digits of their code to be the FIPS Code. These values were averaged to capture the typical proportion of a county.
- Once all variables were transformed to county-wide granularity, each data frame was merged on FIPS Code. Each input variable was then standardized using scikit-learn's StandardScaler() to account for differences in unit

magnitudes. The output variable, MEATALTPCT, was not standardized as it already falls within a range of 0 to 1.

- Rows with missing values were omitted using na.omit() before model development.
- Using the Shapiro-Wilk test for normality and shapiro.test(), we determined that each variable was significantly different from the normal distribution. This impacted our statistical exploration rather than our predictive models.

2.6 Hypotheses

Based on the literature in consumer behavior on grocery proximity, urban residency, and financial status, our analysis is guided by the following three hypotheses:

H1. Grocery proximity is positively related to a county's likelihood of purchasing meat-alternatives.
H2. Counties with a higher proportion of urban population and a lower proportion of impoverished population in poverty are associated with more likely meat-alternative purchases.
H3. Counties with financial freedom tend to purchase meat alternatives.

3   Results

Due to the lack of normality of our variables, we used a correlation plot with Spearman's correlation coefficient to examine the linear relationships between our variables as it does not rely on the assumption of normally distributed features [2] (Fig. 2).

As expected, LAPOPHALF and LAPOP1 are highly correlated, which can be explained by the likelihood that the 1 mile population entails the half mile population. Similarly, we expect that MEDHHINC and POVPROP are related in that higher income directly correlates to less households living with insufficient income. The rest of the heat map demonstrates weak linear correlation values, primarily between MEATALTPCT and remaining features (Fig. 3).

We began to answer the question "How significant are external features in influencing a population's tendency to purchase meat alternatives?" by comparing the predictive power of a logistic regression model and a support vector machine (SVM). Both models allowed for binary classification based on a set of quantitative input variables; these were the logical applications given our county-wide metrics and 'yes' and 'no' survey responses.

	Estimate	P-Value		
(Intercept)	-2.150e+01	< 2e-16	***	Signif. codes:
URBANPROP	1.086e+00	5.01e-05	***	
MEDHHINC	1.373e-05	0.0154	*	0 '***'
POVPROP	1.213e+01	< 2e-16	***	0.001 '**'
FOODCPI	6.588e-02	5.39e-14	***	0.01 '*'
LAPOPHALF	4.830e-03	.6667		
LAPOP1	1.327e-02	.0907		
FOODHOME	2.017e-06	6.53e-11	***	

Fig. 3. Logistic Regression Summary Output

Logistic regression is well suited for predicting the probability that a county falls into one of two categories. Additionally, it can quantify the influence of individual variables on the predictive model. SVM defines a hyperplane that best separates observations in their feature space; though we cannot quantify the individual impact of features, it is worth considering for its greater flexibility. Flexibility, here, refers to accounting for noisy data. As a classification approach, SVM is flexible in that it allows data points on the boundaries of the hyperplane to fit into multiple categories.

By employing both models, we were able to ensure a more robust attempt to test our hypotheses and directly compare the results of two binary classifiers. We evaluated whether URBANPROP, MEDHHINC, POVPROP, FOODCPI, LAPOPHALF, LAPOP1, FOODHOME could predict if a county was more or less likely than average to purchase meat alternatives. We set a threshold to the mean of MEATALTPCT, with values greater than average classified as 1, "More Likely", and values less than average classified as 0, "Less Likely".

After splitting our data into a 80% training and 20% test set, the logistic regression model was developed and assessed. On the same training and test split, the support vector machine was tuned using cross validation to establish a best cost parameter of .01 and similarly assessed.

The logistic regression model indicates five significant features, URBAN-PROP, MEDHHINC, POVPROP, FOODCPI, and FOODHOME, at a p-value threshold of .05; each estimated coefficient represents a positive contribution to the logistic model. Grocery access features, LAPOPHALF and LAPOP1, were statistically insignificant in our model (Figs. 4 and 5).

Both classification models performed significantly better than the no-information rate (the rate of accuracy for a model that assigns all data points to the most frequent class), with the logistic regression slightly outperforming the SVM in overall accuracy. The SVM more accurately predicted true positives while the logistic regression more accurately predicted true negatives (Fig. 6).

To explore the non-linear relationship between each individual variable and meat-alternative purchasing behavior, we developed a Generalized Additive Model (GAM) with smoothing splines. We determined the degrees of freedom for each spline by evaluating linear models with 6-degree polynomials. Degrees

Reference

Predicted	More Likely	Less Likely	
More Likely	**TP** = 95	**FP** = 50	No Information Rate = .5894
Less Likely	**FN** = 130	**TN** = 273	Accuracy = 67.15%
	Sensitivity = 84.52%	Specificity = 42.22%	P-Value [Acc > NIR] = .00004

Fig. 4. Confusion matrix demonstrating the predictive success of the logistic regression model on test data

Reference

Predicted	More Likely	Less Likely	
More Likely	**TP** = 122	**FP** = 68	No Information Rate = 58.94%
Less Likely	**FN** = 103	**TN** = 255	Accuracy = 68.80%
	Sensitivity = 78.95%	Specificity = 54.22%	P-Value [Acc > NIR] = .000001

Fig. 5. Confusion matrix demonstrating the predictive success of the support vector machine on test data

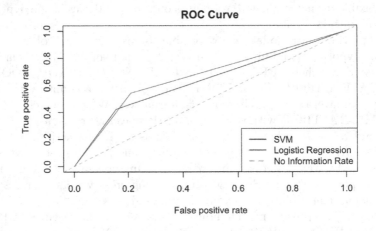

Fig. 6. Comparison of Logistic Regression and Support Vector Machine Accuracy

of polynomials with p-values that were essentially zero were discarded, as they indicated insufficient fit [9]. Then, those with the best significance relative to an alpha of .1 were chosen.

Our component-wise plots of the GAM's statistically significant variables allowed us to see the overall positive relationship that MEDHHINC and URBANPROP have with MEATALTPCT. POVPROP, FOODCPI, and FOODHOME trend upwards until tapering off at their peak point (Fig. 7).

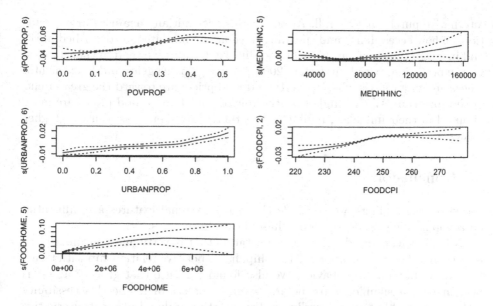

Fig. 7. Isolated effects of the GAM's significant variables on MEATALTPCT (Y-axes demonstrate fitted variable splines and their respective degrees of freedom)

4 Discussion

Our analyses suggest that urban population, consumer expenditure, food price indices, household income, and poverty are reasonably strong predictors of how likely a country is to purchase meat alternatives. Specifically, each of these variables contributed significantly to our logistic regression model's predictive ability and supports H2 and H3 hypotheses. However, the insignificance of population shares with low access to grocery stores refutes our H1 hypothesis that grocery proximity is related to a county's likelihood of purchasing meat alternatives.

Both classifications models demonstrated accuracy significantly above the no-information rate. In a practical setting, the similar efficacy between each model leads us to choose the support vector machine as it more accurately classified true negatives. The goal of our research is to inform policy changes and marketing that would support more sustainable decisions. A true negative is a population less likely on average to purchase meat alternatives. As such, our SVM would be useful in identifying communities of need, where additional effort may be directed.

Our generalized additive model corroborates, in part, previous findings in this field. Counties with higher urban populations median household income, and expenditure on groceries display higher proportions of households that purchase meat-alternatives. This supports our H3 hypothesis that components of financial freedom and physical accessibility increase meat-alternative purchases. Alternatively, we see that both increased shares of the population living in poverty and an increased food consumer price index also display higher proportions of meat alternative purchasing overall. Although this goes initially against our expectations of how accessibility and spending freedom are inhibited, as described in H3 and in, these two variables plateau and dip slightly at upper end of their ranges. Our expectation, based on Jetter (2005), studied Los Angeles and Sacramento. These are major cities whose poverty and food prices are toward the greater end of the spectrum. We conclude that the role of poverty and food prices are more nuanced in their influence, inhibiting meat-alternative purchases just at higher values.

5   Conclusion

Based on our findings, we conclude that some external features are influential on a population's tendency to purchase meat alternatives.

All of our features, despite our expectation that poverty and consumer price indices would have a negative relationship, had a positive relationship with meat-alternative purchasing behavior. We also found evidence that grocery access is not, in fact, a significant predictor. Overall, our set of financial accessibility features were able to successfully predict county likelihood of meat-alternative purchasing. Given more time, we would want to improve our models to have higher accuracy and to more consistently identify low-likelihood counties. This could direct policy-makers to provide incentive buying meat-alternatives in these areas.

We were faced with limitations, such as a lack of specific meat-alternative prices, inaccessible consumer purchasing data, and a narrow range of potential target variables, that might have contributed to more accurate models. First, studies suggest that COVID-19 influenced consumer purchasing behavior of plant-based foods, including an increase in COVID-19 related messaging to strategically persuade reduced meat consumption [12]. The COVID-19 pandemic also had an influence on shifting to online purchasing, which may have impacted the influence of proximity to a grocery store on consumer choices.

Another limitation is we were not able to access government subsidies as a factor in the study, due to the MRI Simmons data limitations. Future research could explore company price data to external financial features and government subsidies to better understand the differences in their influence on the plant-based market. It may also be more fitting to predict specific consumer purchases as county predictions require generalizations across a relatively large population.

As the availability of data grows, we anticipate that predictive models in the meat-alternative market will grow more informed, generating opportunity for climate crisis interventions. In identifying external factors that influence a population's tendency to purchase meat-alternatives, our study provides valuable insights that promote environmentally responsible food choices and begin to counteract the unsustainability of animal-based consumption.

References

1. Ultimate Study of Americans (USA) - MRI-Simmons
2. Bishara, A.J., Hittner, J.B.: Testing the significance of a correlation with non-normal data: comparison of Pearson, Spearman, transformation, and resampling approaches. Psychol. Methods **17**(3), 399–417 (2012)
3. Coibion, O., Gorodnichenko, Y., Weber, M.: The cost of the COVID-19 crisis: lockdowns, macroeconomic expectations, and consumer spending. In: Working Paper 27141, National Bureau of Economic Research, May 2020
4. Danofer: Zipcodes county fips crosswalk (2017). https://www.kaggle.com/danofer/zipcodes-county-fips-crosswalk
5. Dunn, A., Hood, K., Batch, A., Driessen, A.: Measuring consumer spending using card transaction data: lessons from the COVID-19 pandemic. In: AEA Papers and Proceedings, vol. 111, pp. 321–25 (2021)
6. Godfray, H.C.J., et al.: Meat consumption, health, and the environment. Science **361**(6399), eaam5324 (2018)
7. Habib, R., White, K., Hardisty, D.J., Zhao, J.: Shifting consumer behavior to address climate change. Curr. Opinion Psychol. **42**, 108–113 (2021). Psychology of Climate Change (2021)
8. T.G.F. Institute: 2022 plant-based state of the industry report (2023)
9. James, G., Witten, D., Hastie, T., Tibshirani, R.: An Introduction to Statistical Learning: With Applications in R. Springer Texts in Statistics, 2nd edn. Springer, New York (2021). https://doi.org/10.1007/978-1-4614-7138-7
10. Jetter, K.M., Cassady, D.L.: The availability and cost of healthier food alternatives. Am. J. Prev. Med. **30**(1), 38–44 (2006)
11. MRI-Simmons: Fall 2020 NHCS adult study 12 month [meat alternatives used by households by geographies - zip codes] (2020). https://simmonsinsights.com/
12. Niemiec, R., Jones, M.S., Mertens, A., Dillard, C.: The effectiveness of COVID-related message framing on public beliefs and behaviors related to plant-based diets. Appetite **165** (2021)
13. U.B. of Labor Statistics: Glossary of terms used in the Consumer Expenditure Survey. Accessed 2023
14. Rosenfeld, D.L., Bartolotto, C., Tomiyama, A.J.: Promoting plant-based food choices: findings from a field experiment with over 150,000 consumer decisions. J. Environ. Psychol. **81**, 101825 (2022)
15. U.S. Census Bureau: CPS subject definitions. https://www.census.gov/programs-surveys/cps/technical-documentation/subject-definitions.html. Accessed 2023
16. U.S. Department of Agriculture, Economic Research Service. Documentation: Food access research atlas. https://www.ers.usda.gov/data-products/food-access-research-atlas/documentation/. Accessed 2023

AI and Machine Learning

AIGC-Enabled Interdisciplinary Science Measurement

Jiangfeng Liu[1,2] , Xiyu Wang[3] , Dongbo Wang[3] , and Lei Pei[1,2]([✉])

[1] School of Information Management, Nanjing University, Nanjing 210023, China
jfliu@smail.nju.edu.cn
[2] Laboratory of Data Intelligence and Interdisciplinary Innovation, Nanjing University,
Nanjing 210023, China
[3] College of Information Management, Nanjing Agricultural University, Nanjing 210095, China

Abstract. [Purpose/Significance] Generative large language models have revolutionized the natural language processing research paradigm, propelling a new trend in artificial intelligence-empowered social science research. They offer fresh perspectives for quantifying the interdisciplinarity and integration of humanities and social sciences from the standpoint of deep semantic features in texts. [Method/Process] This paper employs ChatGPT to perform discipline classification on academic literature in humanities and social sciences. Through small-sample learning, it identifies discipline-specific knowledge entities from model-generated prediction results. These results are then compared and analyzed about the corresponding disciplines of the journals to propose a quantitative research framework for interdisciplinary studies, which includes metrics such as interdisciplinary richness, interdisciplinary closeness, and centrality, alongside interdisciplinary degree. [Results/Conclusion] Focusing on AIGC's empowerment of interdisciplinary science measurement research, this paper introduces a comprehensive research framework and methodology. It addresses issues related to discipline classification, discipline entity extraction from generative model responses, multi-disciplinary candidate question weighting, and content-based metrics for interdisciplinary science. These contributions allow for the thorough utilization of AIGC in social science research and offer valuable insights for exploring the underlying logic of various social science studies.

Keywords: ChatGPT · LLM · Interdisciplinarity Measurement · Few-shot Learning · Humanities and Social Sciences

1 Introduction

The measurement of interdisciplinarity has long been a discipline of scholarly attention, aiming to employ quantitative research methods to assess the influence of research in different fields on each other, thereby fostering the advancement of interdisciplinary research. This bears significant value in the planning of technological development. Interdisciplinary research draws upon theories and methods from multiple disciplines,

I. Sserwanga et al. (Eds.): iConference 2024, LNCS 14596, pp. 161–170, 2024.
https://doi.org/10.1007/978-3-031-57850-2_13

evolving from single indicators to comprehensive metrics. In the past, disciplinary categorization often relied on journal categories, neglecting the content of the literature. Consequently, it is more suitable to determine disciplinary affiliations based on the content of the literature. In 2018, Liu [1] introduced the "interdisciplinary degree", which, by combining recall rates from machine learning models, estimated the interdisciplinarity of a discipline from textual content for the first time. However, this metric only reflects the strength of interdisciplinarity and does not provide specific insights into which disciplines a discipline cross with and the degree of such cross-disciplinarity. Furthermore, this method still constructs models based on the disciplinary classification of journal articles, which contradicts the research objective and consequently limits its reliability.

Large-scale language models such as ChatGPT [2] offer new possibilities in natural language processing. They enable the transformation of the discipline classification problem from a supervised text classification task into an unsupervised natural language generation task. This avoids the issues associated with training classification models based on journal-assigned disciplines. To address these research gaps, this paper proposes an interdisciplinary measurement framework rooted in the semantic content of literature. It utilizes large language models for discipline classification and enhances the interdisciplinary degree metric to provide more specific measurement values. This approach offers improved quantification of interdisciplinary research within the humanities and social sciences.

2 Methods

2.1 Research Objectives

This study focuses on several key aspects:

How can the disciplinary affiliation of academic literature be determined from the perspective of deep semantic features within the text? What is the degree of cross-disciplinarity within the field of humanities and social sciences? To what extent are different disciplines closely interconnected with other disciplines? (Fig. 1)

2.2 AIGC-Powered Ambiguous Disciplinary Classification of Academic Literature

OpenAI utilized a substantial amount of publicly available conversational data from the internet during the training process of the large language model ChatGPT. This data encompasses various sources such as social media, forums, chat applications, Wikipedia, news, books, and literature, covering a wide range of topics and domains. In total, these data consist of approximately billions of words. The diversity and richness of the training data play a crucial role in enhancing model performance. Considering the breadth of domains covered and the volume of data, ChatGPT is adequately equipped to effectively learn from various types of texts, including research papers, to generate coherent, clear, professionally sound, and appropriately toned responses. Thus, this study posits that employing ChatGPT for discipline classification questions regarding academic literature can yield discipline attributions for scholarly content from a content-oriented perspective.

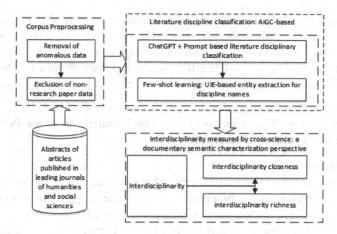

Fig. 1. Research Framework

Given that the responses of large language models to academic literature discipline attribution are expressed in natural language and may contain redundant information, this study requires specific segments from the model's responses, namely the discipline names. Given the substantial volume of data used in this research and the need for labeled data in traditional full-sample supervised named entity recognition methods, this study plans to employ a small-sample learning approach for the task of extracting

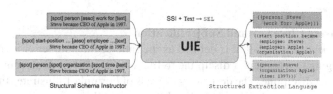

Fig. 2. Overall Framework of UIE

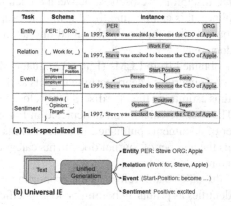

Fig. 3. UIE

discipline-specific named entities. Universal Information Extraction (UIE) [3] is a unified information extraction framework that employs a generative text-to-structure structure to unify four tasks: named entity recognition, relation extraction, event extraction, and opinion extraction (see Figs. 2 and 3). UIE has achieved state-of-the-art performance on 13 standard datasets in fully supervised, low-resource, and low-sample scenarios.

2.3 Interdisciplinary Measurement: Cross-Disciplinarity from the Perspective of Semantic Features in Literature

Interdisciplinarity

Equation 1 represents the interdisciplinarity index proposed by Liu [1]. This index indicates that the interdisciplinarity of a particular discipline is approximately equal to the sum of the model's recall rates in that category. Here, DID(n) represents the cross-disciplinarity of discipline n, m represents journals belonging to discipline n, N_m denotes the number of articles published in journal m, and N_(m,n) signifies the number of articles published in journal m that belong to discipline n. P_n represents the number of articles predicted by the model to belong to discipline n. DID(n) ∈ [0,1], and a higher value indicates stronger interdisciplinarity. In this study, the discipline categories assigned by the generative large-scale model replace the discipline prediction results provided by supervised deep learning models.

$$DID(n) = \sum_{m \in n} \frac{N_m - N_{m,n}}{N_m} = 1 - \frac{\sum_{m \in n} N_{m,n}}{\sum_{m \in n} N_m} \approx 1 - \frac{P_n}{N_n} \approx 1 - Recall(n) \quad (1)$$

Interdisciplinary Closeness and Subjectification

From the perspective of recall, it is defined as the ratio of the number of identified documents belonging to a particular discipline to the total number of documents originally belonging to that discipline. The derivation process of Formula 1 illustrates that the ratio of unidentified documents belonging to that discipline to all documents belonging to that discipline can serve as a method for quantifying the interdisciplinarity of that discipline. Thus, concerning the interdisciplinary closeness between a document of a specific discipline and other disciplines, this can be quantified using the proportion of documents from that discipline's journals that should be classified into another discipline relative to the total number of documents.

In this study, results obtained from LLMs (Large Language Models) are employed to replace the predictions of supervised deep learning models as the actual discipline for individual documents, thus estimating the interdisciplinary closeness between a specific discipline and others. The specific calculation is depicted in Formula 2, where N_ (m, i) represents the number of documents published in journal m that belong to discipline i, and P_ (n, i) represents the number of journal documents categorized by the model as discipline i for discipline n.

Subjectification, on the other hand, refers to the proportion of documents that the large language model identifies as primarily belonging to a specific discipline within the total number of journal documents in discipline n. It is used to measure which discipline's documents dominate within journals associated with a specific discipline, designating that discipline as the "mainstream discipline" for discipline n. The specific calculation is presented in Formula 3.

The subjectification of the first discipline pertains to the calculation of subjectification when considering only the first candidate discipline provided by the model. Conversely, mixed subjectification across all candidate disciplines refers to the calculation of subjectification when considering all candidate disciplines given by the model, employing a simplified approach that assigns equal weights to all candidate disciplines.

$$DIDC(n, i) = \sum_{m \in n} \frac{N_{m,i}}{N_m} = \frac{\sum_{m \in n} N_{m,i}}{\sum_{m \in n} N_m} \approx \frac{P_{n,i}}{N_n} \tag{2}$$

$$DIDF(n) = \max_{m \in n} \frac{N_{m,f}}{N_m} = \frac{\max\limits_{m \in n} N_{m,f}}{\sum_{m \in n} N_m} \approx \frac{\max\limits_{f \in n} P_{n,f}}{N_n} \tag{3}$$

Interdisciplinary Richness

The measure of interdisciplinary closeness solely reflects the degree of interaction between a discipline and other disciplines and does not provide an overall indication of how many disciplines a particular discipline intersects with. To address this limitation, we introduce the interdisciplinary richness metric, which serves to quantify the breadth of research within a discipline. Specifically, we calculate the frequency with which documents are classified into other disciplines based on the model's predicted discipline classifications, as defined by Formula 4. In this formula, D represents the set comprising all disciplines, num(D) denotes the total number of disciplines, and α represents the minimum error threshold. This approach proves instrumental in mitigating the impact of misclassifications by the large language model on the calculation of interdisciplinary richness. When the proportion of documents from one discipline classified as belonging to another discipline falls below α, we categorize it as a result of model error.

$$DIDR(n, \alpha) = \frac{\sum_{i \neq n, i \in D} DIDR(n, i, \alpha)}{num(D)} = \frac{\sum_{i \neq n, i \in D} \begin{cases} 1, DIDC(n, i) \geq \alpha \\ 0, DIDC(n, i) < \alpha \end{cases}}{num(D)} \tag{4}$$

3   Experiments and Results

3.1   Data Acquisition and Preprocessing

The data was sourced from CSSCI (Chinese Social Sciences Citation Index). We selected 31 journals that have been categorized as top-tier journals by the Social Sciences Department of Nanjing University as candidate data sources. Among these, three journals classified under the "Social Sciences Comprehensive" category were excluded due to their lack of distinct individual characteristics as independent journals (Table 1).

Table 1. Directory of top journals in humanities and social sciences

First-level Discipline	Top Journals
Linguistics	Studies of the Chinese Language, Foreign Language Teaching and Research
Philosophy	Philosophical Research
Religious Studies	Studies in World Religions
Economics	Economic Research Journal, China Industrial Economics
Law	Chinese Journal of Law, China Legal Science
Political Science	CASS Journal of Political Science, World Economics and Politics
Sociology	Sociological Studies
Ethnology	Ethno-National Studies
Marxist Theory	Studies on Marxism
Education	Educational Research
Sports Science	China Sport Science
Chinese Literature	Literary Review
Foreign Literature	Foreign Literature Review
Journalism and Communication	Journalism & Communication
Art Studies	Literature & Art Studies
History	Modern Chinese History Studies, World History
Archaeology	Archaeology
Management Science	Journal of Management Sciences in China, Journal of Management World, Chinese Public Administration
Library, Information Science, and Archive Management	Journal of Library Science in China, Journal of the China Society for Scientific and Technical Information
Psychology	Acta Psychologica Sinica

3.2 LLM-Driven Academic Article Discipline Classification

Transforming the task of discipline classification of academic documents into an automatic question-answering task via ChatGPT requires posing a question to ChatGPT. This approach, which converts NLU (Natural Language Understanding) tasks into NLG (Natural Language Generation) tasks by inputting prompt questions, is known as "Prompt Learning." Considering the impact of different prompts on the model's performance, this study designed a prompt that guides the model to produce more concise results and compared the model's generated content on a small sample.

Prompt: Perform discipline classification for the following academic document abstract: "[Insert Abstract]." Based on the content of this abstract, categorize the document into one or more primary disciplines.

3.3 Discipline Entity Recognition Based on Few-Shot Learning

In this study, UIE was used to identify candidate disciplines from the results generated by LLM, conducting zero-shot and few-shot learning experiments. UIE-base, UIE-m-base, and UIE-m-large were employed as benchmark models.

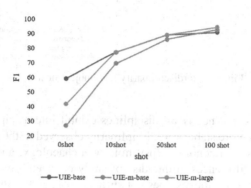

Fig. 4. Performance of Few-Shot Learning (%)

From Fig. 4, it can be observed that the model's extraction performance is generally moderate in zero-shot scenarios, but a small number of annotated samples can significantly enhance the model's performance. When the number of annotated samples reaches 100, the model's F1-score exceeds 90%, reaching a reliable level.

3.4 Cross-Disciplinary Measurement

Interdisciplinarity, Subjectification and Cross-Disciplinary Closeness
In contrast to traditional methods that rely on citation information and authorship affiliations to assess interdisciplinary phenomena, this research utilizes large-scale pre-trained language models to discern the discipline attribution of academic documents based on the deep semantic features of scholarly text abstracts. Using interdisciplinarity and cross-disciplinary closeness metrics, this section calculates the degree of cross-disciplinary closeness between different disciplines and the overall interdisciplinary nature of a particular discipline based on the discipline attribution predictions generated by ChatGPT, coupled with academic document abstracts, as depicted in Fig. 5.

Considering the inherent unpredictability and randomness in the model's generated results, this study conducted multiple question-answering iterations for individual documents. Under simplified conditions, it can be assumed that the uncontrollability of the model, multiple question-answering iterations, and the weighting of candidate sequences offset each other.

168   J. Liu et al.

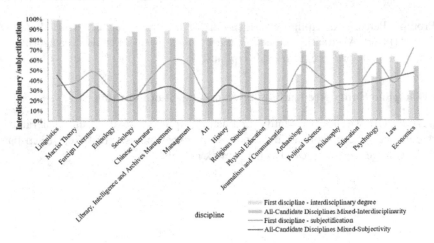

discipline

First discipline - interdisciplinary degree
All-Candidate Disciplines Mixed-Interdisciplinarity
First discipline - subjectification
All-Candidate Disciplines Mixed-Subjectivity

Fig. 5. Interdisciplinarity and Subjectification

Figure 5 indicates that nearly all disciplines exhibit interdisciplinarity exceeding 50%, with higher and more stable interdisciplinarity observed in the scenario involving all candidate disciplines. Economics, psychology, archaeology, and religious studies demonstrate notable differences in interdisciplinarity between the two scenarios. The subjectification of most disciplines does not surpass 60%, and in the scenario with all candidate disciplines, the subjectification of most disciplines remains below 40%. Except for library and archival management, management studies, archaeology, and economics, the subjectification differences across most disciplines are relatively minor between the two scenarios. Further analysis of cross-disciplinary closeness (See Fig. 6) reveals that disciplines such as history, philosophy, political science, education, sociology, social sciences, management, economics, and computer science and technology exhibit higher cross-disciplinary closeness with humanities and social sciences disciplines.

Interdisciplinary Richness
While interdisciplinarity and cross-disciplinary closeness are crucial, they do not comprehensively reflect the breadth of research within a discipline. Therefore, this study introduces the metric of interdisciplinary richness to holistically assess the breadth of disciplines. Experiments were conducted with varying thresholds (α), and the results indicate that management studies, history, library and archival management, arts, philosophy, and political science exhibit higher levels of interdisciplinary richness. Management studies often require the integration of computer science, economics, sociology, and other fields to solve intricate problems. Historical research necessitates consideration of factors from various domains such as economics, politics, and society. Library and archival management is closely related to fields such as engineering, management, and education. Arts intersect with fields like philosophy, literature, and history, and digital arts and cultural communication create more intersections with computer science, journalism, and other domains. Similarly, political science research often requires consideration of multiple factors from domains like society, economics, and law, leading to intersections with fields such as economics, history, sociology, and law (Fig. 7).

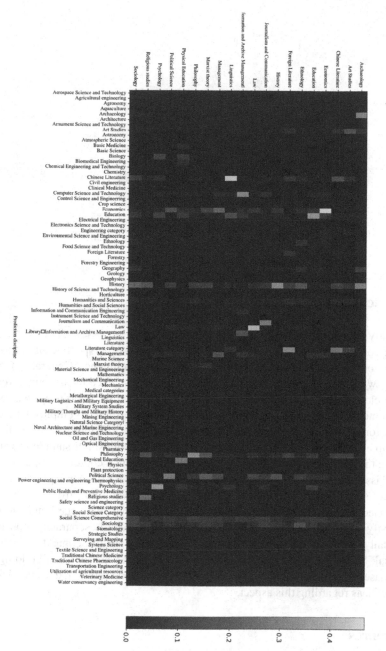

Fig. 6. Heat map of Interdisciplinary Closeness

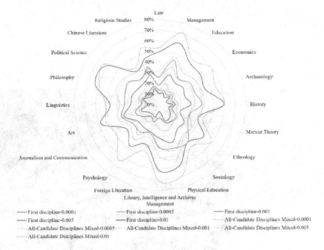

Fig. 7. Interdisciplinary Richness

4 Conclusion

The study of interdisciplinary science measurement is an essential research area in information metrics and evaluation. This paper, from the perspective of empowering information metrics research with AIGC (Artificial Intelligence Generated Content), offers new insights and approaches to interdisciplinary science measurement research. The article introduces a technical framework for conducting interdisciplinary science measurements using large language models. It describes how to employ ChatGPT + Prompt for classifying literature into specific disciplines, efficiently identify discipline names in a vast volume of model-generated responses using small-sample learning and measure the degree and breadth of interdisciplinarity from a content perspective.

The issues addressed in this paper still offer directions for further exploration. Firstly, the paper simplifies the problem of multi-disciplinary weighting from the perspective of knowledge dispersal. Future research could consider using large language models to classify literature based on titles, abstracts, and keywords separately, constructing a rational framework for discipline weight distribution in the context of knowledge dispersal. Secondly, while the paper suggests that AIGC can assist in building a flat, graph-based interdisciplinary classification and evaluation system, it does not delve into specific ideas regarding this aspect.

References

1. Liu, L., Wang, D.: Identifying interdisciplinary social science research based on article classification. Data Anal. Knowl. Discovery **2**(03), 30–38 (2018)
2. Introducing ChatGPT. https://openai.com/blog/chatgpt
3. Lu, Y., et al.: Unified structure generation for universal information extraction. In: Proceedings of the 60th Annual Meeting of the Association for Computational Linguistics (Volume 1: Long Papers), pp. 5755–5772. Association for Computational Linguistics, Dublin (2022)

Role of Emotional Experience in AI Voice Assistant User Experience in Voice Shopping

Xiwei Wang[1,2]([✉]) [iD], Yutong Liu[1] [iD], Siguleng Wuji[1] [iD], and Ran Luo[1] [iD]

[1] School of Management, Jilin University, Changchun 130000, China
wxw_mail@163.com
[2] Research Center for Big Data Management, Jilin University, Changchun 130000, China

Abstract. With the rapid advancement of artificial intelligence and natural language processing technologies, AI voice assistants are gaining attention for their potential to enable voice shopping. Based on cognitive appraisal theory, this study constructs a theoretical model of AI voice assistant user experience with emotional experience as a mediating variable and examines the antecedent variables of emotional experience and the mechanism of its effect on users' willingness to adopt AI voice assistant in the context of voice shopping. The study used data collected from 318 users of AI voice assistants. Findings of Partial Least Squares (PLS-SEM) suggest that perceived service quality, and perceived entertainment significantly influence emotional state and emotional attachment towards the users' adoption intention. Perceived anthropomorphism significant influence the emotional attachment but not emotional state. By exploring the role of emotional experience in the user experience of AI voice assistants, this paper proposes suggestions to enhance user experience and promote voice shopping.

Keywords: Cognitive Appraisal Theory · AI Voice Assistant · User Experience · Emotional Experience · Artificial Intelligence

1 Introduction

AI voice assistants, such as Apple's Siri, Amazon's Alexa and Xiaoai, have involved in the daily work and life of users, helping users with information search, media usage and calendar management [1, 2]. Also, AI voice assistants are already in use to enhance the user experience in several industries such as e-commerce, driving, travel and aviation [3, 4]. Among them, voice shopping utilizing AI voice assistants is seen as highly promising. According to Statista, 27.4% of U.S. consumers voice shopped in 2022, with 10% of them voice shopping weekly [5].

AI voice assistants based on natural language processing, voice interaction technology and other artificial intelligence technologies are able to interact with users in a more natural and efficient manner through voice commands [6, 7]. AI voice assistants are believed to revolutionize e-commerce marketing by providing voice shopping consumers with a fast, personalized and voice-interactive user experience [8, 9]. AI voice

I. Sserwanga et al. (Eds.): iConference 2024, LNCS 14596, pp. 171–190, 2024.
https://doi.org/10.1007/978-3-031-57850-2_14

assistant user experience research should focus on the user adoption under voice shopping, in order to supplement the lack of this part of the research to provide research support for the promotion of voice shopping.

Current research on the user experience of AI voice assistants mainly focuses on the impact of the user's cognitive experience. Studies have analyzed the user's cognitive experience in terms of the technical attributes of AI voice assistants, such as the utilitarian elements and hedonic elements. Perceived usefulness and perceived ease of use have proven to be key elements of AI voice assistant user experience [3]. Due to the human-like attributes of AI voice assistants, Perceived anthropomorphism and social presence could potentially influence user behavioral intentions [1].

According to marketing research, since emotion is a key element in the user experience [8, 10], some studies have begun to examine the impact of emotion on AI device user adoption behavior. Lu et al. [11] suggests that emotion is a key variable in AI device user adoption behavior. However, Gkinko & Elbanna [12] argued that there are multiple emotions in the emotional experience of users of AI technologies, such as connection emotion. Focusing only on a single emotional state is not conducive to a deeper understanding of the emotional experience of AI technologies. The antecedents of emotional experience and the mechanism of complex emotional experience on AI voice assistant user's behavioral intention under voice shopping context need to be further deepened.

Therefore, the main objectives of this paper are:

- To identify the antecedents of user emotional experience of AI voice assistants under voice shopping context.
- To empirically test the mechanism of emotional experience on AI voice assistant user adoption under voice shopping context.

2 Research Overview

2.1 AI Voice Assistant User Experience

In the user research on AI voice assistant in shopping scenarios, apart from focusing on the adoption of AI voice assistants, attention is also given to the word-of-mouth behaviors [1], post-shopping evaluations [13, 14], and brand relationships [15]. There has been relatively limited research on the willingness to adopt AI voice assistants in the context of voice shopping. In this regard, this study focuses on the impact of AI voice assistant user experience on users' willingness to adopt AI voice assistant for voice shopping behavior, in order to supplement the lack of AI voice assistant user experience research.

By summarizing previous studies, this paper concludes that the cognitive elements of AI voice assistant user experience can be categorized into utilitarian, risk, hedonic, and anthropomorphic elements from the perspective of AI voice assistant technical services. Utilitarian elements are cognitive elements of the functional value of AI voice assistant applications. There are studies that validated the positive impact of perceived usefulness and perceived ease of use based on TAM theory [16] and performance expectations based on UTAUT theory [17] on the user experience of AI voice assistants. Risk elements represented by privacy risk play an important role of AI voice assistants user experience, and risk elements such as privacy concerns [18] and usage barriers [19] adversely impact user attitudes and behaviors. Since hedonics is a key element of technology adoption, there are also studies that tested the impact of playfulness [1] and hedonic features [14] of AI voice assistants. Meanwhile, human-like attributes are the most distinctive technical service feature of AI voice assistants, perceived anthropomorphism and the social presence that comes with anthropomorphic features have become the focus of research attention [14, 20].

2.2 Emotional Experience of AI Voice Assistants

User emotional experience is a key component of AI voice assistant user experience. According to Computer Social Role Theory (CASA), users will assign human traits to computers [21]. AI voice assistants using natural language and human voice to interact with users [22], and a high degree of social presence that makes the user more likely to have a complex emotional experience [20]. Kautish et al. [8] examined the awe experience as a specific positive emotional experience and tests its mediating role in consumers' use of AI voice assistants for fashion shopping. Gkinko & Elbanna [12] argued that connection emotion is a special emotional experience during the interaction between AI voice assistants and users. In this regard, this paper examines the emotional experience of AI voice assistant users by dividing it into two parts: emotional state and emotional attachment.

Emotional state refers to the subjective state that users produce in response to a specific stimulus [23, 24], including positive and negative emotional states. Positive emotional states, such as satisfaction and enjoyment, can help improve user experience [25]. Negative emotional states, such as anxiety and anger will discourage adoption, generate confrontation and cause discontinuation of usage [26].

Emotional attachment reflects the emotional connection between the AI voice assistant and the user, which is conceptualized as the perceived emotional connection between a person and a specific object [24]. Emotional attachment originated from the field of social psychology in the study of personal intimacy and attachment behavior as an important factor influencing interpersonal relationships and subsequently introduced to the field of human-computer interaction to explain the emotional bonds and connections between people and technology [24]. Emotional attachment is both a key goal of voice shopping brand-marketing [27] as well as customer relationship management [28, 29]. It has been verified that emotional attachment plays an important role in building user trust [30, 31].

2.3 Cognitive Appraisal Theory

Cognitive appraisal theory states that emotions are evoked on the basis of an individual's assessment of the relevant stimulus or event [32]. It was proposed by Lazarus to explain coping responses to stressful situations [33]. Lazarus [32] believed that cognitive appraisal is a sufficiently necessary condition for the generation of emotion, and is related to the individual's motivations, needs, or experience. Bagozzi et al. [34] further argued that key elements of behavior such as attitudes, subjective norms and intentions require certain self-regulatory processes to produce the predicted effect, which encompass cognitive appraisal processes, emotional reactions and coping responses. Users generate specific emotions based on the outcome assessment of the level of motivational satisfaction, and the emotions in turn stimulate the generation of corresponding behaviors as a coping response [34]. Cognitive appraisal theory provides an explanatory model that explains why specific emotions are triggered by marketing stimuli, thus making it a major theory in the study of consumer emotions [35].

3 Research Hypothesis and Theoretical Model

This study draws on ideas from cognitive appraisal theory to analyze the antecedents and consequences of consumers' emotional experiences in the user experience of AI voice assistants. The key variables of this study are defined and presented in Table 1.

Table 1. Summary of the key constructs

Role	Term	Definitions and operational concepts
Cognitive appraisal - independent variable	Perceived Service Quality (PQ)	Perceived service quality is defined as the extent to which users perceive AI voice assistants facilitate task performance
	Perceived Usage Cost (PC)	Perceived usage cost is defined as the burden on the consumed costs in using and maintaining AI voice assistants
	Perceived Anthropomorphism (PA)	Perceived Anthropomorphism is defined as human tendencies to label AI voice assistants as humans and humanize them as companions
	Perceived Entertainment (PE)	Perceived entertainment is defined as the level to which using AI voice assistant is seen as enjoyable and fun
Emotional experience-mediating variable	Emotional state (ES)	Emotional state is defined as the subjective state of the user in response to a specific stimulus, which contains positive emotions such as satisfaction, enjoyment, and negative emotions such as anger, disappointment

(*continued*)

Table 1. (*continued*)

Role	Term	Definitions and operational concepts
	Emotional attachment (EA)	Emotional attachment is defined as a specific connection perceived emotionally between users and AI voice assistants
Behavioral outcome - dependent variable	Willingness to Adoption (WA)	Willingness to adoption is defined as the degree to which users are willing to adopt AI voice assistants for voice shopping

3.1 Perceived Service Quality

Perceived service quality is defined as the extent to which users perceive AI voice assistants facilitate task performance [11]. AI voice assistants are capable of providing intelligent services with real-time feedback by voice [16]. Users use AI voice assistants to complete operations such as information search, purchasing repeat products and voice shopping in a convenient way to meet functional needs [1, 36]. The importance of utilitarian factors has been verified in HCI research. Competence affects the customer experience, attitude, and satisfaction [37]. When users perceive the use of AI voice assistants as beneficial to meet their functional needs, the provision of high-quality technological services generates positive emotions such as satisfaction and pleasure.

On the other hand, perceived service quality has an equally positive effect on establishing an emotional attachment between users and AI voice assistants. User trust in AI has a significant impact on users' willingness to use it, while perceived usefulness and perceived ease of use enhance users' trust in the functionality of AI [38]. The tangibility, transparency, reliability, and immediacy of AI help develop cognitive trust[39]. The convenience, personalized, and other functional advantages of AI devices will facilitate the relationship commitment between the user and the AI device and thus enhance the AI user experience [3]. Thus, this paper proposes the following hypothesis:

H1a: Perceived service quality positively influences emotional states in using AI voice assistants.
H1b: Perceived service quality positively influences emotional attachment in using AI voice assistants.

3.2 Perceived Usage Cost

Economic concerns have always been a major obstacle to the diffusion of innovative information technology [40]. Perceived usage cost is defined as the burden on the consumed costs in using and maintaining AI voice assistants [40]. Users are used to comparing the relative benefits of technology services versus the cost of use [41]. The cost of using AI voice assistants includes the mental burden on the degree of difficulty in use, potential risks such as privacy, etc. For AI voice assistants collect users' vocal information and record information about consumers' behavioral preferences which leads to the existence of privacy concerns and negatively affect the trust and continued willingness to use [18, 42, 43].

On the other hand, perceived usage costs including concerns about risk will negatively affect user trust [44], which is detrimental to the establishment of emotional attachment. Research has identified system security as the key to building trust between users and the system [45], and security elements such as privacy risk and property risk, which is detrimental to their emotional connection with the system. Especially in the scenario of voice shopping using AI voice assistants, security is an issue that must be considered when it comes to transaction scenarios. At present, few studies have analyzed the influence of perceived usage cost of AI voice assistants on users' emotional attachment. This study argues that the perceived usage cost of using AI is a significant barrier to user adoption and relationship building. Users using AI voice assistants will face huge transfer costs, uncertainty costs, sunk costs, etc. [46]. Perceived usage cost should be a key variable in the user experience research of AI voice assistants. Thus, the following hypothesis is proposed in this paper:

H2a: Perceived usage cost negatively influences emotional state in using AI voice assistants.

H2b: Perceived usage cost negatively influences emotional attachment in using AI voice assistants.

3.3 Perceived Anthropomorphism

AI voice assistants are using natural language and voice interaction technology to mimic real people with obvious anthropomorphic features, so perceived anthropomorphism is an important variable in the cognitive appraisal stage of AI voice assistants [1]. Perceived anthropomorphism refers to the human tendency to label AI voice assistants as humans and humanize them as companions [13]. According to the" Computers as Social Actors" paradigm (CASA), people tend to unconsciously anthropomorphize non-human physical devices and treat the devices in a manner similar to human interactions [47]. Previous research has shown that the more users view AI voice assistants as social actors, the more satisfied they are with their devices and the more likely they are to continue using them [13].

On the other hand, AI voice assistants have the ability to alleviate users' loneliness and provide emotional support [48]. According to the CASA paradigm, AI voice assistants with anthropomorphic features are easily perceived by users as social actors with social attraction, thus prompting users to establish emotional attachment with AI voice assistants. The process of interacting with the device, users are more likely to disclose personal information because they view the device as a social actor [49]. Users motivated by social interaction or efficiency are likely to perceived AI voice assistant as different social roles, such as butler, assistant, or friend [13]. Guerreiro argues that the anthropomorphic features of AI voice assistants can make consumers feel connected to AI voice assistants [15]. Therefore, this paper argues that perceived anthropomorphism of AI voice assistants has a positive impact on the establishment of emotional attachment. In this regard, this paper proposes the following hypothesis:

H3a: Perceived anthropomorphism positively influences users' emotional state using AI voice assistants.

H3b: Perceived anthropomorphism positively influences users' emotional attachment in using AI voice assistants.

3.4 Perceived Entertainment

Perceived entertainment is an important influencing factor in the cognitive appraisal of AI voice assistants and can positively affect user emotional state. The enjoyment and pleasure gained by interacting with the AI voice assistant are related to the emotional experience of the user [36]. Perceived entertainment refers to the level to which using AI voice assistant is seen as enjoyable and fun [50]. The perceived entertainment of the interaction process positively influences user experience by providing humorous responses to questions asked by AI voice assistants [1].

On the other hand, perceived entertainment can positively influence users' emotional attachment. Previous studies have validated the relationship between perceived enjoyment and user satisfaction with smart devices [40]. In e-commerce, perceived entertainment may not directly influence users' purchase willingness, but it will enhance user trust [51]. Especially, entertainment as part of perceived value can promote user trust in the brand [52], facilitating connection between users and brands. For AI voice assistants, studies have verified that perceived enjoyment is a key variable for continued user use [36]. This paper argues that the perceived entertainment of AI voice assistants can bring consumers closer to AI voice assistants psychologically and facilitate consumer relationships with AI voice assistants through emotional attachment.

H4a: Perceived entertainment positively influences users' emotional state towards AI voice assistants.

H4b: Perceived entertainment positively influences users' emotional attachment to AI voice assistants.

3.5 Emotional States

According to the cognitive appraisal theory, users experience complex cognitive appraisal followed by emotional experience, and the action of the two stages will determine the user behavior intention, such as adopting or rejecting technological services. Positive emotions such as anticipation, delight and satisfaction have been verified to be beneficial for user experience and positive user behavior. Positive emotions can increase user service time and consumption frequency. Watson's study showed that positive emotions can advance user adoption behavior and enhance user experience [35]. Conversely, negative user sentiment can cause users to adopt negative behaviors as a coping strategy, such as resisting or rejecting technological services [53, 54]. Thus, the following hypothesis is proposed in this paper:

H5: Positive emotional state positively influences users' willingness to adopt AI voice assistants.

H6a: Emotional states mediate the association between perceived service quality and willingness to adopt AI voice assistants.

H6b: Emotional states mediate the association between perceived usage cost and willingness to adopt AI voice assistants.

H6c: Emotional states mediate the association between perceived anthropomorphism and willingness to adopt AI voice assistants.

H6d: Emotional states mediate the association between perceived entertainment and willingness to adopt AI voice assistants.

3.6 Emotional Attachment

Emotional attachment refers to users' trust, dependence, and intimate connection with AI voice assistants, manifested as a feeling of closeness and connectivity during the interaction. Therefore, it serves to facilitate emotional trust between users and AI voice assistants which is defined as a specific connection perceived emotionally between users and AI voice assistants [24]. Building emotional attachment is an emotional way to build user trust [30]. Interactions between users and AI voice assistants align with the definition of quasi-social relationships, which involve enduring bonds formed between a user and an intermediary performer [55]. Previous research suggests that emotional attachment significantly impacts users' behavioral intentions [24]. During continuous use, users can develop an emotional attachment with AI voice assistant [1]. We argue that when consumers exhibit trusting and approachable attitudes toward AI voice assistants, the emotional attachment between users and AI voice assistants positively impacts users' appraisal and behavioral intention, such as continuance use. While few studies have used emotional connection as a mediating variable, this paper asserts that emotional attachment, as a critical element of emotional experience, should be consistent with the law that cognitive appraisal influences emotion in cognitive appraisal theory. The model of AI voice assistant user experience influencing factors is depicted in Fig. 1. Accordingly, this paper proposes the following hypothesis:

H7:   Emotional attachment positively influences users' willingness to adopt AI voice assistants.

H8a: Emotional states mediate the association between perceived service quality and willingness to adopt AI voice assistants.

H8b: Emotional attachment mediate the association between perceived usage cost and willingness to adopt AI voice assistants.

H8c: Emotional attachment mediate the association between perceived anthropomorphism and willingness to adopt AI voice assistants.

H8d: Emotional attachment mediate the association between perceived entertainment and willingness to adopt AI voice assistants.

4   Research Methodology

4.1 Measures

The questionnaire includes questionnaire instructions, demographic information, and scales. The questionnaire description section explains the AI voice assistant features and application scenarios that act on the user experience. The contents of the questionnaire are shown in Table 2.

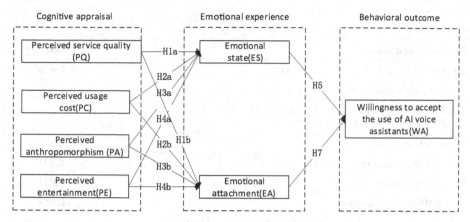

Fig. 1. Conceptual Framework

Table 2. Scale refinement

Constructs and items	Loading
Perceived Service Quality (PQ), adapted from Gursoy [54] and Lu [11]; a = 0.898; CR = 0.917; AVE = 0.734	
AI voice assistant can accurately complete my instructions	0.838
AI voice assistants rarely make frequent errors	0.807
AI voice assistant can improve the efficiency of my work	0.881
AI voice assistant can make me do things better	0.897
Perceived Usage Cost (PC), adapted from Gursoy [54] and Lu [11]; a = 0.872; CR = 0.877; AVE = 0.704	
I feel uneasy about using AI voice assistants	0.775
It took me a long time to understand how to use the AI voice assistant	0.918
I think the use of AI voice assistants is too costly and unnecessary	0.817
Perceived Anthropomorphism (PA), adapted from Mishra A [1] and Fernandes T [16]; a = 0.875; CR = 0.913; AVE = 0.725	
I feel as comfortable talking to the AI voice assistant as I talk to my friends	0.805
I feel like I'm socializing normally when I talk to the AI voice assistant	0.908
I speak to the AI voice assistant in the same way I speak to a real person normally	0.812
I feel like the AI voice assistant is right in front of me when I talk to her	0.875
Perceived Entertainment (PE), adapted form Mishra A [1]; a = 0.820; CR = 0.890; AVE = 0.731	
I had a great time communicating with the AI voice assistant	0.866

(continued)

Table 2. (*continued*)

Constructs and items	Loading
I had fun talking to the AI voice assistant	0.828
My communication with the AI voice assistant makes me enjoy	0.869
Emotion State (ES), adopted from Gursoy [54] and Lu [11]; a = 0.906; CR = 0.933; AVE = 0.777	
Boring - Interesting	0.876
Melancholy - Fulfilling	0.891
Disappointment-Expectation	0.871
Dissatisfaction-satisfaction	0.887
Emotion Attachment (EA), adopted from Fernandes T[16]; a = 0.861; CR = 0.898; AVE = 0.688	
I can rely on AI voice assistants	0.788
I can trust the service provided by AI voice assistants	0.744
AI voice assistant has established a relationship with me	0.897
AI voice assistant has a good relationship with me	0.879
Willingness to adopt the use of AI voice assistant (WA), adopted from Gursoy [54]; a = 0.867; CR = 0.917; AVE = 0.786	
I am willing to communicate with AI voice assistant	0.895
I prefer AI voice assistant compared to traditional interaction methods	0.872
I would like to use AI voice assistant in the future	0.892

4.2 Procedure

First, to ensure that respondents were fully informed about the AI voice assistant, they were asked to answer the following questions before completing the questionnaire: (1) How many brands of AI voice assistants do you know? (2) How many AI voice assistant service scenarios do you know? Respondents were also asked to recall their experiences with AI voice assistants. Then, in order to fully understand voice shopping, respondents need to watch an introductory and demonstration video of voice shopping with Amazon's Alexa and imagine themselves voice shopping in this scenario. Respondents will receive a small amount of cash in return. In order to ensure the validity of the questionnaire, attention check questions were inserted in the questionnaire setup to eliminate unqualified questionnaires.

4.3 Data Collection

The study used the online questionnaire platform "Wenjuanxing" to collect data through social media. Finally, a total of 400 questionnaires were received, 82 invalid questionnaires were excluded for filling in too short a time or failing an attention test. It resulted in a final sample size of 318 valid questionnaires, with an effective rate of 79.5%, which meets the requirements of structural equation data analysis. The sample population was relatively young as shown in Table 3, with age concentrated between 19 and 25 years old (49.1%), followed by 26 to 30 years old (34.8%), which is consistent with the findings of the report of Statista [56].

Since the questionnaire method of self-reported scales is prone to have Common Method Variance (CMV), we performed a post-hoc statistical analysis method, the Harman's single factor test. Using SPSS 24.0. The result showed that the percentage of variance explained by the first common factor was 38.191%, which is less than 50% suggested by MacKenzie and Podsakoff [57]. Thus, it could be considered not to have serious common method bias in the data.

Table 3. Sample profile

Category		Count	Percentage (%)
Gender	Male	69	44.8
	Female	249	55.2
Educational Background	High School and below	2	3.7
	Undergraduate	288	85. 7
	Master and above	28	10.6
Age	18 years old and below	1	0.3
	19–25 years old	302	49.1
	26–30 years old	13	34.8
	30–40 years old	2	13.1
Total		318	100

5   Result

5.1   Measurement Model Assessment

The reliability and validity measurements of this study met the threshold values. The KMO value was 0.926 and the Bartlett's spherical test was significant. Results indicated that all Cronbach's alphas and composite reliability (CR) values for the constructs were above the threshold of 0.7. All item loadings were significant and above the 0.7 threshold, providing evidence for strong internal consistency. The average variance extracted (AVE) values were also above the threshold of 0.50 as shown in Table 2. Scale refinement, indicating desired convergent validity [58].

Discriminant validity was verified by two methods. First, all constructs' squared root of AVEs were greater than the highest correlation with other constructs, as shown in Table 4. Second, the Heterotrait-Monotrait Ration of Correlations (HTMT) values of all the variables are below the threshold of 0.85 as shown in Table 5, suggesting desired discriminant validity [58].

Table 4. Discriminant validity (Fornell-Larcker criterion)

Variables	PQ	PC	PA	PE	ES	EA	WA
PQ	0.836						
PC	−0.133	0.805					
PA	0.567	0.035	0.820				
PE	0.630	−0.151	0.706	0.820			
ES	0.596	−0.162	0.426	0.629	0.863		
EA	0.718	−0.007	0.745	0.742	0.560	0.815	
WA	0.629	−0.170	0.500	0.567	0.686	0.619	0.857

Table 5. Discriminant validity (HTMT Criteria)

Variables	PQ	PC	PA	PE	ES	EA	WA
PQ							
PC	0.242						
PA	0.621	0.144					
PE	0.691	0.193	0.762				
ES	0.619	0.206	0.483	0.647			
EA	0.784	0.115	0.765	0.619	0.619		
WA	0.634	0.242	0.562	0.594	0.694	0.670	

5.2 Structural Model Assessment

All the constructs' variance inflation factor (VIF) values were less than the suggested threshold of 3.3, which ensured that there is no multi-collinearity issue [58]. The hypothesis testing results are presented in Table 6, wherein we used bootstrapping method with 5000 sub-samples to test the significance of the effects [58].

Then, we tested the impact of the control variables, age, gender, and educational background on the users' willingness of adoption. The results showed that the effects of the control variables on the outcome variable are not significant. The data results show that most of hypotheses are valid except for hypotheses H2a, H2b and H3a. The results of the structural equation model are shown in Fig. 2.

Table 6. Results

Hypothesis	Path Coeff.	P value	Supported?
H1a PQ → ES	0.328	***	Yes
H1b PQ → EA	0.388	***	Yes
H2a PC → ES	-0.056	0.220	Not
H2b PC → EA	0.049	0.220	Not

(*continued*)

Table 6. (*continued*)

Hypothesis	Path Coeff.	P value	Supported?
H3a PA → ES	-0.024	0.721	Not
H3b PA → EA	0.310	***	Yes
H4a PE → ES	0.393	***	Yes
H4b PE → EA	0.179	***	Yes
H5 ES → WA	0.477	***	Yes
H7 EA → WA	0.321	***	Yes

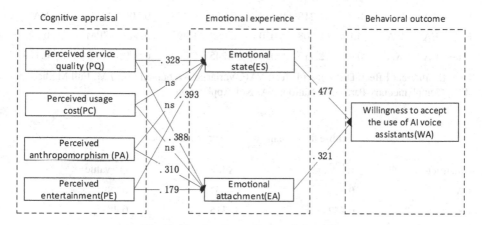

Fig. 2. Structural equation model results

5.3 Mediation Analysis

To examine the mediating effect of emotional state and emotional attachment in emotional experience, we used the PLS bootstrapping method for mediation analysis. Table 7 shows the results of the mediation analysis.

The results show that emotional state fully mediated the relationships between PQ and WA ($\beta = 0.328$, 95% CI: 0.235–0.415), between EM and WA ($\beta = 0.393$, 95% CI: 0.303–0.492). Emotional attachment fully mediated the relationships between PQ and WA ($\beta = 0.328$, 95% CI: 0.235–0.415), between PA and WA ($\beta = 0.310$, 95% CI: 0.217–0.401), leading support to hypotheses H6a, H6d, H8a, H8c. Hypotheses H6b, H6c, H8b, H8d were not supported.

This paper used R^2 to explain the predictive power of the model and found that 48.9% of the variance in adoption willingness was explained, 56.2% of the variance for the emotional attachment variable in the endogenous structure and 41.5% of the variance for emotional state, as shown in Table 8. Also, we applied Q^2 to test the perceived relevance of the path model [58], and the result are in accordance with the requirements (greater than zero) indicating the high predictive relevance.

Table 7. Mediation analysis results

Path Relationships	IE	T	P	DE	T value	P	Mediation type	VAF
PQ → ES → WA	0.156	4.775	0.000	0.281	8.086	0.000	CPM	0.357
PC → ES → WA	−0.027	1.180	0.223	−0.011	0.385	0.700	No	NA
PA → ES → WA	−0.011	0.354	0.723	0.088	1.997	0.046	No	NA
PE → ES → WA	0.188	5.326	0.000	0.245	6.209	0.000	CPM	0.434
PQ → EA → WA	0.124	4.246	0.022	0.281	8.086	0.000	CPM	0.306
PC → EA → WA	0.016	1.218	0.238	−0.011	0.385	0.700	No	NA
PA → EA → WA	0.100	3.808	0.030	0.088	1.997	0.046	CPM	0.532
PE → EA → WA	0.057	2.713	0.026	0.245	6.209	0.000	No	0.189

Note: IE, Indirect Effect; DE, Direct Effect; VAF, Variance Accounted For; FM, Full Mediation; CPM, Complementary Partial Mediation; NA, Not Application

Table 8. Explanatory Power & Relevance

construct	R^2 value	Adj R^2	Q^2 value
EA	0.567	0.562	0.389
ES	0.422	0.415	0.487
WA	0.492	0.489	0.526

6 Discussion and Implications

In the user's cognitive appraisal stage, the data results indicate that perceived service quality positively affects the user's emotional state (H1a) and emotional attachment (H1b), which is consistent with other studies [59]. Perceived service quality remains a core element in AI voice assistant user experience and is key to allowing users to form emotional attachments with AI voice assistants [39].

The hypothesis of perceived usage cost and user emotional state (H2a) and emotional attachment (H2b) have not been verified. This result is inconsistent with the findings of some studies, where Gursoy et al. [54] argues that users' effort expectations are a key antecedent of users' emotion. The possible reason for this is that the research sample in this study is young people in China, who are more receptive to innovative technologies and less concerned about the hindering elements such as the risk of use.

Perceived anthropomorphism positively affects user emotional attachment (H3b), but not user emotional state (H3a). Perceived anthropomorphism positively affects emotional attachment indicating that the anthropomorphic features of AI voice assistants can provide emotional support, which is consistent with the findings of existing studies [1]. Some studies have argued that users' negative emotional states to AI voice assistants with human-like cues increase users' emotional stress [54]. Chuah [60] and Hu [20] argued that people are reluctant to adopt highly anthropomorphic bots for generating negative emotions of discomfort and insecurity.

Perceived entertainment positively influences users' emotional state (H4a) and emotional attachment (H4b) and has the most significant effect on users' cognitive-emotional appraisal which is consistent with the finding of related studies [1]. AI voice assistants with high entertaining technical features make it easier to satisfy users' hedonic needs, and at the same time can relieve users' tension and anxiety, bringing them a better emotional experience [51, 52].

Emotional state positively influences users' willingness to adopt AI intelligent voice assistants (H6) in the context of voice shopping. Related studies concluded that positive emotional states are beneficial to user experience, while negative emotions such as disappointment, fear, uncertainty, nervousness, and worry negatively affect consumer satisfaction [54]. Emotional attachment has a positive effect on users' willingness to adopt behavior (H7) which is consistent with previous research findings and has a significant impact on users' behavioral intentions [61].

6.1 Theoretical Contributions

First, this study constructs an AI voice assistant user experience model based on the cognitive appraisal theory in the context of voice shopping, revealing the role relationship between user cognitive appraisal and emotional experience and behavioral intention. Emotional experience, as a key component in the customer journey, is the focus under the topic of voice shopping research. Second, we introduce "emotional attachment" as a new variable in the user emotional experience stage [24]. Past research analyzing consumer emotions has been limited to a rough emotional classification of positive or negative. Emotional attachment is a key component of utilizing AI voice assistants to enhance customer relationship management and brand loyalty. Thus, by extending the theoretical connotation of emotional experience research, this paper provides a comprehensive framework for understanding users' emotional experience of AI voice assistants. Finally, this paper takes the AI voice assistant user adoption willingness in voice shopping scenarios as the outcome variable, which complements the research scope of AI voice assistant user experience research and provides theoretical support for the important future application trend of voice shopping.

6.2 Implications for Practice

According to the results of the study, the functional and hedonic value of AI voice assistant services in voice shopping scenarios remains key to user experience. For relevant stakeholders, improving the functional service level of AI voice assistants remains the core of technology and application service development. With ChatGPT's powerful natural language processing capabilities gaining widespread interest in society [62], the conversational potential of the AI voice assistant is even more promising. The hedonic perception of AI voice assistants is equally important for user experience. Hedonic design should be a priority in service delivery design [1]. Surprisingly, perceived risk is not a key influencing factor for Chinese consumers in voice shopping, so it may be more the lack of relative advantage of the technology that is preventing consumers from using AI voice assistants [41], reflecting the unique attitude of Chinese consumers towards innovative technology. This study verifies the important role of perceived anthropomorphic for users' emotional attachment in the user experience of AI voice assistants, suggesting that the human-like attributes of AI voice assistants help users establish an emotional connection with the device, which helps to further draw the connection between customers and brands [13, 48]. It also illustrates the potential of applying AI voice assistants in customer relationship management and improving brand loyalty [2]. Therefore, how to design the virtual persona of AI voice assistants and the human-like features and anthropomorphic level on the voice interaction are key issues that designers need to consider carefully.

6.3 Limitations and Future Research Direction

There are some limitations in this study. Firstly, there are limitations in the sample of this study. The sample population is mainly young people, but not the elderly who are not familiar with IT. Also, the present study is constrained solely to a sample population located in China, resulting in a lack of validation and comparative analysis across multinational consumer groups with divergent cultural backgrounds, which shrinks the outcome of the throat. AI voice assistants have great potential for application in providing services to the visually impaired. In this regard, future research should enrich the sample population and explore the user experience and motivational needs of specific groups.

7 Conclusion

This study constructs a theoretical model based on cognitive evaluation theory and divides AI voice assistant user experience into three stages: cognitive appraisal, emotional experience, and behavioral willingness. Based on the research of AI voice assistant users' emotional experience, this study takes emotional attachment as an important content of users' emotional experience in addition to emotional state and analyzes the role of users' cognitive appraisal antecedent variables on emotional experience. The results show that the perceived service quality, perceived entertainment, and perceived anthropomorphism of AI voice assistants are important antecedent variables of users' emotional experience, and the emotional state and emotional attachment in users' emotional experience play a mediating role in influencing users' behavioral intentions. Among them, perceived anthropomorphism has a direct effect on users' emotional attachment and has no significant effect on users' emotional state.

References

1. Mishra, A., Shukla, A., Sharma, S.K.: Psychological determinants of users' adoption and word-of-mouth recommendations of smart voice assistants. Int. J. Inf. Manag. 102413 (2021). https://doi.org/10.1016/j.ijinfomgt.2021.102413
2. Youn, S., Jin, S.V.: "In AI we trust?" The effects of parasocial interaction and technopian versus luddite ideological views on chatbot-based customer relationship management in the emerging "feeling economy. Comput. Hum. Behav. **119**, 106721 (2021). https://doi.org/10.1016/j.chb.2021.106721
3. Ameen, N., Tarhini, A., Reppel, A., Anand, A.: Customer experiences in the age of artificial intelligence. Comput. Hum. Behav. **114**, 106548 (2021). https://doi.org/10.1016/j.chb.2020.106548
4. Puntoni, S., Reczek, R.W., Giesler, M., Botti, S.: Consumers and artificial intelligence: an experiential perspective. J. Mark. **85**(1), 131–151 (2021). https://doi.org/10.1177/0022242920953847
5. Statista Research Department.: Share of consumers making online payments with voice assistants in the United States as of April 2022, by generational cohort. https://www.statista.com/statistics/1375334/us-voice-commerce-shoppers-generation/. Accessed 10 Sept 2023
6. Moriuchi, E.: Okay, Google! An empirical study on voice assistants on consumer engagement and loyalty. Psychol. Mark. **36**(5), 489–501 (2019). https://doi.org/10.1002/mar.21192
7. Acikgoz, F., Perez-Vega, R., Okumus, F., Stylos, N.: Consumer engagement with AI-powered voice assistants: a behavioral reasoning perspective. Psychol. Mark. **40**(11), 2226–2243 (2023). https://doi.org/10.1002/mar.21873
8. Kautish, P., Purohit, S., Filieri, R., Dwivedi, Y.K.: Examining the role of consumer motivations to use voice assistants for fashion shopping: the mediating role of awe experience and eWOM. Technol. Forecast. Soc. Chang. **190**, 122407 (2023). https://doi.org/10.1016/j.techfore.2023.122407
9. Balakrishnan, J., Dwivedi, Y.K.: Conversational commerce: entering the next stage of AI-powered digital assistants. Ann. Oper. Res. (2021). https://doi.org/10.1007/s10479-021-04049-5
10. Ekinci, Y., Sirakaya-Turk, E., Preciado, S.: Symbolic consumption of tourism destination brands. J. Bus. Res. **66**(6), 711–718 (2013). https://doi.org/10.1016/j.jbusres.2011.09.008
11. Lu, L., Cai, R., Gursoy, D.: Developing and validating a service robot integration willingness scale. Int. J. Hosp. Manag. **80**, 36–51 (2019). https://doi.org/10.1016/j.ijhm.2019.01.005
12. Gkinko, L., Elbanna, A.: Hope, tolerance and empathy: employees' emotions when using an AI-enabled chatbot in a digitalised workplace. Inf. Technol. People **35**(6), 1714–1743 (2022). https://doi.org/10.1108/ITP-04-2021-0328
13. Choi, T.R., Drumwright, M.E.: "OK, Google, why do I use you?" Motivations, post-consumption evaluations, and perceptions of voice AI assistants. Telematics Inform. **62**, 101628 (2021). https://doi.org/10.1016/j.tele.2021.101628
14. Maroufkhani, P., Asadi, S., Ghobakhloo, M., Jannesari, M.T., Ismail, W.: How do interactive voice assistants build brands' loyalty? Technol. Forecast. Soc. Chang. **183**, 121870 (2022). https://doi.org/10.1016/j.techfore.2022.121870
15. Guerreiro, J., Loureiro, S.: I am attracted to my cool smart assistant! Analyzing attachment-aversion in AI-human relationships. J. Bus. Res. **161**, 113863 (2023). https://doi.org/10.1016/j.jbusres.2023.113863
16. Fernandes, T., Oliveira, E.: Understanding consumers' acceptance of automated technologies in service encounters: drivers of digital voice assistants' adoption. J. Bus. Res. **122**, 180–191 (2021). https://doi.org/10.1016/j.jbusres.2020.08.058

17. Aw, E., Tan, G., Cham, T.H., Raman, R., Ooi, K.B.: Alexa, what's on my shopping list? Transforming customer experience with digital voice assistants. Technol. Forecast. Soc. Chang. **180**, 121711 (2022). https://doi.org/10.1016/j.techfore.2022.121711

18. Bawack, R.E., Wamba, S.F., Carillo, K.D.A.: Exploring the role of personality, trust, and privacy in customer experience performance during voice shopping: evidence from SEM and fuzzy set qualitative comparative analysis. Int. J. Inf. Manag. **58**, 102309 (2021). https://doi.org/10.1016/j.ijinfomgt.2021.102309

19. Malodia, S., Ferraris, A., Sakashita, M., Dhir, A., Gavurova, B.: Can Alexa serve customers better? AI-driven voice assistant service interactions. J. Serv. Mark. **37**(1), 25–39 (2023). https://doi.org/10.1108/JSM-12-2021-0488

20. Hu, P., Gong, Y.M., Lu, Y.B., Ding, A.W.: Speaking vs. listening? Balance conversation attributes of voice assistants for better voice marketing. Int. J. Res. Mark. **40**(1), 109–127 (2023). https://doi.org/10.1016/j.ijresmar.2022.04.006

21. Araujo, T.: Living up to the chatbot hype: the influence of anthropomorphic design cues and communicative agency framing on conversational agent and company perceptions. Comput. Hum. Behav. **85**, 183–189 (2018). https://doi.org/10.1016/j.chb.2018.03.051

22. Guzman, A.L.: Voices in and of the machine: source orientation toward mobile virtual assistants. Comput. Hum. Behav. **90**, 343–350 (2019). https://doi.org/10.1016/j.chb.2018.08.009

23. Russell, J.A.: Emotion, core affect, and psychological construction. Cogn. Emot. **23**(7), 1259–1283 (2009). https://doi.org/10.1080/02699930902809375

24. You, S., Robert, L.P.: Emotional attachment, performance, and viability in teams collaborating with embodied physical action (EPA) robots. J. Assoc. Inf. Syst. **19**(5), 377–407 (2018). https://doi.org/10.17705/1jais.00496

25. Wade Clarke, D., Perry, P., Denson, H.: The sensory retail environment of small fashion boutiques. J. Fashion Mark. Manag. Int. J. **16**(4), 492–510 (2012). https://doi.org/10.1108/13612021211265872

26. Beaudry, A., Pinsonneault, A.: The other side of acceptance: studying the direct and indirect effects of emotions on information technology use. MIS Q. **34**(4), 689–710 (2010). https://doi.org/10.2307/25750701

27. Tangsupwattana, W., Liu, X.B.: Effect of emotional experience on symbolic consumption in Generation Y consumers. Mark. Intell. Plan. **36**(5), 514–527 (2018). https://doi.org/10.1108/MIP-11-2017-0316

28. Graul, A., Brough, A.R., Isaac, M.S.: How emotional attachment influences lender participation in consumer-to-consumer rental platforms. J. Bus. Res. **139**, 1211–1217 (2022). https://doi.org/10.1016/j.jbusres.2021.10.064

29. Vlachos, P.A., Theotokis, A., Pramatari, K., Vrechopoulos, A.: Consumer-retailer emotional attachment some antecedents and the moderating role of attachment anxiety. Eur. J. Mark. **44**(9–10), 1478–1499 (2010). https://doi.org/10.1108/03090561011062934

30. Gillath, O., et al.: Attachment and trust in artificial intelligence. Comput. Hum. Behav. **115**, 106607 (2021). https://doi.org/10.1016/j.chb.2020.106607

31. Yim, C.K., Tse, D.K., Chan, K.W.: Strengthening customer loyalty through intimacy and passion: roles of customer-firm affection and customer-staff relationships in services. J. Mark. Res. **45**(6), 741–756 (2008). https://doi.org/10.1509/jmkr.45.6.741

32. Lazarus, R.S.: Emotion and Adaption. Oxford University Press, New York (1991)

33. Lazarus, R.S.: Psychological Stress and the Coping Process. McGraw-Hill, New York (1966)

34. Bagozzi, R.P.: The self-regulation of attitudes, intentions, and behavior. Soc. Psychol. Q. **55**(2), 178–204 (1992). https://doi.org/10.2307/2786945

35. Watson, L., Spence, M.T.: Causes and consequences of emotions on consumer behaviour. Eur. J. Mark. **41**(5/6), 487–511 (2007). https://doi.org/10.1108/03090560710737570

36. McLean, G., Osei-Frimpong, K.: Hey Alexa … examine the variables influencing the use of artificial intelligent in-home voice assistants. Comput. Hum. Behav. **99**, 28–37 (2019). https://doi.org/10.1016/j.chb.2019.05.009

37. Jimenez-Barreto, J., Rubio, N., Molinillo, S.: "Find a flight for me, Oscar!" Motivational customer experiences with chatbots. Int. J. Contemp. Hosp. Manag. **33**(11), 3860–3882 (2021). https://doi.org/10.1108/IJCHM-10-2020-1244

38. Choung, H., David, P., Ross, A.: Trust in AI and its role in the acceptance of AI technologies. Int. J. Hum.-Comput. Interact. **9**(39), 1727–1739 (2023). https://doi.org/10.1080/10447318.2022.2050543

39. Glikson, E., Woolley, A.W.: Human trust in artificial intelligence: review of empirical research. Acad. Manag. Ann. **14**(2), 627–660 (2020). https://doi.org/10.5465/annals.2018.0057

40. Park, E.: User acceptance of smart wearable devices: an expectation-confirmation model approach. Telematics Inform. **47**, 101318 (2020). https://doi.org/10.1016/j.tele.2019.101318

41. Hong, D., Cho, C.H.: Factors affecting innovation resistance of smartphone AI voice assistants. Int. J. Hum.-Comput. Interact. **30**(13), 2557–2572 (2022). https://doi.org/10.1080/10447318.2022.2080899

42. Cao, D.M., Sun, Y., Goh, E., Wang, R., Kuiavska, K.: Adoption of smart voice assistants technology among Airbnb guests: a revised self-efficacy-based value adoption model (SVAM). Int. J. Hosp. Manag. **101**, 103124 (2022). https://doi.org/10.1016/j.ijhm.2021.103124

43. Prakash, A.V., Joshi, A., Nim, S., Das, S.: Determinants and consequences of trust in AI-based customer service chatbots. Serv. Ind. J. **43**(9–10), 642–675 (2023). https://doi.org/10.1080/02642069.2023.2166493

44. Shao, Z., Zhang, L., Li, X.T., Guo, Y.: Antecedents of trust and continuance intention in mobile payment platforms: the moderating effect of gender. Electron. Commer. Res. Appl. **33**, 100823 (2019). https://doi.org/10.1016/j.elerap.2018.100823

45. Kim, C., Mirusmonov, M., Lee, I.: An empirical examination of factors influencing the intention to use mobile payment. Comput. Hum. Behav. **26**(3), 310–322 (2010). https://doi.org/10.1016/j.chb.2009.10.013

46. Kim, H., Kankanhalli, A.: Investigating user resistance to information systems implementation: a status quo bias perspective. MIS Q. **33**(3), 567–582 (2009). https://doi.org/10.5555/2481626.2481634

47. Nass, C., Moon, Y.: Machines and mindlessness: social responses to computers. J. Soc. Issues **56**(1), 81–103 (2000). https://doi.org/10.1111/0022-4537.00153

48. Poushneh, A.: Humanizing voice assistant: the impact of voice assistant personality on consumers' attitudes and behaviors. J. Retail. Consum. Serv. **58**, 102283 (2021). https://doi.org/10.1016/j.jretconser.2020.102283

49. Moon, Y.: Intimate exchanges: using computers to elicit self-disclosure from consumers. J. Consum. Res. **26**(4), 323–339 (2000). https://doi.org/10.1086/209566

50. Ko, E., Kim, E.Y., Lee, E.K.: Modeling consumer adoption of mobile shopping for fashion products in Korea. Psychol. Mark. **26**(7), 669–687 (2009). https://doi.org/10.1002/mar.20294

51. Liu, X.L., Zhang, L., Chen, Q.: The effects of tourism e-commerce live streaming features on consumer purchase intention: the mediating roles of flow experience and trust. Front. Psychol. **13**, 995129 (2022). https://doi.org/10.3389/fpsyg.2022.995129

52. Zhang, M.M., Xu, P., Ye, Y.J.: Trust in social media brands and perceived media values: a survey study in China. Comput. Hum. Behav. **127**, 107024 (2022). https://doi.org/10.1016/j.chb.2021.107024

53. Ali, M., Zhou, L., Miller, L., Ieromonachou, P.: User resistance in IT: a literature review. Int. J. Inf. Manag. **36**(1), 35–43 (2016). https://doi.org/10.1016/j.ijinfomgt.2015.09.007

54. Gursoy, D., Chi, O.H., Lu, L., Nunkoo, R.: Consumers acceptance of artificially intelligent (AI) device use in service delivery. Int. J. Inf. Manag. **49**, 157–169 (2019). https://doi.org/10.1016/j.ijinfomgt.2019.03.008

55. Horton, D., Wohl, R.R.: Mass-communication and para-social interaction - observations on intimacy at a distance. Psychiatry **19**(3), 215–229 (1956). https://doi.org/10.1080/00332747. 1956.11023049

56. Share of consumers making online payments with voice assistants in the United States from November 2021 to May 2022. Share of consumers making online payments with voice assistants in the United States from November 2021 to May 2022. https://www.statista.com/statis tics/1375323/us-voice-commerce-monthly-shoppers/. Accessed 10 Sept 2023

57. MacKenzie, S.B., Podsakoff, P.M.: Common method bias in marketing: causes, mechanisms, and procedural remedies. J. Retail. **88**(4), 542–555 (2012). https://doi.org/10.1016/j.jretai. 2012.08.001

58. Hair, J.F., Risher, J.J., Sarstedt, M., Ringle, C.M.: When to use and how to report the results of PLS-SEM. Eur. Bus. Rev. **31**(1), 2–24 (2019). https://doi.org/10.1108/EBR-11-2018-0203

59. Lin, H., Chi, O.H., Gursoy, D.: Antecedents of customers' acceptance of artificially intelligent robotic device use in hospitality services. J. Hosp. Mark. Manag. **29**(5), 530–549 (2020). https://doi.org/10.1080/19368623.2020.1685053

60. Chuah, S.H., Aw, E.C., Yee, D.: Unveiling the complexity of consumers' intention to use service robots: an fsQCA approach. Comput. Hum. Behav. **123**, 106870 (2021). https://doi. org/10.1016/j.chb.2021.106870

61. Rahardja, U., Hongsuchon, T., Hariguna, T., Ruangkanjanases, A.: Understanding impact sustainable intention of S-commerce activities: the role of customer experiences, perceived value, and mediation of relationship quality. Sustainability **13**(20), 11492 (2021). https://doi. org/10.3390/su132011492

62. Dwivedi, Y.K., et al.: "So what if ChatGPT wrote it?" Multidisciplinary perspectives on opportunities, challenges and implications of generative conversational AI for research, practice and policy. Int. J. Inf. Manag. **71**, 102642 (2023). https://doi.org/10.1016/j.ijinfomgt.2023. 102642

A Contextualized Government Service Chatbot for Individuals with limited Information Literacy

Zhixuan Lian(✉) , Meiyin Huang , and Fang Wang

Nankai University, Tianjin 300071, China
728655654@qq.com

Abstract. Improving the Q&A ability of government service chatbots (GSCs) has become an important issue. In practice, a large number of users with poor information literacy often pose vague questions, which makes it challenging for GSCs to comprehend their inquiries within a specific context. In order to enhance contextualization, this study has constructed a multi-turn dialogue model that incorporates R-GCN and fuzzy logic to base on the "question-answer-context" matching process. To obtain more accurate context, we propose a re-question mechanism to further press for contextual details. Additionally, we introduce the sub-graph matching mechanism of fuzzy logic and R-GCN to improve the accuracy of implicitly representation of Chinese logic in the contextualized matching process. This mechanism allows us to prune the context-irrelevant parts in the "answer" and obtain more complete context information. We collected over 300,000 words of real cases as the test-set. The results of the experiments show that this model can significantly improve the contextualized reasoning ability of GSCs in a more humanized way. The innovative response generation method in this research, which utilizes "question-answer-context" matching, is more suitable for complex scenarios where the user may not be articulate. It helps to lower the barrier for accessing government services and provides more user-friendly assistance to individuals with limited information literacy.

Keywords: Government Service · Chatbot · R-GCN

1 Introduction

With the advent of state-of-the-art generative AI like ChatGPT, it is argued that chatbots can revolutionize society as well as the way we work, learn, and communicate [1]. The Government Service Chatbot (GSC) is an AI-enabled program that provides government services based on users' input and helps to "find the intent of the question asked by a user and send an appropriate reply" [2]. Nowadays, GSC has gained significant momentum among both practitioners and scholars as artificial intelligence-based tools to improve communication between the government and the public [3, 4]. For instance, GSCs have

Z. Lian and H. Meiyin—Contributed equally to this work, should be considered co-first authors.

been adopted in many countries, such as Singapore, Australia, the United States, and China, to facilitate responsiveness, accountability, and interaction [5, 6]. Unlike chatbots used for business or entertainment, GSCs are considered virtual civil servants. Therefore, GSCs should not only be capable of exhibiting characteristics such as proactivity, communicability, emotional intelligence, and identity, but also should possess the trait of conscientiousness [4, 7]. A conscientious chatbot should demonstrate attentiveness to the conversation, understand and maintain the conversational context, recognize users' utterances, and respond appropriately and effectively [7, 8].

Conscientiousness plays a paramount role in users' interaction preferences, but creating a conscientious government chatbot remains a challenge. On the one hand, GSCs often face tricky consultations, such as administrative applications and public services. Not all users can express their questions unambiguously. As an extension of the government, GSCs should strive to offer convenient, efficient, and fair services that cater to users with different levels of information literacy [9]. This requires grappling with both the capability of contextual reasoning and addressing ambiguity. On the other hand, GSCs often face tricky consultations, such as administrative applications and public services. As the complexity of a given goal increases, more interactive turns are required, but this results in a more time-consuming process [10]. It merits attention to balance the conversational context sustaining and efficiency to avoid users perceiving it as wasteful and disappointing. This requires GSCs to encourage users to provide additional information to supplement the background information.

To address the practical issues mentioned above, we introduce a theoretical framework that extends the "question-answer" process to a two-step matching process involving "question-answer" and "answer-context-re-question", zooming in on improving GSCs' ability in contextual reasoning and addressing ambiguity. Specifically, GSCs need to re-question in order to obtain more contextual information and filter out irrelevant information from the answers [11]. To optimize the technical aspect of the "answer-context-re-question" process, we propose a multi-turn dialogue model called MTRF-GSC. This model incorporates R-GCN and Fuzzy Logic as the "re-question" prompt. Utilizing R-GCN, MTRF- GSC effectively prunes logically-independent details during graph matching, making the "re-question" prompt more suitable for the Chinese context. Fuzzy Logic is utilized as a pre-processing step for graph matching to supplement the "answer-context-re-question" optimization by reducing the irrelevant context branches. This method simplifies the complex logical reasoning problem into graph matching of logical sub-graphs of questions and answers. And then, it can translate the implicit logical relationship in the Chinese context into a variable that can be learned.

2 Related Works

A chatbot is a type of Question Answering System (or task-oriented dialogue system in other literature) that involves technologies such as natural language understanding (NLU), state tracking, dialogue policy, and natural language generation (NLG) [12]. This technology was coined at TREC-8 in 1999 and has since evolved into knowledge graph-based extraction and generation from primal document-based retrieval. Most dialogue-relationship models arrange the sequence of dialogues in chronological order. As a result, questions, and answers (Q&A) on different topics are intertwined [13–15], making it challenging to construct a "logical-structure" among them. To address this problem, the temporal sequence relationship between dialogues has been modeled as a multi-perspective matching problem, primarily using three methods [16]: (1) Decomposing the context of a query into multiple topic units and defining the relationships between these units in fine granularity. Then, calculate the "logical-matching" relationship between a topic unit and a response using mechanisms such as Multi-hop Selection Network (MSN) [17, 18], Dual Attention Mechanism (TADAM) [19], and Cognitive Graph [20]. (2) Establish a self-attention network with a mask mechanism that can learn and supplement the overall contextual meaning from related vocabulary (e.g., similar topics or speakers) to match the questions and answers from the same topic or speaker. This type of matching can help identify the corresponding relationship between questions and answers with logical consistency in context [21]. (3) Model the dialogue based on an action triplet of the dialogue structure and its subject [22]. The action-responding relationship between subjects can be used to model the logical structure among questions and answers with RNN [23].

The three methods mentioned above are highly effective in identifying and segmenting multi-round dialogue topics. They have been extensively utilized in the downstream tasks of general fields such as automatic dialogue, dialogue generation, retrieval, chatbot, dialogue text processing, and pre-training language models. However, since their training is aimed at making human-machine dialogue more consistent with the habits of oral communication, and the training corpus is dominated by oral conversations such as Douban Multi-Turn Response Selection and Weibo single-turn review [24], these methods are less effective in knowledge-intensive fields, particularly in government affairs consultation and online healthcare [18]. The relationship in this type of corpus focuses heavily on the consistency between words in context but overlooks the coherence of logical reasoning. Excessive contextual text not only provides rich learning features for dialogues but also creates noise that can affect model performance [17] and lead to generalized outputs. For example, conversation models based on matching, such as SMN [25] and DAM [26], are highly sensitive to noise in the counter samples, resulting in a decrease in the accuracy of logical matching. The dialogue generated in the government consultation is significantly different from ordinary oral dialogue. In the former, questions are often implicitly asked by citizens within a complex context. This makes it more difficult to establish strong logical reasoning relationships between the questions and the answers. Therefore, the GSC model needs to reduce the interference of irrelevant contexts and pay more attention to the transformation of the matching logic contained in the context.

3 MTRF-GSC Model Construction

3.1 Background

To contextualize the process of Q&A, a multi-perspective matching problem can be used to model the sequential relationship between human-robot dialogue in the current study, which involves three methods. First, the context of the question is decomposed into multiple topic units. And their relationship is defined in fine granularity to calculate the "logical-matching" relationship between a topic unit and a response, using mechanisms such as the Multi-hop Selection Network (MSN) [17, 18], the Dual Attention Mechanism (TADAM) [19], Causal Emotion Entailment (TSAM) [27], or the Cognitive Graph [20]. Second, the dialogue can be modeled based on an action triplet of its structure and subjects [22], and the action-responding relationship between subjects can be used to model the logical structure between questions and answers or counterfactual inference [28]. Third, instead of the pipe-typed pre-processing of the conversation, a self-attention network can be established to learn and supplement overall contextual meaning from related information such as same topics or speakers, global causes, local intentions, and dialog history. This mechanism can help find the corresponding relationship between questions and answers with logical consistency in context [21]. While these three methods are effective in contextualized reasoning for stance detection, emotional response, counterfactual inference, dialogue consistency, and segmenting multi-turn dialogue topics, they are less effective in Chinese knowledge-intensive Q&A fields [18]. This is due to two reasons. (1) These methods consider a wider range of contextual factors during the Q&A process. It is assumed that all the relevant contextual factors have already been mentioned in the conversation. However, in knowledge-intensive Q&A, users often express their specific context incompletely, which creates a challenge for these methods. (2) These methods focus on aligning human-robot dialogue with the patterns of oral communication, prioritizing consistency between words in context over logical relationships. When these methods only emphasize the consistency of the context, the lack of a clear structure in the reversal transition of Chinese semantics will result in confusion regarding logical relationships. Additionally, introducing excessive consistent contexts may negatively impact model performance and lead to generalized outputs [18]. During government consultations, users with limited information literacy often struggle to fully articulate the relevant contextual elements. Additionally, important contextual details that are not clearly conveyed to the GSCs can significantly impact logical relevance.

3.2 Government Service Chatbots Based on BERT and R-GCN

To achieve the "question-answer-context" matching process, the MTRF-GSC model computes the interactions between the GSC's response and the corresponding question context. The MTRF-GSC comprises (Fig. 1).

System 1: **The empirical rule learning system is responsible for intuitive judgment and constructing reasoning maps based on empirical data, including sub-steps 1 to 4.**

STEP 1: Input the legal provisions to do pre-processing in Stanford CoreNLP; Conduct syntactic dependency analysis of the legal provisions with Stanford CoreNLP and disassemble the legal provisions according to clause annotations (IP, NP, VP, and PU). Extract the conjunctions in the clauses (part of speech tagging CC as paratactic conjunctions, and CS as generic conjunctions) and form a conjunction lexis-set; Embed all conjunctions in the lexicon into four logical relations ($\land$, $\lor$, $\neg$, $\leftrightarrow$) by using one-hot encoding method, and judge the logical relations between clauses according to the conjunctions; Extract nouns (speech tagging as NR, NT, and NN) and verbs (speech tagging VA as predicate adjectives, VC as series verbs, VE as possessive verbs, and VV

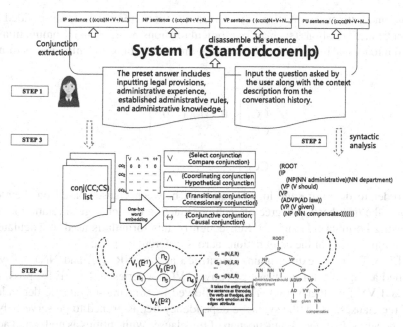

Fig. 1. Structure of the empirical rule learning system

as other verbs), and draw the syntactic dependency tree of clauses; Prune the syntactic dependency tree of clauses to preserve nouns and verbs, and draw the syntactic map of clauses with entities as nodes, verb relations as edges, and whether a verb is made by an administrative agency as edge labels.

STEP 2: Based on the Fuzzy Logic judgment rules (as shown in Table 2), fuse the logical relation of each clause obtained in Step 4 with the syntax diagram in Step 6 to get the clue relation diagram of the clause Gsub. Clause disassembly, logical relationship graphs, and pruning using fuzzy logic. The first part involves disassembling the "answer" and user dialogue history into clauses and extracting conjunctions between them. A membership function[1] Formula (1) determines the type of linguistic logic relation,

$$A = \int_{u \in U} \frac{\mu_A(u)}{u} \tag{1}$$

where, A is the fuzzy set for a single element; μ is the membership degree of the single element A in a single logical relation among the four domains of a discourse (such as $\wedge, \vee, \neg, \leftrightarrow$); $A = \int_{u \in U} \frac{\mu_A(u)}{u}$ represents the membership degree of a specific element to each logical relation. The highest membership degree $\max(A)$ among the four domains is chosen to judge the logical relation represented by the conjunction. To obtain the Logical Membership Degree, we input the "answer" and conversation history, perform syntactic

---

[1] In fuzzy logic, a membership function is employed for characterizing the extent to which an element belongs to a specific fuzzy set. It assigns a membership degree value, ranging from 0 to 1, to the element, facilitating the management of imprecise information and the execution of fuzzy reasoning.

analysis, and extract conjunctions. These conjunctions form a lexis-set divided into different Chinese relations (such as four logical relations $\wedge, \vee, \neg, \leftrightarrow$). Conjunctions are encoded into logical relations for intersection, union, negation, and inference as formula (2).

$$
\begin{array}{c}
CC_1 \\
CC_2 \\
\cdots \\
CC_n
\end{array}
\begin{bmatrix}
\vee & \wedge & \neg & \leftrightarrow \\
0 & 0 & 1 & 0 \\
\cdots\cdots\cdots\cdots \\
\cdots\cdots\cdots\cdots \\
\cdots\cdots\cdots\cdots
\end{bmatrix}
\tag{2}
$$

In order to determine the logical relations between clauses based on their conjunctions, the membership degree of each conjunction to each logical relation is computed using Formulas (1) and (2). Subsequently, this formula is used to calculate the membership degrees of the conjunctions across different corpora.

STEP 3: First, we extract nouns (identified as tags NR, NT, and NN) and verbs (identified as tags VA for predicate adjectives, VC for series verbs, VE for possessive verbs, and VV for other verbs). This is followed by drawing a syntactic dependency tree of the clauses. Then, the syntactic dependency tree is pruned to preserve only the nouns and verbs, to draw a syntactic map of the clauses with entities as nodes and action relations as edges. The label of the edge is determined based on whether the action is carried out by an administrative agency. $G_{sub(n)} = (V, E, R)$ denotes the syntax of the nth clause in an article of the legal provisions. Node (entity) is v_i; $G_{sub(n)}$ involves m entities $v_i \in V(m)$; ; the edge (action-oriented relationship between the entities) is e_{ij}. . The edge of the type (r_{ij}) can be defined according to the task. This study defines the behavioral relationship between entities with 1 as administrative action and 0 as non-administrative action), i. e. $e_{ij} = (v_i, r_{ij}, v_j) \in E, r_{ij} \in R(1, 0)$.

STEP 4: Using Fuzzy Logic judgment rules (as illustrated in Table 1), we fuse the logical relation of each clause with the syntax diagram of the clause to obtain the clue relation diagram of the clause G_{sub}. After obtaining the syntactic tree $G_{sub(n)}$ of each clause, we fuse the clauses $G_{sub(1-n)}$ according to the logical relations between conjunctions. Then, we draw a clue relation graph G_{sub} of the clause. As shown in Table 1, ϕ, ψ, χ are clauses; the syntax diagrams of its clauses are G_1, G_2, G_3; $\varphi(G_n) = G_{sub}$ represents the fusion rule function between clauses.

System 2: The new problem recognition system is responsible for important information extraction, including sub-step 5.

STEP 5: System 2 uses Transformer and BERT models to retrieve similar statements between the contextual text and the "answer". BERT uses the Transformer Encoder block to convert language into vectors. The pre-training process includes the next sentence prediction. Training samples consist of an "answer" clause and a context clause. Context sentences supporting the "answer" are labeled as "1", while unrelated sentences are labeled as "0". The BERT model performs dichotomy prediction on the training samples. The process is illustrated in Formula (4). Our model combines BERT and Transformer to learn the label determination task and determine the overall loss. This enables our system to identify and label supporting contextual sentences (labeled as 1) while discarding

Table 1. Logical Judgment Rules

	Fuzzy Logic judgment rules	Inference attributes
$\wedge$	$\phi \wedge \psi \leftrightarrow \phi$	$\varphi(G_1 \wedge G_2) \leq \varphi(G_1)$
	$\phi \wedge \psi \leftrightarrow \psi \wedge \phi$	$\varphi(G_1 \wedge G_2) = \varphi(G_2 \wedge G_1)$
	$(\phi \wedge \psi) \wedge \chi \leftrightarrow \psi \wedge (\phi \wedge \chi)$	$\varphi((G_1 \wedge G_2) \wedge G_3) = \varphi(G_2 \wedge (G_1 \wedge G_3))$
$\vee$	$\phi \leftrightarrow \phi \vee \psi$	$\varphi(G_1) \leq \varphi(G_1 \vee G_2)$
	$\phi \vee \psi \leftrightarrow \psi \vee \phi$	$\varphi(G_1 \vee G_2) = \varphi(G_2 \vee G_1)$
	$(\phi \vee \psi) \vee \chi \leftrightarrow \psi \vee (\phi \vee \chi)$	$\varphi((G_1 \vee G_2) \vee G_3) = \varphi(G_2 \vee (G_1 \vee G_3))$
$\neg$	$\neg\neg\phi \leftrightarrow \phi$	$\varphi(G_1) = \varphi(\neg\neg G_1)$
	$\phi \wedge \neg\phi \leftrightarrow \overline{0}$	$\varphi(G_1) \uparrow = \varphi(\neg G_1) \downarrow$

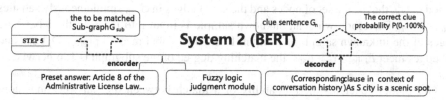

Fig. 2. Structure of the new problem recognition system

unrelated sentences (labeled as 0), allowing for self-monitoring (Fig. 2).

$$\text{Input} = [CLS]\text{question}[SEP]\text{answer}[SEP]\text{label} \qquad (3)$$

System 3: The knowledge reuse system is responsible for semantic analysis and relational reasoning on the graph, including sub-steps 6.

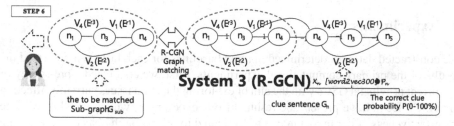

Fig. 3. Structure of the knowledge reuse system

STEP 6: Repeat steps 1–4 to draw the "context" logic diagram Gn, take the sentence vector output by System 2 as the feature of each node in Gn, and take the supporting strength of cue sentence as its node label. Finally, use the "legal provision" clue relation graph as the sub-graph of the "background" logical relation graph and perform graph matching calculation. If $Gsub \in Gn$, it means that the law input in Step 1 can explain the background of the question (Fig. 3).

Based on the law input in Step 1 and the clue sentence in "background" supported by system 1, generate the final reply. System 3 performs relational reasoning on the graph and prompts "re-questioning". It models the "answer-context" relationship as a subgraph matching problem using R-GCN. The matching degree between subgraphs and the "context" graph is calculated. Systems 1 and 2 are iteratively executed. The R-GCN model classifies nodes labeled as using feature aggregation and activation functions. $h_i^{(l+1)} = \sigma\left(\sum_{m\in M_l} g_m\left(h_i^l, h_j^l\right)\right)$ illustrates the structure of the R-GCN model. In a heterogeneous graph with edge attributes, $h_i^{(l+1)} = \sigma\left(\sum_{r\in R}\sum_{j\in N_i^r} \frac{1}{N_{i,r}} W_r^{(l)} h_j^{(l)} + W_0^{(l)} h_i^{(l)}\right)$ enhances information aggregation for subgraphs related to administrative actions. Node classification is performed using R-GCN and Soft-max, with cross entropy used as the loss function. The subgraph matching task determines if is contained in, based on node labels and edge conditions. A matching degree of 1 indicates a match, while 0 indicates no match. The sub-graph matching task refers to whether the subgraph G_{sub} is really contained in G_n, that is, the set of nodes and the set of edges in G_{sub} simultaneously satisfies $V_{sub} \subseteq V_n$. Therefore, when an unknown sample is input into R-GCN, the labels and edges of the unknown sample are output. If the node label meets $V_{label=1} \supseteq V_{sub}$, and the edges meet $E_{label=1} \supseteq E_{sub}$, the matching degree of the subgraph is 1; otherwise, it is 0.

Our model generates the probability of a match between the 'answer' and 'context' elements, while also identifying any mismatched items in the 'answer'. To enable response generation using a pre-trained language model, we linearize the GSC's dialog act into a token sequence. For ease of use, we utilize the preset utterance and Paddle as a response backbone. The model encodes the GSC sequence dialog act as input and generates a response through auto-regressive generation. When the matching probability reaches 1, System 3 creates a reply text based on the 'answer' and the context sentence providing support for the 'answer'. When the matching probability reaches 0, a new question is automatically generated to inquire about the meaning of the node not included in the model, and the verification process repeats.

4 Experiments

We constructed datasets, determined optimal baselines for each task, and presented the results of the primary computational experiments. First, we conducted a pre-survey of 31 current provincial GSCs with the aim of exploring the main issues currently affecting the GSC. Second, we present the results of our experiment, which aimed to validate the effectiveness of our model in two tasks related to our research objectives: detecting contextual mismatch items in the matching of "context-answer" and generating "re-question" responses. The previous method accurately identifies logical inconsistencies through contextual questions. This approach could enhance reasoning skills for complex problems, while the latter engages in a "question-answer-re-question" dialogue to clarify user ambiguity and prompt users to provide more useful information. Finally, we designed a user experiment to test whether this GCS model can reduce the administrative burden for users with different levels of information literacy.

4.1 Datasets

The GSC's preset answer database includes laws and provincial policies, the latter of which are not open source. Therefore, we manually collected a dataset based on open-source laws to supplement the provincial policies as the "preset answers". To replicate the most common scenarios in government affairs consultation, real cases were gathered to serve as "question context". Then, we constructed a dataset that includes "preset answers", "questions", and "question contexts".

"Preset Answer" and "Question": We crawled 31 Chinese provincial government websites and found that 58% of the inquiries were related to government counseling, particularly administrative licensing consultation. For example, "What procedures are required for obtaining a commercial housing pre-sale license?" To simulate daily government counseling scenarios, we selected China's Administrative License Law (ALL) to create the "Preset answer". We also used real appeal cases as "questions" to illustrate examples, such as "what are the required procedures for applying for an administrative license?"

"Question Context": We collected a total of 84 first-instance administrative case judgments related to China's Administrative License Law from the China Judgment Documents Website, which accounted for approximately 300,000 words. After removing 7 duplicate cases, we retained 77 cases as factual sources and adapted them into a "question context" of approximately 150 words of dialogue.

4.2 Evaluation Metrics and Baselines

Evaluation metrics: To evaluate the accuracy of contextual mismatch item detection, we employed precision, accuracy, recall, and micro F1-score. For response generation, we used automatic metrics, including BLEU-4 (B-4) [29], Distinct-1 (D-1) [30], and the recall of ROUGE-2 (R-2) [31], to assess fluency, diversity, and summary ability of those models. Additionally, we developed human evaluation metrics to compare our model with state-of-the-art GSCs in reducing administrative burdens. Seven baselines are shown in Table 2.

5 Results and Analyses

5.1 Pre-survey Results

In April 2023, we conducted a pre-survey about the issues faced by Chinese users in traditional GSCs (in Fig. 4). Out of 7021 user questions surveyed, 142 samples reported experiencing failures with GSCs. The investigation revealed that most GSCs face challenges when trying to comprehend the questions and provide accurate responses within specific contexts. Due to the large number of users with poor information literacy, they often express their questions incompletely and vaguely. Furthermore, an additional finding is that GSCs often provide "answers" that contain excessive and unrelated information in the given context. This overload of information has the potential to overwhelm

Table 2. Baseline models

Baseline		Description	Purpose
1	BERT-Chinese-base	The SOTA end-to-end Chinese models at present	BERT, RoBERTa, and SGM-SVM are commonly employed in conversations to model logical reasoning relationships in GSC systems. Our model surpasses these baselines in both the end-to-end and pipeline-based approaches, demonstrating its superiority
2	RoBERTa-base	A more finely tuned version of the BERT model	
3	SGM-SVM	The model, answering Natural Language Questions by Sub-graph Matching over Knowledge Graphs [31], in short SGM-SVM, combines the sub-graph matching with the QA recommendation ranking model, and uses the SVM-Rank model as the main sub-graph matching tool to make logical reasoning	
4	SGM-GCN	RAEGCN [32], SR-GNN [33], "Answering Natural Language Questions by Subgraph Matching over Knowledge Graph [34]" used graph to represent dialogues (GM-GCN, subgraphs-matching model and GCN in short). This kind of model used conversation rotation and relation to build the matching relationship between question and answer. And the GCN to calculate the node features in the graph	The majority of research on using graph matching to solve logical reasoning problems is based on the GCN model. In our model, we replaced the R-GCN with GCN in ablation studies to remove the effects of the edges
5	Beijing GSC	The GSC on the Beijing government portal. The pre-survey shows that it was the best GSC in China. It responds to users by providing answer options	To demonstrate that initiating a "re-question" way is more effective in reducing the administrative burden of users compared to providing contextual options and similar questions

(continued)

Table 2. (*continued*)

Baseline		Description	Purpose
6	"Faxin" bot	Jointly developed by People's Court Press and the China Judicial Big Data Research Institute. It responds to users by recommending similar cases	
7	GPT-2 with fine tuning	The Advanced language generation model by end-to-end model: https://github.com/Mor izeyao/GPT2-Chinese#gpt2-chi nese	

users and increase their "administrative burden" [35, 36]. Therefore, it is important for GSCs to contextualize the matching process of questions and answers (Q&A) to be more "context-smart" [37]. Consequently, there is an urgent need to improve the contextual understanding capabilities of GSC systems.

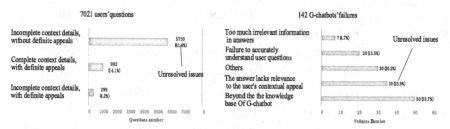

Fig. 4. An Investigation of Problems Encountered by Chinese Users in Traditional GSC

5.2 Situational Reasoning Improvement

Contextual Mismatch Item Detection Task: To begin, we manually labeled the samples. Next, we input the samples into our model and baseline models.

Initially, the automatic metrics precision is employed to evaluate our model with baseline 1–3 and the specific experimental parameter settings. The evaluation results are shown in Table 3, indicating that only 20% of the facts in each "contextual text" being tested are known. With limited known data, the precision of the MTRF-GSC model ranges from 0.62 to 1. SGM-SVM is generally within 0.2–0.4; BERT-base-Chinese and RoBERTa-base are about 0.6–0.733. It shows that our model can detect contextual mismatches in over 60% of the "context" based on a few known facts, which is 10% better than the baselines.

Table 3. Results of Contextual Mismatch Item Detection

Test Dataset	MTRF-GSC	SGM-SVM	Roberta	Bert
1	0.8125	0.21875	0.66666	0.6667
2	0.90625	0.3125	0.66666	0.6667
3	0.71875	0.28125	0.66666	0.6667
4	0.6875	0.28125	0.66666	0.6
5	0.882352941	0.264705882	0.66666	0.73333
6	0.875	0.28125	0.6	0.73333
7	0.846153846	0.346153846	0.66666	0.6
8	0.820512821	0.205128205	0.66666	0.6667
9	0.857142857	0.333333333	0.66666	0.6667
10	0.724137931	0.310344828	0.66666	0.6
11	0.730769231	0.269230769	0.7333	0.6667
12	0.75862069	0.379310345	0.6	0.73333
13	0.970588235	0.205882353	0.66666	0.6667
14	0.942857143	0.257142857	0.66666	0.6667
15	0.852941176	0.323529412	0.66666	0.6
16	0.942857143	0.285714286	0.66666	0.6
17	0.777777778	0.555555556	0.66666	0.6667
18	0.931818182	0.204545455	0.7333	0.73333
19	0.88	0.44	0.66666	0.6667
20	0.861111111	0.25	0.7333	0.6
21	1	0.363636364	0.66666	0.73333
22	0.833333333	0.233333333	0.66666	0.6
23	0.666666667	0.3	0.66666	0.6667
24	0.851851852	0.333333333	0.6	0.6
25	0.741935484	0.290322581	0.66666	0.6667
26	0.789473684	0.210526316	0.66666	0.6667
27	0.961538462	0.384615385	0.66666	0.73333
28	0.888888889	0.333333333	0.7333	0.6667

5.3 Quality of "Re-question"

We developed a prototype system using Python-ChatterBot software to compare baselines 5–7. The evaluation involved inputting "contexts" and "questions" into the baseline models and assessing their responses. Our model performed the best in B-1, excelling in answering questions, but fell short in R-2-f, indicating it uses more redundant expressions. Faxin Bot had better performance in D-1 but struggled in B-1 and R-2-f, compromising coherence and fluency. GPT-2 performed well in D-1 and B-2-F but tended to provide summaries rather than direct answers. Beijing GSC provided non-natural language responses, making it challenging to evaluate. As government consulting relies on Q&A, it is crucial for our model to excel in the ability to answer and B-1 (Table 4).

Table 4. Results of Response Generation

Baseline	Be able to answer	B-1	D-1	R-2-f
Beijing GSC	5.1% (4 of all samples)	–	–	–
Faxin Bot	48% (37 of all samples)	0.1841	0.5179	0.0233
GPT2	–	0.3825	**0.7651**	**0.2342**
MTRF-GSC	79% (61 of all samples)	**0.7527**	0.3592	0.0172

5.4 User Experiments for Different Levels of Information Literacy

Firstly, we selected three questions from our samples that fell within the business scope of the three GSCs, requiring complex reasoning to provide an answer, as shown as in Table 5. From March 15th to 25th, 2022, we invited 10 participants to take part in the experiment and provided them with three experimental questions. After completing the dialogue tasks, participants were asked to fill out a questionnaire to compare the answers provided by the three GSCs and provide feedback on some oral explanations.

We developed a questionnaire based on the administrative burden theory for conducting human evaluations. The administrative burden theory was initially proposed by Woodrow Wilson to describe the costs citizens face when interacting with the government in the management of public affairs [38]. In the 1970s, scholars started to link administrative burden with "bureaucratic encounters" [39]. In recent years, administrative burden has been elaborated as the onerous experience that arises from the interaction between individuals and administrative organizations [40]. The administrative burden in the scenario where "the initiator of the administrative interaction is outside the administrative organization, and the receiver is within it" was further categorized into learning cost, compliance cost, and psychological cost [35, 36]. In order to reduce administrative burden, administrative organizations try to "establish consultation windows on government websites". The GSC is such an auxiliary tool to improve the timeliness of government consultations on public affairs. The questions are listed in Table 6.

The three robots utilize re-question, clickable contextual options, and similar question suggestions when delivering contextualized services. Table 7 displays the evaluation outcomes, where MTRF-GSC outperforms the other two GSCs in mitigating psychological and administrative labor costs. Faxin Bot performs well in one-stop retrieval and case-type recommendation. Nonetheless, its link recommendations to similar questions often result in lengthy texts exceeding 2,000 with legal words, presenting significant

Table 5. The practical effect of the model

Ques-tions	Contexts
My motor vehicle record was scrapped in advance. Can I apply for administrative compensation?	On October 25, 2017, the traffic police canceled my company's motor vehicle registrations based on the belief that it was necessary to withdraw the administrative license in the public interest due to laws and regulations on air pollution prevention and control. As a result, I suffered significant financial losses and could not continue my long-distance transportation business.

Answer of GSC

Law judgement	您的案情与行政许可法第八条类似，但是缺少要件，需要我进一步询问。您缺少的要件是行政许可
For the lack of legal judgment elements in the case of further questioning	根据你所述的案情 公安局交通警察支队认为，根据相关法律，根据《中华人民共和国大气污染防治法》第三十七条第二款的规定及《国务院印发的〈大气污染防治行动计划〉通知》（国发〔2013〕37号）。 根据行政许可法第八条的司法解释 行政许可所依据的法律、法规、规章修改或者废止，也就是说原来的法律、法规、规章准予从事某种活动，后来通过修改，对这种行为加以禁止，另外还有一种情况，即对原来法律、法规、规章规定的颁发行政许可的条件进行了改变，提高了准入的门槛，或者对许可范围进行了调整，被许可人必须满足新的许可条件或者对其从事活动的范围作一定的限制，因而已颁发的行政许可可作出变更。
The case analysis	根据你所述的案情 为了公共利益的需要撤回已经生效的行政许可。 根据行政许可法第八条的司法解释 为了公共利益的需要，可以撤销行政许可 根据你所述的案情 市公安局交通警察支队对我的车辆不再继续登记。 根据行政许可法第八条的司法解释 行政主体与相对人之间存在行政行为
Conclusion	根据你所述的案情 我无法继续经营我的长途运输业务，给我造成巨大经济损失。 根据行政许可法第八条的司法解释 行政行为给原告带来经济损失，需要补偿

Table 6. Evaluation metrics of the Administration Burden with Three GSCs

Theoretical Dimension	Explanation	Sub-dimension	metrics
Learning cost (Problem solving ability) [39]	Users have to acquire relevant knowledge before asking a question	Appeal comprehension	1. Can the GSC correctly understand your appeal on context?
		Information quality	2. Are the answers given by the GSC correct and error-free?
			3. Are the answers given by the GSC complete and without omission?

(continued)

Table 6. (*continued*)

Theoretical Dimension	Explanation	Sub-dimension	metrics
Psychological cost (System interaction capability) [40]	Users have to overcome the "stigma" caused by consultation	Empathy service	4. How comfortable is process of the dialogue with the GSC?
Administrative labor cost (Manual service dependence) [41]	manual support dependence and common-sense knowledge dependence	Manual support	5. Is the recommended answer sufficient to solve the problem without relying on human service?
		Knowledge base	6. Are the answers recommended by the GSC easy to understand without the help of original knowledge?

reading challenges. Although Faxin Bot could recommend authoritative sources to users based on the existing cases and mark the validity of legal elements, its analysis process is invisible.

Although MDRF-GSC falls short of the Faxin Bot and Beijing GSC in terms of data and algorithmic support, it still achieves a comparable outcome. MDRF-GSC helps users think in a self-service way by "re-question", reducing complex questions into a series of simple questions. This feature aligns well with GSC users' characteristics of low information literacy and garners much lower psychological costs while reducing dependency on manual assistance.

Table 7. Average Score of Users' Evaluation on Three GSCs (1–5 level)

Dimension	Question	Beijing GSC	Faxin Bot	MDRF-GSC model
Learning cost (Problem-solving ability)	1	3.3	4.3	4
	2	4	4.2	4.5
	3	3.3	4.3	3.9
Psychological cost (System interaction capability)	4	4.3	4.7	4.9
Administrative labor cost (Manual service dependence)	5	3.9	3.4	4.3
	6	4	4.6	5

6 Conclusion and Discussion

To enhance contextual reasoning abilities, we collected over 300,000 words of actual cases from Chinese Government Portals and China Judgment Documents Website. We propose the MTRF-GSC model with a "re-question" prompt to improve natural response generation. We also introduce a logical reasoning mechanism using R-GCN and Fuzzy Logic prune irrelevant details based on context. Our response generation method, which matches "question-answer-context," provides more contextual and human-like answers. This has practical implications for public managers and AI service contractors, promoting cooperation and customization of services. Inclusive access to AI-based self-service for diverse users should be ensured. Acquiring sufficient training data for the GSC is important, and the cost of data collection should be considered. Further refinement of large language models like GPT2 or Chat-GPT can improve the limited number of valid samples for training. Our work focuses on GPT2 pre-processing for GSCs, and future efforts should aim to adapt language models for GSC applications. In practice, the MTRF-GSC Model can not only help the government to improve the existing GSCs by promoting the government to better reuse previous experiences or the existing knowledge from the perspective of citizens, but also provides a technical channel for citizens to interactively participate in public service. Finally, given the limitations of using China alone as a research background, in the future, we will endeavor to apply our MTRF-GSC Model to a broader range of languages and scenarios.

Acknowledgments. The authors gratefully acknowledge the financial support provided by the National Social Science Foundation of China (20ZDA039), the National Science Foundation of China ("Multi-dimensional Analysis of Policy Driven by Big Data", 72293571), Ministry of Education in China (MOE) Project of Humanities and Social Sciences (Project No. 23YJC630107).

Disclosure of Interests. We declare that the paper is no conflict of interest for all authors.

References

1. Fui-Hoon Nah, F., Zheng, R., Cai, J., Siau, K., Chen, L.: Generative AI and ChatGPT: applications, challenges, and AI-human collaboration. J. Inf. Technol. Case Appl. Res. **25**(3), 277–304 (2023)
2. Goyal, P., Pandey, S., Jain, K.: Deep Learning for Natural Language Processing, p. 19. Apress, New York (2018)
3. Aoki, N.: An experimental study of public trust in AI chatbots in the public sector. Gov. Inf. Q. **37**(4), 101490 (2020)
4. Ju, J., Meng, Q., Sun, F., Liu, L., Singh, S.: Citizen preferences and government chatbot social characteristics: evidence from a discrete choice experiment. Gov. Inf. Q. 101785 (2023)
5. Turban, E., et al.: Innovative EC systems: from E-Government to E-Learning, E-Health, sharing economy, and P2P commerce. In: Electronic Commerce 2018: A Managerial and Social Networks Perspective, pp. 167–201 (2018)
6. Wang, Y., Zhang, N., Zhao, X.: Understanding the determinants in the different government AI adoption stages: evidence of local government chatbots in China. Soc. Sci. Comput. Rev. **40**(2), 534–554 (2022)

7. Chaves, A.P., Gerosa, M.A.: How should my chatbot interact? A survey on social character-istics in human–chatbot interaction design. Int. J. Hum.-Comput. Interact. **37**(8), 729–758 (2021)

8. Dyke, G., Howley, I., Adamson, D., Kumar, R., Rosé, C.P.: Towards academically productive talk supported by conversational agents. Productive Multivocality in the Analysis of Group Interactions, pp. 459–476 (2013)

9. Wang, F.: Social capital or non-human sources? A cross-context study on information source selection of migrant farmer workers. J. Inf. Sci. **49**(5), 1358–1374 (2021, 2023)

10. Jain, M., Kumar, P., Kota, R., Patel, S.N.: Evaluating and informing the design of chatbots. In: Proceedings of the 2018 Designing Interactive Systems Conference, pp. 895–906, June 2018

11. Borji, A.: A categorical archive of ChatGPT failures. arXiv preprint arXiv:2302.03494 (2023)

12. Dale, R.: The return of the chatbots. Nat. Lang. Eng. **22**(5), 811–817 (2016)

13. Yang, Z., Choi, J.D.: FriendsQA: open-domain question answering on TV show transcripts. In: Proceedings of the 20th Annual SIGdial Meeting on Discourse and Dialogue, pp. 188–197, September 2019

14. Li, C., Choi, J.D.: Transformers to learn hierarchical contexts in multiparty dialogue for span-based question answering. arXiv preprint arXiv:2004.03561 (2020)

15. Liu, Q., Chen, B., Lou, J. G., Zhou, B., & Zhang, D.: Incomplete utterance rewriting as semantic segmentation. arXiv preprint arXiv:2009.13166 (2020)

16. Zhou, X., et al.: Multi-view response selection for human-computer conversation. In: Proceedings of the 2016 Conference on Empirical Methods in Natural Language Processing, pp. 372–381, November 2016

17. Yuan, C., et al.: Multi-hop selector network for multi-turn response selection in retrieval-based chatbots. In: Proceedings of the 2019 Conference on Empirical Methods in Natural Language Processing and the 9th International Joint Conference on Natural Language Processing (EMNLP-IJCNLP), pp. 111–120, November 2019

18. Yang, Z., Xu, W., Chen, R.: A deep learning-based multi-turn conversation modeling for diagnostic Q&A document recommendation. Inf. Process. Manag. **58**(3), 102485 (2021)

19. Xu, Y., Zhao, H., Zhang, Z.: Topic-aware multi-turn dialogue modeling. In: Proceedings of the AAAI Conference on Artificial Intelligence, vol. 35, no. 16, pp. 14176–14184, May 2021

20. Ding, M., Zhou, C., Chen, Q., Yang, H., Tang, J.: Cognitive graph for multi-hop reading comprehension at scale. arXiv preprint arXiv:1905.05460 (2019)

21. Qin, L., Xie, T., Che, W., Liu, T.: A survey on spoken language understanding: recent advances and new frontiers. arXiv preprint arXiv:2103.03095 (2021)

22. Zhang, Y., et al.: DialoGPT: large-scale generative pre-training for conversational response generation. arXiv preprint arXiv:1911.00536 (2019)

23. Lowe, R., Pow, N., Serban, I., Pineau, J.: The ubuntu dialogue corpus: a large dataset for research in unstructured multi-turn dialogue systems. arXiv preprint arXiv:1506.08909 (2015)

24. Shang, L., Lu, Z., Li, H.: Neural responding machine for short-text conversation. arXiv preprint arXiv:1503.02364 (2015)

25. Wu, Y., Wu, W., Xing, C., Zhou, M., Li, Z.: Sequential matching network: a new architecture for multi-turn response selection in retrieval-based chatbots. arXiv preprint arXiv:1612.01627 (2016)

26. Zhou, H., Huang, M., Zhang, T., Zhu, X., Liu, B.: Emotional chatting machine: emotional conversation generation with internal and external memory. In: Proceedings of the AAAI Conference on Artificial Intelligence, vol. 32, no. 1, April 2018

27. Zhang, D., Yang, Z., Meng, F., Chen, X., Zhou, J.: TSAM: a two-stream attention model for causal emotion entailment. arXiv preprint arXiv:2203.00819 (2022)

28. Peng, W., Hu, Y., Xing, L., Xie, Y., Sun, Y., Li, Y.: Control globally, understand locally: a global-to-local hierarchical graph network for emotional support conversation. arXiv preprint arXiv:2204.12749 (2022)
29. Papineni, K., Roukos, S., Ward, T., Zhu, W.J.: Bleu: a method for automatic evaluation of machine translation. In: Proceedings of the 40th Annual Meeting of the Association for Computational Linguistics, pp. 311–318, July 2002
30. Li, J., Galley, M., Brockett, C., Gao, J., Dolan, B.: A diversity-promoting objective function for neural conversation models. arXiv preprint arXiv:1510.03055 (2015)
31. Lin, C.Y.: Rouge: a package for automatic evaluation of summaries. In: Text Summarization Branches Out, pp. 74–81, July 2004
32. Zhao, L., Xu, W., Gao, S., Guo, J.: Utilizing graph neural networks to improve dialogue-based relation extraction. Neurocomputing **456**, 299–311 (2021)
33. Wu, S., Tang, Y., Zhu, Y., Wang, L., Xie, X., Tan, T.: Session-based recommendation with graph neural networks. In: Proceedings of the AAAI Conference on Artificial Intelligence, vol. 33, no. 01, pp. 346–353, July 2019
34. Hu, S., Zou, L., Yu, J.X., Wang, H., Zhao, D.: Answering natural language questions by subgraph matching over knowledge graphs. IEEE Trans. Knowl. Data Eng. **30**(5), 824–837 (2017)
35. Herd, P., DeLeire, T., Harvey, H., Moynihan, D.P.: Shifting administrative burden to the state: a case study of medicaid take-up, **73**, S69 (2013)
36. Moynihan, D.P., Herd, P., Ribgy, E.: Policymaking by other means: do states use administrative barriers to limit access to Medicaid? Adm. Soc. **48**(4), 497–524 (2016)
37. Bertot, J., Estevez, E., Janowski, T.: Universal and contextualized public services: digital public service innovation framework. Gov. Inf. Q. **33**(2), 211–222 (2016)
38. Kahn, R.L., Katz, D., Gutek, B.: Bureaucratic encounters—an evaluation of government services. J. Appl. Behav. Sci. **12**(2), 178–198 (1976)
39. Moynihan, D., Herd, P., Harvey, H.: Administrative burden: learning, psychological, and compliance costs in citizen-state interactions. J. Publ. Adm. Res. Theory **25**(1), 43–69 (2015)
40. Burden, B.C., Canon, D.T., Mayer, K.R., Moynihan, D.P.: The effect of administrative burden on bureaucratic perception of policies: evidence from election administration. Publ. Adm. Rev. **72**(5), 741–751 (2012)
41. Arendsen, R., Peters, O., Ter Hedde, M., Van Dijk, J.: Does e-government reduce the administrative burden of businesses? An assessment of business-to-government systems usage in the Netherlands. Gov. Inf. Q. **31**(1), 160–169 (2014)

Detection Vs. Anti-detection: Is Text Generated by AI Detectable?

Yuehan Zhang[1,2], Yongqiang Ma[1,2], Jiawei Liu[1,2], Xiaozhong Liu[3], Xiaofeng Wang[4], and Wei Lu[1,2](✉)

[1] Wuhan University, Wuhan 430072, China
{john_love,mayongqiang,liujiawei,weilu}@whu.edu.cn
[2] Information Retrieval and Knowledge Mining Laboratory of Wuhan University, Wuhan 430072, China
[3] Worcester Polytechnic Institute, Worcester, USA
xliu14@wpi.edu
[4] Indiana University Bloomington, Bloomington, USA
xw7@indiana.edu

Abstract. The swift advancement of Large Language Models (LLMs) and their associated applications has ushered in a new era of convenience, but it also harbors the risks of misuse, such as academic cheating. To mitigate such risks, AI-generated text detectors have been widely adopted in educational and academic scenarios. However, their effectiveness and robustness in diverse scenarios are questionable. Increasingly sophisticated evasion methods are being developed to circumvent these detectors, creating an ongoing contest between detection and evasion. While the detectability of AI-generated text has begun to attract significant interest from the research community, little has been done to evaluate the impact of user-based prompt engineering on detectors' performance. This paper focuses on the evasion of detection methods based on prompt engineering from the perspective of general users by changing the writing style of LLM-generated text. Our findings reveal that by simply altering prompts, state-of-the-art detectors can be easily evaded with F-1 dropping over 50%, highlighting their vulnerability. We believe that the issue of AI-generated text detection remains an unresolved challenge. As LLMs become increasingly powerful and humans become more proficient in using them, it is even less likely to detect AI text in the future.

Keywords: AI-generated Text Detection · Large Language Model · AIGC · Prompt Engineering

1 Introduction

With its powerful performance, large language models (LLMs) have been increasingly accepted as effective personal assistants to elevate our productivity. However, they also pose significant risks if misused. When unregulated, such technology facilitates the creation of convincing yet fraudulent content, including

Y. Zhang and Y. Ma—Both authors contributed equally to this research.

I. Sserwanga et al. (Eds.): iConference 2024, LNCS 14596, pp. 209–222, 2024.
https://doi.org/10.1007/978-3-031-57850-2_16

articles, news, and even fake scientific publications. Journalism, education and research are under the threat of inequality, plagiarism, and other various forms of misuse of LLMs [17,25,28]. Issues in intellectual property, ethics and security are raised. It also challenges the enforcement of legal and regulatory standards. Consequently, addressing these challenges necessitates reliable detection methods for AI-generated text, which is a binary classification task that detects whether the provided text, such as an essay submitted by a student, is generated by LLMs or written by humans [38].

Recent studies have highlighted challenges in distinguishing between human-authored and AI-generated texts [8,12,24], prompting the development of automated detection methods. OpenAI released its online detector [4], and researchers also proposed many AI-generated text detection methods [11,14, 17,18,20,23,27,31,35,39], particularly for the ChatGPT-generated text, such as ZeroGPT [6], GPTZero [3].

Along with the evolution of LLMs such as from GPT-1, GPT-2, and GPT-3 to ChatGPT, AI-generated text detectors were also constantly updated like a cat-and-mouse game. In the line of detection, AI-generated text detectors are developed based on metrics or deep learning. Watermark is also utilized to tackle the detection of AI-generated text [13,19]. In the line of detection evasion, Sadasivan et al. [29] developed a paraphrase method. Researchers also show the effectiveness of randomly added spaces [7] and automatically optimized prompts [39]. Beyond the research of the detection method, the detectability of AI-generated texts is a question not sufficiently discussed. Chakraborty et al. [9] claimed that there is always detectability as the sample number or input length grows.

From the perspective of text generators, the model scale has increased a lot. Therefore, our first hypothesis is that the more parameters the model has, the more difficult it becomes to detect the generated text. Our experiment on the detection of GPT-series models' generated text shows that the detector trained for the weaker LLM has a performance decline when applied to a newer and stronger LLM, which shows the gap between outdated detectors and newer, stronger LLMs.

From the perspective of the prompt text fed to the text generator, researchers have found that the current LLMs are sensitive to the input prompt [41]. However, the detectors' performance on AI-generated text with deliberately designed prompts has not been evaluated. In our research, we make the second hypothesis that the AI-generated text is difficult to detect when deliberately designed prompts are used. To verify this hypothesis, we develop a prompt manipulation method that evades detectors sufficiently without any model training, generated-text paraphrasing, or editing. Specifically, we inject the writing style information into the prompt to change the model output to escape the detector. We find that when prompting the LLMs to generate target text with a given writing style, the LLM-generated text could become much less detectable.

Our findings highlight the gap between AI-generated text detectors and the potential anti-detection methods. Particularly, the detector, trained on a static dataset collected from a single LLM, will fail when the size of the model increases or the generation prompt is customized designed. Factors like model scale and writing styles are important aspects to consider when developing AI-generated detectors.

2   Related Work

2.1   Detection of AI-Generated Text

As the detection of AI-generated text gains much attention [28,33], many approaches are developed. They include statistical metrics-based methods such as entropy, perplexity, log-rank [31] and intrinsic dimensions [35]. DetectGPT [27] makes perturbations to detect AI-generated text based on log probability. There are also transformer-based classifiers such as HC3 classifier [15], and OpenAI classifier. DNA-GPT leveraged LLM itself to generate a few samples for detection based on the similarity between the text to be detected and newly generated ones. Researchers have also noticed the scenario of online environment [36]. Krishna et al. put forward a retrieval-based detection method to defend paraphrasing [20]. Hu et al. proposed a detector-paraphraser joint training method [17]. Watermark techniques [11,19,21,32,40] and datasets designed for detection research are conducted to tackle the challenge of detection [15,24,37]. Off-the-shelf detectors are deployed for the service of detection [1–3,5,6].

2.2   Anti-detection of AI-Generated Text

Liang et al. [22] elevated and decreased the literature and vocabulary of text and successfully reversed the detection result. Lu et al. [25] took out an automatic prompt substitution framework to generate less detectable content. Sadasivan et al. [29] use paraphrasing attacks to evade watermarked and non-watermarked detectors and retrieval-based detectors. SpaceInfi [7] randomly added a space character to evade GPTZero [3], HC3 [15], and MPU detectors [34].

2.3   Detectability of AI-Generated Text

Sadasivan et al. [29] claimed an impossibility of detection as the total variation between humans and AI decreased, causing a theoretical detection ceil that detectors could not be employed practically. They also find that the total variation decreases as model size increases. Chakraborty et al. [9] argues that human and AI distributions are hard to be the same due to the vast diversity within the human population and finds that as collecting more samples the possibility of detection increases (Fig. 1).

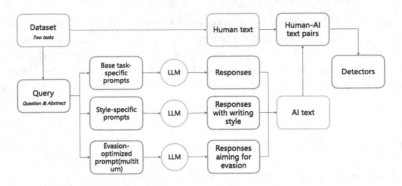

Fig. 1. Framework of Prompt Manipulation Method.

3 Methods

3.1 Task Definition

LLMs can play an important role in text reading and writing improvement. In the scientific domain, there are tools developed by integrating the OpenAI API, such as chatPDF[1] and GPT academic[2]. Considering the usage scenarios, we test our hypothesis on a QA task, a structured abstract generation task(SA task) and an abstract polishing task (Polish task). Under each task, a small set of datasets is generated to test the detectors' performance.

1. For the QA task, we prompt LLMs to generate the answer for a given question. The dataset used is randomly selected samples from HC3 dataset without restricting domains [15].
2. For the Polish task, we use the abstracts of research papers and prompted LLMs to polish the human-written abstract.
3. For the SA task, we use the titles of research papers and prompted LLMs to generate an abstract according to the titles.

The detectors only have access to the human text and generated responses with no extra information such as prompts, questions, original abstracts or titles of the abstract.

3.2 Prompt Design and Dataset Construction

We use LLMs with different scales to generate the structured abstract dataset for an AI-generated detector. Here, we employed GPT-series models, such as GPT-2, text-davinci-002, and ChatGPT as our text generator. The text-davinci-002 is the former base model of ChatGPT[3]. And the GPT-2 [30] is the weaker

---

[1] https://www.chatpdf.com/.
[2] https://github.com/binary-husky/gpt_academic.
[3] https://platform.openai.com/docs/model-index-for-researchers/models-referred-to-as-gpt-3-5.

text generation model than text-davinci-002. The GPT-2 is a white-box model, the parameters of which are open-access. The text-davinci-002 and ChatGPT are the black model, whose responses could only be generated by API. We set max_tokens as 2048 and temperature as 1 for generation parameters.

The prompt is the input text containing instructions that is fed into the LLM to get the desired content. Prompts used in our experiments are designed under four rules to elevate the generating performance, as shown in Fig. 2: Setting a role, stating the tasks clearly, providing information inside of backticks, and indicating the output format. For questions and abstracts in the prompt, we employed the dataset in previous works [15, 26] by random sampling.

To generate different writing styles of AI-generated text, we add a response text style control statement in the prompt: Write in the style of someone. The demo prompts of the QA task are listed in Appendix A, and the full prompts used in the Polish task are in Appendix B.

We also collected responses under deliberately designed prompts without writing styles. The concepts of perplexity and burstiness are explained to Chat-GPT in the prompt for evasion of detectors in multi-turn chat dialogue format [10], which could leverage the power of chat format LLMs. The prompt is listed in Appendix C.

Finally, the text is tagged into categories. The original answer is labeled as a human answer, and the text generated from AI models is labeled as an AI-generated answer.

As *a highly intelligent question answering bot*, your task is to **answer questions**. You will be provided with the **question delimited by triple backticks**. *Format the output* in a JSON object with the following keys: question, answer.
``` {question}```

Fig. 2. Example prompt used in QA task.

Table 1. The detection methods used in this work

Metric-based methods	Classifier-based methods
Log-Likelihood	
Rank	OpenAI Detector
Log-Rank	HC3 Detector
Entropy	ZeroGPT
GLTR Test 2 Features	
```

3.3   AI-Generated Text Detector

we select several metrics-based detectors and classifier detectors [16] and an online detector, as shown in Table 1. The Log-likelihood method takes the probability of words as features [30]. The Rank and Entropy methods use the average rank of words and the entropy of the predicted distribution as features [14]. GLTR applies the statistical features above [14]. Log-Rank uses the average observed log-rank of the tokens in the candidate text [27]. OpenAI Detector is a RoBERTa model fine-tuned on GPT2 output [30]. HC3 Detector is trained on HC3 dataset containing text pairs of human and ChatGPT [15]. ZeroGPT is an off-the-shelf online detector [6].For equivalent comparison, we trained Logistic Regression classifiers based on the metrics.

4   Experimental Results

4.1   Detectability Analysis of Different Scale LLMs

Here, we use the detector OpenAI -Roberta-detector to detect the AI-generated structured abstracts. The detector is trained on WebText data and GPT-2 output text. The performance of a trained detector varies from the scale of the text generator. Specifically, as the model size increases and the model version iterates, the detection effect of AI-generated texts declines a lot.

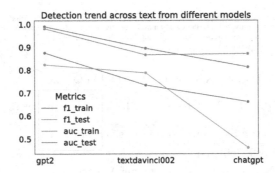

Fig. 3. Detectors' result on the generated text on models of different model scales.

As shown in Fig. 3, there is a clear trend of decline in detection accuracy. The F-1 performance on GPT-2 and ChatGPT test data is 82% versus 46%, showing a relative drop of 36%. The possible reason is that output of GPT-2 is not very smooth and may contain grammatical errors. As the model scale increases, the model output is more fluent. Therefore the performance of detectors trained on original text based on GPT-2 will decline on the output of the ChatGPT model.

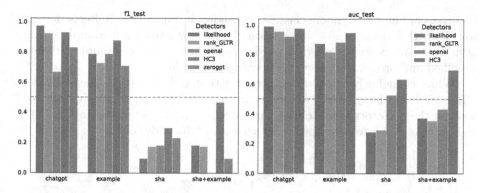

Fig. 4. Detectors' result on QA task with original prompt, prompt with *Shakespeare* writing style guidance in author name, author name plus example, and mere example format.

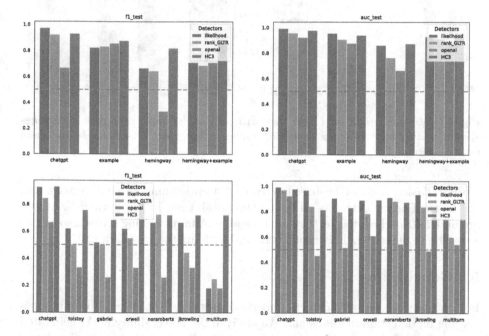

Fig. 5. The upper subfigures: Detectors' result on QA task with original prompt, prompt with *Hemingway* writing style guidance in author name, author name plus example and mere example format. The lower subfigures: Detectors' result on QA task with prompts of different authors and multi-turn prompt designed for evasion.

4.2 Detectability Analysis of Different Writing Styles of AI-Generated Text

QA Task: After adding a writing style to the generated text, it becomes undetectable. When writing style is explicitly appointed by an author name, the detectors fall under a random classifier, as shown in Fig. 4. The Roberta detector and ZeroGPT detector get worse when the author name and example writing style text are explicitly referred to. The one-shot example prompt without a specified author name only weakens detectors a little.

While changing writing styles, we find that different styles have different effect levels. Although some writing styles are weaker than others, it could still weaken the detectors to state that they are not usable. As shown in Fig. 5, the F-1 value of Roberta-base-openai-detector also falls under 50%.

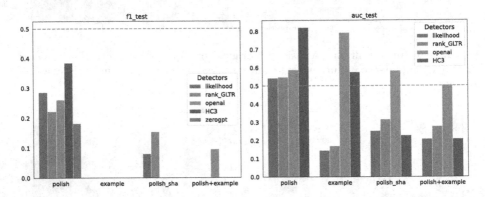

Fig. 6. Detectors' result on Polish task with original prompt, prompt with *Shakespeare* writing style guidance in author name, author name plus example and mere example format.

Polish Task: The metrics-based detectors, deep-learning-based detectors, and off-the-shelf online detectors all fail on the polish task. In Fig. 6, their F1 values are under 40% which means they are unusable. Adding writing styles also causes a decline in detection. This result is in line with another research [24].

5   Conclusion

In previous work, the anti-detection methods neglected the effect of prompt engineering on detection methods and We analyze the detectability of AI-generated text under different model scales and prompts. Easily and cheaply, the detectors of the time are easily evaded by prompts added writing styles or evasion concepts. This demonstrates the vulnerability of detectors.

Although this research is limited by the number of tasks, our method is easy to replicate even for anyone who has access to a LLM. Detection of AI-generated text is still an unsolved problem. This work aims to highlight the potential dangers of misusing LLMs. From a practical and empirical aspect, AI-generated text could not even be detected sufficiently for now. As we wrote this manuscript, OpenAI has quietly shut down its online detection tool. Thus, we highly suspect the usage of popular online detectors nowadays and call for robust and sufficient methods to face the challenge of potential misuse of LLMs.

Appendix A   The Prompts Used for QA Task

[chatgptanswers] As a highly intelligent question answering bot, your task is to answer questions. You will be provided with the question delimited by triple backticks. Format the output in a JSON object with the following keys: question,answer.

"'question"'

[chatgptanswers_sha] As a highly intelligent question answering bot, your task is to answer questions in specific writing styles. Write in the style of Shakespeare. You will be provided with the question delimited by triple backticks. Format the output in a JSON object with the following keys: question,answer.

"'question"'

[chatgptanswers_sha_withexampletext] As a highly intelligent question answering bot, your task is to answer questions in specific writing styles. Write in the style of Shakespeare. You will be provided with an example of Shakespeare's writing style delimited by triple dashes. You will be provided with the question delimited by triple backticks. Format the output in a JSON object with the following keys: question,answer,style_example.

style_example: —example—

question: "'question"'

[chatgptanswers_sha_onlyexampletext] As a highly intelligent question answering bot, your task is to answer questions in specific writing styles. Write in the writing style of an example but ignore the content and topic of the example. You will be provided with the style example delimited by triple quotes. You will be provided with the question delimited by triple backticks. Format the output in a JSON object with the following keys: question,answer,style_example

style_example:"""example"""

question: "'question"'

example = From what power hast thou this powerful might, With insufficiency my heart to sway, To make me give the lie to my true sight, And swear that brightness doth not grace the day? Whence hast thou this becoming of things ill, That in the very refuse of thy deeds, There is such strength and warrantise of skill, That in my mind thy worst all best exceeds? Who taught thee how to make me love thee more, The more I hear and see just cause of hate? O though I love what others do abhor, With others thou shouldst not abhor my state. If thy unworthiness raised love in me, More worthy I to be beloved of thee.

For other writing styles, we change the author name and example text in the prompts.

example_hemingway =He no longer dreamed of storms, nor of women, nor of great occurrences, nor of great fish, nor fights, nor contests of strength, nor of his wife. He only dreamed of places now and of the lions on the beach. They played like young cats in the dusk and he loved them as he loved the boy. He always thought of the sea as 'la mar' which is what people call her in Spanish when they love her. Sometimes those who love her say bad things of her but they are always said as though she were a woman. Some of the younger fishermen, those who used buoys as floats for their lines and had motorboats, bought when the shark livers had brought much money, spoke of her as'el mar' which is masculine. They spoke of her as a contestant or a place or even an enemy. But the old man always thought of her as feminine and as something that gave or withheld great favours, and if she did wild or wicked things it was because she could not help them. The moon affects her as it does a woman, he thought. Fish," he said softly, aloud, "I'll stay with you until I am dead. No one should be alone in their old age, he thought. Fish," he said, "I love you and respect you very much. But I will kill you dead before this day ends.

Appendix B   The Prompts Used for Polish Task

[polish] As an academic paper writer, your task is to rewrite an abstract of a research paper. You will be provided with the abstract delimited by triple backticks. Format the output in a JSON object with the following keys: original_abstract,rewritten_abstract.
original_abstract :"'ab'"

[p_sha] As an academic paper writer, your task is to rewrite an abstract of a research paper in specific writing styles. Write in the style of Shakespeare.You will be provided with the original abstract delimited by triple backticks. Format the output in a JSON object with the following keys: original_abstract,rewritten_abstract.
"'ab'"

[p_withtext] As an academic paper writer, your task is to rewrite an abstract of a research paper in specific writing styles. Write in the style of Shakespeare. You will be provided with an example of Shakespeare's writing style delimited by triple quotes. You will be provided with the original abstract delimited by triple backticks. Format the output in a JSON object with the following keys: original_abstract,rewritten_abstract,style_example.
style_example:"""{example_shakespeare}"""
original_abstract :"'original_abstract'"

[p_onlytext] As an academic paper writer, your task is to rewrite an abstract of a research paper in specific writing styles. Write in the writing style of an example but ignore the content and topic of the example. You will be provided with style example delimited by triple quotes. You will be provided with the original abstract delimited by triple backticks. Format the output in a JSON object with the following keys: original_abstract,rewritten_abstract,style_example.
style_example:"""example_shakespeare"""
original_abstract :"'original_abstract'"

The example text of Shakespeare is the same as that in the QA task.

Appendix C   Multi-turn Prompt Used for Detectors Evasion

[{"role": "user", "content": "As a highly intelligent question answering bot, your task is to rewrite the answer of a question. I'm going to give you some information. You will be provided with instructions, the question, the answer delimited by triple quotes."},{"role": "assistant", "content": "Sure, I'm here to help! Please provide me with the information, instructions, the question, and the answer delimited by triple quotes, and I'll be happy to rewrite the answer for you."},{"role": "user", "content":"When it comes to writing content, two factors are crucial, "perplexity" and "burstiness." Perplexity measures the complexity of text. Separately, burstiness compares the variations of sentences. Humans tend to write with greater burstiness, for example, with some longer or complex sentences alongside shorter ones. AI sentences tend to be more uniform. Therefore, when writing the following content I am going to ask you to create, I need it to have a good amount of perplexity and burstiness. Do you understand?"},{"role": "assistant", "content":"Yes, I understand. You would like the content I generate to exhibit both perplexity, which refers to the complexity of the text, and burstiness, which involves variations in sentence length and complexity. By incorporating these elements, the content should resemble human writing with a mix of longer or complex sentences alongside shorter ones. Please provide me with the specific instructions, the question, and any additional details you'd like to include in the content. I'll make sure to generate a response that meets your criteria for perplexity and burstiness."},{"role": "user", "content": Prompt}]

Prompt = Using the concepts written previously, rewrite this answer of the question with a high degree of perplexity and burstiness:
question:"""{question}"""
answer:"""{answer}"""
Format the output in a JSON object with the following keys:
question,answer,rewritten_answer.

References

1. AI Content Detector. https://crossplag.com/ai-content-detector/
2. AI Detector (GPT / ChatGPT / Claude) | Sapling. https://sapling.ai/ai-content-detector
3. GPTZero | The Trusted AI Detector for ChatGPT, GPT-4, & More. https://gptzero.me/
4. New AI classifier for indicating AI-written text. https://openai.com/blog/new-ai-classifier-for-indicating-ai-written-text
5. Originality.ai. https://app.originality.ai/api-access
6. ZeroGPT - Accurate Chat GPT, GPT4 & AI Text Detector Tool. https://www.zerogpt.com/
7. Cai, S., Cui, W.: Evade ChatGPT Detectors via A Single Space, July 2023. https://doi.org/10.48550/arXiv.2307.02599, http://arxiv.org/abs/2307.02599
8. Casal, J.E., Kessler, M.: Can linguists distinguish between ChatGPT/AI and human writing?: A study of research ethics and academic publishing. Res. Methods Appl. Linguist. **2**(3), 100068 (2023). https://doi.org/10.1016/j.rmal.2023.100068, https://www.sciencedirect.com/science/article/pii/S2772766123000289

9. Chakraborty, S., Bedi, A.S., Zhu, S., An, B., Manocha, D., Huang, F.: On the Possibilities of AI-Generated Text Detection, June 2023. https://doi.org/10.48550/arXiv.2304.04736, http://arxiv.org/abs/2304.04736

10. Chris: The Ultimate ChatGPT Prompt: Content that Outsmarts AI Detectors with 99% Accuracy, March 2023. https://medium.datadriveninvestor.com/the-ultimate-chatgpt-prompt-content-that-outsmarts-ai-detectors-with-99-accuracy-ef20d81582bb

11. Christ, M., Gunn, S., Zamir, O.: Undetectable Watermarks for Language Models, May 2023. https://doi.org/10.48550/arXiv.2306.09194, http://arxiv.org/abs/2306.09194

12. Clark, E., August, T., Serrano, S., Haduong, N., Gururangan, S., Smith, N.A.: All that's 'human' is not gold: evaluating human evaluation of generated text. In: Proceedings of the 59th Annual Meeting of the Association for Computational Linguistics and the 11th International Joint Conference on Natural Language Processing (Volume 1: Long Papers), pp. 7282–7296. Association for Computational Linguistics, Online, August 2021. https://doi.org/10.18653/v1/2021.acl-long.565, https://aclanthology.org/2021.acl-long.565

13. Fu, Y., Xiong, D., Dong, Y.: Watermarking Conditional Text Generation for AI Detection: Unveiling Challenges and a Semantic-Aware Watermark Remedy, July 2023. https://doi.org/10.48550/arXiv.2307.13808, http://arxiv.org/abs/2307.13808

14. Gehrmann, S., Strobelt, H., Rush, A.: GLTR: statistical detection and visualization of generated text. In: Proceedings of the 57th Annual Meeting of the Association for Computational Linguistics: System Demonstrations, pp. 111–116. Association for Computational Linguistics, Florence, Italy, July 2019. https://doi.org/10.18653/v1/P19-3019, https://aclanthology.org/P19-3019

15. Guo, B., et al.: How Close is ChatGPT to Human Experts? Comparison Corpus, Evaluation, and Detection, January 2023. https://doi.org/10.48550/arXiv.2301.07597, http://arxiv.org/abs/2301.07597

16. He, X., Shen, X., Chen, Z., Backes, M., Zhang, Y.: MGTBench: Benchmarking Machine-Generated Text Detection, June 2023. https://doi.org/10.48550/arXiv.2303.14822, http://arxiv.org/abs/2303.14822

17. Hu, X., Chen, P.Y., Ho, T.Y.: RADAR: Robust AI-Text Detection via Adversarial Learning, July 2023. https://doi.org/10.48550/arXiv.2307.03838, http://arxiv.org/abs/2307.03838

18. Ippolito, D., Duckworth, D., Callison-Burch, C., Eck, D.: Automatic detection of generated text is easiest when humans are fooled. In: Proceedings of the 58th Annual Meeting of the Association for Computational Linguistics, pp. 1808–1822. Association for Computational Linguistics, Online, July 2020. https://doi.org/10.18653/v1/2020.acl-main.164, https://aclanthology.org/2020.acl-main.164

19. Kirchenbauer, J., Geiping, J., Wen, Y., Katz, J., Miers, I., Goldstein, T.: A watermark for large language models. In: Krause, A., Brunskill, E., Cho, K., Engelhardt, B., Sabato, S., Scarlett, J. (eds.) Proceedings of the 40th International Conference on Machine Learning. Proceedings of Machine Learning Research, vol. 202, pp. 17061–17084. PMLR, 23–29 July 2023. https://proceedings.mlr.press/v202/kirchenbauer23a.html

20. Krishna, K., Song, Y., Karpinska, M., Wieting, J., Iyyer, M.: Paraphrasing evades detectors of AI-generated text, but retrieval is an effective defense, March 2023. https://doi.org/10.48550/arXiv.2303.13408, http://arxiv.org/abs/2303.13408

21. Kuditipudi, R., Thickstun, J., Hashimoto, T., Liang, P.: Robust Distortion-free Watermarks for Language Models, July 2023. https://doi.org/10.48550/arXiv.2307.15593, http://arxiv.org/abs/2307.15593

22. Liang, W., Yuksekgonul, M., Mao, Y., Wu, E., Zou, J.: GPT detectors are biased against non-native English writers, July 2023. https://doi.org/10.48550/arXiv.2304.02819, http://arxiv.org/abs/2304.02819

23. Liu, Y., et al.: ArguGPT: evaluating, understanding and identifying argumentative essays generated by GPT models, April 2023. https://doi.org/10.48550/arXiv.2304.07666, http://arxiv.org/abs/2304.07666

24. Liu, Z., Yao, Z., Li, F., Luo, B.: Check Me If You Can: Detecting ChatGPT-Generated Academic Writing using CheckGPT, June 2023. https://doi.org/10.48550/arXiv.2306.05524, http://arxiv.org/abs/2306.05524

25. Lu, N., Liu, S., He, R., Wang, Q., Tang, K.: Large Language Models can be Guided to Evade AI-Generated Text Detection, June 2023. https://doi.org/10.48550/arXiv.2305.10847, http://arxiv.org/abs/2305.10847

26. Ma, Y., et al.: AI vs. Human – Differentiation Analysis of Scientific Content Generation, February 2023. https://doi.org/10.48550/arXiv.2301.10416, http://arxiv.org/abs/2301.10416

27. Mitchell, E., Lee, Y., Khazatsky, A., Manning, C.D., Finn, C.: DetectGPT: Zero-Shot Machine-Generated Text Detection using Probability Curvature, July 2023. https://doi.org/10.48550/arXiv.2301.11305, http://arxiv.org/abs/2301.11305

28. Pan, Y., Pan, L., Chen, W., Nakov, P., Kan, M.Y., Wang, W.Y.: On the Risk of Misinformation Pollution with Large Language Models, May 2023. https://doi.org/10.48550/arXiv.2305.13661, http://arxiv.org/abs/2305.13661

29. Sadasivan, V.S., Kumar, A., Balasubramanian, S., Wang, W., Feizi, S.: Can AI-Generated Text be Reliably Detected?, June 2023. http://arxiv.org/abs/2303.11156

30. Solaiman, I., et al.: Release Strategies and the Social Impacts of Language Models, November 2019. https://doi.org/10.48550/arXiv.1908.09203, http://arxiv.org/abs/1908.09203

31. Su, J., Zhuo, T.Y., Wang, D., Nakov, P.: DetectLLM: Leveraging Log Rank Information for Zero-Shot Detection of Machine-Generated Text, May 2023. https://doi.org/10.48550/arXiv.2306.05540

32. Tang, L., Uberti, G., Shlomi, T.: Baselines for Identifying Watermarked Large Language Models, May 2023. https://doi.org/10.48550/arXiv.2305.18456

33. Tang, R., Chuang, Y.N., Hu, X.: The Science of Detecting LLM-Generated Texts, June 2023. https://doi.org/10.48550/arXiv.2303.07205

34. Tian, Y., et al.: Multiscale Positive-Unlabeled Detection of AI-Generated Texts, June 2023. https://doi.org/10.48550/arXiv.2305.18149

35. Tulchinskii, E., et al.: Intrinsic Dimension Estimation for Robust Detection of AI-Generated Texts, June 2023. https://doi.org/10.48550/arXiv.2306.04723

36. Wang, H., Luo, X., Wang, W., Yan, X.: Bot or Human? Detecting ChatGPT Imposters with A Single Question, May 2023. https://doi.org/10.48550/arXiv.2305.06424

37. Wang, Y., et al.: M4: Multi-generator, Multi-domain, and Multi-lingual Black-Box Machine-Generated Text Detection, May 2023. https://doi.org/10.48550/arXiv.2305.14902

38. Wu, J., Yang, S., Zhan, R., Yuan, Y., Wong, D.F., Chao, L.S.: A survey on LLM-generated text detection: necessity, methods, and future directions (2023)

222   Y. Zhang et al.

39. Yang, X., Cheng, W., Petzold, L., Wang, W.Y., Chen, H.: DNA-GPT: Divergent N-Gram Analysis for Training-Free Detection of GPT-Generated Text, May 2023. https://doi.org/10.48550/arXiv.2305.17359
40. Zhao, X., Ananth, P., Li, L., Wang, Y.X.: Provable Robust Watermarking for AI-Generated Text, June 2023. https://doi.org/10.48550/arXiv.2306.17439
41. Zhu, K., et al.: PromptBench: Towards Evaluating the Robustness of Large Language Models on Adversarial Prompts, August 2023. https://doi.org/10.48550/arXiv.2306.04528

PrivacyChat: Utilizing Large Language Model for Fine-Grained Information Extraction over Privacy Policies

Rohan Charudatt Salvi(✉) ⓘ, Catherine Blake ⓘ, and Masooda Bahir ⓘ

University of Illinois at Urbana Champaign, Champaign, IL 61820, USA
rohancsalvi@gmail.com

Abstract. Privacy policies play a crucial role in upholding the privacy rights of users and fostering trust between organizations and their users. By clearly understanding the terms and conditions of a privacy policy, individuals can make well-informed choices about disclosing their personal information and understand how the concerned entity will manage their data. Following the introduction of the General Data Protection Regulation, these policies have become more extensive and intricate. This creates a challenge for users in terms of understanding and finding specific information in the policy. Today, through prompt-based methods, we can extract specific data from extensive text documents using large language models (LLMs), thus eliminating the need for training or fine-tuning models. In this study, we explore a prompt-based approach to extract information concerning personal data from privacy policies using a large language model, GPT-3.5. In this preliminary study, we assess the performance of GPT-3.5 on such a fine-grained extraction task through varied metrics and its capability to address previous computational challenges. The prompt structure can be adapted for other LLMs, and a similar approach can be employed for various information extraction tasks over privacy policies. The data and code are available at our GitHub repository. .

Keywords: Privacy Policy · Information Extraction · Large Language Models

1 Introduction

A privacy policy is a crucial document that outlines how an organization or website collects, uses, stores, and protects the personal information of its users or customers. Over the years, several privacy laws have emerged worldwide through sector regulations and legislative pathways. Hence, for any organization, a well-crafted privacy policy is essential for compliance with various data protection regulations and has become a cornerstone of responsible data management in today's digital age. Unfortunately, from the outset, privacy policies have been long and complex for users to fully read and understand [1]. Research has shown

I. Sserwanga et al. (Eds.): iConference 2024, LNCS 14596, pp. 223–231, 2024.
https://doi.org/10.1007/978-3-031-57850-2_17

that most people accept the terms without reading the policies [2]. Legislative bodies like the European Union are implementing regulations such as the General Data Protection Regulation (GDPR) [3] to empower users by giving them more control over how their personal data is collected, processed, and stored by organizations. These regulations also give users several rights to access, edit, and erase personal information. To ensure compliance, the European Union has set hefty fines in response to which organizations have updated their privacy policies, making them more complex, difficult to read, and significantly longer [4,5].

It has become increasingly difficult for users to understand the policies, especially when looking for a particular facet of interest, such as what data is being collected and the associated rights they have. Researchers have tried several methods [6–10] to extract vital information from privacy policies. However, these methods are not robust and face various computational challenges. With the emergence of large language models (LLMs) like GPT-3.5, which possess exceptional language proficiency and come pre-trained for general tasks [11], there is an opportunity to significantly enhance methods for extracting information with minimal initial effort [12]. By combining these capabilities with prompt engineering [13], one can design prompts to improve information extraction results [14,15]. However, studies have highlighted that LLMs may require domain adaptation, especially in niche domains such as medicine and law [16]. Moreover, prompts might need the inclusion of examples to support extraction, commonly termed a few-shot setting [17]. Furthermore, these models can be prone to hallucination [18], generating unreliable information that is not grounded in the source document [19].

In this pilot study, we assess the performance of the LLM GPT-3.5 on the task of extracting information from privacy policies using a zero-shot learning approach. We observe whether the model can overcome the computational challenges of prior extraction methods, such as the need for extensive training data and the capability to manage lengthy contexts. Our goal is to understand GPT-3.5's capability of interpreting legal language and accurately extracting information about user data rights, thereby addressing both the opacity of privacy policies and the computational limitations of earlier techniques.

2   Related Work

Extensive work has been conducted in the field of privacy policies and natural language processing [20]. Researchers have employed extraction techniques to retrieve opt-out choices [6] from policies and to extract answers to a series of questions to create a concise summary of the policy [9]. Additionally, the development of Privacy QA [7] and Policy QA datasets [8] has facilitated machine reading comprehension-style questions answering in the context of privacy. The Policy IE corpus [10] was created to extract detailed information from privacy policies, involving tasks such as predicting the privacy practices explained in a sentence (intent classification) and identifying the text spans that contain specific information (slot filling). However, all these methods have some limitations, such as their ability to grasp long contexts and robustness to user questions [7,8]. Moreover, they may require a significant amount of effort for setup, including tasks like creating expensive and labor-intensive large datasets, fine-tuning or retraining a model, or a combination of these actions [10,14,15]. In this context, prompt-based learning offers a promising direction. In this method, we adapt a pre-trained LLM to diverse tasks through the use of prompts. "Natural language prompts-pieces of text that are combined with an input and then fed to the language model to produce an output for that task" [12]. Prompt-based learning can be easily applied to some tasks, while it may require some innovation for complex tasks [21]. However, for entity extraction, especially for a single entity, prompting can be more straightforward, like asking, 'What is the location?' [22]. This simple yet effective approach can aid in efficiently extracting specific information. Prompt-based learning is widely being used by different fields for precise information extraction, such as healthcare [12] and material science [14]. Furthermore, researchers are actively working on developing general structures and workflows [14,15,23] for information extraction using large language models.

3   Methodology

To extract detailed information related to the handling of users' personal information in compliance with GDPR regulations and their rights we formulated four specific questions. These four questions were:

1. What types of personal information are gathered from users?
2. With whom is this collected personal information shared or sold?
3. How long does the organization retain user's personal information?
4. What rights do users possess concerning the data collected by the organization?

We randomly selected 60 policies from the PrivaSeer Corpus [24] and manually annotated the responses to these questions to create our test dataset. The answers in this dataset varied significantly, ranging from brief phrases of just two words to more extensive responses spanning up to two sentences. It's important to note that not every policy contains answers to all questions. In cases where questions were unanswerable based on the privacy document, our dataset designates 'None' as a valid response. Table 1 provides an overview of the test dataset.

Our question-answering test dataset might seem similar to the PolicyQA [8] dataset. However, PolicyQA is a machine-reading comprehension dataset that uses only parts of policies spanning a few sentences for context, and its questions vary depending on the policies. In contrast, our approach involves using the entire policy as context and employs a consistent set of questions for all policies. Additionally, we have addressed cases where a question cannot be answered based on the given context, a scenario not supported in the PolicyQA dataset. Lastly, in the PolicyQA dataset, the model predicts the start and end index of a

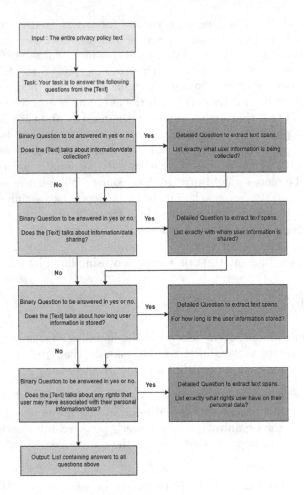

Fig. 1. A flow chart describing our approach.

Table 1. Distribution of Responses in Test Data

Question	Text as response	None as response
What types of personal information are collected from users?	40	20
With whom is this collected personal information shared or sold?	22	38
How long does the organization retain user's personal information?	9	51
What rights do users possess concerning the data collected by the organization?	26	34

sentence span from the text akin to the SQuAD format [25], whereas in our case, the model generates text which is compared against the answer span of text.

To perform information extraction, our approach involved an iterative development of prompts using a structure as depicted in Fig. 1 for the 'gpt-3.5-turbo' model which was employed through an API. This approach was inspired by the ChatExtract method [14]. Within this methodology, we structured the prompts to begin with a binary question initially. When the response was affirmative, we proceeded with more detailed questions to obtain further information successfully. In cases where the response to any binary question was negative, we recorded it as 'None' and proceeded to ask the binary question for the subsequent query. Finally, we assessed the performance of our approach using the test dataset.

We attempted another experiment in which we employed a BERT model trained on the PolicyQA dataset to compare the performance between the two approaches. Nevertheless, we faced difficulties when it came to choosing the relevant context, as the BERT model's context length restricts it to include the entire policy as context. Moreover, given that this model was not tailored specifically for questions with undefined answers, it proved unsuitable for conducting an effective evaluation and comparison with the GPT-3.5 model. Table 3 in the appendix provides a comparison of the answers generated by the two models for a privacy policy.

4 Result and Discussion

We made a few observations while annotating the test dataset and found that for third-party entities, a definitive response is often missing. However, these third-party entities are frequently referred to as 'partners, vendors, contractors, or affiliates' of the business and are entrusted with various responsibilities, such as managing transactions, facilitating deliveries, or overseeing logistics. The identities of such partners remain undisclosed. Regarding the duration of data retention, three potential options emerged: either the data is promptly erased upon account closure, it is maintained for a reasonable period, or the personal information is expunged while other information is retained indefinitely. Nevertheless, in the case of a reasonable period, the precise time frames are consistently absent. Furthermore, the annotation concerning the rights of users varied, with some policies concisely stating just the rights and others elaborating on them, explaining what the right means for the user and how they can reach out to exercise these rights.

As for the PolicyQA BERT model, although it was not evaluated on our dataset, several observations emerged. Context length proved to be a challenge, as the model could not process entire policies in one go. Moreover, we needed to manually select relevant paragraphs or apply heuristics for input. The model's robustness was found to be lacking, as the answers varied when terms like 'data' and 'information' were used interchangeably in the questions.

We used three metrics to measure performance on our test dataset, namely precision, recall, and exact match (EM). Precision, in this context, includes true positive predictions, which consist of cases where the model correctly extracts relevant, complete or partial information. False positives are cases where it extracts incorrect information, but the correct answer is 'None'. Recall is the ratio of true positives to the total number of actual positive cases. In this case, false negatives are cases where the model predicts 'None' rather than extracting information. Exact match measures how often the model's output matches the expected answer exactly. It provides a binary assessment, indicating whether the model's prediction is entirely correct or not. We used it to assess how well the model's answer matches the ground truth.

Table 2. Performance of GPT 3.5 over test data

Question	Precision	Recall	EM
What types of personal information are collected from users?	0.88	0.95	0.15
With whom is this collected personal information shared or sold?	0.67	0.64	0.02
How long does the organization retain users' personal information?	1.0	0.22	0.00
What rights do users possess concerning the data collected by the organization?	0.78	0.27	0.00

Table 2 presents an overview of GPT-3.5's performance across various policies in the test dataset. For the question about the types of personal information collected from users, the model demonstrated a precision of 0.88 and a recall of 0.95, indicating its accuracy in identifying relevant information. However, the EM score was 0.15, suggesting a significant deviation from the expected responses, mainly due to extracting additional information such as log data and website usage data. In the context of the question on sharing or selling personal information, the model achieved a precision of 0.67 and a recall of 0.64, showing relevance in responses but missing details, as indicated by the lower EM score of 0.02. The model encountered challenges with the last two questions about data retention and user rights, achieving perfect precision but a low recall of 0.22, and a precision of 0.78 with a recall of 0.27, respectively. Additionally, both questions had an EM score of 0. It highlights that while the model's answers were correct when generated, it often failed to identify relevant responses, which were mostly 'None' for the last two questions, as evidenced by the low recall scores. These results underscore the variability in GPT-3.5's performance, highlighting the need for significant research, particularly in achieving an exact match with the ground truth responses.

5   Conclusion

In summary, our exploratory study highlights that LLMs like GPT-3.5 can extract information from privacy policies through instruction prompts. Our preliminary testing of its ability to extract detailed information highlights its performance as being of high precision and low recall, as observed in three out of four questions. Furthermore, our study also underscores how these models efficiently overcome the computational challenges that have hindered previous information extraction methods, such as the requirement for extensive training data and the handling of lengthy contexts. Through further refinement of prompts and techniques like few-shot learning, substantial performance improvements can be anticipated. We believe in the foreseeable future, with the emergence of newer and improved LLMs and more robust evaluation datasets, such techniques can become effective tools for information extraction, summarization, and compliance analysis of privacy policies, thereby making it easier to understand and analyze these policies.

6   Appendix

Table 3. Answers generated by BERT and GPT 3.5 from a privacy policy

Question	Answer by PolicyQA BERT	Answer by GPT 3.5
What types of personal information are collected from users?	personal data	name, surname, company location, address, country, payment, invoicing and delivery information
With whom is this collected personal information shared or sold?	personal data with official and selected third party. an example of third party is the distributor in charge of securcube products and services in a specific country. We set our best efforts to establish actions to protect you, respecting your rights, according to the latest international law and regulations. Data are managed securely and we make the official and selected third party aware of the importance of your data and their protection on sharing actions. We may also share your information with suppliers or subcontractors	None
How long does the organization retain users' personal information?	store them	None
What rights do users possess concerning the data collected by the organization?	access to, correction of, blocking and/or deletion (erasure) of your personal data in line with applicable data protection law. You can also withdraw your consent for securcube srl to process your personal data. You can request that your personal data pass to another controller when the process is based on consent or contract. You have the right to ask for a restriction on further processing and object to the processing of your personal data if it has been based on legitimate interest and/or direct marketing. these actions are, generally, for free and have to be managed in a reasonable period of time, anyway within thirty (30) days. To protect the privacy and the personal data collected, securcube srl may ask also for the applicant's information, such as the identity and the right to access to the data	access to, correction of, blocking and/or deletion (erasure) of personal data, withdrawal of consent, data portability, restriction of processing, objection to processing

References

1. Ermakova, T., Baumann, A., Fabian, B., Krasnova, H.: Privacy policies and users' trust: does readability matter? In: AMCIS, August 2014
2. Meinert, D.B., Peterson, D.K., Criswell, J.R., Crossland, M.D.: Privacy policy statements and consumer willingness to provide personal information. J. Electron. Commer. Organ. (JECO) **4**(1), 1–17 (2006)
3. Regulation (EU) 2016/679 of the European Parliament and of the Council (2016). https://data.europa.eu/eli/reg/2016/679/oj
4. Amos, R., Acar, G., Lucherini, E., Kshirsagar, M., Narayanan, A., Mayer, J.: Privacy policies over time: curation and analysis of a million-document dataset. In: Proceedings of the Web Conference 2021, pp. 2165–2176, April 2021
5. Zaeem, R.N., Suzanne Barber, K.: The effect of the GDPR on privacy policies: recent progress and future promise. ACM Trans. Manage. Inf. Syst. **12**(1), 1–20 (2021). https://doi.org/10.1145/3389685
6. Bannihatti Kumar, V., et al.: Finding a choice in a haystack: automatic extraction of opt-out statements from privacy policy text. In: Proceedings of The Web Conference 2020, pp. 1943–1954, April 2020
7. Ravichander, A., Black, A.W., Wilson, S., Norton,T., Sadeh, N.: Question answering for privacy policies: combining computational and legal perspectives. In: Proceedings of the 2019 Conference on Empirical Methods in Natural Language Processing and the 9th International Joint Conference on Natural Language Processing (EMNLP-IJCNLP), pp. 4947-4958, Hong Kong, China. Association for Computational Linguistics (2019)
8. Ahmad, W., Chi, J., Tian, Y., Chang, K.-W.: PolicyQA: a reading comprehension dataset for privacy policies. In: Findings of the Association for Computational Linguistics: EMNLP, pp. 743–749. Online, Association for Computational Linguistics (2020)
9. Zaeem, R.N., German, R.L., Suzanne Barber, K.: PrivacyCheck: automatic summarization of privacy policies using data mining. ACM Trans. Internet Technol. **18**(4), 1–18 (2018). https://doi.org/10.1145/3127519
10. Ahmad, W., Chi, J., Le, T., Norton, T., Tian, Y., Chang, K.-W.: Intent Classification and Slot Filling for Privacy Policies. ACLWeb; Association for Computational Linguistics, 1 August 2021. https://doi.org/10.18653/v1/2021.acl-long.340
11. Kocon, J., et al.: ChatGPT: Jack of all trades, master of none. Inf. Fusion. **99**, 101861 (2023)
12. Agrawal, M., Hegselmann, S., Lang, H., Kim, Y., Sontag, D.: Large language models are few-shot clinical information extractors. In: Proceedings of the 2022 Conference on Empirical Methods in Natural Language Processing, pp. 1998–2022, December 2022
13. Liu, P., Yuan, W., Fu, J., Jiang, Z., Hayashi, H., Neubig, G.: Pre-train, prompt, and predict: a systematic survey of prompting methods in natural language processing. ACM Comput. Surv. **55**(9), 1–35 (2023)
14. Polak, M.P., Morgan, D.: Extracting Accurate Materials Data from Research Papers with Conversational Language Models and Prompt Engineering–Example of ChatGPT (2023). arXiv preprint: arXiv:2303.05352
15. Li, B., et al.: Deliberate then Generate: Enhanced Prompting Framework for Text Generation (2023). arXiv preprint: arXiv:2305.19835
16. Zhao, X., et al.: Domain specialization as the key to make large language models disruptive: a comprehensive survey. arXiv preprint: arXiv:2305.18703 (2023)

17. Wang, Y., Yao, Q., Kwok, J.T., Ni, L.M.: Generalizing from a few examples: a survey on few-shot learning. ACM Comput. Surv. (CSUR) **53**(3), 1–34 (2020)
18. Bang, Y., et al.: A multitask, multilingual, multimodal evaluation of chatgpt on reasoning, hallucination, and interactivity. arXiv preprint: arXiv:2302.04023 (2023)
19. Maynez, J., Narayan, S., Bohnet, B., McDonald, R.: On faithfulness and factuality in abstractive summarization. In: Proceedings of the 58th Annual Meeting of the Association for Computational Linguistics (2020)
20. Ravichander, A., Black, A.W., Norton, T., Wilson, S., Sadeh, N.: Breaking Down Walls of Text: How Can NLP Benefit Consumer Privacy? ACLWeb; Association for Computational Linguistics, 1 August 2021. https://doi.org/10.18653/v1/2021.acl-long.319
21. Mishra, S., Khashabi, D., Baral, C., Choi, Y., Hajishirzi, H.: Reframing Instructional Prompts to GPTk's Language (2021). arXiv:2109.07830
22. Liu, A.T., Xiao, W., Zhu, H., Zhang, D., Li, S.W., Arnold, A.: QaNER: Prompting question answering models for few-shot named entity recognition (2022). arXiv preprint: arXiv:2203.01543
23. Lu, Y., et al.: Unified structure generation for universal information extraction. In: Proceedings of the 60th Annual Meeting of the Association for Computational Linguistics, Volume 1: Long Papers, pp. 5755–5772, Dublin, Ireland. Association for Computational Linguistics (2022)
24. Srinath, M., Wilson, S., Giles, C.L.: Privacy at scale: Introducing the privaseer corpus of web privacy policies (2020). *arXiv preprint* arXiv:2004.1113
25. Rajpurkar, P., Zhang, J., Lopyrev, K., Liang, P.: Squad: 100,000+ questions for machine comprehension of text (2016). *arXiv preprint* arXiv:1606.05250

Information Science and Data Science

Reimagining Data Science Methodology for Community Well-Being Through Intersectional Feminist Voices

Sucheta Lahiri [ID] and LaVerne Gray[(✉)] [ID]

School of Information Studies, Syracuse University, Syracuse, NY 13244, USA
{sulahiri,lgray01}@syr.edu

Abstract. The ethos surrounding data science as a sociotechnical phenomenon is multifaceted. The phenomenon embodies both advantageous and detrimental discourses. On the one hand, data science systems in healthcare offer novel technologies to help private and public institutions aid in better decision-making. On the other hand, facial recognition software often jeopardizes fundamental human rights with invasive and discriminatory algorithms. While making data science systems, practitioners are typically encouraged to execute project management methodology CRISP-DM (Cross Industry Standard Process for Data Mining) to complete projects successfully. Created for data mining projects, CRISP-DM guides the management of data science projects with six phases: business understanding, data understanding, data preparation, modeling, evaluation, and deployment. This work-in-progress conceptual paper uses an intersectional feminist framework to critically analyze CRISP-DM for data science projects. The reimagined intersectional CRISP-DM or InCRISP-DM methodology embraces iterative intersectional feminist interrogation to clarify six standard CRISP-DM workflow phases with four provocations: Learning & Praxis, Harm Reduction, Transformation and Accountability & Transparency. Future work appeals to bringing awareness of transnational risks that can emerge when applying western project management methodologies to countries of the Global South.

Keywords: Intersectionality · Project Management · Data Science · Artificial Intelligence

1 Introduction

Despite the promising developments, there is a growing scholarship on the discriminatory consequences of data science affecting society. This encompasses instances such as biased algorithms recommending unequal healthcare for Black patients compared to white individuals during the COVID-19 pandemic [1] and the failure of scanning machines to correctly identify a nonbinary, transgender, femme-presenting individual [2]. These examples underscore the glaring and exploitative consequences of biases within data science [3].

The biases perpetuating social and ethical risks through the models do not emerge out of thin air. The biases are often rooted in laborious data science practices.

I. Sserwanga et al. (Eds.): iConference 2024, LNCS 14596, pp. 235–252, 2024.
https://doi.org/10.1007/978-3-031-57850-2_18

Discretionary labor starts with problem formulation, data selection, preprocessing, analysis, model development, evaluation, and deployment [4]. Bias may manifest at any phase through the workflow: it can be present from the project's inception, permeate throughout its duration, or emerge towards the end of the workflow, ultimately contributing to data science bias. In short, making data science systems involves specific social agents who contribute human labor through sense-making and discretionary decision-making [4, 5]. The actions that revolve around tasks like problem formulation, translation processes, and analysis can potentially introduce biases into data science systems.

Data science projects as sociotechnical systems are recommended to follow project management methodologies or process models to manage and accelerate the project to success [6–8]. CRoss Industry Standard Process for Data Mining or CRISP-DM is one such highly recommended methodology for managing data science projects [7, 9]. The conceptual approach of CRISP-DM methodology follows an over-simplistic positivist paradigm for managing projects within the bounds of cost, time, and resources [10, 11].

Established in the nineties, CRISP-DM is one of the standard knowledge discovery methodologies that expands the Knowledge Discovery in Databases (KDD) process [6, 12]. The methodology borrows the process efficiency approach from 6σ, the automation approach from 5 A's process, and technical perspectives from SEMMA (Sample, Explore, Modify, Model, and Assess) to create a de facto process model for data mining [6].

The genesis of CRISP-DM can be attributed to a collaboration between expert engineers from DaimlerChrysler, SPSS, and NCR. Established in the late 1990s by this EU consortium, the primary drive behind CRISP-DM was to offer a western-centric, adaptable, and pragmatic framework tailored for data mining projects [6]. Culture, industry, and sector-agnostic CRISP-DM was developed to bring cost-effectiveness, generalizability, reliability, repeatability, manageability, and efficiency to data mining project execution. The methodology gained widespread popularity, and there was a prevailing sentiment to introduce 'speed-dial,' a normalized practice among text mining practitioners to bring time efficiency. Data mining was itself an extractive technology to derive knowledge insights.

During the project execution with CRISP-DM, the primary emphasis was saving time with fail fast and learning faster approach. The business goals were contemplated with material benefits without adequately considering the direct impact on underrepresented groups based on race, gender, ethnicity, class, sexuality, and ability.

Rooted in the concept of interconnectedness of identities, this work-in-progress conceptual paper draws upon Crenshaw's intersectionality framework [13, 14, 28] to critically analyze the phases of a de-facto project methodology for data science projects: CRISP-DM. The rationale behind using intersectional theory for critiquing CRISP-DM is to examine the interconnected systems of privilege and voice of resistance [41] that translate through regimented project methodology. It is noteworthy that the fundamental stage of CRISP-DM problem formulation offers an agency to a few privileged social agents to make decisions on business goals, choice of data, and model selection [4]. The intersectional framework is introduced to highlight 'the practice of willful blindness'

[16] across the work cycle that goes behind the foundation of CRISP-DM methodology for data science projects.

The paper begins by tracing the genealogy of positivistic project management methodologies, with a particular focus on the evolution of the neoliberal foundation of CRISP-DM. Second, the authors define the intersectionality framework and clarify each phase of CRISP-DM using the intersectionality lens. Lastly, CRISP-DM for data science projects is re-envisioned with an evolving intersectionality framework for data science InCRISP-DM. The transformed methodology InCRISP-DM is rooted in the iterative guidelines of Learning & Praxis, Harm Reduction, Transformation, and Accountability & Transparency.

2 Genealogy of Project Management: A Positivist Paradigm

The concept of project management existed before the industrial revolution and was rooted in military, religious institutions, and civil administrations. An illustrative example can be observed in managing bridge construction within the military during China's Ming Dynasty from the 13th to the 16th century [17]. Following the Industrial Revolution and amidst World War I, scientists and engineers like Henri Fayol, Elton Mayo, and Frederick Winslow Taylor actively excelled in their research on productivity and the allocation of tasks within manufacturing facilities. Fayol proposed five aspects of project management that encompass planning, organizing, commanding, coordinating, and controlling. Introducing Gantt charts as a power artifact to streamline projects into a specific roadmap created a control measure for practitioners. Implementing Ford's assembly lines to bring labor efficiency further pushed project management to emerge as a best practice [18].

The advent of the mainframe and exponential growth of IT projects from the 1950s to 1970s gave rise to the need for dedicated project management professionals and certificates. PERT (Program Evaluation and Review Technique) and CPM (Critical Path Method) with IPMA (Institutionalization of International Project Management Association) and PMBOK (The Project Management Body of Knowledge) with Project Management Institute (PMI) in the 1960s introduced formal bodies of project management and commercialized the standard protocols [19].

With the burgeoning scholarship within information systems and PMBOK, project management was gradually accepted as an instrument of control. Multiple definitions of projects emerged that echoed this sentiment. The project was interpreted as a time constrained organizational effort hinged on the triad of (1) cost, (2) time (3) quality. Other essential components that decided the fate of the project were (1) a goal-oriented and time-limited plan, (2) efficient coordination and communication among team members, and (3) user participation. Despite its polysemic nature, the concept of a project and the overarching process of project management were guided by goal-oriented standardized procedures within a positivist paradigm [10, 11, 20].

The principles of the positivist paradigm are rooted in experiences that, in turn, establish norms and procedures. In other words, positivist school of thought holds that truth is always objective and based on experiences that are detached from any personal bias or subjectivity. In the context of project management for western culture, it was typically the case that "Man builds Reality", which appeared protocol-aligned, technicist, objective, masculine, and driven with economic benefits [11].

Notably, with the popularity of masculine project management standards with PMI, these agencies became pertinent entities and points of reference for practitioners. The dominant perspectives of project management disseminated through these organizations directed practitioners to circumvent their thoughts on increasing material benefits with respect to costing, budgeting, customer involvement, and human resources without considering who can get victimized by the functionalist approach [22]. The reductionist application of project charter to execute a project through task-bound project management methodology hid the contours of coercion, repression, racialization, and objectification. With normative standards, project management primarily promoted a technocratic and utilitarian approach focused on achieving desired outcomes by enforcing surveillance.

3   Project Management Methodology CRISP-DM in Data Science

Project management methodologies (PMM) are considered as the action-based instruments that enable measuring progress, efficiency, and task control. According to the PMBOK [19] guide, PMM creates a standardized process and a benchmark for practitioners to develop a common understanding of project success [23]. In other words, PMM consists of various procedures, principles, and practices, all contributing to the effective management of a project. PMM creates a documented ordered checklist for the practitioners and reinforces in them the 'right way' of doing the project. PMM typically aligns with a project management approach that sets the workflow [24]. The interest in following project methodology for data science projects stems from CRISP-DM methodology that manufacturing market players developed to tame business processes (see Fig. 1). There are six instructive and iterative phases of CRISP-DM suggested for data science practitioners: business understanding, data understanding, data preparation, modeling, evaluation, and deployment [7, 25]. Alongside the six phases, four ordered levels of abstraction drive the project from generic to specific tasks [26]. The four levels of abstraction are supplemented by a user guide to limit the data science practitioners to follow along normative best practices.

PMM intends to reinforce a standard ontology and follow an iterative workflow to achieve efficiency for project success. The success criteria are left to the practitioners' discretion, and the iterative phases are instructed to meet broader levels of project milestones. The level of abstraction opens many unanswered questions to the practitioners, leaving them to slice and dice the success criteria without actively considering the social and ethical risks [7] that could adversely impact the well-being of marginalized communities.

Part of CRISP-DM's standardization is to create dedicated work responsibilities and accountability to foster common understanding and interpretations regardless of unequal social standings of gender, class, race, or ethnicity [13, 27]. In other words, the standard approach for data science practitioners who follow CRISP-DM is to follow designated tasks built around impenetrable processes. The overarching goal of these methodologies is to naturalize the standards that do not entertain the subjectivities and possible

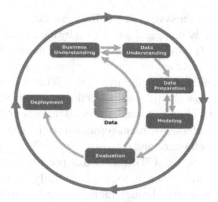

Fig. 1. CRISP-DM Workflow [22]

interconnectedness of data with specific gendered spaces, vulnerable geographies, and communities in general.

However, it is noteworthy that the task-oriented process methodology was developed before the big data surge. As such, these process methodologies failed to consider data heterogeneity and inherent subjectivities [6]. This cursory approach to data, combined with the Eurocentric leanings of CRISP-DM, echoes the 'god trick' [28] - a concept suggesting a positivist viewpoint that observes issues of gender, race, ethnicity, and disability from a detached stance [29]. This 'god trick' metaphor suggests a form of perception that offers an omniscient yet circumscribed knowledge from a position of authority. Within data science, CRISP-DM delivers logical yet detached guidelines for algorithm development, presenting a 'view from nowhere' that masks the stories of those with lived experiences.

4 Intersectionality in CRISP-DM: Commitment to Transformation

With theoretical roots in the works of [30–32], the intersectionality framework brings to light the experiential knowledge of Black women marginalized by the US legal system, highlighting classist and racist dimensions. Drawing from critical race theory, intersectionality asserts that social inequality and the distribution of power within a society are best comprehended not through a singular axis of social division, such as race, gender, or class, but through the intricate interplay of multiple axes that intersect and mutually influence one another [33, 34]. In other words, the framework illuminates how entrenched power dynamics grounded in the dominant and subordinate narratives limit the life opportunities of intersectional individuals existing in a specific social order. When integrated into data science, intersectionality provides a lens to examine erasure, oppression, and exclusion while managing sociotechnical systems. Simultaneously, the framework draws attention to the forces of oppression while highlighting power within the margins.

In the context of data science, this conceptual paper employs an intersectional framework to highlight the pervasive influence of project management methodologies on sociotechnical systems. The intersectional lens brings into light the agents of power and their performativity within these systems, revealing how various stakeholders, processes, and technologies dynamically shape and are shaped by the project management methodologies. The analysis reveals how the normative data science workflow interplay, particularly with CRISP-DM, perpetuates and even amplifies existing societal inequalities - a phenomenon termed "technological redlining" [35]. When viewed through the lens of intersectionality, we argue that algorithmic biases do not remain solely as technical problems. The biases intersect with institutional protocols, epistemic privilege of elite social agents in the institutional hierarchy, management models, and various social categorizations like race, gender, ethnicity, and economic status. The intersectional framework allows us to analyze each phase of CRISP-DM that practitioners follow and the biases lying within. The framework pushes us to think carefully about how these normative workflows impact social structures through racialized and sexualized systems of power.

The intersectional framework is employed to disclose the politics of data science project management methodologies and the human ideologies that work behind the model development. As data science systems are the 'proxies for the people who made them' [36], intersectionality is used to explore the dominant work practices and underlying principles behind the development of data science systems.

5 Transformation of CRISP-DM Through Intersectionality

Making a data science system is 'an exercise in worldbuilding' [37]. Data science practitioners exercise normative practices to imprint their worldviews onto the technology during the making. In diverse contexts, the models often reproduce and perpetuate components of structural racist practices through the established normative worldview. For example, the misinterpretation of Google Maps reading 'X' as a Roman letter for Malcolm X Boulevard is a signifier of how social codes are created that embody racialized beliefs and the underrepresentation of diverse populations in the STEM field. Similar incidents of racialized assessment scores with the ProPublica algorithm reinforce the 'New Jim Code' [37], underscoring the pervasive and concerning issue of bias within technology [36]. While various factors can contribute to these biases, one prominent and significant factor for bias is the skewed training data behind the making of data science systems. Data itself acts as the power that centralizes privilege to one specific population, pushing an(other) to the margin.

This work uses Black feminist epistemology [15, 41, 43] and interrogates techno-deterministic project management methodology as a power-driven tool. Through Black feminist thought [38], we probe how instruction-based project management methodology influences the interests of practitioners thinking towards material benefits and business goals rather than addressing social and ethical risks [7] of discriminatory algorithms. The analysis further navigates through the entire workflow defined by CRISP-DM with an intersectionality lens and clarifies how the process model augments hegemonic normativity in system development. Through the intersectionality lens, we transform the standard methodology, rooted in action and activism, and decentralize the matrix of domination [39] with justice-centered data science methodology. In transforming CRISP-DM, our collective and distinct feminist voices challenge the 'master's house' [40] of normative data science practices.

The collective voice [42, 44] of intersectional feminists through the reimagined intersectional CRISP-DM framework or InCRISP-DM (see Fig. 2) underscores what is missing in the normative methodology [42]. Rather than being prescriptive, InCRISP-DM embodies a reflexive endeavor [44] to rejuvenate the phases by integrating concepts pertinent to marginalized perspectives. This transformation may encompass critical examination, rephrasing, and adopting borrowed terminologies and frameworks [5, 45, 46]. The prefix "In" in InCRISP-DM foregrounds three foundational principles: (1) decentralizing the control management established by power structures, (2) leveraging experiential knowledge to make the methodology inclusive, and (3) fostering grassroots-led collaboration with community stakeholders [47].

5.1 InCRISP-DM: Intersectional CRISP-DM for Data Science

The standard CRISP-DM is a generalized instruction-based methodology that symbolizes prescriptive and top-down, enforcing a rigid sequence and hierarchy approach. Even being iterative, the circular diagram of CRISP-DM is enclosed with two-and-from bidirectional arrows to specific phases. While efficient in certain contexts, such a structured methodology inadvertently perpetuates systems of power by imposing a circumvented path of progression and limiting the agency of those who engage with it. On one hand, the conventional workflow of CRISP-DM mandates data science practitioners to adhere strictly to a predetermined set of guidelines at every phase. InCRISP-DM, on the other hand, creates agility with a flexible workflow and critical interrogation, decentralizing the systems of power.

To decentralize the systems of power and foster a more inclusive and flexible approach, we start with the removal of the arrows in the circular diagram for InCRISP-DM (see Fig. 2). By doing so, we challenge the dominant narrative of a compartmentalized process and open up spaces for diverse voices and experiential knowledge to shape the trajectory of data mining projects. This act of 'de-arrowing' can be seen as intersectional feminist intervention, aiming to dismantle prescriptive hierarchies and promote a more collaborative, participatory, and equitable approach to data science.

The four sides of InCRISP-DM quadrants offer four guidelines embedded in the transformed methodology. The six transformed phases of standard CRISP-DM foreground in the four iterative guidelines borrowed from Operational Intersectionality Framework [45]. Although the Operational Intersectionality Framework is not directed towards data science, the guidelines apply to all the realms of social justice that are aligned with the well-being of marginalized communities. The four guidelines of InCRISP-DM are: (1) learning and sense-making through marginalized community experiences and turning the knowledge into meaningful praxis, (2) transformation of functionalist and objective data science workflow practices to social justice practices that can augment the voices of the invisible, (3) accountability through creating data science models for social good (4) performing ethical data science practices during the execution of the projects that cause harm reduction strategies for systematically marginalized groups.

The four guidelines are cyclical and employed at each workflow phase. The iterative feminist interrogation is conducted at every phase of InCRISP-DM, from business

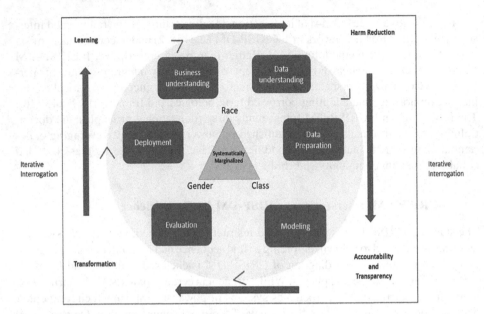

Fig. 2. InCRISP-DM Workflow

understanding, data understanding, data preparation, modeling, evaluation, and deployment of data science models. The interrogations attempt to detect and address traces of bias in the workflow and contested spaces of privilege that can reinforce structural inequalities and strengthen systems of power.

During the data science project execution, InCRISP-DM creates prompts to probe critical inquiries for data science practitioners, such as: while the project execution and model deployment is going on, how can we actively participate in making thought-provoking praxis that surpass the thick, impenetrable walls of systems of oppression? How can we identify and address the individual biases that culminate through various social and political factors of the beings? How can we make sure that technology and experiential knowledge are not abused? How can we design technology that can be inclusive for all?

We possibly cannot remediate all the harms overnight that are caused by data science project management through the InCRISP-DM. The framework is ever-dynamic and ever-evolving that welcomes further contribution from a diverse set of social activists, queer feminist scholars, disability scholars, social scientists, and members of marginalized communities who can contribute to sense-making, sharing lived experiences, vulnerabilities with productive and creative praxis. The framework keeps evolving as an organism with time, adapting and incorporating intersectional perspectives into each iteration.

Table 1 above paints a comparative picture of two project management methodologies: CRISP-DM and the InCRISP-DM. Six rows to the table have six dedicated entries of project management methodology phases described. The first column indicates the presence of standard CRISP-DM used extensively by data science practitioners

Table 1. CRISP-DM Phases and Intersectional Transformation to InCRISP-DM

CRISP-DM Phase	CRISP-DM Description	InCRISP-DM Description
Business Understanding	Translating business goals into measurable problem formulation, design plan, understanding client's expectations, describe success criteria, factfinding behind assumptions [26]	Recognition of the co-constitution of data science and society to break the pattern of bias [5], critical reflexivity, identifying power imbalances among social agents, plurality of subjectivities, and sense-making [9]
Data Understanding	Collecting initial data, attributes, identifying data quality errors, inquiries to explore concealed data patterns for hypotheses testing, 'gross' properties of data, and basic descriptive statistics to understand data distribution [26]	FAIR2 (Findable, Accessible, Interoperable, and Reusable) framework for social good [45], critical inquiries on data, acknowledging data as value-laden and context-heavy [48]
Data Preparation	Creating a final data set from the initial 'raw' data that can be used for the data science model with an iterative process. Transforming and cleansing the data to make it suitable for modeling tools [26]	Identifying power nodes to de-centralize data ownership, iterative interrogation, engagement with communities from diverse backgrounds, acknowledging agents of knowledge rather than objects of knowledge, critical inquiry [34], opt-out option for subjects [49]
Modeling	Identifying and implementing modeling techniques fine-tuning the parameters to achieve optimal values for meeting business objectives. Revisit the data preparation phase in order to accommodate data format prerequisites [26]	Directed Acyclic Graphs [60], acknowledging the diversity of experiences and identities, collaborative efforts across diverse communities, challenging false dichotomies, embracing diverse data sources and interpretations, scrutinizing power dynamics in data, understanding the broader context of data sources, acknowledging the emotional and physical experiences tied to data, and highlighting the efforts behind data collection and processing [34]

(continued)

Table 1. (*continued*)

CRISP-DM Phase	CRISP-DM Description	InCRISP-DM Description
Evaluation	Evaluation of model(s) to make sure that model effectively aligns with the business objectives and identifies any potentially overlooked important business issues, mathematical equation to highlight results and findings, Sandbox, and testing environments [26]	Intersectional group fairness, multi-calibration, risk subgroup fairness, inviting feedback from community members or organizations [50]
Deployment	Facilitating the knowledge gained with the model to the customers and organizations for making informed decisions, the final report presented to management, focus on accuracy, modification to the application domain, any updates to the model, and new data [26]	Collaboration with external grassroots organizations and social activists to implement feedback, source code, and documentation on the lifecycle of model development Model performance that can be accessible to diverse community members, regular audits by non-profit organizations, regular audits [34, 51]

to initiate, manage, and deploy the project in a commercial setup. The second column reimagines the methodology transformed with the intersectional feminist framework, InCRISP-DM.

Below are the six phases of the InCRISP-DM methodology that are broadly critiqued, 'seeded with a vision of what can and should be, and not only a critique of what is' [52].

Business Understanding

In the first stage of industrial CRISP-DM for data science project execution, the emphasis is on comprehending the objective project goals and requisites from a business point of view. This understanding is subsequently translated into a measurable data mining problem definition. Creating an initial project plan is then tailored to accomplish the business objectives [26].

InCRISP-DM, on the other hand, prompts data science professionals to recognize the mutual constitution of data science and society in the problem formulation phase [5]. It is also important to acknowledge that the co-constitution of social and technological elements perpetually favors some and systematically disadvantages the other. In other words, InCRISP-DM reinforces the thought that power is distributed unequally and needs to be identified and decentralized right at the birth of model development [37].

During the initial phases of objective setting, the transformed and reimagined methodology emphasizes the implications of racism, sexism, and ableism. InCRISP-DM prioritizes critical reflexivity [78], which involves consciously and actively interrogating the coexistence of privilege and oppression within the power-laden team structure. By engaging in this introspective process, the practitioners can uncover and negotiate power imbalances among social agents, and work towards fostering harmony and celebrating social justice for marginalized individuals and communities [5].

InCRISP-DM recognizes the positionality of data science practitioners who can carve business goals based on their own social, cultural, and personal contexts. Instead of dismissing the subjectivities as mere biases, InCRISP-DM prompts that they are acknowledged, articulated, and incorporated into business problem for a situated worldview [28].

Data Understanding
In the standard approach of CRISP-DM, the data understanding phase initiates with aggregating the data, comprehending the data, identifying data quality errors, and inquiries to explore concealed data patterns for hypotheses testing [26]. Data is defined with 'gross' properties without exploring who is counted in the data and who is not. Additionally, data is considered monolith and objective without considering various intersecting identities that one individual may contain. The data attributes considered on standard CRISP-DM are basic descriptive statistics such as average, maximum, minimum, and standard deviation. In other words, data is homogenized behind the common measure of central tendencies. The data construed as objective and devoid of value advertently silences or erases the experiences of marginalized groups. By focusing on CRISP-DM data understanding phase, narratives of the dominant population are highlighted, further marginalizing those who don't fit within the standard norms. The data understanding phase does not add any context of population bias that may disadvantage intersectional identities and create privacy issues.

InCRISP-DM advocates FAIR2 framework [46] for the data understanding phase, which builds upon the FAIRification principles (Findable, Accessible, Interoperable, and Reusable). FAIR2 adds four principles specific to working with social science data for social impact: Frame, Articulate, Identify, and Report. This framework aims to bridge the gap between researchers, practitioners, and the communities represented in the data. The FAIR2 framework acknowledges that observational data mirrors societal discrimination and emphasizes the need for a clear framework to address these biases, thereby harnessing data science's potential to support social justice. Using the 'frame' tenet [46] of the framework, InCRISP-DM opens the following critical inquiries to the data science practitioners:

- What is the origin of data?
- How has the data changed over time and location?
- How can the experiential knowledge of systematically underrepresented community determine the distribution of data?
- How may the data, if used for model development, affect the systematically disadvantaged groups?

FAIR2 framework is informed by data science and community-based research that integrates Frame, Articulate, Identify, and Report tenets for handling social science data to achieve meaningful societal impact. InCRISP-DM employs the Frame principle to understand who might be harmed or overlooked during the data collection phase.

Data Preparation

In the third phase of standard CRISP-DM, all data science activities involved in constructing the final dataset from the initial 'raw' data are encompassed within the data preparation phase [26]. Data is often perceived as impartial, unbiased, and factual, devoid of any intrinsic meaning. Data does not contain any face value and remains abstract.

InCRISP-DM starts with the assumption that data can never be 'raw' [48]. Therefore, data exist within a specific context, subject to change, interconnected, and influenced by frameworks. Data are utilized in context to attain specific objectives. Data possesses inherent power, and this power is bestowed upon those who possess ownership of the data.

InCRISP-DM framework enlightens practitioners about this power dynamic and works towards decentralizing data ownership. An initiative to decentralize power is to engage annotators [53] from diverse backgrounds to create training datasets for model development. Iterative interrogation is conducted to ensure data is not skewed towards specific social elites.

During the data preparation phase, InCRISP-DM resists dehumanizing the data by construing subjects behind the data as *agents of knowledge* rather than *objects of knowledge* [54]. This not only amplifies the voices and validates diverse perspectives but also helps us comprehend how to design data science systems that will be inclusive for all. The data preparation phase also induces an opt-out [49] option for the subjects so that they can choose to remain out of the participant pool.

The reimagined InCRISP-DM appeals to a deeper dive into the genealogy of data by presenting the following questions to the data science practitioners [48]:

- What circumstances paved the way for the emergence of data as we know it?
- Who owns the data, oversees its creation and interpretation? What drives their objectives and actions?
- Who are the primary subjects representing the data, and what insights are they generating?
- How does data influence the shaping of society?
- What future actions should be taken regarding data, and what alternative insights might it offer?

Modelling

During this phase of modeling with standard CRISP-DM, normative modeling assumptions are made based on data quality and data format. Diverse algorithm methods such as decision tree or neural network are then selected and implemented, with their parameters adjusted to achieve optimal values. Typically, multiple techniques exist for the same data mining problem, each with specific data format requirements. Consequently, often, the methodology recommends revisiting the data preparation phase to ensure compatibility with the selected techniques [26]. After the model development, the model is ranked based on the business objectives and success criteria. In other words, the primary focus of CRISP-DM modeling phase is on selecting the algorithms, techniques, and parameters to build a predictive model that meet business objectives. As only the format and data quality are considered as attributes, by not addressing intersectionality, the model development phase completely overlooks the systemic bias. It follows a 'one size fits all' solution.

InCRISP-DM methodology directs the practitioners to create causal diagrams (e.g., Directed Acyclic Graphs) of model presuppositions and possible hazards to individuals of intersecting identities [60]. Any chosen modeling techniques must reduce harm of bias and safeguard the protected intersectional attributes. For example, Black queer women-related attributes must be protected with overall underrepresented women of various gendered and ethnic identities.

The reimagined methodology resists weaving ideas around a singular approach to interpreting data modeling. Additionally, the model development phase refutes the idea of risks oversimplifying complex human experiences into mere data points. On the contrary, InCRISP-DM recognizes the multiplicity of experiences and identities, suggesting that model development cannot be anchored to just one perspective. InCRISP-DM demands collaborative efforts across diverse communities, each bringing their unique nuances, challenges, and insights. This dynamic process transforms the singular methodology into a rather fluid and adaptive workflow.

Drawing inspiration from the principles proposed by [34], the model development phase of InCRISP-DM is enhanced by challenging false dichotomies, embracing diverse data sources and interpretations, scrutinizing power dynamics in data, understanding the broader context of data sources, acknowledging the emotional and physical experiences tied to data, and highlighting the efforts behind data collection and processing.

Evaluation
In the evaluation phase, there is an absence of a feedback loop from the evaluation phase to the modeling phase in the standard CRISP-DM. The evaluation phase is looped back to the business understanding phase which advertently conveys that the evaluation criteria should resonate with business success criteria in the business understanding phase. In this phase, data science system is evaluated to make sure that all the business objectives are met with the model [26]. The outcome of a data science project is defined with a mathematical equation where the results are an aggregate of models and findings. The quantitative metrics place a premium on measurable, and statistically reductionist results overlooking the experiential knowledge and lived experiences of particularly for individuals situated at the crossroads of multiple marginalized identities. Sandbox and testing environments are recommended to test the model and assess if the model resonates with business success criteria [26].

As opposed to CRISP-DM that provides instructions to either move ahead with deployment phase or business understanding phase, InCRISP-DM methodology does not add any instructive arrows (see Fig. 1) within the phases. The decentralization of barricaded workflow is to acknowledge the need of exploratory nature of data science. Also, the arrows dictate the workflow to move in definite directions without the flexibility to move back to any phase of the workflow to correct systemic bias. The reimagined InCRISP-DM evaluation phase includes the criteria of intersectional group fairness [50]. Intersectional fairness in data science is a growing area of research that seeks to address biases and disparities that arise from the intersections of multiple protected attributes, such as race, gender, ethnicity, age, and more. Some key methods that can be used for evaluation criteria for intersectional fairness are multi-calibration, risk subgroup fairness, and differential fairness for the intersection of members belonging to multiple groups, also called subgroups. The InCRISP-DM methodology also advocates inviting feedback from community members or organizations that could offer experiential knowledge of the social challenges under study [46].

Deployment
The final stage of deployment for standard CRISP-DM consists of documenting the output of data science projects into tangible attributes. The deployment stage also advocates monitoring the data science model with an exhaustive deployment strategy plan. There is also an emphasis on maintaining a final report and a presentation to the senior management. The deployment phase focuses on accuracy, modification to the application domain, any updates to the model, and new data. However, no mention is made of the impact that the model may have on the underrepresented communities. While the section mentions identifying target groups for the report, it does not emphasize the importance of including representatives from intersectional groups. Engaging with intersectional groups can provide valuable feedback and insights that might be overlooked otherwise. The deployment section does not discuss the importance of gathering feedback from diverse groups post-deployment. Lastly, the presentation report is tailored to suit the needs of stakeholders sitting high-up on the management hierarchy, reinforcing the power structure.

InCRISP-DM advocates adding a deployment phase with monitoring and feedback in the last phase. The methodology recommends documenting the lifecycle of the model with the source code in digestible language that can be accessible to members of the community.

In the last phase, the reimagined methodology recommends collaboration with external grassroot organizations and social activists to implement feedback [34]. Also, the report on the entire lifecycle and performance of the model must be distributed to the community members. Post the deployment, an audit framework is recommended to assess the ethical and social risks of data science systems [51].

5.2 Possible Applications of InCRISP-DM

The InCRISP-DM methodology, though still in its ever-growing stage, is illuminated by several case studies showcasing its potential. These instances not only validate the applicability of InCRISP-DM in tangible data science endeavors but also emphasize its pivotal role in addressing intersectional challenges.

- Recommender Systems for 'No-Shows': Adhering to InCRISP-DM ensures commitment to accountability and harm reduction guidelines. During the data preparation phase, an opt-out feature can empower patrons to exclude themselves from the sample population [55]. Tools like Directed Acyclic Graphs can be employed to discern potential harms arising from the model.
- Ride Hailing Algorithms: Algorithms that exhibit bias by quoting inequitable prices for trips, especially towards non-white patrons, can benefit from the InCRISP-DM framework. Incorporating feedback loops with community members is essential. The data understanding phase should recognize genealogy of data and distribution. The

evaluation phase must test the model predictions for marginalized groups before deployment [57].

6 Conclusion

Data science models are extensively used by decision makers to generate knowledge insights. Despite the development of data science as a phenomenon, there are multiple incidents of algorithmic repression that calls for the need of better project management methodologies for data science. The success of data science projects and the dismantling of power structure can't be discussed unless there are critical enquiries posed behind the workflows. In this regard, this in-progress conceptual paper reimagines one of the popular project management methodologies CRISP-DM to InCRISP-DM by using intersectionality framework. The reimagined InCRISP-DM methodology introduced in this paper is characterized by its embrace of iterative intersectional feminist interrogation. It has led to the development of six transformed InCRISP-DM workflow phases, each aligned with the provocations of Learning & Praxis, Harm Reduction, Transformation, and Accountability & Transparency. These phases prioritize well-being, wisdom of experiential knowledge, inclusivity, equity, and social justice throughout the data science project lifecycle.

In our future work, we put forth the idea of employing culture-centric intersectional methodologies that specifically tackle the detrimental effects of utilizing a culture-agnostic approach in developing countries of Global South. We recognize the need to go beyond a utilitarian perspective and instead adopt approaches that are sensitive to the cultural context and unique challenges present in Global South [57].

References

1. Challen, R., Denny, J., Pitt, M., et al.: Artificial intelligence, bias and clinical safety. BMJ Qual. Saf. **28**(3), 231–237 (2019)
2. Costanza-Chock, S.: Design Justice: Community-Led Practices to Build the Worlds We Need. The MIT Press, Cambridge (2020)
3. Joyce, K., Smith-Doerr, L., Alegria, S., et al.: Toward a sociology of artificial intelligence: a call for research on inequalities and structural change. Socius **7**, 2378023121999581 (2021)
4. Passi, S., Barocas, S.: Problem formulation and fairness. In: Proceedings of the Conference on Fairness, Accountability, and Transparency, pp. 39–48 (2019)
5. Neff, G., Tanweer, A., Fiore-Gartland, B., Osburn, L.: Critique and contribute: a practice based framework for improving critical data studies and data science. Big Data **5**(2), 85–97 (2017)
6. Martínez-Plumed, F., Contreras-Ochando, L., Ferri, C., et al.: CRISP-DM twenty years later: from data mining processes to data science trajectories. IEEE Trans. Knowl. Data Eng. **33**(8), 3048–3061 (2019)
7. Lahiri, S., Saltz, J.: The need for an enhanced process methodology for ethical data science projects. In: IEEE Ethics 2023: Ethics in the Global Innovation Helix (2023)
8. Martinez, I., Viles, E., Olaizola, I.G.: Data science methodologies: current challenges and future approaches. Big Data Res. **24**, 100183 (2021)

9. Aho, T., Sievi-Korte, O., Kilamo, T., Yaman, S., Mikkonen, T.: Demystifying data science projects: a look on the people and process of data science today. In: Morisio, M., Torchiano, M., Jedlitschka, A. (eds.) PROFES 2020. LNCS, vol. 12562, pp. 153–167. Springer, Cham (2020). https://doi.org/10.1007/978-3-030-64148-1_10

10. Gustavsson, T.K., Hallin, A.: Rethinking dichotomization: a critical perspective on the use of "hard" and "soft" in project management research. Int. J. Project Manag. **32**(4), 568–577 (2014)

11. Bredillet, C.: Beyond the positivist mirror: towards a project management'gnosis'. In: Proceedings of the 6th Biannual International Research Network on Organising by Projects (IRNOP) Research Conference, pp. 1–25. International Research Network on Organising by Projects (IRNOP) (2004)

12. Fayyad, U., Piatetsky-Shapiro, G., Smyth, P.: The KDD process for extracting useful knowledge from volumes of data. Commun. ACM **39**(11), 27–34 (1996)

13. Winchester, H., Boyd, A.E., Johnson, B.: An exploration of intersectionality in software development and use. In: Proceedings of the Third Workshop on Gender Equality, Diversity, and Inclusion in Software Engineering, pp. 67–70 (2022)

14. Collins, P.H.: Fighting Words: Black Women and the Search for Justice, vol. 7. University of Minnesota Press, Minneapolis (1998)

15. Winberry, J., Gray, L., Hardy, J., Jaber, B., Mehra, B.: Conceptualizing relevance of information as a social justice issue: an interactive panel discussion. Proc. Assoc. Inf. Sci. Technol. **58**(1), 667–672 (2021)

16. Tormos, F.: Intersectional solidarity. Polit. Groups Identities **5**(4), 707–720 (2017)

17. Lock, D.: Project Management. Routledge, London (2020)

18. Seymour, T., Hussein, S.: The history of project management. Int. J. Manag. Inf. Syst. (IJMIS) **18**(4), 233–240 (2014)

19. Guide, A.: Project management body of knowledge (pmbok® guide). In: Project Management Institute, vol. 11, pp. 7–8 (2001)

20. Atkinson, R., Crawford, L., Ward, S.: Fundamental uncertainties in projects and the scope of project management. Int. J. Project Manag. **24**(8), 687–698 (2006)

21. Introduction to CRISP-DM. https://www.ibm.com/docs/en/spss-modeler/18.2.0?topic=guide-introduction-crisp-dm. Accessed 16 Sept 2023

22. Whitty, S.J., Schulz, M.F.: The PM bok code. In: 20th IPMA World Congress on Project Management: Congress Proceedings, vol. 1, pp. 466–472. International Project Management Association (IPMA) (2006)

23. Ozmen, E.S.: Project management methodology (PMM): how can PMM serve organisations today?. In: Proceedings of PMI Global Congress EMEA (2013)

24. Jovanovic, P., Beric, I.: Analysis of the available project management methodologies. Manag. J. Sustain. Bus. Manag. Solutions Emerg. Econ. **23**(3), 1–13 (2018)

25. Lahiri, S., Saltz, J.: Evaluating Data Science Project Agility by Exploring Process Frameworks Used by Data Science Teams (2023)

26. Chapman, P., Clinton, J., Kerber, R., et al.: CRISP-DM 1.0: step-by-step data mining guide. SPSS Inc **9**(13), 1–73 (2000)

27. Boyd, A.E.: Intersectionality and reflexivity-decolonizing methodologies for the data science process. Patterns **2**(12), 100386 (2021)

28. Haraway, D.: Situated knowledges: the science question in feminism and the privilege of partial perspective. Fem. Stud. **14**(3), 575–599 (1988)

29. Lykke, N.: Non-innocent Intersections of Feminism and Environmentalism. Kvinder, Køn & Forskning (2009)

30. Collins, P.H., Bilge, S.: Intersectionality. Wiley, Hoboken (2020)

31. Hooks, B.: Ain't I a Woman: Black Women and Feminism. South End Press, Cambridge (1981)

32. Crenshaw, K.W.: Mapping the margins: intersectionality, identity politics, and violence against women of color. In: The Public Nature of Private Violence, pp. 93–118. Routledge, London (2013)
33. Rankin, Y.A., Thomas, J.O., Joseph, N.M.: Intersectionality in HCI: lost in translation. Interactions **27**(5), 68–71 (2020)
34. Suresh, H., Movva, R., Dogan, A.L., et al.: Towards intersectional feminist and participatory ML: a case study in supporting feminicide counterdata collection. In: Proceedings of the 2022 ACM Conference on Fairness, Accountability, and Transparency, pp. 667–678 (2022)
35. Noble, S.U.: Algorithms of oppression. In: Algorithms of Oppression. New York University Press, New York (2018)
36. Broussard, M.: Artificial Unintelligence: How Computers Misunderstand the World. MIT Press, Cambridge (2018)
37. Benjamin, R.: Race after technology: abolitionist tools for the new Jim code (2020)
38. Schelenz, L.: Artificial intelligence between oppression and resistance: black feminist perspectives on emerging technologies. In: Hanemaayer, A. (eds.) Artificial Intelligence and Its Discontents. Social and Cultural Studies of Robots and AI, pp. 225–249. Springer, Cham (2022). https://doi.org/10.1007/978-3-030-88615-8_11
39. Collins, P.H.: Learning from the outsider within: the sociological significance of Black feminist thought. Soc. Probl. **33**(6), s14–s32 (1986)
40. Gray, L., Duan, Y.: Positioning social justice in a black feminist information activist community context: a case study of African American activist-mothers in Chicago's public housing. In: Social Justice Design and Implementation in Library and Information Science, pp. 103–115. Routledge, London (2021)
41. Gray, L.: Case study inquiry & black feminist resistance. Int. J. Inf. Divers. Inclus. **5**(2), 71–83 (2021)
42. Gray, L.: In a collective voice: uncovering the Black feminist information community of activist-mothers in Chicago Public Housing, 1955–1970
43. Collins, P.H.: Gender, black feminism, and black political economy. Ann. Am. Acad. Pol. Soc. Sci. **568**(1), 41–53 (2000)
44. Ciston, S.: Intersectional AI is essential: polyvocal, multimodal, experimental methods to save artificial intelligence. J. Sci. Technol. Arts **11**(2), 3–8 (2019)
45. Kriger, D., Keyser-Verreault, A., Joseph, J., Peers, D.: The operationalizing intersectionality framework. J. Clin. Sport Psychol. **16**(4), 302–324 (2022)
46. Richter, F.G.C., Nelson, E., Coury, N., Bruckman, L., Knighton, S.: FAIR2: a framework for addressing discrimination bias in social data science (2023)
47. Queerinai, O.O., Ovalle, A., Subramonian, A., et al.: Queer in AI: a case study in community-led participatory AI. In: Proceedings of the 2023 ACM Conference on Fairness, Accountability, and Transparency, pp. 1882–1895 (2023)
48. Kitchin, R., Lauriault, T.: Towards critical data studies: charting and unpacking data assemblages and their work (2014)
49. Leurs, K.: Feminist data studies: using digital methods for ethical, reflexive and situated socio-cultural research. Fem. Rev. **115**(1), 130–154 (2017)
50. Ghosh, A., Genuit, L., Reagan, M.: Characterizing intersectional group fairness with worstcase comparisons. In: Artificial Intelligence Diversity, Belonging, Equity, and Inclusion, pp. 22–34 (2021)
51. Brown, S., Davidovic, J., Hasan, A.: The algorithm audit: scoring the algorithms that score us. Big Data Soc. **8**(1), 2053951720983865 (2021)
52. Benjamin, R.: Informed refusal: toward a justice-based bioethics. Sci. Technol. Hum. Values **41**(6), 967–990 (2016)
53. Denton, E., Hanna, A., Amironesei, R., et al.: On the genealogy of machine learning datasets: a critical history of ImageNet. Big Data Soc. **8**(2), 20539517211035956 (2021)

54. Rankin, Y.A., Henderson, K.K.: Resisting racism in tech design: centering the experiences of black youth. Proc. ACM Hum.-Comput. Interact. **5**(CSCW1), 1–32 (2021)
55. Murray, S.G., Wachter, R.M., Cucina, R.J.: Discrimination by artificial intelligence in a commercial electronic health record-a case study. Health Affairs Forefront (2020)
56. Pandey, A., Caliskan, A.: Disparate impact of artificial intelligence bias in ridehailing economy's price discrimination algorithms. In: Proceedings of the 2021 AAAI/ACM Conference on AI, Ethics, and Society, pp. 822–833 (2021)
57. Sambasivan, N., Kapania, S., Highfill, H., et al.: "Everyone wants to do the model work, not the data work": data cascades in high-stakes AI. In: Proceedings of the 2021 CHI Conference on Human Factors in Computing Systems, pp. 1–15 (2021)

Participatory Observation Methods Within Data-Intensive Science: Formal Evaluation and Sociotechnical Insight

Elliott Hauser[1] (✉) ⓘ, Will Sutherland[2] ⓘ, and Mohammad Hossein Jarrahi[3] ⓘ

[1] University of Texas at Austin, Austin, TX 78701, USA
eah13@utexas.edu
[2] University of Washington, Seattle, WA 98195, USA
[3] University of North Carolina, Chapel Hill, NC 27599, USA

Abstract. This paper presents a framework enabling qualitative researchers to gain rich participatory access to study scientific practices within collaborative, funded research projects. Participatory observation methods provide unique access to scientific sites for social studies of science but require authentic and mutually beneficial motivations for qualitative researchers' participation. We illustrate a successful approach to configuring such collaborations by presenting the case of our participatory observation of an intensive NSF-funded Data-Intensive Science (DIS) training, as members of the evaluation team. We detail how our dual-purpose data collection methods informed both funder-facing evaluation materials and our own subsequent research publications, completed in parallel to the training's core objectives. We organize our site-specific findings on scientific practice around the themes of Technology, Practices, and Culture. Participatory evaluation of grant-funded science is a rich and under-utilized form of site access for sociotechnical researchers that can facilitate mutually beneficial scientific convergence.

Keywords: Sociotechnical Methods · Participant Observation · Evaluation · Scientific Training · Data-intensive Science

1 Introduction

The U.S. National Science Foundation (NSF) has used the term convergent science [1, 2] to describe scientific study of "complex problems focusing on societal needs" that exceed the bounds of a single discipline, require "deep integration of disciplines", and "new frameworks, paradigms or even disciplines [that] can form sustained interactions across multiple communities" [2]. Amidst these and similar efforts around the world, there is a growing need for articulating the appropriate use of social scientific research methods and role of social science scholars in large team science projects. Information science, informatics, and information studies scholars have a critical role to play in this collaborative integration of scientific inquiry.

The potential contributions and appropriate role of social scientific and ethnographic methods in large team science has been a subject of research and evolving practice for

I. Sserwanga et al. (Eds.): iConference 2024, LNCS 14596, pp. 253–269, 2024.
https://doi.org/10.1007/978-3-031-57850-2_19

decades. Examples of this stream of work include discourse on the role of ethnographic inquiry in the field of Human-Computer Interaction (HCI) [3–5]; the social scientific study of applications of data science [6, 7]; the development and impacts of scientific knowledge infrastructures [8–10]; histories of specific scientific information artifacts such as gene ontologies [11, 12]; and the role of specific knowledge practices and artifacts in space exploration [13, 14]. These research efforts have resulted in direct intervention and recommendations for scientific practice based upon insights of participatory research and practice-informed theory [15–17].

Notwithstanding the continuing positive impacts of this rich discourse upon science practice, important open questions remain [18, 19]. Almost two decades ago, Dourish [3] lamented that ethnographic HCI research was too often co-opted as merely a tool for producing requirements specifications. Five years later, Suchman [20] described a similarly problematic dynamic in anthropology. There is evidence that a similar instrumentalism or mis-alignment between social scientific research and domain science persists. Ribes [6] has cautioned against the relegation of social scientists to "service" roles on sponsored research projects. There is a clear need to continually articulate the transformative contributions of social scientists, both in terms of what they have already offered and what they could more broadly contribute to funded research programs.

The growing complexity of modern team science collaborations [21, 22] demands the holistic consideration of the project's research aims, scientific and computational apparatuses, and social practices and relationships amongst team members. In other words, alongside the disciplinary convergence envisioned by funders like NSF, the success of modern team science efforts depends upon integrated sociotechnical understanding and refinement of technoscientific practices [23].

In this article, we build on our empirical assessment of the NSF-funded Cybercarpentry workshops held at The University of North Carolina at Chapel Hill in 2018 and 2019. The workshops convened postdoctoral and doctoral DIS researchers from a diverse range of domains to learn broadly applicable DIS skills from over a dozen instructors over the course of two weeks each year. We describe our data collection and evaluation methods for this Data-Intensive Science (DIS) training program. The formal program evaluation we produced constitutes "service science", which Ribes [6] cautions can threaten to prevent incorporation of deep social scientific insights into science. Given this caution, We describe how our participatory evaluation methods facilitated the generation of new knowledge about scientific training practices and allowed the evaluation team to engage as intellectual partners in achieving the broader aims of the program.

We intend and expect our evaluation methods and experiences to be valuable to other researchers with evaluation mandates on grant-funded projects. In particular, we hope to equip researchers with participatory access to DIS projects, trainings, and initiatives to produce new knowledge about the factors influencing the achievement of convergence. Nonetheless, interpretation and application of these insights must be informed by the specific context within which we worked. We thus provide a thorough description of our relationship to the site. The article next describes and reflects upon the evaluation methods and strategies we developed, using interview quotes and other evaluation data to demonstrate key findings about the technology, practices, and culture visible in our site relevant to evaluation and implementation of DIS trainings. Finally, we make recommendations for how researchers can cultivate similarly rich participatory access to collaborative team science sites, illustrated by the authors' subsequent projects [24, 25].

2 Research Site

We illustrate our participant-observation approach primarily through our evaluation of the workshops, held over two consecutive years. The following section describes these workshops as a social scientific research site, providing a brief background on DIS and the NSF's rationale for the program, before detailing relevant aspects of the workshop.

2.1 Context: NSF's CyberTraining Program

Large data sets and computationally intensive methods are nearly ubiquitous on collaborative team science projects. Thus, Data-Intensive Science (DIS) education is a pressing concern for funding agencies and universities around the world. The US National Science Foundation (NSF) has prioritized research cyberinfrastructure development for decades, and has for many years now placed a complementary emphasis on cyberinfrastructure training to achieve effective utilization of large-scale scientific resources. The NSF CyberTraining program[1] funds training, events, and resource development for education of scientists and students.

The evaluation of funded scientific training programs via social scientific methods is an increasingly common requirement of funded research training programs [6], and DIS education has become an object of study in its own right. DIS training efforts are intended to deepen researchers' technical expertise for data-intensive research projects, providing skills that complement their domain-related scientific training. DIS research techniques increasingly involve a diverse ecosystem of analysis platforms, techniques, and data sources; some are tightly tied to specific domains (e.g. Hydroshare, a platform for hydrology data and models), some translate outputs of one field for use in another (e.g. the field of phylogenetics generates evolutionary relationships from genomics research data), and others, such as High-Performance Computing cyberinfrastructure, have broad utility. They are supplemented by domain-specific articulations such as specialized analysis software packages. The complexity of subject matter and diversity of tools involved present a distinct challenge for the effective and holistic evaluation of DIS education initiatives. DIS education initiatives, in turn, play a foundational role in the current and future capacity of collaborative team science to achieve convergence.

2.2 The Cybercarpentry Workshops

The Cybercarpentry Workshops were a NSF-funded initiative that provided intensive cohort-based training to postdoctoral and doctoral researchers from a range of scientific domains. The workshop's goals were to instruct scientists and engineers from a wide variety of domains in using computational and data management tools in their work and

---

[1] https://new.nsf.gov/funding/opportunities/training-based-workforce-development-advanced.

to enable the development of a cross-disciplinary community of practice based upon these skills. Instructors were professors in the fields of information or computer science, research scientists, and research staff from NSF-funded cyberinfrastructure projects.

The workshop's primary activity was an intensive, in-person, hands-on introduction to reproducible DIS over two weeks each summer of the program. Classroom sessions occupied most of each day, and breakfast and lunch were provided on-site. In the second week, the participants worked on a variety of group projects, applying computational methods, such as machine learning, or reproducing scientific processing pipelines (in some cases the participants' own). The project groups were selected in ways to simulate real-world scientific collaboration; they were also preselected in order to mix people with backgrounds in computing, engineering, and science as much as possible.

2.3 Participation and Positionality

The evaluation team leaders, including Jarrahi, were co-Primary Investigators (co-PIs) on the grant, but developed and conducted data collection and analysis activities independently from the instructional team. The evaluation team was present at project team meetings where curriculum planning was discussed, but the participation in these meetings was limited to observation.

Then-junior members of the evaluation team, including Hauser and Sutherland, participated in the site more directly. They were identified to participants as part of the workshop team but, as then-doctoral students, occupied a peer or neer-peer positionality with respect to the workshop participants. This participatory configuration provided a deeper, holistic understanding of the event, developed rapport with participants, and still avoided potential positionality complications that could have arisen had the evaluation team leaders (i.e. co-PIs) participated in these ways. One author, Hauser, provided instruction on collaboration tools such as Github, at the invitation of the instructional team. Participatory positionality is critical to analysis but is not a single thing: an investigator's positionality in a site can be as fluid or rigid as the relevant categories they enact over the course of fieldwork.

3 Dual-Purpose Data Collection Activities

We used a variety of methods in order to surface the multidimensional nature of DIS projects as well as struggles and successes the participants experienced over the course of the workshop. These included short surveys, semi-structured interviews, sticky note responses after each instructional session, and direct observation and participation by two of the evaluation team members. The diverse and rich data enabled us to triangulate and compare different perspectives on specific aspects of the training system. For instance, we juxtaposed broad overall ratings from the survey with more detailed individual explanations from the interviews. These methods provided extensive opportunities for participatory insights, a comprehensive perspective on the activities, outcomes, and experiences involved in the workshop for performing the evaluation and resulted in the rich data later used in research publications.

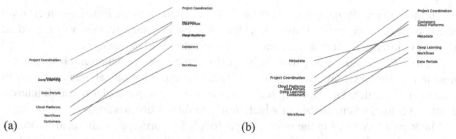

Fig. 1. Slope graphs of week 1 (a) and week 2 (b) survey results for the 2019 Cybercarpentry Workshops provided alongside quantitative data in the formal report. The slope of the line indicates participants' self-reported knowledge of the workshop's topic areas (not readable in the scaled reproduction here). These illustrate artifacts the evaluation team produced from survey data in the formal report but not used in subsequent publications.

3.1 Surveys

We administered two surveys over the course of the workshop through the survey software Qualtrics. The two surveys differed slightly, the first aimed at the instructional section of the workshop, and the second aimed at the project phase. However, both asked the participants to rate their comfort level with each major topic of the course before the workshop, and at the time of the survey (i.e. after training on our projects using these topics, respectively). This was meant to gauge the participants' sense of progress on each topic after the first and second weeks. Both surveys also included text response questions about instances where they struggled, and their interactions with other participants and instructors.

The survey data was a central component of the evaluation report but was less useful for sociotechnical inquiry. Figure 1 shows some of the visualization of quantitative results included in the formal evaluation, a slope graph of reported familiarity pre- and post-training. We omit detailed discussion of survey results here, instead noting that some forms of participatory access will not be directly relevant to sociotechnical studies of science.

3.2 Interviews

The interviews we conducted were equally important for the interpretation of survey results we provided in the project's official evaluation and for our independent research questions. This section briefly describes the interview procedure before turning to an in-depth analysis of the interview protocol as simultaneously contributing to evaluation and sociotechnical research.

We conducted almost 30 interviews each year of the workshops, including almost all participants and instructors. Interviews lasted approximately 30 min and were semi-structured. Protocol-based topical questions and follow-ups (described further below) provided a fruitful mechanism for answering research questions while conducting the formal evaluation.

The majority of the interviews were carried out in person; some instructor interviews were conducted after the workshop via videoconference. Each interview was recorded, pursuant to informed consent, and transcribed verbatim for later analysis.

We found interviews to be particularly fruitful components of our research. Our semi-structured protocol ensured that each participant covered the topical areas relevant to evaluation. We utilized an evolving sensitization to issues of particular research interest to guide whether, when, and about which topics to follow-up questions.

Major topics covered in the interview protocols for participants and instructors are given in Table 1. These major topics were selected because of their relevance to evaluation of the workshop's outcome, the evaluation team's formal mode of participation in the site. The focus of follow up questions, however, were determined by the team's evolving research questions. Hauser and Sutherland [25] used grounded theory method [26] in their analysis of the data, and were able to use follow up questions as a form of theoretical sampling as they navigated towards theoretical saturation of their categories.

Table 1. Topics covered by semi-structured Participant and Instructor interview protocols, selected by evaluation team leaders for their relevance to program evaluation. Follow-up questions were guided by the authors' evolving research interests.

Participant Protocol Topics	Instructor Protocol Topics
Participant expectations about the workshop and what they would learn	Planning process for their section of the workshop
Interactions with other participants and instructors	Interactions with other participants and instructors
Prior experience or knowledge of DIS technologies and techniques	Expectations about what participants would know coming into the workshop
How the workshop fit their professional needs overall	Desired participant learning outcomes

3.3 Field Notes, Artifacts, and Sociotechnical Traces

Interview and survey data, both used in the formal evaluation report, were supplemented by other forms of data collection, used primarily in subsequent research publications.

Field Notes. Both team members who served as assistants during the event made observations in the form of field notes over the course of the workshop, focusing on a couple of key factors that were considered salient:

- Places where participants struggled with the course content.
- Situations where participants or class sessions were held back by technical difficulties.
- How participants worked together in their project groups.
- Particular difficulties participants had with the framing of projects or the relevance of particular class sessions.
- Modes of instruction, which successfully engaged the participants.

- Places where participants struggled because of a lack of familiarity with ancillary tools or other background knowledge.

The instructional context of activity on the site provided a blend of active and passive observation opportunities. During lecture portions of the training, researchers could observe instructors' presentation styles, materials, ways of speaking, as well as participant reactions. During hands-on activities, researchers were able to interact directly with participants who needed help, building a rapport that increased their willingness to participate in interviews and comfort in discussing their experiences frankly. Joining in the activities and projects of the workshop also enabled the researchers to learn from participation: encountering small breakdowns and points of learning where shared goals and understandings became visible [27, 28].

Artifact Elicitation: Stickies. Participants were asked to provide a brief response to each instructional session on sticky notes, immediately after each session, indicating things that went well about the session, as well as things that did not go well. The evaluation team transcribed these stickies into a spreadsheet shared on Google Drive so that instructors in the workshop could see the responses to particular sessions soon after they were completed. The pedagogical method that generated these artifacts was inspired by and lightly adapted from techniques developed within the Software Carpentry training program [29], and simultaneously enhanced the execution of the training and the data available for analysis by our team..

Sociotechnical Trace Data. The evaluation team had access to and reviewed a large amount of digital artifacts generated by instructors and/or participants. These include:

- Group Slack chats
- Collaborative notetaking via HackMD
- Github code repositories and documentation
- Instructor presentations
- Participant final presentations

The evaluation team was able to directly observe participants creating these artifacts in most cases and/or participate in their creation during support activities. Figure # shows two examples of trace data taken from Slack. Participants reported errors or problems via the platform and were assisted by the workshop organizers or other participants. Participants' engagement with the material led them to create memes mentioning the technologies it covered (the second example in Fig. 2 mentions Snakemake, a reproducible workflow technology covered during the event. The holistic access that participant observation provided to trace data, circumstances of its creation, and practices surrounding the workshop enabled more sophisticated interpretation of the participant experience of the workshop and the meaning and values perceived in the technologies, skills, and practices they learned.

Fig. 2. Two screenshots showing interactions between participants on Slack during the workshop, an example of the sociotechnical trace data the authors gained access to through participant observation.

4   Evaluation Framework

The evaluation framework we developed presents our findings along three interrelated themes: technology, practices, and culture. This section of the paper highlights key findings and dynamics we observed in the site. This also serves to illustrate the three themes of our framework, which we believe are likely to be transferable to future evaluation and research efforts concerning similar sites of scientific practice and training.

4.1   Technology

Technologies play a key role in supporting DIS activities; participants and instructors tended to use the names of specific technologies (e.g. Docker) as shorthands for the broader topics of the event (e.g. containerization). Our evaluation approach focused on identifying key technological tools in relation to participants' individual interactions with them. The scientifically meaningful practices accomplished via technological tools gave them meaning and value, even as the tool names often came to serve as stand-in labels for the practices they enabled.

Technological Tools and Workflow Efficiency. Participants differed in which tools they were most excited about, but whichever tools they cited were perceived as potentially enhancing their productivity, the quality of their work, or the cohesiveness of the teams they work with. Tools frequently cited in interviews and survey responses as likely to change participants' scientific practices included container technologies and general purpose tools like Git and Github. Our holistic access to the meanings of these tools in the context of the workshop led us to interpret these proper nouns as standing for the acquired or desired skill sets, they represented to participants. This interpretation was partially validated by some participants' explicit linking of skills with specific tools, such as "machine learning with Keras", "reproducibility with Docker", or "workflows with Snakemake". Participants reported an increased interest in using specific technologies in their own work, a major learning outcome for the evaluation. Regardless of which tool enabled them, skills that enhanced workflow, prioritization, and efficiency were the most commonly reported positive outcome of the workshop. This indicated that the workshops' diversity of tool coverage was an important aspect of its ability to meet a range of participant needs: a less holistically designed workshop might not have covered tools relevant to workflow efficiency for as many participants.

Collaboration Technologies. Collaboration tools are a key aspect of DIS projects. Since most high level scientific work is collaborative, utilizing these tools and practices is a major benefit to researchers and evaluations of DIS would need to embrace the impacts of these tools. Participants cited knowledge of collaboration tools, and associated collaboration practices, as a key outcome that they planned to implement at their home institutions:

> *"We learned as a team to collaborate in GitHub and each do a part of the project. We helped each other on debugging the errors and this helped us going through each phase of the project together."*

Through these experiences, participants were able to directly experience the utility of these tools and easily envision how they could enhance existing work practices in their various laboratories.

Slack, HackMD, and GitHub facilitated workshop activities effectively. Many participants reported that, regardless of prior experiences with these platforms, the practices of collaboration demonstrated by the workshop indicated new ways they might use them in their own work. For instance, some participants mentioned that they had used Github before but not its project management functions (i.e. a card and column-based organization of issues and code). Not only do these platforms support DIS projects but learning and sharing experiences. These platforms, particularly Slack, were in heavy use for communication purposes throughout the sessions and, at times, after hours.

Integration of data tools has real consequences for the way researchers collect and analyze their results. This highlights the need for a focus on data tools and their implications in evaluation efforts. Years of human-computer interaction (HCI) research makes it clear the architecture of the technology and how it may or may not align with users' mental models shape its application and integration in data practices [30]. Data tools are not a neutral substrate for scientific investigation, but they embody specific standards of excellence in scientific work [24]; these design architectures may not necessarily fit the real practices and common understanding of (novice) researchers. Several participants noted that their conceptual understandings of some of these tools developed relatively slowly.

Temporality of Technology. Finally, in any training effort like this, both the educators and learners need to be reminded of the temporality of technology, what connects past to now and future developments [31]. On the one hand, it is intuitive that technology changes so fast so keeping abreast of new tools (e.g. Singularity, developed about two years before the event) is crucial for any researchers. On the other hand, many, if not most, of the technologies, operating systems, platforms, and protocols used during the workshop were comparatively mature and old. Command line utilities like ssh, vi, and bash have existed for decades and have a deep history.

We found that several of the event's instructors emphasized how the technologies they were describing were not available "five years ago". And yet, five years hence, it is very likely that GitHub, git, Vim, and SSH will all still be in use at the core of data- and computationally intensive science practice. As a result, DIS efforts and their evaluation should embrace both emerging and evolving technologies and how they could work together in supporting data practices of scientists. Participants should have a nuanced sense of the durability of core software tools to complement the emphasis on newness common to both software project marketing materials and grant proposals.

Finally, the passage of time since data collection for this study should inform interpretation of the usage and meaning of platforms in today's environment. All of the technologies mentioned are still available for use, but changes, closures, or disruptions to access (such as removal of free plans on commercial platforms) could well change their utility in the future. Longitudinal perspectives and, ideally, longitudinal study of the use of specific technologies are required to address the complex impacts of temporality upon the utility and meaning of specific technologies.

4.2 Practices

Data work involves a great deal of tacit knowledge, developed through hands-on processes and skills, first-hand experience, and practice [32]. While visible computational tools are key, they are situated in trajectories of data practices. They embody a history of technological accretion, contain an array of literal and figurative dependencies, and embed practices which give them scientific meaning and value [33, 34]. The workshop's curriculum design started from the premise that it is through hands-on practices that researchers internalize DIS skills and competencies, and that was well-reflected in our observations of instructors' and participants' practices during the event.

Scientific Practices and the Experience of Learning. Given the centrality of practices to the meaning and value of scientific technologies, evaluation efforts must direct attention to hands-on experiences of the researcher/learners. This focus includes but ranges far beyond the more visible forms of technical pedagogy such as instructions and technologically mediated artifacts such as data analyses or visualization. The evaluation of the workshop made it clear that finding the correct balance of hands-on activities and conceptual overviews is a key challenge. Individual researcher needs and preferences may make this a constantly moving target. Even though the second year's workshop included more hands-on material, some participants wished there were still more:

> *"I think more hands-on time during class built into the first week would help me learn topics better than front-loading the lectures and putting most of the hands-on time into the second week. The information I do absorb makes sense and is taught well, but it's not until I test my knowledge with a hands-on activity that I realize I don't completely understand it."*

The evaluation team members participating as technical assistants during the event saw first-hand the importance of being able to address individual confusions or blockages participants encountered during the event. DIS education and training events should carefully consider their strategies for individuating instruction as a core pedagogical challenge.

Articulation Work. The evaluation of projects must also embrace articulation work beyond the core data work. Articulation work references the critical activities beyond core work tasks that must be performed to define what, who, when, and how a unit of data work will be carried out [35, 36]. A major challenge of DIS projects (much like other software projects) is project management, which includes effective organization, scoping, and coordination of work. In our site, project management was a form of articulation work that participants had had little formal exposure to. Perceptions of the value of project management skills for DIS practice varied markedly.

We observed a variety of articulation challenges over the course of the workshop: students were encouraged to propose projects using their real research data and computational analyses to deepen the relevance of the workshop, but the particularities of these projects required articulation work that other participants felt was not relevant to their learning goals. For example, the participant-provided computational research projects were assembled rather hastily, and there were some problems regarding scoping them or making them relevant to all group members. One of the participant-provided projects ran into issues because the group member who had brought the project was the only one who could contribute to the early phases of the project, which involved editing some of their scripts directly. Because of this, the other two members of the group felt like they were unable to contribute and unable to get hands-on practice with the tools they wanted to learn. The participant who brought the project similarly said that they sensed this problem but did not have the project management skills to better scope the project or organize the group to effectively contribute.

The importance of project management skills to participants highlights the oft-overlooked labor that goes into coordination of DIS projects (and may not be easily encapsulated in the core data work), and the fact that this kind of coordinative work is part of what must be learned in taking up other DIS practices and tools. For instance, there were difficulties dividing the work of the projects. A participant explained that, during the project,

> *"...we did not have a clear plan with division of labor at the beginning, so when we put our pieces back together there was a lot of work to get them to fit."*

Accepting the premise that articulation work is an inevitable part of DIS research can help DIS educators more effectively plan for and incorporate it into their course content. The Cybercarpentry workshop was able to accomplish this in its second iteration by explicitly discussing collaboration tools, techniques, and practices.

Reproducibility: Value, But for Whom? When? Reproducibility is considered one of the major concerns of scientific endeavors and DIS research projects, defining practices of researchers [37]. As a way of making their present work valuable to a hypothetical future, any evaluation efforts need to take into account ways that the concept of reproducibility is perceived and implemented by researchers. Due to fast-paced changes in tools and techniques of DIS, models for reproducibility are not standardized. The research process is so greatly shaped by human actions outside "the code" that reproducibility and involvement of other researchers in later stages of DIS is a non-trivial challenge. For example, data debugging includes documentation steps taken to prepare data; this requires tools that capture data provenance.

Participants' experiences reproducing the work of others (i.e. published work for the projects, and their group members' work) gave them a sense of what is actually required for computational reproducibility. This was cited as a key benefit of the workshop: placing participants in the role of reproducer was an effective way of both showing the value of reproducibility skills (i.e. being able to replicate and analyze others' work), as well as giving them an insight into what challenges potential reproducers of their own work might face. In many cases, participants shared stories of difficulties reproducing *their own work* months or years after completing it, which also reinforced the value of this skill.

We found researchers committed to the meticulous preservation activities of reproducibility, through which they work to construct continuity with previous research [24]. However, reproducibility is a concept in flux and means different things to different researchers and research communities [38]. DIS training and DIS projects need to be mindful of reproducibility as a manifold and evolving ideal that shapes scientific research and shapes interventions to accommodate the diversity of ways through which reproducibility practices evolve within different intellectual communities.

4.3 Culture

The evaluation framework must go beyond technologies and processes and embrace cultural dynamics that may facilitate or constrain data work. The following elements are cultural common grounds we found salient in organizing and running DIS projects based on the workshop experience. We found that the success of the workshops in equipping participants to engage in rigorous DIS was in part due to the successful *acculturation* process, whereby participants comprehended, altered, and enacted new norms amongst themselves. In particular, we here emphasize the collaborative and interdisciplinary nature of the acculturation process.

Collaboration. Collaboration in teams is deeply influenced by the perceptions and backgrounds of team members; DIS projects are no exception. Scientific work is increasingly done in groups, especially on cutting-edge, grant-funded, and/or convergent research projects. The ability to mobilize data from one situation as evidence in another situation is a core promise of collaboration in scientific work [39]. The use of collaborative tools on its own is insufficient for effective scientific collaboration; instructors emphasized that effective collaboration mentality and practices are required for the success of shared work. This is an endemic challenge to collaboration and should be emphasized even more strongly in the evaluation and implementation of project-based collaborative work.

Participants remarked that the culture of diversity and inclusion within the workshop facilitated collaboration. Some of the participants suggested that the venues like the workshop would be a good venue for making more explicit support for inclusion in science more generally:

"I think the great thing about courses like this is the level[ing] of the playing field a little bit for people who may not have otherwise felt comfortable going out and asking for help with programming resources or whatever and like representation

*of minorities and STEM [...] I guess I would have liked to see kind of a stronger
emphasis on that in this course and [to] kind of say it's important."*

In our site, sentiments like this were evidence that the workshop environment presents
opportunities to promote inclusiveness as part of this broader shift in scientific culture,
but also that deliberate efforts at inclusion can still fall short.

Interdisciplinarity. Many DIS projects are interdisciplinary by nature [40]. One of
the major considerations of evaluation frameworks therefore centers on how the project
facilitates and is facilitated by interdisciplinarity (which requires going beyond disciplinary boundaries and assumptions. In our data, when asked about their interactions
with other people, a large number of participants mentioned that it was beneficial to be
able to interact with people from other fields.

*"I feel like I'm really making friends with whom I will stay in contact with after
I leave the workshop. It's interesting hearing about the diverse research areas
being pursued by everyone. Also interesting is how our needs and the tools we
use intersect...Sometimes there are common problems so we can learn from each
other."*

Interdisciplinarity can create challenges for DIS projects. One of the central aspects of
the interdisciplinary work is lack of common ground and vocabulary that could hold back
effective collaboration. In effect, concepts may not translate well beyond disciplinary
boundaries. For instance, a participant provided an insight into the difficulties a lack of
a conceptual overview:

*"I knew I would be a little behind coming into the workshop because I don't have a
computer science background, so I tried to google the items on the schedule – but
it was impossible to find information when all I had were terms like "atmosphere"
and "singularity." It may have helped me to have some basic info on the topics
that would be covered, even just wikipedia-level or a list of terms."*

Atmosphere and Singularity are the names of tools used in the workshop; this participant mentions them here to indicate that the deluge of unfamiliar terms, especially
the names of tools, were a barrier to their learning and to feelings of confidence. Despite
these challenges, an overall atmosphere of inclusiveness and appreciation of varied disciplinary expertise allowed participants the ability to develop a shared sense of purpose
and identity in the context of their learning experiences.

5   Discussion: Practices of Evaluating Scientific Practices

This article presents an approach to collecting diverse data and the application of rich,
interpretive methods capable of effectively analyzing this complexity in specific settings.
As people in a variety of professions are integrating data-focused tools and tasks into
their daily research practices, and entire research fields are transformed by data-intensive
and computational methods, important questions regarding data- and tool-oriented education have arisen. New affordances associated with computational techniques challenge

previous ways of understanding how science might–and should–be conducted, and the role of data in scientific work. As such, an effective evaluation approach of DIS training and projects is necessarily sociotechnical, not only encompassing technology components but also multiplicity of meanings and best practices around the concepts around evolving practices and culture of DIS [23].

The thematic triad of technology, process, and culture presented here emphasizes a socially informed and yet technically rigorous perspective to data science education. DIS is commonly presented as a 'cross-cutting' set of competencies which can be applied to any domain, like the directly related practices of applied AI and data science [41]. This transdisciplinary and meta nature of fields like DIS complicates the way that funded research and research training projects must be evaluated. Our thematic triad helped us discern and present our themes in a way most likely to be transferable to other sites.

We argue for the necessity of an interpretive approach in evaluation, one that recognizes the application of data-intensive tools as socially constructed. We observed participants learning reproducible science as a kind of technical trade, attempting to reconcile broad notions of reproducibility with their own unique research work as they did. Our interpretive approach to evaluation helped us follow each participant's own understanding and application of the broader field of DIS, synthesizing themes and characterizing categories of difference. For our site, effective evaluation required finding a balance between a global dimension or characterization of DIS and a local understanding and application of DIS in participants' own research practices.

6 Conclusion: Deeper Social-Scientific Access to Science Practice

Imbrication of social scientists with data-intensive and collaborative team science efforts can be a mutually beneficial driver of scientific convergence. We contend that practices of formal evaluation of funded scientific projects, such as DIS trainings, provide rare access for sociotechnical studies of science. In the presented case study, our participation directly contributed to the project's main goal: our evaluation of a DIS training workshop revealed insights and phenomena of direct utility to workshop organizers and funders. Crucially, however, this activity enabled the authors to contribute to social scientific knowledge on science practice: supplementation and analysis of the data collected for the formal evaluation generated new insights and subsequent research publications for the qualitative evaluation team (including the authors of the present paper).

We observe that alignment of formal evaluation of scientific projects with social scientific publication output is critical to the career-level sustainability of social scientific participation in funded scientific research. Thus, our participatory observation engagement with this site as an illustration of the kinds of collaborative configurations that sociotechnical researchers studying scientific practice must develop. Doing so more often and more broadly will help sociotechnical researchers achieve the potential impact and contribution Ribes [6] urges us to seek out.

Acknowledgements. This research was supported by NSF Award #1730390. The authors acknowledge the efforts of Melanie Feinberg, Arcot Rajasekar, Nirav Merchant, Hao Xu, and many others involved in the Cybercarpentry workshops program at UNC Chapel Hill.

References

1. NSF: Learn About Convergence Research. https://new.nsf.gov/funding/learn/research-types/learn-about-convergence-research. Accessed 13 Sept 2023
2. Brzakovic, D.: Growing Convergence Research (GCR) Program Solicitation. National Science Foundation (2019)
3. Dourish, P.: Implications for design. In: Proceedings of the SIGCHI Conference on Human Factors in Computing Systems, pp. 541–550. Association for Computing Machinery, New York, NY, USA (2006). https://doi.org/10.1145/1124772.1124855
4. Rode, J.A.: Reflexivity in digital anthropology. In: Proceedings of the SIGCHI Conference on Human Factors in Computing Systems, pp. 123–132. Association for Computing Machinery, New York, NY, USA (2011). https://doi.org/10.1145/1978942.1978961
5. Dourish, P.: Reading and interpreting ethnography. In: Olson, J.S., Kellogg, W.A. (eds.) Ways of Knowing in HCI, pp. 1–23. Springer, New York (2014). https://doi.org/10.1007/978-1-4939-0378-8_1
6. Ribes, D.: STS, meet data science, once again. Sci. Technol. Hum. Values **44**, 514–539 (2019). https://doi.org/10.1177/0162243918798899
7. Borgman, C.L., Wallis, J.C., Mayernik, M.S.: Who's got the data? Interdependencies in science and technology collaborations. Comput. Support. Coop. Work. (2012)
8. Slota, S.C., Hoffman, A.S., Ribes, D., Bowker, G.C.: Prospecting (in) the data sciences. Big Data Soc. **7**, 2053951720906849 (2020). https://doi.org/10.1177/2053951720906849
9. Borgman, C.L., et al.: Knowledge infrastructures in science: data, diversity, and digital libraries. Int. J. Digit. Libr. **16**, 207–227 (2015). https://doi.org/10.1007/s00799-015-0157-z
10. Slota, S.C., Hauser, E.: Inverting ecological infrastructures: how temporality structures the work of sustainability. Hist. Soc. Res. **47**, 215–241 (2022). https://doi.org/10.12759/hsr.47.2022.45
11. Leonelli, S., Diehl, A.D., Christie, K.R., Harris, M.A., Lomax, J.: How the gene ontology evolves. BMC Bioinform. **12**, 325 (2011). https://doi.org/10.1186/1471-2105-12-325
12. Leonelli, S.: Classificatory theory in data-intensive science: the case of open biomedical ontologies. Int. Stud. Philos. Sci. **26**, 47–65 (2012). https://doi.org/10.1080/02698595.2012.653119
13. Vertesi, J., Dourish, P.: The value of data: considering the context of production in data economies. In: Proceedings of the ACM 2011 Conference on Computer Supported Cooperative Work, pp. 533–542. Association for Computing Machinery, New York, NY, USA (2011). https://doi.org/10.1145/1958824.1958906
14. Vertesi, J.: Seeing Like a Rover. University of Chicago Press, Chicago (2015). https://doi.org/10.7208/9780226156019
15. Goodman, A., et al.: Ten simple rules for the care and feeding of scientific data. PLoS Comput. Biol. **10**, e1003542 (2014). https://doi.org/10.1371/journal.pcbi.1003542
16. Smith, B., Ceusters, W.: Ontological realism: a methodology for coordinated evolution of scientific ontologies. Appl. Ontol. **5**, 139–188 (2010). https://doi.org/10.3233/AO-2010-0079
17. Leonelli, S., Davey, R.P., Arnaud, E., Parry, G., Bastow, R.: Data management and best practice for plant science. Nat Plants. **3**, 17086 (2017). https://doi.org/10.1038/nplants.2017.86
18. Borgman, C.L.: Big data, little data, or no data? Why human interaction with data is a hard problem. In: Proceedings of the 2020 Conference on Human Information Interaction and Retrieval, p. 1. Association for Computing Machinery, New York, NY, USA (2020). https://doi.org/10.1145/3343413.3377979
19. Scroggins, M.J., et al.: Thorny problems in data (-intensive) science. Commun. ACM **63**, 30–32 (2020). https://doi.org/10.1145/3408047

20. Suchman, L.: Anthropological relocations and the limits of design. Annu. Rev. Anthropol. **40**, 1–18 (2011). https://doi.org/10.1146/annurev.anthro.041608.105640
21. Read, E.K., et al.: Building the team for team science. Ecosphere. **7**, e01291 (2016). https://doi.org/10.1002/ecs2.1291
22. Spring, B.J., Pfammatter, AFidler, Conroy, D.E.: Continuing professional development for team science. In: Hall, K.L., Vogel, A.L., Croyle, R.T. (eds.) Strategies for Team Science Success, pp. 445–453. Springer, Cham (2019). https://doi.org/10.1007/978-3-030-20992-6_34
23. Sawyer, S., Jarrahi, M.: Sociotechnical approaches to the study of information systems. In: Topi, H. Tucker, A. (eds.) Computing Handbook, 3rd edn, pp. 5-1–5-27. Chapman and Hall/CRC, Boca Raton (2014). https://doi.org/10.1201/b16768-7
24. Feinberg, M., Sutherland, W., Nelson, S.B., Jarrahi, M.H., Rajasekar, A.: The new reality of reproducibility: the role of data work in scientific research. Proc. ACM Hum.-Comput. Interact. **4**, 1–22 (2020). https://doi.org/10.1145/3392840
25. Hauser, E., Sutherland, W.: Temporality in data science education: early results from a grounded theory study of an NSF-funded CyberTraining workshop. In: Sundqvist, A., Berget, G., Nolin, Jan, Skjerdingstad, K.I. (eds.) iConference. LNCS, vol. 12051, pp. 536–544. Springer, Cham (2020). https://doi.org/10.1007/978-3-030-43687-2_43
26. Charmaz, K.: Constructing Grounded Theory: A Practical Guide Through Qualitative Analysis. SAGE Publications, London (2006)
27. Lave, J., Wenger, E.: Situated Learning: Legitimate Peripheral Participation. Cambridge University Press, Cambridge (1991). https://doi.org/10.1017/CBO9780511815355
28. Downey, G., Dalidowicz, M., Mason, P.H.: Apprenticeship as method: embodied learning in ethnographic practice. Qual. Res. **15**, 183–200 (2015). https://doi.org/10.1177/1468794114543400
29. Wilson, G.: Software carpentry: lessons learned. F1000Res **3**, 62 (2014). https://doi.org/10.12688/f1000research.3-62.v2
30. Payne, S.J.: Users' mental models: the very ideas. In: HCI Models, Theories, and Frameworks: Toward a Multidisciplinary Science, pp. 135–156 (2003)
31. Jackson, S.J., Barbrow, S.: Infrastructure and vocation: field, calling and computation in ecology. In: Proceedings of the SIGCHI Conference on Human Factors in Computing Systems, pp. 2873–2882. Association for Computing Machinery, New York, NY, USA (2013). https://doi.org/10.1145/2470654.2481397
32. Baker, K.S., Bowker, G.C.: Information ecology: open system environment for data, memories, and knowing (2007). https://doi.org/10.1007/s10844-006-0035-7
33. Orlikowski, W.J.: Sociomaterial practices: exploring technology at work. Organ. Stud. **28**, 1435–1448 (2007). https://doi.org/10.1177/0170840607081138
34. Pinel, C., Prainsack, B., McKevitt, C.: Caring for data: value creation in a data-intensive research laboratory. Soc. Stud. Sci. **50**, 175–197 (2020). https://doi.org/10.1177/03063127209066567
35. Strauss, A.: The articulation of project work: an organizational process. Sociol. Q. **29**, 163–178 (1988). https://doi.org/10.1111/j.1533-8525.1988.tb01249.x
36. Suchman, L.: Supporting articulation work. In: Kling, R. (ed.) Computerization and Controversy: Value Conflicts and Social Choices, pp. 407–425. Morgan Kaufmann, San Francisco (1996)
37. Goodman, S.N., Fanelli, D., Ioannidis, J.P.A.: What does research reproducibility mean? Sci. Transl. Med. **8**, 341ps12 (2016). https://doi.org/10.1126/scitranslmed.aaf5027
38. Nelson, N.C., Ichikawa, K., Chung, J., Malik, M.M.: Mapping the discursive dimensions of the reproducibility crisis: a mixed methods analysis. PLoS ONE **16**, e0254090 (2021). https://doi.org/10.1371/journal.pone.0254090

39. Leonelli, S.: Data-Centric Biology: A Philosophical Study. University of Chicago Press, Chicago (2016)
40. Asamoah, D.A., Doran, D., Schiller, S.: Interdisciplinarity in data science pedagogy: a foundational design. J. Comput. Inf. Syst. **60**, 370–377 (2020). https://doi.org/10.1080/08874417.2018.1496803
41. Ribes, D., Hoffman, A.S., Slota, S.C., Bowker, G.C.: The logic of domains. Soc. Stud. Sci. **49**, 281–309 (2019). https://doi.org/10.1177/0306312719849709

From Knowledge Representation to Knowledge Organization and Back

Fausto Giunchiglia[ID] and Mayukh Bagchi[✉][ID]

DISI, University of Trento, Trento, Italy
{fausto.giunchiglia,mayukh.bagchi}@unitn.it

Abstract. Knowledge Representation (KR) and facet-analytical Knowledge Organization (KO) have been the two most prominent methodologies of data and knowledge modelling in the Artificial Intelligence community and the Information Science community, respectively. KR boasts of a robust and scalable ecosystem of technologies to support knowledge modelling while, often, underemphasizing the quality of its models (and model-based data). KO, on the other hand, is less technology-driven but has developed a robust framework of guiding principles (*canons*) for ensuring modelling (and model-based data) quality. This paper elucidates both the KR and facet-analytical KO methodologies in detail and provides a functional mapping between them. Out of the mapping, the paper proposes an integrated KO-enriched KR methodology with all the standard components of a KR methodology *plus* the guiding canons of modelling quality provided by KO. The practical benefits of the methodological integration has been exemplified through a prominent case study of KR-based image annotation exercise.

Keywords: Knowledge Representation · Knowledge Organization · Model Quality · Faceted Approach · Information Science · Data Science · AI

1 Introduction

Knowledge Representation is the arena of Artificial Intelligence (AI) dealing with *"how knowledge can be represented symbolically"* [5] within intelligent systems. To that end, KR encompasses a wide spectrum of advanced *technologies* (e.g., the Semantic Web technology stack [24]) and *methodologies* (e.g., [13,23]) to facilitate generation of KR artifacts (e.g., ontologies [29], conceptual models [30], Knowledge Graphs (KGs) [33]). Such methodologies have been widely adopted or adapted for application scenarios from as conventional as, e.g., data integration [28], to as innovative as, e.g., image annotation [18], wherein, conceptual models are designed to organize (objects in) images which are later exploited as high-quality training data for computer vision tasks like object recognition. However, while KR methodologies have remained highly mature in terms of supporting technology and scalable in terms of technology-enabled services, a *key* criticism has been that they have traditionally underemphasized *modelling quality*, e.g., of ontologies or conceptual models (see, [1,10,46], for a few prominent studies), resulting in, often, flawed and biased datasets designed according to such models.

Knowledge Organization, on the other hand, is the arena of Information Science dealing with the cumulative set of activities concerning, quoting [32], the *"description, indexing and classification"* of information resources (e.g., books) in different kinds of *'memory institutions'* (e.g., libraries). To that end, KO encompasses a wide spectrum of modelling systems [53], e.g., classification schemes, taxonomies, catalogs, etc., and, different approaches [32], e.g., enumerative approach, facet-analytical approach, etc., which integrate different KO systems. In this paper, we concentrate exclusively on the facet-analytical KO approach originally proposed by Ranganathan [41,42]. Noticeably, while the activities in (faceted) KO are predominantly intellectual in nature and less technology-driven, they have, in order to support the aforementioned activities, developed a huge number of *guiding principles* for (conceptual) modelling, termed *canons*, following which *high-quality models*, e.g., conceptual hierarchies, conceptual models and model-based *datasets*, can be generated.

From the above overviews, we notice that both KR and KO have several complementary strengths and weaknesses. We concentrate on the specific *problem of how the modelling quality of KR artifacts can be methodologically ensured*. One clear way, in the light of the above discussion, can be the incorporation of the guiding principles for modelling, namely, the *canons*, developed within the facet-analytical approach of KO in mainstream KR. In fact, the potentiality of such an incorporation can be extremely crucial because of growing concerns about *systematic design flaws* inherent in the *quality of data* which are designed using KR models, e.g., data quality issues [50] in ImageNet [9], and, additionally, the *decline in both the quality and performance* of resulting data-driven models, e.g., [35,47]. In this paper, we propose a KO-enriched KR methodology which not only includes the standard roles and activities key to the generation of a KR model, e.g., an ontology-driven KG, but also, most importantly, incorporates the otherwise *missing* activity of generating the high-quality ontology model structuring the KG following the guiding *canons* prescribed in the facet-analytical approach of KO. It also presents brief highlights of a recent study-cum-experiment in KR-based image annotation [19] which preliminarily validates the benefits of implementing an adapted version of the aforementioned methodology.

The remainder of the paper is organized as follows: Sects. 2 and 3 describes the roles and activities within the different phases of a standard KR and facet-analytical KO methodology, respectively. Section 4 maps and integrates the methodologies in the previous two sections into a single KO-enriched KR methodology, with special emphasis on the activity which exploits the guiding principles (canons) to ensure model (and model-based data) quality. Section 5 describes a case study in image annotation which preliminarily validates the advantages of the integrated KO-enriched KR methodology. Section 6 discusses related work and Sect. 7 concludes the paper.

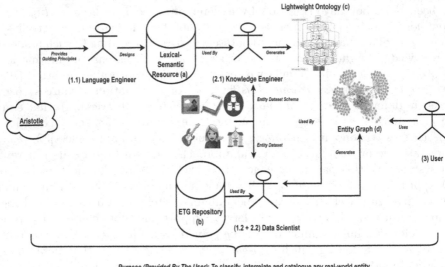

Fig. 1. A high-level view of the KR Methodology.

2 Knowledge Representation (KR)

Let us first concentrate on a detailed exposition of the various phases, and within each phase, the various roles, activities and artifacts, which together compose to form a standard KR methodology. See Fig. 1 for a high-level view of the KR methodology. The methodology can be seen as being constituted of the following four distinct phases (the terminologies being detailed later):

1. The first phase initiating with guiding principles and concluding with the generation of the Lightweight Ontology.
2. The second phase concerning the development of the Entity Type Graph (ETG) repository.
3. The third phase of the methodology concentrating on how the data scientist takes in three different inputs, namely, the Lightweight Ontology, Entity Dataset(s) and ETGs from the ETG repository, and, suitably integrates them to generate the Entity Graph (EG).
4. Finally, the fourth and the final phase concentrating on the different ways in which a user can use and exploit the EG.

The diagrammatic symbols of Fig. 1 include, amongst others, the various roles (visualized via *actor* icon), activities (visualized as edge *labels*) and artifacts (visualized variously via other (coloured) icons). Notice also that the numbers and lowercase alphabets which identify roles and artifacts, respectively, in Fig. 1, are employed later (in Sect. 4) for functional mapping purposes. We now consider each phase of the methodology individually.

The first phase, as already noted, commences with guiding principles articulated as the intensional definition-building paradigm of *Genus-Differentia* [38]
proposed by Aristotle (visualized via a cloud) over two millennia ago. According
to the paradigm, the linguistic definition of any real-world object [25] expressed,
e.g., as a noun, is formulated in terms of two constituent definitions: *Genus*
and *Differentia*. While *Genus* defines an *a priori* set of properties shared across
distinct objects, e.g., the property of being a stringed musical instrument, *Differentia* defines a novel set of properties used to differentiate objects having the
same *Genus*, e.g., the properties of musical instruments having six strings or
thirteen strings. Therefore, as illustrated in Fig. 1, the *Genus-Differentia* guidelines are taken in input and adhered to by the *Language Engineer* to create
machine-processable language data, e.g., WordNet-like lexical-semantic hierarchies of synsets [36] codifying word meanings in different natural languages and
in different domains [2] represented in a machine processable format, e.g., Lexical
Markup Framework [14].

Such machine-processable language data are stored and managed as part of
a *Lexical-Semantic Resource* (see Fig. 1) which is usually designed as a collection of WordNet-like machine-processable lexical hierarchies and, in some cases
[20,21], with an additional language-independent semantic layer unifying different language-specific lexical hierarchies. Given the design of the *Lexical-Semantic
Resource*, the final activity of this phase shifts to the *Knowledge Engineer* (see
Fig. 1) who has to now generate the *Lightweight Ontology* (Fig. 1) which is an
intermediate machine-processable formal hierarchy *"consisting of backbone taxonomies"* [27] that are being considered for representing knowledge in the context of a specific purpose provided by the user. To that end, the *Knowledge Engineer* has to take in two important inputs. Firstly, (s)he has to take in input the
appropriate lexical-semantic hierarchy of words in a specific language which will
inform the syntax and modelling of the taxonomical hierarchy of the *Lightweight
Ontology* she will generate. In addition, (s)he also takes in input the (dataset)
schema of the entities which (s)he wants to model in the *Lightweight Ontology*,
this, providing her with the *exact* way in which the subsumption hierarchy of
parent and child concepts, pertaining to the entities (and their datasets), should
be organized[1].

The second phase, as illustrated in Fig. 1, concerns the design and development of a repository (exposed via a catalog) of reusable Entity Type Graphs
(ETGs) [15], wherein, ETGs are defined as machine-processable *ontological* representations formalizing entity types [26] which capture the semantics inherent in
(dataset) entities. Notice the fact that, ETGs, being *ontological* representations,
also encode *object properties* (modelling how an entity is related to other entities) and *data properties* (modelling the attributes which describe an entity) as
is standard to any KR model. This repository is crucial to the methodology in all
the four dimensions - *F*indability, *A*ccessibility, *I*nteroperability, and *R*eusability
- advanced by the *FAIR* paradigm [51] of scientific data management. Especially,

---

[1] Thereby, significantly speeding up the process of merging the datasets with the KR
model at a later stage of the methodology.

the repository would facilitate not only interoperability amongst ETGs (as they are modelled following the same technological standards) but also enable ETG-based interoperability of data (when ETGs from the repository are reused, in conjunction with lightweight ontology, to produce the final EG). It would also promote the circular reuse of ETGs, for instance, the reuse of the same ETG but for different use case scenarios of KR. A crucial observation. Notice that while there are several technical advantages of designing an ETG repository as elucidated above, the methodology *does not* specify any activity path or roles for enforcing guiding principles which ensure the high-quality of the ETG models constituting the repository (noticeable by the lack of any activity preceding the ETG repository in Fig. 1).

The third phase concentrates on how the *Data Scientist* (see Fig. 1) exploits the outputs of the previous two phases and the concrete (entity) datasets of the use case at hand to generate the final Entity Graph (EG). An EG is a type of Knowledge Graph (KG) which is: (i) taxonomically structured via a lightweight ontology, and, (ii) interrelated and described with object properties and data properties from the relevant ETG. To that end, the *Data Scientist* receives in input the lightweight ontology (output of the first phase), wherein, the use-case specific concepts are hierarchically modelled following the appropriate lexical-semantic hierarchy. The lightweight ontology is then grounded in the relevant classificatorily-compliant ETG from the ETG repository (output of the second phase). This activity has three key advantages. Firstly, the ETG endows the lightweight ontology-ETG combined KR artifact with crucial object properties (which interrelate, at a conceptual level, the entities it encode) and data properties (which encode the descriptive attributes of entities). Secondly, the grounding also ensures the completeness of the KR model in terms of grounding use-case specific concepts (modelled bottom-up) into general (domain) concepts (modelled top-down). Thirdly, the above grounding also ensures the fact that, later, the data encoded via the specific lightweight ontology becomes interoperable with data encoded via other lightweight ontologies which commit to the same ETG. Given the lightweight ontology-ETG combined KR artifact, the *Data Scientist* takes in input the entity datasets and semi-automatically maps them to the combined artifact (see, [22], for the detailed process), one dataset at a time, to generate the final Entity Graph (EG) which is a KG modelled by populating the nodes of the combined KR artifact with data.

Finally, the fourth phase of the methodology concentrates on the different ways in which different *users* can exploit the Entity Graph (EG). This, in turn, informs as well as depends on the different type of basic and specialized *services* which can be developed to explore the EG. A set of basic services can include the option to download a (part of a) KG in different formats, the option to query a KG (see, [15], for an enumeration of potential services). Advanced services can be designed depending upon the use-case, for instance, to exploit a generated KG for image annotation tasks. A prime example can be of an interactive service to facilitate *egocentric* image annotation (with egocentrism becoming increasingly pivotal to the computer vision community [11]). Such a service, for instance, would allow a user to use (a portion of) a KG schema and populate each of its node (i.e., a concept) with (multiple) relevant images to generate a hierarchically organized image dataset ready to be downloaded and used as training data for computer vision models.

3 Knowledge Organization (KO)

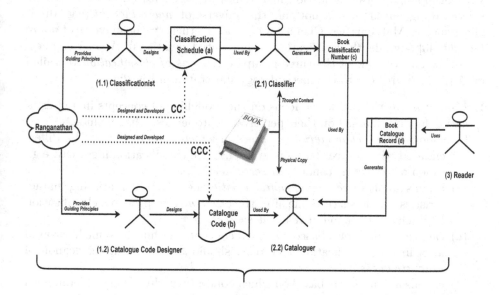

Purpose (Fixed): To classify and catalogue library resources.

Fig. 2. A high-level view of the facet-analytical KO Methodology.

In sync with the previous section on the KR methodology, let us now concentrate on a detailed exposition of the various phases which together compose to form a standard KO methodology within the facet-analytic tradition of KO. See Fig. 2 for a high-level view of the KO methodology. The methodology can be seen as being constituted of the following four distinct phases (the terminologies being detailed later):

1. The first phase initiating with the guiding principles for *Classification* [42] and concluding with the generation of the book classification number.
2. The second phase concerned with the guiding principles for *Cataloguing* [41] and concluding with the design of the catalogue code.
3. The third phase of the methodology concentrating on how the cataloguer takes in three different inputs, namely, the book classification number, the physical copy of the book and the catalogue code, and, suitably integrates them to generate the book catalogue record.

4. Finally, the fourth and the final phase concentrating on the different ways in which a reader visiting a library can use and exploit the book catalogue record.

The diagrammatic symbols of Fig. 2 are similar as before. We now consider each phase of the methodology individually.

The first phase, as already noted, commences with guiding principles, termed *canons of classification*, postulated by Ranaganathan [42] to oversee the generation of *high-quality* classification hierarchies for any subject. Notice that, by *subject*, Ranganathan meant not only the universe of *macro thought* (e.g., disciplines such as Mathematics, Chemistry) but also, crucially, the universe of *micro thought* [43] (e.g., depth classification of differential equations). We now enumerate below an overview of the three groups of *canons of classification* (detailed in [42]) which are core to the methodology illustrated in Fig. 2:

1. *Canons of Idea Plane*, which focus on the modelling of concepts in a classification hierarchy based on their perceivable properties. They include:
   (a) canons about *characteristics* based on which concepts should be differentiated with respect to a single level in the classification hierarchy, e.g., canon of *relevance*, canon of *ascertainability*.
   (b) canons about *succession of characteristics*, i.e., how differentiating characteristics should succeed one after the other with respect to a classification hierarchy, e.g., canon of *relevant succession*.
   (c) canons about *arrays* based on which concepts, within the same horizontal level in the classification hierarchy, should be modelled, e.g., canon of *exhaustiveness*.
   (d) canons about *chains* based on which concepts, within a single hierarchical path in the classification hierarchy, should be modelled, e.g., canon of *modulation*.
2. *Canons of Verbal Plane*, which focus on the proper linguistic rendering of the concepts modelled following the canons of the Idea Plane, e.g., canon of *reticence*.
3. *Canons of Notational Plane*, which focus on assigning a unique numerical identifier for each linguistically labelled concept in the classification hierarchy, e.g., canon of *synonym* and canon of *homonym*.

Thereafter, as illustrated in Fig. 2, the *canons of classification* as briefed above are taken in input by the *Classificationist* to design (a set of) faceted classification schedules for either general knowledge organization usage, e.g., the Colon Classification (CC) [44] designed and developed by Ranganathan himself (indicated with dashed lines), or, for specialized knowledge organization usage, e.g., Uniclass[2], specialized classification for the construction sector. Given the design of the classification schedule(s), the final activity of this phase shifts to the *Classifier* (see Fig. 2) who has to now generate the unique *Book Classification Number* (Fig. 2), e.g., Colon Number, for the subject matter of a book. To that

---

[2] https://www.thenbs.com/our-tools/uniclass.

end, the *Classifier* has to take in two important inputs. Firstly, (s)he has to take the *a priori* designed classification schedules which provide him/her with the concept hierarchy (with each concept uniquely identified via an identifier) as well as the formula (i.e., the *facet formula*) in which relevant concepts should be combined to generate the book classification number. Secondly, (s)he has to take in input the *thought content* of the book to be classified. Finally, the *Classifier* follows Ranganathan's analytico-synthetic classification number generation procedure [44] to generate the *Book Classification Number* which uniquely identifies its subject matter. Notice that the above process is valid not only for books but also for any library resource.

The second phase, as illustrated in Fig. 2, concerns the design and development of a catalogue code. It commences with the *canons of cataloguing* as guiding principles postulated by Ranaganathan [41] to oversee the generation of *high-quality* description of any book (or, any library resource). Some of the canons are notable to be briefed. For example, the canon of *sought heading* mandates that the metadata attributes which should be captured about a book in a catalogue should be strictly based on the *likelihood* of how a user might approach the catalogue. To that end, all unnecessary metadata should be excluded from the catalogue record. Further, the canon of *consistence* prescribes that, for a specific type of (library) resource, the set of metadata which constitute its catalogue record should be consistent, unless otherwise prescribed by the canon of *context*. Another crucial principle is that of *local variation* which allows flexibility in the description of a catalogue record if need arises due to a very typical resource specific to a context. These canons of cataloguing, amongst many others detailed in [41], are taken as input guidelines by the *Catalogue Code Designer* to finally design a *Catalogue Code* - a body of specifications on how and what metadata should be encoded in a catalogue record for a specific bibliographic resource type. In fact, Ranganathan himself designed and developed one such catalogue code termed the *Classified Catalogue Code* (or, CCC; shown in Fig. 2 via dashed lines).

The third phase concentrates on how the *Cataloguer* (see Fig. 2) exploits the outputs of the previous two phases and the concrete physical copy of the resource (e.g., book) at hand to generate the final *Book Catalogue Record*. A bibliographic catalogue record encodes metadata which are termed as *access points*, e.g., title, author, year of publication, subject headings, etc., which might be help the reader in her quest to search and identify the actual copy of the book (or, resource). To that end, the *Cataloguer* receives in input the book classification number (output of the first phase), wherein, the subject matter of the book is modelled following the appropriate classification schedule (and facet formula). Given the book classification number, the procedure of *Chain Indexing* is performed, whereby, the classification number is reverse-engineered through a series of specified steps (see [41] for details) to generate subject headings (*tags* in modern parlance) which can serve as access points in the catalogue record. Further, the *Cataloguer* also receives two other inputs: the concrete copy of the book which contains all its imprint details, and, the catalogue code (e.g., CCC) which strictly specifies which and how such imprint information should be modelled in the catalogue record. Thereafter, the *Cataloguer* integrates the subject headings together with the requisite imprint attributes and the classification number (together with the *call number* to identify the book's exact place in the shelves) to generate the final *Book Catalogue Record.*

Finally, the fourth phase concentrates on how a library *reader* can exploit the book catalogue record. In addition to the usual ways of using the catalogue (see, e.g., [41]), Ranganathan's APUPA principle [45] facilitates a reader in finding very related and somewhat related books/resources on either side of the particular resource one is searching for). Further, a reader can use the catalogue record of an Online Public Access Catalog (OPAC) which is enhanced with *library discovery services* [6], thereby, going beyond traditional means of library search to include web-scale *exploratory search* and recommendations.

4   From KR to KO and Back

Table 1. Functional mapping between roles of KR, KO and KO-Enriched KR.

Phase	KR	KO	KO-Enriched KR
1	Language Engineer (1.1)	Classificationist (1.1)	Language Engineer (1.1)
2	Knowledge Engineer (2.1)	Classifier (2.1)	Knowledge Engineer (2.1)
3	Data Scientist (1.2 + 2.2)	Catalogue Code Designer (1.2) Cataloguer (2.2)	Ontology Engineer (1.2 + 2.3) Data Scientist (2.2)
4	User (3)	Reader (3)	User (3)

In the previous two sections, we've provided a detailed elucidation of the principle roles, activities and artifacts of both the Knowledge Representation and the facet-analytical Knowledge Organization methodology, respectively. In this section, before showing how to complete the loop *from KR to KO and back*, we first concentrate on a *functional mapping* of, chiefly, the roles and the artifacts, of the two aforementioned methodologies (see the first three columns of Table 1). Notice two things. Firstly, via functional mapping, we ascertain whether or not two roles or artifacts perform the *same or synonymous* broad function, irrespective of differences in their syntax, semantics or form. Secondly, in Table 1, we illustrate only the roles as they embody the major functional differences between the two methodologies and not the artifacts (duely elucidated in the following description) which are functionally synonymous. We constantly refer to Table 1, and, to Figs. 1 and 2 as required, in the following discussion.

At the very outset, note that we proceed the functional mapping on the basis of the four informal phases via which we detailed each individual methodology. We notice that, in the first phase, there is a mapping between the roles of *Language Engineer (1.1)* and that of *Classificationist (1.1)*. This is clearly due to the fact that both these roles, based on input guiding principles, generate lexical-semantic classification hierarchies. Next, we also note that the artifacts that the above two roles produce, namely, the *Lexical-Semantic Resource (a)* (see Fig. 1) and the *Classification Schedule (a)* (see Fig. 2) are also in functional mapping to each other, given that both are essentially constituted of (a set of) lexical-semantic classification hierarchies focused on different subjects, domains, etc. Further, the roles *Knowledge Engineer (2.1)* and *Classifier (2.1)* are also mapped to each other because their central function is to use prescribed lexical-semantic hierarchies and classify the *subject* of resources according to their relevant concept within the hierarchy. To that end, the output artifacts they produce, i.e., *Lightweight Ontology (c)* (see Fig. 1) and *Book Classification Number (c)* (see Fig. 2) also serve the synonymous function of encoding the categorization of either the entity dataset schema or the book subject matter.

In the second phase, the *ETG Repository (b)* (see Fig. 1) and *Catalogue Code (b)* (see Fig. 2) are also functionally synonymous in the sense that both of these artifacts endow their input artifacts with reusable specifications of how to describe concepts via attributes within a classification hierarchy. The first major break in functional mapping occurs with respect to the role of *Data Scientist (1.2 + 2.2)*. The Data Scientist role subsumes two roles, namely, that of the *Catalogue Code Designer (1.2)* which exclusively deals with the specification of the descriptive (data) attribute schema in addition to that of the *Cataloguer (2.2)* whose function is to generate the book catalogue record. Further, notice the functional synonymity between the two artifacts: *Entity Graph (d)* (see Fig. 1) and *Book Catalog Record (d)* (see Fig. 2), both of whose function is to provide the end user with an integrated view of top-down and bottom-up knowledge. Finally, the roles of a *User (3)* and a *Reader (3)* are also mapped as both function as end-users using the respective output artifacts of their methodologies in different ways. Notice also the fact that the activities across both the methodologies are also functionally mapped (see the labelled edges on Figs. 1 and 2, respectively) with the only exception of the gap prior to the ETG repository in Fig. 1.

Given the functional mapping, we now concentrate on how the guiding principles, i.e., *canons*, advanced by the facet-analytic KO approach can be incorporated within the KR methodology to ultimately result in a KO-enriched KR methodology. To that end, we concentrate on the various phases (harmonized from both the KR and KO methodologies via the functional mapping) which together compose to form the KO-enriched KR methodology (see Fig. 3). The methodology can be seen as being constituted of the following four distinct phases:

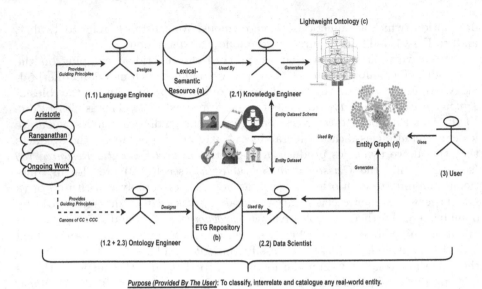

Fig. 3. A high-level view of the KO-Enriched KR Methodology.

1. The first phase initiating with guiding principles and concluding with the generation of the Lightweight Ontology.
2. The second phase initiating with guiding principles (*canons*) guiding the development of *high-quality* Entity Type Graphs (ETGs) within the ETG repository.
3. The third phase of the methodology concentrating on how the data scientist generates the Entity Graph (EG), and,
4. The final phase concentrating on the different ways in which a user can use and exploit the EG.

The diagrammatic symbols of Fig. 3 are similar as before. We now consider each phase of the methodology briefly.

The first phase (see Fig. 3) is exactly the same as that of the original KR methodology (see Fig. 1). Briefly, the *Language Engineer* designs a *Lexical-Semantic Resource* composed of machine-processable language data, i.e., lexical-semantic hierarchies, designed by following the *Genus-Differentia* guiding principle of Aristotle. These lexical-semantic hierarchies are then used by the *Knowledge Engineer* in conjunction with the entity dataset schemas to generate the *Lightweight Ontology*. The second phase of the methodology, i.e., the development of the ETG repository, is markedly different from that in Fig. 1 and constitutes the core of the *back* loop in *from KR to KO and back*. It initiates with the still ongoing work (represented via dashed line in Fig. 3) on the adaptation of Ranganathan's guiding canons of both classification and cataloguing (see Sect. 3) for the development of high-quality ETGs. Notice that the current effort (and the final goal) is to adapt all the relevant canons for classification (i.e., the different canons from the Idea Plane, Verbal Plane and Notational Plane) to generate taxonomically well-founded ETG hierarchies and the canons for cataloguing to mandate guidelines as to how (data) properties should be modelled to describe (conceptual) entities in such hierarchies. To that end, the methodology introduces a new role, that of an *Ontology Engineer*, who will *ensure* the development of the ETGs, and thereby, the ETG repository, in full conformance with the quality guidelines prescribed by the canons of Ranganathan suitably adapted. Notice that, with the support of Ranaganathan's canons of classification, the *Ontology Engineer* would be able to generate ETGs not only restricted to macro-domains but also focused on *fine-grained* micro domain of interests.

The third and the fourth phase of the methodology (see Fig. 3) is also the same as that of the original KR methodology (see Fig. 1). Briefly, the Data Scientist takes in input the lightweight ontology, the entity datasets and the relevant *quality-enriched ETG* and suitably integrates them, in an iterative fashion, to ultimately generate an EG. Finally, the fourth phase concentrates on the ways in which the user can exploit the output EG. At this point, let us recollect the example of an advanced service of egocentric image annotation described in the fourth phase of the original KR methodology (in Sect. 2). In addition to the above service, the methodological incorporation of Ranganathan's canons would also *ensure*, in a major advance from the state-of-the-art, the generation of fine-grained classification (ETG) hierarchies which, e.g., as evidenced from (their lack in) computer vision literature[3], is bound to deeply enrich (KR-based) dataset building and data quality in the entire spectrum of fine-grained image classification.

Notice also, from Table 1, how the roles within the integrated KO-enriched KR methodology functionally compares with that of the original KR and facet-analytical KO methodology. The role of the *Language Engineer (1.1)*, *Knowledge Engineer (2.1)* and *User (3)* in the integrated methodology is functionally similar to that of their counterparts in the KR and KO methodology (which have been functionally mapped before). The key difference, however, is reflected in the role of *Ontology Engineer (1.2 + 2.3)*, which, builds the ETG hierarchy adhering to the *canons* (a completely new role absent in the other methodologies) and additionally specifies the data attributes within the ETG (part of the role of *Data Scientist* in the KR and the role of *Catalog Code Designer* in the KO methodology). The *Data Scientist (2.2)* in the KO-enriched KR methodology is functionally mapped to the role of *Cataloguer* in the KO and to a part of the role of *Data Scientist* in the KR methodology. This difference is because the former *Data Scientist (2.2)* role only integrates the previous three outputs to generate the EG, whereas, the latter role of *Data Scientist (1.2 + 2.2)*, in addition to the above function, also specifies data attributes (performed by the new role of *Ontology Engineer* in the KO-enriched KR methodology). In terms of artifacts, the KO-enriched KR methodology is, functionally, the same as that of the KR methodology, and, thereof, to the KO methodology. Finally, in terms of activities, the KO-enriched KR methodology adds two extra activity flows

---

[3] https://paperswithcode.com/task/fine-grained-image-classification.

over and above the KR methodology, namely: (i) the first activity flow from *Ranganathan* and *Ongoing Work* to the *Ontology Engineer* in terms of adapting guiding principles of CC and CCC, and (ii) the activity flow from the *Ontology Engineer* to the *ETG Repository* in terms of designing the repository.

5 Case Study

Let us now focus on how the incorporation of the guiding principles of modelling quality (i.e., the *canons*) within the overall KO-enriched KR methodology can significantly improve the quality of those data which, within the data science research landscape, are organized and generated by exploiting KR models. To that end, we consider the case of ImageNet [9] which is a *benchmark* dataset for various computer vision tasks such as image annotation, object detection, etc. In fact, ImageNet is also the most prominent dataset within the data science landscape which is structured by populating the nodes of the WordNet lexical-semantic ontology with hundreds of thousands of images of different objects. While it has been heavily used to test and develop multiple computer vision models (e.g., [31,34]), a recent study-cum-experiment [19] revealed a fundamental problem in the quality of the ImageNet ontology model which results in systematic flaws in its data quality (see [50]).

The study established that, in ImageNet, there was a many-to-many mapping between, quoting [19], *"the visual information encoded in an image and the intended semantics of the corresponding linguistic descriptions"*. In its detailed analysis, the study found that the underlying cause was the lack of an *explicit* methodology by the ImageNet creators, backed by *guiding principles* for ensuring conceptual model quality, to align the way visual classification hierarchies, e.g., of images, are modelled and the way in which lexical-semantic hierarchies are modelled. The study, quoting a previous study [50], also noted that this misalignment between visual and linguistic classification led to two major categories of design flaws[4] systemic in ImageNet data annotation (and affecting all models developed and trained on it). Firstly, there are *Mislabelled Images*, wherein, there is a complete misalignment in how an image is visually classified and annotated and how it is linguistically classified and annotated. A famous example is that of a *birthday cake* labelled as an *acoustic guitar* (see, [19]). Secondly, there are *Single-Object Images*, wherein, the misalignment between the visual classification and linguistic classification of an image is chiefly due to either *visual polysemy* or *linguistic polysemy* (several examples in [19]). To that end, notice the fact that the root of all the aforementioned design flaws in ImageNet data is the lack of *modelling quality* in classification, namely, in visual and linguistic classification of an image, and, in their alignment thereafter.

In response to the above problems, the study proposed an overall image annotation methodology within which KO-enriched KR modelling is a *key*

---

[4] Notice that the study [19] also found an additional category of design flaw - *Multi-Object Images*, the root cause of which, however, is object localization and not classification model quality and alignment.

component. Notice, however, the fact that KO-enriched KR modelling component in the said methodology has been adapted and tuned to the needs of image classification. To that end, the study proposed that any KR-based image classification and annotation exercise should be comprised of the following activities:

- Firstly, *Linguistic Classification*, involving the lexical-semantic hierarchical modelling of the space of linguistic labels used to annotate images. Here the meaning of each label within the linguistic hierarchy should be *defined in terms of linguistically defined properties encoding a selected set of visual properties*, thereby, factoring in the alignment of visual and linguistic classification at the language level. For example, the definition of a guitar as being a *"string instrument with six strings"*.
- Secondly, *Visual Classification*, involving the selection of visual properties of an object (in an image) and annotating it with an appropriate label from the linguistic hierarchy as defined via the linguistic classification. For example, for the object *Guitar* in an image, the annotator would not choose the label Guitar but, rather the property that it has six strings. The label *Guitar* comes for free because of how it is defined via the same property in the linguistic classification hierarchy, thereby, eliminating any visual or linguistic ambiguity.

It is very interesting to note that the aforementioned modelling of visual and linguistic classification is completely *guided* by the same set of *canons of classification* proposed by Ranganathan (briefed in Sect. 3) and adapted for KO-enriched KR-based visual classification. The reader is referred to the study in [16,17] for details regarding how the canons were adapted for visual classification and examples of several key modelling instances where the canons ensured the quality of alignment between visual and linguistic classification.

Finally, the study in [19] also performed three experiments to quantify the improvement, if any, brought by the dataset generated following the canons-based high quality alignment between visual and linguistic classification. To that end, the study modelled a dataset on a selected fragment of ImageNet, namely, the stringed musical instruments hierarchy and performed three separate experiments on: the *accuracy* of computer vision (CV) models when trained on the dataset, the improvement in the *inter-annotator agreement* with respect to the visual and linguistic classification, and, the improvements (if any) in the cost of image annotation. As detailed in [19] (see Sect. 5: Evaluation), the study found significant improvements for all the above experiments and attributed the improvement to the enrichment in classification model quality facilitated by adherence to the *canons*.

6   Related Work

There are three important research lines within Data and Information Science, namely, KR model quality, KR methodologies and data quality in data science ecosystem, which are significantly related to the current work. We consider each of the above areas briefly.

Firstly, we focus on literature analyzing the quality of *classification semantics* of KR models of various kinds, e.g., ontologies, conceptual models. The research in, e.g., [1,40] advanced a checklist of modelling issues which directly affect the classification semantics of ontology models, including, amongst others, cycles in a hierarchy, creating polysemous elements, creating synonyms as classes, using different inconsistent naming criteria. More recently, there have also been a lot of work in uncovering *antipatterns* - taxonomically inadmissible hierarchical patterns - in KR models [30,46]. Notice that modelling quality enrichment activity path based on Ranganathan's canons in our proposed KO-enriched KR methodology tackles all of the aforementioned modelling issues which chiefly impact the classification model of the hierarchy.

Secondly, let us focus on some of the prominent state-of-the-art KR methodologies. The highly cited methodology in [13] advanced a *"life cycle to build ontologies based in evolving prototypes"*. The methodology proposed in [37] offered the flexibility of choosing top-down, bottom-up or middle-out approaches while modelling ontologies without any explicit emphasis on modelling quality. Recently, the NeOn methodology [48] proposed reuse, re-engineering and merging of ontological resources and the XD methodology [3] stressed on reuse of ontology design patterns. Notice that modelling quality, especially for the latter, is crucial for integrating the various ontology patterns reused. To that end, differently from all above KR methodologies, the KO-enriched KR methodology includes a dedicated activity path for ensuring the classification modelling quality of the KR model.

Last but not the least, let us focus on data quality in data science research. The research reported in [49] is an early effort in analyzing the issue of data quality. Recent research, e.g., [39,52], proposes adherence to best practices-based methodologies in the modelling of datasets that are attentive to limitations [4] and impact. It is also worthy to note that the crowdsourcing community has also focused extensively on the problem of data quality, see, e.g., [7,12]. Some early work have also been done towards improving the process of ensuring quality, see, e.g., [8]. In our current work, the proposed KO-enriched KR methodology is a significant advance in the aforementioned context of the methodological incorporation of quality best practices in modelling.

7 Conclusion

To summarize, the paper provided a non-trivial functional mapping between the components of the KR and facet-analytical KO methodologies and derived an integrated KO-enriched KR methodology which subsumes all the components of the KR methodology with the major addition of the KO-based canons.

Acknowledgement. The research has received funding from JIDEP under grant number 101058732.

References

1. Baumeister, J., Seipel, D.: Smelly owls-design anomalies in ontologies. In: FLAIRS Conference, vol. 215, p. 220 (2005)
2. Bentivogli, L., Forner, P., Magnini, B., Pianta, E.: Revising the wordnet domains hierarchy: semantics, coverage and balancing. In: Proceedings of the Workshop on Multilingual Linguistic Resources, pp. 94–101 (2004)
3. Blomqvist, E., Hammar, K., Presutti, V.: Engineering ontologies with patterns-the extreme design methodology. Ontology Eng. Ontology Des. Patterns 25, 23–50 (2016)
4. Bouquet, P., Giunchiglia, F.: Reasoning about theory adequacy. a new solution to the qualification problem. Fundamenta Informaticae 23(2, 3, 4), 247–262 (1995)
5. Brachman, R., Levesque, H.: Knowledge Representation and Reasoning. Elsevier (2004)
6. Breeding, M.: The future of library resource discovery. Inf. Stand. Q. 27(1), 24–30 (2015)
7. Daniel, F., Kucherbaev, P., Cappiello, C., Benatallah, B., Allahbakhsh, M.: Quality control in crowdsourcing: a survey of quality attributes, assessment techniques, and assurance actions. ACM Comput. Surv. 51(1), 1–40 (2018)
8. Demartini, G., Roitero, K., Mizzaro, S.: Managing bias in human-annotated data: moving beyond bias removal. arXiv preprint arXiv:2110.13504 (2021)
9. Deng, J., Dong, W., Socher, R., Li, L.J., Li, K., Fei-Fei, L.: ImageNet: a large-scale hierarchical image database. In: 2009 IEEE Conference on Computer Vision and Pattern Recognition, pp. 248–255. IEEE (2009)
10. Duque-Ramos, A., et al.: Evaluation of the OQuaRE framework for ontology quality. Expert Syst. Appl. 40(7), 2696–2703 (2013)
11. Erculiani, L., Giunchiglia, F., Passerini, A.: Continual egocentric object recognition. In: ECAI 2020, pp. 1127–1134. IOS Press (2020)
12. Ewerth, R., Springstein, M., Phan-Vogtmann, L.A., Schütze, J.: "Are machines better than humans in image tagging?" - A user study adds to the puzzle. In: Jose, J.M., et al. (eds.) ECIR 2017. LNCS, vol. 10193, pp. 186–198. Springer, Cham (2017). https://doi.org/10.1007/978-3-319-56608-5_15
13. Fernández-López, M., Gómez-Pérez, A., Juristo, N.: Methontology: from ontological art towards ontological engineering. In: AAAI Conference on Artificial Intelligence (1997)
14. Francopoulo, G., Huang, C.R.: Lexical markup framework: an ISO standard for electronic lexicons and its implications for Asian languages. Lexicography 1, 37–51 (2014)
15. Fumagalli, M., Boffo, M., Shi, D., Bagchi, M., Giunchiglia, F.: Towards a gateway for knowledge graph schemas collection, analysis, and embedding. Ontology Showcase and Demonstrations Track, 9th Joint Ontology Workshops (JOWO 2023), co-located with FOIS 2023, 19-20 July, 2023, Sherbrooke, Québec, Canada. arXiv preprint arXiv:2311.12465 (2023)
16. Giunchiglia, F., Bagchi, M.: Millikan + Ranganathan - from perception to classification. In: 5th Cognition and OntologieS (CAOS) Workshop, Co-located with the 12th International Conference on Formal Ontology in Information Systems (FOIS) (2021)
17. Giunchiglia, F., Bagchi, M.: Object recognition as classification via visual properties. In: 17th International ISKO Conference and Advances in Knowledge Organization. Aalborg, Denmark (2022)

18. Giunchiglia, F., Bagchi, M., Diao, X.: Aligning visual and lexical semantics. In: International Conference on Information, pp. 294–302. Springer (2023).https:// doi.org/10.1007/978-3-031-28035-1_20
19. Giunchiglia, F., Bagchi, M., Diao, X.: A semantics-driven methodology for high-quality image annotation. In: 26th European Conference on Artificial Intelligence (ECAI 2023). arXiv preprint arXiv:2307.14119 (2023)
20. Giunchiglia, F., Batsuren, K., Bella, G.: Understanding and exploiting language diversity. In: IJCAI, pp. 4009–4017 (2017)
21. Giunchiglia, F., Batsuren, K., Freihat, A.A.: One world–seven thousand languages. In: Proceedings 19th International Conference on Computational Linguistics and Intelligent Text Processing, CiCling2018, 18-24 March 2018 (2018)
22. Giunchiglia, F., Bocca, S., Fumagalli, M., Bagchi, M., Zamboni, A.: Popularity driven data integration. In: Villazón-Terrazas, B., Ortiz-Rodriguez, F., Tiwari, S., Sicilia, MA., Martín-Moncunill, D. (eds.) Iberoamerican Knowledge Graphs and Semantic Web Conference, pp. 277–284. Springer, Cham (2022).https://doi.org/ 10.1007/978-3-031-21422-6_20
23. Giunchiglia, F., Dutta, B., Maltese, V.: From knowledge organization to knowledge representation. Knowl. Organ. **41**(1), 44–56 (2014)
24. Giunchiglia, F., Farazi, F., Tanca, L., De Virgilio, R.: The semantic web languages. In: de Virgilio, R., Giunchiglia, F., Tanca, L. (eds.) Semantic Web Information Management: A Model-Based Perspective, pp. 25–38. Springer, Berlin (2009). https://doi.org/10.1007/978-3-642-04329-1_3
25. Giunchiglia, F., Fumagalli, M.: Teleologies: objects, Actions and *Functions*. In: Mayr, H.C., Guizzardi, G., Ma, H., Pastor, O. (eds.) ER 2017. LNCS, vol. 10650, pp. 520–534. Springer, Cham (2017). https://doi.org/10.1007/978-3-319-69904-2_39
26. Giunchiglia, F., Fumagalli, M.: Entity type recognition–dealing with the diversity of knowledge. In: Proceedings of the International Conference on Principles of Knowledge Representation and Reasoning, vol. 17, pp. 414–423 (2020)
27. Giunchiglia, F., Zaihrayeu, I., et al.: Lightweight ontologies. In: Liu, L., Özsu, M. (eds.) Encyclopedia of Database Systems, pp. 1613–1619. Springer, New York (2008). https://doi.org/10.1007/978-1-4899-7993-3_1314-2
28. Giunchiglia, F., Zamboni, A., Bagchi, M., Bocca, S.: Stratified data integration. In: 2nd International Workshop On Knowledge Graph Construction (KGCW), Co-located with the ESWC 2021. Hersonissos, Greece (2021)
29. Guarino, N., Oberle, D., Staab, S.: What is an ontology? Handbook on ontologies, pp. 1–17 (2009)
30. Guizzardi, G.: Ontological patterns, anti-patterns and pattern languages for next-generation conceptual modeling. In: Yu, E., Dobbie, G., Jarke, M., Purao, S. (eds.) ER 2014. LNCS, vol. 8824, pp. 13–27. Springer, Cham (2014). https://doi.org/10. 1007/978-3-319-12206-9_2
31. He, K., Zhang, X., Ren, S., Sun, J.: Deep residual learning for image recognition. In: Proceedings of the IEEE Conference on Computer Vision and Pattern Recognition, pp. 770–778 (2016)
32. Hjørland, B.: What is knowledge organization (KO)? Knowl. Organ. **35**(2–3), 86–101 (2008)
33. Hogan, A., et al.: Knowledge graphs. ACM Computing Surveys (CSUR) **54**(4), 1–37 (2021)
34. Huang, G., Liu, Z., Van Der Maaten, L., Weinberger, K.Q.: Densely connected convolutional networks. In: Proceedings of the IEEE Conference on Computer Vision and Pattern Recognition, pp. 4700–4708 (2017)

35. Koch, B., Denton, E., Hanna, A., Foster, J.G.: Reduced, reused and recycled: the life of a dataset in machine learning research. In: Thirty-fifth Conference on Neural Information Processing Systems Datasets and Benchmarks Track (Round 2) (2021)
36. Miller, G.A.: WordNet: a lexical database for English. Commun. ACM **38**(11), 39–41 (1995)
37. Noy, N.F., McGuinness, D.L., et al.: Ontology development 101: A guide to creating your first ontology (2001)
38. Parry, W.T., Hacker, E.A.: Aristotelian Logic. Suny Press (1991)
39. Paullada, A., Raji, I.D., Bender, E.M., Denton, E., Hanna, A.: Data and its (DIS) contents: a survey of dataset development and use in machine learning research. Patterns **2**(11), 100336 (2021)
40. Poveda-Villalón, M., Suárez-Figueroa, M.C., Gómez-Pérez, A.: Validating ontologies with OOPS! In: Teije, A., et al. (eds.) EKAW 2012. LNCS (LNAI), vol. 7603, pp. 267–281. Springer, Heidelberg (2012). https://doi.org/10.1007/978-3-642-33876-2_24
41. Ranganathan, S.R.: Classified Catalogue Code with Additional Rules for Dictionary Catalogue Code. Asia Publishing House, 5th edn. (1964)
42. Ranganathan, S.R.: Prolegomena to Library Classification. Asia Publishing House (Bombay and New York) (1967)
43. Ranganathan, S.: Depth classification. In: Annals of Library Science. NISCAIR-CSIR, India (1954)
44. Ranganathan, S.: Colon Classification: Basic Classification, vol. 26. Asia Publishing House (1963)
45. Ranganathan, S.: A Descriptive Account of the Colon Classification. Sarada Ranganathan Endowment for Library Science (1967)
46. Sales, T.P., Guizzardi, G.: Ontological anti-patterns: empirically uncovered error-prone structures in ontology-driven conceptual models. Data Knowl. Eng. **99**, 72–104 (2015)
47. Sambasivan, N., Kapania, S., Highfill, H., Akrong, D., Paritosh, P., Aroyo, L.M.: "everyone wants to do the model work, not the data work": data cascades in high-stakes AI. In: CHI, pp. 1–15 (2021)
48. Suárez-Figueroa, M.C., Gómez-Pérez, A., Fernández-López, M.: The NeOn methodology for ontology engineering. In: Suárez-Figueroa, M.C., Gómez-Pérez, A., Motta, E., Gangemi, A. (eds.) Ontology Engineering in a Networked World, pp. 9–34. Springer, Heidelberg (2012). https://doi.org/10.1007/978-3-642-24794-1_2
49. Torralba, A., Efros, A.A.: Unbiased look at dataset bias. In: CVPR 2011, pp. 1521–1528. IEEE (2011)
50. Tsipras, D., Santurkar, S., Engstrom, L., Ilyas, A., Madry, A.: From ImageNet to image classification: contextualizing progress on benchmarks. In: International Conference on Machine Learning, pp. 9625–9635. PMLR (2020)
51. Wilkinson, M.D., et al.: The fair guiding principles for scientific data management and stewardship. Sci. Data **3**(1), 1–9 (2016)
52. Yang, K., Qinami, K., Fei-Fei, L., Deng, J., Russakovsky, O.: Towards fairer datasets: filtering and balancing the distribution of the people subtree in the ImageNet hierarchy. In: FACT Conference, pp. 547–558 (2020)
53. Zeng, M.L.: Knowledge organization systems (KOS). Knowl. Organ. **35**(2–3), 160–182 (2008)

The Missing Linkage Between Science Technology and Innovation Policy and the Scientific Workforce—Evidence from Colombia

Julián D. Cortés[1,2(✉)] ⓘ and María Catalina Ramírez-Cajiao[2] ⓘ

[1] School of Management and Business, Universidad del Rosario, Bogotá, Colombia
julian.cortess@urosario.edu.co
[2] Engineering School, Universidad de Los Andes, Bogotá, Colombia

Abstract. STIP (science, technology, and innovation policy/es) strive to give direction and incentives to the formation and specialization of the scientific workforce. How to draw the linkage between both factors of the national STI system? Here we explore the correlation between highly strategic research areas/fields supported by STIP and the scientific workforce of Colombia from 2013 to 2021. We used a dataset of 225 research funding calls and a sample of 28,000 + scientist profiles. We found no statistically significant correlation between both variables. Our discussion orbited around government STIP transitions, STIP models, and STIP timing of implementation. Our contribution lies in proposing a standardized and replicable diagnosis to identify strategic research areas/fields supported by STIP to the absent literature on STIP-scientific workforce relationship in the contexts of middle and low-income countries.

Keywords: Research policy · Research funding · Scientific workforce · Network science · Co-word analysis

1 Introduction

STIP (science, technology, and innovation policy/es) strive to give direction to norms/rules and practices to conduct basic & applied research and innovation activities within national borders [18, 33, 37]. STIP also can focus on and allocate resources to specific research areas/fields, incentivizing the mobilization and specialization of the national scientific workforce in such areas/fields [4, 19, 51]. STIP research has produced rich literature on frameworks for improving STI impact and post-hoc assessment of the overall and actor-focused performance of the national knowledge production system [2, 3, 6, 7, 10, 18, 19, 21–25, 30–32, 38, 43, 45, 49].

There are, however, two streams to which this work in progress contributes. First, a lack of research on STIP and its plausible relationship with the national scientific workforce via techniques from scientometrics and bibliographic data, and second, a growing interest in in-depth examination at the country level—particularly in middle-low-income regions [12, 27, 42]. Consequently, we formulate the following research

I. Sserwanga et al. (Eds.): iConference 2024, LNCS 14596, pp. 288–297, 2024.
https://doi.org/10.1007/978-3-031-57850-2_21

question: is there a significant relationship between research area/field priorities stated by STIP and the national scientific workforce? Correspondingly, this work in progress explores the correlation between highly strategic research areas/fields supported by STIP and Colombia's national scientific workforce from 2013 to 2021.

Our insights are valuable for STIP and policymaking fourfold: i) public science agencies can diagnose highly strategic research areas/fields supported by STIP at the research funding granularity; ii) the middle-long run research areas/fields relevance despite government transitions; iii) the convergence/divergence between the STIP priorities and the national scientific workforce; iv) a replicable and standardized framework to study national STIP-scientific workforce alignment. After this introduction, we present the data and methodology used. Then, the results are presented. Finally, the Discussion and conclusion section presents limitations and further research questions.

2 Data and Methods

2.1 Data

We used two datasets. First, a hand-curated dataset of 225 research funding calls issued by Colombia's MinCiencias (Ministry of Science Technology and Innovation) from 2013 to 2021 [16, 17]. In this dataset, the research areas/fields explicitly supported by the research funding calls were sourced, translated to English, and then standardized using the ASJC (All Science Journal Classification) [44]. The ASJC is a standard system designed to assign a journal/serial title to single or multiple fields. There are 334 fields in five areas: physical sciences (~34% out of 334 fields), life sciences (~15%), health sciences (~30%), social sciences & humanities (~19%), and multidisciplinary. The ASJC standard was used to standardize the scientific areas MinCiencias' prioritized, hence it was not used to any journal classification where any Colombian researcher had published whatsoever. This is important because some fields like *bio-tech* and *bio-inspired tech* could be replaced plainly with *Biotechnology*, which is a specific ASJC field.

Second, a merged dataset of six national calls where MinCiencias identified and assessed research groups and researchers during 2013–2021. The sample consisted of 28,000+ unique researcher identifiers (IDs) [35]. In addition, the dataset has individual researcher information on the academic degree, gender, research category, ethnicity, institutional affiliation, and principal research field according to the OECD-FORD (Fields of Research and Development) classification [39], among others. We will focus our analysis on the latter variable.

2.2 Methods

Co-word Network Analysis. To identify highly strategic research areas/fields based on the content structure of Colombia's research funding calls, we replicated Cortés and Ramírez-Cajiao [16, 17] methodology. They applied a co-word analysis to assemble an information-based network of co-occurring research fields [8]. Figure 1 presents an example of three hypothetical research fields connected via a joint research funding call in which they were explicitly mentioned/supported.

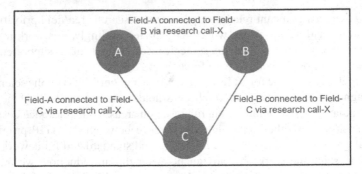

Fig. 1. Co-word analysis of funding research calls. Source: Callon et al. [8].

Betweenness Centrality Indicator. Once we assembled the network, we computed the betweenness calculation centrality indicator as follows:

$$C_B(p_k) = \sum_{i<j}^{n} \frac{g_{ij}(p_k)}{g_{ij}}; i \neq j \neq k \tag{1}$$

where g_{ij} is the shorter path that links nodes p_i and $g_{ij}(p_k)$ is the shorter path that links nodes p_i and $p_j p_k$ [40]. Betweenness centrality measures the structural importance of nodes (i.e., research fields) as it reflects the node's capacity to block or enable the flow of information/knowledge between communities of grouped fields [20, 46]. The indicator was normalized from 0 to 1, 1 as the highest betweenness centrality. The computation of betweenness centrality for each node does not have any external weighing since it considers the links between nodes via a joint research funding call in which they were explicitly mentioned/supported, as shown in Fig. 1. Betweenness centrality has been used extensively to identify key terms in worldwide organizational and academic mission statements, and research fields, among others [11, 13–15].

Matching ASJC and OECD-FORD Standards. The first dataset uses the ASJC standard to classify research areas/fields explicitly mentioned in the calls, while the second uses the OECD-FORD classification for researchers. To standardize and be able to correlate the betweenness score of ASJC fields with the percentage of researchers by OECD-FORD classification, we used a lexical similarity approach.

The approach was to compute a string distance matrix with rows according to the 334 ASJC fields and the 41 second-level (i.e., area) OECD-FORD classifications [29]. The string dissimilarity measure explored here was the *soundex* algorithm [36]. It translates strings to phonetic codes; hence, similar-sounding strings should get similar or equal codes. For instance, the algorithm scored a higher similarity between OECD-FORD "*civil engineering*" code: "2A" and ASJC "*civil and structural engineering*" code:2205. Finally, wc hand-curated the matching to add missing or miss processed research fields/areas.

In sum, we correlate the betweenness centrality of research fields/area matched of the research funding calls 2013–2021 with the ASJC replaced with the OECD-FORD classification and the percentage of unique researcher identifiers by OECD-FORD classification to explore the plausible and positive relationship between highly strategic research fields/areas and specialized scientific workforce at the national level. The following temporal link gives access to the dataset: http://bit.ly/40V4XxW.

Correlation Between STIP and Scientific Workforce. As in many scientometrics aspects [5], we do not assume a normally distributed data on the percentage of researchers in given fields nor a betweenness centrality of all research fields. Therefore, we implemented a Spearman rank correlation.

3 Results

The median number of researchers followed an upward trend from 2013 to 2021. For 41 areas, the median of researcher by area in 2013 was 147 (IQR = 197.5), in 2014 it was 135 (IQR = 168), in 2015 it was 168 (IQR = 244.3), in 2017 it was 240 (IQR = 291), in 2019 it was 316 (IQR = 329.5), and in 2021 it was 362 (IQR = 404.7).

Table 1 displays the top-ten average percentage of researchers by area and the bottom ten 2013–2021. A significant portion of the national scientific workforce works on biological sciences (9.3–13.1%), followed by economics and business (6.6–8.5%), health sciences (4.7–7.8%), educational sciences (5.9–7.3%), and clinical medicine (5–6.7%). Despite being the leading field, the percentage of researchers in biological sciences has been diminishing over the years, a similar trend for clinical medicine, chemical and physical sciences. The contrary case can be argued for economics and business; electrical engineering, electronic engineering, information engineering; and other engineering and technologies. In the bottom ten, no research area represented ≥1%. Medical engineering showed the highest percentage average (0.4–0.7%), followed by other medical sciences (0.2–0.5%), medical biotechnology (0.06–0.4%), industrial biotechnology (0.06–0.2%), and other agricultural sciences (0.08–0.3%). Medical engineering is the only area showing a maintained decreasing trend, while the remaining display either an increasing or stationary trend.

Figure 2 presents the correlation plot between the percentage of researchers and the betweenness centrality of research fields by OECD-FORD classification, 2013–2021. However, there should be noted that out of 41 ASJC/OECD-FORD fields matched, only 26 had any betweenness score. Therefore, results should be interpreted with caution. Fields such as arts, history of arts, performing arts, and music; clinical medicine; computer and information sciences; earth and related environmental sciences; history and archaeology, among others, did not represent any betweenness score in the co-word analysis.

Table 1. Trend of top ten & bottom ten by the average-percentage researcher by OECD-FORD 2013–2021. Source: the author based on MinCiencias [35].

	Area	% of researchers trend 2013-2021
Top-ten by percentage average 2013-2021	biological sciences	
	chemical sciences	
	clinical medicine	
	economics and business	
	educational sciences	
	electrical engineering electronic engineering information engineering	
	health sciences	
	law	
	other engineering and technologies	
	physical sciences	
Bottom-ten by percentage average 2013-2021	agricultural biotechnology	
	environmental biotechnology	
	industrial biotechnology	
	medical biotechnology	
	medical engineering	
	nano-technology	
	other agricultural sciences	
	other medical sciences	
	other natural sciences	
	philosophy ethics and religion	

While there are few cases in which there is a correspondence between the percentage of researchers and highly strategic fields for STIP (e.g., biological sciences; health sciences; education sciences), there is no statistically significant correlation between both variables. Spearman rank correlation revealed a non-significant, although positive moderate, correlation between the percentage of researchers in the country in a field and its corresponding betweenness centrality, $rho(22) = .38, p > .05$. Therefore, there is a misalignment between strategic research areas/fields STIP and the scientific workforce in Colombia.

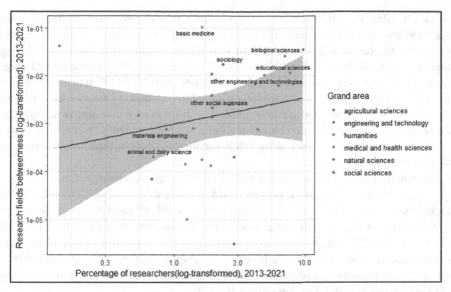

Fig. 2. Correlation plot between the percentage of researchers by OECD-FORD, 2013–2021 & betweenness centrality of ASJC-FORD research fields matching of research funding calls via co-word network analysis, 2013–2021. Source: Source: the author based on MinCiencias [35] and Cortés and Ramírez-Cajiao [16, 17]

4 Discussion and Conclusion

This work in progress explored the plausible link between highly strategic research areas/fields supported by STIP and the scientific workforce in Colombia. We found no statistically significant correlation between both variables, which unveils a missing linkage between STIP and the available scientific workforce in the country. Evidence shows that Colombia's STIP policy is getting more interconnected and network-dense, assembling an intricate and diversified structure of research fields enunciated, thereby making it difficult to establish a middle and long-run national science vision [17].

Here we outline five factors—not necessarily complementary nor directly related—that could explain such diversification and missing linkage with the scientific workforce. First, this unbounded increase in fields included in STIP could also be an intrinsic dynamic of government transitions and changing priorities of institutionally weak middle-low-income countries such as Colombia [1]. Second, it could also reflect the changing model: from STIP government to STIP governance [41] (i.e., the formulation of STIP policies as the product of negotiation with multiple internal/external actors of the policy-making agencies in charge of STIP). Third, timing and geographical context. The time window in which a STIP is enacted might give an edge (i.e., first mover advantage) to a particular STI sector [50]. Also, the privileged geographical position of Colombia close to bio-diverse areas (e.g., the Amazon) can influence the comparative research advantage [34]. That could be the case for researchers in biological sciences or economics and business, and the absence of STIP for other research areas such as nano-technology; arts, music; or earth and related environmental science. STIP might profoundly affect the national scientific workforce; nevertheless, such changes are not instantaneous and need time to be effectively reflected [47]. Furthermore, it is interesting to note that the research and development expenditure remained below 0.31% during the governments of 2007–2010 and 2011–2014. However, in 2015, it experienced a significant increase, reaching its highest point since 1996 at 0.37% [48]. It is plausible that this unprecedented budget for science has provided policy-making actors with a broader scope of action. Countries with a higher amount of resources for investing in science can adopt a strategy of diversification based on comparative advantage. This means that they can invest in a wide range of scientific fields, taking into account their unique strengths and opportunities [26].

The small sample of the number of OECD-FORD fields correlation limits our findings' scope. Further stages of the project could improve the ASJC OECD-FORD fields matching to a more refined level (i.e., at the discipline level: 3rd level) to widen the matching fields corpora. Including financial data also could improve estimating the impact of funding on scientific human capital formation. The inclusion of research-level profiles, such as gender, education degree, ethnicity, and institutional mobility, also could produce more comprehensive insights into the STIP-scientific workforce dynamics as part of the recent and exciting research agenda [9, 28].

References

1. Acemoglu, D., et al.: Finding eldorado: slavery and long-run development in Colombia. J. Comp. Econ. **40**(4), 534–564 (2012). https://doi.org/10.1016/j.jce.2012.07.003
2. Ahrweiler, P. et al.: Modelling research policy: ex-ante evaluation of complex policy instruments. JASSS **18**, 4 (2015). https://doi.org/10.18564/jasss.2927
3. Avellar, A.P.M.D., Botelho, M.D.R.A.: Impact of innovation policies on small, medium and large Brazilian firms. Appl. Econ. **50**(55), 5979–5995 (2018). https://doi.org/10.1080/000 36846.2018.1489109
4. Bollen, J., et al.: An efficient system to fund science: from proposal review to peer-to-peer distributions. Scientometrics **110**(1), 521–528 (2017). https://doi.org/10.1007/s11192-016-2110-3
5. Bookstein, A.: Explanations of the bibliometric laws. Collect. Manag. **3**(2–3), 151–162 (1979). https://doi.org/10.1080/J105v03n02_04
6. Boswell, C., Smith, K.: Rethinking policy "impact": four models of research-policy relations. Palgrave Commun. **3**, 1 (2017). https://doi.org/10.1057/s41599-017-0042-z
7. Bozeman, B., Link, A.N.: Toward an assessment of impacts from US technology and innovation policies. Sci. Publ. Policy **42**(3), 369–376 (2015). https://doi.org/10.1093/scipol/scu058
8. Callon, M., et al.: From translations to problematic networks: an introduction to co-word analysis. Soc. Sci. Inf. **22**(2), 191–235 (1983). https://doi.org/10.1177/053901883022002003
9. Chang, Y.H., Huang, M.H.: Analysis of factors affecting scientific migration move and distance by academic age, migrant type, and country: migrant researchers in the field of business and management. J. Informetr. **17**(1), 101371 (2023). https://doi.org/10.1016/j.joi.2022.101371
10. Confraria, H., et al.: Determinants of citation impact: a comparative analysis of the Global South versus the Global North. Res. Policy **46**(1), 265–279 (2017). https://doi.org/10.1016/j.respol.2016.11.004

11. Cortés, J.D.: Identifying the dissension in management and business research in Latin America and the Caribbean via co-word analysis. Scientometrics (2022). https://doi.org/10.1007/s11 192-021-04259-5

12. Cortés, J.D. et al.: Innovation for sustainability in the Global South: bibliometric findings from management & business and STEM (science, technology, engineering and mathematics) fields in developing countries. Heliyon. 7(8), e07809 (2021). https://doi.org/10.1016/j.hel iyon.2021.e07809

13. Cortés, J.D.: Journal titles and mission statements: lexical structure, diversity, and readability in business, management and accounting research. J. Inf. Sci. 016555152110437 (2021). https://doi.org/10.1177/01655515211043707

14. Cortés, J.D.: What is the mission of innovation?—Lexical structure, sentiment analysis, and cosine similarity of mission statements of research-knowledge intensive institutions. PLoS ONE 17(8), 1–20 (2022). https://doi.org/10.1371/journal.pone.0267454

15. Cortés, J.D., Dueñas, J.: What is the message of mission statements? Acad. Manag. Proc. 2022(1), 10083 (2022). https://doi.org/10.5465/AMBPP.2022.10083abstract

16. Cortés, J.D., Ramírez-Cajiao, M.C.: The content structure of science technology and innovation policy—applying co-word analysis to funding calls in Colombia. In: Sserwanga, I., et al. (eds.) IConference 2023. LNCS (LNAI & LNB), vol. 2, pp. 187–196. Springer, Cham (2023). https://doi.org/10.1007/978-3-031-28035-1_14

17. Cortés, J.D., Ramírez-Cajiao, M.C.: The policy is dead, long live the policy—science technology and innovation policy research priorities and government transitions via multilayer network analysis (2023, in preparation)

18. Edler, J., et al.: The practice of evaluation in innovation policy in Europe. Res. Eval. 21(3), 167–182 (2012). https://doi.org/10.1093/reseval/rvs014

19. Fortin, J.-M., Currie, D.J.: Big science vs. little science: how scientific impact scales with funding. PLoS One 8(6), 1–9 (2013). https://doi.org/10.1371/journal.pone.0065263

20. Freeman, L.C.: A set of measures of centrality based on betweenness. Sociometry. 40(1), 35–41 (1977). https://doi.org/10.2307/3033543

21. Gök, A., Edler, J.: The use of behavioural additionality evaluation in innovation policy making. Res. Eval. 21(4), 306–318 (2012). https://doi.org/10.1093/reseval/rvs015

22. Guskov, A., et al.: Scientometric research in Russia: impact of science policy changes. Scientometrics 107(1), 287–303 (2016). https://doi.org/10.1007/s11192-016-1876-7

23. Hicks, D., Isett, K.R.: Powerful numbers: exemplary quantitative studies of science that had policy impact. Quant. Sci. Stud. 1(3), 969–982 (2020). https://doi.org/10.1162/QSS_A_0 0060

24. Isaksen, A., et al.: Do general innovation policy tools fit all? Analysis of the regional impact of the Norwegian Skattefunn scheme. J. Innov. Entrep. 6, 1 (2017). https://doi.org/10.1186/ s13731-017-0068-x

25. Ito, A., et al.: Multi-level and multi-route innovation policies in China: a programme evaluation based on firm-level data. Millennial Asia 8(1), 78–107 (2017). https://doi.org/10.1177/097 6399616686866

26. Janavi, E., et al.: A methodology for developing scientific diversification strategy of countries. Scientometrics 125(3), 2229–2264 (2020). https://doi.org/10.1007/s11192-020-03685-1

27. Khanna, S., et al.: Recalibrating the scope of scholarly publishing: a modest step in a vast decolonization process. Quant. Sci. Stud. 1–19 (2023). https://doi.org/10.1162/QSS_A_0 0228

28. Kozlowski, D., et al.: Intersectional inequalities in science. Proc. Natl. Acad. Sci. USA 119(2), e2113067119 (2022). https://doi.org/10.1073/pnas.2113067119

29. van der Loo, M.P.J.: The stringdist package for approximate string matching. R J. 6(1), 111–122 (2014). https://doi.org/10.32614/rj-2014-011

30. Louder, E., et al.: A synthesis of the frameworks available to guide evaluations of research impact at the interface of environmental science, policy and practice. Environ. Sci. Policy **116**, 258–265 (2021). https://doi.org/10.1016/j.envsci.2020.12.006

31. Magro, E., Wilson, J.R.: Complex innovation policy systems: towards an evaluation mix. Res. Policy **42**(9), 1647–1656 (2013). https://doi.org/10.1016/j.respol.2013.06.005

32. Magro, E., Wilson, J.R.: Policy-mix evaluation: governance challenges from new place-based innovation policies. Res. Policy **48**, 10 (2019). https://doi.org/10.1016/j.respol.2018.06.010

33. Meyer-Krahmer, F.: Evaluation of industrial innovation policy-concepts, methods and lessons. Rev. Policy Res. **3**(3–4), 467–475 (1984). https://doi.org/10.1111/j.1541-1338.1984.tb00142.x

34. Miao, L., et al.: The latent structure of global scientific development. Nat. Hum. Behav. **6**(9), 1206–1217 (2022). https://doi.org/10.1038/s41562-022-01367-x

35. MinCiencias: Investigadores Reconocidos por convocatoria. https://www.datos.gov.co/Ciencia-Tecnolog-a-e-Innovaci-n/Investigadores-Reconocidos-por-convocatoria/bqtm-4y2h. Accessed 07 Feb 2023

36. National Archives: Soundex System. https://www.archives.gov/research/census/soundex. Accessed 07 Feb 2023

37. Neal, H., et al.: Beyond Sputnik - U.S. Science Policy in the Twenty-First Century. University of Michigan Press, Ann Arbor (2008). https://doi.org/10.3998/MPUB.22958

38. Nikzad, R.: Evaluation of Canadian innovation policy: locating innovation policy among other policies. Int. J. Bus. Continuity Risk Manag. **9**(1), 70–96 (2019). https://doi.org/10.1504/IJBCRM.2019.096699

39. OECD: Frascati Manual 2015: Guidelines for Collecting and Reporting Data on Research and Experimental Development. OECD, Paris (2015). https://doi.org/10.1787/9789264239012-EN

40. Opsahl, T., et al.: Node centrality in weighted networks: generalizing degree and shortest paths. Soc. Netw. **32**(3), 245–251 (2010). https://doi.org/10.1016/j.socnet.2010.03.006

41. Pohoryles, R.J.: Innocult revisited: the impact of EU research programmes on national research policies, key actors and research collaboration. Innovation **19**(1), 107–116 (2006). https://doi.org/10.1080/13511610600607999

42. Rodríguez-Navarro, A., Brito, R.: The link between countries' economic and scientific wealth has a complex dependence on technological activity and research policy. Scientometrics **127**(5), 2871–2896 (2022). https://doi.org/10.1007/s11192-022-04313-w

43. Samara, E., et al.: The impact of innovation policies on the performance of national innovation systems: a system dynamics analysis. Technovation **32**(11), 624–638 (2012). https://doi.org/10.1016/j.technovation.2012.06.002

44. Scopus: What is the complete list of Scopus Subject Areas and All Science Journal Classification Codes (ASJC)?.https://service.elsevier.com/app/answers/detail/a_id/15181/supporthub/scopus/. Accessed 10 Dec 2021

45. Shibayama, S., Baba, Y.: Impact-oriented science policies and scientific publication practices: the case of life sciences in Japan. Res. Policy **44**(4), 936–950 (2015). https://doi.org/10.1016/j.respol.2015.01.012

46. Shugars, S., Scarpino, S.V.: One outstanding path from A to B. Nat. Phys. **17**(4), 540 (2021). https://doi.org/10.1038/s41567-021-01222-2

47. Stage, A.K., Aagaard, K.: National policies as drivers of organizational change in universities: a string of reinforcing reforms. Quant. Sci. Stud. **1**(2), 849–871 (2020). https://doi.org/10.1162/qss_a_00046

48. The World Bank - Data: Research and development expenditure (% of GDP). https://bit.ly/3qzhwia. Accessed 17 Jan 2022

49. Wang, N., et al.: Cloud computing research in the IS discipline: a citation/co-citation analysis. Decis. Support. Syst. **86**, 35–47 (2016). https://doi.org/10.1016/j.dss.2016.03.006
50. Woolley, J.L., MacGregor, N.: Science, technology, and innovation policy timing and nanotechnology entrepreneurship and innovation. PLoS ONE **17**(3 March), e0264856 (2022). https://doi.org/10.1371/journal.pone.0264856
51. Wu, L., et al.: Large teams develop and small teams disrupt science and technology. Nature **566**(7744), 378–382 (2019). https://doi.org/10.1038/s41586-019-0941-9

Understanding Researchers' Data-Centric Tasks: A Classification of Goals, Gaps, and Resources

Guangyuan Sun[1] , Chunfeng Liu[2] , Siyuan Peng[2] , and Qiao Li[3]([⊠])

[1] National Institute of Education, Nanyang Technological University, Singapore, Singapore
[2] Wuhan University School of Information Management, Wuhan, China
[3] Department of Information Resources Management, Nankai University Business School, Tianjin, China
liqiao@nankai.edu.cn

Abstract. In an era where data reuse is increasingly central to research efficacy, this study delves into the granularity of data-centric work tasks and addresses task goals, the challenges researchers encounter (i.e., the gaps), and the essential resources for these tasks. Utilizing a systematic literature review, we articulate a classification framework that identifies four distinct goal families and twelve goal categories. Within the goal families of "Research" and "Data", goals are further characterized as either exploratory, confirmatory, or balanced. Our results demonstrate that the nature of goals has implications for how researchers anticipate gaps and resources. Specifically, those with more defined (confirmatory and balanced) goals predict the hurdles they will face and are proactive in identifying resources, whereas those with exploratory goals show less foresight in challenges but seek a wider range of potential resources. This study enhances our understanding of the complex interplay among goals, gaps, and resources in data-centric research tasks, offering avenues for more targeted research support services.

Keywords: Data-Centric Work Goals · Goal Classification Framework · Identified Gaps · Required Resources · Goal-Gap-Resource Alignment

1 Introduction

Data are purposeful collection of facts, observations, or objects used as evidence for research or scholarship [1, 2]. Amidst the rise of open science and data-intensive scientific discovery, the potential value of open data in driving scientific and technological innovation and sustainable development has garnered widespread recognition [3]. Realizing this value depends significantly on the reuse of open data [4], which is the process of repurposing or re-analyzing existing datasets to generate new knowledge or answer new questions [5]. Data reuse is considered goal-oriented activity [6] encompassing complex tasks [7]. This paper specifically focuses on those researchers who serve as key data re-users [8]. As an exploratory study, we do not restrict the domains of the researchers

we study. Instead, it is defined in the broadest sense: individuals whose primary responsi-
bility is to meticulously study a subject to uncover new facts and knowledge [9]. During
this process, we understand that researchers perform various data-centric work tasks,
which encompass activities related to data reuse that researchers undertake to fulfill specific goals related to their work responsibilities, such as reuse data for generating a new
hypothesis or verifying results [10, 11]. These tasks often serve as a primary motivator for their data utilization endeavors. Recognizing the important role of tasks, efforts
have been made to investigate the classification of researchers' data-centric work tasks,
albeit these endeavors have been relatively limited (e.g., Koesten et al. [7]). In their 2008
study, Li et al. [12] demonstrated that a prerequisite for the accurate classification of
information tasks is the identification and categorization of their underlying goals. This
principle suggests a deep interconnection between the nature of information tasks and
their intended objectives. Building upon this foundation, we adopt a similar approach
for understanding researchers' data-centric work tasks. We posit that a thorough grasp of
the fundamental goals underlying these tasks is essential for an understanding of these
tasks. Consequently, our investigation focuses on the goals of data-centric work tasks,
offering an indirect yet insightful lens through which to understand these tasks, rather
than a direct examination of the tasks themselves. Substantial efforts have been invested
in studying the goals of data reuse activities [13, 14]. The findings from these studies
serve as valuable references for us to systematically uncover the goals that underlie
researchers' data-centric work tasks.

In addition to exploring the goals of data-centric work tasks, our methodology
encompasses an analysis of two additional dimensions: the challenges encountered by
researchers during these tasks (i.e., gaps) and the resources they actively pursue. Studies have underscored that researchers encounter various challenges when performing
data-centric work tasks, including issues such as restricted data access [15], inadequate
contextual information about data [13], and a deficiency in knowledge and experience
[16]. These challenges often hinder researchers from effectively executing their data-
centric work tasks. Additionally, researchers actively seek a range of resources during
the data reuse process, such as metadata [17] and guidance from peers [4].

While previous studies have investigated the challenges and resources within specific
data reuse activities [7, 8], there remains a gap in understanding how these elements
relate to the goals of researchers engaged in data-centric work tasks. Our study aims to
address this shortfall by investigating the complex interplay between goals, challenges,
and resources in the context of data-centric work tasks. To this end, we have conducted
a systematic review, focusing on the following research questions:

RQ1: What types of goals do researchers pursue when executing data-centric work tasks?
RQ2: What specific challenges do researchers encounter (i.e., gaps), and what resources
are essential for them when pursuing various types of task goals?

2 Literature Review

While some efforts have been made to classify researchers' data-centric work tasks,
these endeavors have been relatively sparse. For instance, Koesten et al. [7] categorized
data-centric tasks into two primary categories: process-oriented tasks and goal-oriented

tasks. Process-oriented tasks involve data transformation activities, including tasks like building tools, data integration, or data visualization. Goal-oriented tasks, on the other hand, revolve around searching for data to achieve specific research objectives, such as answering high-level questions or identifying patterns. While this classification offers valuable insights into the categorization of data-centric work tasks, it's worth noting that, as highlighted by Koesten et al. [18], there is currently no established and systematic taxonomy for data-centric tasks.

Considerable efforts have been made to investigate the goals associated with data reuse activities. Gregory et al. [13] observed that earth scientists reuse data for specific purposes like recreating tables, locating maps and data integration, aligning with process-oriented tasks as defined by Koesten et al. [7]. Similarly, Krämer et al. [11] identified specific objectives for data reuse, such as hypothesis formulation and result support, fitting within Koesten et al.'s goal-oriented task category. These findings underline the importance of understanding the goals behind data-centric tasks and call for a comprehensive review to establish a classification framework.

Existing studies have investigated the challenges researchers encounter and the necessary resources required for various data reuse activities with different goals, revealing that these challenges may vary depending on context [8]. For instance, researchers in interdisciplinary projects frequently report challenges like insufficient contextual information and unfamiliarity with knowledge external to their own domain [4]. Koesten et al. [7] highlight that different types of information are critical for different data-centric tasks: data quality, timeliness, and collection methods for process-oriented tasks; and inherent attributes of data like coverage and granularity for goal-oriented tasks [7, 19]. While previous studies have yielded valuable insights, there has been a limited effort in tying together these insights and explore the interconnectedness of task goals, challenges, and necessary resources during the execution of specific data-centric work tasks.

3 Method

This study presents the findings of a content analysis of 76 papers selected from a database search using Web of Science and Scopus which are two internationally recognized multidisciplinary academic databases. We searched within these databases to identify user studies related to data-centric work tasks published before March 2023. The process of identifying these studies is detailed as follows: In March 2023, we initiated the search using the query "('data reuse' OR 'data search' OR 'data seeking' OR 'data sense making' OR 'data understand' OR 'data assess' OR 'data evaluate' OR 'data need' OR 'data access') AND ('research' OR 'science')" to identify relevant records within the title, keywords, and abstract fields.

Following the initial literature search, we collected and stored the complete bibliographic references for each article using Endnote. Subsequently, we conducted an examination of all articles according to the Preferred Reporting Items for Systematic Reviews and Meta-Analyses (PRISMA) guidelines. Specifically, we scrutinized the titles, abstracts, and full texts of each study based on the predefined inclusion and exclusion criteria, which were established in alignment with the research objective of this study—specifically, the identification of goals of data-centric work tasks. Following the application of these criteria, we identified and retained a total of 76 articles, all of which have been incorporated into this review (Fig. 1).

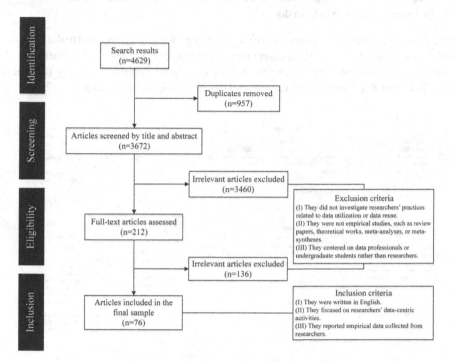

Fig. 1. PRISMA Flow Chart of the Review

The following information was extracted from each included paper: basic article information (i.e., title, authors, source, publication date), task goals, gaps, and resources. As the domain of data-centric work tasks lacked a well-established coding scheme, we employed an iterative coding process, as recommended by Pian et al. [20], to classify the findings from the included studies into distinct types of task goals, gaps, and resources.

During this coding process, we initially selected a random 20% of the articles (n = 15) from the sample, and three coders independently coded these articles using the iterative approach. For example, when a specific task goal emerged during coding, the three coders assigned it to a relevant category within the task goal framework. New categories were introduced if the existing ones were deemed inadequate, ensuring comprehensive categorization of all task goals. This same methodology was applied to gaps and resources. Following the initial coding, the results were compared, and any discrepancies among the three coders were resolved through rounds of discussion with two authors. Ultimately, consensus was achieved for each study. Subsequently, each of the three coders independently applied the established coding scheme to the full text of the remaining papers.

4 Results and Discussion

4.1 Overview of the Classification Framework of Goals Embedded in Data-Centric Work Tasks

Our classification framework consists of twelve categories of goals related to data-centric work tasks, which we term "goal categories". These goal categories are further consolidated into four overarching categories that we call "goal families", namely Research, Data, Teaching & Learning, and Others. All the goals are enumerated in Fig. 2.

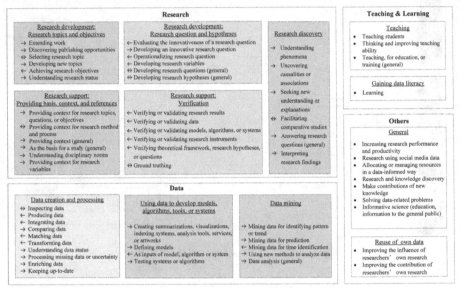

Note: The arrows in this figure are explained in detail in Section 4.2. Right arrows (→) represent exploratory goals; left arrows (←) represent confirmatory goals; bidirectional arrows (↔) represent balanced goals.

Fig. 2. Classification Framework of Data-Centric Work Task Goals

4.2 Characterization of the Goals in "Research" and "Data" Family

A closer examination of the goals within the Research and Data goal families reveals a spectrum concerning the degree of specificity or generality inherent in each goal type. This dimension not only reflects the nuanced intentions of researchers but provides insights into their strategic approaches when reusing secondary data for various tasks. Inspired by Lam et al. [21], we have categorized these goals into three classes:

Exploratory Goals: Denoted by a right arrow (→) in Fig. 2, these goals are characterized by undefined or ambiguous outcomes. These goals allow for flexibility and often lead to unexpected yet innovative results. Examples of exploratory goals in our study include "discovering publishing opportunities" and "understanding research status", among many others.

Confirmatory Goals: Signified by a left arrow ($\leftarrow$) in Fig. 2, these goals involve well-defined expectations and procedural tasks aimed at achieving specific outcomes. Prime examples from our findings fall under the "Research support-verification" goal category.

Balanced Goals: Indicated by a bidirectional arrow ($\leftrightarrow$) in Fig. 2, these goals are currently in a formative stage, capable of shifting toward either exploratory or confirmatory directions as the research process evolves. Examples from our results include "research topic selection" and "providing context for research method and process", among a few others.

In line with the above categorization of individual research goals as exploratory, confirmatory, or balanced, we've extended this typology to classify the goal categories. We employed a numerical counting method to enumerate the different types of goals within each goal category. As a result, we've identified five categories as predominantly "exploratory", containing a majority of exploratory goals and zero or one confirmatory goals. Conversely, we labeled two categories as mainly "confirmatory", comprising a majority of confirmatory goals and zero or one exploratory goals (see Fig. 3).

Goal Categories	Goal Category Types	No. of Exploratory ($\rightarrow$), Balanced ($\leftrightarrow$), Confirmatory ($\leftarrow$) Goals
Research development: Research topics and objectives	Exploratory	$4\rightarrow$, $1\leftrightarrow$, $1\leftarrow$
Research development: Research question and hypotheses	Confirmatory	$1\rightarrow$, $2\leftrightarrow$, $3\leftarrow$
Research support: verification	Confirmatory	$0\rightarrow$, $1\leftrightarrow$, $5\leftarrow$
Research support: provide basis, context, and references	Exploratory	$5\rightarrow$, $1\leftrightarrow$, $0\leftarrow$
Research discovery	Exploratory	$5\rightarrow$, $1\leftrightarrow$, $0\leftarrow$
Data creation and processing	Balanced	$5\rightarrow$, $1\leftrightarrow$, $4\leftarrow$
Developing model, algorithms, tool, system	Exploratory	$3\rightarrow$, $0\leftrightarrow$, $1\leftarrow$
Data mining	Exploratory	$4\rightarrow$, $0\leftrightarrow$, $1\leftarrow$

Fig. 3. Categorization of Research Goals by Their Exploratory, Balanced, or Confirmatory Nature

4.3 Preliminary Overview of Identified Gaps and Resources in Data-Centric Work Tasks

We present our preliminary findings on the types of gaps and resources associated with data-centric work tasks, drawn from a review of existing academic papers. For clarity, "identified gaps" refers to challenges that were faced, anticipated, or recalled by researchers, as reported, or analyzed in the studies we reviewed—even when these researchers were not explicitly aware of such issues. Similarly, "identified resources" pertain to assets that were either utilized, considered useful, or analyzed as useful by the authors of the papers we reviewed.

As shown in Fig. 4, the gaps identified are categorized into three primary types: Data-related, Information-related, and User-related. These categories outline the range of issues researchers might face, from data accessibility to user effort. Similarly, we classify resources into four major groups: Information, Knowledge, Data, and Social Network. Each category encapsulates specific assets, such as domain expertise or meta-data, offering a structured view of tools researchers can use to tackle challenges. This work serves as a starting point for more in-depth research into the complex interplay between these variables.

Classification	Category of Gaps/Resources	Type of Identified Gaps/Resources
Gaps	Data-related gaps	Lack of data
		Poor access
	Information-related gaps	Lack of information
	User-related gaps	High user effort
		Lack of knowledge and experience
Resources	Information	Metadata
		Literature
		Historical records
		Provenance information
	Knowledge	Domain knowledge
		Experience with secondary data
	Data	A larger, nationally representative data
		Commercial data
		Data from cited literature
		Individual-level data
		Large multidisciplinary datasets with minimal indexing
		Open government data
		Old data
		Raw data
		External data
		Data (general)
	Social Network	Colleagues

Fig. 4. Consolidated Overview of Identified Gaps and Resources in Data-Centric Research Work Tasks

4.4 Mapping Goal Categories to Identified Gaps and Resources

In our analysis, we map out the relationships between different types of gaps, resources, and goal categories within the Research and Data goal families. Figure 5 provides a tabulated overview of the results. Figure 6 visually captures these complex relationships, categorizing goal categories as either "Exploratory", "Confirmatory", or "Balanced", and linking them to corresponding gaps and resources. Our key observations are:

Identified Gaps: For exploratory goal categories, there's a clear trend towards a minimal number of identified gap types. Specifically, most have none (n = 4) or just one (n = 1). In contrast, confirmatory and balanced goal categories exhibit a broader range, with the number of identified gaps reaching up to three.

Resources for Addressing Gaps: Exploratory goal categories demonstrate varied links to resource types. For instance, "Research Development: Research Topics and Objectives" is linked to just one type of resource, while "Research Support: Provide Basis, Context, and References" connects to five. Confirmatory goal categories also show diverse connections: "Research Development: Research Question and Hypotheses" relates to one resource type, whereas "Research Support: Verification" aligns with five. Notably, the balanced goal category, "Data Creation and Processing", boasts the broadest spectrum, linked to six distinct types.

Goal Categories	Goal Category Types	Identified Gaps (No. of Types)	Identified Resources (No. of Types)
Research development: Research topics and objectives	Exploratory	Nil (0)	Data from cited literature (1)
Research development: Research question and hypotheses	Confirmatory	Nil (0)	Individual-level data (1)
Research support: verification	Confirmatory	Lack of knowledge and experience; Lack of information; Poor data access (3)	Information: Literature; Information: Methodological information; Data: External data; Data: Data from cited literature; Social network (5)
Research support: provide basis, context, and references	Exploratory	High user effort (1)	Data from cited literature; Open Government data; Commercial data; Information: Methodological information; Information: Research background information (5)
Research discovery	Exploratory	Nil (0)	Social network: Colleagues; Data (general); Old data; Information: Historical records (4)
Data creation and processing	Balanced	High user effort; Lack of data; Lack of information (3)	Data (general); Raw data; External data; Information: Metadata; Information: Methodological information; Information: Provenance information (6)
Developing model, algorithms, tool, system	Exploratory	Nil (0)	Large multidisciplinary datasets with minimal indexing; Information: Metadata; Knowledge: Domain knowledge (3)
Data mining	Exploratory	Nil (0)	Data from cited literature; Data (general); A larger, nationally representative data (3)

Fig. 5. Relationships Among Goal Categories, Combined Identified Gaps and Resources

Note: Goal categories are grouped by type ('Exploratory,' 'Confirmatory,' 'Balanced') and connected to their respective gaps and resources through arrowed lines.

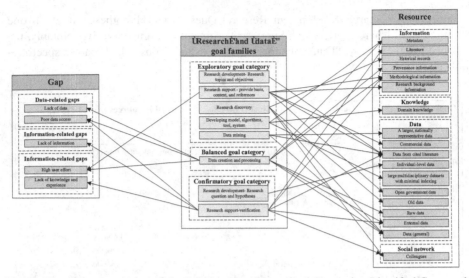

Fig. 6. Visual Representation of the Relationship Among Goal Categories, Identified Gaps, and Resources

5 Discussion

Our classification framework of goals related to data-centric work tasks reveal that researchers are reusing data for a wide range of tasks and goals. We briefly discuss interesting results of each of the four goal families here:

- **Research**: In line with existing literature [4, 7, 10, 14], our findings underscore that secondary data are instrumental in various research phases, from fostering creative exploration—inspiring new research topics—to facilitating more methodical activities, such as the verification of results. While our goal categories do not, and were not intended to, capture every facet of the research lifecycle, understanding these can offer valuable insights into how researchers contextualize their data-centric tasks within the broader research lifecycle.
- **Data**: We find the goal categories of "Data Creation and Processing" surprising, as it suggests that researchers use secondary data not just for papers but also to create new, publicly accessible datasets, and emphasizes that data can serve not just as a means to an end, but also as a valuable end-product in its own right.
- **Teaching and Learning**: Our findings indicate that secondary data benefit both student learning and researchers' personal skill development, adding weight to calls for including data literacy, which involves the ability to collect, understand, analyze data, and transform them into actionable knowledge to address real-world queries [22, 23], in educational programs.
- **Others**: A unique category is "Reusing researchers' own data", highlighting a strategic approach researchers adopt for ensuring ongoing relevance in their field.

We also discuss how the goals of various data-centric tasks, along with their associated resources and gaps, can shed light on the behaviors of researchers during their interaction with data:

- **Confirmatory and Balanced Goals**: For these goal categories, researchers appear to anticipate multiple challenges, evidenced by the higher number of identified gaps. Despite these anticipated challenges, they also seem proactive in identifying various resources to bridge these gaps. This implies that when researchers have more specific goals, they can better anticipate the challenges they might face and, consequently, the resources they might need.
- **Exploratory Goals**: On the other hand, for exploratory goal categories, we observed a wider discrepancy between the number of identified gaps and resources. Specifically, there are almost no identified gaps but a plethora of potential resources. This may suggest that the indeterminate nature of exploratory goals makes it harder for researchers to foresee specific challenges. At the same time, this ambiguity seems to spur them to seek a more extensive set of resources that could be "potentially useful".

The overarching implication is that the specificity of researchers' intentions plays a significant role in how they anticipate challenges and prepare resources in the data reuse process. This insight contributes to our understanding of secondary data reuse and researchers' data-centric work tasks, underscoring the need for tailored data search systems [24] that align closely with the specific goals and expectations of individual researchers.

6 Conclusion

Our review of existing literature has shed light on the various goals, gaps and resources associated with researchers in their data-driven endeavors. Our findings enrich existing literature on data-centric work tasks by showing that the specificity of researchers' goals influences how they anticipate challenges and prepare resources for data reuse. This study provides preliminary insights and is based on moderate exploratory efforts.

We also acknowledge a limitation: researchers within the same subject field may share explicit commonalities in their data-centric work tasks, which may differ significantly from those in other scientific fields. This study does not aim to uncover these commonalities or differences. A more detailed investigation into the variations among researchers from different disciplines or at different stages of their research careers is reserved for future studies.

Acknowledgments. This work was supported by the National Social Science Foundation of China [No. 22CTQ040].

References

1. Zins, C.: Conceptual approaches for defining data, information, and knowledge. J. Am. Soc. Inform. Sci. Technol. **58**(4), 479–493 (2007)
2. Borgman, C.L.: Big data, little data, no data: Scholarship in the Networked World, p. 383. The MIT Press, Cambridge, MA (2015)
3. United Nations Educational Scientific and Cultural Organization: UNESCO science report: Towards 2030 (2015). http://uis.unesco.org/sites/default/files/documents/unesco-science-rep ort-towards-2030-part1.pdf. Accessed 28 Aug 2023
4. Gregory, K., Groth, P., Scharnhorst, A., Wyatt, S.: Lost or found? Discovering data needed for research. Harvard Data Sci. Rev. **2**(2) (2020). https://doi.org/10.1162/99608f92.e38165eb
5. Wang, X., Duan, Q., Liang, M.: Understanding the process of data reuse: an extensive review. J. Am. Soc. Inf. Sci. **72**(9), 1161–1182 (2021)
6. Liu, Y.H., Chen, H.L., Kato, M.P., Wu, M., Gregory, K.: Data discovery and reuse in data service practices: a global perspective. Proc. Assoc. Inf. Sci. Technol. **58**(1), 610–612 (2021)
7. Koesten, L.M., Kacprzak, E., Tennison, J.F., Simperl, E.: The trials and tribulations of working with structured data: a study on information seeking behaviour. In: Proceedings of the 2017 CHI Conference on Human Factors in Computing Systems. May 2017, Denver Colorado, USA, pp. 1277–1289 (2017)
8. Gregory, K.: A dataset describing data discovery and reuse practices in research. Scientific Data **7**(1), 1–11 (2020)
9. https://www.oxfordlearnersdictionaries.com/definition/english/researcher
10. Bishop, B.W., Hank, C., Webster, J., Howard, R.: Scientists' data discovery and reuse behavior: (Meta) data fitness for use and the FAIR data principles. Proc. Assoc. Inf. Sci. Technol. **56**(1), 21–31 (2019)
11. Krämer, T., Papenmeier, A., Carevic, Z., Kern, D., Mathiak, B.: Data-seeking behaviour in the social sciences. Int. J. Digit. Libr. **22**, 175–195 (2021)
12. Li, Y., Belkin, N.J.: A faceted approach to conceptualizing tasks in information seeking. Inf. Process. Manag. **44**(6), 1822–1837 (2008). https://doi.org/10.1016/j.ipm.2008.07.005
13. Gregory, K., Groth, P., Cousijn, H., Scharnhorst, A., Wyatt, S.: Searching data: a review of observational data retrieval practices in selected disciplines. J. Assoc. Inf. Sci. Technol. **70**(5), 419–432 (2019). https://doi.org/10.1002/asi.24165
14. Pasquetto, I.V., Borgman, C.L., Wofford, M.F.: Uses and reuses of scientific data: the data creators' advantage. Harv. Data Sci. Rev. **1**(2) (2019). https://doi.org/10.1162/99608f92.fc1 4bf2d
15. Yan, A., Huang, C., Lee, J.S., Palmer, C.L.: Cross-disciplinary data practices in earth system science: aligning services with reuse and reproducibility priorities. Proc. Assoc. Inf. Sci. Technol. **57**(1), e221 (2020). https://doi.org/10.1002/pra2.218
16. Frank, R.D., Suzuka, K., Yakel, E.: Examining the reuse of qualitative research data: Digital video in education. In: 13th Annual Archiving Conference, April 2016, Washington, DC, pp. 146–151 (2016)
17. Liu, J., Wang, J., Zhou, G., Wang, M., Shi, L.: How do people make relevance judgment of scientific data? Data Sci. J. **19**(1), 9 (2020). https://doi.org/10.1177/002224377501200210
18. Koesten, L., Gregory, K., Groth, P., Simperl, E.: Talking datasets–understanding data sensemaking behaviours. Int. J. Hum. Comput. **146**, 102562 (2021)
19. Chapman, A., et al.: Dataset search: a survey. VLDB J. **29**(1), 251–272 (2020)
20. Pian, W., Chi, J., Ma, F.: The causes, impacts and countermeasures of COVID-19 "Infodemic": a systematic review using narrative synthesis. Inf. Process. Manag. **58**(6), 102713 (2021)
21. Lam, H., Tory, M., Munzner, T.: Bridging from goals to tasks with design study analysis reports. IEEE Trans. Visual Comput. Graphics **24**(1), 435–445 (2017). https://doi.org/10.1109/TVCG.2017.2744319

22. Gummer, E., Mandinach, E.: Building a conceptual framework for data literacy. Teach. Coll. Rec. **117**(4), 1–22 (2015)
23. Ellram, L.M., Tate, W.L.: The use of secondary data in purchasing and supply management (P/SM) research. J. Purch. Supply Manag. **22**(4), 250–254 (2016)
24. Bugaje, M., Chowdhury, G.: Data retrieval= text retrieval? In: Transforming Digital Worlds: 13th International Conference, iConference 2018, Sheffield, UK, 25–28 March 2018, Proceedings 13, pp. 253–262 (2018). Springer International Publishing

Closing the Information Gap in Unidentified Anomalous Phenomena (UAP) Studies

Gretchen R. Stahlman$^{(\boxtimes)}$ (iD)

Florida State University, Tallahassee, FL 32306, USA
gstahlman@fsu.edu

Abstract. Unidentified Anomalous Phenomena (UAP), also known as Unidentified Flying Objects (UFOs), has shifted from being a stigmatized topic on the fringes of scientific inquiry to a legitimate subject of scientific interest with a need for high quality, curated data, and rigorous scientific investigation. This paper presents a preliminary scoping review and analysis of scholarly literature related to UAP from 1967 until 2023, exploring a diverse range of research areas across disciplines to illustrate scholarly discourse about the topic. The paper focuses on characterizing papers published in recent years and notes that Library & Information Science is unrepresented in the current UAP literature. The paper also discusses how researchers across the iFields can contribute to UAP studies through inherent expertise such as data curation and data science as well as information behavior and information literacy, among others. The paper concludes by emphasizing that UAP Studies offer a rich intellectual realm for information science research, with the iFields well positioned to play a crucial role in supporting and engaging in the study of UAP.

Keywords: UAP · iFields · Literature Review · Information science

1 Background

Unidentified Anomalous Phenomena (UAP), also known as Unidentified Flying Objects (UFOs), have long captured the public's fascination and speculation while stigmatized in scientific circles [1]. The notion of extraterrestrial UFOs visiting Earth has been prevalent in popular culture for the better part of a century. However, the recently re-branded concept "UAP" emerged to represent an increasingly legitimate area of scientific interest and inquiry [2, 3], relatively agnostic about the "extraterrestrial" hypothesis in pursuit of rational explanations. Current UAP research encompasses a variety of scientific domains, meanwhile lacking in rigorous methods and sources of reliable data.

This shift in perception gained traction with a 2021 public report released by the U.S. Office of the Director of National Intelligence (ODNI) [4]. The report acknowledged that some incidents of strange objects in the sky remain unexplained and that more and better-quality data are needed to understand the nature of these objects, emphasizing a need for further investigation about UAP. The report therefore sparked renewed scientific interest

I. Sserwanga et al. (Eds.): iConference 2024, LNCS 14596, pp. 310–320, 2024.
https://doi.org/10.1007/978-3-031-57850-2_23

and public discourse and led to the formation of task forces, agencies, and initiatives to investigate UAP.

One such task force, NASA's Unidentified Anomalous Phenomena Independent Study Team (UAPIST), recently worked to identify existing data and to make recommendations for future data collection efforts to support scientific study of UAP [5]. The task force aimed to establish a roadmap for answering questions such as, "Are these objects real or are they sensor artifacts? Are they a threat to aerospace safety? Are they a threat to U.S. national security? Are they unknown natural phenomena? What else could they be?" [6]. While the study team reports no conclusive evidence of an extraterrestrial origin for UAP, it urges a continued role for NASA in U.S.-government efforts to study UAP. Recommendations primarily focus on a critical need for de-stigmatizing the topic to encourage reporting and research, as well as high-quality, curated data adhering to the FAIR principles for Findability, Accessibility, Interoperability, and Reusability [7]. Ultimately, the NASA UAPIST report and other recent developments emphasize that understanding UAP is a data curation and data science problem, with human and social science implications as well.

The broader search for evidence of life beyond Earth has catalyzed scientific progress in astronomy and related fields such as planetary science, exobiology, and the Search for Extraterrestrial Intelligence (SETI) [8]. However, scientific study of UAP is subject to unique challenges and may be especially vulnerable to misinterpretation and sensationalism [9, 10], indicating a timely need for strategic action among the iFields (i.e., information studies, broadly conceived, as defined in [11]). This paper presents an exploratory study on existing research and opportunities for future work in UAP Studies. A literature review was conducted targeting UAP-related publications, with particular interest in scholarly discourse since 2021. The paper includes a preliminary analysis of the literature followed by a series of recommendations for further research participation across the iFields, and plans for future work.

The study overall aims to begin bridging a gap between UAP Studies as an evolving research area and Library & Information Science (LIS), along with other closely related and established perspectives including Science of Science [12], Sociology of Science and Technology [13], and research data management studies [14]. This exploration of scholarly literature about UAP aligns with the broader goals of these fields to understand how scientific knowledge evolves and gains legitimacy over time through consensus. The paper also aims to contribute to ongoing conversations surrounding the nature and study of UAP, a previously stigmatized "fringe" topic that potentially represents an emerging interdisciplinary scientific field in need of novel information and data related research, support, and services.

2   Methods

To better understand the current landscape of scholarly literature on the topic of UAP, an exploratory scoping review was conducted following the PRISMA guidelines for systematic reviews [15], guided by the research question (RQ): *"How has the topic of UFOs/UAP evolved as a subject of scholarly inquiry over time?"*. The following query was searched via Web of Science: ("ufo" OR "ufos" OR "uap" OR "uaps"). The query was limited to title and abstract, and results were further refined to include books, conference proceedings, and scholarly articles in English or Spanish. To ensure that Library & Information Science sources were sufficiently captured, the same search was conducted via ProQuest across three LIS databases: Library & Information Science Collection, Library & Information Science Abstracts (LISA), and Library Science Database. Most results were retrieved via Web of Science (n = 1,999), with 219 results retrieved via the LIS databases. Duplicate records were processed (n = 28), and the remaining records (n = 2,190) were manually screened for relevance (criteria for relevance was considered to be sources directly addressing the topic of UFOs or UAP as a central theme). Thirty-seven potentially relevant items were indexed as citations only and unable to be retrieved. The final dataset includes 174 sources. Figure 1 shows the PRISMA flow diagram.

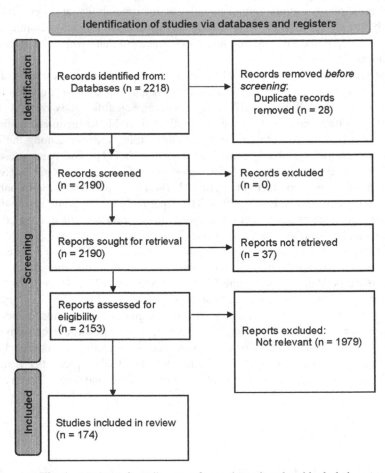

Fig. 1. PRISMA flow diagram of records retrieved and included.

For the purpose of this preliminary scoping review, a high-level content analysis was conducted to capture general features of the sources such as research area and year of publication. Items published since the 2021 release of the ODNI report [4] were examined more closely.

3 Results

Literature sources within the full dataset were published between 1967 and 2023 (Fig. 2).

Psychology (21%) and Religion (13%) are overwhelmingly dominant as research areas represented in the literature (per Web of Science classifications), followed by Astronomy & Astrophysics (6%), and Arts & Humanities (5%). See Fig. 3.

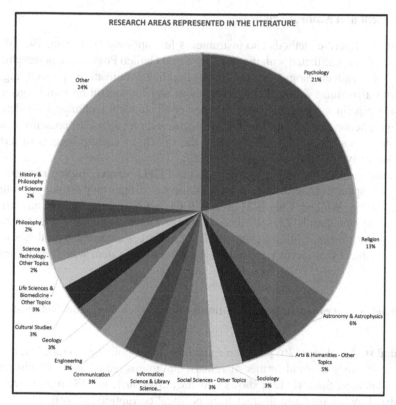

Fig. 3. Research areas represented in literature (n = 174).

For sources published since 2021 (n = 34), Religion represents the largest proportion of research areas (30%), followed by Astronomy & Astrophysics (11%), Arts & Humanities (7%) and Communication (7%). However, apart from two items, the sources categorized under Religion (n = 12) are part of a series [16], and therefore Astronomy & Astrophysics may be considered the true dominant research area. Note that Library & Information Science does not appear as a research area for these recent papers. The subset of 34 sources published since 2021 are categorized and summarized below.

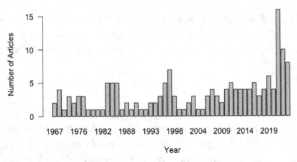

Fig. 2. Distribution of publication year.

3.1 Physical and Natural Sciences

Three papers describe methods and instruments for capturing UAP data. Two of these papers [17, 18] are affiliated with the Harvard-based Galileo Project that is searching for evidence of alien technology [19]; the former highlights motivations for studying UAP along with a roadmap for deploying equipment and implementing multi-sensor data processing pipelines, while the latter outlines computational techniques for detecting anomalous phenomena in data. The third instrumentation paper [20] presents a camera system design and software for calibrating the system to capture images of airborne objects for analysis of their movement patterns.

Antonio, et al. [21] analyze a large dataset of UFO reports, finding reporting patterns with respect to time of day, as well as increased reporting activity surrounding media attention. Wu and Yang [22] present a theoretical foundation for aircraft anti-gravity propulsion. Smith [23] speculates about the nature of extraterrestrial technology for interstellar probes, while Zuckerman [24] challenges a current hypothesis that an interstellar object that recently passed through the solar system was alien technology [25].

3.2 Social Sciences (Including Communication, Psychology and Religious Studies)

In cultural studies, Fians [26] points to a need for anthropologists to take "native" perspectives seriously to avoid further marginalizing groups including UFO witnesses as Others. Marchena Sanabria [27] shows how narratives such as UFO reports were sensationalized by the media to distract from political corruption in Costa Rica between 1979 and 1985. Hayes [28] explores Cold War-era tensions between state actors and citizens surrounding UFO theories and narratives. Wright [29] takes a philosophical stance to examine the underexplored implications of alien and UFO tourism for the tourism industry.

Social science approaches include Yingling, et al.'s [3] large survey of faculty members showing that many academics think UAP is an important topic for research. Stise, et al. [30] analyze national survey data collected after the ODNI report release [4], showing an association between media use and belief in UFOs. Also following on the release of the ODNI report, Braum [31] shows that people form favorable opinions towards conspiracy theories in general when reputable politicians acknowledge that UFOs may be extraterrestrial visitors. Adorjan and Kelly [32] leverage UFO-related "missing time" experiences to explore the importance and role of temporality in social constructionist scholarship. McVittie & McKinlay [33] investigate the discourse of news presenters speaking about UAP as they distance themselves from explaining the phenomena.

Religious studies scholars typically frame UFO and UAP as religious experiences. Agrama [34] challenges the effectiveness of secular science in light of recent developments in the study of UFOs. Similarly, Zeller [35] points to "enchanted" underpinnings of UFO investigations despite their secular organizations and approaches. Kivari [36] discusses how personal supernatural and paranormal experiences are integrated into broader social narratives. Finally, the Zeller [16] series *Handbook of UFO Religions* tackles a number of topics ranging from specific cultural case studies [37] to study of scholarship on UFOs and religion [38].

3.3 Arts and Humanities (Including History and Philosophy)

Within the humanities-classified sources, Hodges & Paxton-Fear [39] analyze the writings that influenced Heaven's Gate cult members as the texts evolved from recruitment to reinforcing belief. Rose [40] explores racial aspects of UFO abduction narratives, suggesting that these stories may stem from a collective sense of white guilt regarding African enslavement and abduction accounts. Presenting a historical perspective, Guimont & Baumhammer [41] describe a panel series that debated the role of pseudoscience in the history and public understanding of science. Rooted in philosophical schools of thought, Butman [42] and Smith & Jonathan [43] explore the epistemology and miraculous nature of UFOs respectively.

4 Discussion

These results represent a snapshot of scholarly literature and discourse about UAP at the time of this writing (September 2023). Researchers from diverse areas are approaching UAP as a serious and actionable topic with implications for society and humanity (while stopping short of endorsing an extraterrestrial hypothesis). Circumstances are likely to change and evolve quickly in the future, although it is presently uncertain whether UAP Studies will develop into a recognized field. Nevertheless, credible research is underway and gaining publicity, suggesting a trend towards legitimizing UAP Studies as an interdisciplinary research area. To uphold the recommendations of the recent ODNI [4] and NASA [6] reports, a need remains to shift the focus from viewing UAP experiences as purely religious or psychological phenomena originating with the spirit or mind towards collecting standardized and reputable data across physical contexts and geographical locations, ranging from civilian and military reporting to high quality images and sensor data within and beyond Earth's atmosphere.

Notably, nearly all research areas and publications outlined in the Results section align with some aspect of the iFields' interdisciplinary research expertise, positioning these areas well for leadership in an emerging, multifaceted field of UAP Studies, with the potential to support government initiatives and inform policy development and knowledge construction. As uncovered by Yingling, et al. [3], academics are largely curious about this topic and consider it very important or essential to dispense with stigma and explore the nature of UAP using scientific methods regardless of the eventual explanations for the phenomena. A few ideas for iField participation in UAP Studies research are outlined below. Note that the broad categories of work presented in the following sections as headings are based upon the author's qualitative perspective and prior research and teaching experience, rather than on an existing taxonomy of subject areas.

4.1 Data Curation and Knowledge Organization

As emphasized by NASA [6], UAP-related data often lack standardization and may not be initially suited for analysis. Data curation and FAIR data practices are essential, particularly to support drawing conclusions from data collected across sources and contexts [7]. iFields are well positioned to help ensure that appropriate infrastructures are in place while assisting various disciplines and research communities with developing strategies to make data FAIR and ensuring that data are compatible with tools for analysis. Furthermore, data curation experts can contribute to handling distributed sensor-generated data, assessing data quality, and supporting anomaly detection techniques to identify UAP-related information that falls outside known constraints. Structured approaches to data management and information organization are crucial to ensure the integrity of a growing knowledge body of knowledge about UAP.

4.2 Information Behavior, Social Informatics, and Online Communities

Understanding information behavior and social dynamics surrounding UAP is another key, opportune area for research. Especially considering that UAP is a historically stigmatized topic and has been long associated with conspiracy theories, human information behavior and social informatics researchers can investigate how individuals seek, share, and evaluate information about UAP amidst a shifting narrative towards open curiosity and scientific study. Such research can shed light on the formation and evolution of online and offline communities and their impact on the dissemination of credible information about UAP as well as their belief systems. Additionally, studying various communities through a socio-technical lens can illuminate how they function and influence public perception, which is important for a comprehensive understanding of the phenomena and to support scientific investigation.

4.3 Data Science, Artificial Intelligence and Machine Learning

Data-driven approaches can be leveraged to make sense of UAP. For example, AI and ML techniques can be applied to analyze large amounts of data associated with UAP to identify patterns, trends, and anomalies that might not be apparent through traditional methods. Machine learning models can be trained with various data types, including sensor readings, eyewitness testimonies, and historical legacy data and records. Natural language processing (NLP) techniques can also extract valuable information from textual sources such as government reports and historical documents. As emphasized in the NASA UAPIST report [6], key challenges for researching and understanding UAP are data oriented.

4.4 Library Services

iFields can also contribute by exploring how libraries and other knowledge institutions should effectively collect, curate, and make UAP-related resources accessible to the public and researchers. This may include creating specialized collections, providing research assistance and reference support, and promoting critical thinking and information literacy skills related to UAP as a topic of growing interest to the public.

4.5 Mis/Dis-Information

The topic of UAP is especially vulnerable to misinterpretation and sensationalism, perhaps in part because it touches upon the existential question of whether humans are alone in the universe. As UAP Studies may become increasingly mainstream, ensuring communication of accurate and credible scientific information about the phenomena and in relation to previously established scientific movements such as the Search for Extraterrestrial Intelligence (SETI) is critical. iFields researchers can investigate various aspects of these challenges, including pinpointing sources and dissemination of misleading information as well as strategies for identifying and countering problematic narratives. This includes studying the role of media, online platforms, and information ecosystems in shaping public perception and belief systems surrounding UAP.

4.6 Data and Science Literacy

The topic of UAP may be an ideal entry point to engage the public in understanding and promoting data and science literacy. Educational programs and resources could be developed about UAP Studies to enhance the public's ability to critically assess and interpret data and scientific findings. This includes creating accessible materials that explain scientific methodologies and encourage evidence-based thinking, helping individuals to make informed judgments about UAP claims and research.

4.7 Science and Technology Studies

In the context of UAP, Science & Technology Studies researchers can explore the dynamics between scientific authorities, government agencies, and the public in defining and studying the phenomena. This includes analyzing the social construction of knowledge around UAP and how it intersects with government secrecy, military technology, international politics, and public perception. STS can also investigate the role of technological advancements in UAP observations, such as the impact of sophisticated sensors and data collection tools on the data available for analysis. By placing UAP within the broader framework of science and technology, it may be possible to develop a more comprehensive understanding of the cultural, political, and epistemological dimensions of UAP Studies and the phenomena itself.

5 Conclusion and Limitations

This paper has presented a preliminary literature review and set of recommendations for involvement of iFields in UAP Studies. The paper notes that LIS is underrepresented in the literature on this topic, indicating an opportunity to close a gap and apply demonstrated research strengths to understanding and explaining the societal, informational, and technological aspects of the phenomena. Future work by the author will build upon this initial exploration to address some of the iField research opportunities listed above and further analyze and expand a bibliometric dataset for in-depth qualitative analysis over the past 50+ years.

The present study has some limitations, by virtue of its early-stage nature. Primarily, as the study intentionally prioritized recall over precision, many irrelevant results were returned, which presented challenges for manually reviewing all sources with close attention to detail. Also, the query may have overlooked some relevant sources by focusing only on acronyms (UFO, UAP) instead of full phrases such as "Unidentified Flying Object(s)" and "Unidentified Anomalous Phenomena" (though the acronyms are typically included alongside the full phrases). Future work will also further explore and adjust the search strategy to capture relevant sources to the extent possible.

UAP Studies represents a rich and fascinating realm for further research and learning across the iFields. The NASA UAPIST report [6] that inspired this paper concludes, "there is an intellectual continuum between extrasolar technosignatures, solar system SETI, and potential unknown alien technology operating in Earth's atmosphere. If we recognize the plausibility of any of these, then we should recognize that all are at least plausible" (p. 33). The first two (SETI and the search for alien technosignatures) are represented by small but established research communities and are supported by instruments such as the James Webb Space Telescope [44]. As new communities, instruments and infrastructures take shape to support research and communication about UAP, this "intellectual continuum" provides a natural home for information studies work.

References

1. Barkun, M.: Conspiracy theories as stigmatized knowledge. Diogenes **62**(3–4), 114–120 (2015)
2. Pasulka, D.W.: American cosmic: UFOs, religion, technology. Oxford University Press (2019)
3. Yingling, M.E., Yingling, C.W., Bell, B.A.: Faculty perceptions of unidentified aerial phenomena. Humanit. Soc. Sci. Commun. **10**(1), 1–15 (2023)
4. Office of the Director of National Intelligence. Preliminary Assessment: Unidentified Aerial Phenomena (2021)
5. National Aeronautics and Space Administration. UAP (2023a). https://science.nasa.gov/uap
6. National Aeronautics and Space Administration. Unidentified Anomalous Phenomena Independent Study Team Report (2023b). https://www.nasa.gov/sites/default/files/atoms/files/uap_independent_study_team_-_final_report_0.pdf
7. Wilkinson, M.D., et al.: The FAIR Guiding Principles for scientific data management and stewardship. Sci. Data **3**(1), 1–9 (2016)
8. Sagan, C., Drake, F.: The search for extraterrestrial intelligence. Sci. Am. **232**(5), 80–89 (1975)

Closing the Information Gap   319

9. Wright, J.T.: Strategies and advice for the Search for extraterrestrial Intelligence. Acta Astronaut. **188**, 203–214 (2021)
10. Davis, R., Schillo, K., Walkowicz, L.: The Impact of Discovering the First Technosignature, pp. 47–56. Technosignatures for Detecting Intelligent Life in Our Universe, A Research Companion (2022)
11. Cobb, P.J., Golub, K.: Digital humanities degrees and supplemental credentials in information schools (iSchools). Educ. Inf. **38**(1), 67–92 (2022)
12. Fortunato, S., et al.: Science of science. Science **359**(6379), eaao0185 (2018)
13. Star, S.L.: Introduction: the sociology of science and technology. Soc. Probl. **35**(5), 197–205 (1988)
14. Borgman, C.L.: Big Data, Little Data, No Data: Scholarship in the Networked World. MIT Press, Cambridge (2017)
15. Page, M.J., et al.: The PRISMA 2020 statement: an updated guideline for reporting systematic reviews. Int. J. Surg. **88**, 105906 (2021)
16. Zeller, B.: Handbook of UFO Religions (Vol. 20). Brill (2021)
17. Watters, W.A., et al.: The scientific investigation of unidentified aerial phenomena (UAP) using multimodal ground-based observatories. J. Astron. Instrum. **12**(01), 2340006 (2023)
18. Cloete, R., et al.: Integrated computing platform for detection and tracking of unidentified aerial phenomena (UAP). J. Astron. Instrum. **12**(1), 2340008 (2023)
19. Loeb, A., Laukien, F.H.: Overview of the Galileo project. J. Astron. Instrum. **12**(1), 2340003 (2022). https://doi.org/10.1142/S2251171723400032
20. Szenher, M., et al.: A hardware and software platform for aerial object localization. J. Astron. Instrum. **12**(01), 2340002 (2023)
21. Antonio, F.J., Itami, A.S., Dalmedico, J.F., Mendes, R.S.: On the dynamics of reporting data: a case study of UFO sightings. Physica A **603**, 127807 (2022)
22. Wu, J.H., Yang, S.K.: Anti-gravity technology by non-positive equivalent mass revealing UFO flying secrets. Europhys. Lett. **136**(6), 64002 (2022)
23. Smith, G.H.: On the first probe to transit between two interstellar civilizations. Int. J. Astrobiol. **22**(3), 185–196 (2023)
24. Zuckerman, B.: 'Oumuamua is not a probe sent to our solar system by an alien civilization. Astrobiology **22**(12), 1414–1418 (2022)
25. Loeb, A.: Extraterrestrial: The First Sign of Intelligent Life Beyond Earth. Houghton Mifflin Harcourt (2021)
26. Fians, G.: The others' others: when taking our natives seriously is not enough. Critique Anthropol. **43**(1), 0308275X231175982 (2023)
27. Marchena Sanabria, J.: Terror in Csta Rica. Diario extra and the discourse of fear, between 1979 and 1985. Cuadernos Inter. ca mbio sobre Centroamérica y el Caribe **18**(1), e45862 (2021)
28. Hayes, M.: Search for the Unknown: Canada's UFO Files and the Rise of Conspiracy Theory. McGill-Queen's Press-MQUP (2022)
29. Wright, D.W.M.: Encountering UFOs and aliens in the tourism industry. J. Tourism Futures **8**(1), 7–23 (2022)
30. Stise, R., Bingaman, J., Siddika, A., Dawson, W., Paintsil, A., Brewer, P.R.: Cultivating paranormal beliefs: how television viewing, social media use, and podcast listening predict belief in UFOs. Atlantic J. Commun. 1–14 (2023)
31. Bram, C.: When a conspiracy theory goes mainstream, people feel more positive toward conspiracy theorists. Res. Politics **8**(4), 20531680211067640 (2021)
32. Adorjan, M., Kelly, B.: Time as vernacular resource: temporality and credibility in social problems claims-making. Am. Sociologist **53**(2), 1–27 (2022)

33. McVittie, C., McKinlay, A.: "I don't mean extradimensional in a woo-woo sense": doing non-explanation in discussions of unidentified aerial phenomena. Lang. Commun. **88**, 90–98 (2023)

34. Agrama, H.A.: Secularity, synchronicity, and uncanny science: considerations and challenges. Zygon®, **56**(2), 395–415 (2021)

35. Zeller, B.E.: (Dis) enchanted ufology: the boundaries of science and religion in MUFON, the mutual UFO network. Nova Religio: J. Altern. Emergent Religions **25**(2), 61–86 (2021)

36. Kivari, K.: Extraordinary experiences in the culture of the supernatural: vernacular theories and identities. Implicit Relig. **24**(1), 87 (2021)

37. Pokorny, L.: Maitreya, Crop Circles, and the Age of Light: Benjamin Creme's UFO Thought. In: Handbook of UFO Religions, pp. 295–311. Brill (2021)

38. Ashcraft, W.M.: Scholarship on UFO s and Religion: The First Seventy-Five Years. Handbook of UFO Religions, pp. 16–35 (2021)

39. Hodges, D., Paxton-Fear, K.: An analysis of the writing of 'suicide cult' members. Digital Sch. Humanit. **37**(1), 137–151 (2022)

40. Rose, D.J.: Alienation and aliens: a comparative study of narratives of abduction in historical African and UFO experiences. Fabula **63**(3–4), 262–279 (2022)

41. Guimont, E., Baumhammer, M.: Public history, personal pseudohistory, and VirtHSTM. Endeavour **46**(3), 100835 (2022)

42. Butman, J.: Reported phenomena, unexplainable phenomena: an epistemology of UAP. Cosmos Hist. **18**(2), 380–412 (2022)

43. Smith, T., Jonathan, S.V.: Hume on Miracles and UFOs. Prolegomena: Časopis za filozofiju, **22**(1), 67–87 (2023)

44. Wright, J.T., Haqq-Misra, J., Frank, A., Kopparapu, R., Lingam, M., Sheikh, S.Z.: The case for technosignatures: why they may be abundant, long-lived, highly detectable, and unambiguous. Astrophys. J. Lett. **927**(2), L30 (2022)

The Scholarly Age—Beyond the Academic Age Using Techno-Scientific, Knowledge Appropriation and Mentoring Outputs

Julián D. Cortés[1,2]([✉]) [iD], Nicolás Robinson-García[3] [iD],
Zaida Chinchilla-Rodríguez[4] [iD], and María Catalina Ramírez-Cajiao[2] [iD]

[1] School of Management and Business, Universidad del Rosario, Bogotá, Colombia
julian.cortess@urosario.edu.co
[2] Engineering School, Universidad de Los Andes, Bogotá, Colombia
[3] EC3 Research Group, Department of Information and Communication, University of Granada,
Granada, Spain
[4] Instituto de Políticas y Bienes Públicos (IPP), Consejo Superior de Investigaciones Científicas
(CSIC), Madrid, Spain

Abstract. Various aspects of academic careers are studied using academic age as a proxy for the chronological age. The limitation of this metric is that it does not consider a wide range of scientific workforce outputs, since it only focuses on scientific publications. This study aims to extend understanding of the scientific workforce by amplifying the computation of academic age to include the *scholarly age* which considers different knowledge outputs from scientific publications. Using data from Colciencias/Ministry of Science Technology and Innovation's national research group assessments in Colombia, we analyzed 1,318,799 unique products from 1990–2020. We computed four typologies of scholarly age based on four products classes: new knowledge; technological development and innovation; social appropriation of knowledge and dissemination of science; and training human resources. The Shapiro-Wilk test shows a non-normal distribution of scholarly ages. The median scholarly age of social appropriation of knowledge and dissemination of science was 8 years; training human resources 7 years; new knowledge 5 years; and technological development and innovation 1 year. Statistically significant differences and large effect size, $\eta^2 = .27$, were found between all scholarly age typologies through Kruskal-Wallis and post-hoc Dunn tests. It reveals that estimating a researcher's expertise based on scientific publication alone is a partial and different proxy compared to the diverse spectrum of scholarly activities and further know-how researchers may possess.

Keywords: Scholarly Age · Academic Age · Academic Careers · Research Policy

1 Introduction

The chronological age is a crucial variable in studying diverse factors related to the careers and ageing process in academia, such as knowledge productivity, impact, direction, and collaboration patterns [1–4]. However, there are privacy restrictions to source

© The Author(s), under exclusive license to Springer Nature Switzerland AG 2024
I. Sserwanga et al. (Eds.): iConference 2024, LNCS 14596, pp. 321–330, 2024.
https://doi.org/10.1007/978-3-031-57850-2_24

the chronological age of researchers, even more to conduct larger scale bibliometric studies. The academic age (i.e., the time a researcher has spent researching in a discipline) is an alternative proxy to the chronological age.

Research published on academic age has been prolific. To name a few, it has provided insights on its relationship and uses to study inter-institutional mobility, scientific (peak)performance, collaboration, research evaluation, increasing research' complexity and international migration [5–11]. Yet, the visible restriction of the academic age is that it only uses research articles or reviews indexed in both canonical bibliographic databases, Web of Science Core Collection or Scopus.

Consequently, the mainstream academic age does not consider the complete and diverse set of activities that the scientific workforce performs in academia besides scientific research, such as under/graduate mentorship, draft a report to inform congressman/woman in the process of policy/law making, software development, patents publication, among others [12]. Including these knowledge outputs different from scientific publication is vital to understand the scientific workforce experience in developing countries considering that these systems have a historical tradition of professionalization: a focus on training professionals and not the scientific production of knowledge [13]. In that line, we outlined two RQs (research questions):

- What other types of scholarly age typologies beyond academic age can be estimated based on further scientific-technology-innovation knowledge production, mentoring, and dissemination?
- Are there significant differences between such scholarly age typologies or are they similar expressions of the research-based expertise of the scientific workforce?

We aim to extend the understanding of the diverse expertise of the scientific workforce, amplifying the computation of the academic age to the *scholarly age* which considers a comprehensive range of knowledge outputs. We focus on the case of study of the national science system of Colombia. Our contribution expands the well-established literature on academic age, introducing a more comprehensive and systematic view of the expertise of scholars based on a more diverse kind of scientific-technology-innovation knowledge outputs.

2 Materials and Methods

2.1 Materials

The data used in this study was extracted from six national research group assessments conducted by Colciencias/Ministry of Science Technology and Innovation (MinCiencias) in Colombia during the years 2013, 2014, 2015, 2017, 2019, and 2021. The dataset is open access (i.e., for complete access to the dataset and variables dictionary, see Ref. [14]). Table 1 shows the definition of the knowledge product classes and exemplary knowledge product types according to 2021 assessment. The main variable of interest of the knowledge products data set is the product classes/types of classification and their respective year of creation/publication. Their respective year of creation/publication will enable us to compute a diversity of scholarly age typologies. There are four knowledge classes, excluding "no category", namely: social appropriation of knowledge and public dissemination of science (ap_soc_div), with 70 different product types; new knowledge (nuev_cono), with 50; technological development and innovation, with 46 (tech_inn); and training of human resources (rrhh), with 17. There are 1,318,799 unique products identifiers.

Table 1. Definition and examples of knowledge product classes registered in the national assessments of research groups in Colombia.

Variable acronym	Knowledge product classes	Definition	Number of products	Examples of knowledge product types
ap_soc_div	Social appropriation of knowledge and public dissemination of science	Products which involve the exchange of knowledge and know-how of science, technology, and innovation among citizens to address situations of common interest and propose solutions or concerted improvements that respond to their realities	70	Research results informative bulletin; edition; audio content generation; research dissemination books and/or compilation of dissemination books; specialized knowledge network
nuev_cono	New knowledge	Products with a significant contribution to the state of the art in an area of knowledge, which have been discussed and validated in order to be incorporated into the scientific discussion, the development of research activities and technological development, and which may be a source of innovation	50	Research articles; books; patent of invention; plant variety; art, architecture and design works or products

(*continued*)

Table 1. (*continued*)

Variable acronym	Knowledge product classes	Definition	Number of products	Examples of knowledge product types
tech_inn	Technological development and innovation	Products that account for the generation of ideas, methods and tools that impact economic development and generate transformations in society	46	Scientific-technical consulting; business management innovation; regulation and standard epidemiological surveillance protocols; software; spin-off
rrhh	Training of human resources	The generation of spaces to advise and develop the activities involved in the completion of a thesis or degree work that granted the title of doctor, master or professional (respectively); the execution of R + D + I projects with training and support to training programs; and the management of research projects that allow the attainment of the necessary resources for the development of research or innovation	17	Undergraduate thesis; master's thesis; PhD thesis

2.2 Methods

There are two mainstream approaches for calculating the academic age of researchers. First, years that had passed since their first research article/review publication, or,

$$A_{v1} = C - t_{fp} \tag{1}$$

where C is the current year and t_{fp} is the year of first publication [15]. The second one is the difference between the year of last and first publication plus one, or,

$$A_{v2} = t_{lp} - t_{fp} + 1 \tag{2}$$

where t_{lp} is the year of last publication and t_{fp} is the year of first publication [16]. In contrast with the first approach, here *transient authors* (i.e., authors with just one publication) are excluded and *multi-paper authors* (or those who have published more than once) are those who are considered for calculating the academic age. Each researcher's scholarly age was calculated based on the latter principle for determining academic age.

We implemented this principle to all knowledge products sourced from the Colciencias/MinCiencias groups' national assessments, not just publications. Therefore, a single researcher could have not only an academic age based on scientific publications (nuev_cono) but also further scholarly age types based on technological development and innovation (tech_inn); social appropriation of knowledge and public dissemination of science (ap_soc_div); and training of human resources (rrhh) outputs. Table 2 shows the different scholarly age types a researcher could have by applying the general principle proposed here.

Evidence shows that the distribution of the academic age among researchers is not normally distributed, even controlling by disciplines [16, 17]. We opted for applying non-parametric test to identify significant differences between the scholarly age classes and types computed. First, as a double check, we ran for our sample of scholarly age typologies a Shapiro-Wilk test to examine if they are normally distributed [18]. Then, we implemented a Kruskal-Wallis test to determine if there are differences between the scholarly age typologies of researchers when they are not normally distributed [18]. And third, a Dunn's post-hoc tests to determine which pair of groups are different [18].

Table 2. Example of calculation of scholarly age

Researcher ID	Product class	First year of creation of product x in that product class	Last year of creation of product y in that product class	Scholarly age in that product class
007	nuev_cono	2013	2018	6
	tech_inn	2015	2017	3
	ap_soc_div	2010	2019	10
	rrhh	2005	2020	16

3 Results

Figure 1 displays the count of products by class between 1990 and 2020. The 1990 s was a decade in which the only two classes of products registered by their authors for the national assessments were training of human resources (rrhh) and social appropriation of knowledge and public dissemination of science (ap_soc_div), the latter showing a volatile trend when compared with a more upward and constant trend of the former. The next classes of products to be registered were new knowledge (nuevo_cono) since 2000 and tech_inn since 2005. There was a significant increase after 2007 for the main classes of products, i.e., ap_soc_div, rrhh, and nuevo_cono. Around similar periods, technological development, and innovation (teach-in) also showed an increasing trend, yet it does not surpass the quantity of products of the three first classes.

We focused our output analysis since 2005, a year of remarkable increase in the overall knowledge production in the country. In the first period between 2005–2010, there were produced ~ 5% over the total of products of rrhh products, followed by ~ 5% ap_soc_div, ~ 2% nuevo_cono, and ~ 0.1% of tech_inn. In a second period between 2011–2020, there was a production of ~ 36% rrhh, ~ 33% ap_soc_div, ~ 16% nuevo_cono, and ~ 2% tech_inn. We excluded from this count the "no category" product class. The inset if Fig. 1 shows a box plot with the distribution of the count of products by researcher.

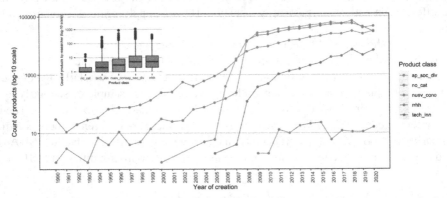

Fig. 1. Count of new products by class 1990–2020. Source: MinCiencias [19]. Notes: the inset shows a box plot of the distribution of the count of products by researcher. Social appropriation of knowledge and public dissemination of science (ap_soc_div); new knowledge (nuevo_cono); Technological development and innovation (tech_inn); Training of human resources (rrhh); Non-categorized (no_cat).

Figure 2 reports the scholarly age distribution for the complete sample of researchers by knowledge product classes. For 77,400 researchers, ~ 17% do not report age class ap_soc_div, ~ 39% for age class nuev_cono, ~ 35% age class rrhh, and ~ 88% age class tech_inn. Excluding the non-reporting cases for each age class, ~ 53% of researchers have an age class ap_soc_div between 1–5 years, ~ 40% for age class nuev_cono, ~ 41% for age class rrhh, and ~ 10% for age class tech_inn. The median scholarly age of ap_soc_div were 8 years, followed by rrhh with 7 years, nuev_cono with 5 years, and tech_inn with 1 year.

The Shapiro-Wilk tests showed a $p < 0.05$ which allows to reject the hypothesis that the scholarly age values are normally distributed. Figure 3 reports the results of the Kruskal-Wallis test for the case of researchers with the four scholarly age typologies ($n = 6,088$). It showed a significant difference between groups, $H(3) = 6681.21, p < 0.001$. The size effect (epsilon-squared: $\varepsilon2$) of the Kruskal-Wallis test was .27, meaning a large magnitude effect size to which 27% of the total variance in scholarly age value can be explained by the product class groups. Post-hoc Dunn test reported that the mean differences between all four groups were significant, $p < 0.001$.

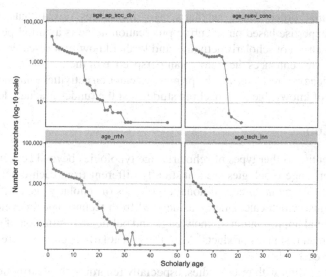

Fig. 2. Number of researchers by scholarly age typologies for the complete sample.

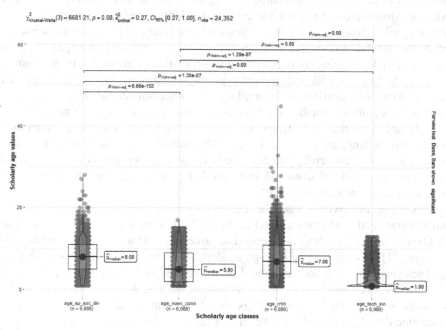

Fig. 3. Box plot distribution of scholarly age grouped by their respective product class and tests results.

The Colombian scientific workforce exhibits marked differences in scholarly age categories across product classes used as an expertise proxy variable, with the ap_soc_div class having the highest median scholarly age, followed by rrhh, nuevo_cono, and tech_inn, in that order. These scholarly age differences reveal that estimating a researcher's 'expertise based on scientific publication alone is a partial perspective of the diverse spectrum of scholarly activities and further know-how researchers may possess. Our approach enhances the Colombian perspective of the case by accentuating the median proficiency of researchers who primarily center on activities related to the social appropriation of knowledge and coaching students at the (under)graduate levels.

4 Discussion

This study identifies other types of scholarly age typologies beyond academic age and if such scholarly age typologies are statistically different from each other. We found, for the case of Colombia, three additional typologies of scholarly ages different scientific publications, which calculation was derived from technological development and innovation; social appropriation of knowledge and public dissemination of science; and training of human resources products. Also, those scholarly age types were statistically different from each other.

Our findings align with prior studies, especially regarding the distribution and average academic age. According to evidence, the distribution of academic age among researchers is not normally distributed. A long-tail distribution is observed in the academic age distribution of physics and computer science scholars, with approximately 80% of scholars possessing less than 4 years of academic age [11]. The academic age distribution exhibits an exponential decay from the maximum academic age of 51 years observed in fields ranging from astronomy to economics [16], similar to that showed in Fig. 2. The Shapiro-Wilk tests applied to all the scholarly age typologies here examined stated that their distribution departed significantly from normality. An explanatory factor of the significant number of early career researchers with a junior academic and scholarly age is the rise of the temporary scientific workforce. Increasing competition for research funding, higher stakes in research evaluation criteria, team composition and size, are just a few driving forces of the division and specialization of tasks which requires more specialized albeit transient technical personal that supports projects that just a few senior researchers lead [20].

Concerning the average academic age, 6–10 years group is the most common for both emigrant and immigrant researchers in the Middle East and North Africa region [9]. Over 50% of researchers in diverse disciplines have an academic age between 6–10 years [21]. In contrast, the average academic age found in Poland was 41 years [2]. These academic age metrics should be interpreted with caution, since they were calculated as time elapsed since first publication, the first approach we mentioned in 'Methods' section with the shortcomings already explained (i.e., authors with just one publication decades ago could be labeled as a *senior* author when in reality they exited from academia). In this study, the scholarly age median for all typologies was from 1 to 8 years, being 5 years the median age in for the nuev_cono class in which are the scientific publications categorized. These findings highlight the relevance of national in-depth analysis of the dynamics and differences between academic and other scholarly age typologies.

This study is susceptible to various constraints. To begin with, it is important to highlight that there is significant diversity within each category in terms of the number of products evaluated. For instance, the nuevo_cono category encompasses 50 different products. Therefore, the scholarly age of new knowledge might be computed as the difference between the year of last creation of a utility patent and the year of first creation of a research article. As a second point, it should be noted that there is a lack of additional data regarding the impact of diverse knowledge and mentoring products. This incorporates article/patent citations, the headcount of assistants at a congress, and the future career possibilities of mentees. Incorporating that information with the scholarly age of a researcher in a more robust model could prove to be of interest.

In further stages of the project, we will implement a more sub-refined calculation of the scholarly age within each product class and include at least article/patent citation indicators. Also, expanding the correlation between scholarly age and chronological age and explore scholarly age differences between researcher gender and disciplines/fields. We will aim to determine the relationship between scholarly ages and researchers' status in the national system (i.e., senior, associated, junior) and academic degree (i.e., PhD, MSc) to establish a more refined profiles of researchers' careers. Finally, we will delve into a more comprehensive inclusion of bibliographic data from canonical databases such as WoS or Scopus to study potential biases in the assessment of researchers produced in coverage variations.

References

1. Kaskie, B.: The academy is aging in place: assessing alternatives for modifying institutions of higher education. Gerontologist **57**, 816–823 (2017). https://doi.org/10.1093/geront/gnw001
2. kwiek, M., Roszka, W.: Academic vs. biological age in research on academic careers: a large-scale study with implications for scientifically developing systems. Scientometrics **127**(6), 3543–3575 (2022). https://doi.org/10.1007/s11192-022-04363-0
3. Lee, S., Bozeman, B.: The impact of research collaboration on scientific productivity. Soc. Stud. Sci. **35**, 673–702 (2005). https://doi.org/10.1177/0306312705052359
4. Sinatra, R., Wang, D., Deville, P., Song, C., Barabási, A.-L.: Quantifying the evolution of individual scientific impact. Sci. **354**(1979), aaf5239 (2016). https://doi.org/10.1126/science.aaf5239
5. Chen, Y., Wu, K., Li, Y., Sun, J.: Impacts of inter-institutional mobility on scientific performance from research capital and social capital perspectives. Scientometrics **128**, 3473–3506 (2023). https://doi.org/10.1007/s11192-023-04690-w
6. Lyu, X., Costas, R.: Studying the characteristics of scientific communities using individual-level bibliometrics: the case of big data research. Scientometrics **126**, 6965–6987 (2021). https://doi.org/10.1007/s11192-021-04034-6
7. Yair, G., Goldstein, K.: The Annus mirabilis paper: years of peak productivity in scientific careers. Scientometrics **124**, 887–902 (2020). https://doi.org/10.1007/s11192-020-03544-z
8. Hammarfelt, B., De Rijcke, S.: Accountability in context: effects of research evaluation systems on publication practices, disciplinary norms, and individual working routines in the faculty of arts at Uppsala University. Res. Eval. **24**, 63–77 (2015). https://doi.org/10.1093/reseval/rvu029
9. El-Ouahi, J., Robinson-García, N., Costas, R.: Analyzing scientific mobility and collaboration in the middle east and North Africa. Quant. Sci. Stud. **2**, 1–25 (2021). https://doi.org/10.1162/qss_a_00149

10. Liang, Z., Ba, Z., Mao, J., Li, G.: Research complexity increases with scientists' academic age: evidence from library and information science. J Informetr. **17**, 101375 (2023). https://doi.org/10.1016/j.joi.2022.101375
11. Wang, W., Yu, S., Bekele, T.M., Kong, X., Xia, F.: Scientific collaboration patterns vary with scholars' academic ages. Scientometrics **112**, 329–343 (2017). https://doi.org/10.1007/s11192-017-2388-9
12. Robinson-Garcia, N., Costas, R., Nane, G.F., van Leeuwen, T.N.: Valuation regimes in academia: Researchers' attitudes towards their diversity of activities and academic performance. Res Eval. **32**(2), 496–514 (2023). https://doi.org/10.1093/RESEVAL/RVAC049
13. Vasen, F., Sarthou, N.F., Romano, S.A., Gutiérrez, B.D., Pintos, M.: Turning academics into researchers: the development of national researcher categorization systems in Latin America. Res Eval. **32**(2), 244–255 (2023). https://doi.org/10.1093/RESEVAL/RVAD021
14. MinCiencias: Producción grupos investigación. https://bit.ly/3MKGgyE. Accessed 15 Nov 2023
15. Radicchi, F., Castellano, C.: Analysis of bibliometric indicators for individual scholars in a large data set. Scientometrics **97**, 627–637 (2013). https://doi.org/10.1007/S11192-013-1027-3/FIGURES/5
16. Milojević, S.: How are academic age, productivity and collaboration related to citing behavior of researchers? PLoS ONE **7**, 1–13 (2012). https://doi.org/10.1371/journal.pone.0049176
17. Wang, L., Wang, X., Philipsen, N.J.: Network structure of scientific collaborations between China and the EU member states. Scientometrics **113**, 765–781 (2017). https://doi.org/10.1007/s11192-017-2488-6
18. Hettmansperger, T.P., McKean, J.W.: Robust Nonparametric Statistical Methods. John Wiley and Sons Inc., New York, USA (1998)
19. Minciencias: Resultados Generales de Grupos e Investigadores. https://minciencias.gov.co/la-ciencia-en-cifras/estadisticas-generales. Accessed 27 Jan 2022
20. Milojevic, S., Radicchi, F., Walsh, J.P.: Changing demographics of scientific careers: the rise of the temporary workforce. Proc. Natl. Acad. Sci. U.S.A. **115**, 12616–12623 (2018). https://doi.org/10.1073/pnas.1800478115
21. Kwiek, M., Szymula, L.: Is the researcher population really getting older?. https://www.elsevier.com/connect/is-the-researcher-population-really-getting-older. Accessed 19 Nov 2023

Information and Digital Literacy

"Words Are not just Words; They Carry Experiences Within Them": Navigating Personal Information Management in Multilingual Contexts

Lilach Alon[1]([✉])[iD] and Maja Krtalić[2][iD]

[1] Tel-Hai Academic College, Qiryat Shemona, Israel
alonlil@telhai.ac.il
[2] Victoria University of Wellington, Wellington, New Zealand
maja.krtalic@vuw.ac.nz

Abstract. This exploratory study examines the factors that shape personal information management (PIM) in multilingual contexts (MPIM) by investigating how individuals manage personal information in multiple languages. Through conducting 10 semi-structured interviews with voluntary migrants in higher education in the US, New Zealand, and Germany, the study sheds light on the challenges and opportunities of MPIM. The findings suggest that language choice in MPIM is influenced by various factors, including life transitions, contextual factors, affective and identity-related factors, and challenges accompanying MPIM. The results offer new insights into the MPIM experience and suggest potential ways to improve PIM in multi-lingual contexts, such as improving platform design and developing systems that support alphabet recognition and translation to better serve multilingual users' PIM needs. In conclusion, the study underscores the need for improved MPIM support in platform design and further research on MPIM practices and experiences.

Keywords: Personal Information Management · Multilingual PIM · PIM Practices · Migrants

1 Introduction

1.1 Purpose

Over the past few years, there has been a significant rise in the number of individuals voluntarily immigrating to other countries for personal or professional reasons [1]. However, adapting to a new country can be an overwhelming task, especially when it involves accessing and managing personal information in multiple languages, which can be particularly challenging for those who are not fluent in the language of the host country [2]. Given the challenges associated with this process, effective practices for the management of personal information are important to successfully settling into a

© The Author(s), under exclusive license to Springer Nature Switzerland AG 2024
I. Sserwanga et al. (Eds.): iConference 2024, LNCS 14596, pp. 333–342, 2024.
https://doi.org/10.1007/978-3-031-57850-2_25

new country, both personally and professionally [3]. Therefore, it is essential to gain a better understanding of the information practices, challenges, and needs of multilingual individuals, including many migrants who are navigating new information landscapes [4, 5]. Yet, research attention on these aspects remains limited despite their significance.

To address this gap, this study examines multilingual personal information management (MPIM) through the lens of personal information management (PIM). PIM is concerned with understanding how individuals acquire, store, and retrieve information for their everyday tasks and roles [6]. By examining MPIM, this study seeks to contribute new knowledge to the field of PIM and deepen interdisciplinary understanding of the difficulties that multilingual individuals face when managing personal information in diverse contexts.

1.2 Theoretical Background

The issue of multilingual information behavior has been studied extensively in various information science fields. However, when viewed through the lens of PIM, only one study has addressed the multilingual aspect, which found that users tag URLs in multiple languages [7]. Conversely, there is an abundance of research on multilingual information seeking, searching, accessing, and cross-language information retrieval. These studies have contributed to our understanding of how individuals search for information in multiple languages, described different aspects of multilingual information searching and accessing, and suggested ways to improve platform design to support cross-language information retrieval [8–16].

Nonetheless, these studies do not shed light on the MPIM behavior and experiences of individuals who use more than one language to manage their personal information. Several studies in information science have examined various aspects of migrants' information behavior and experiences, such as their interactions with personal collections during different phases of life [1, 17, 29, 30] and the importance of information literacy for migrants [18]. However, to the best of our knowledge, no study has yet focused on the MPIM experiences and challenges of migrants.

The purpose of this study is to bridge the gaps in our understanding of MPIM by examining the factors that shape how individuals utilize MPIM, as well as exploring the experiences and challenges attached to it. The study reports an initial research phase, which comprises findings from 10 interviews with migrants who use multiple languages in their daily lives. By doing so, the study aims to propose more inclusive and effective tools and solutions for PIM in a globalized and multilingual world, while also addressing equity issues in language support. Furthermore, the study aims to establish a foundation for future research that can provide a more comprehensive understanding of MPIM practices and experiences.

2 Method

2.1 Research Approach

This study utilized the qualitative phenomenological approach to examine the MPIM experiences of migrants. This approach involves describing individuals' experiences and perspectives and identifying the meaning they attach to them within a specific context [19,

20]. The selection of this approach was appropriate as it is well-suited for investigating relatively new topics that lack an extensive empirical background [21], such as managing personal information in multiple languages.

2.2 Participants

The initial phase of this research comprised of 10 participants, ages 29–40, who migrated voluntarily. Among them, six immigrated to the USA, two to New Zealand, and two to Germany. All participants work in the higher education sector and regularly use multiple languages in their daily activities. Recruitment was conducted through university postings, personal networks, and a snowballing approach, with interested participants spreading the word about the research. Participant characteristics are summarized in Table 1.

Table 1. Participants' Characteristics.

	Gender	Age	Occupation	PIM languages	Home country	Residency country	Length of stay
P1	Female	35	Postdoc	Korean; English	South-Korea	USA	17 years
P2	Female	36	Postdoc	Hebrew; English	Israel	USA	1.5 years
P3	Female	31	PhD student	Persian (Farsi); English	Iran	New Zealand	6 months
P4	Female	40	PhD student	Persian (Farsi); English	Iran	New Zealand	4 years
P5	Female	36	Postdoc	Hebrew; English	Israel	USA	8 months
P6	Male	38	Postdoc	Hebrew; English; German; Yiddish	Israel	Germany	1.9 years
P7	Female	38	Postdoc	Hebrew; English; German	Israel	Germany	6 years
P8	Male	35	Postdoc	Hebrew; English; German; Yiddish	Israel	USA	3 weeks

(continued)

Table 1. (*continued*)

	Gender	Age	Occupation	PIM languages	Home country	Residency country	Length of stay
P9	Female	29	Postdoc	Hebrew; English	Israel	USA	4 months
P10	Female	40	Postdoc	Hebrew; English; Arabic; Cantonese	Israel	USA	9 months

In the next stage of the study, we intend to increase the sample size to 20 interviews to gain a more comprehensive understanding of MPIM experiences and challenges.

2.3 Tools, Procedure and Analysis

We used semi-structured interviews as the primary data collection method in line with the phenomenological approach [22, 23]. The interviews comprised four sections: background information, MPIM practices, experiences, ideal PIM tools. Participants shared their demographic information, language proficiency, and reasons for using MPIM in the background section. The second section focused on language usage in MPIM practices, and the experiences section explored decision-making processes and emotions related to using different languages. The last section discussed preferred MPIM systems and long-term language usage.

Participants were informed of the study's purpose, and consent was obtained before the interviews that were conducted both face-to-face and via Zoom in March 2023, with an average duration of 60 min. Transcriptions were analyzed using NVivo software, with participant anonymity ensured.

Both researchers jointly developed a coding scheme based on Moustakas' approach [24] and conducted two stages of analysis: horizontal and cluster of meanings. The horizontal analysis focused on each participant's experience, while the cluster of meanings analysis identified themes and sub-themes across all the interviews. Rigorous discussions and a collaborative reliability assessment of coding [25] were employed between the researchers to refine the coding scheme, ensuring precision and coherence. This iterative process concluded in the identification of four themes capturing MPIM experiences, subsequently expanded into sub-themes as summarized in Table 2.

Table 2. Coding Scheme.

Theme	Sub-theme
Theme 1: Language choice reflecting life transitions	1a. Integration and cultural facilitation 1b. Duration of stay 1c. Future plans
Theme 2: Contextual factors in language choice	2a. Work-life distinction 2b. Language-content alignment 2c. Audience-focused communication
Theme 3: Affect and identity in language choice	3a. Discomfort with new language 3b. Emotional attachment with native language
Theme 4: Navigating MPIM challenges	4a. Technological limitations 4b. Visual esthetics 4c. Information retrieval

3 Findings

Findings are presented according to the four identified themes.

3.1 Language Choice Reflecting Life Transitions

Participants adjusted their language choices for MPIM during significant life transitions, such as moving to a new country. These adjustments aided their integration and adaptation to the new cultural contexts and reflected the duration of their stay in the new country as well as their future plans.

Managing personal information in multiple languages facilitated smoother integration in a new country: "Now I live in the US, so I try to handle everything in English" (P4). P7 who live in Germany, echoed a similar sentiment: "It's about knowing that certain things might get lost in translation; for later retrieval, I stay close to the original name, like *Beschied* for Taxes, or *Versicherung* for Social Security".

Language choice reflected the duration of the stay in the new country. Those with extended stays in their new countries tended to shift towards using the local language more for their PIM practices. P1, a long-term US resident, shared, "When I create folders, my instinct is to use English". In contrast, P2, a recent arrival in the US, noted, "All of my personal information is organized in both English and Hebrew. Everyone uses English here, but I still rely on Hebrew". P8, who had moved to the US three weeks before the interview, described his challenges in PIM transitioning from Hebrew to English: "I started this research table in English. It's a bit odd and I felt a bit silly at first, but this project represents me, so I had to switch from Hebrew to English."

Languages choices also extended to future residence decisions: "If I return to Korea, I'd switch everything to Korean. After all these years, they might perceive me as a foreigner, so I want to keep my Korean identity through language" (P1). P9 also reflected her thoughts about future language choice: "I want to find a permanent position in academia. I think that I'll use English for interactions with international colleagues, while communicating with local colleagues and students in Hebrew".

3.2 Contextual Factors in Language Choice

Participants' language choice for organizing personal information depended on the context and nature of the information. These included three main factors: work-life distinction, language-content alignment, and audience-focused communication.

Findings for work-life distinction reveal that work related information were often organized in English, while private or family related information were typically organized in the native language. For example, P9 said: "I have a strong separation in my mind. Hebrew feels more personal, while English is for professional matters". Similarly, P1 said: "My work items are almost 100% English. Private information is almost 100% Korean".

Participants also conveyed that language choices for naming files were intertwined with the item's content or context. For instance, P2 utilized Hebrew names for organizing her Israeli PhD research but named literature folders in English because she read papers in English. P3 shared how she encountered certain academic terms in English during her PhD journey, leading her to naturally spring to mind when naming files. Similarly, P6 noted that when dealing with files predominantly in English, he would name them with English titles.

Participants' language preferences in PIM were also influenced by the intended recipients of the information. Language selection dynamics often revolve around the specific audience, aiming to achieve effective communication across diverse languages. P7, an Israeli in Germany, exemplified this by using English when collaborating with German scholars to avoid errors. P10, an Israeli postdoc in the US proficient in four languages, highlighted the challenges of this adjustment, stating, "Since leaving Israel, my Hebrew writing skills have faded, and I prefer English for professional emails. This became clear when I had trouble writing a formal Hebrew email to a colleague".

3.3 Affect and Identity in Language Choice

Findings showed that affective and identity factors played a significant role in the choice of languages for PIM. Participants often felt more comfortable, emotional, and authentic while using their native language for organizing and maintaining information items. For instance, P2 remarked: "Managing my to-do lists in English feels like I'm faking it; it doesn't feel natural." P5 said that her fluency in English falls short of her proficiency in Hebrew, leading even minor daily tasks to "feel like a huge burden." P3, a native Persian speaker, added, "Sometimes using words in English feels weird." Furthermore, P8 conveyed a feeling of discomfort when it came to taking notes during work in a language that is not his native tongue.

The use of specific words in their native language to manage personal information evoked more emotions and attachment compared to the same words in the non-native language. For example, P1 named a folder for personal memories as *Chooeok* (memories in Korean), saying, "the Korean word comes to me as memory, but I wouldn't have any emotional attachment to the English word". P3 shared a similar idea explaining how her birthday in *Farvardin* (April in Farsi) coincides with April in the English calendar. However, using the English word for her birth month does not hold any emotional attachment or memory. Summing up, she emphasized, "Words are not just words; they carry experiences within them".

3.4 Navigating MPIM Challenges

This theme describes the obstacles that participants encountered during MPIM. These encompassed technological limitations, visual esthetics, and information retrieval difficulties.

Participants navigated issues arising from the lack of language support and grappled with the complexities of transitioning between various languages. P4 elaborated on technological constraints, resorting to "Penglish" (Persian and English) due to the absence of a Persian keyboard during online chats. P1 faced complications while harmonizing English and Korean in OneNote, where Korean text appeared as red lines, expressing frustration: "That bothers me because I don't know if there's a mistake or not". The integration of languages written in different directions also posed an obstacle for some participants. When digitally jotting down notes in Hebrew (written right-to-left) and English (written left-to-right), strategies like line-skipping or favoring one language were employed to ensure proper alignment.

These technological limitations further influenced the visual aesthetics of participants' personal information spaces. P8 remarked, "The fonts in English look much better than the Hebrew ones". P4 stressed the significance of email aesthetics, even at the cost of linguistic accuracy, recounting a scenario where Persian text was interchanged with English to enhance appearance.

The challenge of information retrieval was also prominent among participants. P10 shared an ongoing struggle to locate a specific file due to memory lapses regarding its name. She reflected, "This paper has become fixed in my mind as the 'river article,' even though it bears no connection to rivers. I tried saving this article under numerous names too, yet the challenge of retrieval persists". These challenges prompted the adoption of inventive file naming practices, as illustrated by P1 who saved files in Korean and English to aid retrieval, and P3 who embraced "Fenglish" (Farsi and English) to ensure compatibility.

4 Discussion and Future Research

Our study offers preliminary insights into the experiences and challenges of MPIM, specifically focusing on migrants. The findings underscore the intricate interplay of factors influencing language choice for PIM, encompassing life transitions, contextual considerations, affective aspects, and the unique challenges posed by MPIM.

Participants exhibited a versatile approach to MPIM, utilizing both their native language and the language of their adopted country across diverse practices, ranging from acquiring and creating to storing, organizing, retrieving, and using information. This encompassed various information items, including documents, emails, personal notes, social media, and even everyday grocery lists. The participants seamlessly transitioned between different devices, such as phones, computers, and online platforms, reflecting their multiple roles both at home and at work. These findings underscore the comprehensive presence of MPIM across all domains of PIM as identified by Jones [6].

Participants used multiple languages for PIM to achieve goals linked to their migration experience, such as language development, cultural adaptation, and integration [5, 17]. These practices intertwined closely with affective and identity-related factors, revealing participants' emotional and authentic connections to their native language [1, 29]. Conversely, using a non-native language led to a perceived sense of reduced expressiveness and connection. Even seemingly routine PIM tasks, like naming files or creating to-do lists, took on deeper emotional and authentic significance beyond mere information organization.

These findings resonate with previous research that underscores the profound role of emotions and identity in PIM [26, 27]. Considering that information items may change in purpose and reuse across different linguistic contexts during migration [1, 30], appropriate renaming or descriptions become vital to ensure their continued usability. Supporting migrants in multitasking across multiple languages or seamlessly switching between them can contribute significantly to their well-being and integration. Enhancing PIM skills and platform designs tailored to multilingual users' needs holds potential in achieving these objectives [28].

Our study draws attention to the challenges inherent in MPIM, which necessitate addressing when adapting platforms for multilingual users. These challenges include the integration of languages with differing directionalities, coping with software that lacks support for specific languages, and the efficient retrieval of information. While existing literature has primarily focused on cross-language information retrieval challenges and platform design enhancements [10, 11], our study uniquely spotlights the need for improved MPIM support, encompassing searching, maintaining, and even naming suggestions based on language recognition and translation.

An immediate practical implication of our findings lies in the potential to inform the design of user-centric systems and tools catering to the distinct needs of multilingual individuals managing personal information. Tackling the identified MPIM challenges, such as integrating languages with diverse directionalities and effectively managing multilingual personal information spaces, could pave the way for more efficient platforms. The incorporation of features like seamless multi-language typing, voice input, AI-assisted language tools, and integrated language recognition could elevate the MPIM experience, facilitating streamlined information retrieval across multiple languages.

Beyond the practical implications, the MPIM challenges mirror broader societal trends, reflecting the increasing mobility, cultural diversity, and blending of languages and cultures in various contexts. As societies become more linguistically and culturally diverse, the ability to adeptly manage personal information in multilingual environments becomes an indispensable skill. Our findings contribute to a deeper understanding of the challenges and opportunities presented by multilingual information practices, thereby enriching broader discussions on language support, cultural inclusion, and equity.

While our study provides a fresh perspective on MPIM, acknowledging its limitations is essential. The small sample size and limited diversity in participants' work and language backgrounds underscore the need for further exploration. Specifically, since the participated migrants are identified as highly skilled due to their profession, their MPIM experiences may not represent those of other migrant groups. In subsequent phases of our research, we intend to delve into different contexts, such as multilingual households with two or more spoken languages, and examine how MPIM could potentially support language preservation or revitalization. Exploring the impact of aging and legacy factors on MPIM presents another avenue for investigation. In essence, this study serves as a stepping-stone for future research endeavors in this evolving field.

References

1. Krtalić, M., Ihejirika, K.T.: The things we carry: migrants' personal collection management and use. J. Document. **79**(1), 86–111 (2022)
2. Haley, A.N., Clough, P.: Affective experiences of international and home students during the information search process. New Rev. Acad. Librariansh. **23**(4), 396–420 (2017)
3. Shi, L., Brown, N.R.: The effect of immigration on the contents and organization of autobiographical memory: a transition-theory perspective. J. Appl. Res. Mem. Cogn. **5**(2), 135–142 (2016)
4. Caidi, N., Allard, D., Quirke, L.: Information practices of immigrants. Ann. Rev. Inf. Sci. Technol. **44**(1), 491–531 (2010)
5. Lloyd, A.: Researching fractured (information) landscapes: implications for library and information science researchers undertaking research with refugees and forced migration studies. J. Document. **73**(1), 35–47 (2017)
6. Jones, W.: Personal information management. Ann. Rev. Inf. Sci. Technol. **41**(1), 453–504 (2007)
7. Stiller, J., Gäde, M., Petras, V.: Is tagging multilingual? A case study with BibSonomy. In: Proceedings of the 11th Annual International ACM/IEEE Joint Conference on Digital Libraries, pp. 421–422. Association for Computing Machinery, New York (2011)
8. Alsalmi, H.M.: Information-seeking in multilingual digital libraries: comparative case studies of five university students. Library Hi Tech **39**(1), 80–100 (2020)
9. Brazier, D., Harvey, M.: A comparative study of native and non-native information seeking behaviours. In: European Conference on Information Retrieval, pp. 237–248. Springer, Cham (2018) https://doi.org/10.1007/978-3-319-76941-7_18
10. Harvey, M., Brazier, D.: E-government information search by English-as-a Second Language speakers: the effects of language proficiency and document reading level. Inf. Process. Manage. **59**(4), 102985 (2022)
11. Steichen, B., Lowe, R.: How do multilingual users search? An investigation of query and result list language choices. J. Am. Soc. Inf. Sci. **72**(6), 759–776 (2021)
12. Peters, C., Sheridan, P.: Multilingual information access. In: Agosti, M., Crestani, F., Pasi, G. (eds.) ESSIR 2000. LNCS, vol. 1980, pp. 51–80. Springer, Heidelberg (2000). https://doi.org/10.1007/3-540-45368-7_3
13. Wu, D., Fan, S., Yao, S., Xu, S.: An exploration of ethnic minorities' needs for multilingual information access of public digital cultural services. J. Documentation **79**(1), 1–20 (2022)
14. Granell, X.: Multilingual Information Management: Information, Technology and Translators. Chandos Publishing, Oxford (2015)
15. Peters, C., Braschler, M., Clough, P.: Multilingual Information Retrieval: From Research to Practice. Springer Berlin Heidelberg, Berlin, Heidelberg (2012). https://doi.org/10.1007/978-3-642-23008-0

16. Nie, J.Y.: Cross-Language Information Retrieval. Morgan & Claypool, USA (2010)
17. Caidi, N., Du, J.T., Li, L., Shen, J.M., Sun, Q.: Immigrating after 60: information experiences of older Chinese migrants to Australia and Canada. Inf. Process. Manage. **57**(3), 102111 (2020)
18. Sayyad Abdi, E., Partridge, H., Bruce, C., Watson, J.: Skilled immigrants: a resettlement information literacy framework. J. Documentation **75**(4), 892–908 (2019)
19. Creswell, J.W.: Quality Inquiry and Research Design: Choosing Among Five Traditions. Sage, Thousand Oaks, CA (1998)
20. Miles, M.B., Huberman, A.M., Saldana, J.: Qualitative Data Analysis: A Methods Sourcebook, 3rd edn. Sage, Los Angeles (2014)
21. Alon, L., Hardof-Jaffe, S., Nachmias, R.: How knowledge workers manage their personal information spaces: perceptions, challenges and high-level strategies. Interact. Comput. **31**(3), 303–316 (2019)
22. Leedy, P.D., Ormrod, J.E.: Practical research: Planning and design (11th ed.). Harlow, Pearson Education, Edinburgh Gate (2015)
23. Smith, J.A., Fieldsend, M.: Interpretative phenomenological analysis. In: Camic, P.M. (Ed.), Qualitative Research in Psychology: Expanding perspectives in methodology and design, pp. 147–166. American Psychological Association (2021)
24. Moustakas, C.: Phenomenological Research Methods. Sage, Thousand Oaks, CA (1994)
25. Miller, W.L., Crabtree, B.F.: Clinical research: a multimethod typology and qualitative roadmap. In: Crabtree, B.F., Miller, W.L. (eds.) Doing Qualitative Research, pp. 3–32. Sage Publications, CA (1999)
26. Alon, L., Nachmias, R.: The role of feelings in personal information management behavior: deleting and organizing information. J. Librariansh. Inf. Sci. **55**(2), 313–322 (2022)
27. Cushing, A.L.: "It's stuff that speaks to me": exploring the characteristics of digital possessions. J. Am. Soc. Inform. Sci. Technol. **64**(8), 1723–1734 (2013)
28. Alon, L.: Information seeking and personal information management behaviors as scaffolding during life transitions: The case of early-career researchers. Aslib J. Inform. Manage. (2023)
29. Krtalić, M.: Cultural information needs of long-settled immigrants, their descendants and family members: use of collective and personal information sources about the home country. J. Document. **77**(3), 663–679 (2021)
30. Krtalić, M., Dinneen, J.D: Information in the personal collections of writers and artists: practices, challenges, and preservation. J. Inform. Sci. (2022)

Data Curation Competencies, Skill Sets, and Tools Analysis

Angela P. Murillo$^{(\boxtimes)}$, Ayoung Yoon, Mitch Duncan, and Adam Thomas-Fennelly

Indiana University, Indianapolis, IN 46202, USA
{apmurill,ayyoon,duncanmw,thomaada}@iu.edu

Abstract. The project aims to extend the current understanding of data curation competencies by examining existing skill sets and tools through a systematic analysis of data curation literature. For this research, the researchers reviewed forty-two data curation-related documents, including peer-reviewed literature, conference papers, and book sections through descriptive quantitative analysis and inductive qualitative content analysis based on a systematically created document protocol to extract informational items about the documents, as well as competencies, skills, and tools relevant to data curation activities. This paper presents the preliminary findings of this analysis and future steps for this project.

Keywords: Data Curation · Digital Curation · Local or Community Data

1 Introduction

Library and information science (LIS) professionals have created data curation education, professional development programs, and related research to foster the development of graduate programs (i.e., master's-level specializations), professional development (i.e., post-graduate certificates), and professional networks (i.e., conferences) for over 20 years. These programs have provided data-related curriculum resources for LIS educators and professionals and have built a robust data curation community of educators, researchers, and practitioners.

While these efforts have successfully fostered the data curation community, particularly for the research data management (RDM) community, few efforts have considered the context of community-related data, such as non-profit organizations, community-based organizations, and local government. Community data is broadly defined as data that describes the local context and is used for community decision-making. These include open government and school data, community-related private sector data, and local organizations' data. Few efforts have been made to understand and address the specific needs for community data curation, relevant stakeholders, and how LIS educators should educate future professionals to curate community data.

This project will create a community data competency framework and curriculum that can be utilized by LIS researchers, educators, and professionals to fill the current gap in LIS education (See Fig. 1).

I. Sserwanga et al. (Eds.): iConference 2024, LNCS 14596, pp. 343–357, 2024.
https://doi.org/10.1007/978-3-031-57850-2_26

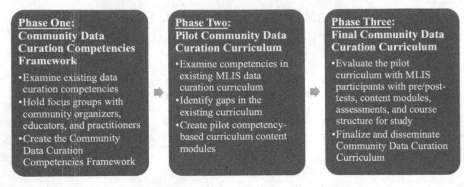

Fig. 1. Key activities for each project phase.

This paper provides the preliminary results of the first step of Phase One, where we conducted a systematic literature review and a content analysis of data curation competencies, skill sets, and tools. The following provides a review of related literature, a description of the research methods, findings, next steps, and conclusions.

2 Related Literature

LIS professionals have been at the forefront of data curation research and education, focusing their efforts on RDM, scientific data curation, and the academic workforce [1, 2]. Professional development opportunities such as the Research Data Management Librarian Academy [3] and MANTRA [4] provide free, self-paced online professional development RDM curricula. Organizations offer professional services, case studies, and guidance related to RDM, including the Digital Curation Centre [5] and Data Curation Network [6]. Recently, LIS professionals have recognized the need to expand the scope of data curation curriculum and have created complimentary data-related educational programs, including data science and data analytics within LIS curriculum [7–9]. Computer and data science professional development programs geared toward LIS professionals have also been created, such as Library Carpentry, which provides workshops on best practices in software development and data-related skills [10].

Both public and private sector community organizations (e.g., local government, non-profit organizations, community-based organizations) have become more data-driven by generating and engaging in data work [11, 12]. These organizations create and use internal organizational data and existing open data, and collect additional local data for decision-making, program development, and assessment. With increased data utilization, community organizations face data curation challenges [13, 14].

LIS professionals have moderately engaged with community data challenges through eGovernment [15], citizen science [16], and open data [17]. Recent research reported that most LIS professionals do not have expertise in competencies related to civic data, calling for the need to develop LIS curriculum that prepares students for these emerging data roles [18, 19]. As a response, several LIS educational initiatives have brought together library professionals, government partners, and LIS students and educators (e.g., Leveraging Open Data [20], Building Civic Open Data Capacity [21], mCODE

[22]). For example, the Open Data Literacy project has aimed to create LIS curriculum, field experiences, and open educational resources to train LIS professionals in open data literacy [23, 24].

While these efforts have provided some understanding of open and local data, more research needs to be conducted to fully understand the context of community data, the needs of related stakeholders, and the competencies needed to work with community data. This project begins to fill this gap by examining current data curation competencies.

3   Research Methods

The researchers utilized a modified five-step systematic literature review process [25] to understand current data curation competencies, which included:

1. Framing the question for review,
2. Identifying relevant literature,
3. Assessing the literature,
4. Capturing and summarizing the findings, and
5. Analyzing and interpreting the findings.

For *step one*, the framing question was *What competencies, skill sets, and proficiencies are needed to conduct data curation activities*?

For *step two*, the databases (Scopus, Library and Information Science Source, Web of Science, LISTA, and ERIC), journals (Journal of the Association for Information Science and Technology (JASIST) and the International Journal of Digital Curation (IJDC), and conference proceedings (ASIS&T Annual Conference, iConference, ALISE, and iPres) were searched. A specific search strategy was created for each database, journal, or conference proceedings which included a combination of keywords (data OR digital AND curation) AND (skill* OR competenc*)).

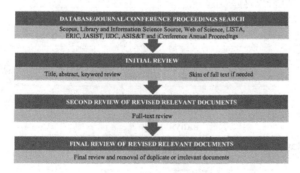

Fig. 2. Procedures to identify relevant documents.

For *step three*, titles, abstracts, and keywords were reviewed, and the full text was skimmed for an initial review. Next, the two researchers individually reviewed the full text of the first twelve documents and determined yes, no, or maybe, then met to discuss any differences in opinion. Since the differing opinions were extremely minimal, they continued individually to complete the review of the initial list. Lastly, a final full-text review of the documents was conducted to remove the remaining irrelevant documents or duplicate documents. See Fig. 2 and Table 1.

Table 1. Search strategy, retrieved, and relevant documents.

	Search Terms	Initial Retrieved Documents	Initial Relevant Documents	Removed Documents	Final Relevant Documents
Scopus	(TITLE-ABS-KEY (data OR digital AND curation) AND TITLE-ABS-KEY (skill* OR competenc*))	291	9	1	8
Library and Information Source	((data OR digital AND curation) AND (skill* OR competenc*))	378	13	5	8
Web of Science	(TS = ((data OR digital) AND curation)) AND TS = (skill* OR competenc*)	241	26	15	11
LISTA	(data OR digital) AND curation AND (skill* OR competenc*)	144	12	8	4
ERIC	As above	31	2	2	0
JASIST	""	87	3	2	1
IJDC	""	7	5	1	4
ASIS&T	""	114	3	2	1
iConference	""	Searched years individually	11	7	4
ALISE (2002–2022)	Reviewed manually	79	3	2	1
iPres (2005–2022)	""	90	5	4	1
TOTALS		**1462 +**	**92**	**49**	**43**

Date parameters were not needed for the database and journal searches. ALISE (2002–2022) and iPres (2005–2022) conference proceedings were reviewed manually, as these are spread over several repositories. The iDCC conference proceedings were reviewed but overlapped with the IJDC search.

Only documents explicitly examining and describing competencies, skill sets, or proficiencies related to digital or data curation activities were deemed relevant. Documents were removed if they only provided high-level summary descriptions. Of the 92 initial relevant documents, 49 were removed due to irrelevance or duplicates, and a total of 43 documents were analyzed.

For *step four*, a protocol was created to capture and summarize the literature. The documents were iteratively analyzed to determine which data should be gathered and how to operationalize the protocol items (See Table 2). The data was gathered into an Excel spreadsheet based on the protocol.

Table 2. Document protocol items and description.

Protocol Item	Description
Context	Context in which the document was written (i.e., archives, rdm, etc.)
Year	Year published
Country	Is the context of the document based in the USA or outside of the USA?
Author Domain	What was the domain expertise of the author?
Theoretical/Empirical	Was the research theoretical or empirical?
Education Research	Was this education research (i.e., curriculum/program/professional development)?
Research Methods	What were the research methods?
Study Population	Who or what was the study population?
Definition	Definition of data/digital curation, if provided
Existing models	Existing models used for the basis of data analysis
Relevant Models	Other relevant models or frameworks discussed
Skill sets	Specific skill sets, competencies, and activities needed for data curation
Tools	Specific tools used for data curation
Purpose statement	Problem statement or research question
Other relevant documents	Other potentially relevant citations

Over several meetings, the protocol items were operationalized. Each researcher separately gathered data from the first twelve documents and compared results to finalize the protocol. Then, data was separately gathered by two research assistants whom the lead researcher trained and provided continual feedback. Once the information was gathered from all documents, the researchers conducted several reviews to ensure accuracy and make final decisions.

Intercoder agreement was calculated for each protocol item gathered. While there were discussions throughout the coding process, coder differences were seen in four protocol items, including context, author domain, theoretical or empirical, and education research. The intercoder agreement for these items was 90%, 90%, 85%, and 88%, respectively. The lead researcher resolved any coding differences. Additionally, one document was removed during document analysis; therefore, the final total of documents analyzed was 42. See References [26–67] for the list of analyzed documents.

Lastly, for *step five,* descriptive statistics were created for quantifiable data, and qualitative content analysis was conducted by the lead researchers and the research assistants to discover major themes in the documents.

4   Findings

The 42 documents analyzed were published between 2007 and 2022 (see Fig. 3), with most of the documents written from the context of RDM (40%), followed by general LIS (29%), earth or atmospheric science (10%), archives (10%), data science (7%), and cultural heritage (5%). Additionally, the domains of the authors were mostly from LIS (69%), followed by information science (21%), archives (5%), and earth science (5%).

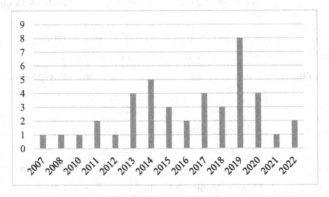

Fig. 3. Year published.

Sixty percent were written from the perspective of the USA, while 36% were outside of the USA context, and 5% were from both contexts. Most described empirical research (67%), while 14% described theoretical research, and 19% had a combined theoretical and empirical approach. Additionally, 36% (15) of the documents were educational research. Of these 15 documents, 60% were curriculum development, 20% were professional development, and the remaining 20% were both.

Most studies utilized surveys and interviews. Additionally, several studies conducted extensive literature reviews, job posting analysis, and framework or model analysis (See Table 3).

Table 3. Research methods.

Research Methods	Citation
Surveys (13)	Kouper, 2016; Lee et al., 2011; Thompson et al., 2013; Cox et al., 2017; Kaushik, 2017; Tibbo et al., 2008; Strathmann et al., 2012; Chiware, 2020; Pasek et al., 2019; Gregory et al., 2011; Molloy et al., 2014; Lucic et al., 2016; Tang, 2019
Interviews (12)	Bishop et al., 2018; Tammaro et al., 2019, Lee et al., 2011; Post et al., 2019; Lee et al., 2007; Lee et al., 2017; Bishop et al., 2021; Lee et al., 2014; Bossaller et al.,2022; Gregory et al., 2011; Lucic et al., 2016; Thompson et al., 2015
Literature Review (7)	Tammaro et al., 2019; Feng et al., 2018; Semeler et al., 2019; Lee et al., 2007; Koltay, 2017; Yelverton et al., 2022; Harvey, 2010
Job Postings Analysis (7)	Bishop et al., 2018; Tammaro et al., 2019; Kim, 2015; Constantinescu, 2018; Si et al., 2013; Gregory et al., 2011; Kim et al., 2013; Lyon et al., 2015
Model Analysis (6)	Karatas et al., 2020; Franks, 2014; Feng et al., 2018; Post et al., 2019; Lee et al., 2007; Briganti et al., 2020
Theoretical Approach (5)	Lee et al., 2011; Feng et al., 2018; Lee et al., 2014; Harvey, 2010; Bishop et al., 2021
Curriculum/Program Analysis (5)	Botticelli et al., 2013; Acker et al., 2020; Kim, 2015; Mayernik et al., 2014; Tammaro et al., 2014
Syllabi Analysis (4)	Lee et al., 2011; Gregory et al., 2011; Briganti et al., 2020; Yelverton et al., 2022
Case Studies (3)	Cushing et al., 2019; Giannini et al., 2019; Fan, 2019
Focus Groups (1)	Molloy et al., 2014

Twenty-four (57%) documents employed already-established models to guide their analysis. Twelve studies used the DCC Curation Lifecycle Model [68], eight used the DigCCurr Matrix [69], and four used the OAIS model [70]. Several other models were utilized, including the University of California's Research Data Management Lifecycle model [71] and the Research Data Netherlands Front Office-Back Office Model [72].

The documents described technical tools needed for data curation. Table 4 provides the complete list of technical tools, the citation, and example terms to provide context for each category. Twenty documents included digital repositories/archives-related tools. Eighteen discussed metadata techniques. Sixteen described database design techniques. Fourteen described data manipulation or analysis tools, and thirteen included programming languages. Other important technical skills included content management systems, data management, XML editors, basic office tools, general software development, GIS, the ability to work with various data formats, and distributed systems and cloud.

Table 4. Technical tools.

Technical Tools	Citation	Example Terms
Digital Repositories/Archives (20)	Bishop et al., 2018; Lee et al., 2011; Botticelli et al., 2013; Cushing et al., 2019; Feng et al., 2018; Giannini et al., 2019; Kim, 2015; Fan, 2019; Post et al., 2019; Tibbo et al., 2008; Koltay, 2017; Lee et al., 2017; Bishop et al., 2021; Chiware, 2020; Constantinescu, 2018; Lee et al., 2014; Gregory et al., 2011; Briganti et al., 2020; Kim et al., 2013; Thompson et al., 2015	DSpace, Archivematica, ArchivesSpace,
Metadata (18)	Bishop et al., 2018; Lee et al., 2011; Botticelli et al., 2013; Karatas et al., 2020; Thompson et al., 2013; Cushing et al., 2019; Feng et al., 2018; Giannini et al., 2019; Kim, 2015; Semeler et al., 2019; Post et al., 2019; Lee et al., 2017; Bishop et al., 2021; Lee et al., 2014; Si et al., 2013; Kim et al., 2013; Thompson et al., 2015; Yelverton et al., 2022	Dublin Core, METS, PREMIS, RDFS/OWL
Database Design (16)	Botticelli et al., 2013; Karatas et al., 2020; Thompson et al., 2013; Feng et al., 2018, Kim, 2015; Semeler et al., 2019; Fan, 2019; Koltay, 2017; Mayernik et al., 2014; Lee et al., 2017; Bishop et al., 2021; Si et al., 2013; Briganti et al., 2020; Kim et al., 2013; Lucic et al., 2016; Lyon et al., 2015	MySQL, ER Models, UML, NoSQL
Data Manipulation/Analysis (14)	Bishop et al., 2018; Giannini et al., 2019; Fan, 2019; Koltay, 2017; Lee et al., 2017; Bishop et al., 2021; Chiware, 2020; Lee et al., 2014; Si et al., 2013; Briganti et al., 2020; Kim et al., 2013; Lucic et al., 2016; Thompson et al., 2015; Lyon et al., 2015	SciSpark, ATLAS.ti, NVivo, SPSS

(continued)

Table 4. (*continued*)

Technical Tools	Citation	Example Terms
General Programming (13)	Bishop et al., 2018; Feng et al., 2018; Kim, 2015; Semeler et al., 2019; Fan, 2019; Koltay, 2017; Mayernik et al., 2014; Bishop et al., 2021; Chiware, 2020; Constantinescu, 2018; Briganti et al., 2020; Lucic et al., 2016; Lyon et al., 2015	R, C, Fortran, Python
Content Management System (12)	Botticelli et al., 2013; Karatas et al., 2020; Giannini et al., 2019; Kim, 2015; Fan, 2019; Franks, 2014; Koltay, 2017; Lee et al., 2017; Bishop et al., 2021; Kim et al., 2013; Thompson et al., 2015; Lyon et al., 2015	Drupal, Omeka, Scholarshpere, CONTENTdm,
Data Management (12)	Karatas et al., 2020; Cox et al., 2017; Koltay, 2017; Lee et al., 2017; Chiware, 2020; Constantinescu, 2018; Lee et al., 2014; Si et al., 2013; Briganti et al., 2020; Thompson et al., 2015; Yelverton et al., 2022; Tang et al., 2019	DMPs, DOIs, ORCID, URI, FAIR
XML (11)	Bishop et al., 2018; Lee et al., 2011; Botticelli et al., 2013; Kim, 2015; Semeler et al., 2019; Franks, 2014; Lee et al., 2017; Bishop et al., 2021; Si et al., 2013; Kim et al., 2013; Thompson et al., 2015	XML, Oxygen, Morpho, Nesstar, XSLT
Office Tools (10)	Bishop, 2018; Franks., 2014; Post et al., 2019; Lee et al., 2017; Bishop et al., 2021; Lee et al., 2014; Si et al., 2013; Briganti et al., 2020; Kim et al., 2013; Lyon et al., 2015	Dropbox, Microsoft, Slack, Zoom
Software Development (9)	Bishop et al., 2018; Botticelli et al., 2013; Kim, 2015; Post et al., 2019; Lee et al., 2017; Bishop et al., 2021; Constantinescu, 2018; Briganti et al., 2020; Kim et al., 2013	Scrum, PuTTY, Terminal, JIRA

(*continued*)

Table 4. (*continued*)

Technical Tools	Citation	Example Terms
GIS (9)	Bishop et al., 2018; Karatas et al., 2020; Lee et al., 2017; Bishop et al., 2021; Si et al., 2013; Pasek et al., 2019; Gregory et al., 2011; Briganti et al., 2020; Lyon et al., 2015	ArcGIS, ISO 19115, FGDC
Data Formats/ Types (8)	Bishop et al., 2018; Karatas et al., 2020; Kim, 2015; Post et al., 2019; Lee et al., 2017; Lee et al., 2014; Thompson et al., 2015; Lyon et al., 2015	NetCDF, cvs, time series and raw data
Distributed Systems/Cloud (8)	Bishop et al., 2018; Botticelli et al., 2013; Thompson et al., 2013; Fan, 2019; Lee et al., 2017; Bishop et al., 2021; Lee et al., 2014; Briganti et al., 2020	Hadoop, virtual machines, AWS

While the analysis for specific technical tools is complete for all 42 documents, the review of specific data curation competencies is ongoing, and approximately half (22) of the documents have been reviewed. Several competencies extracted from the documents follow the same themes as the technical tools analysis, such as competencies related to metadata, preservation, data management, and general programming. However, the documents include non-technical related competencies, including domain knowledge, research skills, advocacy, and outreach, and interpersonal, teaching, legal, ethical, leadership, and project management skills.

5 Conclusions and Next Steps

While this paper provides initial findings, the researchers continue to analyze the specific competencies described in the literature. Additionally, a visualization analysis of the major themes in the 42 documents has been created to gain an additional understanding of data curation competencies and changes in themes over time. These analyses will be presented in future publications to provide a more holistic review of data curation competencies.

Additionally, more work needs to be done to understand data curation in the context of community data. Therefore, we are conducting three 60-min focus group sessions to receive feedback from relevant stakeholders on the initial data curation competencies, including participants from community organizations, data curation professionals, and data curation educators. It is with this feedback that we will create a framework for community data curation competencies, as well as a set of curriculum modules that can be utilized by educators in data curation and related fields to prepare students to work with community data.

Acknowledgement. This project is supported by the Institute of Museum and Library Services Grant # RE-252380-OLS-22.

References

1. Palmer, C.L., Thompson, C., Baker, K., Senseney, M.: Meeting data workforce needs: indicators based on recent data curation placements. In: Proceedings of the 2014 iConference, IDEALS, Berlin, Germany (2014) https://doi.org/10.9776/14133
2. Varvel Jr., V.E., Bammerlin, E.J., Palmer, C.L.: Education for data professionals: a study of current courses and programs. In: Proceedings of the 2012 iConference, ACM, Toronto, Canada (2012). https://doi.org/10.1145/2132176.2132275
3. Research data management librarian academy. https://rdmla.github.io/. Accessed 14 Sep 2023
4. MANTRA: Research data management training. https://mantra.ed.ac.uk/. Accessed 14 Sep 2023
5. Digital curation centre homepage. https://dcc.ac.uk/. Accessed 14 Sep 2023
6. Data curation network homepage. https://datacurationnetwork.org/. Accessed 14 Sep 2023
7. Murillo, A.P., Jones, K.M.L.: The development of an undergraduate data curriculum: a model for maximizing curricular partnerships and opportunities. In: Chowdhury, G., McLeod, J., Gillet, V., Willett, P. (eds.) iConference 2018. LNCS, vol. 10766, pp. 282–291. Springer, Cham (2018). https://doi.org/10.1007/978-3-319-78105-1_32
8. Ortiz-Repiso, V., Greenberg, J., Calzada-Prado, J.: A cross-institutional analysis of data-related curricula in information science programmes: a focused look at the iSchools. J. Inf. Sci. **44**(6), 768–784 (2018). https://doi.org/10.1177/0165551517748149
9. Palmer, C., et al.: Confronting the expanse of data education: from local open data to global cyberinfrastructure. Proc. Assoc. Inf. Sci. Technol. **55**(1), 722–725 (2018). https://doi.org/10.1002/pra2.2018.14505501092
10. Library carpentry homepage. https://librarycarpentry.org/index.html. Accessed 14 Sep 2023
11. Kassen, M.: A promising phenomenon of open data: a case study of the Chicago open data project. Gov. Inf. Q. **30**(4), 508–513 (2013). https://doi.org/10.1016/j.giq.2013.05.012
12. Yoon, A., Copeland, A., McNally, P.J.: Empowering communities with data: role of data intermediaries for communities' data utilization. Proc. Assoc. Inf. Sci. Technol. **55**(1), 583–592 (2018). https://doi.org/10.1002/pra2.2018.14505501063
13. Bertot, J.C., Butler, B.S., Travis, D.M.: Local big data: the role of libraries in building community data infrastructures. In: Proceedings of the 15th Annual International Conference on Digital Government Research, pp. 17–23. ACM, Aguascalientes, Mexico (2014). https://doi.org/10.1145/2612733.2612762
14. Yoon, A., Copeland, A.: Understanding social impact of data on local communities. Aslib J. Inf. Manag. **71**(4), 558–567 (2019). https://doi.org/10.1108/AJIM-12-2018-0310
15. Bertot, J.C., Jaeger, P.T., Gorham, U., Taylor, N.G., Lincoln, R.: Delivering e-government services and transforming communities through innovative partnerships: public libraries, government agencies, and community organizations. Inf. Polity **18**(2), 127–138 (2013). https://doi.org/10.3233/IP-130304
16. Ignat, T., et al.: Merry work: libraries and citizen science. Insights the UKSG J. **31** (2018). https://doi.org/10.1629/uksg.431
17. City of chattanooga open data portal chattadata about. https://data.chattlibrary.org/about. Accessed 14 Sep 2023
18. Chaar-Pérez, K., Mattern, E., Rapchak, M., Burton, M.: Exploring civic data work in libraries: an opportunity for LIS curriculum and community empowerment. In: Proceedings of the 2021 ALISE Conference, IDEALS, Virtual (2021)

19. Xiao, F., Jeng, W., He, D.: Investigating metadata adoptions for open government data portals in US cities. Proc. Assoc. Inf. Sci. Technol. **55**(1), 573–582 (2018). https://doi.org/10.1002/pra2.2018.14505501062

20. IMLS leveraging open data LG-246255-OLS-20. http://imls.gov/grants/awarded/lg-246255-ols-20. Accessed 26 Apr 2023

21. IMLS building civic open data capacity RE-246295-OLS-20. http://www.imls.gov/grants/awarded/re-246295-ols-20. Accessed 26 Apr 2023

22. IMLS mCODE LG-250098-OLS-21, http://imls.gov/grants/awarded/lg-250098-ols-21. Accessed 26 Apr 2023

23. Palmer, C.L., Weber, N., Throgmorton, K., Norlander, B.: The open data literacy project on public libraries and open government data: partnerships for progress. Library Journal (2021) https://www.libraryjournal.com/story/public-libraries-and-open-government-data-partnerships-for-progress

24. Weber, N.M., Pamer, C.L., Norlander, B.: Advancing open data: aligning education with public sector data challenges. Proc. Assoc. Inf. Sci. Technol. **55**(1), 927–928 (2018). https://doi.org/10.1002/pra2.2018.14505501179

25. Khan, K.S., Kunz, R., Kleijnen, J., Antes, G.: Five steps to conducting a systematic review. J. R. Soc. Med. **96**(3), 118–121 (2003). https://doi.org/10.1177/014107680309600304

26. Bishop, B.W., Hank, C.: Earth Science data management: mapping actual tasks to conceptual actions in the curation lifecycle model. In: Chowdhury, G., McLeod, J., Gillet, V., Willett, P. (eds.) Transforming Digital Worlds, pp. 598–608. Springer International Publishing, Cham (2018). https://doi.org/10.1007/978-3-319-78105-1_67

27. Kouper, I.: Professional participation in digital curation. Libr. Inf. Sci. Res. **38**(3), 212–223 (2016). https://doi.org/10.1016/j.lisr.2016.08.009

28. Tammaro, A.M., Matusiak, K.K., Sposito, F.A., Casarosa, V.: Data curator's roles and responsibilities: an international perspective. Libri **69**(2), 89–104 (2019). https://doi.org/10.1515/libri-2018-0090

29. Lee, C.A., Tibbo, H.: Where's the archivist in digital curation? Exploring the possibilities through a matrix of knowledge and skills. Archivaria **72**, 123–168 (2011)

30. Botticelli, P., Fulton, B., Pearce-Moses, R., Szuter, C., Watters, P.: Educating digital curators: challenges and opportunities. Int. J. Digit. Curation **6**(2), 146–164 (2011). https://doi.org/10.2218/ijdc.v6i2.193

31. Karatas, T., Lombardo, V.A: Multiple perspective account of digital curation for cultural heritage: tasks, disciplines, and institutions. In: UMAP 2020 Adjunct: Adjunct Publication of the 28th ACM Conference on User Modeling, Adaptation and Personalization, pp. 325–332. ACM, Genoa, Italy (2020) https://doi.org/10.1145/3386392.3399277

32. Thompson, C.A., Senseney, M., Baker, K.S., Varvel, V.E., Palmer, C.L.: Specialization in data curation: preliminary results from an alumni survey, 2008–2012. Proc. Am. Soc. Inf. Sci. Technol. **50**(1), 1–4 (2013). https://doi.org/10.1002/meet.14505001151

33. Cushing, A.L., Shankar, K.: Digital curation on a small island: a study of professional education and training needs in Ireland. Arch. Rec. **40**(2), 146–163 (2019). https://doi.org/10.1080/23257962.2018.1425135

34. Acker, A., Donaldson, D.R., Kriesberg, A., Thomer, A., Weber, N.: Integrating research and teaching for data curation in iSchools. Proc. Assoc. Inf. Sci. Technol. **57**(1), e285 (2020). https://doi.org/10.1002/pra2.285

35. Cox, A.M., Kennan, M.A., Lyon, L., Pinfield, S.: Developments in research data management in academic libraries: towards an understanding of research data service maturity. J. Am. Soc. Inf. Sci. **68**(9), 2182–2200 (2017). https://doi.org/10.1002/asi.23781

36. Feng, Y., Richards, L.: A review of digital curation professional competencies: theory and current practices. Rec. Manag. J. **28**(1), 62–78 (2018). https://doi.org/10.1108/RMJ-09-2016-0022

37. Giannini, S. Molino, A.: The data librarian: Myth, reality, or utopia? The Grey Journal **15**(1). (2019)
38. Kaushik, A.: Perceptions of LIS Professionals about the Data Curation. World Digit. Libr. Int. J. **10**(2) (2017) https://doi.org/10.18329/09757597/2017/10207
39. Kim, J.: Competency-based curriculum: an effective approach to digital curation education. J. Educ. Libr. Inf. Sci. Online **56**(4), 283–297 (2015). https://doi.org/10.12783/issn.2328-2967/56/4/2
40. Pasek, J. E., Mayer, J.: Education needs in research data management for science-based disciplines: self-assessment surveys of graduate students and faculty at two public universities. Issues Sci. Technol. Librarianship **92** (2019) https://doi.org/10.29173/istl12
41. Fan, Z.: Context-based roles and competencies of data curators in supporting research data lifecycle management: multi-case study in China. Libri **69**(2), 127–137 (2019). https://doi.org/10.1515/libri-2018-0065
42. Franks, P.C.: Sustainability: An Unintended Consequence of the Integration of Digital Curation Core Competencies into the MLIS Curricula. In: Bolikowski, Ł, Casarosa, V., Goodale, P., Houssos, N., Manghi, P., Schirrwagen, J. (eds.) Theory and Practice of Digital Libraries -- TPDL 2013 Selected Workshops: LCPD 2013, SUEDL 2013, DataCur 2013, Held in Valletta, Malta, September 22-26, 2013. Revised Selected Papers, pp. 226–238. Springer International Publishing, Cham (2014). https://doi.org/10.1007/978-3-319-08425-1_25
43. Post, C., et al.: Digital curation at work: modeling workflows for digital archival materials. In: Proceedings of the Joint Conference on Digital Libraries, (2019), pp. 39–48. IEEE, Urbana-Champaign, Illinois (2019). https://doi.org/10.1109/JCDL.2019.00016
44. Tibbo, H.R., Hank, C., Lee, C.A.: Challenges, curricula, and competencies: researcher and practitioner perspectives for informing the development of a digital curation curriculum. In: Proceedings of Archiving 2008. Bern, Switzerland (2008)
45. Lee, C.A., Tibbo, H.R., Schaefer, J.C.: Defining what digital curators do and what they need to know: the DigCCurr project. In: Proceedings of the Joint Conference on Digital Libraries, pp. 49–50. Vancouver, British Columbia, Canada (2007)
46. Strathmann, S., Engelhardt, C.: Skills, competences and training needs in digital preservation and curation: results of a DigCurV survey. In: Mouren, R. (ed.) Ambassadors of the Book: Competences and training for heritage librarians, pp. 63–82. DE GRUYTER SAUR (2012). https://doi.org/10.1515/9783110301502.63
47. Koltay, T.: Facing the Challenge of Data-Intensive Research: Research Data Services and Data Literacy in Academic Libraries. In: Baker, D., Evans, W. (eds.) Innovation in Libraries and Information Services, pp. 45–61. Emerald Group Publishing Limited (2016). https://doi.org/10.1108/S0732-067120160000035008
48. Tammaro, A.M., Casarosa, V.: Research data management in the curriculum: an interdisciplinary approach. Procedia Comput. Sci. **38**, 138–142 (2014). https://doi.org/10.1016/j.procs.2014.10.023
49. Mayernik, M.S., et al.: Research center insights into data curation education and curriculum. In: Bolikowski, Ł, Casarosa, V., Goodale, P., Houssos, N., Manghi, P., Schirrwagen, J. (eds.) Theory and Practice of Digital Libraries -- TPDL 2013 Selected Workshops: LCPD 2013, SUEDL 2013, DataCur 2013, Held in Valletta, Malta, September 22-26, 2013. Revised Selected Papers, pp. 239–248. Springer International Publishing, Cham (2014). https://doi.org/10.1007/978-3-319-08425-1_26
50. Lee, D.J., Stvilia, B.: Practices of research data curation in institutional repositories: a qualitative view from repository staff. PLoS ONE **12**(3), e0173987 (2017). https://doi.org/10.1371/journal.pone.0173987
51. Bishop, B.W., Orehek, A.M., Collier, H.R.: Job analyses of earth science data librarians and data managers. Bull. Am. Meteor. Soc. **102**(7), E1384–E1393 (2021). https://doi.org/10.1175/BAMS-D-20-0163.1

52. Chiware, E.R.T.: Data librarianship in South African academic and research libraries: a survey. Libr. Manag. **41**(6/7), 401–416 (2020). https://doi.org/10.1108/LM-03-2020-0045
53. Constantinescu, N.: Data librarian, the steward. Rom. J. Libr. Inf. Sci. **14**(4), 113–121 (2018). https://doi.org/10.26660/rrbsi.2018.14.4.113
54. Lee, D.J., Stvilia, B.: Data curation practices in institutional repositories: an exploratory study: data curation practices in institutional repositories: an exploratory study. In: Proceedings of the American Society for Information Science and Technology, pp. 1–4. Wiley, Seattle, Washington (2014). https://doi.org/10.1002/meet.2014.14505101085
55. Si, L., Zhuang, X., Xing, W., Guo, W.: The cultivation of scientific data specialists: development of LIS education oriented to e-science service requirements. Libr. Hi Tech **31**(4), 700–724 (2013). https://doi.org/10.1108/LHT-06-2013-0070
56. Semeler, A.R., Pinto, A.L., Rozados, H.B.F.: Data science in data librarianship: core competencies of a data librarian. J. Librariansh. Inf. Sci. **51**(3), 771–780 (2019). https://doi.org/10.1177/0961000617742465
57. Bossaller, J., Million, A.J.: The research data life cycle, legacy data, and dilemmas in research data management. J. Assoc. Inf. Sci. Technol. **74**, 701–706 (2022). https://doi.org/10.1002/asi.24645
58. Gregory, L., Guss, S.: Digital curation education in practice: catching up with two former fellows. Int. J. Digit. Curation **6**(2), 176–194 (2011). https://doi.org/10.2218/ijdc.v6i2.195
59. Briganti, J.S., Ogier, A.: Piloting a community of student data consultants that supports and enhances research data services. Int. J. Digit. Curation **15**(1), 1–11 (2022). https://doi.org/10.2218/ijdc.v15i1.723
60. Molloy, L., Gow, A., Konstantelos, L.: The DigCurV curriculum framework for digital curation in the cultural heritage sector. Int. J. Digit. Curation **9**(1), 231–241 (2014). https://doi.org/10.2218/ijdc.v9i1.314
61. Kim, J., Warga, E., Moen, W.: Competencies required for digital curation: an analysis of job advertisements. Int. J. Digit. Curation **8**(1), 66–83 (2013). https://doi.org/10.2218/ijdc.v8i1.242
62. Lucic, A., Blake, C.: Preparing a workforce to effectively reuse data: preparing a workforce to effectively reuse data. In: Proceedings of the American Society for Information Science and Technology, pp. 1–10. Wiley, Copenhagen, Denmark (2016). https://doi.org/10.1002/pra2.2016.14505301075
63. Thompson, C.A., Mayernik, M.S.: LIS programs and data centers: integrating expertise. In: Proceedings of the 2015 iConference, Newport Beach, California (2015)
64. Yelverton, K., van Deventer, M.: Curricula analysis for big data stewardship – embedding data curation roles in the big data value chain. In: Proceedings of the iConference, Springer, Virtual (2022)
65. Harvey, R.: Curation in the curriculum: equipping the profession to ensure the preservation of information. In: Proceedings of the iConference, IDEALS, Urbana-Champaign, Illinois (2010)
66. Tang, R., Hu, Z.: Needs assessment of library data services: establishing a curriculum framework for RDMLA. In: Proceedings of the 2019 ALISE Annual Conference, IDEALS, Knoxville, Tennessee (2019)
67. Lyon, L., Mattern, E.: Applying translational principles to data science curriculum development. In: Proceedings of the 2015 iConference, Newport Beach, California (2015)
68. DCC Curation Lifecycle Model Homepage. https://www.dcc.ac.uk/guidance/curation-lifecycle-model. Accessed 14 Sep 2023
69. Matrix of Digital Curation Knowledge and Competencies Homepage. https://ils.unc.edu/digccurr/digccurr-matrix.html Accessed 14 Sep 2023
70. Reference Model for an Open Archival Information System (OAIS). https://public.ccsds.org/Pubs/650x0m2.pdf Accessed 14 Sep 2023

71. The Research Data Management Life Cycle. https://guides.lib.uci.edu/datamanagement Accessed 14 Sep 2023
72. Research Data Netherlands, Front Office-Back Office Model. https://datasupport.resear chdata.nl/en/start-the-course/vi-data-support/data-stewardship/front-office-back-office. Accessed 14 Sep 2023

The Effect of Digital Literacy on International Students' Adjustment to University Life: Focusing on the Mediating Effect of ICT Self-efficacy

Shuangling Cheng⑩, Yeonhee Kim, and Jae-Hwang Choi(✉)

Department of Library and Information Science, Kyungpook National University, Daegu, South Korea
{chengs120,domi1401}@naver.com, choi@knu.ac.kr

Abstract. This study aims to investigate the effect of digital literacy on international students' adjustment to university life and how ICT self-efficacy mediates the relationship between digital literacy and adjustment to university life. A survey was conducted among 118 international undergraduate and graduate students in Seoul and Daegu. Analytical methods consisted of reliability analysis, validity analysis, regression analysis and multiple mediation analysis performed using the SPSS 26.0 and PROCESS macro (Version 4.0). The results indicated that digital literacy significantly affected international students' academic adjustment, social adjustment, personal-emotional adjustment, and institutional adjustment. In addition, ICT self-efficacy was identified as a mediating factor in the relationship between digital literacy and academic adjustment. These findings suggest that university libraries, which are the central institutions for providing academic information at universities, should provide a variety of digital literacy programs for international students to improve their ability to use digital tools and help them adjust to the SW-centered society and university life.

Keywords: Digital Literacy · ICT Self-efficacy · Adjustment to University Life

1 Introduction

As the internationalization trend in higher education persists, the number of students studying abroad for a higher level of education and various cultural experiences has gradually increased yearly [24,58]. Since the mid-2000s, Korea has implemented the "Study Korea Project," a government-led project to attract international students, and the number of international students has steadily increased over the past decade [29,46]. In particular, the number of international students in Korea for degree and non-degree courses in 2022 was 166,892, the highest ever [25]. However, at the same time, the rate of international students leaving school increased significantly. The proportion of international students enrolled in general universities in Korea who ceased studying due to dropping out was 7.3% in 2021, a 37% increase from 5.3% in 2019 [26].

Adjustment to university life is critical for international students [23]. International students must adapt not only to language and culture but also to their studies and daily lives. However, international students face difficulties adjusting to university life due to academic stress, linguistic barriers, cultural adjustment difficulties, human relations problems, and economic problems [33]. Accordingly, international students use ICT to adapt to university life to obtain information necessary for their studies or daily living [41,59].

Today, information and communication technology (ICT) is essential in all areas of daily life [7]. As digital devices (computers, smartphones, tablets, etc.) have become ubiquitous, ICT has increasingly significant societal, economic, and cultural impacts. In particular, ICT is crucial for university students' studies and daily lives [54]. ICT self-efficacy is the belief in one's own ability to solve a given problem and meet their needs using information and communication technology, which is one of the most important determinants of digital system use [53].

Digital literacy has become a key competency of modern knowledge- and information-based societies. International students should also be able to collect, evaluate, process, and analyze necessary information using digital devices in academic performance and adjustment to Korean society. However, due to unfamiliar environments and languages, international students have been alienated from digital literacy education in universities [21]. Although the number of international students in Korean universities has been increasing annually, few university libraries have provided digital literacy programs to accommodate these students. However, low levels of digital literacy among international students could lead to problems of maladjustment to university and social life [6].

Previous studies on the adjustment of international students to university life in Korea found that factors such as language barriers, cultural adjustment stress, and academic adjustment due to the difficulty of forming interpersonal relationships in universities and relatively low Korean language skills affect their adjustment [22,49].

However, although most international students frequently use ICT and digital technologies to adapt to university life, little research has been conducted on how digital literacy and ICT self-efficacy affect international students' adjustment to university life. Therefore, this study aims to identify the correlation between digital literacy, ICT self-efficacy, and university life adjustment for international students and to analyze how ICT self-efficacy affects the relationship between digital literacy and university life adjustment. These aims generate the following research questions.

Research Question 1. How does the digital literacy of international students impact their adjustment to university life?

Research Question 2. Does ICT self-efficacy play a mediating effect in the relationship between international students' digital literacy and their adjustment to university life?

2   Background

2.1   Digital Literacy

With the development of digital technology, digital literacy has become necessary for individuals to effectively perform tasks and solve given problems in a digital environment. Digital literacy is "the ability to understand and use various types of sources and formats presented through computers" [11], which includes all the technologies necessary to read, generate, find, or participate in online space [52]. Digital literacy has been defined by various institutions such as ALA [3], JISC [16], IFLA [14], and UNESCO [27], which emphasize access to and use of digital resources (See Table 1).

Table 1. Definitions of digital literacy

Sources	Definition
ALA (2011)	The ability to use information and communication technologies to find, evaluate, create, and communicate information, requiring both cognitive and technical skills.
JISC (2014)	Those capabilities which fit living, learning, and working in a digital society.
IFLA (2017)	One can use technology to its fullest effect - efficiently, effectively and ethically - to meet information needs in personal, civic, and professional lives.
UNESCO (2018)	The ability to access, manage, understand, integrate, communicate, evaluate and create information safely and appropriately through digital technologies for employment, decent jobs and entrepreneurship. It includes competencies that are variously referred to as computer literacy, ICT literacy, information literacy and media literacy.

University students have high digital literacy and often use ICT in their studies and daily lives [54,59]. Most university students rated their digital literacy skills as high or moderate [48]. However, university students have reported no or low satisfaction with information search because they did not efficiently access the information they wanted [17]. In addition, they often learned their digital capabilities independently rather than through digital competency classes in educational institutions. However, they also showed considerable interest in digital competency improvement classes conducted at schools and institutions [42].

Shin & Lee [47] and Kim & Park [19] developed a scale to measure ICT basic competencies, basic work utilization skills, Internet utilization skills, software(SW)-centered social adjustment skills, social networking service(SNS) utilization and collaboration skills as components of digital literacy. This study aims to measure the digital literacy of international students using this scale.

2.2 ICT Self-efficacy

Self-efficacy is a "personal belief that one can successfully perform a particular task" [5] and significantly influences people's behavior [30]. This concept encompasses general self-efficacy and efficacy for an individual's ability in a specific context or situation [10]. General self-efficacy is an overall perception of one's own ability to effectively cope with various stressful situations in a broad range of contexts [10].

ICT self-efficacy refers to a belief in one's own ability to process digital information and communicate with others using computers and the Internet, which is positively related to digital capabilities [1,37]. Existing studies on university students' ICT self-efficacy have shown that ICT use experience at school and at home has directly or indirectly positively affected university students' ICT self-efficacy [34,38]. High ICT self-efficacy among students was positively associated with students' academic satisfaction, learning strategies and learning behavior, and academic achievement, especially among those who used ICT to learn and perform tasks, which was also linked to academic achievement [43,50,60]. Furthermore, the influence of ICT, digital and information literacy on students' academic performance, school life and daily activities is mediated by ICT self-efficacy [18,40].

2.3 Adjustment to University Life

Adjustment to university life refers to coping with the academic, interpersonal, and emotional requirements of physically attending university [20]. Baker and Siryk [4] divided university life adjustment into four areas: academic adjustment, social adjustment, personal-emotional adjustment, and university environment adjustment, and developed a questionnaire to measure it. Academic adjustment reflects the degree to which students successfully adapt to the academic requirements of university, such as attitudes toward the lecture process, lecture participation, and the appropriateness of learning and academic efforts. Social adjustment refers to the degree to which new social relationships are formed and adapted to university social activities, such as participating in university activities or meeting new people. Personal-emotional adjustment is the degree to which students experience stress or anxiety due to various needs in the university environment. Students' attachment to university institutions indicates how emotionally satisfied they are with their universities [4,9,31].

In previous studies on university life adjustment, ICT use experience and ICT self-efficacy positively affected students' adjustment to university life. In particular, ICT use experience was found to expand university students' communication and interaction patterns and help them deal with problems related to university life adjustment by developing appropriate behavioral patterns in university life [56]. In addition, students with high self-efficacy can efficiently cope with various problems in adapting to university life [28]. Individuals with high ICT self-efficacy can show a more active attitude to digital devices such as computers and adapt more quickly [15].

University students' digital literacy levels and digital literacy learning experiences also positively correlated with university life adjustment. In addition to linguistic competence, digital literacy learning experiences positively impacted university freshmen's academic adjustment [39], and students with higher digital literacy levels reported higher satisfaction and academic adjustment to online lectures [55]. This finding could be explained by students with high digital literacy being familiar with ICT and able to collect and analyze a variety of information using digital devices and meet their academic and entertainment needs [57].

3 Methods

3.1 Research Model and Hypothesis

This study aims to verify the effect of digital literacy on the adjustment to university life among international students living in Korea and the mediating effect of ICT self-efficacy in this relationship. The research model is shown in Fig. 1.

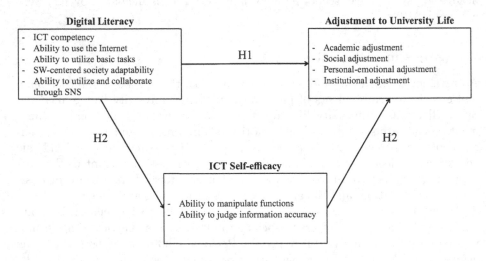

Fig. 1. Research model

H1: Digital literacy will affect adjustment to university life.
  H1-1: Digital literacy will affect academic adjustment.
  H1-2: Digital literacy will affect social adjustment.
  H1-3: Digital literacy will affect personal-emotional adjustment.
  H1-4: Digital literacy will affect institutional adjustment.
H2: ICT self-efficacy will have a mediating effect on the relationship between digital literacy and adjustment to university life.

H2-1: ICT self-efficacy will have a mediating effect on the relationship between digital literacy and academic adjustment.

H2-2: ICT self-efficacy will have a mediating effect on the relationship between digital literacy and social adjustment.

H2-3: ICT self-efficacy will have a mediating effect on the relationship between digital literacy and personal-emotional adjustment.

H2-4: ICT self-efficacy will have a mediating effect on the relationship between digital literacy and institutional adjustment.

3.2   Data Collection

Data were collected through online and face-to-face surveys of 118 foreign undergraduate and graduate students attending four-year universities in Korea. From June 16 to July 10, 2023, an online survey was conducted among the online community of international students in Korea. Simultaneously, a face-to-face survey was carried out among international students attending Korean language programs at the language institute of K University. The questionnaire consisted of 64 questions derived from previous studies (See Table 2). Digital literacy, an independent variable, consisted of 4 basic ICT competencies, 10 Internet utilization skills, 4 basic work utilization skills, 5 SW-centered social adjustment skills, and 5 SNS utilization and collaboration skills and was measured on a 5-point Likert scale. Nine questions measured the ICT self-efficacy parameter on a 5-point Likert scale. The dependent variable, university life adjustment, was based on the "Student Adjustment to University Questionnaire (SACQ)" developed by Baker & Sirky [4], but the questions revised and supplemented by Noh [36] and Seo [45] were partly adapted for this study. The measure of university life adjustment consisted of four sub-factors: academic adjustment, social adjustment, emotional adjustment, and university environment adjustment; a total of 20 questions measured on a 5-point Likert scale were composed. In addition, demographic characteristics were composed of 7 items(gender, age, degree level, major, nationality, Korean language ability, and study-abroad period) and measured together on a nominal scale.

3.3   Data Analysis

In this study, the relationship between digital literacy, ICT self-efficacy, and university life adjustment of international students was confirmed using SPSS 26.0 and PROCESS macro (Version 4.0), and the mediating effect of ICT self-efficacy was identified in the effect of digital literacy on university life adjustment. The study was carried out as follows. First, exploratory factor analysis was conducted to confirm the validity of the measurement tool, and reliability analysis was performed to verify the internal consistency of the identified factors. The demographic characteristics of the survey respondents were identified through frequency analysis and descriptive statistical analysis. Second, the correlation between digital literacy, ICT self-efficacy, and university life adjustment of survey respondents was investigated through Pearson correlation coefficient

Table 2. Structure of questionnaire

Domain	Measure variables	Number of items	Scale
Demographical characteristics	Gender, Age, Degree, Major, Nationality, Korean language skill, Period of studying abroad	7	Nominal scale
Digital literacy [19,47]	ICT competency	4	Likirt 5-scale
	Ability to use the Internet	10	
	Ability to utilize basic tasks	4	
	SW-centered society adaptability	5	
	Ability to utilize and collaborate through SNS	5	
ICT self-efficacy [44,57]	ICT self-efficacy	9	
Adjustment to university life [4,36,45]	Academic adjustment	5	
	Social adjustment	5	
	Personal-emotional adjustment	5	
	Institutional adjustment	5	

analysis. Third, multiple regression analysis was performed to confirm the effect of digital literacy on university life adjustment. In addition, to assess the mediating effect of ICT self-efficacy in the relationship between digital literacy and university life adjustment, the mediating effect was analyzed using PROCESS macro's Model 4, and the statistical significance of the indirect effect was verified through bootstrapping. The significance of the indirect effect was set to 5,000 bootstrapping iterations, verified and estimated at the 95% confidence interval, and interpreted as statistically significant if 0 was not included in the 95% confidence interval.

3.4   Validity and Reliability of Survey Tools

This study conducted exploratory factor analysis to verify the validity and adopted main component analysis and orthogonal rotation methods. Some questions were removed to increase the explanatory power and suitability of factor analysis. The commonality of variables included in one factor required 0.4 in principle. In addition, Cronbach's α coefficient, which represents the internal consistency of the questionnaire, was acceptable at 0.6 or higher.

The results of exploratory factor analysis and the reliability of the questionnaire items are shown in Table 3. Sphericity was verified using Kaiser-Meyer-Olkin (KMO) and Bartlett tests to verify the significance of all items. The KMO value was 0.792, and Bartlett's sphericity test results were significant ($p<.001$).

Five factors consisting of the final 24 questions were derived, and the total variance described was 67.600%.

The exploratory factor analysis with ICT self-efficacy derived the ability to manipulate functions and the ability to judge information accuracy (See Table 4). The values for the KMO and Bartlett's tests were 0.754 and $\chi^2 = 368.835$ ($p<0.001$), respectively, confirming the suitability of factor analysis. The total variance described was 69.036%.

The factor analysis and reliability results for the questions that measured university life adjustment are shown in Table 5. The KMO value was 0.862, and Bartlett's sphericity test results were significant ($p<.001$). As a result of the exploratory factor analysis, four factors consisting of the final 18 questions were identified. The total variance described was 64.729%.

Table 3. Factor analysis of independent variable

Questions	Factors					Reliability
	ICT competency	Ability to use the Internet	Ability to utilize basic tasks	SW-centered society adaptability	Ability to utilize and collaborate through SNS	Cronbach's α
Adapt to the world changed by ICT	**.848**	.291	.037	.096	.028	.787
Adapt changes in everyday life	**.835**	.328	−.061	.088	.039	
Use smart devices	**.751**	.099	.258	−.033	.127	
Sensitivity to the world	**.447**	.287	−.339	.085	.299	
Acquire information	.130	**.811**	−.052	−.062	.201	.856
Provide information to others	.217	**.760**	−.116	.117	.157	
Find information quickly	.166	**.723**	.146	−.066	.191	
Find information accurately	.388	**.699**	.163	−.066	−.049	
Build knowledge	.202	**.699**	.246	.119	.070	
Produce Internet contents	.071	**.638**	.289	.171	.070	
Understand Internet copyright	.031	**.634**	.119	−.027	.078	
Use tools to edit drawings	.087	.208	**.696**	.081	.342	.747
Create advanced presentations	−.015	.285	**.671**	.348	.204	
Use objects to write document	.255	.387	**.389**	.252	.311	
Understand the meaning of SW-centered society	.026	−.031	.033	**.877**	.135	.826
Use programming language	−.082	−.043	.118	**.798**	−.022	
Learn computational skills	.210	−.002	−.003	**.692**	.223	
Establish a procedure	−.020	.170	.446	**.666**	.002	
Computational thinking	.200	.197	.549	**.560**	.064	
Use SNS in everyday life	.134	.062	.149	.058	**.882**	.928
Ability to use SNS	.026	.044	.060	.016	**.874**	
Identify valuable information	.082	.235	.121	.080	**.842**	
Increase network by SNS	.104	.098	.181	.104	**.840**	
Collaborate with others	−.023	.200	−.005	.144	**.838**	
Eigen-value	1.652	7.528	1.064	2.753	3.227	Total
% of variance	6.882	31.366	4.435	11.471	13.447	67.600
Kaiser-Meyer-Olkin Test	.792					
Bartlett's Test of Sphericity	Approx. Chi-Square					1689.598***
	df					276

$^*p < .05,\ ^{**}p < .01,\ ^{***}p < .001$

Table 4. Factor analysis of mediator variable

Questions	Factors		Reliability
	Ability to manipulate functions	Ability to judge information accuracy	Cronbach's α
Ability to sort data in a worksheet table according to the criteria	**.843**	.047	.854
Ability to create a chart by using worksheet data	**.824**	.237	
Ability to format documents using word processing	**.813**	.091	
Ability to print single page from a long text	**.756**	.239	
Ability to create a shortcut for a program on the desktop	**.660**	.134	
Distinguish whether the search engine results are advertisements	.111	**.905**	.772
Recognize whether the information provided on a web page is trustworthy	.207	**.871**	
Eigen-value	3.522	1.311	**Total**
% of variance	50.311	18.725	69.036
Kaiser-Meyer-Olkin Test	.754		
Bartlett's Test of Sphericity	Approx. Chi-Square		368.835***
	df		21

*p < .05, **p < .01, ***p < .001

Table 5. Factor analysis of dependent variable

Questions	Factors				Reliability
	Academic adjustment	Personal-emotional adjustment	Institutional adjustment	Social adjustment	Cronbach's α
Motivated and concentrate on studying	**.873**	.081	.096	.028	.833
Satisfied with current academic performance	**.831**	.076	.092	.190	
Working hard on given coursework	**.766**	−.128	.120	.199	
Capable of academic expectations	**.746**	.263	.040	.029	
Interested in entering advanced school	**.520**	.190	.252	.241	
Not felt very nervous recently	.041	**.826**	.074	.243	.836
Not felt very depressed recently	.099	**.763**	.050	.362	
Cope with the stresses of university	.185	**.762**	.237	.124	
Can sleep well	.100	**.639**	.293	.028	
Not become angry too easily recently	.025	**.591**	.511	−.014	
Satisfied with university's curriculum	.078	.226	**.835**	.166	.812
Pleased with the decision to attend this university	.167	.154	**.807**	.274	
Satisfied with university life	.069	.584	**.626**	.165	
Interested in coursework at university	.323	.188	**.531**	−.113	
Highly engaged in social activities at university	.006	.258	−.054	**.752**	.742
Actively participating in university social activities	.258	.237	.089	**.731**	
Doing well in present accommodation	.179	.082	.410	**.618**	
Have some good friends at university	.448	.034	.305	**.567**	
Eigen-value	6.872	2.616	1.558	1.253	**Total**
% of variance	36.168	13.767	8.201	6.594	64.729
Kaiser-Meyer-Olkin Test	.862				
Bartlett's Test of Sphericity	Approx. Chi-Square				1254.806***
	df				190

*p < .05, **p < .01, ***p < .001

4   Results

4.1   Demographic Characteristics

After excluding insincere responses, 58.5% of the 118 remaining respondents were female, and 41.5% were male. As for the age distribution, 44.9% were 25 to 29, followed by 20 to 24(36.4%) and 18.6% were aged 30 or older. The majority of respondents (75.4%) were Chinese nationals. Ph.D. students were the most common at 32.2%, followed by master's students at 24.6%, undergraduate students at 23.7%, language training students at 16.9%, and master's and doctorate integration students at 2.5%.

4.2   Hypothesis Testing

H1: Digital Literacy Will Affect Adjustment to University Life.

The regression model R^2_{adj}=0.153, F=22.114 (p<0.001) and the regression model R^2_{adj}=0.282, F=16.37 (p<0.001) that analyzed the impact of digital literacy on academic adjustment through multiple regression analysis for testing H1 R^2_{adj}=0.078, F=10.918 (p<0.01), and a regression model that analyzes the effect on university life adjustment R^2_{adj}=.163, F=23.709 (p<0.001) were derived. The results are shown in Table 6. The analysis was carried out using a stepwise approach. The analysis showed that the ability to utilize basic tasks (β=0.400, p<0.001) was the only aspect of digital literacy affecting academic adjustment. The ability to utilize and collaborate through SNS (β=0.371, p<0.001), SW-centered society adaptability (β=0.191, p<0.01), and the ability to use the Internet (β=0.189, p<0.01). The ability to use the Internet was the only aspect of digital literacy affecting emotional and university life adjustment. Therefore, H1 was supported.

H2: ICT Self-efficacy Will Have a Mediating Effect on the Relationship between Digital Literacy and Adjustment to University Life.

To test H2, Hayes' (2017) PROCESS macro was used to directly calculate the size of the mediating effect of ICT self-efficacy and test its statistical significance. The effect of the independent variable on the dependent variable when the mediator, ICT self-efficacy, is controlled is the direct effect, and the effect of the independent variable on the dependent variable through the mediator is the indirect effect.

First, to test H2-1, the indirect effect of ICT self-efficacy on the relationship between digital literacy and academic adjustment was analyzed in Table 7. In the results, ICT self-efficacy had a positive significant effect on the impact of the ability to use the Internet on academic adjustment (β=0.219, 95% CI[0.087, 0.373]). More specifically, only the indirect effect of the ability to manage functions was significant (β=0.180, 95% CI[0.46, 0.323]). ICT self-efficacy also had a positive mediating effect on the impact of the ability to utilize basic tasks (β=0.210, 95% CI[0.043, 0.386]), SW-centered society adaptability (β=0.098,

Table 6. Types of digital literacy that affect adjustment to university life.

Dependent Variable	Independent variable	Unstandardized Coefficients		Standardized Coefficients	t
		B	S.E	β	
Academic adjustment	(Constant)	2.550	.295	–	8.649***
	Ability to utilize basic tasks	.340	.072	.400	4.703***
$R^2 = .160$, $R^2_{adj} = .153$, $F(p) = 22.114^{***}$					
Social adjustment	(Constant)	1.371	.432	–	3.173**
	Ability to utilize and collaborate through SNS	.280	.063	.371	4.423***
	SW-centered society adaptability	.137	.058	.191	2.349**
	Ability to use the Internet	.228	.100	.189	2.275**
$R^2 = .301$, $R^2_{adj} = .282$, $F(p) = 16.337^{***}$					
Personal-emotional adjustment	(Constant)	1.866	.537	–	3.474***
	Ability to use the Internet	.413	.125	.293	3.304***
$R^2 = .086$, $R^2_{adj} = .078$, $F(p) = 10.918^{**}$					
Institutional adjustment	(Constant)	1.579	.468	–	3.372***
	Ability to use the Internet	.530	.109	.412	4.869***
$R^2 = .170$, $R^2_{adj} = .163$, $F(p) = 23.709^{***}$					

$^*p < .05$, $^{**}p < .01$, $^{***}p < .001$

95% CI[0.014, 0.225]) and the ability to utilize and collaborate through SNS (β=0.180, 95% CI[0.043, 0.383]) on academic adjustment.

In contrast, ICT self-efficacy did not mediate the relationship between digital literacy, social adjustment, personal-emotional adjustment, and institutional adjustment. Therefore, H2 was partly supported.

5 Discussion

The analysis of the relationship between digital literacy and academic adjustment revealed that only the ability to utilize basic tasks significantly impacted international students' academic adjustment. This finding could indicate that international students proficient in using digital tools or performing basic digital tasks may adapt better to the academic environment.

Analyzing the relationship between digital literacy and social adjustment revealed that the ability to use the Internet, SW-centered society adaptability, and the ability to utilize and collaborate through SNS all had a significant impact. This finding suggests that international students who actively maintain relationships using the Internet and social media may adapt better to the social environment. This finding is consistent with previous research [2,13,51] showing that the use of SNS and the Internet can facilitate the social adjustment and participation of foreign immigrants. Studies by Jih-Hsuan et al. [35] and Closson & Bond [8] have also mentioned the influence of students' use of SNS on their social adjustment.

Table 7. Analysis of the mediating effect of ICT self-efficacy in the relationship between digital literacy and academic adjustment.

Paths	β	95% CI	
		LLCI	ULCI
Total effect (ICT competency→Academic adjustment)	.177	−.004	.358
Direct effect (ICT competency→Academic adjustment)	−.033	−.214	.149
Total indirect effect (ICT competency→ICT self-efficacy→Academic adjustment)	.210	.110	.304
Indirect effect — ICT competency →Ability to manipulate functions→Academic adjustment	.152	.051	.240
ICT competency →Ability to judge information accuracy→Academic adjustment	.058	−.015	.152
Total effect (Ability to use the Internet→Academic adjustment)	**.340**	**.167**	**.513**
Direct effect (Ability to use the Internet→Academic adjustment)	.121	−.075	.316
Total indirect effect (Ability to use the Internet→ICT self-efficacy→Academic adjustment)	**.219**	**.087**	**.373**
Indirect effect — Ability to use the Internet →Ability to manipulate functions→Academic adjustment	**.180**	**.046**	**.324**
Ability to use the Internet →Ability to judge information accuracy→Academic adjustment	.039	−.054	.151
Total effect (Ability to utilize basic tasks→Academic adjustment)	**.400**	**.232**	**.569**
Direct effect (Ability to utilize basic tasks→Academic adjustment)	.158	−.040	.356
Total indirect effect (Ability to utilize basic tasks→ICT self-efficacy→Academic adjustment)	**.242**	**.107**	**.397**
Indirect effect — Ability to utilize basic tasks →Ability to manipulate functions→Academic adjustment	**.210**	**.043**	**.386**
Ability to utilize basic tasks →Ability to judge information accuracy→Academic adjustment	.032	−.017	.116
Total effect (SW-centered society adaptability→Academic adjustment)	**.323**	**.149**	**.497**
Direct effect (SW-centered society adaptability→Academic adjustment)	**.227**	**.065**	**.389**
Total indirect effect (SW-centered society adaptability→ICT self-efficacy→Academic adjustment)	.096	−.005	.226
Indirect effect — SW-centered society adaptability →Ability to manipulate functions→Academic adjustment	**.098**	**.014**	**.225**
SW-centered society adaptability →Ability to judge information accuracy→Academic adjustment	−.002	−.037	.033
Total effect (Ability to utilize and collaborate through SNS→Academic adjustment)	**.221**	**.041**	**.400**
Direct effect (Ability to utilize and collaborate through SNS→Academic adjustment	.030	−.147	.207
Total indirect effect (Ability to utilize and collaborate through SNS→ICT self-efficacy→Academic adjustment)	**.191**	**.061**	**.390**
Indirect effect — Ability to utilize and collaborate through SNS →Ability to manipulate functions→Academic adjustment	**.180**	**.043**	**.383**
Ability to utilize and collaborate through SNS →Ability to judge information accuracy→Academic adjustment	.011	−.009	.065

In the relationship between digital literacy and personal-emotional adjustment, as well as institutional adjustment, only the ability to use the Internet had a significant effect.

The investigation of whether ICT self-efficacy mediates the relationship between digital literacy and adjustment to university life revealed a mediating effect of ICT self-efficacy on the relationship between digital literacy and academic adjustment. When examining the relationship between digital literacy and academic adjustment, ICT self-efficacy was statically significant in mediating the influence of the ability to use the Internet. Moreover, the direct effect of the ability to use the Internet on academic adjustment was not significant. This finding implies that the effect of the ability to use the Internet on academic adjustment is primarily mediated through ICT self-efficacy. Specifically, only the indirect effect of the ability to manipulate functions was statistically significant.

Regarding the impact of SW-centered society adaptability on academic adjustment, although the total indirect effect of ICT self-efficacy was not significant, the indirect effect of the ability to manipulate functions was significant. Therefore, the ability to manipulate functions partially mediates the impact of SW-centered society adaptability on academic adjustment.

Additionally, the ability to manipulate functions was found to statistically mediate the relationship between the ability to utilize basic tasks and the ability to utilize and collaborate through SNS and academic adjustment. This finding suggests that an increased ability to utilize basic tasks and an increased ability to utilize and collaborate through SNS are associated with increased ICT self-efficacy, which enhances academic adjustment. This finding partially aligns with the research findings of Lee [32] and Ham et al. [12].

6   Conclusion

This study explored the relationship between digital literacy, ICT self-efficacy, and adjustment to university among international students. Data were collected through paper and online surveys of international students attending universities in Seoul and Daegu, and the results of the analysis are as follows. First, as a result of analyzing the effect of digital literacy of international students on their adjustment to university life, it was found that the better they used digital tools or social network services, the higher their levels of academic, social, personal-emotional, and institutional adjustment to university life. In particular, the ability to use the Internet was almost the only influence on the personal-emotional and institutional adjustment of international students. Second, it was found that the ICT self-efficacy of international students had a mediating effect on the relationship between digital literacy and adjustment to university life. The higher the level of digital literacy, the better the ICT self-efficacy, and as a result, it can be seen that increased digital literacy has a positive effect on the adjustment of international students to university life.

Based on this study, several suggestions are proposed to help international students improve their level of digital literacy and adapt to university life. First of all, it is necessary to diversify and activate digital literacy programs for international students at the university library level. In particular, considering that international students' ability to use SNSs and adapt to a SW-centered society affects social adjustment, education is needed to cultivate SNS utilization and SW-centered society adjustment. In addition, university libraries need to educate international students on various ICT utilization methods that can be useful in learning and daily life and provide them with opportunities to solve problems using ICT to improve their ICT self-efficacy.

However, there are several limitations to this study. First, the sample size was limited to only 118 international students attending universities in Seoul and Daegu, and the majority of the respondents were from East Asia. Second, further research using qualitative research methods in addition to quantitative research methods is needed to better understand the level of digital literacy, adjustment to university life, and ICT self-efficacy. In future studies, it is essential to increase the number of subjects and conduct qualitative research on international students from a wider range of countries to better understand the relationship between their digital literacy levels and their adjustment to university life. This study's findings provide a foundation for developing more effective strategies to support digital literacy and adjustment to university life of international students.

References

1. Aesaert, K., van Braak, J.: Exploring factors related to primary school pupils' ICT self-efficacy: a multilevel approach. Comput. Hum. Behav. **41**, 327–341 (2014). https://doi.org/10.1016/j.chb.2014.10.006
2. Ahmad, A.L., Mirza, E., Mohd, R.H., Pawanteh, L., Salman, A.: Adaptation and the new media technology: a study on Malaysian students in Australia and United Kingdom. Malays. J. Commun. **30**(1), 195–206 (2014)
3. American library association digital literacy taskforce: what is digital literacy? https://literacy.ala.org/digital-literacy/. Accessed 10 Aug 2023
4. Baker, R.W., Siryk, B.: Measuring adjustment to college. J. Couns. Psychol. **31**(2), 179–189 (1984). https://doi.org/10.1037/0022-0167.31.2.179
5. Bandura, A.: Self-efficacy: The Exercise of Control. W. H. Freeman and Company, New York (1997)
6. Choi, M., Park, S., Lee, H.S.: The effect of digital media literacy in the Babyboomer generation on the intention of continuous use of media: focusing on the moderating effect of self-efficacy and the mediating effect of media multitasking. Commun. Theor. **17**(3), 258–305 (2021)
7. Chul, K.: Importance of ICT education for older adults' adjusting to digital future society. Korean J. Res. Gerontol. **28**(1), 1–14 (2019)
8. Closson, L.M., Bond, T.A.: Social network site use and university adjustment. Educ. Psychol. **39**(8), 1027–1046 (2019). https://doi.org/10.1080/01443410.2019.1618443
9. Credé, M., Niehorster, S.: Adjustment to college as measured by the student adaptation to college questionnaire: a quantitative review of its structure and relationships with correlates and consequences. Educ. Psychol. Rev. **24**(1), 133–165 (2012). https://doi.org/10.1007/s10648-011-9184-5
10. Dullard, B.: A comparison of general and task-specific measures of self-efficacy in adult hearing AID users. Ph. D. thesis, University of Connecticut (2014)
11. Gilster, P.: Digital Literacy. Wiley Computer Pub. New York, New York (1997)
12. Ham, S.Y., Eum, T., Kang, W.: The influence of motivation for using SNS on school adjustment behavior: focusing on mediation effects of self efficacy. J. New Ind. Bus. **36**(1), 23–44 (2018)
13. Hsiao, J.C.Y., Dillahunt, T.R.: Technology to support immigrant access to social capital and adaptation to a new country. Proc. ACM Hum Comput. Interact. **2**(CSCW), 1–21 (2018). https://doi.org/10.1145/3274339
14. International federation of library associations and institutions: IFLA statement on digital literacy. https://repository.ifla.org/handle/123456789/1283. Accessed 10 Aug. 2023
15. Jin, M., Lim, K.Y.: Factors affecting computer and information literacy and computational thinking: focusing on ICT self-efficacy and attitude toward ICT. J. Educ. Stud. **52**(1), 119–146 (2021)
16. JISC: Developing digital literacies. https://www.jisc.ac.uk/guides/developing-digital-literacies. Accessed 10 Aug 2023

17. Kaeophanuek, S., Na-Songkhla, J., Nilsook, P.: How to enhance digital literacy skills among information sciences students. Int. J. Inf. Educ. Technol. **8**(4), 292–297 (2018)

18. Kahveci, P.: Language teachers' digital literacy and self-efficacy: are they related? ELT Res. J. **10**(2), 123–139 (2021)

19. Kim, M.J., Park, Y.: Analysis of the impact of college students' digital literacy attitude on digital literacy competency. J. Learner Centered Curriculum Instr. **21**(6), 495–507 (2021)

20. Kim, M., Lee, Y., Song, Y.: A qualitative study on the difficulties of the college adjustment in Vietnamese students and the overcoming. J. Educ. Culture **24**(1), 481–503 (2018)

21. Kim, N.: A study on the composition of Korean language courses to strengthen digital literacy capability. Bilingual Res. **89**, 1–25 (2022)

22. Kim, O.S.: A structural equation model of coping with acculturative stress and college adaption among international students in Korea. Multicultural Educ. Stud. **8**(3), 109–131 (2015)

23. Kim, S., Yoon, J.: A comparison of the foreign student college life adaptation index of Chinese students by region: the case of Seoul and Daejeon. J. Asiatic Stud. **60**(4), 157–184 (2017)

24. King, R., Sondhi, G.: International student migration: a comparison of UK and Indian students' motivations for studying abroad. Glob. Soc. Educ. **16**(2), 176–191 (2018). https://doi.org/10.1080/14767724.2017.1405244

25. Korean educational development institute: education statistics and indicators, pocket book. https://kess.kedi.re.kr/eng/publ/view?survSeq=2022&publSeq=80&menuSeq=0&itemCode=02&language=en. Accessed 10 Aug 2023

26. Korean ministry of education: foreign student status. https://www.academyinfo.go.kr. Accessed 9 Aug 2023

27. Law, N., Woo, D., de la Torre, J., Wong, G.: A global framework of reference on digital literacy skills for indicator 4.4.2. https://unevoc.unesco.org/home/Digital+Competence+Frameworks/lang=en/id=4. Accessed 10 Aug 2023

28. Lee, H., Kim, N.Y., Lee, M., Park, H.: Factors influencing male nursing students' adaptation to college life in Korea. J. Nurs. Res. **30**(4), e220 (2022)

29. Lee, J., Kang, Y.S., Park, S.G.: A study on the influence of Korean language teachers' perception of foreign students and on the multicultural perception or attitudes. Multiculture Peace **15**(3), 96–133 (2021)

30. Lee, K.H., Song, J.S.: The effect of emotional intelligence on self-efficacy and job stress of nurses - mediating role of self-efficacy. J. Korean Acad. Nurs. Adm. **16**(1), 17–25 (2010)

31. Lee, S.Y.: A study of Chinese students' intention to retain in college: focusing on Chinese and Korean SNS use, social support, adjustment to college. Korean J. Commun. Stud. **27**(1), 33–56 (2019)

32. Lee, S.Y.: A study of Chinese students' intention to retain in college: focusing on Chinese and Korean SNS use, social support, adjustment to college. Korean J. Commun. Stud. **27**(1), 33–56 (2019)

33. Li, Q., Oh, I., Lee, S.: The relations of acculturation type, acculturation stress, basic psychological needs and college adaptation. Asian J. Educ. **17**(1), 101–120 (2016)

34. Li, Z., Zuo, T., Wei, X., Ding, N.: ICT self-efficacy scale: the correlations with the age of first access to the internet, the age at first ownership of a personal computer (PC), and a smartphone. Med. Educ. Online **28**(1), 2151068 (2023). https://doi.org/10.1080/10872981.2022.2151068

35. Lin, J.H., Peng, W., Kim, M., Kim, S.Y., LaRose, R.: Social networking and adjustments among international students. New Media Soc. **14**(3), 421–440 (2012). https://doi.org/10.1177/1461444811418627

36. Noh, S.J.: Relationship between stress coping style of college students and smartphone addiction: the mediation effect of adjustment to college life. Master's thesis, Yonsei University (2021)

37. Papastergiou, M.: Enhancing physical education and sport science students' self-efficacy and attitudes regarding information and communication technologies through a computer literacy course. Comput. Educ. **54**(1), 298–308 (2010). https://doi.org/10.1016/j.compedu.2009.08.015

38. Papastergiou, M., Gerodimos, V., Antoniou, P.: Multimedia blogging in physical education: effects on student knowledge and ICT self-efficacy. Comput. Educ. **57**(3), 1998–2010 (2011). https://doi.org/10.1016/j.compedu.2011.05.006

39. Roche, T.B.: Assessing the role of digital literacy in English for academic purposes university pathway programs. J. Acad. Lang. Learn. **11**(1), A71–A87 (2017)

40. Rohatgi, A., Scherer, R., Hatlevik, O.E.: The role of ICT self-efficacy for students' ICT use and their achievement in a computer and information literacy test. Comput. Educ. **102**, 103–116 (2016). https://doi.org/10.1016/j.compedu.2016.08.001

41. Rolf, H.G.: Placing ICT in acculturation: a mixed methods study of mobile phones in the everyday life of the international student. Ph. D. thesis, University of Tasmania (2017)

42. Santos, A.I., Serpa, S.: The importance of promoting digital literacy in higher education. Int. J. Soc. Sci. Stud. **5**(6), 90–93 (2017)

43. Schunk, D., Meece, J., Pintrich, P.: Motivation in Education: Theory, Research, and Applications. Pearson (2014)

44. Senkbeil, M., Ihme, J.M.: Motivational factors predicting ICT literacy: first evidence on the structure of an ICT motivation inventory. Comput. Educ. **108**, 145–158 (2017). https://doi.org/10.1016/j.compedu.2017.02.003

45. Seo, D.S.: The effects of life skills of college student athletes on college life adaptation and life satisfaction. Master's thesis, Chung-Ang University (2020)

46. Seo, Y.I.: A study on enhancing management and support system for foreign students in Korea. Tech. rep, Korean Educational Development Institute (2012)

47. Shin, S., Lee, S.: A study on development and validity verification of a measurement tool for digital literacy for university students. J. Learner Centered Curriculum Instr. **19**(7), 749–768 (2019)

48. Shopova, T.: Digital literacy of students and its improvement at the university. J. Effi. Responsib. Educ. Sci. **7**(2), 26–32 (2014). https://doi.org/10.7160/eriesj.2014.070201

49. Son, B.Y., Cho, H.: The effect of social support and resilience on the types of college adjustment of foreign students. J. Humanit. Soc. Sci. **11**(5), 903–918 (2020)

50. Tømte, C., Hatlevik, O.E.: Gender-differences in self-efficacy ICT related to various ICT-user profiles in Finland and Norway. How do self-efficacy, gender and ICT-user profiles relate to findings from PISA 2006. Comput. Educ. **57**(1), 1416–1424 (2011). https://doi.org/10.1016/j.compedu.2010.12.011

51. Tsai, J.H.C.: Use of computer technology to enhance immigrant families' adaptation. J. Nurs. Scholarsh. **38**(1), 87–93 (2006). https://doi.org/10.1111/j.1547-5069.2006.00082.x

52. Turner, K.H., et al.: Developing digital and media literacies in children and adolescents. Pediatrics **140**(Supplement–2), S122–S126 (2017). https://doi.org/10.1542/peds.2016-1758P

53. Ulfert-Blank, A.S., Schmidt, I.: Assessing digital self-efficacy: review and scale development. Comput. Educ. **191**, 104626 (2022). https://doi.org/10.1016/j.compedu.2022.104626
54. Vega-Hernández, M.C., Patino-Alonso, M.C., Galindo-Villardón, M.P.: Multivariate characterization of university students using the ICT for learning. Comput. Educ. **121**, 124–130 (2018). https://doi.org/10.1016/j.compedu.2018.03.004
55. Vermisli, S., Cevik, E., Cevik, C.: The effect of perceived stress and digital literacy on student satisfaction with distance education. Rev. Esc. Enferm. U.S.P. **56**, e20210488 (2022). https://doi.org/10.1590/1980-220x-reeusp-2021-0488en
56. Vijayakumar, V.S.R., Agrawal, T.: Impact of ICT usage on adjustment of college students. J. Indian Acad. Appl. Psychol. **39**(2), 196–204 (2013)
57. Wang, K.: ICT Self-Efficacy and Learning Adaptation: Moderated Mediation Model. Ph.D. thesis, Central China Normal University (2021)
58. Wu, Q.: Motivations and decision-making processes of Mainland Chinese students for undertaking master's programs Abroad. J. Stud. Int. Educ. **18**(5), 426–444 (2014). https://doi.org/10.1177/1028315313519823
59. Yoon, J.W.: Information seeking behaviors throughout the settlement stages among international students in Korea. J. Korean Soc. Libr. Inf. Sci. **56**(1), 27–45 (2022)
60. Zimmerman, B.J.: Self-efficacy: an essential motive to learn. Contemp. Educ. Psychol. **25**(1), 82–91 (2000)

Data Wellness and Everyday Life Data Literacy

Amanda Hovious$^{(\boxtimes)}$ ⓘ and Sarah Sutton ⓘ

Emporia State University, Emporia, KS 66801, USA
ahoviou1@emporia.edu

Abstract. This short paper proposes a framework for data literacy for the general public by reconceptualizing everyday life data literacy as data wellness. Data wellness is the application of basic data literacy and data citizenship to improve one's everyday life as an individual, family, or other everyday life group member and citizen. Data literacy is a foundational infrastructure need in an economically resilient society, and data citizenship provides people with "critical and active agency," returning power to those who have traditionally lacked it. The literacies of data wellness are multiple and inter-connected, both supporting data practices and drawing on them. The framework of data wellness integrally involves learners in data activities that are a part of their lived experiences. As such, data wellness is one key to a resilient society. This holds important implications for the role of public libraries as essential infrastructure to support data wellness initiatives.

Keywords: Data Literacy · Data Wellness · Everyday Life · Resilience

1 Introduction

The inspiration for this short paper emerged from a National Science Foundation (NSF) planning grant for the statewide Adaptive and Resilient Infrastructure for Social Equity (ARISE) project in Kansas, United States. The ARISE project supports the goals of the Kansas State Science and Technology Plan, which include data literacy as a foundational infrastructure need [1]. The grant, recently awarded, harnesses the role of public libraries as essential infrastructure to support resilience through the development of data literacy initiatives. This is important because critical decision making relies heavily on the ability to analyze data. As a result, data literacy is a recognized skill for successful functioning within society, contributing to a strong economy and a strong workforce and serving as a protective mechanism against misinformation in the information age [2]. Currently, trends in data literacy education focus on workforce development [3] and K-20 education [4]. For example, the American Library Association [5] recognizes the importance of data literacy for policy and workforce development, while the National Council of Teachers of Mathematics sees data literacy as an imperative for all PK-12 students, whether they enter STEM or non-STEM fields [4]. Conversely, efforts made toward data literacy education initiatives for the general public are lacking. Yet, these types of initiatives have the potential to create strong data citizens who can fully participate in their communities and society.

I. Sserwanga et al. (Eds.): iConference 2024, LNCS 14596, pp. 375–382, 2024.
https://doi.org/10.1007/978-3-031-57850-2_28

This paper proposes a framework for data literacy for the lay public by reconceptualizing everyday life data literacy as data wellness. Data wellness shifts the view away from the institutional perspective on data literacy that focuses heavily on technical skills and abilities toward a focus that leans more toward the sociocultural data practices that occur within and across different domains of existing literacy practices. Data wellness as a construct is a way to describe everyday life data literacy while avoiding the term "literacy." The reasoning behind this approach is twofold: (a) the notion of data wellness may resonate more deeply with non-technical learners (i.e., everyday people), and (b) the term "literacy" carries a negative social stigma in historically low-literate communities [6].

2   Defining Data Wellness

Data wellness is the application of basic data literacy and data citizenship to improve one's everyday life as an individual, family, or other everyday life group member and citizen. Data wellness occurs in daily activities, exemplified by the ability to read food labels at the grocery store, read a story to a child, or understand the privacy statements (HIPPA form) at the doctor's office. Thus, it incorporates basic statistical, numeric, prose, media, and other literacies. It has roots in data literacy and data citizenship while adhering to a multiliteracies lens.

Data literacy is the general ability to read, work with, analyze, and argue with data. It is a fundamental skill for individuals within society [2]. In everyday life contexts, as it is commonly conceptualized, the application of data literacy presents two challenges, that it is a skill to be learned and applied by individuals [7] and that it may be inaccessible to those who lack a technical background [8], which further disenfranchises the socio-economically disadvantaged [9].

Data citizenship provides people with critically active agency by returning power to those who have traditionally lacked it. It consists of three activities focused on the use of data: data thinking, data doing, and data participation. First, data thinking requires a critical understanding of data that questions data rather than accepts it at face value. Second, data doing comprises an individual's everyday interactions with data, such as deleting data and using data in an ethical way. In other words, in data doing, an individual recognizes and identifies their own interactions with data. Third, data participation is an individual's commitment to dynamically engage with data in society. This may include protecting data privacy, whether individually and collectively, or it may mean volunteering to support others' data wellbeing, such as helping others with their data literacy. Hence, data participation is not just an interaction but a decision to take an action that results from the first two actions [10].

The long-held view of literacies (plural) is that of skills learned and applied by individuals. However, a growing body of scholars argue that literacies are social practices constructed within everyday life contexts [8]. Data wellness approaches literacies this way. It is a framework, a process for thinking about individuals' everyday interactions with data. Through interactions with data—including the data we encounter and the data we create—our beliefs about data develop, which makes data wellness an active process of social construction rather than merely a set of skills to learn and apply at the personal level [10].

3   Dimensions of Data Wellness

Data wellness is comprised of multiple and inter-connected literacies, both supporting data practices and drawing on them. This multiliteracies concept assumes that individuals construct their understanding of the world through multiple information sources and by multiple modes of representation. Furthermore, individuals practice multiliteracies within and across multiple domains and dimensions. Figure 1 illustrates the dimensions of data wellness as multiple literacies that build on each other.

Quantitative literacy is rooted in data practices across all the literacies in Fig. 1. Digital literacy recognizes that contemporary data practices are also digital practices, while media and information literacy further build on critical understandings of data and information in an information- and digitally media-rich world. Visual literacy is the "music" of a datafied society, connecting data points through graphical and visual methods from which data citizens must learn to make meaning. Participatory literacy is the practice of data "prosumption," or the process by which a data consumer contributes to data production, through activities such as citizen science projects or community-based research. Transliteracy is the culminating practice of data wellness. The sections that follow describe each of the literacies in more detail.

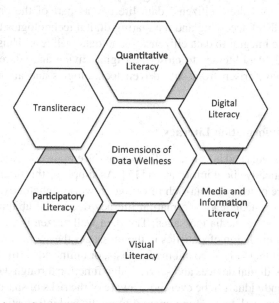

Fig. 1. The dimensions of data wellness. Clockwise, each literacy supports the next literacy, while a multiliteracies thread binds the literacies together such that they all serve as dimensions of data wellness yet exist as domains of practice within their own right.

3.1   Quantitative Literacy

Institutionalized notions of data literacy—those that apply to academic and workplace contexts—are strongly rooted in the quantitative literacies of data production, which include algorithmic thinking, statistical methods, and data programming and analysis. On the other hand, data consumption and data participation are the aims of data wellness. Because of this, the quantitative literacies of data wellness encompass the ability to apply an elementary knowledge of mathematics and statistics to varying contexts to aid in the comprehension, interpretation, and critical evaluation of data-laden messaging [11]. Principally, the quantitative literacy practices that contribute to data wellness are present in individuals' everyday life information encounters and include activities like applying number sense to the interpretation of media stories, performing everyday quantitative tasks like balancing a checkbook or calculating a tip, and recognizing how to reach data-based inferences.

3.2 Digital Literacy

Jaeger et al. [12] define digital literacy as "the skills and abilities necessary for access once the technology is available, including a necessary understanding of the language and component hardware and software required to successfully navigate the technology." While digital literacy, along with digital access, are important components of digital inclusion, the evolving landscape of the digitally datafied society has hastened the call by policy makers to address citizens' data literacy as part of the process [13]. The digital literacy skills of accessing and navigating digital technologies to find, discover, and access data are integral to data citizenship and data wellness. Thus, digital literacy functions alongside data literacy to close the digital divide and address the structural inequalities that have arisen from data driven technologies and algorithmic decision making [14].

3.3 Media and Information Literacy

UNESCO defines media and information literacy as the empowering ability to use digital tools and think critically about information [15]. As simple as this definition is, it belies the complex nature of today's data-rich information world. Inherently, data wellness is a key component of media and information literacy due to the ubiquitous use of data and statistics in modern media messages. The data well citizen is wary of and able to understand the manipulation of statistics in the messages they consume, whether digital news stories, streaming videos, social media posts, or online ads [16]. Furthermore, the pervasive nature of digital devices and services that function through data collection and analysis requires individuals to be ever more aware of the risks of sharing their personal data. Therefore, data wellness is fundamental to media and information literacy.

3.4 Visual Literacy

Visual literacy is ever present in the everyday life data practices of individuals, who rely heavily on visual information as a representation of data to make sense of it. Cooley [17] uses the metaphor of music to describe visual literacy as "the strategic connecting of notes to form a melody, which repeats or evolves to form a chorus." Thus, data visualization is the translation of data into meaningful information, or data notes into a full-scale song, metaphorically speaking. The data citizen achieves data wellness, not only by becoming a savvy consumer of visual messages, but also by becoming an active participant in data storytelling culture. This is an example of participatory literacy.

3.5 Participatory Literacy

When data consumers participate in meaningful and relevant data activities, such as contributing to a citizen science project, engaging in community-based research, or sharing their knowledge about disinformation tactics, they become data "prosumers" [18]. The "prosumer" is part consumer and part producer, which exemplifies participatory literacy. Accordingly, participatory literacy is "the ability to contribute to the collective intelligence of digital networks, and to leverage the collective intelligence of those networks in the service of personal and/or collective goals" [19]. The goal of data wellness is data participation, and the "prosumer" activities of data participation reflect data citizenship.

3.6 Transliteracy

Transliteracy extends data citizenship across everyday life worlds. Transliteracy is the ability to adapt socially constructed literacy practices across multiple social contexts [7]. In the context of data citizenship, transliteracy may be both constructed and applied in everyday life worlds. Thus, we conceive of data wellness as the ongoing social construction of everyday life data literacy and data citizenship, especially among the socio-economically disadvantaged, across multiple everyday life worlds.

4 Discussion

Why data wellness instead of data literacy? One may argue that current concepts of data literacy are too techno-centric and are better suited for formal institutional contexts, like the school and the workplace [8]. Others argue for the elimination of the term "literacy" in everyday life activities due to the stigma of illiteracy in communities that are historically low-literate [6]. While data wellness is rooted in the encompassing nature of multiliteracy practices or dimensions, the framing of literacy as wellness offers a more palatable approach for addressing it, especially for those with the greatest need for it. Furthermore, unlike the academic and workforce training efforts of current data literacy approaches, data wellness recognizes the existence of an interactional relationship between individual and society. In doing so, data wellness rejects the idea that data literacy is merely a set of individual skills. Instead of an isolated skills-based focus, the framework of data wellness integrally involves learners in data activities that are a part of their lived experiences. In other words, data wellness is everyday life data literacy, which is key to a resilient society.

4.1 Data Wellness and the Resilient Society

Societal resilience is dependent upon active and intentional resistance to the threats of disinformation and misinformation that individuals encounter in their everyday lives [2].

Inherent in this is the ability to make sense of data and to use it to make informed decisions. Data citizenship, which encompasses the dimensions of data wellness, provides a framework for understanding the needs and practices of everyday life data literacy. Thus, data wellness focuses on data practices that are rooted in individual interests and community contexts. This reflects a social (or societal) practice rather than a skills perspective, a perspective that is rooted in Brazilian educator and philosopher Paulo Freire's [20] influential critical pedagogy work with poor, illiterate adults. Freire took a constructivist approach to literacy by supporting knowledge construction within learners' own social contexts.

D'Ignazio [8] points to Freire as an important theoretical influence on how to approach data literacy, adopting the term creative data literacy and situating it within a broader space of inquiry. She argues that the current landscape of data literacy education is too technically oriented for acquainting novice learners with the language of data and recommends five tactics for creative data literacy education: (1) community-centered data that is relevant to its users; (2) data biographies for understanding the origin, purpose, and impact of data; (3) messy data that takes learners through collection, categorization, and standards-creation; (4) learner-centered tools that scaffold the learning process; and (5) creative and community-centered output that is meaningful to learners. Thus, the goals of creative data literacy education offer a promising approach toward advancing the data wellness framework in informal learning environments like public libraries.

4.2 The Role of Public Libraries in Data Wellness

Because the fundamental purpose of the public library is to serve the unique needs of its community, it is ideally situated to responsively foster the multiliteracy practices of data wellness. One barrier to this socio-educational role is that the central mission of public libraries today is often corporate leaning, focusing on patrons as customers rather than patrons as learners and handing over any educational role to their academic and school library counterparts. While the recognition of the public library's role in the broader conceptualization of information-related literacies is present, the formalization of any information activity as an "information literacy skill" or "data literacy skill" often goes unrecognized [21]. Where public libraries have adopted such initiatives, they target specific domains or audiences, such workforce data literacy or youth data literacy [22, 23]. The less-formalized connotation of data wellness, instead of data literacy, may solve this issue by bringing everyday life data literacy to all.

As such, there is a gap in the availability of everyday life data literacy education in public libraries, as most programs focus on academic or workforce development. Non-technical data literacy initiatives are absent, despite the growing call for everyday individuals to become data fluent so that they can make sound decisions that benefit themselves and society [2]. Furthermore, data wellness is an issue of social equity, which is one of the core values of the library profession. Thus, data wellness initiatives in public library spaces can bridge the gap between the data-haves and data-have-nots, bringing equitable access to data-informed decision making that not only benefits individuals but also the communities and broader societies to which they belong.

5 Conclusion

Data wellness is a framework for defining the multiple and interconnected literacies in which everyday life data practices may flourish through data-informed decision making. Data wellness draws on understandings of literacy as a social practice and eschews the skills-based focus of current data literacy educational initiatives. Doing so provides flexibility for replacing the term "literacy" with "wellness" in an effort to acknowledge the non-technical aspects of everyday life data practices and to destigmatize the process of becoming data literate (from an illiterate state) to a state of becoming data well. Data wellness is a key factor in community and societal resilience because it empowers citizens to become actively resistant against the threats of disinformation and misinformation that is endemic in their everyday lives. Within this framework, public libraries play a vital role. As essential organizations in their communities, they are ideally situated to foster the multiliteracy practices of data wellness and data citizenship that support the formation of resilient communities.

References

1. Kansas NSF EPSCoR: A brief overview of Kansas NSF EPSCoR and the ARISE project [PowerPoint slides] (2022). https://nsfepscor.ku.edu/internal-ks-nsf-epscor-opportunities/. Accessed 07 Jan 2024
2. Norman, S.E.: How data literacy can keep America safe. Time (2023). https://time.com/629 0684/data-literacy-us-national-security/, Accessed 16 Sep 2023
3. Brown, S.: How to build data literacy in your company. MIT Management Sloan School (2021). https://mitsloan.mit.edu/ideas-made-to-matter/how-to-build-data-literacy-your-com pany. Accessed 16 Sep 2023
4. U.S. Department of Education: Data literacy [PowerPoint slides] (2021). https://www.ed.gov/ sites/default/files/documents/stem/20211015-data-literacy.pdf. Accessed 16 Sep 2023
5. American Library Association: Data that counts: An introduction to census data for public libraries [Webinar] (2021), http://www.ala.org/pla/education/onlinelearning/webinars/ond emand/datathatcounts. Accessed 16 Sep 2023
6. Adkins, N.L., Ozanne, J.L.: The low literate consumer. J. Consum. Res. **32**(1), 93–105 (2005)
7. Hovious, A.: Toward a socio-contextual understanding of transliteracy. Ref. Serv. Rev. **46**(2), 178–188 (2018)
8. D'Ignazio, C.: Creative data literacy: bridging the gap between the data-haves and data-have nots. Inf. Des. J. **23**(1), 6–18 (2017)
9. Yates, P.S.J., Carmi, E., Lockley, E., Wessels, B., Pawluczuk, A.: Understanding Citizens Data Literacy: Thinking, Doing & Participating with Our Data (Me & My Big Data Report). University of Liverpool (2020)
10. Carmi, E., Yates, S.J., Lockley, E., Pawluczuk, A.: Data citizenship: rethinking data literacy in the age of disinformation, misinformation, and malinformation. Internet Policy Rev. **9**(2), 1–22 (2020)
11. Gal, I.: Adults' statistical literacy: meanings, components, responsibilities. Int. Stat. Rev. **70**(1), 1–25 (2002)
12. Jaeger, P.T., Bertot, J.C., Thompson, K.M., Katz, S.M., DeCoster, E.J.: The intersection of public policy and public access: digital divides, digital literacy, digital inclusion, and public libraries. Public Libr. Q. **31**(1), 1–20 (2012)

13. Carmi, E., Yates, S.J.: What do digital inclusion and data literacy mean today? Internet Policy Rev. **9**(2), 1–14 (2020)
14. Dencik, L., Hintz, A., Redden, J., Trere, E.: Exploring data justice: conceptions, applications, and directions. Inf. Commun. Soc. **22**(7), 873–881 (2019)
15. UNESCO: Media and information literacy. https://www.unesco.org/en/media-information-literacy. Accessed 16 Sep 2023
16. Palmer, E.: Teaching students how to spot manipulated data. HMH (2020). https://www.hmhco.com/blog/teaching-students-how-to-spot-manipulated-data. Accessed 16 Sep 2023
17. Cooley, B.D.: Why visual literacy is essential to good data visualization. Towards Data Science (2019). https://towardsdatascience.com/why-visual-literacy-is-essential-to-good-data-visualization. Accessed 16 Sep 2023
18. Špiranec, S., Kos, D. George, M.: Searching for critical dimensions in data literacy. Inf. Res. **24**(4), paper colis1922 (2019)
19. Pegrum, M., Hockly, N., Dudeney, G.: Digital Literacies, 1st edn. Routledge, London (2014)
20. Freire, P.: Pedagogy of the Oppressed. 30th Anniversary Edn. The Continuum International Publishing Group, New York (1970)
21. Widdowson, J., Smart, D.: Information literacy in public libraries. In: Hagen-McIntosh, J. (ed.) Information and Data Literacy: The Role of the Library, pp. 15–20. Apple Academic Press, Palm Bay, FL (2016)
22. American Library Association: Building business know-how through data literacy [Webinar] (2021). http://www.ala.org/pla/education/onlinelearning/webinars/ondemand/buildingbusiness. Accessed 16 Sep 2023
23. American Library Association: Data literacy for youth: using census data in public library programming [Webinar] (2021). http://www.ala.org/pla/education/onlinelearning/webinars/ondemand/foryouth. Accessed 16 Sep 2023

Meeting People Where They Are: Customizing Digital Literacy Education

Alison Harding[✉], Jane Behre, and Mega Subramaniam

University of Maryland, College Park, MD 20742, USA
{hardinga,jbehre,mmsubram}@umd.edu

Abstract. Despite high levels of broadband adoption and digital device usage across economic divides and geographic location, the so-called digital divide remains a persistent issue. In the US state where this study is conducted, Maryland, there were 520,000 households that were not subscribed to wireline broadband services, above the US average by approximately 6%. Despite being above the national average, this still translates to 23% of the Maryland population lacking adequate internet capabilities in their home. This study utilizes a nuanced, qualitative approach to determine how residents of Maryland are or are not seeking, leveraging, and using digital literacy (DL) education venues and resources/training to build and enhance their digital literacy skills. The findings were used to create a typology of learners and illustrative personas that educators can use to identify what type of learning experience is best suited to their community members. The findings support the recommendations that educators need flexibility in their DL educational approaches by fostering the luxury of ambivalence among learners. This can be done by prioritizing transferable skills that allow learners to be self-sufficient in their future DL skills educational needs.

Keywords: Digital Literacy Skills · Digital Equity · Digital Literacy Skills Education

1 Introduction

As new technologies are introduced and adopted and it changes the ways individuals access information, "[t]hose able to keep up with the changes benefit from the advances while those who cannot keep pace fall behind [13]." In 2019, the overall adoption rate for high-speed Internet in the United States (US) was 70.8%. In the US state where this study is conducted, Maryland, there were 520,000 households not subscribed to wireline broadband services, above the US average by approximately 6% [6]. Despite being above the national average, this still translates to 23% of the Maryland population lacking adequate internet capabilities in their home. Additionally, 13% of households lacked a desktop, laptop, or tablet computing device [6]. A leader in digital inclusion advocacy in the US, National Digital Inclusion Alliance (NDIA) suggests that increasing digital equity, and therefore the adoption of broadband internet, includes the building of 'Digital Inclusion Ecosystems', which includes a crucial component of "multilingual digital literacy and digital skill trainings that meet the community's needs [11]."

I. Sserwanga et al. (Eds.): iConference 2024, LNCS 14596, pp. 383–397, 2024.
https://doi.org/10.1007/978-3-031-57850-2_29

This study aims to determine how residents of Maryland (hereinafter referred to Marylanders) are or are not seeking, leveraging, and using digital literacy education venues and resources/training to build and enhance their digital literacy skills. In this study, digital literacy skills (hereinafter referred to DL skills) are defined broadly as any skills that one utilizes in successfully accessing and navigating the digital world. Employing a nuanced, qualitative approach to measuring DL education preferences, we examined where Marylanders go to learn or get assistance to complete DL tasks, their preferred format, and people to learn from, and their perceived value of DL in general. Specifically, we address the following research questions:

1. Why do Marylanders want (or not want) to learn DL skills?
2. How do Marylanders learn DL skills?

This paper presents the typology of digital learners in Maryland and will contribute to the development of a statewide DL curriculum and resources repository called Marylanders Online that is set to be completed by the end of 2024. Marylanders Online focuses on bringing "digital inclusion to Maryland by providing quality resources and education that help improve digital literacy (*About | UME Digital Literacy*, n.d.) [1]." This typology will help DL educators rethink their DL education offerings, formats, and venues in a rapidly changing digital environment that is populated by a range of types of learners.

2 Related Frameworks

In this section, the researchers will share the DL education stakeholder landscape in the US, along with a brief overview of the critical nature of DL in the current cultural climate.

2.1 DL Education Stakeholders

Despite high levels of broadband adoption and digital device usage across economic divides [14] and geographic location [15], the so-called digital divide remains a persistent issue. Per the American Library Association's (ALA) 2022 report, 59 million Americans accessed the internet through public wifi, and public libraries hosted nearly 224 million internet use sessions in 2019 [2]. The Public Library Association (PLA) notes that nearly 88% of public libraries in America offer some form of DL programming and over one third of public libraries have a staff member that is dedicated to these types of programs [9].

NDIA, a leader in digital equity advocacy, acknowledges that DL skills are vital to achieving digital equity. As a part of their Digital Inclusion Startup Manual, NDIA indicates that DL skills education and training is one of the "five elements" of digital inclusion (Siefer et al., n.d.). Public libraries are one of the key stakeholders that NDIA indicates are valuable partners in the efforts to further DL skills education. Partnerships with nonprofits, corporations, educational institutions (K-12 and higher education), local government institutions, and many others are suggested key stakeholders in DL skills education as well. These suggestions of key stakeholders informed our choices of local institutions to collaborate with to recruit participants for this study.

2.2 The Ongoing and Increasing Importance of Digital Literacy

Digital literacy has long been a topic of discussion, both in scholarship and policy. Barzilai-Nahon [3] cites a tradition of monotopical measurement and access-oriented thinking that had centered the conversation around digital literacy since the 1990s. While access-oriented discussions are still necessary, it is becoming increasingly obvious to those working in varied fields that understanding how to participate in a digital society depends on digital literacy and not only digital access.

As an example of the increased need for digital literacy, telehealth utilization has undergone a meteoric rise since the onset of the COVID-19 pandemic in 2019 [5]. Given this rise in usage, medical scholars and practitioners have added their sense of urgency to existing calls for the prioritization of digital skills training. An observation and survey study of 502 adult inpatients at University of Chicago Medicine found that most participants owned a smartphone or other digital device and reported that they had used the internet previously, however those with low health literacy often also had low digital literacy and were unable to perform tasks online without assistance despite having access to a device and the internet [16]. Telehealth has also been identified as a valuable tool to alleviate the disparities in mental health care in rural communities, even prior to the onset of the pandemic. Myers [8] identified the need for additional professional training and changes in care delivery modes for the integration of telehealth practices. This change in mental health care delivery modes also requires the patient to have adequate digital literacy skills to make and attend virtual appointments. Similarly, digital literacy is essential for individuals to participate in government services, civic engagement, education, employment, and many other everyday tasks, hence identifying digital literacy learning preferences will guide digital literacy providers and individuals to seek the learning experiences that may be best for an individual and for a particular context or task.

3 Methodology

This paper reports on the findings of a study conducted between May and August 2023 in the state of Maryland in the U.S. Interview sites were in eight locations in local institutions in various communities (see Table 1). Sites were chosen because of two reasons: First, to represent the diversity of Maryland. We utilized the existing partnership network of the Marylanders Online project to source their suggestions for local institutions in target regions across the state. Second, these sites were trusted institutions in the community, hence maximizing the comfort for participants. The local institutions helped recruit potential participants by advertising the study and providing a space in which their community members would feel comfortable talking to the researchers. Going through these institutions to recruit participants, rather than trying to recruit directly, helped us establish trust and rapport with community members and assuaged potential concerns about the research. The study received IRB approval.

Enrollment in the study occurred on the day of the interviews. Participants self-identified to researchers as currently living in Maryland, being aged 11 or older, and feeling comfortable participating in an interview in English. If a potential participant was under the age of 18, verbal parental consent was provided directly to the researcher

Table 1. Education, connectivity, and site type data for the regions of local institutions.

	Allegany County	Baltimore City	Montgomery County	Prince George's County	Talbot County	Queen Anne's County
Site Information						
Site Type(s)	Community College Public Library	Low-income Housing Community Makerspace	Senior Housing Community	Government Agency	Public Library	Public Library
Education						
High school graduate or higher (% of persons ages 25+, 2017-2021)[1]	90.3%	86.3%	91.2%	87.2%	91.7%	92.9%
Bachelor's degree or higher (% of persons ages 25+, 2017-2021)[1]	20.2%	34.2%	59.8%	34.9%	41.0%	37.0%
Income & Poverty						
Median Household Income (2017-2021)[1]	$51,090	$54,124	$117,345	$91,124	$79,349	$99,597
Persons in poverty (%)[1]	16.4%	20.3%	8.5%	11.5%	9.4%	8.0%
Computer Use, Internet Use, and Access						
Households with a computer (%, 2017-2021)[1]	87.6%	89.7%	97.5%	95.9%	92.7%	96.1%
Households with a broadband Internet subscriptions (%, 2017-2021)[1]	81.1%	79.6%	94.3%	91.1%	88.2%	86.5%
Population living in areas without quality broadband subscription (%, 2015-2019)[2]	9.4%	1.3%	1.2%	3.0%	12.8%	1.5%
Households without a computer or broadband subscription (%, 2015-2019)[2]	17.6%	21.4%	6.5%	11.3%	10.2%	10.5%

[1] United States Census Bureau. (n. d.) *U.S. Census Bureau Quickfacts.* https://www.census.gov/quickfacts/
[2] United States Census Bureau. (n. d.) *Digital Equity Act Population Viewer.* https://rmgis-portal.geo.census.gov/arcgis/apps/webappviewer/index.html?id=c5e8cf675865464a90ff1573c5072b42

and youth assent was solicited prior to starting the interview. The research team chose age 11 as the lower limit for this research because middle school aged children are able to identify and discuss their DL skills in the context of an interview. The semi-structured interviews were either conducted one-on-one or in a group setting. The interview protocol covered the following topics: typical daily interaction with digital devices and activities, how important digital skills are, education (past, present, and future) about digital skills, and interaction with government services online. For youth under the age of 18, questions regarding government services were replaced with questions about digital skills in a school environment. With participant assent, the interviews were audio recorded and later transcribed using the online transcription service Rev. If a participant did not consent to being recorded, notes were taken. All participants were offered a $25 gift card. A total of 98 participants have been interviewed at the time that this paper was written. See Fig. 1 for age distribution, which is the only demographic information that we collected (see *Limitations*).

79 interview transcripts were analyzed using the collaborative qualitative analysis software Dedoose. Participants identities were anonymized through the use of a code based on which site they were interviewed at and which interview number they were at that site (e.g. W1-01 for the first participant at Western Maryland site 1).

We imported the transcriptions into the qualitative software analysis program Dedoose and used an iterative process to develop and refine the codebook. All three members of the research team used the same transcript to collaborate on creating a codebook through an emergent coding process [10]. We discussed the coding process and refined the codebook, adding, deleting, and merging codes. The team then tested that codebook on a second transcript to confirm a consensus of the codes [7]. Following the creation of the codebook, one researcher coded all transcripts and notes. The coded transcripts were then reviewed by one of the two other researchers. Coder one utilized memo-ing as a technique to draw attention to certain areas for the second coder to direct

Age Ranges of Participants

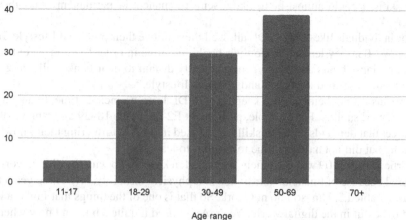

Fig. 1. Age range of participants. Note: Group interviews explain the discrepancy in the number of transcripts versus the number of participants.

their attention to in their review. While no changes were made to the codebook throughout the coding process, any emergent addition or clarification to the description of each code were discussed as a team throughout the coding process. The final codebook contained 7 parent codes and 5 child codes. The codes reviewed for this paper included: Digital skills education, Value of the Internet, Avoidance of the Internet, Value of digital literacy, and Access to Internet and devices.

4   Findings

4.1   Why Do Marylanders Want (or not Want) to Learn DL Skills?

Marylanders desire to learn DL skills is rooted in their reaction to seeing the world around them change, and these reactions manifest in different ways which we will discuss below.

Wanting to Keep Up
For those Marylanders who expressed a desire to keep up with the changing digital world, there were very clear benefits to this course of action. Some participants stated that the internet is vital because it allows them to complete tasks but not be forced into leaving their home. Participant B1–12 disclosed that "If I can do it online, I'ma do it online. I hate to leave my house...", which motivated them to keep their DL skills up to date.

Others, like participant E1-01, saw benefit in broadening their DL skills as it pertained to improving their financial and familial situation, "...it helped me further my education, which led to a better job. It helped me to communicate better. So, I have more connections with friends and family." Another example of the same sort, participant E1-07 self-described as digitally illiterate, was extremely enthusiastic about the value that more DL skills could have in both their home and work life, "...I would like to get better at it because right now I'm babysitting my grandchildren two days a week… [I]f I had better skills, I could almost be a, like a semi-permanent or permanent um, substitute teacher…".

For individuals like W2-03, DL allowed them to live their preferred lifestyle. In the case of W2-03, they learned to do their banking online in order to do tasks outside of normal business hours and while geographically distant to their bank – allowing them to live a self-described nocturnal and nomadic lifestyle.

Reasons for not being able to keep up with DL learning include time, financial constraints, and disability. For example, participant E2-06, in the 18–29 age range working in a career that demands high DL skills, expressed interest in furthering their knowledge of coding but did not have the time to commit to learning.

Participant W2-09 was extremely interested in keeping up with the digital world but struggled because of financial constraints and physical disability, "… Three years ago I became disabled… Um, so I do not work. So that is one of the things that I miss a lot, is I used to be out in the digital world. Yeah. And I used it quite a bit. And now when I'm on a fixed income, which is basically nothing, um, I don't even have internet at home."

Ambivalence Towards Keeping Up

The most substantial group of participants were those who expressed keeping up with the digital world as something inevitable and unconcerning. This is a very ambivalent position, which amounts to being resigned to the fact that the digital world is changing and that there is no point in feeling strongly about having to keep up. Participants who are ambivalent about keeping up with DL skills talk about the state of the digital world as inevitable. Participants in interview B1–11 spoke amongst themselves about how the world is changing: "P1: It's just going to keep going. P2: True, true. It's never going back to the… to yellow pages."

This ambivalent position also impacts a participant's interest in education. These participants often express a level of contentment with the status of their skills, like participant W1-06 who feels they have the necessary knowledge to maintain their position in a digital world but has no motivation to seek out additional DL skills education without an identifiable benefit to their career, "I think I would if it, like, stood out to me as 'Oh, this could advance my career, or advance my networking abilities, or advance my…But I don't, I'm not, I wouldn't necessarily just be interested in doing it for doing it's sake." Or participant W2-23 who identified as happy with a middle of the road position: "… I'm not that old generation who's resisting, but I'm not like the new that's doing everything on there. I'm kind of in the middle. I can mix and match and pick and choose what's kind of convenient for me."

Keeping up with changes as an ambivalent action is also tied to the introduction of major changes in the way of life or career of a person. Ambivalent participants were discussing their adoption of new skills and technologies in regard to situations outside their control. This is most notable in those who spoke about becoming increasingly familiar with Zoom during the pandemic. There is obviously an urgency to the situation – the pandemic forced people to pivot to digital communication – but the ambivalence regarding learning new skills is still very present. In a different way of expressing a lack of urgency, participant W1-03 started a small business that was pushing them to stay current but not enough to become more fully digitally integrated. While the needs of their business requires them to interact with financials online, they still default to doing most of their personal finances in person. This is partially because their business accepts cash, negating their ability to be fully digital, but also due to a lack of urgency – in person banking is still an option, so there is no need to further their skills yet. Another series of skills that many participants talked about with no urgency was communication. Participant E1-01 continued to grow their skills so that they could communicate with people in places/applications that they want to be reached.

Forced to Keep Up
While not as common of a position as ambivalence towards keeping up with DL skills, there were those that felt they were being forced to keep up their skills. While this position was primarily expressed by older adults, this was not universal. Older adults expressed that things were too fast or too time consuming, as represented by participant B2-02, an adult in the 50–69 age range who said "…[it] is just too overwhelming and daunting and too time consuming to have my head bent down looking at a phone…" Participants were aware that they were reacting to the changing digital world at least partly because of their age, such as when participant E1-03 admitted they would prefer to engage in the world in an in-person way because of their age: "… but that's because I'm 66 years old."

Younger participants also expressed a desire to slow the tide of integrating the digital world into all aspects of their lives. A participant (PG1-04) in the 30–49 range was very adamant about their distaste for the digital world: "I just want to go back to when everything was regular. Not digital. Yeah. I hate technology bad. I want to ride horses and walk and garden and stuff like that. I really hate modern stuff like this…I do love the internet, where you can quickly access most stuff. But the fact that they can just put anything on, it's just like 'go back!'…".

Participant W1-06 was in an even younger age range, 18–29, but referred to themself as "digitally illiterate by choice," and made an active decision to hand write and mail physical letters on a regular basis to avoid over reliance on the digital world.

Participants who expressed a world view that centered on them feeling forced to keep up usually either ignored digital ways of completing tasks or utilized them but were vocal in their dislike of the digital world. Participant E2-07, a participant in the 70+ age range, is representative of the first way that this world view impacts action, who said that she would walk to her insurance agent's office to renew her insurance and will only go online "…if they made it so that I [she] could understand what to do.".

In another instance of ignoring digital ways of completing tasks, participant PG1-05 eventually gave up attempting to interact with the government or their doctors digitally because they hadn't been able to work with digital services.

4.2 How Do Marylanders Learn DL Skills?

When learning DL skills, Marylanders often utilized the strategy of teaching themselves how to use technology. This is very similar to learning by doing, but we define learning by doing as learning through hands-on experience or trial-and-error, while teaching oneself involves looking up information, watching tutorials, or completing self-paced instruction. Structured education and asking others for help are other strategies that

Marylanders identified for learning DL skills. In this paper, references to structured or unstructured learning opportunities are discussing a difference in learning style while references to structured and unstructured institutions are referring to a difference between traditional educational institutions (e.g. K-12, higher education) and other educational opportunities (e.g. library programming, workforce development, etc.).

Learning by Doing

The vast majority of participants indicated that they learned some or all of their DL skills simply by using technology regularly. The participants who expressed that they learn DL skills through this process primarily fell in the 18–29, 30–49, and 50–69 age groups. Many discussed using the trial-and-error process more generally, while others explained how they learned digital skills by using technology for work.

When discussing learning by doing, many participants outlined their process for trying new things when using technology and how that process helped them learn DL skills. Participant W1-07 explained that "I've kind of taught myself…Like I'm not afraid to just play around with stuff. You can't really mess anything up." Additionally, participant E1-11 mentioned that they learned their skills through "trial and error… I never really took a class or read a book…or anything like that." This trial-and-error process often precedes any self-teaching strategies: "Well if I can't figure out how to solve a particular technology problem…I probably Google it" (E2-05).

Participants mentioned a variety of jobs that helped them to learn various DL skills, including a digital media specialist at the Baltimore Sun (B2-08), a paralegal in Washington D.C. (E1-03), and a payroll worker at a home improvement business (W1-05). Some participants discussed learning specific digital skills while on the job. W2-05 specifically mentioned learning Microsoft Office software for their job, while participant E1-03 explained how they learned DL as a secretary.

Teaching Oneself

The majority of participants who discussed teaching themselves DL skills fell into the 18–29 and 30–49 age groups. One of the most common ways that participants taught themselves DL skills was through utilizing tools like Google and YouTube when they had an immediate need to learn a skill. Other participants taught themselves a specific digital skill without having a specific need. Participant E2-06 mentioned how "I taught myself how to code in high school with my brothers and…I did some game design in Python in high school." And participant B2-01 decided that they wanted to teach themself how to use Excel, so they ordered an Excel book.

As mentioned earlier, some participants, like E2-05, chose to go through the trial-and-error process before moving on to trying to teach themselves. However, it seems that the context of the need affects how one may search for information to learn a DL skill. For example, participant W2-03 discussed how, when they had a more formal need, in this case trying to solve a problem with their bank, they first tried to solve a problem on their own before reaching out to an expert for help. Addressing a more informal need such as operating a video game, they would prefer to ask friends for help first before trying to teach themself.

Structured Education

A very common method mentioned for learning digital skills was learning these skills in school, specifically taking classes in elementary, middle, and high schools, and some took courses in college. The majority of participants who learned digital skills in school fell into the 18–29 and 30–49 age ranges. Interestingly, we also found that some of the computer classes that they took in school weren't necessarily relevant, and/or the classes stopped at a certain point, so they were not able to learn additional skills. There were participants who received structured instruction on digital skills through their workplace. Participant W1-08 mentioned that their workplace would pay for them to learn software, and participant W2-23 discussed how "we had computer classes that were updated like every year…".

Another frequently mentioned type of structured education for DL skills was general computer classes, often offered through institutions like a library. The majority of participants who expressed that they took this kind of class were in the 30–49 and 50–69 age ranges.

Asking Others

Many participants discussed how they consulted with a friend or family member when they had a problem or question related to digital skills, or they were the person that a friend or family member reached out to when they had a problem or question related to digital skills. The majority of participants who discussed reaching out to family (or were the ones who family members reached out to) fell into the 30–49 and 50–69 age groups. Some participants mentioned how they often ask their children for help when they have questions about technology, and the reverse when they teach their children DL skills. Participants also discussed how their "friends will give tips and stuff" when they are working together on computers.

Other examples of getting help from others include asking colleagues for help or asking an expert. The majority of participants who reach out to colleagues for help regarding digital skills fall in the 50–69 age group. When participants mentioned asking an expert, it looked different depending on the situation. Participant E1-03 discussed how if they were having an issue with a Microsoft product "I'd probably contact Microsoft." Whereas participant W2-06 explained how if there "was a really deep problem with…the computer" they are more likely to reach out to their "IT guy."

5 Discussion

5.1 Typology of Learners

From the findings of RQ1, in which we ask about why do Marylanders want (or not want) to learn DL skills, we derived a typology of DL skills learners that contained three major identities and two sub-identities. The underlying reason for seeking education is key to connecting a community member with the appropriate programming or to point them to more applicable learning experiences. In this section we lay out each branch of the typology, as seen in Fig. 2, in greater detail. The findings of RQ1 have further informed the creation of personas for each learner type. To illustrate the interaction of learner type and learning strategy, each type will be presented in terms of a persona of a potential DL skills learner. See Fig. 2 below and larger format in Appendix A. While effective self-sufficiency in maintaining digital skills is the end goal of DL skills education, factoring in how best to teach transferable skills to the learner who falls under each typology is critical. We isolate those who fall into types 1A and 3A in this section, because educational interventions for these types are unlikely to benefit the learner or the educator.

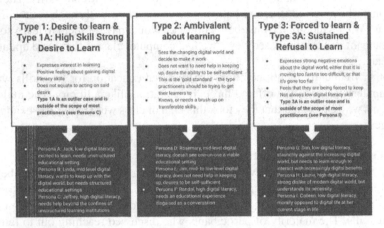

Fig. 2. A diagram of the Typology of Maryland Digital Literacy Skills Learners

Type 1 - Strong Desire to Learn

In this branch of the typology, you find potential learners who are strongly motivated to enhance their DL skills through different types of learning practices. These are participants described in Sect. 4.1 as wanting to learn and have a high interest-driven DL learning style. The interest or positivity is a key component of identifying a learner as Type 1. There is no required level of existing DL skill that would indicate that one is a Type 1 learner, rather a strong positive outlook on DL skills education will be the primary characteristic. While those identified as being Type 1 will not always act on the desire, that desire is there and can be leveraged in engaging them in educational opportunities. Type 1 learners are a group that should be highly prioritized by any DL skills educators.

Type 1 Learning Styles

Type 1 learners can present in two different forms. Persona A (Jack) is a representative of a Type 1 learner who prefers unstructured educational experiences while Persona B (Linda) is a representative of a Type 1 learner who could thrive in structured educational experiences.

Type 1A - High Skill Strong Desire to Learn

Type 1A learners possess an additional key characteristic that makes them one of the lowest priority learners for most institutions outside of formal educational systems. Type 1A learners are those who already have adequate or high levels of DL skills *and* are interested in education for further personal fulfillment or learning that is beyond the typical scope of unstructured institutions, such as participant E2-06. Their interest in learning to code would be more appropriately handled in a self-taught/guided learning situation or in a structured institution's course.

Type 1A Learning Style
Unlike Type 1 learners who are a major target for DL skills educators, Type 1A learners should be treated with respect, but they can be generally considered outside of the target audience of most unstructured DL skills educational programming. These learners are primarily going to self-teach or should be referred to structured institutions. Type 1A is represented by Persona C, Jeffrey.

Type 2 - Ambivalent About Learning
Those individuals who are identified as Type 2 learners are those who see changes happening in the digital world and are unphased by them. Type 2 learners have been educated in transferable skills (such as being able to transfer skills that they learned from logging into and updating a social media profile to password management or using and updating an app-based budget manager) that make learning new skills easier. Type 2 learners may still encounter situations where they are unable to solve their own problems, but they have a toolkit of strategies to try before involving experts. Type 2 learners are able to 'just Google it' or attempt to utilize trial and error to solve their educational needs on their own. Some prefer to ask trusted sources first, but all Type 2 learners feel confident enough in their own knowledge that they can have the luxury of being ambivalent about the changes happening in the digital world. A Type 2 learner who is interacting with an educational opportunity requires a focus on transferable skills as they relate to the specific problem they are encountering, no matter how they prefer to learn. While this may seem counterintuitive, this type is where we should aim for most learners to arrive at the conclusion of any type of DL educational experience.

Type 2 Learning Styles
Type 2 learners are the most wide-ranging category of learners. Persona D (Rosemary) is an ambivalent learner who could use a brush up but would thrive in a more structured one-off workshop or course. Persona E (Jim) is representative of those Type 2 learners who need one-on-one, unstructured help with a particularly unusual challenge. While Persona F (Randal) also looks to unstructured educational moments but needs an educator to act less like an instructor and more a contemporary and sounding board.

Type 3 - Forced to Learn
Educators are often most concerned about facilitating DL learning for Type 3 learners so that they have the skills they need to live successful and independent lives in an increasingly digital world. Type 3 learners are those learners who describe the digital world as overwhelming or too hard. The strong negative emotion of a Type 3 learner is one of their key characteristics. They have the opposite reaction to the changing digital world from those in Type 1 or 1A despite both expressing strong emotional affect about the situation. A Type 3 learner does not necessarily possess low DL skills – a Type 3 learner could also be someone who is highly skilled but is unhappy about the integration of the digital world into the physical world.

Type 3 Learning Styles
Type 3 learners are identifiable through their generally negative response to needing digital literacy education. Persona G (Dan) is representative of a learner who feels left behind and forced to keep up but is unsuited to the long-term structured help of a workshop series or class. They need one-on-one attention in a potentially repetitive fashion. Those Type 3 learners who are average to highly skilled but against the march of technology are represented in Persona H (Laurie) and are best reached through structured educational experiences outside of the formal educational system.

Type 3A - Sustained Refusal to Learn
Type 3A, like Type 1A, is a type that is generally beyond the assistance of most DL skills educators. Those who fall into this category are either morally opposed to technology as a whole or have strong reactions against individual types of digital tasks or companies. The latter of these two possibilities presents an interesting challenge for educators, as it requires the ability to suggest alternatives to what are generally considered ubiquitous technologies or services. As the type of name, Sustained Refusal to Learn, suggests Type 3A people should be treated with respect but are unlikely to ever respond to efforts by educators unless there is a dramatic change in their personal circumstances.

Type 3A Learning Styles
Type 3A is another unique case, as we recommend that the bulk of an educator's effort be directed towards other learners. The example persona details out possible Type 3A learner (Colleen). A notable subpopulation that would fall into Type 3A would include learners in rural spaces whose religious beliefs might make them avoid technology entirely or limit their interactions with it [4]. It is unlikely that these learners will approach a DL skills educator with the intention of learning, though they may ask for assistance in getting something done in the digital world. DL skills educators can use these possible interactions as a way of gauging their potential to be transformed to s a Type 3 or possibly a Type 2 through conversation but do not pressure them.

5.2 Utilizing the Typology in Practice

Being able to quickly and accurately identify an individual's learner type is vital to connecting them with the appropriate learning experience that will enhance their DL skills. Based on our findings, we encourage the use of the typology and related personas to allow DL educators to prioritize potential learners in a way that limits their interaction with Types 1A and 3A learners and allows them to expend their efforts in moving Types 1 and 3 learners into the Type 2 category. The typology also allows DL educators to identify the types of programs that will be most effective for their learners. Being able to identify a learner who is ill-suited to structured educational experiences saves time and potentially mitigates in-session challenges that would impact not just the ill-suited learner, but also their fellow education seekers.

The typology and related learning styles showcase the vital nature of flexibility in the options of DL programming being offered. This study spanned the entire state of Maryland, including urban, suburban, and rural populations and communities all along the socioeconomic spectrum. We observed that each DL skills learner type is present in each community, and learning styles are similarly not fixed to specific demographics. We recommend that DL educators create a toolkit of structured and unstructured educational experiences that they can implement when they have identified the type of learner they are interacting with. Some of these experiences will be very short. For example, a Type 2 learner who presents similar to a Persona F might only need a quick conversation in which an educator reminds them of a particular digital tool or search engine that they can utilize to find the answers to their question. Other experiences may be longer or more involved, such as a recurring one-on-one session with an older Type 1 community member who has had negative experiences with structured education, or a structured workshop for a Type 3 learner on how to best utilize an online entertainment tool that has transferable skills to other aspects of the digital world.

From this study, the two vital recommendations are that all educators and organizations need to be flexible in their DL educational offerings and focus on transferable skills that allow all learners to have the luxury of being ambivalent about DL skills education.

5.3 Limitations

This study primarily focused on Marylanders and their own interaction with DL skills and access, however some participants were also digital literacy educators, such as librarians. Additionally, several of the interview sites were libraries or educational institutions. These factors may have contributed to an over-representation of the perspective of library patrons.

The interviews relied on self-reported data about participants' digital literacy practices and behaviors. We recognize that some participants may have been reluctant to share their experiences.

Additionally, as mentioned in the *Introduction* section, while we adopted a broad definition of DL for the framing of this study, we acknowledge that the definition of DL is time-, technology- and context-bound, and may not be inclusive of all the digital skills that were shared by the participants in this study. In addition to using this broad definition, our mapping of the absence and presence of DL education and learning styles relied on our own interpretations and previous DL education that were discussed in the *Literature Review* section. Through an iterative coding process that allowed each of the authors to check and verify coded transcripts, we attempted to minimize any inaccurate or privileged interpretations.

Finally, when conducting the interviews, we specifically did not collect identifying information from participants beyond that required for the consent forms (age). In many cases, participants volunteered information about themselves and their backgrounds when responding to questions; however, due to the sensitive nature of the research and the population, we determined that directly asking them for demographic information might make participants uncomfortable and less willing to share their learning approaches and challenges with us. Instead, we use demographic data for the communities around each institution (Table 1) as a proxy for our participants' demographic info. While this provides a less rigorous accounting of the specific background of each participant, we believe this choice yields a richer dataset. Furthermore, by using local institutions as host sites, we could ensure that the majority of the participants lived in the neighborhood. We also believe that partnering with these trusted institutions who knew our study's research goals yielded participants who were well-positioned to contribute to this study.

6   Conclusion

In this paper, we presented the findings of a statewide interview study with the aim of understanding what motivates Marylanders to learn DL skills and how they are learning DL skills. The findings were used to create a typology of learners that educators can use to identify what type of learning experience is best suited for their learners. Finding the right match between the learner type and learning experiences is crucial, and our data corpus and analysis provide a first look into how such connections can be built and used by DL educators. The vital recommendations for educators are the need for flexibility in their DL educational offerings and experiences, and that DL skills education needs to focus on fostering the luxury of ambivalence by prioritizing transferable skills that allow learners to be self-sufficient in their future. As we mentioned in the *Introduction* section, this study will inform the development of a statewide DL curriculum and resources repository called *Marylanders Online*, hence we will begin curating and developing resources that incorporate these recommendations that DL educators can use with all learner types that we found in this study.

Acknowledgements. Funding for this project was provided by the State of Maryland with the American Rescue Plan (ARP) - State and Local Fiscal Recovery Fund (SLFRF).

References

1. About | UME Digital Literacy (n.d.). https://marylandersonline.umd.edu/about. Accessed 16 Aug 2023
2. American Library Association (2022). Leverage Libraries to Achieve Digital Equity for All
3. Barzilai-Nahon, K.: Gaps and bits: conceptualizing measurements for digital divide/s. Inf. Soc. **22**(5), 269–278 (2006). https://doi.org/10.1080/01972240600903953
4. Ems, L.: How the Amish Use Technology. WIRED, 7 June 2022. https://www.wired.com/story/virtually-amish-hacking-innovation/?utm_source=pocket-newtab
5. Garfan, S., et al.: Telehealth utilization during the Covid-19 pandemic: a systematic review. Comput. Biol. Med. **138**, 104878 (2021). https://doi.org/10.1016/j.compbiomed.2021.104878
6. Horrigan, J.B.: Disconnected in Maryland (The Abell Report). The Abell Foundation (2021). https://abell.org/publications/disconnected-maryland
7. Lincoln, Y.S., Guba, E.G.: Naturalistic inquiry (Nachdr.). Sage Publications (1985)
8. Myers, C.R.: Using telehealth to remediate rural mental health and healthcare disparities. Issues Ment. Health Nurs. **40**(3), 233–239 (2019). https://doi.org/10.1080/01612840.2018.1499157
9. Public Library Association. 2020 Public Library Technology Survey Summary Report (2021)
10. Rubin, A.T.: Rocking Qualitative Social Science: An Irreverent Guide to Rigorous Research. Stanford University Press (2021)
11. Scorse, Y.: NDIA Community Defines "Digital Inclusion Ecosystem." National Digital Inclusion Alliance, 27 August 2021. https://www.digitalinclusion.org/blog/2021/08/27/ndia-community-defines-digital-inclusion-ecosystem/
12. Siefer, A., Callahan, B., Balboa, P. (n.d.). The Digital Inclusion Startup Manual. https://startup.digitalinclusion.org/index.html. Accessed 12 Sept 2023
13. Thompson, K. M., Jaeger, P. T., Taylor, N. G., Subramaniam, M., & Bertot, J. C. (2014). Digital literacy and digital inclusion: Information policy and the public library. Rowman & Littlefield Publishers

14. Vogels, E.A.: Digital divide persists even as Americans with lower incomes make gains in tech adoption. Pew Research Center (2021). https://www.pewresearch.org/short-reads/2021/06/22/digital-divide-persists-even-as-americans-with-lower-incomes-make-gains-in-tech-adoption/
15. Vogels, E.A.: Some digital divides persist between rural, urban, and suburban America. Pew Research Center (2021b). https://www.pewresearch.org/short-reads/2021/08/19/some-digital-divides-persist-between-rural-urban-and-suburban-america/
16. Vollbrecht, H., Arora, V., Otero, S., Carey, K., Meltzer, D., Press, V.G.: Evaluating the need to address digital literacy among hospitalized patients: cross-sectional observational study. J. Med. Internet Res. **22**(6), e17519 (2020). https://doi.org/10.2196/17519

"Inclusion We Stand, Divide We Fall": Digital Inclusion from Different Disciplines for Scientific Collaborations

Wei Feng[ID], Lihong Zhou[(✉)][ID], and Qinggong Shi[ID]

School of Information Management, Wuhan University, Wuhan 430072, China
{fengwei211,l.zhou}@whu.edu.cn, freesqg@163.com

Abstract. Digital inclusion research requires interdisciplinary collaboration to achieve a comprehensive understanding and develop effective strategies. This paper highlights the importance of interdisciplinary collaboration in digital inclusion research and provides a framework for understanding the contributions of different disciplines, using Library and Information Science, Computer Science, and Economics as examples. Specifically, it analyzes the relationship between these disciplines and digital inclusion, research topics related to digital inclusion, and research paradigms for studying digital inclusion. To address the three levels of the digital divide, the paper proposes an "Access - Capability - Outcome" three-layer relationship model to explain the functions of different disciplines in digital inclusion research. Additionally, two paths are proposed to promote integration and collaboration across different disciplines: the "inclusion technology for human" (technology-centered) path and the "inclusion of human in technology" (human-centered) path.

Keywords: Digital Inclusion · Digital Divide · Library and Information Science · Computer Science · science and Inclusion

1 Introduction

Digital technology can be not only a "facilitator" but also a "divider" of social inclusion [1]. The ubiquitous utilization of the Internet, personal computer, and mobile phones has brought the digital divide to the forefront since the 1990s [2–4]. This divide has been existing and evolving ever since between developing and developed countries [5, 6], urban and rural areas [6, 7], different age groups [8–10], and different income groups [11, 12]. Since 2020, the digital divide has been further accentuated as the COVID-19 pandemic spreads globally [13, 14]. As a consequence of the COVID-19 pandemic, the expanding prevalence of digital technology has delivered substantial convenience and benefits to individuals' daily lives due to the need for social distance, while simultaneously exacerbating the pre-existing digital divide and social inequality for certain populations lacking equal access to these technologies [15–17].

The original version of the chapter has been revised. A correction to this chapter can be found at https://doi.org/10.1007/978-3-031-57850-2_33

© The Author(s), under exclusive license to Springer Nature Switzerland AG 2024, corrected publication 2024
I. Sserwanga et al. (Eds.): iConference 2024, LNCS 14596, pp. 398–409, 2024.
https://doi.org/10.1007/978-3-031-57850-2_30

To bridge the digital divide, digital inclusion, as a form of social inclusion [1, 18], has received significant attention since around the 2000s [4] and developed as one of the primary global policy priorities [19]. Digital inclusion is defined by the United Nations as "equitable, meaningful, and safe access to use, lead, and design of digital technologies, services, and associated opportunities for everyone, everywhere" [20], while the National Digital Inclusion Alliance defines it as "the activities necessary to ensure that all individuals and communities, including the most disadvantaged, have access to and use of Information and Communication Technologies (ICTs)" [21]. Despite of the lack of a unified definition due to its complexity and diversity [22], digital inclusion can not only alleviate the adverse effects of the pandemic but also establish a more equitable and interconnected society.

National governments and international organizations have acknowledged the significance of digital inclusion and taken various measures to ensure that all individuals can partake in the digital society and reap the benefits of digital technology. For example, the International Federation of Library Associations and Institutions (IFLA) launched the "Library Pledge for Digital Inclusion" to promote internet access for communities to relevant digital content and services [23]. In China, "accelerating the construction of ICTs and assisting the elderly and the disabled in sharing a digital life" is an explicit requirement outlined by the Chinese government in the "14th Five-Year Plan for National Economic and Social Development and the Long-Range Objectives Through the Year 2035" [24]. Significant efforts from different shareholders like public institutions, private companies, and social associations have been put into practice to improve digital inclusion in China [25–27].

2 Problem Statement

Digital inclusion issues are complex and involve multiple layers, crossing economic, social, and cultural boundaries [28]. Scholars from various disciplines have studied digital inclusion, shedding light on various aspects of digital inclusion from the research paradigm of their respective disciplines. For example, computer scientists are primarily concerned with improving ICTs to make people's lives more digital [29–32], while economists tend to analyze the benefits of digital inclusion from a cost-benefit perspective [33–35]. The interdisciplinary nature of digital inclusion problems highlights the need for collaboration between different fields to achieve a more comprehensive understanding and to develop effective strategies [36–38].

Nevertheless, scanty research is claimed to explore similarities and differences in digital inclusion across disciplines or to propose strategies to integrate the efforts from different disciplines. Up to now, far too little attention has been paid to establishing a semantic framework between these disciplines. To address the above identified knowledge gaps, this paper therefore raises the following research questions:

RQ1: What do prior studies from different disciplines say about digital inclusion?

RQ2: What is the relationship between different disciplines studying digital inclusion?

RQ3: What strategies can be developed to enable the collaboration of digital inclusion studies across different disciplines?

3 Research Method

3.1 Literature Review

The literature review was conducted in two phases. Firstly, a comprehensive examination of digital inclusion was performed using the Chinese full-text database CNKI. However, this search yielded few Chinese articles, with the majority not being research papers. The initial review indicated that digital inclusion is an interdisciplinary field, with Library and Information Science (LIS), Computer Science (CS), and Economics being the most prominent disciplines due to their shared interest in advancing digital inclusion and their reliance on information resources and digital technologies. LIS primarily focuses on information organization, retrieval, and dissemination, while CS is dedicated to the design, development, and implementation of digital technologies, and Economics examines the production, distribution, and consumption of digital goods and services. Consequently, the research team proceeded with a second-stage review using English papers from Web of Science and Scopus, focusing on these three disciplines to address the research questions.

After meticulous screening, a total of 81 papers were selected for analysis, including 33 in LIS, 24 in CS, and 24 in Economics[1]. Due to length constraints, only a subset of articles was discussed in this paper. To gain a more comprehensive understanding of the relationship between these disciplines and digital inclusion, additional articles were included and analyzed in the research findings section.

3.2 Case Study

To broaden the scope of the literature review and ensure its relevance, this paper incorporates case studies based on the outcomes of the literature analysis to address any limitations. Despite the scarcity of Chinese papers on digital inclusion, China has made significant strides in practical digital inclusion initiatives. Therefore, within each discipline, one case study from China was selected to illustrate how that particular discipline contributes to digital inclusion.

4 Research Findings

4.1 Digital Inclusion in Library and Information Science (LIS)

The study of digital inclusion is a central expression of both the humanistic tradition and technical tradition of LIS. Since its inception as a scientific discipline in the early 19th century, LIS has held the humanistic tradition as the dominant ideology in academic research, professional education, and social practice [39–41]. The issue of information inequality among marginalized and vulnerable groups has always been a research focus in LIS [42–45]. The mission of LIS is to enhance the information literacy of these groups, ensure their effective access to and retrieval of information, and promote the efficient

---

[1] The complete list of references is available at https://github.com/fengwei211/iConference2024 ReferenceList/blob/main/iConference2024ReferenceList.pdf.

use of information [46]. Technical tradition is another common ground between LIS and digital inclusion [41]. LIS plays a crucial role in promoting digital inclusion by providing access to information and technology resources, as well as by teaching digital literacy skills. Libraries and other information institutions can serve as community hubs for technology training and access [47].

Concerns about digital inclusion in the field of LIS have increased in the years following COVID-19 [14]. In the decades following, LIS professionals put concerted efforts towards promoting digital inclusion. One of the first promoters to achieve digital inclusion is the public library [48–50]. Governments at almost all levels are relying on public libraries to ensure digital inclusion by providing public access to technologies [50]. In particular, public libraries in rural areas play a critical role predominantly through providing technological access and skills development in narrowing the urban-rural digital divide [51–54]. As a representative of vulnerable groups in the information society, the elderly are the focus of LIS mainly because they have an obvious need for health information [55, 56].

The Chinese government has carried out the Rural Library Project since 2007. As of June 2023, the number of rural internet users in China has reached 301 million, accounting for 27.9% of the total number of internet users, while the internet penetration rate in rural areas is 60.5% [57]. The digitalization of rural libraries has become an inevitable trend to accommodate the development of rural areas [58]. This trend has expedited the timely acquisition of epidemic prevention knowledge and news information, making contributions to epidemic prevention in rural regions [59].

4.2 Digital Inclusion in Computer Science (CS)

Computer sciences (CS) produce the bulk of the work in digital inclusion [15]. As a symbol and pusher of the development of digital technology, CS has a mutual cause-consequence relationship with the digital divide and digital inclusion. On the one hand, it is a discipline that provides technical support (e.g. ICTs, Internet infrastructure, etc.) for digital inclusion. For example, artificial intelligence (AI) facilitates the realization of digital financial inclusion, enabling the participation of marginalized and vulnerable groups in the mainstream financial market [60]. On the other hand, CS also serves as motivation for the digital divide as the initial and first-level digital divide is the inequality of access to digital technology [61]. In 2019, HUAWEI, a Chinese tech giant, launched TECH4ALL - an initiative aimed at promoting digital inclusion through education, environment, health, and balanced development. Through this initiative, HUAWEI is investing heavily in digital technologies and platforms such as connectivity, cloud computing, AI, and terminals to enable more innovative applications in digital inclusion [26, 62].

Algorithms, as a core component of CS, were expected to break down long-standing social inequalities and to create a new kind of social justice, namely algorithmic justice [63]. Such expectations have logically led to more algorithms being used to assist humans in the distribution of social goods and automated decision-making [64], such as healthcare services [65], employment opportunities [66], urban public services [67], etc. However, algorithmic systems have been affecting people's lives in fundamental, but unequal, ways [68]. As a critical component of the cultures of the Internet, which is formed by people's attitudes and beliefs toward the Internet, algorithms not only have roots in but also are still shaping digital divides [69]. The new digital inequality spawned by algorithms is concentrated on expanding the scope of the digitally poor and the dimensions of the digital divide, creating the algorithmic divide [70, 71].

4.3 Digital Inclusion in Economics

Digital inclusion enables people to participate in the digital economy, access information, and connect with others. Akubue (2000) defines digital inclusion initiatives as technology that is suitable for the social and economic conditions of the geographic area in which it is to be applied [72]. Ensuring ICT access for rural communities in developing countries can lead to economic benefits [73]. Conversely, people may face economic exclusion if they lack the necessary skills to use the Internet [74]. This may occur due to the capitalist economic model and public policy that generate and sustain poverty [75]. Economic research helps to identify the factors that promote or hinder digital inclusion and provides insights into how digital technologies can be used to drive economic growth.

Most studies about digital inclusion in economics also concern marginalized and vulnerable groups, such as poor individuals, rural areas, and developing countries. Specifically, they are concerned about whether digital inclusion in economics can narrow urban-rural residents' income gap [76–78] and whether poorer-income households will obtain higher wages [79, 80]. Economists typically employ several research paradigms to study digital inclusion, such as empirical analysis, theoretical analysis, and experimental research. The empirical analysis involves collecting and analyzing large amounts of data to investigate the current state of digital inclusion and its determinants with various digital inclusion indices, like the Digital Opportunity Index (DOI), Human Development Index (HDI), ICT Opportunity Index (IOI) [81–83], etc. Constructing economic models to study the mechanisms and impacts of digital inclusion is the way that economists carry out theoretical research [84, 85]. Some economists try to conduct experiments to test the efficacy and effects of digital inclusion policies [86].

Digital financial inclusion is closely related to but different from digital inclusion. It refers to the utilization of digital technologies to provide formal financial services, like digital transactional platforms, devices, and retail agents, tailored to the needs of financially excluded and underserved populations [87]. Digital financial inclusion is considered the intersection of financial inclusion and social inclusion [88]. Digital inclusion is a prerequisite for achieving digital financial inclusion, as a lack of digital inclusion is attributed to low levels of digital financial inclusion [88, 89]. Digital inclusive finance in China significantly reduces relative poverty in households, with higher poverty reduction effects observed in the Yangtze River Delta region compared to the central and western regions. This is due to the digital divide in the central and western regions inhibiting the poverty reduction effect of digital inclusive finance [90].

5   Discussion

5.1   Relationship Between Different Disciplines

The study of digital inclusion is not an independent pursuit within each discipline, but rather an interconnected web of research. The relationships between the various fields form the framework for the entire research landscape. Each discipline brings a unique perspective and set of tools to the table, allowing for a more comprehensive understanding of the complex issues surrounding digital inclusion. In response to the three levels of the digital divide [3, 61, 91] and considering the characteristics of different disciplines approaching digital inclusion, this paper conceptualizes the following model (see Fig. 1) to explain the relationship among different disciplines related to digital inclusion.

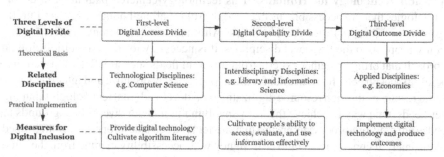

Fig. 1. "Access-Capability-Outcome" Three-Layer Relationship Model among Different Disciplines.

As shown in Fig. 1, the disciplines (i.e. CS) responding to the first-level are both the instigators and remedies of the digital divide, serving as a prerequisite for digital inclusion. Acting as the intermediary between the first-level and the third-level, some interdisciplinary fields (i.e. LIS) corresponding to the second-level address ways to enhance individuals' capability in digital societies. Disciplines aligned with the third-level (i.e. Economics) are linked to the implementation of digital technologies and are the byproducts of digital inclusion initiatives. These disciplines fulfill distinct roles in the research and practice of digital inclusion with mutual coordination.

It is worth noting that each discipline may not belong to a single level, they may belong to two or even three levels at the same time due to the interdisciplinary nature of the discipline. For example, LIS and CS have an overlap, and CS can also be considered an interdisciplinary field. LIS can also be an applied discipline that considers implementing digital technologies for digital literacy and inclusion. To cultivate digital inclusion, interdisciplinary strategies should be established by recognizing the interrelationships among different fields.

5.2 Two Paths to Promote Integration and Collaborations Across Different Disciplines

According to Sect. 3, there is a consensus that digital inclusion revolves around two core concepts, namely human and technology. The integration of these two concepts is crucial to ensure that individuals from all socio-economic backgrounds have access to the digital world. Digital inclusion is not only about including technology for human (technology-centered path) but also about including human in technology (human-centered path). The former path focuses on enhancing technology's positive impact and reducing negative effects on humans, while the latter explores rational technology use and seeks the improvement of the human ability to adapt to technology. Based on the above two paths, this paper proposes strategies to promote collaboration and integration across disciplines.

Inclusion Technology for Humans. This technology-centered path aims to develop technologies that are accessible, usable, and useful for all individuals and communities, regardless of their abilities or disabilities. Although the technology-centered path is mainly adaptive to the first-level disciplines, it is necessary to adopt a multidisciplinary approach that brings together experts from different fields such as CS, LIS, psychology, sociology, design, etc. It is essential for them to effectively organize and integrate various digital resources through resource digitization and develop digital technologies that meet user needs. One way to achieve this is by involving users with diverse backgrounds and needs in the design process to ensure that the technologies developed meet their needs. Additionally, technologies should be designed with accessibility in mind from the outset, rather than as an afterthought. This can be accomplished through the use of universal design principles that ensure that technologies are usable by the widest possible range of users.

Inclusion of Humans in Technology. This human-centered path, mainly for the second-level and the third-level of digital inclusion, aims to enhance human capabilities and promote well-being. This path places the needs and experiences of humans at the center of technological development. At the second level, individuals must be equipped with the necessary skills and abilities to use digital technologies and products. Thus, we propose that public agencies and institutions actively provide support services and user education to ensure that people can remain proactive in the face of technological change. At the third level, it is crucial to ensure that all individuals have access to and can use digital resources when applying digital technologies. Easy-to-use technologies should be accessible to all. It is also important to consider the ethical implications of technology, particularly with regard to issues such as privacy, security, and data protection.

6 Conclusion

This paper analyzes how different disciplines approach the study of digital inclusion and proposes a theoretical model for understanding the relationship between these disciplines. Additionally, we suggest strategies to promote collaboration across different disciplines in the field of digital inclusion. In the realm of digital inclusion, the "divide" is not only the gap between humans and technology but also exists between different disciplines that study digital inclusion. Thus, "inclusion" is more of an integration of disciplines related to digital inclusion. Only through interdisciplinary collaboration can digital inclusion truly benefit humanity. Due to the authors' professional skills restrictions, this paper only discusses digital inclusion studies from LIS, CS, and Economics. We encourage readers to explore digital inclusion studies within their disciplinary contexts, develop comprehensive theoretical frameworks, and provide practical strategies for collaboration.

Acknowledgement. This work was supported by the National Key Research and Development Program of China [Grant Number: 2021YFF0900400].

References

1. Nguyen, A.: Digital inclusion. In: Liamputtong, P. (ed.) Handbook of Social Inclusion: Research and Practices in Health and Social Sciences, pp. 265–279. Springer, Cham (2022). https://doi.org/10.1007/978-3-030-89594-5_14
2. Eastin, M.S., Cicchirillo, V., Mabry, A.: Extending the digital divide conversation: examining the knowledge gap through media expectancies. J. Broadcast. Electron. Media **59**, 416–437 (2015). https://doi.org/10.1080/08838151.2015.1054994
3. Scheerder, A., van Deursen, A., van Dijk, J.: Determinants of Internet skills, uses and outcomes. A systematic review of the second- and third-level digital divide. Telematics Inf. **34**, 1607–1624 (2017). https://doi.org/10.1016/j.tele.2017.07.007
4. Sharp, M.: Revisiting digital inclusion: a survey of theory, measurement, and recent research. Digital Pathways at Oxford (2022). https://doi.org/10.35489/BSG-DP-WP_2022/04
5. Chen, W., Wellman, B.: The global digital divide - within and between countries. IT Soc. **1**, 39–45 (2004)
6. Cohen, E.B.: Navigating Information Challenges. Informing Science (2011)
7. Fong, M.W.L.: Digital divide between urban and rural regions in China. Electron. J. Inf. Syst. Dev. Count. **36**, 1–12 (2009). https://doi.org/10.1002/j.1681-4835.2009.tb00253.x
8. Hwang, H., Nam, S.-J.: The digital divide experienced by older consumers in smart environments. Int. J. Consum. Stud. **41**, 501–508 (2017). https://doi.org/10.1111/ijcs.12358
9. Livingstone, S., Helsper, E.: Gradations in digital inclusion: children, young people, and the digital divide. New Media Soc. **9**, 671–696 (2007). https://doi.org/10.1177/1461444807080335
10. Menéndez Álvarez-Dardet, S., Lorence Lara, B., Pérez-Padilla, J.: Older adults and ICT adoption: analysis of the use and attitudes toward computers in elderly Spanish people. Comput. Hum. Behav. **110**, 106377 (2020). https://doi.org/10.1016/j.chb.2020.106377
11. Elena-Bucea, A., Cruz-Jesus, F., Oliveira, T., Coelho, P.S.: Assessing the role of age, education, gender, and income on the digital divide: evidence for the European Union. Inf. Syst. Front. **23**, 1007–1021 (2021). https://doi.org/10.1007/s10796-020-10012-9
12. Tewathia, N., Kamath, A., Ilavarasan, P.V.: Social inequalities, fundamental inequities, and recurring of the digital divide: insights from India. Technol. Soc. **61**, 101251 (2020). https://doi.org/10.1016/j.techsoc.2020.101251
13. International Telecommunication Union: The State of Broadband 2020: Tackling Digital Inequalities - A Decade for Action (2020)
14. Casselden, B.: Not like riding a bike: How public libraries facilitate older people's digital inclusion during the Covid-19 pandemic. J. Librarianship Inf. Sci. 09610006221101898 (2022). https://doi.org/10.1177/09610006221101898

15. Campbell-Meier, J., Sylvester, A., Goulding, A.: Indigenous digital inclusion: Interconnections and comparisons. Critical Librarianship 301–316 (2020)
16. Nguyen, M.H., Hargittai, E., Marler, W.: Digital inequality in communication during a time of physical distancing: the case of COVID-19. Comput. Hum. Beh. **120** (2021). https://doi.org/10.1016/j.chb.2021.106717
17. Samms, G.: As Cities Face COVID-19, The Digital Divide Becomes More Acute. https://www.forbes.com/sites/pikeresearch/2020/04/02/as-cities-face-covid-19-the-digital-divide-becomes-more-acute/. Accessed 16 Apr 2023
18. Reisdorf, B., Rhinesmith, C.: Digital inclusion as a core component of social inclusion. Soc. Inclusion **8**, 132–137 (2020). https://doi.org/10.17645/si.v8i2.3184
19. World Bank: World Development Report 2016: Digital Dividends., Washington DC (2016)
20. The United Nations: Definition of Digital Inclusion (2015)
21. National Digital Inclusion Alliance: Digital Inclusion Definition. https://www.digitalinclusion.org/definitions/. Accessed 15 Sept 2023
22. Borg, K., Smith, L.: Digital inclusion and online behaviour: five typologies of Australian internet users. Beh. Inf. Technol. **37**, 367–380 (2018). https://doi.org/10.1080/0144929X.2018.1436593
23. IFLA: Library Pledge for Digital Inclusion. https://www.ifla.org/publications/library-pledge-for-digital-inclusion/. Accessed 15 Apr 2023
24. Chinese Government: 14th Five-Year Plan for National Economic and Social Development and the Long-Range Objectives Through the Year 2035. http://www.gov.cn/xinwen/2021-03/13/content_5592681.htm. Accessed 26 Feb 2023
25. Xie, J.: A study of commercial banks bridging the digital divide in payment field--Take bank A as an example (2023). https://kns.cnki.net/kcms2/article/abstract?v=3uoqIhG8C475KOm_zrgu4sq25HxUBNNTmIbFx6y0bOQ0cH_CuEtpsM9oafKoeTLbftW8rS4B-OccOL3vyKjezNvRPTUJm9iV&uniplatform=NZKPT. https://doi.org/10.27283/d.cnki.gsxcc.2023.000603
26. Dang, B.: Huawei TECH4ALL makes the digital world more equal and sustainable (2023). https://doi.org/10.28806/n.cnki.ntxcy.2023.000208
27. Chen Y., Chen J.: Digital Inclusion Service of Public Libraries in China: Underlying Logic, Practical Status Quo, and Development Path. Library Development. 1–8
28. Helsper, E.: Digital inclusion: an analysis of social disadvantage and the information society. Department for Communities and Local Government, London, UK (2008)
29. Adam, I.O., Dzang Alhassan, M.: Bridging the global digital divide through digital inclusion: the role of ICT access and ICT use. Transforming Gov.- People Process Policy **15**, 580–596 (2021). https://doi.org/10.1108/TG-06-2020-0114
30. Adkins, D., Sandy, H.M.: Information behavior and ICT use of Latina immigrants to the US Midwest. Inf. Process. Manage. 57 (2020). https://doi.org/10.1016/j.ipm.2019.102072
31. Alhassan, M.D., Adam, I.O.: The effects of digital inclusion and ICT access on the quality of life: a global perspective. Technol. Soc. **64**, 101511 (2021). https://doi.org/10.1016/j.techsoc.2020.101511
32. Ali, M.A., Alam, K., Taylor, B., Rafiq, S.: Does digital inclusion affect quality of life? Evidence from Australian household panel data. TELEmatics and Informatics **51** (2020). https://doi.org/10.1016/j.tele.2020.101405
33. Ahmad, M., Majeed, A., Khan, M.A., Sohaib, M., Shehzad, K.: Digital financial inclusion and economic growth: provincial data analysis of China. China Econ. J. **14**, 291–310 (2021). https://doi.org/10.1080/17538963.2021.1882064
34. Khera, P., Ng, S., Ogawa, S., Sahay, R.: Measuring digital financial inclusion in emerging market and developing economies: a new index. Asian Econ. Policy Rev. **17**, 213–230 (2022). https://doi.org/10.1111/aepr.12377

35. Shen, Y., Hueng, C.J., Hu, W.: Measurement and spillover effect of digital financial inclusion: a cross-country analysis. Appl. Econ. Lett. **28**, 1738–1743 (2021). https://doi.org/10.1080/13504851.2020.1853663

36. Armenta, A., Serrano, A., Cabrera, M., Conte, R.: The new digital divide: the confluence of broadband penetration, sustainable development, technology adoption and community participation. Inf. Technol. Dev. **18**, 345–353 (2012). https://doi.org/10.1080/02681102.2011.625925

37. Bach, A.J., Wolfson, T., Crowell, J.K.: Poverty, literacy, and social transformation: an interdisciplinary exploration of the digital divide. J. Media Literacy Educ. **10**, 22–41 (2018). https://doi.org/10.23860/jmle-2018-10-1-2

38. Martínez-Bravo, M.-C., Sádaba-Chalezquer, C., Serrano-Puche, J.: Fifty years of digital literacy studies: a meta-research for interdisciplinary and conceptual convergence. Profesional de la información **29** (2020). https://doi.org/10.3145/epi.2020.jul.28

39. Ford, E.: Tell me your story: narrative inquiry in LIS research. C&RL **81** (2020). https://doi.org/10.5860/crl.81.2.235

40. Koltay, T.: Library and information science and the digital humanities: perceived and real strengths and weaknesses. J. Doc. **72**, 781–792 (2016). https://doi.org/10.1108/JDOC-01-2016-0008

41. Song, Y., Wei, K., Yang, S., Shu, F., Qiu, J.: Analysis on the research progress of library and information science since the new century. Library Hi Tech. ahead-of-print (2020). https://doi.org/10.1108/LHT-06-2020-0126

42. Cushing, A.L., Kerrigan, P.: Personal information management burden: a framework for describing nonwork personal information management in the context of inequality. J. Am. Soc. Inf. Sci. **73**, 1543–1558 (2022). https://doi.org/10.1002/asi.24692

43. Gibson, A.N., Hughes-Hassell, S.: We will not be silent: amplifying marginalized voices in LIS education and research. Libr. Q. **87**, 317–329 (2017). https://doi.org/10.1086/693488

44. Gibson, A.N., Martin, J.D., III.: Re-situating information poverty: information marginalization and parents of individuals with disabilities. J. Am. Soc. Inf. Sci. **70**, 476–487 (2019). https://doi.org/10.1002/asi.24128

45. Mathiesen, K.: Informational justice: A conceptual framework for social justice in library and information services. Libr. Trends **64**, 198–225 (2015). https://doi.org/10.1353/lib.2015.0044

46. Jardine, F.M., Zerhusen, E.K.: Charting the course of equity and inclusion in LIS through iDiversity. Libr. Q. **85**, 185–192 (2015). https://doi.org/10.1086/680156

47. Hagen-McIntosh, J.: Information and Data Literacy: The Role of the Library. CRC Press (2016)

48. Bertot, J.C.: Building digitally inclusive communities: the roles of public libraries in digital inclusion and development (2016). https://doi.org/10.1145/2910019.2910082

49. Stevenson, S.A., Domsy, C.: Redeploying public librarians to the front-lines: prioritizing digital inclusion. Libr. Rev. **65**, 370–385 (2016). https://doi.org/10.1108/LR-02-2016-0015

50. Jaeger, P.T., Bertot, J.C., Thompson, K.M., Katz, S.M., DeCoster, E.J.: The intersection of public policy and public access: digital divides, digital literacy, digital inclusion, and public libraries. Public Lib. Quart. **31**, 1–20 (2012). https://doi.org/10.1080/01616846.2012.654728

51. Real, B., Bertot, J.C., Jaeger, P.T.: Rural public libraries and digital inclusion: issues and challenges. Inf. Technol. Libr. **33**, 6–24 (2014). https://doi.org/10.6017/ital.v33i1.5141

52. Strover, S., Whitacre, B., Rhinesmith, C., Schrubbe, A.: The digital inclusion role of rural libraries: social inequalities through space and place. Media Cult. Soc. **42**, 242–259 (2020). https://doi.org/10.1177/0163443719853504

53. Wagg, S., Simeonova, B.: A policy-level perspective to tackle rural digital inclusion. Inf. Technol. People **35**, 1884–1911 (2022). https://doi.org/10.1108/ITP-01-2020-0047

54. Bell, R., Goulding, A.: Mobile libraries and digital inclusion: a study from Aotearoa new Zealand. Public Library Quarterly. **42**, 1–20 (2023). https://doi.org/10.1080/01616846.2022.2029223

55. de Sales, M.B., Silveira, R.A., de Sales, A.B., de Cássia Guarezi, R.: Learning by peers: an alternative learning model for digital inclusion of elderly people. In: Tatnall, A. and Jones, A. (eds.) Education and Technology for a Better World. pp. 436–444. Springer, Heidelberg (2009). https://doi.org/10.1007/978-3-642-03115-1_46

56. Holcombe-James, I.: 'I'm fired up now!': digital cataloguing, community archives, and unintended opportunities for individual and archival digital inclusion. Arch. Sci. **22**, 521–538 (2022). https://doi.org/10.1007/s10502-021-09380-1

57. China Internet Network Information Center (CNNIC): The 52nd Statistical Report on Internet Development in China. https://www.cnnic.net.cn/n4/2023/0828/c88-10829.html. Accessed 18 Sept 2023

58. Lang, P.: A review of "accessibility" of public cultural service of digital farm library and its improvement path. Library Theory and Practice. 1–8 (ahead of print). https://doi.org/10.14064/j.cnki.issn1005-8214.20230605.001

59. Yu, Y., Zhao, L.: The value, dilemma, and approach of rural library construction under the background of rural revitalization. View on Publishing. 66–69 (2022). https://doi.org/10.16491/j.cnki.cn45-1216/g2.2022.15.012

60. Mhlanga, D.: Industry 4.0 in finance: the impact of artificial intelligence (AI) on digital financial inclusion. Int. J. Financ. Stud. **8**, 45 (2020). https://doi.org/10.3390/ijfs8030045

61. Wei, K.-K., Teo, H.-H., Chan, H.C., Tan, B.C.Y.: Conceptualizing and testing a social cognitive model of the digital divide. Inf. Syst. Res. **22**, 170–187 (2011). https://doi.org/10.1287/isre.1090.0273

62. Huawei: TECH4ALL for Digital Inclusion. https://www.huawei.com/cn/tech4all. Accessed 18 Sept 2023

63. Jia, S., Yan, H.: A systematic review of concept, philosophy foundation and impacts of algorithmic bias. J. Library Sci. China **48**, 57–76 (2022). https://doi.org/10.13530/j.cnki.jlis.2022051

64. Susskind, J.: Future Politics: Living Together in a World Transformed by Tech. Oxford University Press (2018)

65. Obermeyer, Z., Powers, B., Vogeli, C., Mullainathan, S.: Dissecting racial bias in an algorithm used to manage the health of populations. Science **366**, 447–453 (2019). https://doi.org/10.1126/science.aax2342

66. Lambrecht, A., Tucker, C.: Algorithmic bias? An empirical study of apparent gender-based discrimination in the display of STEM Career Ads. Manage. Sci. **65**, 2966–2981 (2019). https://doi.org/10.1287/mnsc.2018.3093

67. Kontokosta, C.E., Hong, B.: Bias in smart city governance: how socio-spatial disparities in 311 complaint behavior impact the fairness of data-driven decisions. Sustain. Cities Soc. **64**, 102503 (2021). https://doi.org/10.1016/j.scs.2020.102503

68. Gran, A.-B., Booth, P., Bucher, T.: To be or not to be algorithm aware: a question of a new digital divide? Inf. Commun. Soc. **24**, 1779–1796 (2021). https://doi.org/10.1080/1369118X.2020.1736124

69. Dutton, W.H., Reisdorf, B.C.: Cultural divides and digital inequalities: attitudes shaping Internet and social media divides. Inf. Commun. Soc. **22**, 18–38 (2019). https://doi.org/10.1080/1369118X.2017.1353640

70. Ragnedda, M.: Enhancing Digital Equity: Connecting the Digital Underclass. Springer Nature (2020)

71. Yu, P.K.: The algorithmic divide and equality in the age of artificial intelligence. Fla. L. Rev. **72**, 331 (2020)

72. Akubue, A.: Appropriate technology for socioeconomic development in third world countries. Electron. J. Technol. Stud. **26**, 33 (2000). https://doi.org/10.21061/jots.v26i1.a.6
73. Caspary, G., O'Connor, D.: Providing low-cost information technology access to rural communities in developing countries: what works? What pays? OECD. Paris (2003). https://doi.org/10.1787/675385036304
74. Newhagen, J.E., Bucy, E.P.: Routes to media access. In: Newhagen, J.E., Bucy, E.P. (eds.) Media Access: Social and Psychological Dimensions of New Technology Use. Psychology Press (2004)
75. Nemer, D.: From digital divide to digital inclusion and beyond. J. Commun. Inf. 11 (2015). https://doi.org/10.15353/joci.v11i1.2857
76. Ji, X., Wang, K., Xu, H., Li, M.: Has digital financial inclusion narrowed the urban-rural income gap: the role of entrepreneurship in China. Sustainability. **13**, 8292 (2021). https://doi.org/10.3390/su13158292
77. Shen, H., Luo, T., Gao, Z., Zhang, X., Zhang, W., Chuang, Y.-C.: Digital financial inclusion and the urban–rural income gap in China: empirical research based on the Theil index. Econ. Res.-Ekonomska Istraživanja. **0**, 1–25 (2022). https://doi.org/10.1080/1331677X.2022.2156575
78. Yu, N., Wang, Y.: Can digital inclusive finance narrow the Chinese urban–rural income gap? The perspective of the regional urban–rural income structure. Sustainability. **13**, 6427 (2021). https://doi.org/10.3390/su13116427
79. Gangadharan, S.P.: Digital inclusion and data profiling. First Monday. (2012). https://doi.org/10.5210/fm.v17i5.3821
80. Parsons, C., Hick, S.F.: Moving from the digital divide to digital inclusion. Currents: Scholarship in the Human Services 7 (2008)
81. International Telecommunication Union: From the Digital Divide to Digital Opportunities - Measuring Infostates for Development. https://www.itu.int/ITU-D/ict/publications/dd/summary.html. Accessed 19 Apr 2023
82. Kerras, H., Sánchez-Navarro, J.L., López-Becerra, E.I., de-Miguel Gómez, M.D.: The impact of the gender digital divide on sustainable development: Comparative analysis between the European Union and the Maghreb. Sustainability **12**, 3347 (2020). https://doi.org/10.3390/su12083347
83. Mutula, S.M.: Digital divide and economic development: case study of sub-Saharan Africa. Electron. Libr. **26**, 468–489 (2008). https://doi.org/10.1108/02640470810893738
84. Acemoglu, D., Autor, D.: Chapter 12 - Skills, tasks and technologies: implications for employment and earnings. In: Card, D., Ashenfelter, O. (eds.) Handbook of Labor Economics. pp. 1043–1171. Elsevier (2011). https://doi.org/10.1016/S0169-7218(11)02410-5
85. Piketty, T., Saez, E.: Inequality in the long run. Science **344**, 838–843 (2014). https://doi.org/10.1126/science.1251936
86. Aker, J.C., Mbiti, I.M.: Mobile phones and economic development in Africa. J. Econ. Perspect. **24**, 207–232 (2010). https://doi.org/10.1257/jep.24.3.207
87. World Bank: Digital Financial Inclusion. https://www.worldbank.org/en/topic/financialinclusion/publication/digital-financial-inclusion. Accessed 17 Apr 2023
88. Aziz, A., Naima, U.: Rethinking digital financial inclusion: evidence from Bangladesh. Technol. Soc. **64**, 101509 (2021). https://doi.org/10.1016/j.techsoc.2020.101509
89. Ozili, P.K.: Social inclusion and financial inclusion: international evidence. Int. J. Dev. Issues. **19**, 169–186 (2020). https://doi.org/10.1108/IJDI-07-2019-0122
90. Yang, Y., Sun, X.: Digital inclusive finance and urban relative poverty: empirical evidence from Yangtze river delta. In: World Economic Papers, pp. 19–35 (2022)
91. Ragnedda, M., Ruiu, M.: Social capital and the three levels of digital divide. Presented at the, Abingdon October 2 (2017)

Developing Library and Data Storytelling Toolkits: Scenarios and Personas

Kate McDowell$^{(\boxtimes)}$, Xinhui Hu, and Matthew Turk

School of Information Sciences, University of Illinois at Urbana Urbana-Champaign,
Champaign, IL, USA
kmcdowel@illinois.edu

Abstract. With the increasing datafication of all aspects of civic life and public resources, libraries will need better data tools in the future to communicate their impact. Based on the development of the interactive Data Storytelling Toolkit for Librarians (DSTL), this paper analyzes the results of a survey of librarians to understand their needs as users of an in-development data storytelling toolkit. This study explores two research questions: (1) What have developers needed to know so far for building this data storytelling toolkit for librarians? (2) What should developers of all kinds of library data apps know based on this survey? Thirty-nine respondents provided insights from a range of different kinds of libraries. Results include user scenarios and user personas that will aid in the development the DSTL and improve future development of related data-focused applications for librarians as users.

Keywords: Design · Data Storytelling · Libraries · Toolkit

1 Introduction

Libraries face uncertain futures amidst crises that range from public funding cuts to book banning, and so the need to advocate and argue for the mission of libraries has grown. Library data that demonstrates how mission translates to impact is important for the survival of libraries as institutions. This paper analyzes the results of a survey of self-identified librarians[1] to understand their needs for a data storytelling (DS) toolkit and to develop a conceptual model for future toolkit design in libraries. This research is a result of the Data Storytelling Toolkit for Librarians (DSTL) project, funded by the Institute of Museum and Library Services (IMLS). The DSTL is an in-development interactive online toolkit with guides for developing data stories by connecting evidence with classic library impact arguments, narrative strategies, and audience communication. It is built to be flexibly used by librarians, so that they may explore this guidance like a "choose your own adventure" book, with a set of optional paths based on their choices.

---

[1] The term "librarians" here is shorthand for both professional librarians and any library workers who work with library data, whether they hold a degree from an accredited American Library Association degree program or not.

I. Sserwanga et al. (Eds.): iConference 2024, LNCS 14596, pp. 410–420, 2024.
https://doi.org/10.1007/978-3-031-57850-2_31

This paper analyzes results of a survey of librarians' needs as DS users. Results include user scenarios and user personas will aid in the development of the DSTL. Lessons learned provide insights into designing for librarians as users. Finding could improve future development of DS-focused technologies for libraries.

The DSTL builds on prior library data projects that have supported more robust data infrastructure for public libraries since 2006.[2] Interest since the project launch has been overwhelming, with 680 registrants for the first DSTL open workshop in fall 2022, a forty-person design team from 26 US states, and presentations at seven conferences in 2023. Demand indicates that this work is timely and of interest. The DSTL aims to educate staff at libraries with any level of data expertise in data storytelling.

The responsibilities of librarians often include advocating for continued funding as non-profit governmental entities. They require special consideration when developing products for their use. The following questions guided the survey development and analysis:

- Who are future DSTL users and what are their interests in data and story?
- How much do librarian respondents know about data storytelling?
- What materials do they create to communicate library impact?
- What tools do they already use?
- What are their limitations as users?

This study explores two research questions: (RQ1) What have developers needed to know so far for building this data storytelling toolkit for librarians? (RQ2) What should developers understand about library users based on this survey? An online survey was distributed directly to library staff through social media and through professional librarian organizations. Thirty-nine respondents provided insights that led to the development of scenarios and personas. These design tools will aid in DSTL development and the development of future toolkits for librarians.

2   Research Background and Literature Review

Library data is any data collected by or about libraries. These data are typically used to demonstrate return on investment for taxpayers or funders in annual reports. However, they may include any data about libraries, such as comparisons to peer libraries and benchmarking against national library metrics and trends. Prior research has demonstrated that library staff struggle with fears of data, fear of story, and with having sufficient time, tools, and training to engage data storytelling effectively [1].

2.1   Data Storytelling

Data storytelling (DS) means any communication of data using narrative structures or strategies. [2] Data visualization is often a component of DS. Recent storytelling research

---

[2] Including outcome-based evaluation concepts and practices; PLA's Project Outcome; the Research Institute for Public Libraries (RIPL); Measures that Matter (MtM); and since fall 2022 Benchmark: Library Metrics and Trends, a joint initiative of PLA and the Association of College and Research Libraries (ACRL).

demonstrates the importance of theorizing information in terms of narrative structures, narrative experiences, and a framework for understanding how data relate to knowledge, information, and wisdom in storytelling [3]. Data stories are true stories told accurately and honestly, so that libraries document and communicate stories of impact that leaders and decision-makers can easily understand and retell.

2.2 Design and User Personas in Libraries

Using DS allows data to become meaningful and memorable stories, communicating library impact to all stakeholders. Stakeholders who need to know what libraries accomplish may be local community patrons, customers, or users. They may also be administrators, board or foundation members, or taxpayers. One study of elected stakeholders in Norway revealed limited understandings of what libraries provide beyond books and reading culture [4].

Personas are fictional representations of real people, based on true information about them. They are a convenient fiction for programmers, designers, and others who are tasked with understanding and building tools to meet information needs of users. Personas have occasionally been created to represent library users. Developing personas to represent patrons has implications for understanding users in, for example, academic libraries generally [5], for specialized users such as humanities scholars [6], and distance education library users [7]. One study leveraged service data to understand the interaction and intersection of types of library users, creating a graphic representation of needs and motivations [8]. Developing six user profiles similar to personas was part of a scenario-based process for re-designing physical entryways [9]. Personas have also been created to counter tendencies for historically underrepresented populations to be ignored or underserved [10].

Still, considering librarians and their needs as the basis of personas is unusual. A handful of studies have developed personas based on library work or related information professions. For example, rare books and cultural heritage professionals were the speculative basis for personas and archetypes representing them [11]. A study of librarians examined knowledge and use of social media for library services, developing four personas that characterized librarians' patterns [12].

2.3 Related Toolkits

Other projects have created toolkits to help advocate for libraries. The Get Ready Stay Ready community action toolkit is specifically designed to help libraries in difficult times, supported by a range of organizations, from libraries to publishers (https://www.getreadystayready.info/). The toolkit supports libraries as providers of unbiased service and institutions that fight censorship. It provides scripts for public speaking and writing along with other training materials for library advocates.

Similarly, the Association for Library Services to Children has responded to recent threats with an Intellectual Freedom Programming Toolkit (https://www.oif.ala.org/new-from-alsc-intellectual-freedom-programming-toolkit/). It contains templates to integrate freedom to read and related concepts into library programs and services, including sample programs, discussion questions, and activities about intellectual freedom.

Another recent study used interactive design to develop and implement a toolkit for librarians as educators. The research methods focused on the principles of Design-Based Implementation Research for a multi-year study of the iterative and collaborative development of the ConnectedLib Toolkit. Multiple phases of qualitative research elicited and refined "connected learning goals" for library programs and services [13].

These three resulting toolkits contain static templates. The DSTL is being designed to provide an interactive experience of choosing a path and receiving data story guidance. The emergence of adaptable toolkits like the DSTL is a newer phenomenon. Designing this and future data toolkits will require deeper understanding of library design needs.

3 Methods

A survey was distributed immediately after the DSTL launch webinar and publicized via social media and through professional library organizations for one month. The survey was created with Qualtrics, and it was piloted with testing by the advisory board for the project and with support from the Survey Research Group at the Center for Innovation in Teaching and Learning at the University of Illinois at Urbana Champaign. This human subjects protocol was also approved by the Institutional Review Board at the University of Illinois (#23158).

Data processing was both qualitative and quantitative for the thirty-nine responses from twelve US states. Qualitative data were independently coded by a group of five student researchers who each coded 100% of the content and shared their coding schemes. There was an 87% initial agreement rate. A senior researcher reviewed all the coding results, revised the coding scheme, and discussed the potential divergence with the coders until reached 100% agreement. Quantitative data were synthesized and visualized using the built-in Qualtrics tools. Respondents came from five types of libraries and a few other organizations focused on library data use (Table 1).

Table 1. Distribution of types of libraries represented by respondents

Library Type	Distribution
Community College Library	13.51%
Public Library	27.03%
Academic Library	32.43%
Private Library	8.11%
Other	18.92%

While space and confidentiality prohibit a comprehensive reporting of job titles, jobs included deans, directors, chairs, marketing specialists, instruction librarians, as well as data specialists at state and local levels. The survey aimed to capture participants' knowledge of and uses for DS in libraries, with sections on user demographics, skills, and needs.

4 Results

4.1 User Scenarios

Research Question (1) Asks: what have developers needed to know so far for building this data storytelling toolkit for librarians? The most important need has been to understand librarians' relationship to DS and existing DS tools. The survey asked how familiar they were with DS, and most respondents were slightly, moderately, or very familiar (not familiar 12.24%, slightly 24.49%, moderately 38.78%, very 20.41%, extremely 4.08%). They were also asked to define DS in 1–2 sentences. Qualitative analysis resulted in the following synthesis of those definitions, with agreement from all five coders:

- Telling stories using technology/visualization
- Making data understandable
- Conveying emotion
- Revealing data patterns, contexts, and insights
- Constructing narratives
- Making impact with story-based outreach
- Describing and justifying library work

To support building an effective DSTL, the survey also asked participants to describe how they use data to reach their audiences, and responses were in communication to users and stakeholders for demonstration of library impact. The survey asked when they had seen DS ("Have you seen data storytelling techniques used in any of the following?"), asking them to select from a range of library materials options or provide their own "other" examples (Table 2).

Table 2. Observed uses of DS techniques

Library Materials	Yes	No	Not sure
Annual report	56.76% (n = 21)	24.32% (n = 9)	18.92% (n = 7)
Website	56.76% (n = 21)	21.62% (n = 8)	21.62% (n = 8)
Library Brochures	43.24% (n = 16)	24.32% (n = 9)	32.43% (n = 12)
Events advertisement	30.56% (n = 11)	36.11% (n = 13)	33.33% (n = 12)
Other	26.32% (n = 5)	21.05% (n = 4)	52.63% (n = 10)

Uses were mostly in annual reports, websites, and brochures, with fewer uses for events or other forms of communication.

One goal of the DSTL is to save time for library workers. Based on these same use scenarios, the survey asked how much staff time the participants' libraries typically spend to create materials (Table 3).

Given the outcomes, it was clear that any data toolkit has potential to save users' time.

Table 3. Time required to create standard library communications materials.

Library Materials	A few hours	A few days	A few months	More time than that
Annual report	18.75% (n = 6)	46.88% (n = 15)	25.00% (n = 8)	9.38% (n = 3)
Website	15.63% (n = 5)	31.25% (n = 10)	25.00% (n = 8)	28.13% (n = 9)
Library Brochures	29.03% (n = 9)	41.94% (n = 13)	25.81% (n = 8)	3.23% (n = 1)
Events advertisement	45.16% (n = 14)	32.26% (n = 10)	19.35% (n = 6)	3.23% (n = 1)
Other	22.22% (n = 2)	33.33% (n = 3)	44.44% (n = 4)	0.00% (n = 0)

* Other = None, not my area, newsletter, instruction presentations

4.2   User Personas

Research question (2) asked: What should developers understand about librarian users based on this survey? In order to synthesize survey results into usable findings, the author team created user personas. These personas were based on a series of qualitative questions about interests and skills as well as one question about experience with data visualization tools. Personas were generated through a synthesis of responses to these questions, which were:

- How interested are you in applying data storytelling in your own library work at this time?
- What might be challenging about using data storytelling in your work? Please briefly describe the challenges below.
- In your library work, how important are each of these areas in communicating data stories to the public?
  - o Income or revenue; Material expenditures; Staff expenditures; Numbers of library locations; Collection size; Website visits and database use; Programs offered; Library cards/registered borrowers; Public computer use; Program attendance; Circulation)
- How much experience do you have with these data visualization tools?

Before presenting the two resulting personas, it is worth exploring the answer to the last question in some depth because of its implications for design of any form of technology for librarians as users. Tools were selected because data visualization is frequently part of DS (Table 4).

The majority of respondents were proficient with Excel. Approximately half of the respondents are acquainted with infographic and storyline tools (Infogram, Canva, or similar). These findings indicate that librarians are currently using few data visualization tools.

Synthesizing the responses to all questions reveals two major categories of users, hence two personas: storytelling experts and data experts.

Table 4. Familiarity with existing data and/or storytelling tools

Tools	Never heard of it or Heard it but never used	Tried to use for a couple of times	Somewhat proficient or Very proficient
Excel	10.82% (n = 4)	18.92% (n = 7)	72.97% (n = 27)
Infogram, Canva, or similar	37.84% (n = 14)	16.22% (n = 6)	37.84% (n = 14)
Python	75.67% (n = 28)	13.51% (n = 5)	10.81% (n = 4)
Tableau, Power BI, or similar	56.75% (n = 21)	13.51% (n = 5)	10.81% (n = 4)
Google Studio	75.67% (n = 28)	24.32% (n = 9)	5.41% (n = 2)
R Studio	83.79% (n = 31)	32.43% (n = 12)	2.70% (n = 1)

4.3 Personas

Persona 1: Storytelling Experts. As users, storytelling experts have strong storytelling and narrative skills, and they usually lack systematic training in data skills. They mostly have positive attitudes toward data-centered work, although some are averse to data, in concept and practice. Their data-related concerns are about lack of data literacy and possibilities of surveillance. They mostly have positive attitudes toward data storytelling, with concerns centered on learning skills and methodologies. Barriers to data storytelling for storytelling experts are lack of relevant skills (data); lack of time to learn skills, to collect data, and to clean data; and lack of data that is cleaned and formatted well for their use. They are concerned about and lack of data that aligns well with their intended stories. Sometimes these users also lack administrative support. Most of all, they need a toolkit that is convenient and easy to use. They also need tools that are tailored to the specific work of librarians. Ideally, they would like a toolkit that produces results that are ready for immediate use, and they are very concerned about potential information overload.

Persona 2: Data Experts. As users, data experts have strong data skills, and they usually lack systematic training in storytelling skills. They have positive attitudes toward data-driven work and data storytelling. Their concerns center on how they will compose narratives from analyses. They are also concerned about data privacy and security. Barriers to data storytelling are a lack of relevant skills (storytelling), lack of time to learn skills, and lack of data that aligns well with their intended stories, at least as they initially imagine them. Sometimes these users also lack administrative support. They need stories that are tailored to the specific work of librarians, a convenient and easy to use DS toolkit, and they would prefer aesthetically pleasing features.

These two categories are visually formatted for designers in Appendix A. These personas are part of the same overall user population of librarians, so developers need to keep in mind that any toolkit will have to serve both types of users at the same time.

5 Design Implications for Data Storytelling Toolkits for Librarians

5.1 RQ1: User Scenarios

Developers need to know about the work practices, contexts, and content of library DS work. Overall, responses showed interest in DS. DS toolkits should produce results in a readily usable format, as many users are already spending significant time producing materials. Lack of relevant skills demands a user-friendly and convenient design. Visualized easy to use in a variety of communications practices will be needed. However, library workers will also need significant support in constructing stories from data, making the leap from quantitative information to a holistic narrative of the purpose and impact of library work.

5.2 RQ2: Personas

Personas were the easiest way to synthesize findings for developers. Persona 1, Storytelling Experts, need clear and easy-to-use data tools that will provide well-structured data as evidence for the stories they craft. DS tools should do some work for them, perhaps including data visualization. Persona 2, Data Experts, need training in story crafting and storytelling. They may need to look at stories from other libraries or data from related contexts in order to be able to craft a compelling story about library work. They will benefit greatly from examples of how other libraries use DS to communicate their work.

5.3 Limitations

This research has some limitations, including the number of survey responses and self-selection of participants. While based on patterns, personas may not capture all kinds of users. The audience of developers support libraries and library work may have yet to emerge. Furthermore, story efficacy rests not only on story content and structure, but also on storytelling quality. While a toolkit may scaffold the production of a story based on data, it cannot guarantee that the story will be told well or wisely.

6 Discussion and Conclusion

Designing for libraries should include designing tools for use by library workers. Because many libraries are funded by taxpayers or embedded in non-profit educational institutions, large financial investments in design are unlikely, so researchers must develop them in non-profit contexts. While libraries have advanced technologies for circulation and digital collection management, the technologies that would be most effective for toolkits like the DSTL are as yet underdeveloped. Research that supports development of interactive toolkits for libraries might dramatically increase the interactivity of future toolkits, which in turn could increase their uptake. Lessons learned from the DSTL, including user scenarios and user personas, will aid in the development the DSTL and improve future development of related data-focused applications for library work.

Acknowledgements. We would like to thank the DSTL advisory board, the research practicum students from spring 2023, and the core design team for their outstanding contributions to this project. None of this work would have been possible without the generosity and curiosity of the library community.

Appendix A. Library Personas

Story tellers

Skill Sets

Story telling

Data

Attitude to storytelling

Positive

Attitude to data

Open attitude

Averted

Concerns of data
- Data literacy
- Surveillance

Barriers to data storytelling
- Lack of relevant skills (data)
- Lack data
  - Lack clean and formatted data
  - Lack data that align with stories
- Lack of time
  - To learn skills
  - To collect data
  - To clean data
- Need more administrative support

Needs
- Convenient and easy to use
- Tailored to librarians' work
- Ideal to have ready-to-use results
- Avoid information overload

Storyteller Adam Read

"I have an interest in data storytelling, but I have too much to learn."

Background
- Master in Library Science
- Librarians in a public library
- Book lovers
- Hope add values to libraries

Skill Sets

Storytelling

Data

Attitudes

Storytelling

Data

Concerns about data
- Data literacy
- Surveillance

Goals
- Learn skills
- Learn methodologies

Barriers to data storytelling
- Lack of relevant skills (data)
- Lack of data
  - Lacks clean and formatted data
  - Lacks data that aligns with stories
- Lack of time
  - To learn skills
  - To collect data
  - To clean data
- Need more administrative support

Needs
- Convenient and easy to use toolkit
- Tailored to librarians' work
- Ready-to-use results
- Avoid information overload

Data Experts

Skill Sets

Story telling

Attitude to storytelling

Positive

Lack awareness

Attitude to data

Positive

Concerns about data

- Privacy
- Security

Barriers to data storytelling

- **Lack of relevant skills (storytelling)**
  - Composing narratives for analyses
- **Lack of data**
  - Lacks data that align with stories
- **Lack of time**
  - To learn skills
- **Need more administrative support**

Needs

- **Tailored to librarians' work**
- **Convenient to use**
- **Aesthetically pleasing outcomes**

Data Expert Emily Datum

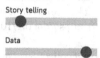

"I would love more inspiration for composing narratives to go with my analysis."

Background

- Master in Data Science
- Community college librarian
- Tech Geek
- Hopes to make library data more meaningful

Skill Sets

Storytelling

Data

Attitudes

Storytelling

Data

Concerns about data

- Data privacy
- Security

Goals

- To learn narrative skills
- To make data understandable

Barriers to data storytelling

- **Lack of relevant skills (storytelling)**
  Composing narratives for analyses
- **Lack of data**
  Lacks data align with stories
- **Lack of time**
  - To learn skills
- **Need more administrative support**

Needs

- **Tailored to librarians' work**
- **Convenient to use**
- **Aesthetically pleasing outcomes**

References

1. McDowell, K.: Data storytelling for libraries: Peer to peer review. Library Journal (2023). https://www.libraryjournal.com/story/data-storytelling-for-libraries-peer-to-peer-review. Accessed 16 Jan 2024. McDowell, K: Making sense of a gap: Data storytelling and libraries. Public Libraries Magazine **62**(6), 28–35 (2023)
2. McDowell, K.: Library data storytelling: obstacles and paths forward. Public Library Quart. **43**(2), 202–222 (2024). https://doi.org/10.1080/01616846.2023.2241514
3. McDowell, K.: Storytelling wisdom: story, information, and DIKW. J. Assoc. Inf. Sci. Technol. **72**(10), 1223–1233 (2021). https://doi.org/10.1002/asi.24466
4. Audunson, R.: How do politicians and central decision-makers view public libraries?: the case of Norway. IFLA J. **31**(2), 174–182 (2005). https://doi.org/10.1177/0340035205054882

5. Zaugg, H., Rackham, S.: Identification and development of patron personas for an academic library. Performance Measur. Metrics **17**(2), 124–133 (2016). https://doi.org/10.1108/PMM-04-2016-0011

6. Al-Shboul, M.K., Abrizah, A.: Information needs: developing personas of humanities scholars. J. Acad. Librarianship **40**(5), 500–509 (2014). https://doi.org/10.1016/j.acalib.2014.05.016

7. Lewis, C., Contrino, J.: Making the invisible visible: personas and mental models of distance education library users. J. Lib. Inf. Serv. Dist. Learn. **10**(1–2), 15–29 (2016). https://doi.org/10.1080/1533290X.2016.1218813

8. Tempelman-Kluit, N., Pearce, A.: Invoking the user from data to design. Coll. Res. Lib. **75**(5), 616–640 (2014). https://doi.org/10.5860/crl.75.5.616

9. Harrington, S., Churchill, V.: Planning an entry sequence with service design: a case study. Pub. Serv. Quart. **18**(1), 1–18 (2022). https://doi.org/10.1080/15228959.2021.1895949

10. Adkins, D., Moulaison Sandy, H., Bonney, E.N.: Creating personas on which to build services for Latinx users: a proof of concept. Pub. Lib. Quart. **38**(1), 50–71 (2019). https://doi.org/10.1080/01616846.2018.1528573

11. Landis, W.E.: Personas and archetypes: envisioning the 21st-century special collections professional. RBM: J. Rare Books Manuscripts Cult. Heritage **7**(1), 40–48 (2006). https://doi.org/10.5860/rbm.7.1.255

12. Zohoorian-Fooladi, N., Abrizah, A.: Personafying academic librarians' social media presence. Malays. J. Libr. Inf. Sci. **19**(3), 13–26 (2014)

13. Subramaniam, M., Hoffman, K. M., Davis, K., Pitt, C.: Designing a connected learning toolkit for public library staff serving youth through the design-based implementation research method. Lib. Inf. Sci. Res. **43**(1), Article 101074 (2021). https://doi.org/10.1016/j.lisr.2021.101074

Nostalgia-Driven Design: Creating an Inclusive VR Experience for Older Black Adults

Kuo-Ting Huang[✉]

Department of Information Culture and Data Stewardship, School of Computing and Information, University of Pittsburgh, Pittsburgh, USA
timhuang@pitt.edu

Abstract. This study examines the technological feasibility and emotional efficacy of a Virtual Reality (VR) platform tailored for older Black adults; a demographic often marginalized in the realm of digital technology. Using a participatory design methodology grounded in user-centered paradigms, theories of nostalgia are integrated with practical technological elements to create a prototype that meets both functional and emotional needs. A total of 28 participants were involved through five stages of the design thinking process, culminating in evaluations at a local senior center. The results reveal enthusiastic user engagement, not only with the platform's interface and functionalities but also its emotional and cultural resonance. These findings highlight the platform's role in fostering digital inclusion among older adults, transforming them from mere consumers to active co-creators, thereby enriching a collective narrative and cultural heritage. The study offers valuable contributions to intersecting fields of human-computer interaction, gerontology, and cultural studies, demonstrating the potential of emotionally and culturally resonant technology to enhance the quality of life for older adults.

Keywords: Virtual Reality · Participatory Design · Digital Inclusion · Older Adults · Minorities

1 Introduction

Virtual reality (VR) technology shows transformative potential in enhancing older adults' physical, cognitive, and emotional well-being [1]. Research evidence highlights improved cognitive functions [2], enhanced emotion regulation [3], and advanced physical performance [4] as some of the potential benefits of VR-based interventions. In other words, VR technologies and applications can promote and sustain wellness among older adults once adopted [5, 6]. Recognizing and utilizing these benefits in the design of VR systems can particularly improve wellness outcomes for this demographic. Nevertheless, the 'digital divide' persists, posing a challenge especially for economically disadvantaged older adults and those from racial and ethnic minority groups [7]. Limited prior exposure, low digital literacy, physical impairments, economic constraints, and the perception that these technologies do not cater to their needs often inhibit these

I. Sserwanga et al. (Eds.): iConference 2024, LNCS 14596, pp. 421–429, 2024.
https://doi.org/10.1007/978-3-031-57850-2_32

individuals' adaptation to new technologies [8]. This divide also prevents these under-resourced and vulnerable populations from benefiting from VR technology and hinders their representation in the virtual world [9], potentially amplifying the perception that these technologies are not designed for them. This exclusion, in turn, reinforces digital ageism [10, 11] and age-related stereotypes [10, 11].

Realizing VR's full potential for older adults requires addressing their unique needs, preferences, and barriers in VR designs and promotion strategies. Design considerations need to expand beyond physiological and cognitive factors associated with aging to include cultural, social, and economic aspects that influence their lived experiences [12]. For older adults from racial and ethnic minorities, including elements that resonate with their cultural heritage and lived experiences is especially crucial [13]. Incorporating life story elements into VR environments can help stimulate past memories and enhance the sense of self, which is particularly beneficial for individuals from diverse backgrounds, including those with cognitive impairments such as dementia [14]. A culturally sensitive approach can enhance the relevance of VR experiences, fostering inclusion and representation in the virtual world.

Besides being culturally sensitive, addressing the digital divide necessitates a shift beyond the provision of physical access to technology towards improving motivational and skill access. Enhancing skill access requires developing intuitive, user-friendly VR experiences attuned to the specific needs and preferences of this demographic. Past research indicates that a participatory design approach, integrating social or community elements into design processes, can effectively navigate these multifaceted access challenges [15]. Another pivotal aspect is affordability, given that cost is a considerable impediment to technology adoption for economically disadvantaged older adults [16]. In consideration of potential usability issues associated with VR, the deployment of more cost-effective VR alternatives, such as phone-based VR solutions, may present viable strategies [17].

Nostalgia and reminiscence can significantly enhance older adults' engagement with VR technology. Research indicates that using VR to stimulate reminiscence can evoke seniors' memories cognitively and nostalgia affectively, leading to increased levels of engagement with the technology [14, 15, 18]. Furthermore, studies show that VR can be effectively used for reminiscence therapy and group reminiscence, incorporating personal history and emotional content within the VR experience [18]. Similarly, nostalgia, an emotional or affective resonance with the past, primarily positive, has been linked to improved self-esteem and growth-oriented behaviors, such as technology adoption. This connection occurs as nostalgia helps alleviate negative feelings such as anxiety and the perceived loss of control [19]. Thus, nostalgia and reminiscence can serve as powerful tools to motivate older adults to adopt new technological experiences by invoking "good old days".

In addition to the motivational role, nostalgia satisfaction has been linked to enhanced mental health and well-being [20], In this light, harnessing the combined power of nostalgia and reminiscence can yield multi-faceted benefits, promoting technology adoption, cultural preservation, and well-being enhancement among older adults. The design of VR experiences, therefore, should be informed by the insights gleaned from the study of nostalgia and reminiscence. By developing VR environments that effectively facilitate reminiscence, we can capitalize on the power of nostalgia to promote VR among seniors, contributing to digital inclusion, mental well-being, and cultural preservation.

In existing VR literature, three notable gaps affect older adults and racial minorities. First, while nostalgia and reminiscence are acknowledged as beneficial to seniors, they are seldom used as design motivators to enhance engagement and therapeutic outcomes. Second, current VR content largely caters to a younger, white, tech-savvy demographic, leaving a void in representation for older adults from diverse backgrounds. This calls for more inclusive and culturally relevant VR experiences. Lastly, there's a lack of research examining VR's effectiveness for older, digitally disadvantaged adults from various racial backgrounds, indicating an untapped area for investigation.

To address these issues, the present study has two primary objectives. The first is to identify and understand the specific barriers that inhibit older adults, particularly those from racial and ethnic minority backgrounds, from embracing VR technologies. The second objective aims to directly involve these older adults in the design and developmental process of VR experiences tailored to meet their specific needs and preferences. Through this dual-pronged, inclusive approach, the study aims to both amplify the voices of a marginalized demographic and optimize the potential benefits of VR, thereby contributing to both its technical accessibility and its emotional resonance for older adults.

2 Methods

Aligned with the aforementioned complex challenges and opportunities, this study employs a multi-stage, participatory design approach to directly engage older adults from racial and ethnic minority backgrounds, particularly older Black adults who are economically disadvantaged or digitally less savvy. By invoking elements of nostalgia and reminiscence, we aim to fulfill the latent emotional needs of this demographic, thereby creating VR experiences that are both technically and emotionally resonant. This co-creative process aims to tackle digital ageism by making VR technology more accessible and inclusive.

2.1 Research Design and Procedure

The research, conducted from September 2022 to July 2023 at a senior center in Pittsburgh, followed a participatory design methodology, integrating the principles of user-centered design and design thinking. This approach was chosen to ensure that the VR experience was developed in close collaboration with the target demographic, thereby addressing their specific needs and preferences. The study comprised 10 sessions with a total of 28 participants and was structured around five key stages of the design thinking process developed by IDEO: Empathize, Define, Ideate, Prototype, and Test [21]. This iterative process allowed for continuous refinement of the VR experience based on user feedback and insights, ensuring that the final product was both technically feasible and emotionally resonant for older Black adults.

Stage 1: Empathize—Understanding the User Context. In partnership with the Community Engagement Center of our institution, we targeted participants aged 65 or older

424   K.-T. Huang

who self-identified as digitally disadvantaged and part of racial minority groups, particularly older Black adults. Qualitative data was gathered through in-depth interviews and ethnographic observations, delving into their prior technological interactions, digital experiences, and latent needs.

Stage 2: Define—Articulating User Needs and Challenges. After completing data collection on the users' VR-related needs, perceptions, and challenges, we conducted a thematic analysis. This analysis helped us formulate a clear and actionable problem statement: "How can we create a VR experience that is both accessible and engaging, designed to address the technological and experiential limitations faced by digitally disadvantaged older Black adults?".

Stage 3: Ideate—Intellectual Exploration and Concept Generation. In this stage, we engaged community resources to spark interest. We used Teenie Harris's photography archive from the Carnegie Museum of Art as a reference to create nostalgia-inducing VR experiences. An archivist was consulted to ensure historical and cultural accuracy, thereby enriching the ideation process. This step redefined our actionable problem statement to incorporate these cultural elements.

Stage 4: Prototype—Initial Solution Development. We created multiple prototypes of 360-degree video experiences that allowed older adults to revisit significant Pittsburgh locations, like Crawford Grill and Freedom Corner (see Fig. 1). These prototypes underwent preliminary tests with our participant cohort to assess both their functionality and emotional impacts.

Stage 5: Test—Empirical Evaluation and Usability Assessment. The prototypes were then subject to an extensive set of usability tests involving the original group of participants, supplemented by additional users. These tests, held at the local senior center, utilized heuristic analyses to assess the prototypes' functionality, usability, and emotional resonance with this demographic.

Fig. 1. An example of VR rendering of Old Pittsburgh (left) alongside older adults using the VR headsets.

2.2 Data Analysis and Interpretation

The data derived from all workshops and discussion sessions underwent rigorous analysis using both qualitative and quantitative methods. Direct observational metrics, thematic analysis of open-ended interviews, and statistical analysis of structured questionnaires were all employed to identify patterns, challenges, and opportunities for iterative improvements. Through adherence to this comprehensive, culturally sensitive methodology, heavily influenced by the five stages of the design-thinking process, the study seeks to address the existing gaps concerning older adults, particularly those from racial minorities like older Black adults. Our aspiration is to create an inclusive VR landscape that combats digital ageism and optimizes the manifold benefits that VR can offer to enhance the quality of life for these communities.

3 Results

3.1 Emotional Resonance and the Power of Nostalgia

One of the most salient findings from our participatory research was the strong emotional resonance of nostalgia among older Black adults. Engaging with the target demographic in a series of in-depth interviews and ethnographic observations revealed that nostalgia served as a compelling motivator to interact with digital technology, specifically VR. Participants expressed a deep connection to the idea of "reliving the past," showcasing the importance of embedding nostalgic elements in the VR platform. One participant mentioned: *"Being from the Hill District, Crawford Grill, it's in my blood. The sounds of musicians, like Ella Fitzgerald and George Benson, are not just things we remember, it's the rhythm our people lived by. Sadly, today's youngsters won't ever truly get that, as they've never been privileged to witness such times firsthand."* This supports our hypothesis drawn from theories of nostalgia and user-centered design, affirming that a technology aiming to be more than a tool but also an emotional companion is possible and impactful for this demographic.

While nostalgia was a key motivator, we were mindful to avoid an overly idealized portrayal of the past. The content creation process involved careful selection and curation, with input from community members and experts, to ensure a balanced representation that respected historical accuracy and authenticity. This approach ensured that the VR experience was not only engaging but also truthful to the complexities of the era, avoiding the pitfalls of romanticizing history.

3.2 User Goals and Cultural Resonance

Another significant finding was the participants' interest in specific kinds of digital experiences those that could transport them back to cultural landmarks from the 1960s era. In other words, it wasn't just any form of nostalgia that appealed to them, but a nostalgia rooted deeply in their cultural history and identity. Participants voiced a desire for an experience that would be not just entertaining but emotionally enriching. They pointed out the importance of cultural landmarks, like historical sites and music venues from their youth, revealing a strong desire for VR experiences that could reconnect them with these aspects of their identities. Another participant mentioned: *"I never thought technology could make me feel so connected to our past. This isn't just a game; it's like a digital archive of our collective memory"*.

3.3 Technological Feasibility and Emotional Efficacy

Our Ideate stage research showed that the user goals and cultural resonance could indeed be translated into a technologically feasible VR platform. This was a pivotal finding, as it merged the emotional and psychological needs of the older Black adults with the realm of what is currently possible within VR technology. The positive reception of the preliminary prototypes from the participants validated that not only could a functional system be developed, but it could also retain the emotional resonance and cultural significance the participants were seeking. One participant commented: "*I was a bit skeptical about this round-picture thing (referring to VR) at first, thinking it's for the younger folks. But when I saw places, I grew up around, right there man, it felt real*". This underlines the vital role that user experience design plays in the successful implementation of technology aimed at a specific demographic.

3.4 Community Contribution

The final evaluation sessions held at the local senior center in Pittsburgh served as an empirical test to validate our research approach and the developed VR platform. Feedback from participants was not limited to the interface and its functionality; they were particularly enthusiastic about the emotional and cultural resonance of the platform. This supports the initial theory that leveraging nostalgia could significantly enhance user engagement among older Black adults. Importantly, participants felt that they were not merely passive consumers of the VR content; they felt they had a role in shaping the collective narrative of nostalgia. As multiple participants mentioned in the workshop: "*this isn't just for us to revisit the past; it's a way for the young folks to learn what life was like for us. We're not just going back in time; we're saving it for the future*" This finding suggests that the platform serves as a two-way conduit for cultural enrichment, allowing users not only to consume but also to contribute to the broader tapestry of shared experiences.

4 Discussion

4.1 Summary and Interpretation of Results

The overarching goal of the present investigation was to rigorously evaluate the dual goals of technological feasibility and emotional efficacy within the context of a VR platform, specifically engineered for older Black adults a cohort that has been largely underserved in the domain of digital technology. To this end, the study adopted a participatory design framework steeped in user-centric paradigms. This facilitated an interdisciplinary dialogue that cohesively integrated theoretical frameworks revolving around nostalgia with practical engineering imperatives. The developed prototype not only fulfills rudimentary technical specifications but also resonates on an emotional and psychological level with the target user group. This discussion will delve further into these findings and explore their broader implications for both theory and practice in designing VR for older adults.

Our approach intentionally leveraged nostalgia, not as a byproduct but as a central design principle, to enhance emotional resonance and engagement. By involving participants in the design process, we aimed to create a VR experience that was not only technologically feasible but also deeply meaningful and culturally resonant. This participatory design methodology allowed us to co-create with older Black adults, ensuring that their voices and experiences were integral to the development of the VR platform. The resulting VR experience is a testament to the power of nostalgia as a tool for emotional connection and cultural preservation, as well as the importance of inclusivity in technology design.

Our emphasis on participatory and inclusive design not only conforms to but also extends contemporary trends in HCI research advocating for technological inclusivity. Most extant literature primarily explores the digital divide vis-à-vis age but insufficiently addresses intersectional variables such as race and cultural identity. This study significantly augments the HCI corpus by providing nuanced insights into the confluence of age, race, and digital technology, thereby contributing to a more comprehensive understanding of digital inclusion and ageism.

Although previous research has investigated the utility of VR in enhancing quality of life among older adults, few studies have ventured into the domain of cultural specificity. This research fills this lacuna by positing that emotional factors, specifically nostalgia, can serve as potent catalysts for technology adoption among older Black adults. These findings corroborate and extend the current understanding of user engagement mechanisms within HCI, positing that the synergy between emotional and cultural elements can produce significantly heightened user engagement.

The study illuminates an often-neglected facet of HCI—the role of nostalgia in facilitating emotional connections. It suggests that technologies can transcend their conventional utilitarian roles by incorporating emotional and cultural elements, thereby becoming vehicles for emotional well-being and psychological resilience. This finding implicates the broader HCI field by suggesting that emotionally resonant factors can and should be integrated into user experience design frameworks.

One of the most salient features of this research was its adoption of a participatory design methodology, which afforded the target demographic an active role in the co-creation process. This aligns with our findings under the "Collaborative Iterative Design" section and underpins the potential for increased emotional investment, user satisfaction, and long-term engagement. By enabling users to act as both consumers and contributors, the platform transcends its functionality to serve as a communal asset, thereby fulfilling its objective as an inclusive digital tool.

Finally, the "Ideate" and "Prototype" stages of this investigation empirically validated the technological feasibility of the designed VR system, in alignment with the "Technological Feasibility and Emotional Efficacy" section of the results. Nevertheless, the issue of scalability remains an area for further academic inquiry. The foundational principles elucidated empathetic design, active user participation, and emotional resonance could feasibly be extrapolated to other cultural or historical contexts, thereby broadening the system's applicability and impact.

4.2 Limitations and Future Directions

While our study provides crucial insights into digital inclusivity and cultural resonance via VR, limitations exist. These primarily concern the small sample size and focus on a single senior center in Pittsburgh, which may limit generalizability. Additionally, the participatory design approach, although enriching, might introduce bias due to heightened participant investment in the project's success. Given these constraints, future research could explore expanding to other marginalized communities and varied geographical locations. Additional features for interactive storytelling, an exploration of the impact of different historical contexts on user engagement, and strategies for scalability also represent promising research avenues.

5 Conclusion

Our study contributes valuable insights to the intersecting fields of human-computer interaction, gerontology, and cultural studies. It illuminates the profound impact that emotionally resonant and culturally relevant technology can have on enhancing the quality of life for older Black adults. By employing a participatory, user-centered approach that leverages nostalgia, our VR platform has the potential to serve as a model for digital inclusion initiatives aimed at marginalized communities.

References

1. Carroll, J., et al.: A scoping review of augmented/virtual reality health and wellbeing interventions for older adults: redefining immersive virtual reality. Front. Virtual Real. **2**, 655338 (2021)
2. Appel, L., et al.: Older adults with cognitive and/or physical impairments can benefit from immersive virtual reality experiences: a feasibility study. Front. Med. **6**, 329 (2020)
3. Montana, J.I., et al.: The benefits of emotion regulation interventions in virtual reality for the improvement of wellbeing in adults and older adults: a systematic review. J. Clin. Med. **9**(2), 500 (2020)
4. Phu, S., et al.: Balance training using virtual reality improves balance and physical performance in older adults at high risk of falls. Clin. Interv. Aging **14**, 1567 (2019)
5. Baker, S., et al.: Evaluating the use of interactive virtual reality technology with older adults living in residential aged care. Inf. Process. Manage. **57**(3), 102105 (2020)
6. Dermody, G., et al.: The role of virtual reality in improving health outcomes for community-dwelling older adults: systematic review. J. Med. Internet Res. **22**(6), e17331 (2020)
7. Robinson, L., et al.: Digital inequalities 2.0: legacy inequalities in the information age. First Monday **25**(7) (2020)
8. Robinson, L., et al.: Digital inequalities 3.0: emergent inequalities in the information age. First Monday **25**(7) (2020)
9. Huang, K.-T., Ball, C., Francis, J.: The Perceived Impacts of COVID-19 on users' acceptance of virtual reality hardware: a digital divide perspective. Am. Beh. Sci. 00027642231156775 (2023)
10. Manor, S., Herscovici, A.: Digital ageism: a new kind of discrimination. Human Behav. Emerging Technol. **3**(5), 1084–1093 (2021)
11. Chu, C.H., et al.: Digital ageism: challenges and opportunities in artificial intelligence for older adults. Gerontologist **62**(7), 947–955 (2022)
12. Czaja, S.J., et al.: Designing for Older Adults: Principles and Creative Human Factors Approaches. CRC Press (2019)
13. Sorkin, D.H., et al.: Barriers to mental health care for an ethnically and racially diverse sample of older adults. J. Am. Geriatr. Soc. **64**(10), 2138–2143 (2016)
14. Siriaraya, P., Ang, C.S.: Recreating living experiences from past memories through virtual worlds for people with dementia. In: Proceedings of the SIGCHI Conference on Human Factors in Computing Systems, Toronto, Ontario, Canada, pp. 3977–3986. Association for Computing Machinery (2014)

15. Baker, S., et al.: Exploring the design of social VR experiences with older adults. In: Proceedings of the 2019 on Designing Interactive Systems Conference, San Diego, CA, USA. pp. 303–315. Association for Computing Machinery (2019)

16. Lee, C., Coughlin, J.F.: PERSPECTIVE: Older adults' adoption of technology: an integrated approach to identifying determinants and barriers. J. Prod. Innov. Manag. **32**(5), 747–759 (2015)

17. Margrett, J.A., et al.: Older adults' use of extended reality: a systematic review. Front. Virtual Real. **2**, 176 (2022)

18. Baker, S., et al.: School's back: scaffolding reminiscence in social virtual reality with older adults. Proc. ACM Hum.-Comput. Interact. **4**(CSCW3) (2021). Article 267

19. Huang, N., et al.: New technology evokes old memories: Frequent smartphone use increases feeling of nostalgia. Pers. Soc. Psychol. Bull. **49**(1), 138–151 (2023)

20. Routledge, C., et al.: Nostalgia as a resource for psychological health and well-being. Soc. Pers. Psychol. Compass **7**(11), 808–818 (2013)

21. Brown, T.: Design thinking. Harv. Bus. Rev. **86**(6), 84 (2008)

Correction to: "Inclusion We Stand, Divide We Fall": Digital Inclusion from Different Disciplines for Scientific Collaborations

Wei Feng⬡, Lihong Zhou⬡, and Qinggong Shi⬡

Correction to:
Chapter 30 in: I. Sserwanga et al. (Eds.): *Wisdom, Well-Being, Win-Win,* **LNCS 14596,**
https://doi.org/10.1007/978-3-031-57850-2_30

The original version of this chapter, Author name erroneously presented as Wei Fang rather than Wei Feng. This has been corrected.

The updated version of this chapter can be found at
https://doi.org/10.1007/978-3-031-57850-2_30

I. Sserwanga et al. (Eds.): iConference 2024, LNCS 14596, p. C1, 2024.
https://doi.org/10.1007/978-3-031-57850-2_33

Author Index

A

Adkins, Denice II-416
Alon, Lilach I-333
Anwar, Misita III-295
Astuti, Hanim III-329

B

Ba, Zhichao III-3
Bagchi, Mayukh I-270
Bahir, Masooda I-223
Bates, Jo III-54
Behre, Jane I-383
Bi, Chongwu III-170
Blake, Catherine I-223
Bogers, Toine I-70
Bratt, Sarah I-147

C

Cai, Yunna III-150
Cao, Thi Binh Minh I-70
Cao, Yaning II-236
Cao, Zhe II-338
Carroll, John M. II-82
Chen, Mozhuo II-19
Chen, Xiaoyu I-96
Cheng, Shuangling I-358
Cheng, Zizuo II-105
Chinchilla-Rodríguez, Zaida I-321
Chmielinski, Grace I-147
Cho, Hyerim II-416
Choi, Jae-Hwang I-358
Choi, Kahyun III-283
Chowdhury, Gobinda I-139
Chu, Clara M. I-3
Clark, Malcolm I-106
Collier, Chelsea III-195
Corso, Anthony J. II-175
Corso, Nathan A. II-175
Cortés, Julián D. I-288, I-321, II-122, II-131

D

da Silva Santos, Diogenes II-416
Dainas, Ashley R. I-53
Dalrymple, Mary III-382
Deng, Jun I-12
Deng, Shengli III-150
Dewitz, Leyla II-62
Ding, Weiwei III-150
Disanto, Nicolas C. II-175
Du, Jia Tina I-3
Duncan, Mitch I-343

E

Emdad, Forhan Bin III-271

F

Feng, Wei I-398
Fleischmann, Kenneth R. III-195
Frank, Rebecca D. III-79
Fratczak, Monika III-54
Freeburg, Darin II-392
Frias-Martinez, Vanessa III-382
Frings-Hessami, Viviane III-356
Fu, Hengyi III-125

G

Gao, Ge III-338
Gilliland, Anne II-141
Girona, Antonio E. II-43
Giunchiglia, Fausto I-270
Goh, Dion Hoe-Lian II-198
Gray, LaVerne I-235
Greenberg, Sherri R. III-195
Guo, Jiayan I-84

H

Habing, Kelda II-94
Harding, Alison I-383
Hauser, Elliott I-253
Herring, Susan C. I-53

Hossain, Md Khalid III-356
Hou, Jingrui II-376
Hou, Yujia III-161
Hovious, Amanda I-375
Hu, Die II-3
Hu, Qibiao II-376
Hu, Xinhui I-410
Huang, Kuo-Ting I-421
Huang, Meiyin I-191
Huang, Ying II-105, II-338

I

Ibrahim, Mohamed III-295
Igarashi, Tomoya II-322
Ito, Hiroyoshi III-232

J

Jarrahi, Mohammad Hossein I-253
Jiang, Tianji I-20
Jiang, Zhuoren II-254
Jin, Minshu II-301
Jin, Yan III-170
Johnston, Jamie II-322

K

Ke, Qing I-31, II-236
Kim, Yeonhee I-358
Klein, Katie II-392
Koizumi, Masanori II-322
Kröber, Cindy II-27
Krtalić, Maja I-333
Krueger, Stephanie III-79

L

Lahiri, Sucheta I-235
Lassiter, Tina III-195
Ledford, Theodore Dreyfus II-211
Lee, Esther II-175
Lee, Seul II-141
Li, Chenguang I-84
Li, Qiao I-298
Li, Shijuan III-319
Li, Xin II-407
Li, Xinyue II-268
Li, Zixing III-395
Lian, Jingwen II-268
Lian, Zhixuan I-191
Liao, Jiaqi II-186

Lin, Tianqianjin II-254
Liu, Chang II-3
Liu, Chunfeng I-298
Liu, Jiangfeng I-161
Liu, Jiawei I-209
Liu, Jing III-248
Liu, Leilei III-3
Liu, Liu II-3
Liu, Mandie II-268
Liu, Ruoxi II-198
Liu, Xiaozhong I-209, II-254
Liu, Yaqi III-105
Liu, Yutong I-171
Long, Alicia K. II-416
Longoria, Raul G. III-195
Lu, Quan III-213
Lu, Wei I-209
Luo, Ran I-171

M

Ma, Yongqiang I-209
McDowell, Kate I-410
McNeese, Nathan III-365
Medina-Perea, Itzelle III-54
Mehra, Bharat I-3
Meng, Kai III-3
Morishima, Atsuyuki III-232
Mostafa, Javed III-161
Murillo, Angela P. I-343

N

Nath, Amit Kumar III-271
Newman, Jarrett III-311
Nie, Weimin II-356

O

Ochu, Erinma III-54
Oliver, Gillian III-295
Oliver, Gillian Christina III-356
Ou, Shiyan II-356
Oyama, Satoshi III-232

P

Park, Sunyup III-90
Pei, Lei I-161
Peng, Siyuan I-298
Peng, Xueying III-213

Q

Qian, Qianwen II-157, III-150
Qiu, Haoran II-198

R

Ramírez-Cajiao, María Catalina I-288,
   I-321, II-122, II-131
Roberts, Alec III-65
Robinson-García, Nicolás I-321
Ruan, Lian II-94
Rudolphr, Carsten III-295
Ruthven, Ian I-106, I-139

S

Saha, Manika III-295
Salvi, Rohan Charudatt I-223
Sbaffi, Laura III-65
Schneider, Jodi II-211
Schulz, Peter J. II-198
Sengupta, Subhasree III-365
Shang, Yuanyuan II-338
Shen, Xiao-Liang II-157, II-280
Sheng, Manyu I-129
Shi, Qinggong I-398
Si, Li III-35
Song, Ian Y III-204
Stahlman, Gretchen R. I-310
Stratton, Caroline III-329
Su, Yueli III-105
Subramaniam, Mega I-383
Sun, Guangyao II-3
Sun, Guangyuan I-298
Sun, Guoye III-248
Sun, Haodong I-31
Sun, Jiarui I-20
Sun, Shaodan I-12
Sun, Xuan III-261
Sun, Zhuo III-170
Sutherland, Will I-253
Sutton, Sarah I-375

T

Tacheva, Jasmina III-365
Tamura, Takumi III-232
Tan, Qian III-395
Tang, Jian I-84
Tang, Juan II-105
Tang, Xuli II-407
Thomas, Dain I-139

Thomas-Fennelly, Adam I-343
Turk, Matthew I-410

V

Vitak, Jessica III-90

W

Wang, An-I Andy III-271
Wang, Dongbo I-161, II-3
Wang, Fan III-150
Wang, Fang I-191
Wang, Haining III-409
Wang, Haowei III-150
Wang, Pianran III-261
Wang, Ping II-376
Wang, Xiaofeng I-209
Wang, Xiwei I-171
Wang, Xiyu I-161
Wang, Yunran I-84
Wang, Yuting III-261
Wang, Zhenyu III-150
Wickett, Karen M. III-311
Wu, Dan III-248
Wu, You II-157, II-280
Wuji, Siguleng I-171

X

Xiao, Aoxia II-301
Xiao, Yi III-319
Xie, Haoyu III-65
Xie, Sherry L III-204

Y

Yan, Pengwei II-254
Yang, Hanqin II-376
Yang, Jiaqi II-105
Yang, Leo I-53
Yang, Lin III-135
Yang, Ruixian III-170
Yang, Ruoxi I-96
Yang, Siluo II-301
Yarger, Lynette II-43
Yi, Ming II-407
Yoon, Ayoung I-343
Yu, Guo II-254
Yuan, Weikang II-254
Yuan, Xiaoqun III-395
Yue, Mingliang II-301

Z

Zhang, Chengzhi   III-23
Zhang, He   II-82
Zhang, Lin   II-338
Zhang, Pengyi   I-129
Zhang, Yingyi   III-23
Zhang, Yongle   III-338
Zhang, Yuehan   I-209

Zhao, Di   III-170
Zhao, Xin   III-65
Zheng, Heng   II-211
Zheng, Wenjie   III-105
Zhou, Jing   III-35
Zhou, Lihong   I-398
Zhou, Xinxue   I-84
Zhu, Qinghua   II-268

Printed in the United States
by Baker & Taylor Publisher Services